A MIRROR FOR MAGISTRATES

Over the six decades it remained in print in Tudor and Stuart England, William Baldwin's collection of tragic verse narratives, *A Mirror for Magistrates*, captivated readers and led numerous poets and playwrights to create their own *Mirror*-inspired works on the fallen figures of England's past. This modernized and annotated edition of Baldwin's collection – the first such edition ever published – provides modern readers with a clear and easily accessible text of the work. It also provides much-needed scholarly elucidations of its contents and glosses of its most difficult lines and unfamiliar words. The volume permits students of early modern literature and history to view Baldwin's work in a new light, allowing them to reassess its contents and its poems' appeal to several generations of early modern readers and authors, including William Shakespeare, Michael Drayton, and Samuel Daniel.

SCOTT C. LUCAS is Professor of English Literature at The Citadel, the Military College of South Carolina. He is the author of *'A Mirror for Magistrates' and the Politics of the English Reformation* (2009).

T0381923

A MIRROR FOR MAGISTRATES

A Modernized and Annotated Edition

EDITED BY

SCOTT C. LUCAS

CAMBRIDGE
UNIVERSITY PRESS

CAMBRIDGE
UNIVERSITY PRESS

University Printing House, Cambridge CB2 8BS, United Kingdom

One Liberty Plaza, 20th Floor, New York, NY 10006, USA

477 Williamstown Road, Port Melbourne, VIC 3207, Australia

314-321, 3rd Floor, Plot 3, Splendor Forum, Jasola District Centre, New Delhi - 110025, India

103 Penang Road, #05-06/07, Visioncrest Commercial, Singapore 238467

Cambridge University Press is part of the University of Cambridge.

It furthers the University's mission by disseminating knowledge in the pursuit of education, learning and research at the highest international levels of excellence.

www.cambridge.org
Information on this title: www.cambridge.org/9781009224390
DOI: 10.1017/9781139626910

First published 2019
First paperback edition 2022

A catalogue record for this publication is available from the British Library

ISBN 978-1-107-04001-4 Hardback
ISBN 978-1-009-22439-0 Paperback

Contents

Illustrations

Acknowledgments

It is a pleasure to recognize and to express my thanks to the many people and institutions who aided me during the preparation of this edition. I am grateful to Mike Pincombe and Jennifer Richards for first suggesting to me the idea of a new edition of the original texts of *A Mirror for Magistrates*, and to John N. King for championing the project when the time came to propose it to Cambridge University Press. I am equally grateful to Sarah Stanton of Cambridge University Press for guiding me during the first several years I devoted to the edition, and to Emily Hockley, who took over the project on behalf of the Press after Sarah's retirement and saw the work to publication.

Research for this edition was aided by the generosity of several institutions and their members. My first vote of thanks is to my college, The Citadel, and to The Citadel Foundation, which supplied valuable financial support and sabbatical leave time as I worked on it. I thank in particular Provost Samuel Hines, Dean Bo Moore, and Professor David Allen, former Head of the Department of English, Fine Arts, and Communications, for all the assistance they have given me. Libraries and archives, of course, were instrumental in furthering this edition, and I wish to recognize the generous help of the administrators and staff of the Huntington Library, the Folger Shakespeare Library, the British Library, the National Archives, the London Metropolitan Archives, and the university and college libraries of Cambridge and Oxford Universities. A special thanks goes to the Inter-Library Loan librarians of The Citadel's Daniel Library, who were always willing to help me with any request I might have. Finally, a one-month fellowship awarded me by the University of Texas's Ransom Center allowed me to consult the many useful volumes of the Center's Pforzheimer Collection and to enjoy both the time and a congenial working community in which to advance my project.

Several scholars generously agreed to read annotated poems and/or prose passages from my edition and to offer responses to them. These include Erin Ashworth-King, Kathryn DeZur, Katie Forsyth, Rachel Hile, Denna Iammarino, Roger Kuin, Michael Livingston, Melanie Lo, Ben Lowe, John McDiarmid, Ernest Rufleth, Cathy Shrank, Rachel Stenner, and Matthew Woodcock. People to whom I've turned over the course of the project for advice, answers, and/or general support include David Allen, Harriet Archer, Amy Blakeway, James Broaddus, Paul Cavill, Anne Curry, Joel Davis, Kelly DeVries, Alyson Eggleston, Thomas Freeman, Andrew Hadfield, Thomas Herron, Stuart Kinsella, Roger Kuin, Michael Livingston, Daniel Lochman, Peter Marshall, Steven May, Tricia McElroy, James Nohrnberg, Mike Pincombe, Anne Lake Prescott, Beth Quitslund, Jon Quitslund, Robert Reid, Nicola Royan, Sara Saylor, and Jessica Winston.

I was fortunate to have begun my project at a time when three excellent scholars of my acquaintance were also deeply engaged with the literature of the mid-Tudor period. I was helped immensely over the course of creating this edition by the aid and good fellowship of Jason Powell, J. Christopher Warner, and Matthew Woodcock. In addition to their willingness as a group to tackle any question of interpretation I might put their way, Jason Powell's meticulous editing of Sir Thomas Wyatt's works was an inspiration and guide to my own editorial endeavours, while Chris Warner's broad knowledge of mid-Tudor verse forms taught me much about the metrical choices of the *Mirror* authors. Finally, my good friend Matt Woodcock's close study of the life and writings of *Mirror* contributor Thomas Churchyard proved to be a superb resource for understanding the literary culture of the mid-Tudor period in general and that of the *Mirror* authors in particular.

Outside of academic circles, my friends and family have long provided support, encouragement, and general good cheer. I thank in particular my mother, Elizabeth Lucas, my sister Lisanne Lucas, my brother Stephen Lucas and his family (Joanne, Mark, and Meghan), my parents-in-law Tony and Anna Marie Martinovich, as well as my friends Jay Cahan, Derry Casey, and especially George K. Deukmejian, as close, generous, and valuable a friend as anyone may ever hope to have. Finally, I dedicate this book to the nearest members of my own family, my wife Stephanie and my daughters Charlotte and Caroline. They have lived with this project for many years, and their support and love throughout the whole process have been a source of great happiness and inspiration.

Abbreviations

Aesop	Aesop, *Aesopi Phrygis et vita … et fabellae* (London, 1535; *STC* 171)
Calvin, *Institutes*	John Calvin, *Institutes of the Christian Religion*, 2 vols., ed. John McNeill, trans. Ford Battles (Philadelphia: Westminster Press, 1960)
Curtius, *History of Alexander*	Quintus Curtius Rufus, *Quintus Curtius, with an English Translation (History of Alexander)*, 2 vols., trans. John Rolfe (Cambridge, Mass.: Harvard University Press, 1946)
Douay-Rheims Bible	*The Holie Bible faithfully translated into English* (Douai, 1609; *STC* 2207)
Fabyan; *Fabyan's Chronicle*	Robert Fabyan, *The New Chronicles of England and France*, ed. Henry Ellis (London, 1811) (Modern edition comprising the texts of the early modern editions of 1516, 1533, 1542, and 1559 (*STC* 10659–64))
Froissart, 1; Froissart's *Chronicles*, 1	Jean Froissart, *Here begynneth the first volum of sir Iohan Froyssart of the cronycles*, trans. John Bourchier, Lord Berners (London, 1523; *STC* 11396) (English translation of Jean Froissart's *Chroniques*, written *c.* 1370–1405)
Froissart, 2; Froissart's *Chronicles*, 2	Jean Froissart, *Here begynneth the thirde and fourthe boke of sir Iohn Froissart of the cronycles*, trans. John Bourchier, Lord Berners (London, 1525; *STC* 11397)
Geneva Bible	*The Bible and Holy Scriptures* (Geneva, 1560; *STC* 2093)
Great Bible	*The Byble in Englyshe* ([Paris and] London, 1539; *STC* 2068)

Hall; *Hall's Chronicle*	Edward Hall, *Hall's Chronicle*, ed. Henry Ellis (London, 1809) (based on the early modern editions of 1548 and 1550; *STC* 12721–3a). Original title *The Union of the Two Noble and Illustre Famelies of Lancastre & Yorke*.
Hardyng; *Hardyng's Chronicle*	John Hardyng, *The Chronicle of John Hardyng*, ed. Henry Ellis (London, 1812 (based on the two early modern editions of 1543, both of which print the 'Yorkist' version of the metrical chronicle Hardyng composed and revised *c.* 1436–65); *STC* 12766.7–7)
Herodotus	*Herodotus, with an English Translation*, 4 vols., trans. A. D. Godley (Cambridge, Mass.: Harvard University Press, 1920–30)
Livy, *History of Rome*	Livy, *Livy, With an English Translation* (*History of Rome*), 14 vols., trans. B. O. Foster et al. (London: Heinemann, 1919–59)
Lucas, *'A Mirror for Magistrates'*	Scott C. Lucas, *'A Mirror for Magistrates' and the Politics of the English Reformation* (Amherst: University of Massachusetts Press, 2009)
Lucas, '"Let none such office take"'	Scott C. Lucas, '"Let none such office take, save he that can for right his prince forsake": *A Mirror for Magistrates*, Resistance Theory, and the Elizabethan Monarchical Republic', *The Monarchical Republic of Early Modern England: Essays in Response to Patrick Collinson*, ed. John McDiarmid (Aldershot: Ashgate, 2007), 91–107
Lydgate, *Tragedies*	John Lydgate, *The Tragedies, gathered by Jhon Bochas, of all such Princes as fell from theyr estates* (*The Fall of Princes*) (London: J. Wayland, [1554]; *STC* 3178)
OED	*Oxford English Dictionary*
Ovid, *Metamorphoses*	Ovid, *Metamorphoses with an English Translation*, 2 vols., trans. Frank Justus Miller (Cambridge, Mass.: Harvard University Press, 1960)
Plutarch's Lives	Plutarch, *Plutarch's Lives*, 11 vols., trans. Bernadotte Perrin (Cambridge, Mass.: Harvard University Press, 1914)
PROME	Chris Given-Wilson, ed., *The Parliament Rolls of Medieval England, 1275–1504*, 16 vols. (Woodbridge: Boydell Press, 2005)

Ross, *Edward IV*	Charles Ross, *Edward IV* (Berkeley: University of California Press, 1974)
STC	A. W. Pollard, et al., *A Short Title Catalogue of Books Printed in England, Scotland, and Ireland, and of English Books Printed Abroad, 1475–1640*, 2nd edn, 3 vols. (London: Bibliographical Society, 1976–91) (citations to the *STC* are to entry number)
NA	National Archives, Kew, Surrey
Valerius	Valerius Maximus, *Memorable Doings and Sayings*, 2 vols., ed. and trans. D. R. Shackleton Bailey (Cambridge, Mass.: Harvard University Press, 2000)
Virgil, *Aeneid*	Virgil, *Virgil, with an English Translation*, 2 vols., trans. H. Rushton Faircloth (London: Heinemann, 1930)

Introduction

Scholars have long recognized *A Mirror for Magistrates* as one of the most widely read and influential works of English poetry of the entire Tudor and Jacobean periods. For more than sixty years, this collection of tragic verse narratives spoken in the voices of ghosts from Britain's past remained almost constantly in print, appearing in numerous ever-expanding editions between 1559 and 1610 and in several reissues of earlier editions between 1575 and 1621. Its poems' style and subject matter inspired a host of early modern authors, including such figures as William Shakespeare, Edmund Spenser, and Michael Drayton. In addition, it led numerous poets not connected with the original group of *Mirror* contributors to try their own hands at tragic verse narratives in the *Mirror* tradition. A number of these poems were added to the earliest gatherings of *Mirror* tragedies in new editions of the text, swelling the number of *Mirror* poems from nineteen in 1559 to ninety-one by 1610. Few Tudor works inspired such adulation and emulation as *A Mirror for Magistrates*; the full extent of its appeal to and influence on early modern readers remains still to be assessed.[1]

The Origins of *A Mirror for Magistrates*, 1554–*c*. 1556

The work that would become *A Mirror for Magistrates* began its life in 1554 under the title *A Memorial of Such Princes, as since the time of King Richard the Second have been unfortunate in the realm of England*. The text was an unlikely collaboration between a religiously conservative (and soon to be openly Catholic) printer John Wayland (d. *c*. 1571–3) and his evangelical Protestant employee William Baldwin (1526/7–1563). In the reign of England's reformist monarch Edward VI (1547–1553), William Baldwin had worked in the print shop of Edward Whitchurch, perhaps the most prolific printer of Reformation texts in England. King Edward died in 1553, however, and he was succeeded by his Catholic sister Mary I (1553–1558), whose new government was hostile to the activities of those who had advanced religious reform under her brother. In the months after Mary's accession, many evangelical printers thus either voluntarily left their trade or were removed from it. Among the latter group was Whitchurch. While it allowed Whitchurch to maintain ownership of his printing house, Mary's government forced him to accept a new man, John Wayland, as his shop's overseer. Wayland took control of Whitchurch's employees and presses for a specific purpose: to use them to print a new, ultimately Catholic version of the church's most popular book of private devotion, the English primer.[2]

Wayland received permission to print the Marian primer in October 1553, and he installed himself in Whitchurch's shop in the months thereafter. Unfortunately, church leaders had not yet agreed on a text for this revised devotional manual, and Wayland had no sense of when that decision might be made. Therefore, to bring in money and to keep his print servants employed while he waited, he decided to release new editions of venerable literary works from England's past. The first text to which he turned was Stephen Hawes's *Pastime of Pleasure* (1509), which came off his presses in June 1554; as the *Pastime* was being prepared, he determined to follow this publication with a new printing of John Lydgate's *The Fall of Princes* (c. 1431–7), a massive poetic work which recounts in voluminous detail the downfalls of historical figures stretching from Adam and Eve to King John II of France (d. 1364).

To make his edition of *The Fall* more appealing to contemporary readers, Wayland commissioned a supplement to the poem, one which would continue Lydgate's narrative plan of recording in verse the falls of famous men and women (a genre scholars have termed *de casibus* tragedy), but which would focus solely on fallen English, Scottish, and Welsh figures of the previous two centuries. Wayland assigned this project to Baldwin, who during his time with Whitchurch had become both an expert printer and a celebrated author. Reluctant to take on the task alone, Baldwin gathered seven 'learned men' to assist him.[3] Evidence suggests that this group of contributors initially met sometime between 20 April and 21 May 1554. Reading through copies of two Tudor chronicles, Robert Fabyan's *Fabyan's Chronicle* (first printed in 1516) and Edward Hall's *Union of the Two Noble and Illustre Families of Lancaster and York* (first printed in 1548), the men planned a series of individual poems, each telling the story of a British figure who endured tragedy sometime after the narratives included in Lydgate's *Fall* ended, in the mid fourteenth century.[4]

While they used the *Fall* as their general literary model, the *Memorial* poets modified Lydgate's style of recording his historical tragedies. In composing his poem, Lydgate had offered chiefly a paraphrase of his prose source, Giovanni Boccaccio's *De Casibus Virorum Illustrium* (*Concerning the Falls of Illustrious Men*) (1355–74), which Lydgate knew through a French translation (Laurence de Premierfait's *De Cas de Noble Hommes et Femmes* (1400–9)). In his text, Boccaccio had presented the ghosts of famous figures from the past as coming before him to tell their woeful tales. Lydgate, by contrast, in most cases only summarized in his own voice how the ghosts interacted with Boccaccio (or 'Bochas', as Lydgate called him). The *Memorial* authors chose to replace Lydgate's paraphrastic presentation with a more dramatic one, in which each spirit would rise before William Baldwin to narrate his own tragic verse narrative himself. The result was a poetic form of immediate and often intense emotional power, which invited readers to imagine hearing the actual voices of some of the most famous men of fourteenth- and fifteenth-century Britain relating in tones of personal grief, regret, or outrage the course of their lives and the events that led to their tragic ends.

The poets spent the summer of 1554 composing their historical verse tragedies, and they met at least once more in late August or early September to share with each other the poems they had created.[5] Baldwin evidently took notes at both the initial gathering and at this later one, and he then combined his records of the two meetings into a fictionalized running prose narrative that provided means of transition between the various tragedies of *A Memorial of Such Princes*. For the prose links, Baldwin created the fiction that the *Memorial* contributors all gathered on a single evening, in which they read accounts from the chronicles and, in a burst of extemporaneous inspiration, immediately composed poems in the voices of the fallen subjects they found most worthy of comment. The result was a prose frame for the collection unique in English literature of the time, one that purported to share with readers a record of the authors' actual comments on their own and others' contributions, as well as their thoughts on a wide range of other topics related to the poems' contents.

After arranging the collection into a form suitable for printing, Baldwin took the *Memorial* to Wayland's shop and had it printed at the end of the new *Fall of Princes* edition. Unfortunately, someone in Wayland's shop (most likely Wayland himself) detected controversial matter in the *Memorial* poems and brought the newly printed work to Mary I's lord chancellor, Stephen Gardiner, for review. Gardiner found enough of the contents of the *Memorial* objectionable to order the entire work suppressed before publication. The *Memorial* was never allowed to appear in Mary's reign, and most of its pages were simply scrapped. As a result, copies of only a single leaf of text and two title pages relating to the 1554

1. Title page of the prohibited *Fall of Princes-Memorial of Such Princes* volume (London, John Wayland, [1554]; STC 3177.5). © Victoria and Albert Museum. Reproduced by permission.

Memorial now survive (see Illustrations 1 and 2). Although his methods were harsh, Gardiner's suspicions were not in fact unfounded, for some of the *Memorial* indeed contained controversial political content, including assertions of the right to actively oppose unjust rulers and elements that could be read as composed to admonish and/or allusively indict some of the chief rulers of the Marian regime.[6]

Despite the government's suppression of the 1554 *Memorial*, Baldwin remained determined to publish some sort of *de casibus* tragedy collection in the 1550s. To that end, in about late 1555 or early 1556 he commissioned new poems in the style of the original *Memorial* contributions. Whereas the original *Memorial* had sought to present the ghosts of figures from Richard II's reign (1377–1399) to that of Edward IV (1461–1483), Baldwin's new gathering of tragedies, informally called the 'Second Part' of the *Memorial*, would recount the falls of men and women who suffered under Edward V and Richard III (1483–1485). Baldwin received several poems for this collection, and he acquired as well George Ferrers's tragedy 'Edmund Duke of Somerset', which belonged with the original set of *Memorial* tragedies, and at least part of Humphrey Cavell's 'Blacksmith', which was intended for a planned third volume of tragedies covering the falls of Tudor subjects. Now wiser with experience, Baldwin took the precaution of presenting his *de casibus* tragedy idea to members of Queen Mary's privy council before attempting to put his collection into print. Unfortunately for Baldwin, Mary's officers forbade the publication of this second literary attempt, despite its relative lack of controversial political content, just as Chancellor Gardiner had prohibited the first one. It would not be until Elizabeth's reign that any of the Marian poems Baldwin had collected could see publication.[7]

A Mirror for Magistrates, 1559

The death of Mary I in November 1558 finally allowed Baldwin the opportunity to guide *A Memorial of Such Princes* into print. Through the assistance of his fellow *Memorial* contributor Lord Henry Stafford, Baldwin received in early 1559 a licence from the Elizabethan regime to release *A Memorial of Such Princes*, now lightly re-edited and retitled *A Mirror for Magistrates* (see Illustration 3). In a newly composed dedication 'to the nobility and all other in office', Baldwin no longer presented his collection as a supplement to Lydgate's *Fall* but as an admonitory 'mirror' designed specifically to dissuade England's highest officers from the sort of political misbehaviour its tragedies portray. 'For here as in a looking glass,' Baldwin told England's rulers in his dedication, 'you shall see (if any vice

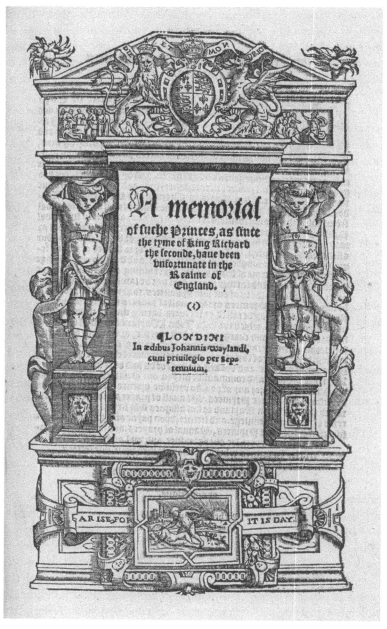

2. Internal title page of the suppressed *A Memorial of Such Princes* (London,
John Wayland, [1554]; STC 1246), sig. [GG4r]. Reproduced by permission of the
Folger Shakespeare Library, under a Creative Commons Attribution Share-Alike
4.0 International Licence.

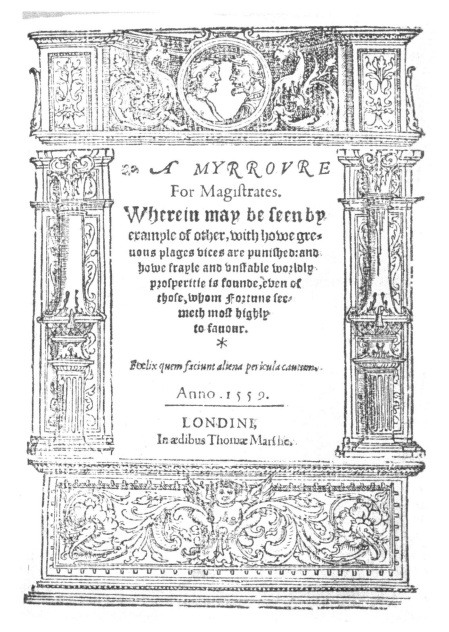

A MYRROVRE

For Magiſtrates.

Wherein may be ſeen by
eraumple of other, with howe gre=
uous plages bices are puniſhed: and
howe frayle and bnſtable woꝛldly
pꝛoſperitie is founde, even of
thoſe, whom Foꝛtune ſee=
meth moſt highly
to fauour.

*

Fœlix quem faciunt aliena pericula cautum.

Anno . 1 5 5 9.

LONDINI,
In ædibus Thomæ Marſhe.

3. Title Page of *A Mirror for Magistrates* (London, Thomas Marshe, 1559; STC 1247).
Reproduced by permission of the Huntington Library, San Marino, California.

be in you) how the like hath been punished in other heretofore; whereby admonished, I trust it will be a good occasion to move you to the sooner amendment. This is the chiefest end why it was set forth, which God grant it may attain.'

While Baldwin made the politically admonitory purpose of many of his collection's poems clear, one *Memorial* tragedy evidently remained too controversial to publish, even in the wake of Mary I's death. This was George Ferrers's poem 'Good Duke Humphrey Murdered and Eleanor Cobham his Wife Banished', which appeared in the table of contents of the 1559 *Mirror* but not in the text itself (see Appendix 1). That poem, eventually revised and split into two separate tragedies, did not come before the public until 1578 (see Tragedy 28 and Tragedy 29, as well as their associated prose links).[8]

A Mirror for Magistrates, 1563

In the early 1560s, Stafford encouraged Baldwin to publish the poems he had gathered in or around 1556 for his unpublished 'Second Part' of *A Memorial of Such Princes*. At some point in this project, Baldwin decided not merely to print his manuscript of Marian *de casibus* tragedies and prose links but to revise it, adding new, Elizabethan creations composed by himself and others to augment and, it seems likely, in some cases to replace the poems he had received years ago.

Baldwin was still at work on his new *Mirror for Magistrates* project when he passed away suddenly in September 1563. Left with only a partially revised manuscript, *Mirror* printer Thomas Marshe released what he had, combining Baldwin's partly revised Elizabethan manuscript with the remaining original material from the Marian collection. This additional material contained eight new poems that were on the whole much longer than the original works gathered for the *Memorial*. Among those works were George Ferrers's 'Edmund Duke of Somerset', which Ferrers had intended for the original *Memorial* but did not finish in time, and the poem 'Blacksmith', which would likely have been saved for a planned third volume of *Mirror* tragedies. Also included in this edition were two poems that were to help to ensure the enduring success of *A Mirror for Magistrates* for decades to come: Thomas Churchyard's oft-imitated 'Shore's Wife' and Thomas Sackville's lengthy tour de force of flowing verse, classical allusion, and high tragic emotion, 'The Induction and Complaint of Henry Duke of Buckingham'.

A Mirror for Magistrates, 1571–1621

William Baldwin did not live to see the full success of his long-troubled *de casibus* tragedy collection. Such was the enduring popularity of his work that a third edition of the *Mirror* appeared in 1571, which revised and in some cases rearranged several of the poems and prose pieces in the collection. Unlike the edition of 1563, this offering mentioned Humphrey Duke of Gloucester and Eleanor Cobham in its table of contents, but it now presented what had been described as a single poem in the 1559 edition as two different texts, one in each of the voices of the fallen pair. Despite this listing, neither Humphrey's nor Eleanor's tragedy appeared in the edition itself.

A fourth offering of the *Mirror* appeared in 1574, with a companion volume of tragedies by the poet John Higgins – not a member of Baldwin's original gathering of contributors – presenting fallen men and women of Britain's mythic past.[9] The 1574 text was reissued in a new printing of 1575, followed by a fifth edition of Baldwin's work in 1578. It was in the first released version of the 1578 *Mirror* that a poem in the voice of Humphrey, duke of Gloucester, finally appeared. Sometime after this edition was published, the printer Marshe added as a cancel to unsold copies a new poem in the voice of Eleanor Cobham. With both Gloucester's and Cobham's poems now published, all the poems originally compiled for *A Memorial of Such Princes* in 1554 were finally, at least in some form, in print. Many questions, however, still remain concerning the poems 'Gloucester' and 'Eleanor Cobham' and their precise relation to Ferrers's original hybrid 'Gloucester–Cobham' tragedy included in the suppressed *Memorial* text.[10]

In 1587 yet another edition of the *Mirror* appeared, this one combining Baldwin's gathered poems with those of John Higgins, as well as adding new poems by various hands, including a tragedy by Thomas Churchyard in the voice of Thomas Cardinal Wolsey (d. 1530). In 1610 the seventh and final edition of the *Mirror* came before the public, conjoining Baldwin's and Higgins's editions with poems by one Thomas Blenerhasset, who in 1578 had released an independent collection of *de casibus* tragedies titled *The Second Part of the Mirror for Magistrates.* The editor of the 1610 edition, Richard Niccols, added a new induction to the work and several tragedies of his own, and he removed all the prose links of the previous editions. Niccols's offering of this now fifty-year-old text was the last in the early modern period. Copies of this edition were reissued in 1619, 1620, and 1621 and thereafter the text ended its six decades before the eyes of early modern readers. Despite its troubled beginning, few literary texts in early modern England proved themselves to be as long-lived, earnestly admired, and widely influential as William Baldwin's *A Mirror for Magistrates*.

Known Authors of Baldwin's *A Mirror for Magistrates* (1559 and 1563 Editions)

Although the titles of twenty poems appear in the table of contents of the 1559 *Mirror for Magistrates*, only nineteen are actually included in the text itself. Of those nineteen, eight are credited to three particular authors, while a single surviving leaf of the suppressed 1554 edition identifies Sir Thomas Chaloner as the author of the poem 'Richard II'. Ten tragedies in the 1559 *Mirror* are anonymous, though evidence points to Henry, tenth Baron Stafford, as the author of one of them. By contrast, the 1563 edition clearly identifies by last name each of the authors of the eight poems added to it, though more than one hand evidently took part in at least one of the tragedies, namely Tragedy 27, 'The Blacksmith'. The known authors of Baldwin's *A Mirror for Magistrates* are as follows.

Authors of the 1559 Mirror for Magistrates

WILLIAM BALDWIN (author of at least Tragedies 4, 6, 8, 13, 18, 20, 23, and perhaps others, as well as creator of all the prose sections of the text) William Baldwin, the compiler, editor, and chief contributor to the first two editions of *A Mirror for Magistrates*, was born in London sometime between 15 January 1526 and 14 January 1527.[11] Nothing certain is known of his life before the year 1547, when he published his earliest extant work, a commendatory sonnet attached to a medical text printed by Edward Whitchurch (Baldwin's is the first sonnet known to have been printed in England). Baldwin's next work, a collection of wise sayings attributed to ancient thinkers titled *A Treatise of Moral Philosophy* (January 1548), was an immediate and lasting success, going through four editions in Edward VI's reign and a remarkable twenty over the course of the succeeding 100 years. In 1549 Baldwin followed his *Treatise* with a metrical paraphrase of the Song of Songs, *The Canticles or Ballads of Solomon*. Baldwin printed this work himself in the shop of Edward Whitchurch.

In the 1550s Baldwin's writings became more controversial. Near the opening of the decade Baldwin released anonymously his translation of Pier Paolo Vergerio's scabrous anti-papal satire *Wonderful News of the Death of Paul III*, and he likely took part, as the pseudonymous 'Western Wyll', in the 1551 public flyting (exchange of poetic invective) occasioned by future

Mirror poet Thomas Churchyard's allusive attack, in his broadside poem *Davy Dycar's Dream*, on the unpopular government of John Dudley, earl of Warwick. By 1552 Baldwin had become close enough to future *Mirror* contributor George Ferrers to have Ferrers bring him to court to assist in mounting Christmas-time entertainments for Edward VI. Baldwin used his service at court as the scene for the opening of his next major work, the comedic prose narrative *Beware the Cat* (composed 1553), which some have called the first English novel.

The anti-Catholic content Baldwin built into both *Beware the Cat* and his 1553 poem *The Funerals of Edward VI* ensured that neither could be printed after Edward VI's July 1553 death and the accession of Mary I to the throne. Under Mary, Baldwin continued to work in Edward Whitchurch's printing house, and it was for that shop's new government-imposed supervisor John Wayland that he undertook the creation of *A Memorial of Such Princes*.

On Queen Elizabeth's accession (November 1558), Baldwin quickly moved to bring his prohibited *Memorial of Such Princes* into print as *A Mirror for Magistrates*. He then released his other long-suppressed works, *The Funerals of Edward VI* (printed 1560) and *Beware the Cat* (printed 1561). At the same time, Baldwin took holy orders, becoming in 1560 a minister in the English church. By early 1561 he was in service to Lord Henry Stafford as his chaplain, and he continued to serve the bibliophile Stafford even after gaining in June 1561 the benefice of St Michael le Querne church, which stood directly across from the principal locus of the London book trade, the churchyard of St Paul's cathedral. It is a testament to the respect London diocesan leaders held for Baldwin that they invited him in September 1563 to preach the Sunday sermon at Paul's Cross, an event that often attracted thousands of auditors, including some of the highest of the realm.

Baldwin would not live to capitalize on his growing success. Within a week of his appearance at Paul's Cross he succumbed to the plague, leaving unfinished his revision of new material for the 1563 *Mirror* and also a planned new English chronicle he intended to compose with the antiquarian John Stow. He died at just 37 years of age.

GEORGE FERRERS (Tragedies 1, 3, 26, 28, 29)   George Ferrers (*c.* 1510–1579) was born to a prominent family of St Albans, Hertfordshire.[12] According to his admirer John Leland, he began his personal rise to fame when he entered the service of Thomas Cromwell, likely in the late 1520s.[13] By the early 1530s Ferrers had left Cromwell's employ to pursue the study of law, almost certainly beginning at an unknown Inn of Chancery (where law students at the time traditionally commenced their studies) before moving to Lincoln's Inn in 1534. In that same year the antiquarian Ferrers released the first printed English translation of *Magna Carta*, publishing it with a host of other medieval legal documents he translated from Latin and Anglo-Norman French.[14]

Ferrers returned to Cromwell's service in the later 1530s, and was declared fit to be a 'daily waiter' in Cromwell's house. In 1539 he transferred his service to the king himself, becoming first a member of Henry VIII's personal bodyguard and then, by 1542, a page of the chamber. Ferrers also began in 1542 a parliamentary career that would extend well into the reign of Elizabeth I.

On the accession of Edward VI, Ferrers apparently continued to hold some position as a crown officer, though in 1548 he was described as having entered the personal service of the powerful and charismatic protector of the realm, Edward Seymour (d. 1552), duke of Somerset. In the wake of Somerset's removal from power in October 1549 by a group of powerful nobles led by John Dudley, earl of Warwick, and Thomas Wriothesley, earl of Southampton, Ferrers was understood to have remained loyal to his patron. In March 1550, following Somerset's pardon in the previous month for alleged crimes committed as protector, Ferrers was arrested, along with Sir Thomas Chaloner's two younger brothers and other 'ffyne wytted yong men' associated with King Edward's court, on suspicion of writing against the newly ascendant Warwick and his allies in government.[15] Ferrers ultimately escaped without any formal charge against him. In later years he would make Edward Seymour's troubles, both those imposed upon him by others and those of his own creation, allusive topics of reference in several of his *Mirror* tragedies.

If Ferrers had earned the suspicion of high officers in 1550, that suspicion was not shared by his monarch. It was apparently Edward VI himself who in 1551 invited Ferrers to mount Christmas entertainments as the court's annual lord of misrule. Together with future *Mirror* author Sir Thomas Chaloner, Ferrers created performances so entertaining that he was brought back again – this time with William Baldwin as his assistant – as the Christmas-time lord of misrule for the 1552/3 season.

In Mary's reign, Ferrers served in the parliaments of 1553 and 1554 and as a justice of the peace for Hertfordshire, where he held the large and valuable manor of Markyate. He assisted the privy council in defending London against the 1554 rebellion of Sir Thomas Wyatt the younger, and in 1555 he supplied evidence against the Catholic priest (and former adherent of John Dudley) John Dee, whom he accused of using sorcery to calculate the deaths of Queen Mary and her husband King Philip. After 1555 he retired from public life, concentrating on managing his estates in Hertfordshire.

In the years after Elizabeth's accession, Ferrers apparently became close to Robert Dudley, first earl of Leicester, and was involved with Leicester's plan to make Mary, Queen of Scots, Elizabeth I's heir. He continued to support Mary Stuart's claim to the English crown even as he served in the parliament of 1571. According to John Stow, Ferrers composed in the 1560s an account of Mary I's reign for the chronicler Richard Grafton; in 1575 he helped mount the earl of Leicester's famous entertainments for Queen Elizabeth at Kenilworth. He died in 1579.

SIR THOMAS CHALONER (Tragedy 5) Thomas Chaloner (1520/1–1565) was born to a prosperous London mercer who served as a teller of the exchequer under Henry VIII and Edward VI.[16] After studying at Cambridge, Chaloner returned to London, where, like George Ferrers, he entered both Lincoln's Inn and Thomas Cromwell's service. After time abroad in the service of the Tudor diplomat Sir Henry Knyvett, Chaloner joined his father in 1544 in the exchequer. The next year he became a member of parliament and a clerk of the privy council, the latter position allowing him close access to some of the most important political figures of the mid-Tudor period. Through an advantageous marriage, he also began to acquire extensive former monastery lands in the north of England.

Chaloner's career continued to advance under Edward VI. He maintained his position as clerk of the privy council and, in September 1547, he joined Protector Somerset's expedition into Scotland as Somerset's secretary. It was Somerset who knighted Chaloner in the field for his service. Having a strong humanist bent, the learned Chaloner published several translations during the 1540s, including the first English version of Erasmus's celebrated *Praise of Folly*. In 1551–2 he joined George Ferrers in mounting Christmas entertainments for Edward VI, and he spent the last years of King Edward's reign as one of the three English ambassadors to the French court.

Following Queen Mary's accession, Chaloner was recalled from his foreign post. He thereafter spent most of Mary's rule on his lands in Yorkshire and Cumberland, serving as a member of the Council of the North and as a representative in negotiations with Scotland. On the accession of Elizabeth, Chaloner was selected for ambassadorial service, first at the Imperial court and then, in 1561, at that of the Spanish (and former English) King Philip II. Although generally unhappy in Spain, Chaloner used his time abroad to devote himself to the composition of much neo-Latin verse. Throughout the Elizabethan period he remained in touch through letters with his fellow *Mirror* authors George Ferrers and Thomas Sackville. He died in October 1565; William Cecil served as his chief mourner and oversaw the publication of all of Chaloner's unpublished Latin poetry.

HENRY, TENTH BARON STAFFORD (Tragedy 2)   Unlike Baldwin, Ferrers, and Chaloner, Henry Lord Stafford (1501–1563) is not mentioned by name in either *A Mirror for Magistrates* or the surviving leaf of text from *A Memorial of Such Princes*. Nevertheless, strong circumstantial evidence points to his authorship of Tragedy 2, 'The Two Rogers'.[17]

Stafford was the eldest son of Edward Stafford (d. 1521), third duke of Buckingham, and for twenty years he enjoyed an elevated status as heir to the wealthiest noble in Henry VIII's England.[18] His privileged life collapsed, however, in 1521, when his father was condemned and executed on treason charges that the younger Stafford never accepted as true. As a consequence of Buckingham's treason conviction, all the Stafford lands, goods, and titles were confiscated by the crown, leaving Henry Stafford to live in very straitened – and sometimes desperate – circumstances. After much petitioning and pleading, Stafford finally convinced parliament in 1547 to grant him the least of his family's historical titles, baron of Stafford. He received with it, however, none of his family's lands or former wealth.

It was in that same year of his elevation that Stafford made the acquaintance of future *Mirror* contributor George Ferrers, whose Markyate manor Stafford proposed to (and, it seems, did) rent from Ferrers. The two men shared an interest in antiquarian endeavour, Stafford's shaped not merely by a love of learning but also by his zeal to find historical precedents to contest the legality of condemning noblemen without proper trial or response to charges, a method commonly used in passing parliamentary bills of attainder of the sort posthumously used against his own father in 1523.

In February 1554 Stafford successfully petitioned Queen Mary to grant him the office of chamberlain of the exchequer. His new post gave him not only a steady income but also access to the store of long-unconsulted medieval government records held in the Tower of London. Both Stafford and Ferrers availed themselves of the Plantagenet rolls of parliament kept in the Tower archive to inform their poems in *A Memorial of Such Princes* and *A Mirror for Magistrates*.

Under Elizabeth, Stafford worked to calendar and index the Tower's medieval documents, and he made William Baldwin his chaplain. Although he never recovered the bulk of his family's wealth and property, the learned Stafford was able to live comfortably until the end of his life, overseeing his lands, expanding his impressive personal library, and assisting and encouraging Baldwin in bringing the Marian *Memorial of Such Princes* material into print as *A Mirror for Magistrates*. He died in early 1563.

JOHN SKELTON (Tragedy 19)   An anonymous *Mirror* poet ends the 1559 collection by providing a version of the poem 'Of the Death of the Noble Prince King Edward IV', which he attributes to John Skelton (*c.* 1460–1529). The work first appeared in print about the year 1545 in the collection *Here After Followeth Certain Books, Compiled by Master Skelton* (*STC* 22598); the version included in the *Mirror* is based on that of this edition, with a new title supplied by William Baldwin and some slight emendations.[19]

Authors of Poems Added to the 1563 Edition

In addition to William Baldwin, who takes credit for two poems printed in the 'Second Part of the *Mirror for Magistrates*' (the gathering of Marian and Elizabethan poems and prose links added to those of the 1559 *Mirror* in the second edition), and George Ferrers, who composed one of that text's offerings, five new men contributed verse to the 1563 'Second Part'. Of these, two composed their poems in Queen Mary's reign, two created their tragedies in that of Elizabeth, and one, Thomas Sackville, apparently composed parts of his hybrid 'Induction and Complaint of Henry Duke of Buckingham' both in the Marian and Elizabethan periods.

Marian Contributors

THOMAS CHURCHYARD (Tragedy 25)   The prolific poet Thomas Churchyard was born in Shrewsbury about the year 1529.[20] After serving as a page in the household of Henry Howard, poet earl of Surrey, Churchyard began a lengthy career as a solider and poet, often journeying abroad to fight and then returning to England to make a living as best he could as an author. The public flyting over his poem *Davy Dycar's Dream* may have first brought him to William Baldwin's attention, but it is George Ferrers who is credited with bringing Churchyard's tragedy 'Shore's Wife' to Baldwin for the planned 'Second Part' of *A Memorial of Such Princes* (see Prose 21). On its publication in the 1563 *Mirror*, Churchyard's poem became an instant success, inspiring numerous imitators and making its speaker Elizabeth (dubbed by later authors Jane) Shore one of the most familiar female figures in Elizabethan and Jacobean historical literature.

Unfortunately, the impecunious Churchyard was never able to replicate the success of 'Shore's Wife' and, over the course of his long life, he published numerous works of verse and prose that brought him little in the way of remuneration. Churchyard never lost his interest in *A Mirror for Magistrates* or the *de casibus* tragedy tradition. In 1575 he released 'Sir Simon Burley's Tragedy', which told – in the manner of Ferrers's Tragedy 1, 'Robert Tresilian' – the downfall of one of King Richard II's favourites, and in 1587 he contributed a new poem in the voice of Thomas Cardinal Wolsey (d. 1530) and two prose links to the sixth edition of *A Mirror for Magistrates*. In 1593 he returned to his ever-popular 'Shore's Wife', composing an expanded version of the work and defending his authorship of the poem against the many who, he claimed, denied his composition of it. Issued in that year as well was another *de casibus* work, 'The Earl of Morton's Tragedy'. Still composing verse until almost the end of his life, Churchyard passed away in 1604.

HUMPHREY CAVELL (Tragedy 27)   The career of the parliamentarian and Inns of Court man Humphrey Cavell (1525–1558) would seem to indicate a closeness with George Ferrers, but it was in fact Baldwin who solicited Cavell's contribution to the *circa* 1556 'Second Part' of the *Memorial of Such Princes*. Cavell was born to a junior branch of an important Cornish family. He joined the Middle Temple in or before 1546, and it may have been his fellow member of that Inn of Court, Henry Lord Stafford, who brought Cavell to Baldwin's attention. Under Mary I, Cavell enjoyed a successful legal career and sat in three Marian parliaments. Mike Pincombe persuasively argues that Cavell supplied only the middle section of Tragedy 27, 'The Blacksmith', leaving Baldwin to compose the remainder.[21] Cavell died on 17 November 1558, the last day of Queen Mary's reign.[22]

Marian-Elizabethan Contributor

THOMAS SACKVILLE (Tragedy 22)   Evidence suggests that Thomas Sackville (*c.* 1536–1608) provided new verse to both the Marian 'Second Part' of *A Memorial of Such Princes* and to the Elizabethan section of the 'Second Part of the *Mirror for Magistrates*'. In Prose 23, Baldwin describes Sackville as having contributed Tragedy 22b, 'Henry, Duke of Buckingham', to the 'Second Part' of the *Memorial*. On hearing that the Marian privy council would not permit Baldwin to print the 'Second Part', Sackville took all the tragedies composed in the voices of figures who fell before Buckingham and set out to write his own *Memorial*-like *de casibus* tragedy collection, moving backwards in English history to the time of William the Conqueror. To begin this new sole-author project, Sackville crafted an 'induction' or introductory framing poem (Tragedy 22a), which he then attached to the previously written 'Buckingham'. Eventually abandoning his own *de casibus* tragedy project, Sackville gave Baldwin the joint 'Induction and Complaint of Henry Duke of Buckingham' poem for inclusion in the second edition of *A Mirror for Magistrates*. Although the date of Sackville's 'Induction' is not certainly known, Paul Bacquet argues that it is a work of the Elizabethan period, and that Sackville employed the lengthy description of the heavenly bodies at the opening of the poem to pinpoint the date on which the action of his 'Induction' is set, 23 November 1560.[23]

Sackville was the son and heir of the wealthy royal servant Sir Richard Sackville, a man who in 1560 would help William Baldwin to his first clerical living.[24] Said to have been educated at Oxford University, Sackville joined the Inner Temple in November 1554, and he was praised by Jasper Heywood in 1560 for the sonnets (now lost or unidentified) he wrote while a student there. The flowing iambic verse, powerful imagery, and high emotion of Sackville's 'Induction' soon made it the most widely admired and imitated piece of poetry in *A Mirror for Magistrates*, and its author's reputation as an artist only grew through his part in composing England's first blank verse tragedy, *Gorboduc* (1561). Sackville, however, quickly left literature as a calling and commenced a decades-long career as a diplomat, crown officer, and privy councillor. In 1567 Queen Elizabeth named him Baron Buckhurst; in 1604 James I made him first earl of Dorset. Sackville died at the privy council table at Whitehall on 19 April 1608.

Elizabethan Contributors

JOHN DOLMAN (Tragedy 21) It was the printer Thomas Marshe who in Elizabeth's reign found two new poets to contribute to the 1563 *Mirror* project (see Prose 21). The first, John Dolman (1540/1–1602 or after), was a younger son of a prosperous Berkshire clothier.[25] He attended Oxford University and entered the Inner Temple in 1560. In the following year he published a translation of Cicero's *Tusculan Disputations* printed by Thomas Marshe, and it was no doubt this work that led Marshe to recommend him for Baldwin's expansion of *A Mirror for Magistrates*. Dolman's contribution, 'Lord Hastings' (Tragedy 21), has proven itself to be the most aesthetically controversial poem in Baldwin's collection: Lily B. Campbell calls it perhaps the worst piece of poetry in the *Mirror*, while John Thompson praises it as among the best the collection has to offer.[26] Both perspectives are at least partly correct. Dolman's tragedy mixes forbidding stanzas filled with convoluted word order and unclear referents with lines offering some of the most direct, vibrant, and exciting poetry of the mid-Tudor period. Dolman's introduction of a number of innovations into the *Mirror* tradition, including offering multiple voices in his poem, full stops in the middle of lines, and frequent enjambment appears to have influenced Baldwin's own experimentations with these techniques in Tragedy 20, 'Anthony Woodville, Lord Rivers and Scales'. 'Hastings' is Dolman's last known literary work; after its publication, he evidently devoted himself almost solely to what became a long and distinguished career in law.

FRANCIS SEAGER (Tragedy 24)   Almost certainly the son of the Dutch-born Cambridge stationer Seager Nicholson (who witnessed Francis's will), Francis Seager (d. 1565), a scrivener by trade, established himself as an author as early as Edward VI's reign.[27] After publishing in 1549 a revised and expanded version of William Caxton's translation of Alain Chartier's *Le Curial,* Seager (whose name appears in contemporary writings variously as Seager, Seagar, Segar, Seagars, and 'Nycholson, *alias* Seager') released *Certain Psalms Select out of the Psalter of David, and Drawn into English Metre* (1553), which presented metrical psalm paraphrases in the style of Thomas Sternhold's immensely popular *Certain Psalms Chosen Out of the Psalter of David, and Drawn Into English Metre* (1549). Seager also released a poetic compendium of moral instruction titled *The School of Virtue* (1557 or before), which became so popular that it continued to be reprinted well into the seventeenth century. Thomas Marshe, who brought to Baldwin Seager's 'Richard III', is not known to have been a printer of any of Seager's works; he could have become acquainted with Seager, however, during the time the two men were concurrently members of the Stationers' Company (1557–9).[28] Seager wrote his will on 22 January 1565 and died soon thereafter. He left several children who came to prominence under Elizabeth and James, including Sir William Segar, Garter King of Arms; Jane Segar, author of the manuscript poetry collection 'Divine Prophecies of the Ten Sybils' (1589); and Francis Segar, a well-known gentleman servant to the Landgrave of Hesse.[29]

Interpreting Baldwin's *Mirror*

For much of the twentieth century *Mirror* scholars chiefly treated Baldwin's collection as a more or less univocal expression of uncontroversial 'Tudor ideas', a storehouse of contemporary beliefs that they could extract from the text and apply to the study of later, better-known works of Elizabethan literature. When such scholars found difficulty in reducing the lengthy and complex *Mirror* to a simple exemplary display of doctrinal statements, many of them declared it to be a failure, since it did not achieve the task they claimed it was created to achieve.[30]

Given earlier scholars' inability to account for how such a 'failed' work could have gained the wide admiration and influence it enjoyed in its own time, many later students of the text have rejected the totalizing assumptions of earlier *Mirror* critics and have instead asserted the radical multivocality of Baldwin's *Mirror* editions. Baldwin's editions comprise twenty-seven poems and twenty-nine prose links, with as many as fourteen poets taking a hand in the composition of these sections. Similarly, Baldwin represents numerous authors, friends, and 'furtherers' as sharing their thoughts with one another in the prose links, and he records a remarkably wide variety of opinions and assertions in the prose sections he offers. It is little wonder, then, that many later *Mirror* scholars have called for the study of each *Mirror* poem as an individual work of art in itself and for an understanding of the text's numerous prose links as works of fundamentally unsettled and dynamic dialogic exchange.[31]

Moreover, each *Mirror* poem is offered in the voice of a specific ghostly figure of the fourteenth or fifteenth century, and it is not always clear when a represented speaker is meant to be understood as expressing the views of his/her creator and when he/she is meant to be read as speaking 'in character', offering opinions appropriate to the figure him/herself and not necessarily those endorsed by that character's creator.[32] Finally, as the notes to this edition demonstrate, several *Mirror* authors take great liberty with their historical sources, at times to create more powerfully affective works of art but at others to turn contemporary readers' attention away from the medieval protagonists they portray to reflect instead on recent and ongoing political actions of the mid-Tudor period. The possibility of topical allusion must be taken into account when reviewing any of the 1559 *Mirror* tragedies, though not all, of course, pursue such a project. Each individual section of *A Mirror for Magistrates*, in other words, demands careful analysis from a variety of perspectives, each of which may provide fruitful avenues of interpretive investigation.

The Verse of the *Mirror*

Baldwin's *Mirror* has traditionally been faulted not only for its allegedly 'failed' content but also for its prosody, which a number of critics have condemned for its inability to emulate the regular iambic rhythms of later English poetry. It is important to remember, however, that the majority of *Mirror* authors never set out to write in iambic pentameter, a form that was to dominate English verse only after the tragedies of Baldwin's *Mirror* were composed (and which, indeed, was helped to prominence by two widely admired *Mirror* poems, Sackville's 'Induction and Complaint of Henry Duke of Buckingham' and Churchyard's 'Shore's Wife'). Certainly, several generations of Elizabethan and Jacobean readers found the *Mirror* tragedies' versification not only entirely satisfactory but even admirable. Most notably, in the 1580s no less a judge of English poetry than Sir Philip Sidney lauded the *Mirror* as 'meetely furnished of beautiful parts', and he held the collection to be worthy of honour above almost any other work of English-language verse.[33] In their tragedies, the *Mirror* authors employ a variety of both traditional and innovative poetic styles; so variegated are the poets' metrical choices that one critic has hailed the collection as 'an extraordinary museum of metre', one worthy of close analysis rather than curt dismissal.[34]

The majority of the *Mirror* tragedies are written in the formal manner of John Lydgate's *Fall of Princes*, that is, in seven-line rhyme royal stanzas of accentual verse. Lydgate did not write in iambs; instead, he aimed for five stressed 'beats' per line, placing from zero to two unstressed syllables between each of his five stressed syllables. This was the dominant metre in the late medieval period for what Martin Duffell calls 'long-line' verse, that averaging ten or more syllables per line.[35] While many of the *Mirror* authors follow Lydgate's general example, they usually seek a line length more uniform than that of Lydgate's *Fall*, rarely offering fewer than ten or more than eleven syllables per five-stress line.

Not all *Mirror* authors follow Lydgate's metrical example, however. George Ferrers emulates the traditional four-beat line of John Skelton's Tragedy 19, 'King Edward IV', in composing his own Tragedy 3, 'Thomas of Woodstock', and he and Francis Seager employ the 'tumbling verse' (poetry of no fixed rhythm) familiar in medieval romances and popular poetry for two *Mirror* contributions (Tragedies 1 and 24). For their part, Sir Thomas Chaloner and the author of Tragedy 17, 'King Henry VI', reject models of the past and create new stanzaic forms for their poems, while Sackville, Churchyard, and Dolman emulate the poet earl of Surrey's striking experiments in iambic verse – a form Duffell terms 'iambic *vers de dix*' – in their own *Mirror* contributions. As with the content of the *Mirror*, the metrics of the various tragedies of the collection and their effect on shaping readers' responses to each poem have yet fully to be explored.[36]

The Text of this Edition

The text of this edition of Baldwin's *Mirror for Magistrates* is based on the copies of the 1559, 1563, and 1578 editions held by the Huntington Library. They have been collated with the copies of these texts in the British

Library and checked against others at the Folger Shakespeare Library, the University of Texas's Harry Ransom Center, the Bodleian Library, and the University and Trinity College Libraries of Cambridge University. All textual variants are noted in the apparatus, with the exception of the unique content of one sheet included in the Trinity College 1563 copy, which was apparently a proof sheet accidently included in that text.[37] I have corrected obvious printing errors in the text, silently in the case of those listed in the original editions' errata sheets and with reference in the textual apparatus to the original renderings when making alterations on my own.

In this edition the entire contents of Baldwin's two *Mirror* editions have been modernized, with the exception of usages with no direct modern equivalent (e.g. I preserve archaic past tenses such as 'drave' and 'be' in place of 'drove' and 'been') and words whose early modern rendering allows the possibility of more than one meaning (e.g. 'sournamed' (*surnamed*) is preserved in its original spelling in Tragedy 18 to keep the possible pun on the word 'sour'). Quotes in the Explanatory Notes from other early modern texts are kept in original spelling, though orthography has been modernized ('i' is rendered as 'j' and 'v' as 'u' where appropriate, and contractions have been silently expanded).

To aid in the reading of the *Mirror* authors' verse, I have added accents to show where syllables usually silent in modern usage are apparently meant to be pronounced (as in the voiced '-ed' ending and in unusual pronunciations such as the trisyallbic 'marrìage' that appears in several of the tragedies). For the same reason, I have also indicated when words are spelled in the original with fewer syllables than they are in modern orthography (e.g. 'en'my' instead of 'enemy' when the word is rendered as two syllables in the original).

The rhythm of each line will indicate the pronunciation of most other words in the text. Readers should note that words such as 'tower', 'flower', and 'power' are usually monosyllabic in the *Mirror*. Terms such as 'over', 'never', and 'even' can be one or two syllables, as can the word 'naked'. The terminal 'e' in 'the' before a vowel – and sometimes in other words – is frequently elided ('the one' is often pronounced 'th'one', even if it is not spelled as such), and a terminal 'y' before an initial vowel sound in the succeeding word may be combined with that vowel sound ('many a' is usually meant to be pronounced 'man-ya'). Words whose first syllable ends in an 'e' can have that 'e' pronounced or not pronounced ('flattery' is in many cases 'flatt'ry', 'shouldest' is often 'should'st'), while the '-eth' suffix may have its 'e' understood to be silent and – in Tragedy 21 in particular – even the entire suffix understood to be silent.

Some scholars have called attention to the fact that both Baldwin in 1554 and Thomas Marshe's compositors in 1559 and 1563 set the prose passages of the *Memorial* and *Mirror* in a typeface somewhat larger than that of the poems.[38] Sherri Geller has argued that the prose sections' larger typeface was Baldwin's bid to call readers' primary attention away from the poems themselves and to focus it on the prose passages linking them; for Geller, Lily B. Campbell's choice in her 1938 edition of *A Mirror for Magistrates* not similarly to place the prose links in a larger typeface thus 'significantly misrepresents the early *Mirrors* and thereby contributes inadvertently to critics' misdirected privileging of the complaints and underestimation of the frame story [that is, the prose links]'.[39]

These scholars' arguments rest on the belief that a larger typeface automatically connoted to early modern readers a sense of increased importance for the passages so rendered. There is, however, no evidence for this assumption. That the evangelical printer John Day, for instance, often chose to use a type for scriptural quotations smaller than that of the main text in his editions of John Foxe's *Actes and Monuments* does not indicate that Day held the Bible to be a work of lesser status than Foxe's writings. Similarly, that in printing John Calvin's *Institutes* Reyner Wolfe and Richard Harrison chose to put Calvin's preface to the reader in a type larger than that used for the body of text speaks more to the printers' desire for aesthetic variety than to their sense that Calvin's short preface was somehow of more importance than the primary contents of Calvin's famous work.[40] Finally, if Baldwin did seek to indicate by means of type size the primacy of the prose passages over the poems, early modern *Mirror* readers completely missed this cue: while extracts from the poems of the 1559 and 1563 *Mirror* may be found in a number of extant Tudor and Stuart commonplace books and printed collections, I am not aware of any similar extensive extraction of material from the prose offerings of the *Mirror*. For his part, *Mirror* editor Richard Niccols expressed no reservations at all in printing only poems from *A Mirror for Magistrates* and none of its prose links in his 1610 edition of the work. I thus acknowledge here the slight disparity of typeface sizes in the original *Mirror* editions, but I choose to employ, as earlier editors did, a uniform font size for all sections of Baldwin's work.

Except where noted, I follow for historical names, titles, dates, and facts information provided in the various articles of the *Oxford Dictionary of National Biography* (online edition). My edition's orthography and definitional glosses rely chiefly on matter in the *Oxford English Dictionary* (online edition).

This is the first annotated edition of *A Mirror for Magistrates*, and I hope its notes and glosses will prove useful to scholars as they approach what has long been viewed as a difficult and forbidding literary work. Much of the *Mirror* handles political events of the fourteenth and fifteenth centuries, as filtered both through the beliefs and prejudices of the medieval and early modern chroniclers the authors use as their sources and also, in several places, through the poets' own projects of rewriting the past allusively to 'mirror' political events of their own time, the mid-Tudor period, a time still relatively unfamiliar to many students of early modern English literature. As a work of the mid-Tudor period, furthermore, *A Mirror for Magistrates* often couches its subject matter in language closer to Middle English than the early modern English used later in the sixteenth century. For this reason, the poems of the *Mirror* often resist easy comprehension even for students of the later Tudor literature. It is my hope that the glosses and annotations of this edition will help readers as they negotiate the poems and prose links of the collection and thereby spur further critical interest in Baldwin's still understudied two *Mirror* editions.[41]

Issues of space have constrained me to aim this edition's glosses chiefly at advanced students of early modern literature. Elucidations in the text are thus, for the most part, confined to difficult passages and the most unfamiliar words. Words that suggest their modern equivalents I have not glossed (e.g. 'valiantise', when the context points to its meaning 'valiancy'; and 'bewray', whose sound suggests its meaning of 'betray'), nor have I always defined early modern aphaeretic usages if their meaning seems sufficiently clear by sound and/or context (e.g. 'scape' for 'escape', 'prive' for 'deprive', 'gin' for 'begin'). Most archaic past tenses, such as 'brake' for 'broke' and 'sware' for 'swore', I have listed at the end of this volume but have not defined in the text itself. Finally, rather than elucidate in the text itself modern words that possessed in the early modern period meanings beyond those most familiar to readers today (words often termed 'false friends' for their immediate suggestion of an inapplicable modern connotation different from the intended early modern one), I have instead created a single glossary of such terms, which is located at the end of the book. Readers should remind themselves of the various early modern meanings of the terms defined in the Glossary, in addition to the words' familiar modern connotations, before approaching the content of the *Mirror*.

Notes

1. On the admiration for and influence of the *Mirror* in the early modern period, see W. F. Trench, *'A Mirror for Magistrates': Its Origin and Influence* (Edinburgh, 1898), 71–137; Willard Farnham, 'The Progeny of *A Mirror for Magistrates*', *Modern Philology* 29.4 (1932): 395–410; and Homer Nearing, *English Historical Poetry, 1599–1641* (Philadelphia: University of Pennsylvania Press, 1945). See also the headnotes offered before each *Mirror* tragedy's explanatory notes, which are placed at the end of the book.

2. The evidence for the Marian government's installation of Wayland in Whitchurch's shop is presented in Peter Blayney, *The Stationers' Company and the Printers of London, 1501–1557*, 2 vols. (Cambridge University Press, 2013), 2:756–65; and Scott Lucas, '"An Auncient Zelous Gospeller [...] Desirous to Do Anything to Common Good": Edward Whitchurch and the Reformist Cause in Marian and Elizabethan England', *Reformation* 21.1 (2016): 50–2. Parliament returned England to the Catholic faith on 1 January 1555.

3. See 'Baldwin's Dedication' below. While these seven men are usually referred to as the 'company of authors' or the poets of the *Mirror*, it should be noted that Baldwin never refers to the group by either of those two names. While he indeed credits the members of the company with producing matter for the *Mirror* poems, it is possible that some of these men supplied only historical information about the subjects of the collection's tragedies and not the actual verse in which that information was displayed. The language of the prose passages preceding Tragedies 7 and 14 in particular may suggest that some of the company contributed only ideas and 'notes' to Baldwin, matter which Baldwin himself then put into verse (see Prose 7 and Prose 14). That such an arrangement existed could help to make sense of Baldwin's suggestion in the dedicatory epistle of the 1563 *Mirror* that the bulk of the poetry in the 1559 *Mirror* was of his own creation ('Baldwin's Dedication').

4. For the conception and creation of *A Memorial of Such Princes*, see Prose 1 and John Wayland's printer's note in Appendix 1. The approximate date of the contributors' initial meeting in 1554 is indicated by the participation in this London-based project of Sir Thomas Chaloner, a resident of the north during Mary's reign. According to his own account book, Chaloner left his Yorkshire residence for London on 16 April 1554, a journey that took him a minimum of four days to complete. He was once more at his Yorkshire residence on 25 May and would not return to London until August (see British Library, Lansdowne MS 824, fo. 50r).

5. Chaloner left Yorkshire in 1554 for his second visit to London on 17 August and was back on his Yorkshire lands by 13 September (British Library, Lansdowne MS 824, fos. 51v, 54r).

6. For the suppression of the *Memorial* and the politically allusive matter that may have sparked Gardiner's decision to prohibit it, see Lucas, *'A Mirror for Magistrates'*, 20–3, 49–201. For general studies of the often controversial political content of the *Memorial* and 1559 *Mirror*, see Andrew Hadfield,

Literature, Politics and National Identity (Cambridge University Press, 1994), 91–107; Lucas, '*A Mirror for Magistrates*'; and Lucas, '"Let none such office take"'.

7. For a fuller discussion of the Marian origins of Baldwin's *Mirror*, see Lucas, '*A Mirror for Magistrates*', 18–23, 237–44.

8. On the politically controversial content of Ferrers's Tragedy 28, 'Gloucester', see Lucas, '*A Mirror for Magistrates*', 90–105.

9. Higgins drew all of his British examples from Geoffrey of Monmouth's fabulous account of Britain's supposed earliest rulers *Historia Regum Britanniae* (*c.* 1136).

10. For some of these questions, see Lily B. Campbell, 'Humphrey Duke of Gloucester and Elianor Cobham his Wife in the *Mirror for Magistrates*', *Huntington Library Bulletin* 5 (1934): 119–55; and Cathy Shrank, '"Hoysted high vpon the rolling wheele": Elianor Cobham's *Lament*', *A Mirror for Magistrates' in Context: Literature, History, and Politics in Early Modern England*, ed. Harriet Archer and Andrew Hadfield (Cambridge University Press, 2016), 109–25.

11. For detailed treatments of Baldwin's biography, see Lucas, '*A Mirror for Magistrates*', 36–41, and Scott Lucas, 'The Birth and Later Career of the Author William Baldwin (d. 1563)', *Huntington Library Quarterly* 79.1 (2016): 149–62.

12. Except where noted, this account of Ferrers's life draws on H. R. Woudhuysen, 'Ferrers, George (*c.* 1510–1579)', *Oxford Dictionary of National Biography*, 7 December 2017, http://www.oxforddnb.com/view/10.1093/ref:odnb/978019 8614128.001.0001/odnb-9780198614128-e-9360; and Lucas, '*A Mirror for Magistrates*', 41–6 (though the latter biography's claims that Ferrers attended Cambridge University and received a university degree are mistaken).

13. John Leland, '*Ad Georgium Ferrarium*', in *Principum, ac Illustrium Aliquot et Eruditorum in Anglia Virorum* (London, 1589; *STC* 15447), 99. Just how Ferrers came to Cromwell's attention is unknown, though it is perhaps significant that his half-brother Loye Ferrers was successively sub-prior and prior of St Albans monastery in the 1520s, the very period in which Cromwell's master Thomas Cardinal Wolsey held that monastery's office of abbot (NA PROB 11/32/269; Oxford University, Jesus College Library, MS 77, fo. 313r; C. W. Boase, ed., *Register of the University of Oxford*, 2 vols. (Oxford, 1885), 1:102; William Dugdale, *Monasticon Anglicanum*, 6 vols. (London, 1846), 3:327).

14. *The Boke of Magna Carta*, trans. and ed. George Ferrers (London, 1534; *STC* 9272).

15. Susan Brigden, ed., 'The Letters of Richard Scudamore to Sir Philip Hoby, September 1549–March 1555', *Camden Miscellany 30*, Camden Society, 4th series, 39 (London: Royal Historical Society, 1990), 125.

16. For Chaloner's biography, this section draws on Clarence Miller's introduction to Sir Thomas Chaloner, *The Praise of Folie*, ed. Clarence Miller (Oxford University Press, 1965), xxix–xlix; 'Chaloner, Thomas (1521–65)', *The History of Parliament: The House of Commons, 1509–1558*, 3 vols., ed. S. T. Bindoff (London: Secker & Warburg, 1982), 1:611–12; and John Baker, *Men of Court*,

1440–1550: A Prosopography of the Inns of Court and Chancery, 2 vols. (London: Selden Society, 2012), 1:451–2.

17. See Scott C. Lucas, 'Henry Lord Stafford, "The Two Rogers", and the Creation of _A Mirror for Magistrates, 1554–1563_', _Review of English Studies_ 66 (2015): 843–58.

18. For Stafford's life, see C. S. L. Davies, 'Stafford, Henry, tenth Baron Stafford (1501–1563), nobleman', _Oxford Dictionary of National Biography_, 7 December 2017, http://www.oxforddnb.com/view/10.1093/ref:odnb/9780198614128.001 .0001/odnb-9780198614128-e-26205; Lucas, 'Henry Lord Stafford'.

19. While some scholars have challenged Skelton's authorship of this poem, A. S. G. Edwards finds no compelling grounds for overturning the early modern belief that Skelton was its creator. See his 'John Skelton and "A Lamentable of Kyng Edward IIII"', _Notes & Queries_ 61.2 (2014): 203–4.

20. The best study of Churchyard's life and writings is Matthew Woodcock, _Thomas Churchyard: Pen, Sword, and Ego_ (Oxford University Press, 2016).

21. Mike Pincombe, 'William Baldwin, Humphrey Cavell, and the Authorship of The Tragedy of the Blacksmith in the 1563 _Mirror for Magistrates_', _Notes & Queries_ 56.4 (2009): 515–21.

22. For Cavell, see 'Cavell, Humphrey (by 1525–68)', in Bindoff, ed., _History of Parliament_, 1:596–7; Baker, _Men of Court_, 1:445.

23. Paul Bacquet, _Un Contemporain d'Elisabeth I: Thomas Sackville, L'Homme et L'Oeuvre_ (Geneva: Droz, 1966), 151–7.

24. Lucas, 'Birth and Later Career', 153. For Sackville, see Bacquet, _Contemporain_; and Rivkah Zim, 'Sackville, Thomas, first Baron Buckhurst and first earl of Dorset (_c._ 1536–1608), poet and administrator', _Oxford Dictionary of National Biography_, 7 December 2017, http://www.oxforddnb.com/view/10.1093/ ref:odnb/9780198614128.001.0001/odnb-9780198614128-e-24450

25. For Dolman, see Lily B. Campbell, 'John Dolman', _ELH_ 4.3 (1937): 192–200.

26. Lily B. Campbell, ed., _The Mirror for Magistrates: Edited from the Original Texts in the Huntington Library_ (Cambridge University Press, 1938), 45; John Thompson, _The Founding of English Metre_ (New York: Columbia University Press, 1961), 56–61.

27. There exists no fully reliable biography of Francis Seager. For Seager's works published during his lifetime, see _STC_ 2728, 5058, and 22134.5–5. Seager's will, which was probated on 24 February 1565, is in London Metropolitan Archives DL/C/B/005/MS09172/006A, number 36.

28. Edward Arber, ed., _A Transcript of the Registers of the Company of Stationers of London, 1554–1640 AD_, 5 vols. (London, 1875), 1:69; 'The Common Paper: Subscriptions to the Oath, 1417–1613', _Scriveners' Company Common Paper 1357–1628 With a Continuation to 1678_, ed. Francis W Steer (London: London Record Society, 1968), 20–49. _British History Online_, 22 May 2017, http:// www.british-history.ac.uk/london-record-soc/vol4/pp20–49

29. Anthony R. J. S. Adolph, 'Segar, Sir William (_c._ 1554–1633), herald', _Oxford Dictionary of National Biography_, 7 December 2017, http://

www.oxforddnb.com/view/10.1093/ref:odnb/9780198614128.001.0001/
odnb-9780198614128-e-25033

30. See Lucas, '*A Mirror for Magistrates*', 4–9. For an overview of the first eighty
years of twentieth-century *Mirror* criticism, see Jerry Leith Mills, 'Recent
Studies in *A Mirror for Magistrates*', *English Literary Renaissance* 9.2 (1979):
343–52.

31. See, among others, Lucas, '*A Mirror for Magistrates*', 8–12; and Jessica Winston,
*Lawyers at Play: Literature, Law, and Politics at the Early Modern Inns of Court,
1558–1581* (Oxford University Press, 2016), 127–48.

32. This point is particularly emphasized by Jennifer Richards in 'Transforming
A Mirror for Magistrates', *Renaissance Transformations*, ed. Margaret Healy and
Thomas Healy (Edinburgh University Press, 2009), 48–63.

33. Sir Philip Sidney, *An Apologie for Poetrie* (London, 1595; *STC* 22534), sig. I4r–v.
Only the poetry of Chaucer, Henry Howard, earl of Surrey, Edmund Spenser,
and the authors of *Gorboduc* (Thomas Sackville and Thomas Norton) receives
similar praise in his text.

34. Thompson, *Founding*, 37. The most influential and perhaps harshest
condemnation of the verse of the *Mirror* is that of C. S. Lewis in *English
Literature in the Sixteenth Century, Excluding Drama* (Oxford University Press,
1954), 240–4, 467.

35. Martin Duffell, *A New History of English Metre* (London: Legenda, 2008),
102–4.

36. Ibid., 122–5. For an analysis of the prosody of several *Mirror* tragedies, see
Thompson, *Founding*, 37–61.

37. See the Cambridge University, Trinity College Library, copy Capell R.13 of *A
Myrrour for Magistrates* (London, 1563; *STC* 1248), sigs. Bb7v–8r.

38. It is likely that in 1554 the experienced printer Baldwin oversaw the production
of the *Memorial* in the print shop in which he was employed. By contrast, the
relatively sloppy production of the 1559 *Mirror*, which occasioned a number of
notable errors in both the text and the foliation, suggests that Baldwin simply
gave Marshe an amended copy of the printed *Memorial of Such Princes* and
allowed Marshe's own compositors to set the type (one indication that Marshe's
men worked in 1559 from the printed *Memorial* is the table of contents, which
fits not the *Mirror* but the suppressed *Memorial* (see Appendix 2)). That the
1563 *Mirror* went to press with its 'Second Part' only about half revised almost
certainly suggests that Baldwin had passed away before the second edition was
printed. He thus could have had no hand in its production in Marshe's shop.

39. Sherri Geller, 'What History Really Teaches: Historical Pyrrhonism in William
Baldwin's *A Mirror for Magistrates*', *Opening the Borders: Inclusivity in Early
Modern Studies: Essays in Honor of James V. Mirollo* (Newark: University of
Delaware Press, 1999), 150. See also Geller, 'Editing Under the Influence of
the Standard Textual Hierarchy: Misrepresenting *A Mirror for Magistrates* in
the Nineteenth- and Twentieth-Century Editions', *Textual Cultures* 2.1 (2007):
43–77; Winston, *Lawyers at Play*, 133–4; Archer and Hadfield, 'Introduction',
'*A Mirror for Magistrates' in Context*, 4.

40. See, for instance, John Foxe, *Actes and Monuments* (London, 1563; *STC* 11222), 928; John Calvin, *The Institution of Christian Religion* (London, 1561; *STC* 4415), sig. A2r–v.

41. While much work remains to be performed in the study of Baldwin's *Mirror* and its influence on early modern culture, book-length engagements with the text already undertaken include Paul Budra, *'A Mirror for Magistrates' and the Shape of De Casibus Tragedy* (University of Toronto Press, 2000); Lucas, *'A Mirror for Magistrates'*; Archer and Hadfield, eds., *'A Mirror for Magistrates' in Context*; and Harriet Archer, *Unperfect Histories: 'A Mirror for Magistrates', 1559–1610* (Oxford University Press, 2017). Two other valuable long-form studies are Mike Pincombe's *'A Mirror for Magistrates, 1559'*, and *'A Mirror for Magistrates, 1563'*, in the online database The Origins of Early Modern Literature: Recovering Mid-Tudor Writing for a Modern Readership, ed. Cathy Shrank et al., www.hrionline.ac.uk/origins/frame.html.

❧ A MIRROR FOR MAGISTRATES.

Wherein may be seen by
example of other with how grievous plagues vices are punished, and
how frail and unstable worldly
prosperity is found, even of
those whom Fortune see-
meth most highly to favour.

*

Foelix quem faciunt aliena pericula cautum

Anno 1559

Londini,

In aedibus Thomae Marshe.

10. ***Foelix quem faciunt aliena pericula cautum***: 'Happy is he who is made wary by the dangers of others', a phrase often ascribed in the medieval and early modern periods to the Roman poet Horace (d. 8 BC).   **13–14. *Londini*, In aedibus Thomae Marshe**: London, In the house of Thomas Marshe.

[1] *1563*: ¶ *A* [9] *1563*: ❧ [11] *1563*: Anno. 1563 [13–14] *1563*: ¶ Imprinted at London in   Fleet Street near to Saint Dunstan's Church by Thomas Marshe

I

[Baldwin's Dedication]

Love and Live.

᠅ To the nobility and all other in office,
God grant wisdom and all things needful
for the preservation
of their estates.
Amen.

Plato, among many other of his notable sentences concerning the government of a commonweal, hath this: 'Well is that realm governed, in which the ambitious desire not to bear office'.⁴² Whereby you may perceive, right honourable, what offices are where they be duly executed, not gain-
5 ful spoils for the greedy to hunt for but painful toils for the heedy to be charged with. You may perceive also by this sentence that there is nothing more necessary in a commonweal than that officers be diligent and trusty in their charges. And sure in whatsoever realm such provision is made that officers be forced to do their duties, there is as hard a matter to get an of-
10 ficer as it is in other places to shift off and put by those that with flattery, bribes, and other shifts sue and press for offices. For the ambitious (that is to say, prowlers for power or gain) seek not for offices to help other, for which cause offices are ordained, but with the undoing of other to prank up themselves. And therefore bar them once of this bait and force them to
15 do their duties, and they will give more to be rid fro their charges than they did at the first to buy them, for they seek only their commodity and ease.

And, therefore, where the ambitious seek no office, there, no doubt, offices are duly ministered, and where offices are duly ministered, it cannot be chosen but the people are good, whereof must needs follow a good

Heading . **Love and Live**: William Baldwin's personal motto.   **12. prowlers**: persons who seek gain by dishonourable means.   **13–14. prank up**: glorify (lit. decorate).

[Heading] *1563*: ¶ TO

2

20 commonweal, for if the officers be good, the people cannot be ill. Thus, the goodness or badness of any realm lieth in the goodness or badness of the rulers. And therefore not without great cause do the holy apostles so earnestly charge us to pray for the magistrates, for indeed the wealth and quiet of every commonweal, the disorder also and miseries of the same,

25 come specially through them.[43]

I need not go either to the Romans or Greeks for proof hereof, neither yet to the Jews or other nations, whose commonweals have alway flourished while their officers were good and decayed and ran to ruin when naughty men had the regiment. Our own country stories, if we read and

30 mark them, will show us examples enow: would God we had not seen mo than enow! I purpose not to stand here upon the particulars, because they be in part set forth in the tragedies, yet by the way this I note, wishing all other to do the like, namely, that as good governors have never lacked their

35 deserved renown, so have not the bad escaped infamy, besides such plagues as are horrible to hear of.

For God, the ordainer of offices, although he suffer them for punishment of the people to be often occupied of such, as are rather spoilers and Judases than toilers or justices (whom the scripture therefore calleth hypocrites), yet suffereth he them not to scape unpunished, because they

40 dishonour him, for it is God's own office, yea, his chief office, which they bear and abuse.[44] For as justice is the chief virtue, so is the ministration thereof the chiefest office, and therefore hath God established it with the chiefest name, honouring and calling kings and all officers under them by his own name, gods. Ye be all gods, as many as have in your charge any

45 ministration of justice. What a foul shame were it for any now to take upon them the name and office of God and in their doings to show themselves devils. God cannot of justice but plague such shameless presumption and hypocrisy, and that with shameful death, diseases, or infamy.[45]

How he hath plagued evil rulers from time to time in other nations, you

50 may see gathered in Bochas's book intituled *The Fall of Princes*, translated into English by Lydgate.[46] How he hath dealt with some of our countrymen your ancestors for sundry vices not yet left, this book named *A*

---

30. enow: enough.   **50. Bochas's book**: Giovanni Boccaccio's *De Casibus Virorum Illustrium*, as metrically paraphrased and translated by John Lydgate under the title *The Fall of Princes*.

[26] *1563*: for the proof

Mirror for Magistrates can show, which therefore I humbly offer unto your honours, beseeching you to accept it favourably. For here as in a looking
55 glass, you shall see (if any vice be in you) how the like hath been punished in other heretofore, whereby admonished, I trust it will be a good occasion to move you to the sooner amendment. This is the chiefest end why it is set forth, which God grant it may attain.

The work was begun and part of it printed four year ago but hindered
60 by the lord chancellor that then was; nevertheless, through the means of my Lord Stafford, lately perused and licenced.[47] When I first took it in hand, I had the help of many granted, and offered of some, but of few performed, scarce of any, so that where I intended to have continued it to Queen Mary's time I have been fain to end it much sooner, yet so that it
65 may stand for a pattern till the rest be ready, which with God's grace (if I may have any help) shall be shortly.[48]

In the meanwhile, my lords and gods (for so I may call you), I most humbly beseech you favourably to accept this rude mirror and diligently to read and consider it. And although you shall find in it that some have
70 for their virtue been envied and murdered, yet cease not you to be virtuous but do your offices to the uttermost. Punish sin boldly, both in yourselves and other, so shall God (whose lieutenants you are) either so maintain you that no malice shall prevail or, if it do, it shall be for your good and to your eternal glory both here and in heaven, which I beseech God you may covet
75 and attain. Amen.

Yours most humble,
William Baldwin

In the 1563 edition, Baldwin replaced the words of the penultimate paragraph
(as presented above) of the 1559 dedication with these lines:
80 The work was begun and part of it printed in Queen Mary's time, but hindered by the lord chancellor that then was. Nevertheless, through the means of my Lord Stafford, the first part was licensed and imprinted the first year of the reign of this our most noble and virtuous queen and dedicate

---

60. **lord chancellor**: Stephen Gardiner (d. 1555).   61. **Lord Stafford**: Henry Stafford (d. 1563), tenth Baron Stafford.   83. **first ... queen**: the first regnal year of Queen Elizabeth I (17 November 1558–16 November 1559).

[59–66] *1563: see the penultimate paragraph of the 1563 dedication, printed in this edition above at the end of the 1559 dedication text*   [68] *1563:*   beseech your honours favourably   [71] *1563:* uttermost: suppress sin   [72] *1563:* (whose officers you are)   [74] *1563:* may both covet

then to your honours with this preface. Since which time, although I have
85 been called to another trade of life, yet my good Lord Stafford hath not
ceased to call upon me to publish so much as I had gotten at other men's
hands, so that through his lordship's earnest means I have now also set forth
another part containing as little of mine own as the first part doth of other
men's, which, in the name of all the authors, I humbly dedicate unto your
90 honours, instantly wishing that it may so like and delight your minds that
your cheerful receiving thereof may encourage worthy wits into enterprise
and perform the rest.[49] Which, as soon as I may procure, I intend through
God's leave and your favourable allowance to publish with all expedition.

90. **instantly**: fervently.

[Prose 1]

❡ A brief Memorial

of sundry unfortunate Englishmen

William Baldwin
to the Reader

When the printer had purposed with himself to print Lydgate's book of
the *Fall of Princes* and had made privy thereto many both honourable and
worshipful, he was counselled by divers of them to procure to have the story
continued from whereas Bochas left unto this present time, chiefly of such as
5 Fortune had dallied with here in this island, which might be as a mirror for
all men as well noble as others, to show the slippery deceits of the wavering
lady and the due reward of all kind of vices. Which advice liked him so well
that he required me to take pains therein. But because it was a matter passing
my wit and skill and more thankless than gainful to meddle in, I refused
10 utterly to undertake it, except I might have the help of such as in wit were
apt, in learning allowed, and in judgement and estimation able to wield and
furnish so weighty an enterprise, thinking even so to shift my hands.

But he, earnest and diligent in his affairs, procured Atlas to set under
his shoulder, for, shortly after, divers learned men whose many gifts need
15 few praises consented to take upon them part of the travail. And when
certain of them to the number of seven were through a general assent at
an appointed time and place gathered together to devise thereupon, I resorted unto them, bearing with me the book of Bochas, translated by Dan
Lydgate, for the better observation of his order, which, although we liked
20 well, yet would it not comelily serve, seeing that both Bochas and Lydgate
were dead, neither were there any alive that meddled with like argument,
to whom the unfortunate might make their moan.

To make therefore a state meet for the matter, they all agreed that I
should usurp Bochas's room and the wretched princes complain unto me,
25 and took upon themselves every man for his part to be sundry personages

---

1. **the printer**: John Wayland (d. *c.* 1571). 1–2. **Lydgate's book of the *Fall of Princes*:** John Lydgate's *Fall of Princes*
(*c.* 1431–9). 4. **Bochas**: Giovanni Boccaccio (d. 1375), author of the Latin prose work that Lydgate paraphrased,
translated, and put into metre as *The Fall of Princes*. 12. **shift my hands**: evade fulfilment of my charge. 13–14:
procured Atlas to set under his shoulder: i.e., he induced me to take on this weighty task. 18. **Dan**: an honorific
title. 19. **order**: arrangement; practice. 20. **comelily**: properly. 24. **room**: role.

and in their behalves to bewail unto me their grievous chances, heavy destinies, and woeful misfortunes.

30 This done, we opened such books of chronicles as we had there present, and Master Ferrers, after he had found where Bochas left, which was about the end of King Edward III's reign, to begin the matter, said thus:[50]

'I marvel what Bochas meaneth to forget among his miserable princes such as were of our nation, whose number is as great as their adventures wonderful. For to let pass all both Britons, Danes, and Saxons and to come to the last conquest, what a sort are they and some even in his own time?
35 As, for example, King Richard I, slain with a quarrel in his chief prosperity, also King John his brother, as some say, poisoned – are not their histories rueful and of rare example?[51] But as it should appear, he being an Italian, minded most the Roman and Italic story, or else perhaps he wanted our country chronicles. It were therefore a goodly and a notable matter to
40 search and discourse our whole story from the first beginning of the inhabiting of the isle.

'But seeing the printer's mind is to have us follow where Lydgate left, we will leave that great labour to other that may intend it and, as blind Bayard is alway boldest, I will begin at the time of Richard II, a time as
45 unfortunate as the ruler therein.[52] And forasmuch, friend Baldwin, as it shall be your charge to note and pen orderly the whole process, I will so far as my memory and judgement serveth, somewhat further you in the truth of the story.[53] And therefore, omitting the ruffle made by Jack Straw and his meiny, and the murder of many notable men which thereby happened
50 (for Jack, as ye know, was but a poor prince),[54] I will begin with a notable example which within a while after ensued. And although he be no great prince, yet sithens he had a princely office, I will take upon me the miserable person of Sir Robert Tresilian, chief justice of England, and of other which suffered with him, thereby to warn all of his authority and profes-
55 sion to take heed of wrong judgements, misconstruing of laws, or wresting the same to serve the prince's turns, which rightfully brought them to a miserable end, which they may justly lament in the manner ensuing.'

---

29. Master Ferrers: George Ferrers (d. 1579).   **33–4. For … time**: 'For passing over all of the fallen Britons, Danes and Saxons in English history in order to consider only those who have suffered since the last conquest [the Norman invasion], how numerous they are, and some of them lived and died even in Boccaccio's own time!'   **35. quarrel**: arrow.   **43–4. blind Bayard**: the impetuous bay horse ('bayard') of the proverbial phrase 'as bold as blind Bayard', which was applied to those inclined to act without considering the consequences.   **48. ruffle**: commotion; **Jack Straw**: one of the leaders of the 1381 Peasants' Revolt.   **49. meiny**: rabble.   **52. sithens**: since.

[Tragedy 1]

The Fall of Robert Tresilian, Chief Justice of England, and Other his Fellows, for Misconstruing the Laws and Expounding Them to Serve the Prince's Affections

In the rueful register of mischief and mishap,
Baldwin we beseech thee with our names to begin,
Whom unfriendly Fortune did train unto a trap,
When we thought our state most stable to have been,
So lightly leese they all which all do ween to win.   [5]
Learn by us, ye lawyers and judges of the land,
Uncorrupt and upright in doom alway to stand.

And print it for a precedent to remain forever,
Enrol and record it in tables made of brass,
Engrave it in marble that may be razed never, [55]   [10]
Where judges and justicers may see as in a glass
What fee is for falsehood and what our wages was
Who, for our prince's pleasure, corrupt with meed and awe,
Wittingly and wretchedly did wrest the sense of law.[56]

A change more new or strange seldom hath be seen,   [15]
Than from the bench above to come down to the bar;
Was never state so turned in no time as I ween,
As they to become clients that counsellors erst were.
But such is Fortune's play, which featly can prefer
The judge that sat above full low beneath to stand   [20]
At the bar a prisoner holding up his hand.

---

3. **train**: lure. **5. leese**: lose. **11. justicers**: high-court judges. **13. meed**: corrupt gains; **awe**: submissive reverence (for King Richard). **16. bar**: the wooden rail before the judicial bench at which prisoners stood during arraignment, trial, or sentencing. **19. featly can prefer**: neatly can promote (used ironically).

[21] *1563*: bar as prisoner

Which in others' cause could stoutly speak and plead,
Both in court and country, careless of the trial,
Stand mute like mummers without advice or rede,
Unable to utter a true plea of denial,⁵⁷ [25]
Which have seen the day when that for half a rial
We could by very art have made the black seem white
And matters of most wrong to have appeared most right.

Behold me unfortunate foreman of this flock,
Tresilian sometime chief justice of this land, [30]
By descent a gentleman; no stain was in my stock.
Lockton, Holt, and Bealknap, with other of my band⁵⁸
Which the law and justice had wholly in our hand,
Under the second Richard, a prince of great estate,
To whom froward fortune gave a foul checkmate. [35]

In the common laws our skill was so profound,
Our credit and authority such and so esteemed,
That whatso we concluded was taken for a ground,
Allowed was for law whatso to us best seemed.
Life, death, lands, goods, and all by us was deemed, [40]
Whereby with easy pain so great gain we did get,
That everything was fish that came unto our net.

At sessions and at sizes we bare the stroke and sway,
In patents and commissions of quorum alway chief,
So that to whether side soever we did weigh, [45]
Were it right or wrong it passed without reprief:
We let hang the true man somewhiles to save a thief.
Of gold and silver our hands were never empty;
Offices, farms, and fees fell to us in great plenty.

---

22. Which: Those who. **24. mummers**: persons unable to speak. **26. rial**: coin worth fifteen shillings. **29. foreman**: leader (with an echo of the chief man of a jury). **42. everything ... net**: everything that came to us was for our profit (a proverbial saying). **43. At ... sway**: At trials and at assizes we held chief authority and power (**assizes**: legal sessions held periodically in English counties by judges of the higher courts). **44. In ... chief**: In the letters patent and official documents designating the quorum, our names took the most important places (**quorum**: a group of eminent judges, the presence of one or more of whose members on shire peace commissions was necessary to make rulings valid). **46. reprief**: reproof. **49. farms**: annual payments; **fees**: rewards; bribes.

[26] *1563*: when for half

But what thing may suffice unto the greedy man?   [50]
The more he hath in hold, the more he doth desire.
Happy and twice happy is he that wisely can
Content himself with that which reason doth require
And moileth for no more than for his needful hire,
But greediness of mind doth never keep the size,   [55]
Which, though it have enough, yet doth it not suffice.

For like as dropsy patients drink and still be dry,
Whose unstaunched thirst no liquor can allay,
And drink they never so much, yet still for more they cry,
So covetous catchers toil both night and day,   [60]
Greedy and ever needy, prowling for their prey.
Oh endless thirst of gold, corruptor of all laws,
What mischief is on mould whereof thou are not cause?

Thou madest us forget the faith of our profession,
When serjeants we were sworn to serve the common law,   [65]
Which was that in no point we should make digression
From approved principles in sentence nor in saw.⁵⁹
But we unhappy wretches without all dread and awe
Of the judge eternal, for world's vain promotion,
More to man than God did bear our whole devotion.   [70]

The laws we interpreted and statutes of the land
Not truly by the text but nully by a gloze,
And words that were most plain when they by us were scanned
We turned by construction like a Welshman's hose,⁶⁰
Whereby many one both life and land did lose,   [75]
Yet this we made a mean to mount aloft on mules:
To serve kings in all points, men must somewhile break rules.⁶¹

Thus climbing and contending alway to the top,
From high unto higher and then to be most high,
The honeydew of Fortune so fast on us did drop   [80]
That of King Richard's counsel we came to be full nigh,

---

54. **moileth**: strives.   55. **size**: proper limits.   58. **liquor**: liquid.   63. **mould**: earth.   67. **sentence nor in saw**: neither in judicial rulings nor decrees.   72. **nully**: incorrectly, in a legally invalid manner (evidently a nonce coined on the model of 'null', meaning without legal force); **gloze**: false exposition.   80. **honeydew**: manna.

To creep into whose favour we were full fine and sly,
Alway to his profit, where any word might sound,
That way (all were it wrong) the sense we did expound.

So working law like wax, the subject was not sure   [85]
Of life, land, nor goods, but at the prince's will,
Which caused his kingdom the shorter time to dure.
For claiming power absolute both to save and spill,
The prince thereby presumed his people for to pill,
And set his lusts for law, and will had reason's place: [90]
No more but hang and draw, there was no better grace.

The king thus transcending the limits of his law,
Not reigning but raging by youthful insolence,
Wise and worthy persons did fro the court withdraw:
There was no grace ne place for ancient prudence.   [95]
Presumption and pride, with excess of expense,
Possessed the palace, and pillage the country,
Thus all went to wrack, unlike of remedy.

The barony of England, not bearing this abuse,
Conspiring with the commons assembled by assent,   [100]
And seeing neither reason nor treaty could induce
The king in anything his rigour to relent,
Maugre all his might they called a parliament
Frank and free for all men without check to debate,
As well for weal public as for the prince's state.[62]   [105]

In which parliament, much things was proponed
Concerning the regaly and rights of the crown,
By reason King Richard, which was to be moaned,
Full little regarding his honour and renown,
By sinister advice had turned all upside down.   [110]
For surety of whose state, them thought it did behove
His corrupt counsellors from him to remove.

---

89. pill: rob.   **100. conspiring with**: combining with in a joint purpose (not necessarily in a negative sense).   **101. treaty**: entreaty.   **106. proponed**: put forward.   **107. regaly**: kingship.

[103] *1563*: Maugre his might   [111] *1563*: whose estate

Among whom Robert Vere, called duke of Ireland,
With Michael de la Pole, of Suffolk new made earl,
Of York also the archbishop dispatched were out of hand,   [115]
With Brembre of London mayor, a full uncourteous churl.[63]
Some learned in the law in exile they did hurl,
But I, poor Tresilian, because I was the chief,
Was damned to the gallows most vilely as a thief.[64]

Lo the fine of falsehood, the stipend of corruption!   [120]
Fie on stinking lucre, of all unright the lure!
Ye judges and ye justicers let my most just punition
Teach you to shake off bribes and keep your hands pure.
Riches and promotion be vain things and unsure;
The favour of a prince is an untrusty stay,   [125]
But justice hath a fee that shall remain alway.

What glory can be greater before God or man
Than by the paths of equity in judgement to proceed,
So duly and so truly the laws always to scan
That right may take his place without reward or meed?   [130]
Set apart all flattery and vain worldly dread.
Take God before your eyes, the just judge supreme:
Remember well your reckoning at the day extreme.

Abandon all affray, be soothfast in your saws;
Be constant and careless of mortal men's displeasure.   [135]
With eyes shut and hands close you should pronounce the laws;
Esteem not worldly hire; think there is a treasure
More worth than gold or stone a thousand times in valure
Reposed for all such as righteousness ensue,
Whereof you cannot fail: the promise made is true.   [140]

If some in latter days had called unto mind
The fatal fall of us for wresting of the right,
The statutes of this land they should not have defined
So wilfully and wittingly against the sentence quite.

---

115. dispatched: dismissed.   **118. chief**: i.e. the worst among the corrupt justices.   **120. lo**: behold; **fine**: end; penalty.   **126. fee**: reward.   **128. equity**: fairness.   **133. day extreme**: judgement day.   **134. affray**: fear; **soothfast**: truthful, just.   **138. valure**: value.   **139. ensue**: follow.

But though they scaped pain, the fault was nothing light.   [145]
Let them that come hereafter both that and this compare
And, weighing well the end, they will I trust beware.

[Prose 2]

When Master Ferrers had finished this tragedy, which seemed not unfit for
the persons touched in the same,[65] another, which in the meantime had
stayed upon Sir Roger Mortimer, whose miserable end, as it should appear,
was somewhat before the others, said as followeth:

5   'Although it be not greatly appertinent to our purpose, yet, in my
judgement, I think it would do well to observe the times of men and,
as they be more ancient, so to place them. For I find that before these of
whom Master Ferrers here hath spoken, there were two Mortimers, the
one hanged in Edward III's time out of our date, another slain in Ireland
10   in Richard II's time, a year before the fall of these justices, whose history,
sith it is notable and the example fruitful, it were pity to overpass it.[66]
And, therefore, by your licence and agreement, I will take upon me the
personage of the last, who, full of wounds, miserably mangled, with a pale
countenance and grisly look, may make his moan to Baldwin as followeth':

2. another: Lord Henry Stafford.   **3. Sir Roger Mortimer**: Sir Roger Mortimer (d. 1398), fourth earl of March.   **9. one hanged**: Sir Roger Mortimer (d. 1330), first earl of March; **out of our date**: not within the historical period on which we agreed; **another**: the fourth earl of March.   **11. sith**: since.

[Tragedy 2]

How the Two Rogers Surnamed Mortimers for their Sundry Vices Ended their Lives Unfortunately

Among the riders of the rolling wheel
That lost their holds, Baldwin forget not me,
Whose fatal thread false Fortune needs would reel
Ere it were twisted by the sisters three.
All folk be frail, their blisses brittle be;   [5]
For proof whereof, although none other were,
Suffice may I, Sir Roger Mortimer.

Not he that was in Edward's days the Third,
Whom Fortune brought to boot and eft to bale,
With love of whom the king so much she stirred   [10]
That none but he was heard in any tale.⁶⁷
And whiles she smooth blew on this merry gale,
He was created earl of March, alas,
Whence envy sprang, which his destruction was.⁶⁸

For wealth breedeth wrath in such as wealth do want,   [15]
And pride with folly in such as it possess.
Among a thousand shall you find him scant
That can in wealth his lofty heart repress.
Which in this earl due proof did plain express,
For where he somewhat haughty was before,   [20]
His high degree hath made him now much more.

For now alone he ruleth as him lust,
Ne recketh for rede, save of King Edward's mother,

1. **the rolling wheel**: the wheel of Fortune.   3. **fatal thread**: the thread spun out by the mythological Fates that determines a person's life; **reel**: take up on a reel.   4. **Ere ... three**: Before it might be spun out into a (strong) cord by the three Fates.   9. **to boot and eft to bale**: to advantage and afterwards to harm.   23. **recketh**: concern himself.

Which forcèd envy foulder out the rust
That in men's hearts before did lie and smother. [25]
The peers, the people, as well the one as the other,
Against him made so heinous a complaint
That for a traitor he was taken and attaint.

Then all such faults as were forgot before
They scour afresh, and somewhat to them add, [30]
For cruel envy hath eloquence in store
When Fortune bids to worse things meanly bad.
Five heinous crimes against him soon were had:[69]
First, that he caused the king to yield the Scot,
To make a peace, towns that were from him got [35]

And therewithal the charter called Ragman;
That of the Scots he bribèd privy gain;[70]
That through his means Sir Edward of Carnarvan
In Berkeley Castle traitorously was slain;
That with his prince's mother he had lain; [40]
And, finally, with polling at his pleasure
Had robbed the king and commons of their treasure.[71]

For these things, lo, which erst were out of mind
He was condemned and hangèd at the last,
In whom Dame Fortune fully showed her kind: [45]
For whom she heaves she hurleth down as fast.
If men to come would learn by other past,
This cousin of mine might cause them set aside
High climbing, bribing, murd'ring, lust, and pride.

The final cause why I this process tell [50]
Is that I may be known from this other,
My like in name, unlike me though he fell,

---

24. foulder out: flash or thunder forth. **28. attaint**: condemned to death. **32. When ... bad**: When Fortune seeks to make worse things that are only moderately bad. **37. bribed**: obtained through taking bribes. **45. kind**: nature. **50. final cause**: ultimate reason; **process**: account, narrative.

[30] *1559, 1563*: The scour ('The' apparently an uncorrected error for 'They')

Which was, I think, my grandsire or his brother.[72]
To count my kin, Dame Philip was my mother,
Dear daughter and heir of doughty Lionel,   [55]
The second son of a king that did excel.

My father hight Sir Edmund Mortimer,
True earl of March, which I was after earl;[73]
By just descent, these two my parents were,
Of which the one of knighthood bare the ferle,[74]   [60]
Of womanhood the other was the pearl,
Through their desert so called of every wight,
Till death them took and left in me their right.

For why the attainder of my elder Roger
(Whose shameful death I told you but of late)   [65]
Was found to be unjust and passèd over
Against the law, by those that bare him hate,
For whereby law the lowest of free estate
Should personally be heard ere judgement pass,
They barred him this, wherethrough destroyed he was.[75]   [70]

Wherefore by doom of court in parliament,
When we had proved our cousin ordered thus,
The king, the lords, and commons of assent
His lawless death unlawful did discuss
And both to blood and good restorèd us: [75]
A precedent most worthy showed and left,
Lords' lives to save that lawless might be reft.

While Fortune thus did further me amain,
King Richard's grace the second of the name
(Whose dissolute life did soon abridge his reign)   [80]
Made me his mate in earnest and in game.
The lords themselves so well allowed the same
That, through my titles duly coming down,
I was made heir apparent to the crown.[76]

---

64. **For why the attainder**: Because the conviction for treason (which entailed Roger Mortimer's loss of title and the dispossession of his heirs). **66. passed over**: put into execution. **71. Wherefore**: For which reason. **73. and commons of assent**: with the agreement of the members of parliament's lower house. **74. His ... discuss**: They examined the illegalities surrounding his unlawful death. **75. And ... us**: And they restored our family both in blood and in possessions (as legally recognized descendants of and heirs to Roger the elder). **78. amain**: with full force.

[56] *1563*: king who did

Who then but I was everywhere esteemed? [85]
Well was the man that might with me acquaint.
Whom I allowed, as lords the people deemed.
To whatsoever folly had me bent,
To like it well, the people did assent.
To me as prince attended great and small, [90]
In hope a day would come to pay for all.

But seldom joy continueth trouble-void;
In greatest charge cares greatest do ensue.
The most possessed are ever most annoyed;
In largest seas sore tempests lightly brew. [95]
The freshest colours soonest fade the hue;
In thickest place is made the deepest wound.
True proof whereof myself too soon have found.

For whiles that Fortune lulled me in her lap
And gave me gifts mo than I did require, [100]
The subtle quean behind me set a trap,
Whereby to dash and lay all in the mire.
The Irishmen against me did conspire
My lands of Ulster fro me to have reft,
Which heritage my mother had me left.[77] [105]

And whiles I there, to set all things in stay
(Omit my toils and troubles thitherward),
Among mine own with my retinue lay,
The wilder men whom little I did regard
(And had therefore the reckless man's reward), [110]
When least I thought set on me in such number
That fro my corpse my life they rent asunder.

87. **allowed**: praised.   90–1. **To ... all**: people of high and low station alike attended on me as if I were a prince, in hope that one day they would be recompensed.   92. **trouble-void**: untroubled.   94. **The most possessed**: those who possess most.   95. **lightly**: easily.   101. **quean**: impudent woman (a term of insult).   105. **heritage**: inherited property.   106. **in stay**: in order.   109. **The wilder men**: The 'wild Irish', the Gaelic-speaking inhabitants of Ireland who lived outside of English control.

[99] *1563*: whiles fair Fortune   [100] *1563*: gifts more than

Nought might avail, my courage nor my force,
Nor strength of men which were, alas, too few;
The cruel folk assaulted so my horse　　　　　　　　　[115]
That all my helps in pieces they to hew.
Our blood distained the ground as drops of dew:
Nought might prevail to flee nor yet to yield,
For whom they take they murder in the field.[78]

They know no law of arms nor none will learn;　　　　[120]
They make not war (as other do) a play.
The lord, the boy, the galloglass, the kern:
Yield or not yield, whom so they take they slay.
They save no prisoners for ransom nor for pay;
Their chiefest boot they count their bodoh's head,　　[125]
Their end of war to see their en'my dead. [79]

Amongst these men – or rather savage beasts –
I lost my life, by cruel murder slain.
And therefore, Baldwin, note thou well my geasts
And warn all princes rashness to refrain.　　　　　　[130]
Bid them beware their en'mies when they feign
Nor yet presume unequally to strive:
Had I thus done, I had been man alive.

But I despised the naked Irishmen
And for they flew, I fearèd them the less:　　　　　　[135]
I thought one man enough to match with ten,
And through this careless unadvisedness
I was destroyed – and all my men, I guess –
At unawares assaulted by our foen
Which were in number forty to us one.[80]　　　　　　[140]

See here the stay of fortunate estate,
The vain assurance of this brittle life,

---

115. horse: mounted soldiers.　**121. play**: game.　**122. galloglass**: soldier in the retinue of an Irish chief; **kern**: lightly armed Irish soldier of lesser degree than a galloglass.　**125. bodoh's**: see explanatory note 79.　**130. geasts**: gests, notable actions.　**134. naked**: unarmoured.

[139] *1563*: unwares

For I, but young, proclaimèd prince of late,
Right fortunate in children and in wife,[81]
Lost all at once by stroke of bloody knife.   [145]
Whereby assured, let men themselves assure
That wealth and life are doubtful to endure.

[Prose 3]

After that this tragedy was ended, Master Ferrers said, 'Seeing it is best to place each person in his order, Baldwin take you the chronicles and mark them as they come, for there are many worthy to be noted, though not to be treated of. First, the Lord Morif, a Scottishman, who took his death's wound through a stroke lent him by the earl of Nottingham, whom he challenged at the tilt.[82] But to omit him, and also the fat prior of Tiptree, pressed to death with throng of people upon London Bridge at the Queen's entry,[83] I will come to the duke of Gloucester, the king's uncle, a man much minding the commonweal and yet at length miserably made away. In whose person, if ye will give ear, ye shall hear what I think meet to be said.'

[Tragedy 3]

How Sir Thomas of Woodstock, Duke of Gloucester, Uncle to King Richard the Second, was Unlawfully Murdered

Whose state is stablished in seeming most sure
And so far from danger of Fortune's blast,
As by the compass of man's conjecture
No brazen pillar may be fixed more fast,
Yet, wanting the stay of prudent forecast, [5]
When froward Fortune list for to frown
May in a moment turn upside down.

In proof whereof, oh Baldwin, take pain
To hearken awhile to Thomas of Woodstock,
Addressed in presence his fate to complain, [10]
In the forlorn hope of the English flock.
Extract by descent from the royal stock,
Son to King Edward third of that name
And second to none in glory and fame.

This noble father to maintain my state [15]
With Buckingham earldom did me endow.[84]
Both nature and Fortune to me were grate,
Denying nothing which they might allow.
Their sundry graces in me did so flow,
As beauty, strength, high favour, and fame; [20]
Who may of God more wish than the same?

Brothers we were to the number of seven,
I being sixth and youngest but one.

10. **Addressed ... complain:** Prepared and present to complain of his fate.   11. **In ... flock:** In the vanguard (or among the most woeful) of those Englishmen who have come to complain (**forlorn hope:** the men at the very front of a military attack, a term often used figuratively to denote woeful or suffering persons).   17. **grate:** agreeable, pleasing.

[18] *1563:* Denying me nothing

A more royal race was not under heaven
More stout or more stately of stomach and person,   [25]
Princes all peerless in each condition,
Namely Sir Edward called the Black Prince:
When had England the like before either since?[85]

But what of all this any man to assure,
In state uncareful of Fortune's variance?   [30]
Sith daily and hourly we see it in ure
That where most cause is of affiance
Even there is found most weak assurance.
Let none trust Fortune but follow reason,
For often we see in trust is treason.   [35]

This proverb in proof over-true I tried,
Finding high treason in place of high trust,
And most fault of faith where I most affied,
Being by them that should have been just
Traitorously entrapped ere I could mistrust.   [40]
Ah, wretched world, what it is to trust thee
Let them that will learn now hearken to me.

After King Edward the Third's decease,
Succeeded my nephew Richard to reign,
Who for his glory and honour's increase   [45]
With princely wages did me entertain,
Against the Frenchmen to be his chieftain.
So, passing the seas with royal puissance,
With God and St. George I invaded France.

Wasting the country with sword and with fire,   [50]
Overturning towns, high castles and towers,
Like Mars god of war inflamed with ire,
I forced the Frenchmen to abandon their bowers.
Wherever we matched, I won at all hours,
In such wise visiting both city and village   [55]
That alway my soldiers were laden with pillage.

---

25. stout: splendid; valiant; **stomach**: temperament.   **27. Namely**: Above all.   **31. sith**: since; **in ure**: in practice.   **32. affiance**: trust.   **36. I tried**: I ascertained through trial that this proverb was all too true.   **38. affied**: trusted.   **46. entertain**: retain, keep in service.

With honour and triumph was my return;
Was none more joyous than young King Richard
Who, minding more highly my state to adorn,
With Gloucester dukedom did me reward.[86]   [60]
And after in marriage I was preferred
To a daughter of Bohun, an earl honourable,
By whom I was of England high constable.[87]

Thus hoisted so high on Fortune's wheel
As one on a stage attending a play   [65]
Seeth not on which side the scaffold doth reel
Till timber and poles and all flee away,
So fared it by me, for day by day
As honour increased I looked still higher,
Not seeing the danger of my fond desire.   [70]

For when Fortune's flood ran with full stream,
I, being a duke descended of kings,
Constable of England, chief officer in the realm,
Abused with esperance in these vain things,
I went without feet and flew without wings,   [75]
Presuming so far upon my high state
That, dread set apart, my prince I would mate.[88]

For whereas all kings have counsel of their choice
To whom they refer the rule of their land,
With certain familiars in whom to rejoice,   [80]
For pleasure or profit, as the case shall stand,
I, not bearing this, would needs take in hand,
Maugre his will, those persons to disgrace
And such as I thought fit to appoint in their place.[89]

But as an old book saith, whoso will assay,[90]   [85]
About the cat's neck to hang on a bell
Had first need to cut the cat's claws away,
Lest if the cat be curst or not tamed well
She haply with her nails may claw him to the fell.

---

61. preferred: brought to marriage, advanced in status.   **65. stage**: raised platform; **attending**: watching.
66. scaffold: raised platform constructed out of poles and trestles.   **71. stream**: flow.   **74. esperance**: hopeful
expectation.   **77. mate**: overpower.   **88. curst**: vicious.   **89. haply**: possibly.   **89. fell**: the flesh beneath the skin.

For doing on the bell about the cat's neck, [90]
By being too busy I caught a sore check.

Read well the sentence of the rat of renown,
Which Piers the Plowman describes in his dream,
And whoso hath wit the sense to expound
Shall find that to bridle the prince of a realm [95]
Is even (as who saith) to strive with the stream.
Note this, all subjects, and construe it well,
And busy not your brain about the cat's bell.

But in that ye be lieges learn to obey,
Submitting your wills to your prince's laws.[91] [100]
It sitteth not a subject to have his own way;
Remember this byword of the cat's claws.
For princes, like lions, have long and large paws
That reach at random and, whom they once twitch,
They claw to the bone before the skin itch. [105]

But to my purpose: I being once bent
Towards the achieving of my attemptate,
Four bold barons were of mine assent
By oath and alliance fastly confederate.
First, Henry of Derby, an earl of estate, [110]
Richard of Arundel and Thomas of Warwick,
With Mowbray earl marshal, a man most warlike.

At Radcot bridge assembled our band,
The commons in clusters came to us that day
To daunt Robert Vere, then duke of Ireland, [115]
By whom King Richard was ruled alway.
We put him to flight and brake his array, [92]
Then, maugre the king, his leave, or assent,
By constable's power we called a parliament,[93]

Where not in robes but with bastards bright [120]
We came for to parle of the public weal,

---

91. busy: vigorously active; meddlesome in matters that are not one's concern.   **96. strive with the stream**: fight against the current.   **101. It sitteth not**: It is not proper.   **104. twitch**: pull at.   **109. fastly**: steadfastly.   **117. brake his array**: dispersed his military force.   **120. bastards**: swords.

Confirming our quarrel with main and with might,
With swords and no words we tried our appeal,
Instead of reason declaring our zeal.
And whom so we knew with the king in good grace   [125]
Plainly we deprived him of power and of place.⁹⁴

Some with short process were banished the land,
Some executed with capital pain,
Whereof whoso list the whole to understand
In the parliament roll it appeareth plain.⁹⁵   [130]
And, further, how stoutly we did the king strain
The rule of his realm wholly to resign
To the order of those whom we did assign.

But note the sequel of such presumption:
After we had these miracles wrought,   [135]
The king, inflamed with indignation
That to such bondage he should be brought,
Suppressing the ire of his inward thought
Studied nought else but how that he might
Be highly revenged of his high despite.   [140]

Aggrieved was also this latter offence
With former matter his ire to renew,
For once at Windsor I brought to his presence
The mayor of London with all his retinue
To ask a reckoning of the realm's revenue,⁹⁶   [145]
And the soldiers of Brest were by me made bold
To claim entertainment, the town being sold.⁹⁷

These griefs remembered, with all the remnant,
Of hate in his heart hoarded a treasure,
Yet openly in show made he no semblant   [150]
By word nor by deed to bear displeasure.
But lovedays dissembled do never endure,

---

122. **Confirming ... might**: adding force to our quarrel with physical strength and armed might.   131. **strain**: constrain.   138. **Suppressing**: hiding.   140. **despite**: insulting treatment.   141. **Aggrieved**: exacerbated.   147. **entertainment**: support.   148–9. **These ... treasure**: these remembered griefs, along with all the rest of his grievances, built up a store of hatred in his heart.   152. **lovedays**: days appointed to settle disputes.

And whoso trusteth a foe reconciled
Is for the most part always beguiled.

For as fire ill quenched will up at a start,   [155]
And sores not well salved do break out of new,
So hatred hidden in an ireful heart,
Where it hath had long season to brew,
Upon every occasion doth easily renew,
Not failing at last, if it be not let,   [160]
To pay large usury besides the due debt.[98]

Even so it fared by this friendship feigned,
Outwardly sound and inwardly rotten.
For when the king's favour in seeming was gained,
All old displeasures forgiven and forgotten,   [165]
Even then at a sudden the shaft was shotten
Which pierced my heart void of mistrust –
Alas that a prince should be so unjust!

For lying at Pleshey myself to repose,
By reason of sickness which held me full sore,   [170]
The king, espying me apart from those
With whom I confedered in band before,
Thought it not meet, to tract the time more
But, glad to take me at such advantage,
Came to salute me with friendly visage.   [175]

Who, having a band bound to his bent,
By colour of kindness to visit his eme
Took time to accomplish his cruel intent
And, in a small vessel down by the stream,
Conveyed me to Calais out of the realm   [180]
Where, without process or doom of my peers,
Not nature but murder abridged my years.[99]

This act was odious to God and to man,
Yet, rigour to cloak in habit of reason,

---

156. of new: anew.   **160–1. Not … debt**: If it (i.e. hatred hidden in an angry heart) is not checked, it will not fail to pay back those who stirred it with harm much greater than that of the original hurt.   **173. tract**: delay.   **177. eme**: uncle.   **184. Yet … reason**: Yet in order to make their cruelty to appear to be an act of reason (**habit**: garb).

By crafty compass devise they can   [185]
Articles nine of right heinous treason.
But doom after death is sure out of season,
For whoever saw so strange a precedent
As execution done before judgement?[100]

Thus hate harboured in depth of mind   [190]
By sought occasion burst out of new,
And cruelty abused the law of kind,
When that the nephew the uncle slew.
Alas, King Richard! sore mayest thou rue,
Which by this fact preparedest the way   [195]
Of thy hard destiny to hasten the day.

For blood asketh blood as guerdon due,
And vengeance for vengeance is just reward.
Oh righteous God, thy judgements are true!
For look what measure we other award,   [200]
The same for us again is prepared.
Take heed, ye princes, by examples past:
Blood will have blood, either first or last.[101]

185. **compass**: contrivance.

[Prose 4]

When Master Ferrers had ended this fruitful tragedy, because no man was
ready with another, I, having perused the story which came next, said,
'Because you shall not say, my masters, but that I will in somewhat do
my part, I will, under your correction, declare the tragedy of the Lord
5   Mowbray, the chief worker of the duke's destruction.[102] Who, to admonish
all counsellors to beware of flattering princes or falsely envying or accusing
their paregals, may lament his vices in manner following':

2. **story**: historical account.   7. **paregals**: peers.

[2] *1563*: with any other

How the Lord Mowbray, Promoted by King Richard the Second,
was by him Banished the Realm and Died miserably in Exile

Though sorrow and shame abash me to rehearse
My loathsome life and death of due deserved,
Yet that the pains thereof may other pierce
To leave the like, lest they be likely served,
Ah Baldwin, mark! I will show thee how I swerved: [5]
Dissembling, envy, and flattery, bane that be
Of all their hosts, have showed their power on me.

I blame not Fortune, though she did her part,
And true it is she can do little harm.
She guideth goods; she hamp'reth not the heart: [10]
A virtuous mind is safe from every charm.
Vice, only vice, with her stout strengthless arm
Doth cause the heart to evil to incline,
Which I, alas, do find too true by mine.

For where by birth I came of noble kind,   [15]
The Mowbrays' heir, a famous house and old,
Fortune, I thank her, was to me so kind
That of my prince I had what so I would,
Yet neither of us was much to other hold,
For I through flattery abused his wanton youth   [20]
And his fond trust augmented my untruth.

He made me first the earl of Nottingham
And marshal of the realm, in which estate¹⁰³

---

4. **likely**: similarly.   **12. stout strengthless**: powerful, though it possesses no physical strength.   **19. hold**: loyal, gracious.   **21. untruth**: dishonesty; lack of fidelity.

The peers and people jointly to me came,
With sore complaint against them that, of late   [25]
Made officers, had brought the king in hate
By making sale of justice, right, and law
And living nought without all dread or awe.[104]

I gave them aid these evils to redress
And went to London with an army strong,   [30]
And caused the king against his will oppress
By cruel death all such as led him wrong.
The lord chief justice suffered these among,
So did the steward, of his household head;
The chancellor scaped, for he aforehand fled.[105]   [35]

These wicked men thus from the king removed,
Who best us pleased succeeded in their place,
For which both king and commons much us loved,
But chiefly I with all stood high in grace.
The king ensued my rede in every case,   [40]
Whence self-love bred, for glory maketh proud,
And pride ay looketh alone to be allowed.[106]

Wherefore to th'end I might alone enjoy
The king's good will, I made his lust my law
And where of late I laboured to destroy   [45]
Such flattering folk as thereto stood in awe,
Now learned I among the rest to claw,
For pride is such, if it be kindly caught,
As stroyeth good and stirreth up every nought.

Pride pricketh men to flatter for the prey,   [50]
To oppress and poll for maintenance of the same,
To malice such as match uneaths it may,
And, to be brief, pride doth the heart inflame
To fire what mischief any fraud may frame

---

28. nought: wickedly.   **32. cruel**: painful.   **40. rede**: counsel.   **48. kindly caught**: thoroughly contracted (in the manner of a disease).   **49. nought**: wicked thing.   **50. prey**: spoils.   **52. To ... may**: [Pride may lead men to] harm those who are no match for (or rival to) them (**uneaths**: scarcely, hardly).   **54. To ... frame**: To inspire the heart to pursue the ill deeds to which fraud might direct it, whatsoever they might be.

And ever at length the evils by it wrought [55]
Confound the worker and bring him unto nought.

Behold in me due proof of every part,
For pride first forced me my prince to flatter
So much, that whatsoever pleased his heart,
Were it never so evil, I thought a lawful matter, [60]
Which caused the lords afresh against him clatter,
Because he had his holds beyond sea sold
And seen his soldiers of their wages polled.

Though all these ills were done by my assent,
Yet such was luck that each man deemed no; [65]
For see the duke of Gloucester for me sent
With other lords, whose hearts did bleed for woe
To see the realm so fast to ruin go.
In fault whereof, they said the two dukes were,
The one of York, the other of Lancaster.[107] [70]

On whose remove fro being about the king
We all agreed and sware a solemn oath,
And while the rest provided for this thing,
I, flatter I, to win the praise of troth,
Wretch that I was brake faith and promise both, [75]
For I bewrayed the king their whole intent,
For which unwares they all were tane and shent.[108]

Thus was the warder of the commonweal
The duke of Gloucester guiltless made away,
With other mo, more wretch I so to deal, [80]
Who through untruth their trust did ill betray,
Yet, by this means, obtained I my prey.

65. Yet ... no: Yet fortunately enough no man thought it to be so. **70. one of York**: Edmund of Langley (d. 1402), first duke of York; **other of Lancaster**: John of Gaunt (d. 1399), first duke of Lancaster. **74. flatter**: flatterer; **troth**: loyalty. **77. shent**: ruined. **80. With ... deal**: with other more, so much more was I a wretch in acting as I did.

[74] *1563*: I flatterer I

Of king and dukes I found for this such favour
As made me duke of Norfolk for my labour.

But see how pride and envy jointly run: [85]
Because my prince did more than me prefer
Sir Henry Bolingbroke, the eldest son
Of John of Gaunt, the duke of Lancaster,
Proud I, that would alone be blazing star,
Envied this earl for nought save that the shine   [90]
Of his deserts did glister more than mine.[109]

To the end therefore his light should be the less,
I slyly sought all shifts to put it out,
But as the peise that would the palm tree press
Doth cause the boughs spread larger round about,   [95]
So spite and envy causeth glory sprout,
And aye the more the top is overtrod
The deeper doth the sound root spread abroad.[110]

For when this Henry earl of Harforde[111] saw
What spoil the king made of the noble blood,   [100]
And that without all justice, cause, or law,
To suffer him so he thought not sure nor good.
Wherefore to me, two facèd in a hood,
As touching this, he fully brake his mind
As to his friend that should remedy find.   [105]

But I, although I knew my prince did ill
So that my heart abhorrèd sore the same,
Yet mischief so through malice led my will
To bring this earl from honour unto shame
And toward myself my sovereign to enflame   [110]
That I bewrayed his words unto the king
Not as a rede but as a most heinous thing.

---

94. **peise**: weight.   103. **two faced in a hood**: duplicitous, a reference to the proverbial saying 'he bears two faces under one hood'.

[103] *1563*: in hood

Thus where my duty bound me to have told
My prince his fault and willed him to refrain,
Through flattery, lo, I did his ill uphold, [115]
Which turned at length both him and me to pain.
Woe, woe to kings whose counsellors do feign!
Woe, woe to realms where such are put in trust
As leave the law, to serve the prince's lust!

And woe to him that by his flattering rede [120]
Maintaineth a prince in any kind of vice;
Woe worth him eke for envy, pride, or meed
That misreports any honest enterprise.
Because I, beast, in all these points was nice,
The plagues of all together on me light, [125]
And due, for ill illdoers doth acquite.

For when the earl was charged with my plaint,
He flat denied that any part was true
And claimed by arms to answer his attaint,
And I, by use that warly feats well knew, [130]
To his desire incontinently drew,
Wherewith the king did seem right well content,
As one that passed not much with whom it went.[112]

At time and place appointed we appeared,
At all points armed to prove our quarrels just, [135]
And when our friends on each part had us cheered,
And that the heralds bade us do our lust,
With spear in rest we took a course to just.
But ere our horses had run half their way,
A shout was made; the king did bid us stay. [140]

And for to avoid the shedding of our blood
With shame and death, which one must needs have had,
The king through counsel of the lords thought good
To banish both, which judgement straight was rad.

---

124. nice: punctilious, precise.   **126. And … acquite**: And appropriately so, for harm requites evildoers for their malign deeds.   **129. And … attaint**: And he moved to challenge my imputation of his honour by means of trial by combat.   **130. warly**: martial.   **138. just**: joust.   **144. rad**: read.

[140] *1563*: king commanded stay

No marvel then though both were wroth and sad, [145]
But chiefly I, that was exiled for ay,
My en'my stranged but for a ten-years' day.

The date expired, when by this doleful doom
I should depart to live in banished band,
On pain of death to England not to come, [150]
I went my way. The king seized in his hand
My offices, my honours, goods, and land
To pay the due, as openly he told,
Of mighty sums, which I had from him polled.[113]

See Baldwin, see, the salary of sin; [155]
Mark with what meed vile vices are rewarded!
Through pride and envy I lose both kith and kin,
And, for my flattering plaint so well regarded,
Exile and slander are justly me awarded.
My wife and heir lack lands and lawful right, [160]
And me their lord made Dame Diana's knight.[114]

If these mishaps at home be not enough,
Adjoin to them my sorrows in exile;
I went to Almain first, a land right rough,
In which I found such churlish folk and vile [165]
As made me loath my life each otherwhile.
There, lo, I learned what it is to be a guest
Abroad and what to live at home in rest.[115]

For they esteem no one man more than each;
They use as well the lackey as the lord, [170]
And like their manners churlish is their speech,
Their lodging hard, their board to be abhorred.
Their pleated garments herewith well accord:
All jagged and frounced, with divers colours decked,
They swear, they curse, and drink till they be flecked. [175]

---

145. though: if. **146. for ay**: forever. **147. stranged**: banished. **157. kith**: native country. **158. plaint**: accusation. **161. made Dame Diana's knight**: condemned to forced chastity. **164. Almain**: Germany. **166. each otherwhile**: frequently. **169. each**: every other. **174. frounced**: gathered up in folds. **175. flecked**: spotted, blemished.

They hate all such as these their manners hate,
Which reason would no wise man should allow;
With these I dwelt, lamenting mine estate,
Till at the length they had got knowledge how
I was exiled because I did avow   [180]
A false complaint against my trusty friend,
For which they named me traitor still unend

That what for shame and what for weariness
I stale fro thence and went to Venice town,
Whereas I found more ease and friendliness   [185]
But greater grief, for now the great renown
Of Bolingbroke, whom I would have put down,
Was waxed so great in Britain and in France
That Venice through each man did him advance.

Thus, lo, his glory grew through great despite,   [190]
And I thereby increasèd in defame.
Thus envy ever doth her host aquite
With trouble, anguish, sorrow, smart, and shame
But sets the virtues of her foe in flame,
To water like, which maketh clear the stone,   [195]
And soils itself, by running thereupon.

Or ere I had sojourned there a year,
Strange tidings came he was to England gone,
Had tane the king and, that which touched him near,
Imprisoned him with other of his foen   [200]
And made him yield him up his crown and throne.
When I these things for true by search had tried,
Grief gripped me so I pined away and died.[116]

Note here the end of pride; see flattery's fine;
Mark the reward of envy and false complaint.   [205]

---

182. still unend: endlessly.   **188. Britain**: Brittany.   **189. That ... advance**: That throughout Venice each man extolled him.   **190. despite**: hatred.   **192. aquite**: acquit, repay.   **195. To water like**: In the same manner as water.   **197. Or ere**: Before.

[195–6] *1563*: Like water waves, which cleanse the muddy stone / And soils themselves by beating thereupon

And warn all princes from them to decline
Lest likely fault do find the like attaint.
Let this my life be to them a restraint:
By other's harms who listeth take no heed
Shall by his own learn other better rede.   [210]

---

206. **decline**: turn away.   207. **likely**: similar; **attaint**: condemnation.

---

[206] *1563*: all people from   [208] *1563*: life to them be a

---

[Prose 5]

This tragical example was of all the company well liked; howbeit a doubt
was found therein, and that by means of the diversity of the chronicles.
For whereas Master Hall, whom in this story we chiefly followed, maketh
5   Mowbray accuser and Bolingbroke appellant, Master Fabyan reporteth the
matter quite contrary (and that by the report of good authors), making
Bolingbroke the accuser and Mowbray the appellant.[117] Which matter, sith
it is more hard to decise than needful to our purpose, which mind only to
dissuade from vices and exalt virtue, we refer to the determination of the
heralds or such as may come by the records and registers of these doings,
10   contented in the meanwhile with the best allowed judgement and which
maketh most for our foreshowed purpose.[118]

This doubt thus let pass, 'I would', quoth one of the company, 'gladly
say somewhat for King Richard. But his personage is so sore entangled as I
think few benefices be at this day, for, after his imprisonment, his brother
15   and divers other made a masque, minding by Henry's destruction to have
restored him, which masquers' matter so runneth in this, that I doubt
which ought to go before.[119] But seeing no man is ready to say ought in
their behalf, I will give whoso listeth leisure to think thereupon and, in
the meantime to further your enterprise, I will in the king's behalf recount
20   such part of his story as I think most necessary. And therefore imagine,
Baldwin, that you see him all-to bemangled, with blue wounds, lying pale
and wan all naked upon the cold stones in Paul's church, the people standing round about him and making his moan in this sort':[120]

---

4. **appellant**: a mistake for 'appellee' (the person accused in an appeal of treason).   6. **sith**: since.   13. **personage**: personal identity; **entangled**: fraught with difficulties and embarrassments.   14. **benefices**: kindnesses.   21. **all-to bemangled, with blue wounds**: completely lacerated, with bruises.   22. **stones in Paul's church**: floor slabs in St Paul's Cathedral, London.

How King Richard the Second was for his evil Governance
Deposed from his Seat and miserably Murdered in Prison

Happy is the prince that hath in wealth the grace
To follow virtue, keeping vices under.
But woe to him whose will hath wisdom's place,
For whoso renteth right and law asunder
On him at length, lo, all the world shall wonder.   [5]
High birth, choice fortune, force, nor princely mace
Can warrant king or kaiser fro the case:
Shame sueth sin, as raindrops do the thunder;
Let princes therefore virtuous life embrace,
That wilful pleasures cause them not to blunder.   [10]

Behold my hap, see how the seely rout
Do gaze upon me, and each to other say:
'See where he lieth for whom none late might rout.
Lo how the power, the pride, and rich array
Of mighty rulers lightly fade away.   [15]
The king, which erst kept all the realm in doubt,
The veriest rascal now dare check and lout.
What mould be kings made of but carrion clay?
Behold his wounds, how blue they be about,
Which, while he lived, thought never to decay.'   [20]

Methinks I hear the people thus devise,
And, therefore, Baldwin, sith thou wilt declare

---

7. **Can ... case**: can protect king or emperor from the consequences of debilitating right and law.   8. **sueth**: follows as a consequence.   11. **seely rout**: simple, low-born crowd.   13. **for ... rout**: whom none previously might ever threaten (**rout for**: approach with the intention to attack).   16. **doubt**: dread, fear.   17. **The ... lout**: the lowest of the rabble now may beat and mock.   18. **mould**: matter; **carrion clay**: flesh subject to decay (with 'clay' echoing the biblical idea that humans are made of dust and will return to dust once more (Genesis 2:7, 3:19)).   22. **sith**: since.

How princes fell, to make the living wise,
My vicious story in no point see thou spare,
But paint it out that rulers may beware   [25]
Good counsel, law, or virtue to despise.
For realms have rules, and rulers have a size
Which, if they keep not, doubtless say I dare
That either's griefs the other shall agrise,
Till the one be lost, the other brought to care.   [30]

I am a king that rulèd all by lust,
That forcèd not of virtue, right, or law,
But alway put false flatterers most in trust,
Ensuing such as could my vices claw,
By faithful counsel passing not a straw.   [35]
What pleasure pricked, that thought I to be just:
I set my mind to feed, to spoil, to just.
Three meals a day could scarce content my maw,
And all to augment my lecherous mind that must
To Venus' pleasures alway be in awe.¹²¹   [40]

For maintenance whereof my realm I polled,
Through subsidies, sore fines, loans, many a prest,
Blank charters, oaths, and shifts not known of old,¹²²
For which my subjects did me sore detest.
I also made away the town of Brest,   [45]
My fault wherein because mine uncle told
(For princes' vices may not be controlled),
I found the means his bowels to unbreast,
The peers and lords that did his cause uphold
With death, exile, or grievous fines oppressed.¹²³   [50]

Neither lacked I aid in any wicked deed,
For gaping gulls whom I promoted had
Would further all in hope of higher meed.

---

24. vicious: vice-ridden.   **27. size**: a proper limit to behaviour.   **29. agrise**: fill with horror.   **32. forced not of**: cared nothing for.   **34. Ensuing**: following the guidance of; **claw**: gratify.   **37. just**: joust.   **42. many a prest**: many a charge, duty, and/or tax.   **43. blank charters**: see explanatory note 122.   **48. unbreast**: free or take from the breast (either a reference to wounding so that the bowels spill from the body or to the early modern practice of removing abdominal organs from a corpse to prepare it for burial).   **52. gaping gulls**: greedy hangers-on (gulls were thought to be particularly greedy, ravenous birds).

A king can never imagine ought so bad
But most about him will perform it glad,   [55]
For sickness seldom doth so swiftly breed
As vicious humours grow the grief to feed.
Thus kings' estates of all be worst bested,
Abused in wealth, abandonèd at need,
And nearest harm when they be least adread.   [60]

My life and death the truth of this can try,
For while I fought in Ireland with my foes
Mine uncle Edmund, whom I left to guide
My realm at home, right trait'rously arose
To help the Percies plying my depose   [65]
And called from France Earl Bolingbroke, whom I
Condemnèd ten years in exile to lie,[124]
Who cruelly did put to death all those
That in mine aid durst look but once awry –
Whose number was but slender, I suppose.   [70]

For when I was come back this stir to stay,
The earl of Worcester whom I trusted most
(Whiles we in Wales at Flint our castle lay,
Both to refresh and multiply mine host)
Did in my hall in sight of least and most   [75]
Bebreak his staff, my household office stay,
Bade each man shift and rode himself away.[125]
See princes, see the power whereof we boast:
Whom most we trust at need do us betray,
Through whose false faith my land and life I lost.   [80]

For when my traitorous steward thus was goen,
My servants shrank away on every side,

56–7. **For … feed**: For sicknesses seldom grow to cause grief as quickly as depraved inclinations do.   **58. bested**: constituted.   **60. adread**: reverenced, feared.   **65. plying my depose**: working to depose me.   **66. Earl Bolingbroke**: Henry Bolingbroke (d. 1413), first duke of Hereford and later King Henry IV (the title 'earl' is evidently an unconscious error; cf. line 85).   **68–70. Who … suppose**: Who put cruelly to death all those who offered me even a little bit of support – a small number of subjects, I have to believe (**look … awry**: cast an oblique glance).   **76. my household office stay**: the prop, buttress of my household's offices (the steward was the chief officer of the royal household).

[77] *1563*: each make shift [**make shift**: bestir himself]

That caught I was and carried to my foen,
Who for their prince a prison did provide
And therein kept me, till Duke Henry's pride   [85]
Did cause me yield him up my crown and throne,
Which shortly made my friendly foes to groan.
For Henry, seeing in me their falsehood tried,
Abhorred them all and would be ruled by none,
For which they sought to stop him straight a tide.[126]   [90]

The chief conspired by death to drive him down,
For which exploit a solemn oath they swore,
To render me my liberty and crown
Whereof themselves deprivèd me before.
But salves help seld an overlong suff'red sore;   [95]
To stop the breech no boot to run or rown,
When swelling floods have overflown the town.
Till sails be spread, the ship may keep the shore;
The anchors weighed, though all the freight do frown,
With stream and steer perforce it shall be bore.   [100]

For though the peers set Henry in his state,
Yet could they not displace him thence again,
And where they easily put me down of late,
They could restore me by no manner pain:
Things hardly mend but may be marred amain.   [105]
And when a man is fall'n in froward fate,
Still mischiefs light one in another's pate,
And well-meant means his mishaps to restrain
Wax wretched moans, whereby his joys abate:
Due proof whereof in me appeareth plain.   [110]

For when King Henry knew that for my cause
His lords in mask would kill him if they might,[127]

87. **friendly foes**: those who had accepted Henry Bolingbroke's victory but still sympathized with the deposed Richard.   90. **straight a tide**: straightway.   96–7. **To … town**: It is useless to run or to hold a discussion once floods have overwhelmed the town (**rown**: round, in the sense of 'talk about or discuss something').   99–100. **The … bore**: Once the anchor is weighed, the current and helmsman will guide the ship along, no matter how much the passengers may frown (**freight**: those who paid for passage on the ship).   105. **Things … amain**: Things are put right only with difficulty, but they can be damaged very quickly.   106–9. **And … abate**: And when a man has fallen into an adverse fate, troubles continually descend on him, one on top of the other, and well-meant attempts to lessen his misfortunes only increase the wretched moans that end his joys.

[107] *1563*: on one another's

To dash all doubts, he took no farther pause
But sent Sir Pierce of Exton, a trait'rous knight,
To Pomfret Castle, with other armèd light, [115]
Who causeless killed me there against all laws.[128]
Thus lawless life to lawless death ay draws,
Wherefore bid kings be ruled and rule by right:
Who worketh his will and shunneth wisdom's saws
In flattery's claws and shame's foul paws shall light. [120]

117. **ay**: ever.

[Prose 6]

When he had ended this so woeful a tragedy, and to all princes a right worthy instruction, we paused, having passed through a miserable time full of
piteous tragedies. And seeing the reign of Henry the Fourth ensued, a man
more ware and prosperous in his doings, although not untroubled with wars
5 both of outforth and inward enemies, we began to search what peers were
fallen therein, whereof the number was not small. And yet, because their
examples were not much to be noted for our purpose, we passed over all the
masquers (of whom King Richard's brother was chief) which were all slain
and put to death for their traitorous attempt.[129] And finding Owen Glendour
10 next, one of fortune's own whelps, and the Percies his confederates, I thought
them unmeet to be overpassed, and therefore said thus to the silent company: 'What, my masters, is every man at once in a brown study? Hath no man
affection to any of these stories? You mind so much some other belike, that
these do not move you: and to say the troth there is no special cause why they
15 should. Howbeit Owen Glendour, because he was one of fortune's darlings,
rather than he should be forgotten, I will tell his tale for him under the privilege of Martin Hundred,[130] which Owen, coming out of the wild mountains
like the image of death in all points (his dart only excepted), so sore hath
famine and hunger consumed him, may lament his folly after this manner.'

1. **he**: Sir Thomas Chaloner. 4. **ware**: cautious. 9. **Owen Glendour**: Owain Glyn Dŵr (d. *c.* 1416), Welsh rebel
leader. 10. **Percies**: Henry Percy (d. 1408), first earl of Northumberland, and his kinsmen. 12. **in a brown study**:
lost in gloomy reflection. 18. **dart**: light spear. (The image of a personified, skeletal death and his dart was familiar
in early modern England.)

[1] *1554*: When Master Chaloner had [1–2] *1554*: a right   (as the Welshmen take me in hand) my pedigree is de-
notable and worthy [4] *1554*: a man more prosperous, al-   scended, although he be but a slender prince, yet rather
though [5] *1554*: what princes [14] *1554*: and to say troth   **[take me in hand**: lead me to believe] [17] *1554*: coming
[15–16] *1554*: because he is a man of that country whence   naked out [19] *1554*: him, lamenteth his infortune after

[Tragedy 6]

How Owen Glendour, Seduced by False Prophecies, Took Upon Him to be Prince of Wales and was by Henry, then Prince Thereof, Chased to the Mountains, where he Miserably Died for Lack of Food

I pray thee Baldwin, sith thou dost intend
To show the fall of such as climb too high,
Remember me, whose miserable end
May teach a man his vicious life to fly.
Oh Fortune, Fortune, out on her I cry!   [5]
My body and fame she hath made lean and slender,
For I, poor wretch, am starvèd Owen Glendour.

A Welshman born and of a gentle blood,
But ill brought up, whereby full well I find
That neither birth nor lin'age make us good,   [10]
Though it be true that cat will after kind.
Flesh gend'reth flesh, so doth not soul or mind:
They gender not but fouly do degender,
When men to vice from virtue them do surrender.

Each thing by nature tendeth to the same   [15]
Whereof it came and is disposèd like.
Down sinks the mould, up mounts the fiery flame;
With horn the hart, with hoof the horse doth strike;
The wolf doth spoil, the subtle fox doth pike;
And generally no fish, flesh, fowl, or plant   [20]
Doth any property that their dame had want.

But as for men, sith severally they have
A mind whose manners are by learning made,

Title: **Henry**: Henry of Monmouth (d. 1422), prince of Wales and the future King Henry V.   **1. sith**: since.   **11. a cat will after kind**: a cat will act according to its nature (a proverbial saying).   **12. gend'reth**: engenders.   **13. gender**: reproduce; **degender**: degenerate.   **17. mould**: soil, earth.   **19: pike**: steal ('pick').   **22. severally**: each individually.

[2] *1554*: falls
[10] *1554*: make men good

[14] *1554*: do render; *1563*: them surrender

40

Good bringing up alonely doth them save
In virtuous deeds, which with their parents fade, [25]
So that true gentry standeth in the trade
Of virtuous life, not in the fleshly line,
For blood is brute, but gentry is divine.[131]

Experience doth cause me thus to say
And that the rather for my countrymen, [30]
Which vaunt and boast their selves above the day,
If they may strain their stock for worthy men:
Which let be true, are they the better then?
Nay far the worse, if so they be not good,
For why they stain the beauty of their blood. [35]

How would we mock the burden-bearing mule
If he would brag he were an horse's son?
To press his pride (might nothing else him rule),
His boast to prove, no more but bid him run.
The horse for swiftness hath his glory won, [40]
To which the mule could never the more aspire,
Though he should prove that Pegas was his sire.

Each man may crack of that which is his own;
Our parents' virtues theirs are and not ours.
Who therefore will of noble kind be known [45]
Ought shine in virtue like his ancestors.
Gentry consisteth not in lands and towers:
He is a churl though all the world be his,
Yea Arthur's heir, if that he live amiss.

For virtuous life doth make a gentleman [50]
Of her possessor, all be he poor as Job,
Yea though no name of elders show he can.

24–5. **Good … fade**: Good bringing-up in virtuous deeds alone will preserve them (in honour), since the good their parents performed will eventually fade away. **32. strain their stock**: insist on their ancestry. **35. For why**: Because. **38. press**: suppress. **42. Pegas**: Pegasus. **43. crack**: boast. **49. Yea … amiss**: Even if he is King Arthur's heir, he is a churl if he lives amiss. **51. all be he**: even though he be.

[31] *1554, 1563*: boast themselves [32] *1563*: stock fro worthy [38] *1563*: press the pride [39] *1563*: his boasts to [42] *1554*: Pegas were his; *1563*: Pegas is his [43] *1563*: which was his [49] *1559*: He Arthur's (an uncorrected fault in the 1559 edition for 'Yea Arthur's', which is the 1563 reading)

For proof take Merlin fathered by an hob.
But who so sets his mind to spoil and rob,
Although he come by due descent fro Brute, [55]
He is a churl, ungentle, vile, and brute.[132]

Well thus did I for want of better wit,
Because my parents noughtly brought me up,
For gentle men (they said) was nought so fit
As to attaste by bold attempts the cup [60]
Of conquest's wine, whereof I thought to sup,
And therefore bent myself to rob and rive,
And whom I could of lands and goods deprive.

For Henry the Fourth did then usurp the crown,
Despoiled the king, with Mortimer the heir, [65]
For which his subjects sought to put him down.[133]
And I, while Fortune offered me so fair,
Did what I might his honour to appair
And took on me to be the prince of Wales,
Enticed thereto by many of Merlin's tales. [70]

For which, such idle as wait upon the spoil
From every part of Wales unto me drew,
For loit'ring youth untaught in any toil
Are ready ay all mischief to ensue.
Through help of these so great my glory grew [75]
That I defied my king through lofty heart
And made sharp war on all that took his part.

See luck, I took Lord Reynold Grey of Rithen
And him enforced my daughter to espouse,
And so unransomed held him still. And sithen [80]
In Wigmore land through battle rigorous
I caught the right heir of the crownèd house
The earl of March, Sir Edmund Mortimer,
And in a dungeon kept him prisoner.[134]

---

53. hob: hobgoblin.   **62. rive**: pillage.   **68. appair**: impair.   **71. idle**: idlers.   **74. ay**: always.   **80. still**: perpetually; **sithen**: afterwards.

[53] *1554*: Merlin, whose father was an hob

Then all the marches longing unto Wales   [85]
By Severn west I did invade and burn,
Destroyed the towns in mountains and in vales,
And rich in spoils did homeward safe return:
Was none so bold durst once against me spurn.
Thus prosperously doth Fortune forward call   [90]
Those whom she minds to give the sorest fall.¹³⁵

When fame had brought these tidings to the king
(Although the Scots then vexèd him right sore),
A mighty army against me he did bring,
Whereof the French King being warned afore,   [95]
Who mortal hate against King Henry bore,
To grieve our foe he quickly to me sent
Twelve thousand Frenchmen armed to war and bent.

A part of them led by the earl of March
Lord James of Bourbon, a valiant tried knight,   [100]
Withheld by winds to Wales-ward forth to march,
Took land at Plymouth privily on a night,
And when he had done all he durst or might,
After that a many of his men were slain,
He stole to ship and sailèd home again.   [105]

Twelve thousand mo in Milford did arrive
And came to me, then lying at Denbigh
With armèd Welshmen thousands double five,
With whom we went to Worcèster well nigh
And there encamped us on a mount on high   [110]
To abide the king, who shortly after came
And pitched his field on a hill hard by the same.

There eight days long our hosts lay face to face,
And neither durst the other's power assail,
But they so stopped the passages the space   [115]

86. **Severn**: a river of Wales and west England. 101. **to Wales-ward**: towards Wales. 112. **pitched his field**: positioned his troops for battle.

[88] *1554*: And with rich; *1563*: spoils had

That vitals could not come to our avail,
Wherethrough constrained, our hearts began to fail
So that the Frenchmen shrank away by night,
And I with mine to the mountains took our flight:

The king pursued us, greatly to his cost,   [120]
From hills to woods, fro woods to valleys plain,
And by the way his men and stuff he lost,
And when he see he gainèd nought save pain,
He blew retreat and got him home again.
Then with my power I boldly came abroad,   [125]
Taken in my country for a very god.

Immediately after fell a jolly jar
Between the king and Percy's worthy bloods,
Which grew at last unto a deadly war,
For like as drops engender mighty floods   [130]
And little seeds sprout forth great leaves and buds,
Even so small strifes, if they be suffered run,
Breed wrath and war and death or they be done.

The king would have the ransom of such Scots
As these the Percies had tane in the field,   [135]
But see how strongly lucre knits her knots:
The king will have; the Percies will not yield.
Desire of goods soon craves but granteth seld.
Oh cursèd goods! desire of you hath wrought
All wickedness that hath or can be thought.[136]   [140]

The Percies deemed it meeter for the king
To have redeemed their cousin Mortimer –
Who in his quarrel all his power did bring
To fight with me that took him prisoner –
Than of their prey to rob his Soldìer   [145]
And therefore willed him see some mean were found
To quit forth him whom I kept vilely bound.

---

116. vitals: victuals.   128. Percy's worthy bloods: worthy men of the Percy lineage (at the time the dominant noble family in the north of England).   133. or: before.   141–5. The ... Soldier: The Percies deemed it fitter for Henry IV to redeem their kinsman Mortimer, who on the king's behalf had marshalled all his forces to fight me (i.e. Glendour), than to 'rob' a man who fought in the king's service (his Soldier: Sir Henry Percy) of his family's spoils of war.
147. quit forth: set free.

Because the king mislikèd their request,
They came themselves and did accord with me,
Complaining how the kingdom was oppressed [150]
By Henry's rule, wherefore we did agree
To put him down and part the realm in three:
The North part theirs, Wales wholly to be mine,
The rest to rest to th'earl of March's line.[137]

And for to set us hereon more agog, [155]
A prophet came (a vengeance take them all!)
Affirming Henry to be Gogmagog,[138]
Whom Merlin doth a mouldwarp ever call,
Accursed of God, that must be brought in thrall
By a wolf, a dragon, and a lion strong, [160]
Which should divide his kingdom them among.

This crafty dreamer made us, three such beasts,
To think we were these foresaid beasts indeed,
And for that cause our badges and our crests
We searchèd out, which scarcely well agreed; [165]
Howbeit the heralds, ready at such a need,
Drew down such issues from old ancestors
As proved these ensigns to be surely ours.

Ye crafty Welshmen, wherefore do you mock
The noble men thus with your feignèd rhymes? [170]
Ye noble men, why fly you not the flock
Of such as have seduced so many times?
False prophecies are plagues for divers crimes,
Which God doth let the devilish sort devise
To trouble such as are not godly wise. [175]

And that appeared by us three beasts in deed,
Through false persuasion highly borne in hand
That in our feat we could not choose but speed
To kill the king and to enjoy his land,
For which exploit we bound ourselves in band [180]
To stand contented each man with his part,
So fully folly assured our foolish heart.

---

158. **mouldwarp**: mole.   176. **in deed**: in actual practice.   177. **borne in hand**: deluded.

But such they say as fish before the net
Shall seldom surfeit of the prey they take;
Of things to come the haps be so unset   [185]
That none but fools may warrant of them make.
The full assured success doth oft forsake,
For Fortune findeth none so fit to flout
As suresby sots which cast no kind of doubt.

How sayest thou Henry Hotspur, do I lie?   [190]
For thou right manly gavest the king a field
And there was slain because thou wouldst not fly.
Sir Thomas Percy thine uncle, forced to yield,
Did cast his head (a wonder seen but seld)
From Shrewsbury town to the top of London Bridge: [195]
Lo, thus fond hope did their both lives abridge.¹³⁹

When Henry King this victory had won,
Destroyed the Percies, put their power to flight,
He did appoint Prince Henry, his eldest son,
With all his power to meet me if he might,   [200]
But I, discomfit through my partners' fight ,
Had not the heart to meet him face to face
But fled away, and he pursued the chase.

Now Baldwin mark, for I, called prince of Wales
And made believe I should be he indeed,   [205]
Was made to fly among the hills and dales,
Where all my men forsook me at my need:
Who trusteth loiterers seld hath lucky speed,
And when the captain's courage doth him fail
His soldiers' hearts a little thing may quail.   [210]

And so Prince Henry chasèd me that, lo,
I found no place wherein I might abide,
For as the dogs pursue the seely doe,
The brach behind the hounds on every side,
So traced they me among the mountains wide,   [215]

---

189. **suresby sots**: over-confident fools.   191. **a field**: a battle.   213. **seely**: innocent.   214. **brach**: scent hound.

Whereby I found I was the heartless hare
And not the beast Coleprophet did declare.

And at the last – like as the little roach
Must either be eat or leap upon the shore
Whenas the hungry pickrel doth approach   [220]
And there find death which it escaped before –
So double death assaulted me so sore
That either I must unto my en'my yield
Or starve for hunger in the barren field.

Here shame and pain a while were at a strife: [225]
Pain prayed me yield, shame bade me rather fast;
The one bade spare, the other spend my life,
But shame (shame have it) overcame at last.
Then hunger gnew that doth the stone wall brast
And made me eat both gravel, dirt, and mud,   [230]
And, last of all, my dung, my flesh, and blood.[140]

This was mine end, too horrible to hear,
Yet good enough for a life that was so ill.
Whereby (O Baldwin) warn all men to bear
Their youth such love to bring them up in skill.   [235]
Bid Princes fly Coleprophet's lying bill
And not presume to climb above their states,
For they be faults that foil men, not their fates.

---

217. **Coleprophet**: false prophet (the false prophet of line 156).   218. **roach**: a small freshwater fish.   220. **pickrel**: pike.   228. **shame have it**: an obscure phrase: perhaps 'as shame would have it'.   229. **gnew**: gnawed.   235. **in skill**: in accordance with what is right.

[Prose 7]

When starved Owen had ended his hungry exhortation, it was well-enough liked. Howbeit, one found a doubt worth the moving, and that concerning this title 'earl of March': for, as it appeareth, there were three men of three divers nations together in one time entitled by that honour.
5   First, Sir Edmund Mortimer, whom Owen kept in prison, an Englishman; the second, the Lord George of Dunbar, a valiant Scot, banished out of his

---

5. **Mortimer**: Sir Edmund Mortimer (d. 1425), fifth earl of March.   6. **George of Dunbar**: George Dunbar (d. between 1416 and 1423), ninth earl of March.

country and well esteemed of Henry the Fourth; the third, Lord James of
Bourbon, a Frenchman, sent by the French king to help Owen Glendour.
These three men had this title all at once, which caused him to ask how
10   it was true that every one of these could be earl of March. Whereto was
answered that every country hath marches belonging unto them, and those
so large that they were earldoms, and the lords thereof intituled thereby, so
that Lord Edmund Mortimer was earl of March in England, Lord James
of Bourbon of the Marches of France, and Lord George of Dunbar earl
15   of the Marches in Scotland.[141] For otherwise neither could have interest in
other's title.

   This doubt thus dissolved, Master Ferrers said, 'if no man have affection to the Percies, let us pass the times both of Henry the Fourth and the
Fifth and come to Henry the Sixth, in whose time Fortune (as she doth
20   in the minority of princes) bare a great stroke among the nobles. And yet
in Henry the Fourth's time are examples which I would wish Baldwin
that you should not forget, as the conspiracy made by the bishop of York
and the Lord Mowbray, son of him whom you late treated of, pricked
forward by the earl of Northumberland, father to Sir Henry Hotspur, who
25   fled himself, but his partners were apprehended and put to death, with
Baynton and Blinkinsops, which could not see their duty to their king but
took part with Percy that banished rebel.'[142]

   As he was proceeding, he was desired to stay by one which had pon-
dered the story of the Percies, who briefly said, 'to the end, Baldwin, that
30   you may know what to say of the Percies, whose story is not all out of my
memory (and it is a notable story), I will take upon me the person of Lord
Henry, earl of Northumberland, father of Henry Hotspur, in whose behalf
this may be said:

---

18. the Percies: Henry Percy (d. 1408), first earl of Northumberland, and his son Sir Henry Percy (d. 1403), called
'Hotspur'.   **20. bare a great stroke**: wielded great influence.   **23. son of him**: son of Thomas Mowbray (d. 1399),
first duke of Norfolk, speaker of Tragedy 3.   **24. earl of Northumberland**: Henry Percy (d. 1408), first earl of
Northumberland;   **Sir Henry Hotspur**: Sir Henry Percy (d. 1403), called 'Hotspur'.   **27. banished**: driven away.

How Henry Percy, Earl of Northumberland, was for his Covetous and Traitorous Attempt Put to Death at York

Oh moral Senec, true find I thy saying
That neither kinsfolk, riches, strength, or favour
Are free from Fortune but are ay decaying.
No worldly wealth is aught save doubtful labour;
Man's life in earth is like unto a tabor,   [5]
Which now to mirth doth mildly men provoke,
And straight to war with a more sturdy stroke.[143]

All this full true I, Percy, find by proof,
Which whilom was earl of Northumberland,
And therefore, Baldwin, for my peers' behoof,   [10]
To note men's falls sith thou hast tane in hand,
I would thou shouldest my state well understand,
For fewè kings were more than I redoubted,
Through double Fortune lifted up and louted.

As for my kin, their nobleness is known,   [15]
My valiantise were folly for to praise,
Wherethrough the Scots so oft were overthrown
That who but I was doubted in my days?
And that King Richard found at all assays,
For never Scots rebellèd in his reign   [20]
But through my force were either caught or slain.

A brother I had was earl of Worcester,
Always in favour and office with the king,[144]

---

4. **aught save**: anything but.   11. **sith**: since.   13. **fewe**: few (disyllabic); **redoubted**: respected.   14. **Through … louted**: Through duplicitous Fortune first raised up and then forced to stoop.   18. **doubted**: dreaded.   19. **assays**: martial attempts.

And by my wife Dame Eleanor Mortimer
I had a son, which so the Scots did sting   [25]
That, being young and but a very spring,
Sir Henry Hotspur they gave him to name,
And though I say it, he did deserve the same.[145]

We three triumphèd in King Richard's time,
Till Fortune ought both him and us a spite,   [30]
But chiefly me, whom clear from any crime
My king did banish from his favour quite
And openly proclaimed a traitorous knight –
Wherethrough false slander forcèd me to be
That which before I did most deadly flee.[146]   [35]

Let men beware how they true folk defame,
Or threaten on them the blame of vices nought,
For infamy breedeth wrath, wreck followeth shame,
Eke open slander oftentimes hath brought
That to effect that erst was never thought.   [40]
To be misdeemed men suffer in a sort,
But none can bear the grief of misreport.

Because my king did shame me wrongfully,
I hated him and indeed became his foe,
And, while he did at war in Ireland lie,   [45]
I did conspire to turn his weal to woe,
And through the duke of York and other mo
All royal power from him we quickly took
And gave the same to Henry Bolingbroke.[147]

Neither did we this alonely for this cause   [50]
But, to say truth, force drave us to the same,
For he, despising God and all good laws,
Slew whom he would, made sin a very game.
And seeing neither age nor counsel could him tame,
We thought it well done for the kingdom's sake   [55]
To leave his rule that did all rule forsake.

24. Eleanor Mortimer: the poet's error for Northumberland's actual first wife Margaret Neville (d. 1372).   **26. a very spring**: a true youth.   **30. Till … spite**: Until Fortune dealt harm to both King Richard and us.   **37. vices nought**: non-existent vices.   **41. to be misdeemed**: to be looked on unfavourably; to be thought evil of.

But when Sir Henry had attained his place,
He straight became in all points worse than he,
Destroyed the peers and slew King Richard's grace,
Against his oath made to the lords and me.[148]   [60]
And, seeking quarrels how to disagree,
He shamelessly required me and my son
To yield him Scots, which we in field had won.[149]

My nephew, also, Edmund Mortimer,
The very heir apparent to the crown,   [65]
Whom Owen Glendour held as prisoner
Vilely bound, in dungeon deep cast down,
He would not ransom but did felly frown
Against my brother and me that for him spake,
And him proclaimèd traitor for our sake.[150]   [70]

This foul despite did cause us to conspire
To put him down as we did Richard erst,
And that we might this matter set on fire,
From Owen's jail our cousin we remerced
And unto Glendour all our griefs rehearsed,   [75]
Who made a bond with Mortimer and me
To prive the king and part the realm in three.[151]

But when King Henry heard of this device,
Toward Owen Glendour he sped him very quick,
Minding by force to stop our enterprise.   [80]
And, as the devil would, then fell I sick;
Howbeit, my brother and son, more politic
Than prosperous, with an host fro Scotland brought,
Encountered him at Shrewsbury, where they fought.

The one was tane and killed, the other slain,   [85]
And shortly after was Owen put to flight,
By means whereof, I forcèd was to feign
That I knew nothing of the former fight.
Fraud oft avails more than doth sturdy might,

68. felly: fiercely.   **74. remerced**: redeemed.   **77. prive**: deprive.   **82. politic**: crafty.

For by my feigning I brought him in belief   [90]
I knew not that wherein my part was chief.[152]

And while the king thus took me for his friend,
I sought all means my former wrong to wreak,
Which that I might bring to the sooner end
To the bishop of York I did the matter break,   [95]
And to th'Earl Marshal likewise did I speak,
Whose father was through Henry's cause exiled;
The bishop's brother with traitorous death defiled.

These straight assented to do what they could,
So did Lord Hastings and Lord Fauconbridge,   [100]
Which altogether promisèd they would
Set all their power the king's days to abridge.[153]
But see the spite: before the birds were flidge,
The king had word and seasoned on the nest,
Whereby, alas, my friends were all oppressed.   [105]

The bloody tyrant brought them all to end
Excepted me, which into Scotland scaped
To George of Dunbar, th'earl of March, my friend,
Who in my cause all that he could ay scraped.
And, when I had for greater succour gaped   [110]
Both at the Frenchmen and the Flemings' hand
And could get none, I took such as I fand.

And, with the help of George my very friend,
I did invade Northumberland full bold,
Whereas the folk drew to me still unend,   [115]
Bent to the death my party to uphold.
Through help of these full many a fort and hold,
The which the king right manfully had manned,
I eas'ly won and seizèd in my hand.[154]

Not so content (for vengeance drave me on),   [120]
I entered Yorkshire, there to waste and spoil

---

93. wreak: revenge.   **103. flidge:** fledged.   **104. seasoned on:** dug his claws into (said of a bird or beast of prey).   **112. fand:** found (northern dialect).

But, ere I had far in the country gone,
The sheriff thereof, Rafe Rekesby, did assoil
My troubled host of much part of our toil.
For he, assaulting freshly, took through power   [125]
Me and Lord Bardolf both at Bramham Moor,

And thence conveyed us to the town of York
Until he knew what was the king's intent.
There, lo, Lord Bardolf, kinder than the stork,[155]
Did lose his head, which was to London sent,   [130]
With whom for friendship mine in like case went.[156]
This was my hap, my fortune, or my fawte:
This life I led, and thus I came to nought.

Wherefore, good Baldwin, will the peers take heed
Of slander, malice, and conspiracy,   [135]
Of covetise whence all the rest proceed,
For covetise joint with contumacy
Doth cause all mischief in men's hearts to breed.
Add therefore this to *Esperance,* my word:
Who causeth bloodshed shall not scape the sword.[157]   [140]

---

123. assoil: set free, discharge.   **129. lo**: behold, see.   **132. fawte**: fault, failing.

[Prose 8]

By that this was ended, I had found out the story of Richard, earl of
Cambridge, and, because it contained matter in it, though not very notable, yet for the better understanding of the rest I thought it meet to
touch it and, therefore, said as followeth: 'You have said well of the Percies
5 and favourably, for indeed, as it should appear, the chief cause of their
conspiracy against King Henry was for Edmund Mortimer their cousin's
sake, whom the king very maliciously proclaimed to have yielded himself
to Owen colourably, whenas indeed he was taken forcibly against his will
and very cruelly ordered in prison.[158] And, seeing we are in hand with
10 Mortimer's matter, I will take upon me the person of Richard Plantagenet,

---

1. Richard: Richard (d. 1415), first earl of Cambridge.   **8. colourably**: in appearance but not in reality (see Tragedy 7, n. 150); **whenas**: when.

earl of Cambridge, who for his sake likewise died. And, therefore, I let pass
Edmund Holland, earl of Kent, whom Henry the Fourth made admiral
to scour the seas, because the Bretons were abroad, which earl (as many
things happen in war) was slain with an arrow at the assault of Briake,
15 shortly after whose death this king died and his son Henry the fifth of that
name succeeded in his place. In the beginning of this Henry the Fifth's
reign died this Richard and, with him, Henry the Lord Scrope and others,
in whose behalf this may be said.[159]

[17] *1563*: other

How Richard, Earl of Cambridge, Intending to the King's Destruction, was Put to Death at Southampton

'Haste maketh waste' hath commonly been said,
And secret mischief seld hath lucky speed;
A murdering mind with proper peise is weighed:
All this is true; I find it in my creed.
And therefore, Baldwin, warn all states take heed   [5]
How they conspire any other to betrap,
Lest mischief meant light in the miner's lap.

For I, Lord Richard, heir Plantagenet,
Was earl of Cambridge and right fortunate,
If I had had the grace my wit to set   [10]
To have content me with mine own estate.
But oh false honours, breeders of debate,
The love of you our lewd hearts doth allure
To leese ourselves by seeking you unsure.

Because my brother Edmund Mortimer,   [15]
Whose eldest sister was my wedded wife –
I mean that Edmund that was prisoner
In Wales so long through Owen's busy strife –
Because, I say, that after Edmund's life
His rights and titles must by law be mine   [20]
(For he ne had nor could increase his line),[160]

Because the right of realm and crown was ours,
I searchèd means to help him thereunto

---

3. **peise**: heaviness, burden (of guilt). **5. all states**: members of every class. **7. miner**: underminer, literally a soldier charged with setting explosives to undermine walls; used figuratively to mean a secret assailant bent on destruction. **14. leese**: lose.

And, where the Henrys held it by their powers,
I sought a shift their tenures to undo,   [25]
Which being force, sith force or sleight must do,
I, void of might, because their power was strong,
Set privy sleight against their open wrong.

But sith the deaths of most part of my kin
Did dash my hope, throughout the father's days   [30]
I let it slip and thought it best begin
Whenas the son should dread least such assays,
For force through speed, sleight speedeth through delays,
And seld doth treason time so fitly find
As when all dangers most be out of mind.[161]   [35]

Wherefore while Henry of that name the Fift
Prepared his army to go conquer France,
Lord Scrope and I thought to attempt a drift
To put him down, my brother to advance.
But, were it God's will, my luck, or his good chance,   [40]
The king wist wholly whereabout we went
The night before the king to shipward bent.[162]

Then were we straight as traitors apprehended;
Our purpose spied, the cause thereof was hid.
And, therefore, lo, a false cause we pretended,   [45]
Wherethrough my brother was fro danger rid.
We said for hire of the French king's coin we did
Behight to kill the king, and thus with shame
We stained ourselves to save our friend fro blame.[163]

When we had thus confessed so foul a treason,   [50]
That we deserved we suffered by the law.
See, Baldwin, see, and note (as it is reason)
How wicked deeds to woeful ends do draw.
All force doth fail; no craft is worth a straw

---

24. **Henrys**: Henry IV and Henry V.   25. **tenures**: possession of the crown.   26. **being force**: was necessary; **sith**: since.   30. **father's**: i.e. Henry IV's.   33. **force ... delays**: force finds success through rapid execution; plots succeed through delays.   48. **Behight**: vow.

[42] *1563*: before to shipward he him bent

To attain things lost, and therefore let them go,   [55]
For might ruleth right, and will though God say no.

[Prose 9]

When stout Richard had stoutly said his mind, 'belike', quoth one, 'this
Richard was but a little man or else little favoured of writers, for our
chronicles speak very little of him. But, seeing we be come now to King
Henry's voyage into France, we cannot lack valiant men to speak of, for
5   among so many as were led and sent by the king out of this realm thither, it
cannot be chosen but some, and that a great sum, were slain among them,
wherefore to speak of them all I think not needful. And therefore to let
pass Edward, duke of York, and the earl of Suffolk slain both at the battle
of Agincourt,¹⁶⁴ as were also many other, let us end the time of Henry the
10   Fifth and come to his son Henry the Sixth, whose nonage brought France
and Normandy out of bondage and was cause that few of our noblemen
died aged. Of whom to let pass the number, I will take upon me the person of Thomas Montagu, earl of Salisbury, whose name was not so good
at home (and yet he was called the good earl) as it was dreadful abroad,¹⁶⁵
15   who, exclaiming upon the mutability of fortune, justly may say thus:

2. **little man**: person of no great importance.   3–4. **King Henry's voyage**: Henry V's 1415 invasion of France.

[Tragedy 9]

How Thomas Montagu, the Earl of Salisbury, in the mids of his Glory was Chanceably Slain with a Piece of Ordnance

What fools be we to trust unto our strength,
Our wit, our courage, or our noble fame,
Which time itself must needs devour at length,
Though froward Fortune could not foil the same.
But seeing this goddess guideth all the game, [5]
Which still to change doth set her only lust,
Why toil we so for things so hard to trust?

A goodly thing is surely good report,
Which noble hearts do seek by course of kind.
But seen the date so doubtful and so short, [10]
The ways so rough whereby we do it find,
I cannot choose but praise the princely mind
That presseth for it, though we find oppressed
By foul defame those that deserve it best.

Concerning whom, mark Baldwin what I say, [15]
I mean the virtuous hindered of their bruit,
Among which number reckon well I may
My valiant father John Lord Montacute,
Who lost his life, I judge, in just pursuit.
I say the cause and not the casual speed [20]
Is to be weighed in every kind of deed.[166]

This rule observed, how many shall we find
For virtue's sake by infamy oppressed?
How many again, through help of fortune blind,
For ill attempts achieved with honour blest? [25]

9. **course of kind**: by their very nature.   10. **seen**: seeing; **date**: duration.   20. **the casual speed**: the chance success.

Success is worst oft-times when cause is best.
Therefore say I God send them sorry haps
That judge the causes by their afterclaps!

The end indeed is judge of everything,
Which is the cause or latter point of time. [30]
The first true verdict at the first may bring;
The last is slow or slipper as the slime,
Oft changing names of innocence and crime.
Duke Thomas's death was justice two years long
And ever since sore tyranny and wrong.[167] [35]

Wherefore I pray thee, Baldwin, weigh the cause
And praise my father as he doth deserve.
Because Earl Henry, king against all laws,
Endeavourèd King Richard for to starve
In jail, whereby the regal crown might swarve [40]
Out of the line to which it then was due
(Whereby God knows what evil might ensue),[168]

My Lord John Holland, duke of Exeter,
Which was dear cousin to this wretched king,
Did move my father and the earl of Gloucester, [45]
With other lords, to ponder well the thing.
Who, seeing the mischief that began to spring,
Did all consent this Henry to depose
And to restore King Richard to the rose.[169]

And while they did devise a pretty train [50]
Whereby to bring their purpose better about,
Which was, in mask, this Henry to have slain,
The duke of Aumale blew their counsel out.
Yet was their purpose good, there is no doubt:
What cause can be more worthy for a knight [55]
Than save his king and help true heirs to right?[170]

---

28. That … afterclaps: who judge the worthiness of a cause by the results it produced.   **29. end**: purpose of an action; result of an action.   **31. The … bring**: The first named (i.e. the cause) may immediately provide the true judgement concerning the action in question.   **45. earl of Gloucester**: Thomas (d. 1400), second Lord Despenser and, until November 1399, first earl of Gloucester.   **49. rose**: figuratively, the rule of England (the English rose as a symbol of the country).   **50. train**: stratagem.

For this with them my father was destroyed
And buried in the dunghill of defame.[171]
Thus evil chance their glory did avoid,
Whereas their cause doth claim eternal fame. [60]
When deeds therefore unluckily do frame,
Men ought not judge the authors to be naught,
For right through might is often overraught.

And God doth suffer that it should be so,
But why, my wit is feeble to decise, [65]
Except it be to heap up wrath and woe
Upon their heads that injuries devise.
The cause why mischiefs many times arise
And light on them that would men's wrongs redress
Is for the rancour that they bear, I guess. [70]

God hateth rigour, though it further right,
For sin is sin however it be used,
And therefore suffereth shame and death to light
To punish vice, though it be well abused.
Who furthereth right is not thereby excused, [75]
If through the same he do some other wrong:
To every vice due guerdon doth belong.

What preach I now: I am a man of war,
And that my body, I dare say, doth profess.
Of cured wounds beset with many a scar, [80]
My broken jaw unhealed can say no less.
Oh Fortune, Fortune, cause of all distress!
My father had great cause thy fraud to curse,
But much more I, abusèd ten times worse.

Thou never flattered'st him in all his life, [85]
But me thou dandled'st like thy darling dear.

---

59. avoid: make void. 63. overraught: overpowered. 65. decise: decide. 73. light: descend (upon some-one). 74. well abused: used improperly but for good ends. 77. guerdon: requital. 78. What preach I now: What I now proclaim.

[67] *1563*: On wicked heads   [86] *1563*: like the darling

Thy gifts I found in every corner rife;
Wherever I went I met thy smiling cheer,
Which was not for a day or for a year
But through the reign of three right worthy kings   [90]
I found thee forward in all kind of things.

The while King Henry conquerèd in France,
I sued the wars and still found victory;
In all assaults so happy was my chance,
Holds yield or won did make my en'mies sorry.   [95]
Dame Prudence eke augmented so my glory
That in all treaties ever I was one
When weighty matters were agreed upon.[172]

But when this king, this mighty conqueror,
Through death unripe was both his realms bereft,   [100]
His seely infant did receive his power,
Poor little babe full young in cradle left,
Where crown and sceptre hurt him with the heft,
Whose worthy uncles had the governance,
The one at home, the other abroad in France.[173]   [105]

And I, which was in peace and war well skilled,
With both these rulers greatly was esteemed,
Bare rule at home as often as they willed
And fought in France when they it needful deemed.
And everywhere so good my service seemed   [110]
That Englishmen to me great love did bear;
Our foes, the French, my force fulfilled with fear.

I always thought it fitly for a prince
And such as have the regiment of realms
His subjects' hearts with mildness to convince,   [115]
With justice mixed, avoiding all extremes.
For like as Phoebus with his cheerful beams

---

88. cheer: countenance.   **90. three right worthy kings**: Henry IV, Henry V, and Henry VI.   **91. forward**: ready, eager.   **92. King Henry**: King Henry V.   **93. sued**: followed.   **94. happy**: successful.   **96. Dame Prudence**: good sense, discretion.   **101. seely**: helpless, innocent.

Doth freshly force the fragrant flow'rs to flourish,
So rulers' mildness subjects' love doth nourish.

This found I true, for through my mild behaviour   [120]
Their hearts I had with me to live and die,
And in their speech for to declare their favour
They called me still good earl of Salisbury.
The lords confessed the commons did not lie,
For virtuous life, free heart, and lowly mind   [125]
With high and low shall always favour find.[174]

Which virtues chief become a man of war,
Whereof in France I found experience,
For in assaults due mildness passeth far
All rigour, force, and sturdy violence,   [130]
For men will stoutly stick to their defence
When cruel captains covet them to spoil
And, so enforced, oft give their foes the foil.

But when they know they shall be friendly used,
They hazard not their heads but rather yield;   [135]
For this, my offers never were refused
Of any town, or surely very seld.
But force and furies fit be for the field,
And there indeed I usèd so the same:
My foes would fly if they had heard my name.[175]   [140]

For when Lord Stewart and Earl Vantadore
Had cruelly besiegèd Cravant town,
Which we had wan and kept long time before,
Which lieth in Auxerre on the river Yonne,
To raise the siege the regent sent me down,   [145]
Where, as I used all rigour that I might,
I killèd all that were not saved by flight.[176]

When the earl of Bedford, then in France lord regent,
Knew in what sort I had removed the siege,

---

118. freshly force: vigorously impel.   **148. earl of Bedford**: duke of Bedford.

[122] *1563*: speech bewrayer of their (**bewrayer of**: discloser of)   [132] *1563*: covet after spoil

In Brie and Champagne he made me vicegerent   [150]
And lieutenant for him and for my liege,
Which caused me go to Brie and there besiege
Montaiguillon with twenty weeks' assault,
Which at the last was yielded me for naught. [177]

And for the duke of Britain's brother, Arthur,   [155]
Both earl of Richmond and of Ivery,[178]
Against his oath from us had made departure
To Charles the Dolphin, our chief enemy,
I with the regent went to Normandy
To take his town of Ivery, which of spite   [160]
Did to us daily all the harm they might.

They at the first compounded by a day
To yield, if rescues did not come before.
And, whiles in hope to fight, we at it lay,
The Dolphin gathered men two thousand score,   [165]
With earlès, lords, and captains jolly store,
Of which the duke of Alençon was guide,
And sent them down to see if we would bide.[179]

But they left us and down to Verneuil went,
And made their vaunt they had our army slain,   [170]
And through that lie that town from us they hent,
Which shortly after turnèd to their pain,
For there both armies met upon the plain
And we eight thousand, whom they flew not slew before,
Did kill of them ten thousand men and more.[180]   [175]

When we had taken Verneuil thus again,
To drive the Dolphin utterly out of France
The regent sent me to Anjou and to Maine,
Where I besieged the warlike town of Mawns.
There lord of Toyser's, Baldwin's, valiance   [180]
Did well appear, which would not yield the town,
Till all the towers and walls were battered down.[181]

158. **Dolphin**: Dauphin.   162–3. **They ... before**: They made terms to surrender if relief (supplied by the Dauphin) did not come by a certain appointed day.   164. **we at it lay**: we lay in siege (at Ivry).   166. **jolly store**: in admirably great supply.   171. **hent**: seized.   174. **flew**: fled from.   180. **lord of Toyser's**: seigneur de Tucé's.

But hear now, Baldwin; take it in good part:
Though that I brought this Baldwin there to yield,
The lion fierce for all his noble heart   [185]
Being overmatched is forced to fly the field.
If Mars himself had there been with his shield
And in my storms had stoutly me withstood,
He should have yield or else have shed my blood.

This worthy knight, both hardy, stout, and wise,   [190]
Wrought well his feat, as time and place require.
When fortune fails, it is the best advice
To strike the sail, lest all lie in the mire.
This have I said to th'end thou take no ire,
For, though no cause be found, so nature frames,   [195]
Men have a zeal to such as bear their names.[182]

But to return, in Maine wan I at length
Such towns and forts as might either help or hurt;
I manned Mayenne and Suzannes, towns of strength,
Fort Barnarde, Thanceaux, and S. Cales the curt,   [200]
With Lile sues Bolton, standing in the dirt;
Eke Gwerland, Suszè, Louplande, and Mountsure,
With Malicorne, these wan I and kept full sure.[183]

Besides all this, I took near forty holds,
But those I razèd even with the ground,   [205]
And for these deeds, as seely sheep in folds
Do shrink for fear at every little sound,
So fled my foes before my face full round.
Was none so hardy durst abide the fight,
So Mars and Fortune furthered me their knight.   [210]

I tell no lie, so ghastful grew my name
That it alone discomfited an host.

188. storms: artillery assaults.   **189. should have yield:** would have yielded.   **199. Mayenne:** Mayenne-la-Juhez; **Suzannes:** Sainte-Suzanne.   **200. Fort Barnard:** La Ferté-Bernard; **Thanceaux:** Château L'Hermitage; **S. Cales:** Saint-Calais; **curt:** large house or castle ('court'); short.   **201. Lile sues Bolton:** l'Isle sous Brûlon.   **202. Gwerland:** Château de Gallerande; **Susze:** La Suze-sur-Sarthe ('Susze' is disyllabic in the poem); **Mountsure:** Montsûrs.   **203. Malicorne:** Malicorne-sur-Sarthe.   **206. seely:** simple-minded.

[186] *1563*: to flee

The Scots and Frenchmen will confess the same,
Else will the town which they like cowards lost.
For when they siegèd Bewron with great boast,	[215]
Being forty thousand Britains, French, and Scots,
Five hundred men did vanquish them like sots.

For while the Frenchmen did assault them still,
Our Englishmen came boldly forth at night,
Crying 'Saint George! Salisbury! Kill, kill, kill!',	[220]
And offered freshly with their foes to fight,
And they as Frenchly took themselves to flight,
Supposing surely that I had been there:
See how my name did put them all in fear.

Thus was the Dolphin's power discomfited,	[225]
Four thousand slain, their camp tane as it stood,
Whereby our town and soldiers profited,
For there were victuals plentiful and good.[184]
This while was I in England, by the rood,
To appease a strife that was right foul befall,	[230]
Between Duke Humphrey and the Cardinal.[185]

The duke of Exeter shortly after died,
Which of the king at home had governance,
Whose room the earl of Warwick then supplied,
And I took his and sped me into France.	[235]
And, having a zeal to conquer Orlyaunce,
With much ado I gat the regent's aid
And marched thither and siege about it laid.[186]

But in the way I took the town of Yayn,
Where murdered were for stoutness many a man;	[240]
But Beaugency I took with little pain,
For which to show them favour I began.
This caused the towns of Mewne and Jargeman,

---

215. Bewron: Beuvron.   **216. Britains**: Bretons.   **226. tane**: taken.   **229. by the rood**: by the cross (an oath).   **236. Orlyaunce**: Orléans.   **239. Yayn**: Janville.

[218] *1563*: freshly assaulted still

That stood on Loire, to proffer me the keys
Ere I came near them, well nigh by two days.[187]   [245]

See here how Fortune forward can allure,
What baits she layeth to bring men to their ends!
Who having hap like this but would hope sure
To bring to bail whatever he intends?
But soon is sour the sweet that Fortune sends: [250]
When hope and hap, when health and wealth is high'st,
Then woe and wrack, disease, and need be nigh'st.

For while I, suing this so-good success,
Laid siege to Orlyaunce on the river side,
The Bastard (cuckold Cawny's son, I guess,   [255]
Though thought the duke's), who had this town in guide,[188]
Came fiercely forth, when he his time espied,
To raise the siege but was beat back again
And hard pursued both to his loss and pain.

For there we won the bulwark on the bridge   [260]
With a mighty tower standing fast thereby.
Ah, cursèd tower that didst my days abridge,
Would God thou hadst been further, either I!
For in this tower a chamber stands on high,
From which a man may view through all the town   [265]
By certain windows, iron grated, down.[189]

Where on a day (now Baldwin note mine end)
I stood in viewing where the town was weak,
And, as I busily talkèd with my friend,
Shot fro the town, which all the grate did break,   [270]
A pellet came and drove a mighty flake
Against my face and tare away my cheek,
For pain whereof, I died within a week.[190]

---

248. hap: good luck.   249. bring to bail: bring into his power.   260. bulwark: fortification (including the bridge's gatehouse and tower).   271. pellet: cannonball; flake: fragment.

[247] *1563*: their end   [248] *1563*: but hopeth sure

See Baldwin, see the uncertainty of glory,
How sudden mischief dasheth all to dust! [275]
And warn all princes by my broken story
The happiest fortune chiefly to mistrust.
Was never man that alway had his lust.
Then such be fools, in fancy more than mad,
Which hope to have that never any had. [280]

---

277. **happiest fortune**: most favourable set of circumstances.

[Prose 10]

This strange adventure of the good earl drave us all into a dump, inwardly
lamenting his woeful destiny, out of which we were awaked after this sort:

'To what end', quoth one, 'muse we so much on this matter? This earl is
neither the first nor the last whom Fortune hath foundered in the height of
5   their prosperity. For all through the reign of this unfortunate King Henry
we shall find many which have been likewise served, whose chances, sith
they be martial and therefore honourable, may the better be omitted. And,
therefore, we will let go the Lords Morlines and Poynings, slain both at the
siege of Orléans shortly after the death of this earl.[191] Also the valiant earl
10   of Arundel, destroyed with a bullet at the assault of Gerbory, whose stories
nevertheless are worth the hearing.[192] And to quicken up your spirits, I will
take upon me a tragical person indeed; I mean King Jamie, slain by his
servants in his privy chamber, who, although he be a Scot, yet seeing he
was brought up in England, where he learned the language, his example
15   also so notable, it were not meet he should be forgotten.

And therefore mark, Baldwin, what I think he may say:

---

1. **good earl**: Thomas Montagu (d. 1428), fourth earl of Salisbury, the speaker of the previous tragedy.   5. **King Henry**: Henry VI.   6. **sith**: Since.   12. **King Jamie**: King James I (d. 1437) of Scotland.

[1] *1563*: dump   [15] *1563*: meet it should
[3] *1563*: on the matter

How King James the First, for Breaking his Oaths and Bonds, was by God's Sufferance Miserably Murdered of his own Subjects

If for example's sake thou write thy book,
I charge thee Baldwin thou forget me not,
Whom Fortune always frowardly forsook,
Such was my luck, my merit, or my lot.
I am that James, King Robert's son, the Scot   [5]
That was in England prisoner all his youth,
Through mine Uncle Walter's traitorous untruth.

For when my father, through disease and age,
Unwieldy was to govern well his land,[193]
Because his brother Walter seemèd sage,   [10]
He put the rule thereof into his hand.[194]
Then had my father, you shall understand,
Of lawful bairns me and one only other,
Nempt Davy Rothsay, who was mine elder brother.

This Davy was prince of Scotland, and so take,   [15]
Till his adultery causèd men complain;
Which that he might by monishment forsake,
My father prayed mine uncle take the pain
To threaten him, his vices to refrain.
But he, false traitor, butcherly murd'ring wretch,   [20]
To get the crown began to fetch a fetch

And, finding now a proffer to his prey,
Devisèd means my brother to devour

---

7. **untruth**: disloyalty. 13. **bairns**: children (chiefly Scottish). 14. **nempt**: named (chiefly Scottish); **Davy Rothsay**: David Stewart (d. 1402), first duke of Rothesay. 15. **and so take**: take it as a fact. 21. **fetch a fetch**: devise a stratagem. 22. **proffer**: apparently used here to mean opening or means (though the *OED* records no such usage).

And for that cause conveyed him day by day
From place to place, from castle unto tower, [25]
To Falkland fort, where like a tormenter
He starvèd him and put to death a wife
Whom through a reed he sucked to save his life.[195]

Oh wretched death! Fie, cruel tyranny!
A prince in prison lost for fault of food? [30]
Was never en'my wrought such villainy:
A trusted brother stroy his brother's blood.
Woe worth foe friendly! Fie on double-hood!
Ah, wretched father, see thy son is lost,
Starved by thy brother, whom thou trusted'st most. [35]

Of whom when some began to find the fraud
(And yet the traitor made himself so clear
That he should seem to have deservèd laud,
So woeful did he for his death appear),
My doubtful father, loving me full dear, [40]
To avoid all danger that might after chance,
Sent me away, but nine years old, to France.

But winds and weather were so contrary
That we were driven to the English coast,
Which realm with Scotland at that time did vary, [45]
So that they took me prisoner, not as host,
For which my father, fearing I were lost,
Conceivèd shortly such an inward thought
As to the grave immediately him brought.[196]

Then had mine uncle all the regiment [50]
At home, and I in England prisoner lay,
For to himself he thought it detriment
For my release any ransom for to pay,
For, as he thought, he had possessed his prey,

31–2. **Was … blood**: There was never before an enemy who practised such villainy as a trusted brother's destruction of his brother's blood kindred.   33. **double-hood**: duplicity.   54. **prey**: that for which he had hunted; plunder.

[33] *1563*: worth so friendly

And therefore wished I might in durance dure   [55]
Till I had died, so should his reign be sure.

But good King Henry, seeing I was a child
And heir by right unto a realm and crown,
Did bring me up, not like my brother, wild,
But virtuously in feats of high renown,   [60]
In liberal arts, in instrumental sowne,
By mean whereof when I was after king,
I did my realm to civil order bring.[197]

For ere I had been prisoner eighteen year –
In which short space two noble princes died,   [65]
Whereof the first in prudence had no peer,
The other in war most valiant throughly tried,
Whose room his son, babe Henry, eke supplied –
The peers of England, which did govern all,
Did of their goodness help me out of thrall.   [70]

They married me to a cousin of their king,
The duke of Somerset's daughter, rich and fair,
Released my ransom save a trifling thing,
And after I had done homage to the heir
And sworn my friendship never should appair,   [75]
They brought me kingly furnished to my land,
Which I receivèd at mine uncle's hand.[198]

Whereof my lords and commons were full glad,
So was mine uncle chiefly (as he said),
Who in his mouth no other matter had   [80]
Save punish such as had my brother trayed,
The fault whereof apparently he laid
To good Duke Murdo, his elder brother's son,
Whose father died long ere this deed was done.

My cursèd uncle, slier than the snake,   [85]
Which would by craft unto the crown aspire,

---

55. **in durance dure**: remain in forced constraint. 57. **King Henry**: Henry IV. 61. **sowne**: music (lit. sound;
chiefly a Scottish usage). 65. **two noble princes**: Henry IV and Henry V. 67. **throughly tried**: thoroughly prov-
en. 68. **babe Henry**: King Henry VI. 74. **heir**: Henry VI. 75. **appair**: diminish. 77. **my uncle's**: 'Walter',
duke of Albany's. 81. **trayed**: betrayed. 82. **apparently**: openly; in appearance only.

Because he saw this Murdo was a stake
That stayèd up the stop of his desire
(For his elder brother was Duke Murdo's sire),
He thought it best to have him made away, [90]
So was he sure, I gone, to have his prey.

And by his crafts the traitor brought to pass
That I destroyed Duke Murdo and his kin,
Poor innocents, my loving friends, alas!
Oh kings and princes, what plight stand we in: [95]
A trusted traitor shall you quickly win
To put to death your kin and friends most just.
Take heed, therefore, take heed whose rede you trust.[199]

And at the last to bring me whole in hate
With God and man at home and eke abroad, [100]
He counselled me for 'surance of my state
To help the Frenchmen, then nigh overtrode
By Englishmen, and more to lay on load,
With power and force all England to invade,
Against the oath and homage that I made.[200] [105]

And though at first my conscience did grudge
To break the bonds of friendship knit by oath,
Yet after proof (see mischief) I did judge
It madness for a king to keep his troth.
And semblably with all the world it go'th: [110]
Sins oft assayed are thought to be no sin,
So sin doth soil the soul it sinketh in.

But as diseases, common cause of death,
Bring danger most when least they prick and smart,
Which is a sign they have expulsed the breath [115]
Of lively heat which doth defend the heart,[201]
Even so such sins as felt are on no part

---

103. **and more to lay on load**: and further to harm.   106. **did grudge**: showed itself unwilling.   108. **Yet after proof (see mischief)**: Yet after putting it to the proof (regard this as evildoing).   110. **semblably**: in a similar manner.   115–16. **the breath of lively heat**: the breath (*spiritus*) of life-giving heat (see explanatory note 201).

[112] *1563*: So soileth sin the

Have conquered grace and, by their wicked ure,
So killed the soul that it can have no cure.

And grace agate, vice still succeedeth vice, [120]
And all to haste the vengeance of the first.
I arede therefore all people to be wise
And stop the brack when it begins to burst.
Attaste no poison (vice is venom worst:
It mates the mind); beware eke of too much: [125]
All kill through muchness, some with only touch.

When I had learned to set my oath at nought,
And through much use the sense of sin exiled,
Against King Henry what I could I wrought –
My faith, my oath, unjustly foul defiled. [130]
And while sly Fortune at my doings smiled,
The wrath of God, which I had well deserved
Fell on my neck, for thus, lo, was I served.

Ere I had reignèd fully fifteen year,
While time I lay at Pertho at my place, [135]
With the queen my wife and children me to cheer,
My murd'ring uncle with the double face
That longèd for my kingdom and my mace,
To slay me there subornèd Robert Graham,
With whom his nephew Robert Stuart came. [140]

And when they time fit for their purpose found,
Into my privy chamber they astart,
Wherewith their swords they gave me many a wound,
And slew all such as stuck my part.
There, lo, my wife did show her loving heart, [145]
Who, to defend me, fellèd one or twain
And was sore wounded ere I could be slain.²⁰²

---

118. ure: regular exercise, practice. **120. agate**: going away. **122. arede**: advise. **123. stop the brack**: fill the break. **124. Attaste**: taste; **vice … worst**: vice is worse than posion. **125. mates**: kills. **126. All … touch**: All things kill through overindulgence; some kill simply by mere contact. **142. astart**: start up; appear suddenly.

[141] *1563*: for the purpose

See Baldwin, Baldwin, the unhappy ends
Of such as pass not for their lawful oath,
Of those that causeless leave their faith or friends   [150]
And murder kinsfolk through their foes' untroth.
Warn, warn all princes all like sins to loathe
And chiefly such as in my realm be born,
For God hates highly such as are forsworn.

151. **untroth**: treachery.

[154] *1563*: highly all that are

[Prose 11]

When this was said, 'Let King Jamie go', quoth Master Ferrers, 'and return we to our own story and see what broils were among the nobility in
the king's minority, how the Cardinal Beaufort maligneth the estate of
good Duke Humphrey, the king's uncle and protector of the realm, and by
5 what drifts he first banisheth his wife from him, and, lastly, how the good
duke is murderously made away through conspiracy of Queen Margaret
and other, both whose tragedies I intend at leisure to declare, for they be
notable.'203

'Do so I pray you', quoth another, 'but take heed ye demur not upon
10 them. And I to be occupied the meantime, will show what I have noted in
the duke of Suffolk's doings, one of the chiefest of Duke Humphrey's de-
stroyers, who, by the providence of God, came shortly after in such hatred
of the people that the king himself could not save him from a strange and
notable death, which he may lament after this manner.'

3. **the king's**: Henry VI's; **Cardinal Beaufort**: Henry Beaufort (d. 1447), cardinal and bishop of Winchester.
4. **Duke Humphrey**: Humphrey (d. 1447), first duke of Gloucester.   5. **his wife**: Eleanor, née Cobham (d. 1452),
duchess of Gloucester.   6. **Queen Margaret**: Queen Margaret of Anjou (d. 1482), Henry VI's wife.

How Lord William de la Pole, Duke of Suffolk, was worthily Punished for Abusing his King and Causing the Destruction of Good Duke Humphrey

Heavy is the hap whereto all men be bound,
I mean the death, which no estate may fly,
But to be banished, headed so, and drowned
In sink of shame from top of honours high
Was never man so served I think but I.   [5]
And therefore, Baldwin, fro thy grave of grief
Reject me not, of wretched princes chief.

My only life in all points may suffice
To show how base all baits of Fortune be,
Which thaw like ice through heat of envy's eyes   [10]
Or vicious deeds which much possessèd me.
Good hap with vices cannot long agree,
Which bring best fortunes to the basest fall
And happiest hap to envy to be thrall.

I am the prince Duke William de la Poole[204]   [15]
That was so famous in Queen Margaret's days,
That found the mean Duke Humphrey's blood to cool,
Whose virtuous pains deserve eternal praise.
Whereby I note that Fortune cannot raise
Anyone aloft without some other's wrack: [20]
Floods drown no fields before they find a brack.

But as the waters which do break their walls
Do lose the course they had within the shore,

Title. **his king**: King Henry VI; **Duke Humphrey**: Humphrey (d. 1447), first duke of Gloucester.   **1. hap**: lot.
4. sink: pool for collecting sewage.   **8. My only life**: My life by itself.   **12. Good hap**: success, prosperity.
14. happiest hap: most fortunate; most pleasing situation in life.   **21. brack**: breech.

[Title] *1563*: Worthily Banished for
[23] *1563*: lose their course

And, daily rotting, stink within their stalls
For fault of moving, which they found before, [25]
Even so the state that over high is bore
Doth lose the life of people's love it had
And rots itself until it fall to bad.

For while I was but earl, each man was glad
To say and do the best by me they might, [30]
And Fortune, ever since I was a lad,
Did smile upon me with a cheerful sight,
For when my king had dubbèd me a knight
And sent me forth to serve at war in France,
My lucky speed mine honour did enhance.[205] [35]

Where to omit the many feats I wrought
Under others' guide, I do remember one
Which with my soldiers valiantly was fought,
None other captain save myself alone,
I mean not now the apprinze of Pucelle Joan [40]
In which attempt my travail was not small,
Though the Duke of Burgoyne had the praise of all.[206]

But the siege of Aumerle is the feat I praise,
A strong-built town, with castles, walls, and vaults,
With men and weapon armed at all assays, [45]
To which I gave nigh five times five assaults
Till at the last they yielded it for naughts,
Yet Lord Rambures, like a valiant knight,
Defended it as long as ever he might.[207]

But what prevailèd it these towns to win, [50]
Which shortly after must be lost again?
Whereby I see there is more glory in
The keeping things than is in their attain:
To get and keep not is but loss of pain.

---

24. **stalls**: standing places. 40. **apprinze**: apprehension (apparently a neologism). 44. **castles**: strongholds. 45. **at all assays**: ready at all times.

Therefore ought men provide to save their winnings   [55]
In all attempts, else lose they their beginnings.

Because we could not keep the towns we won
(For they were more than we might easily wield),
One year undid what we in ten had done,
For envy at home and treason abroad did yield   [60]
King Charles his realm of France, made barren field,
For bloody wars had wasted all increase,
Which caused the pope help poverty sue for peace.

So that in Touraine at the town of Tours
Duke Charles and other for their prince appeared,   [65]
So did Lord Ross and I, then earl, for ours,
And when we showed wherein each other dered
We sought out means all quarrels to have cleared,
Wherein the lords of Germany, of Spain,
Of Hungary, and Denmark took exceeding pain.²⁰⁸   [70]

But sith we could no final peace induce
(For neither would the other's covenants hear),
For eighteen months we did conclude a truce
And, while as friends we lay together there,
Because my warrant did me therein bear   [75]
To make a perfect peace and through accord,
I sought a marriage for my sovereign lord.²⁰⁹

And for the French king's daughters were too small,
I fancied most Dame Margaret his niece,
A lovely lady, beautiful and tall,   [80]
Fair spoken, pleasant, a very princely piece,
In wit and learning matchless hence to Greece—
Duke Rainer's daughter, of Anjou, king by style
Of Naples, Jerusalem, and of Sicil Isle.

But ere I could the grant of her attain,   [85]
All that our king had of her father's lands,

<hr />

61. **King Charles**: King Charles VII.   67. **And ... dered**: And when we showed each other what troubled us.   71. **sith**: since.   76. **through**: thorough.   83. **king by style**: titular king.

As Mauntes the city, the county whole of Maine,
And most of Anjou duchy in our hands
I did release him by assurèd bands
And, as for dowry, with her none I sought: [90]
I thought no peace could be too dearly bought.²¹⁰

But when this marriage throughly was agreed,
Although my king were glad of such a make,
His Uncle Humphrey abhorred it indeed,
Because thereby his pre-contract he brake, [95]
Made with the heir of the earl of Arminake,
A noble maid with store of goods endowed,
Which more than this, with loss, the duke allowed.²¹¹

But love and beauty in the king so wrought
That neither profit or promise he regarded [100]
But set his uncle's counsel still at nought,
And for my pains I highly was rewarded:
Thus virtue starves, but lustfood must be larded.
For I, made marquess, went into France again
And brought this bride unto my sovereign.²¹² [105]

At whom because Duke Humphrey ay repined,
Calling their marriage adultery (as it was),
The Queen did move me, erst thereto inclined,
To help to bring him to his requiem mass,
Which, sith it could for no crime come to pass [110]
(His life and doings were so right and clear),
Through privy murder we brought him to his bier.²¹³

Thus righteousness brought Humphrey to rebuke,
Because he would no wickedness allow,
But for my doings I was made a duke, [115]
So Fortune can both bend and smooth her brow
On whom she list, not passing why nor how.
Oh Lord, how high, how soon she did me raise,
How fast she filled me both with preys and praise!

---

87. Mauntes: Le Mans, capital of Maine; **county**: territory traditionally subject to a count. **93. make**: wife. **96. earl of Arminake**: count of Armagnac. **98. allowed**: declared. **103. lustfood**: matter that maintains lust; **larded**: fattened. **119. preys**: plunder, goods.

The lords and commons both of like assent   [120]
Besought my sovereign, kneeling on their knees,
To record my doings in the parliament
As deeds deserving everlasting fees,
In which attempt they did no labour leese,
For they set not my praise so fast in flame   [125]
As he was ready to reward the same.²¹⁴

But note the end: my deeds so worthy deemed
Of king, of lords, and commons altogether
Were shortly after treasons false esteemed,
And all men cursed Queen Margaret's coming hither,   [130]
For Charles the French king, in his feats not lither,
When he had rendered Rainer Mauntes and Maine,
Found mean to win all Normandy again.²¹⁵

This made the people curse the marrìage,
Esteeming it the cause of every loss,   [135]
Wherefore at me with open mouth they rage,
Affirming me to have brought the realm to moss.
When king and queen saw things thus go across,
To quiet all a parliament they called
And causèd me in prison to be thralled   [140]

And, shortly after, brought me forth abroad,
Which made the commons more than double wood,
And some with weapons would have laid on load,
If their grand captain Bluebeard, in his mood,
Had not in time with wisdom been withstood.   [145]
But though that he and mo were executed,
The people still their worst against me bruited²¹⁶

And so applied the parliament with bills
Of heinous wrongs and open trait'rous crimes
That king and queen were forced against their wills   [150]
Fro place to place to adjourn it divers times.

---

124. **leese**: lose. 125. **fast**: firmly. 131. **lither**: sluggish. 137. **to moss**: to decay. 138. **go across**: go awry.
143. **laid on load**: committed violent acts.

For princes' power is like the sandy slimes,
Which must perforce give place unto the wave
Or sue the windy surges when they rave.

Their life was not more dear to them than I,   [155]
Which made them search all shifts to save me still,
But ay my foes such faults did on me try
That to preserve me from a worser ill
The king was fain, full sore against his will,
For five years' space to send me in exile,   [160]
In hope to have restored me in a while.[217]

But mark how vengeance waiteth upon vice:
As I was sailing toward the coast of France,
The earl of Devonshire's bark, of little price,
Encountered me upon the seas by chance,   [165]
Whose captain took me by his valiance,
Let pass my ships with all the freight and load
But led me with him into Dover road,

Where, when he had recounted me my faults,
As murd'ring of Duke Humphrey in his bed,   [170]
And how I had brought all the realm to naughts
In causing the king unlawfully to wed,
There was no grace but I must lose my head,
Wherefore he made me shrive me in his boat,
On the edge whereof my neck in two he smote.[218]   [175]

A piteous end, and therefore Baldwin warn
All peers and princes to abhor untroth,
For vicious grain must come to foul end's barn.
Who breweth breach of lawful bond or oath
God will, ere long, cause all the world to loathe.   [180]
Was never prince that other did oppress
Unrighteously but died in distress.[219]

---

152. **sandy slimes**: littoral sandy mud.   154. **sue**: follow.   157. **ay**: ever; **on me try**: prove against me.   164. **price**: worth, esteem.   168. **Dover road**: sheltered water near Dover, Kent, where ships could rest at anchor.   174. **shrive me**: make my confession (in the religious sense).   177. **untroth**: unfaithfulness.

[Prose 12]

When this was said, every man rejoiced to hear of a wicked man so mar-
vellously well punished, for though Fortune in many points be injurious to
princes, yet in this and such like she is most righteous and only deserveth
the name of a goddess, when she provideth means to punish and destroy
5   tyrants.

And when we had a while considered the drifts of the king and queen
to have saved this duke, and yet they could not, 'it is worth the labour',
said one, 'to weigh the works and judgements of God, which, seeing they
are known most evidently by comparing contraries, I will touch the story
10   of Jack Cade in order next following, whom King Henry with all his puissance was no more able for a while to destroy (yet was he his rebellious
enemy) than he was to preserve the duke of Suffolk his dearest friend, by
which two examples doth appear how notably God disposeth all things
and that no force stretcheth farther than it pleaseth him to suffer. For this
15   Cade, being but base born, of no ability and less power, accompanied
with a few naked Kentishmen, caused the king with his army at all points
appointed to leave the field and to suffer him to do whatsoever he lusted;
in whose behalf, seeing he is one of Fortune's whelps, I will trouble you a
while to hear the process of his enterprise, which he may declare in manner
20   following:

16–17. **naked**: without armour;   **at all points appointed**: completely equipped.   18. **one of Fortune's whelps**: one
of Fortune's offspring (a man fully under Fortune's control).   19. **process**: narrative.

[Tragedy 12]

❧ How Jack Cade, Traitorously Rebelling Against his King, was for his Treasons and Cruel Doings Worthily Punished

Shall I call it Fortune or my froward folly
That lifted me and laid me down below?
Or was it courage that me made so jolly,
Which of the stars and bodies' 'greement grow?
Whatever it were, this one point sure I know,   [5]
Which shall be meet for every man to mark:
Our lust and wills our evils chiefly wark.

It may be well that planets do incline
And our complexions move our minds to ill,
But such is reason that they bring to fine   [10]
No work unaided of our lust and will,
For heaven and earth are subject both to skill:
The skill of God ruleth all, it is so strong;
Man may by skill guide things that to him long.

Though lust be sturdy and will inclined to nought   [15]
(This forced by mixture, that by heaven's course),
Yet through the skill God hath in reason wrought
And given man, no lust nor will so coarse
But may be stayed or swagèd of the source,

3–4. **Or … grow**: Or was it my courage that made me so high-spirited and presumptuous, courage which grows from the astrological affinity of the stars and other heavenly bodies? (**courage**: inherent spirit of liveliness, vigour).   7. **lust and wills**: fleshly appetites and mental inclinations.   8–9. **It … ill**: It may well be that the influence of astrological bodies and our own natural constitutions impel us toward the commission of evil (**complexions**: specific combinations of bodily humours understood to influence a person's temperament and disposition).   10. **fine**: conclusion.   12. **skill**: moral discrimination, sense of what is right.   13. **skill of God**: God's moral certainty; God's expertness in his tasks.   14. **skill**: conscience; **long**: belong. 15–21. See explanatory note 220.   15. **sturdy**: vigorous, robust; **nought**: wickedness.   17. **skill**: the power of moral discernment; **wrought**: incorporated, worked (into).   19. **swaged**: pacified.

[Title] *1563*: [no fleuron]

So that it shall in nothing force the mind   [20]
To work our woe or leave the proper kind.²²⁰

But though this skill be given every man
To rule the will and keep the mind aloft,
For lack of grace full fewè use it can,
These worldly pleasures tickle us so oft.   [25]
Skill is not weak, but will strong; flesh is soft
And yields itself to pleasure that it loveth
And hales the mind to that it most reproveth.

Now if this hap whereby we yield our mind
To lust and will be fortune, as we name her,   [30]
Then is she justly callèd false and blind
And no reproach can be too much to blame her,
Yet is the shame our own when so we shame her,
For sure this hap, if it be rightly known,
Cometh of ourselves, and so the blame our own.   [35]

For who so liveth in the school of skill
And meddleth not with any world's affairs,
Forsaketh pomps and honours that do spill
The mind's recourse to grace's quiet stayers,
His state no fortune by no mean appairs,   [40]
For Fortune is the folly and plague of those
Which to the world their wretched wills dispose.

Among which fools – mark, Baldwin! – I am one
That would not stay myself in mine estate.
I thought to rule but to obey to none,   [45]
And therefore fell I with my king at bate
And to the end I might him better mate
John Mortimer I caused myself be called,
Whose kingly blood the Henries nigh had thralled.²²¹

This shift I used the people to persuade   [50]
To leave their prince, on my side more to stick,

---

21. proper kind: mode of action proper for humans.   **22. skill:** power of moral discernment.   **23. aloft:** dominant; fixed on highest matters.   **24. grace:** inner virtue, goodness; **fewe:** few (disyllabic).   **25. tickle:** stir, excite.   **26. Skill:** conscience.   **28. hales:** draws.   **29. hap:** determiner of events.   **36. For ... skill:** For whoso follows the instruction of conscience.   **38. spill:** destroy.   **39. quiet stayers:** calming restraints.   **40. fortune:** happenstance; **appairs:** weakens.   **42. dispose:** give over.   **46. at bate:** into contention.   **47. mate:** defeat.   **49. nigh had thralled:** all but kept captive.

Whereas indeed my father's name was Cade,
Whose noble stock was never worth a stick,
But, touching wit, I was both ripe and quick,
Had strength of limbs, large stature, comely face,   [55]
Which made men ween my lin'age were not base.

And seeing stoutness stuck by men in Kent,
Whose valiant hearts refuse none enterprise,
With false persuasions straight to them I went
And said they suffered too-great injuries,   [60]
By mean whereof I causèd them to rise
And battlewise to come to Blackheath plain
And thence their griefs unto the king complain,

Who being deaf, as men say, on that ear,
For we desired release of subsidies,   [65]
Refusèd roughly our requests to hear
And came against us as his enemies.
But we, to trap him, sought out subtleties,
Removed our camp, and back to Senock went,
After whom the Staffords with their power were sent.[222]   [70]

See here how Fortune setting us afloat
Brought to our nets a portion of our prey,
Forwhy the Staffords with their army hot
Assailèd us at Senock where we lay,
From whence alive they parted not away,   [75]
Which when the king's retinue understood,
They all affirmed my quarrel to be good.[223]

Which caused the king and queen, whom all did hate,
To raise their camp and suddenly depart,
And that they might the people's grudge abate   [80]
To imprison some full sore against their heart.
Lord Sayes was one, whom I made after smart,
For after the Staffords and their host was slain,
To Blackheath field I marchèd back again.

---

53. **stock**: lineage (with a play on 'wood, stump').   62. **battlewise**: ordered for battle.   73. **Forwhy**: because.

[68] *1563*: to tray him [**tray**: trouble]

And where the king would nothing hear before,   [85]
Now he was glad to send to know my mind,
And I thereby enflamèd much the more
Refused his grants, so folly made me blind.
For this, he flew and left Lord Scales behind
To help the town and strengthen London Tower,   [90]
Towards which I marchèd forward with my power²²⁴

And found there all things after my desire.
I entered London, did there what I list,
The treasurer, Lord Sayes, I did conspire
To have condemnèd: whereof, when I missed   [95]
(For he by law my malice did resist),
By force I took him in Guildhall fro the heap
And headed him before the cross in Cheap.

His son-in-law James Cromer, shrive of Kent,
I caught at Mile End, whereas then he lay,   [100]
Beheaded him and on a pole I sent
His head to London, where his father's lay.
With these two heads I made a pretty play,
For pight on poles I bare them through the street
And for my sport made each kiss other sweet. ²²⁵   [105]

Then brake I prisons, let forth whom I would,
And used the city as it had be mine,
Took from the merchants money, ware, and gold,
From some by force, from other some by fine.
This at the length did cause them to repine,   [110]
So that Lord Scales, consenting with the mayor,
Forbade us to their city to repair.

For all this while mine host in Southwark lay,
Who, when they knew our passage was denied,
Came boldly to the bridge and made a fray,   [115]

---

97. **the heap**: the crowd (at Guildhall).   99. **shrive**: sheriff.   100. **Mile End**: a village close to east London.   102. **father's**: father-in-law's.   104. **pight**: set in place.   112. **repair**: return.   115. **the bridge**: London Bridge.

[90] *1559*: Mo help [an uncorrected printer's error]   [107] *1563*: had been mine

For in we would, the townsmen us defied.
But, when with strokes we had the matter tried,
We won the bridge and set much part on fire;
This done, to Southwark back we did retire.²²⁶

The morrow after came the chancellor   [120]
With general pardon for my men half gone,
Which heard and read, the rest within an hour
Shrank all away, each man to shift for one.
And when I saw they left me post alone,
I did disguise me like a knight of the post   [125]
And into Sussex rode away in post.²²⁷

And there I lurkèd, till that cursèd coin,
That restless beagle, sought and found me out,
For straight the king by promise did enjoin
A thousand mark to whosoever mought   [130]
Apprend my corse, which made men seek about,
Among the which one Alexander Iden
Found out the hole wherein the fox was hidden,

But ere he took me, I put him to his trumps,
For yield I would not while my hands would hold,   [135]
But hope of money made him stir his stumps
And to assault me valiantly and bold.
Two hours and more our combat was not cold,
Till at the last he lent me such a stroke
That down I fell and never after spoke.²²⁸   [140]

Then was my carcass carried like a hog
To Southwark borough where it lay a night;
The next day drawn to Newgate like a dog,
All men rejoicing at the rueful sight.

---

123. **shift for one**: look out for himself.   124. **post alone**: all by myself.   125. **knight of the post**: falsifier, duplicitous person (**post**: whipping post).   126. **in post**: with great haste.   128. **restless beagle**: unwearying tracking hound.   129. **enjoin**: grant (lit. impose).   130. **mark**: marks (coins worth two-thirds of an English pound); **mought**: might.   131. **apprend my corse**: seize my body (whether living or dead).   134. **But ... trumps**: But before he took me, I pushed him to his limits.   136. **stir his stumps**: act briskly (lit. move his legs).

[131] *1563*: made them seek

Then were on poles my parboiled quarters pight   [145]
And set aloft for vermin to devour:
Meet grave for rebels that resist the power.[229]

Full little know we wretches what we do,
When we presume our princes to resist.
We war with God, against his glory too,   [150]
That placeth in his office whom he list.
Therefore was never traitor yet but missed
The mark he shot and came to shameful end,
Nor never shall, till God be forced to bend.

God hath ordained the power; all princes be   [155]
His lieutenants or debities in realms.
Against their foes still therefore fighteth he,
And, as his en'mies, drives them to extremes;
Their wise devices prove but doltish dreams.
No subject ought for any kind of cause   [160]
To force the lord, but yield him to the laws.

And therefore Baldwin warn men follow reason,
Subdue their wills and be not Fortune's slaves;
A troublous end doth ever follow treason.
There is no trust in rebels, rascal knaves,   [165]
In Fortune less, which worketh as the waves,
From whose assaults, who list to stand at large
Must follow skill and fly all worldly charge.

---

147. **Meet … power**: fitting resting place for rebels who strive against those in authority.   149. **princes**: sovereigns, governors.   156. **debities**: deputies.   158. **extremes**: utmost hardships.   159. **wise devices**: clever stratagems.   161. **lord**: governor; God.   167. **at large**: in freedom.   168. **skill**: conscience; **worldly charge**: worldly dictates; troublesome matters.

[Prose 13]

'By Saint Mary', quoth one, 'if Jack were as well learned as you have made
his oration, whatsoever he was by birth I warrant him a gentleman by his
learning.[230] How notably and philosopher-like hath he described Fortune
and the causes of worldly cumbrance? How uprightly also and how like
a divine hath he determined the states both of officers and rebels?[231] For
indeed officers be God's deputies, and it is God's office which they bear,
and it is he which ordaineth thereto such as himself listeth, good when he
favoureth the people and evil when he will punish them. And, therefore,
whosoever rebelleth against any ruler either good or bad rebelleth against
GOD and shall be sure of a wretched end, for God cannot but maintain
his deputy.[232]

'Yet, this I note by the way concerning rebels and rebellions: although
the devil raise them, yet God always useth them to his glory, as a part of his
justice, for when kings and chief rulers suffer their under-officers to misuse
their subjects and will not hear nor remedy their people's wrongs when
they complain, then suffereth GOD the rebel to rage and to execute that
part of his justice which the partial prince would not.[233] For the Lord Sayes,
a very corrupt officer and one whom notwithstanding the king always
maintained, was destroyed by this Jack, as was also the bishop of Salisbury
(a proud and covetous prelate) by other of the rebels.[234] And, therefore,
whatsoever prince desireth to live quietly without rebellion must do his
subjects right in all things and punish such officers as grieve or oppress
them: thus shall they be sure from all rebellion. And for the clearer opening hereof, it were well done to set forth this Lord Sayes's tragedy.'

'What need that', quoth another, 'seeing the like example is seen in the
duke of Suffolk, whose doings are declared sufficiently already? Nay, rather
let us go forward, for we have a great many behind that may not be omitted, and the time, as you see, passeth away. As for this Lord Sayes, whom
Cade so cruelly killed and spitefully used after his death, I dare say shall
be known thereby what he was to all that read or hear this story, for God
would never have suffered him to have been so used, except he had first
deserved it. Therefore, let him go and, with him, the bishop and all other
slain in that rebellion, which was raised, as it may be thought, through
some drift of the duke of York,[235] who shortly after began to endeavour all

---

4. **cumbrance**: trouble, distress.   17. **partial**: biased.   23–4. **opening**: disclosing.   25. **another**: George Ferrers.
26. **duke of Suffolk**: see Tragedy 11.

[10] *1563*: wicked end

35 means to attain the crown and therefore gathered an army in Wales and
marched toward London. But the king with his power tarried and met him
at St. Albans, where, while the king and he were about a treaty, the earl of
Warwick set upon the king's army and slew the duke of Somerset, the earl
of Northumberland, the Lord Clifford, and other and, in conclusion, got
40 the victory, and the duke was made lord protector, which so grieved the
queen and her accomplices that privy grudges and open dissembling never
ceased till the duke and his allies were glad to fly the field and realm, he into
Ireland, they to Calais.²³⁶ Whence they came again with an army, whereof
the earl of Salisbury was leader, and marched toward Coventry, where the
45 king then was and had gathered an army to subdue them and encountered
them at Northampton and fought and lost the field and was taken himself,
the duke of Buckingham, the earl of Shrewsbury, the Viscount Beaumont,
the Lord Egremont, and many other of his retinue slain.²³⁷ If no man have
any mind to any of these noble personages, because they were honourably
50 slain in battle, let some man else take the book, for I mind to say somewhat
of this duke of Somerset.'²³⁸

ᶓ While he was devising thereon, and every man seeking farther notes,
I looked on the chronicles and, finding still field upon field, and many
noble men slain, I purposed to have overpassed all, for I was so weary that
55 I waxed drowsy and began indeed to slumber, but my imagination, still
prosecuting this tragical matter, brought me such a fantasy:²³⁹ me thought
there stood before us a tall man's body full of fresh wounds but lacking a
head, holding by the hand a goodly child, whose breast was so wounded
that his heart might be seen, his lovely face and eyes disfigured with drop-
60 ping tears, his hair through horror standing upright, his mercy-craving
hands all-to bemangled, and all his body imbrued with his own blood.
And, when through the ghastfulness of this piteous spectacle, I waxed
afeared and turned away my face, me thought there came a shrieking voice
out of the weasand pipe of the headless body, saying as followeth:

---

36. tarried: awaited. **53. still field upon field**: continually battle after battle. **61. all-to bemangled**: completely
lacerated. **64. weasand pipe**: trachea.

[42] *1563*: glad to flee

How Richard Plantagenet, Duke of York, was Slain Through his
Overrash Boldness, and his Son the Earl of Rutland for his
Lack of Valiance

'Trust Fortune', quoth he, in whom was never trust:
Oh folly of men that have no better grace!
All rest, renown, and deeds lie in the dust
Of all the sort that sue her slipper trace.
What meanest thou Baldwin for to hide thy face?　　　　[5]
Thou needest not fear, although I miss my head,
Nor yet to mourn for this my son is dead.

The cause why thus I lead him in my hand,
His skin with blood and tears so sore bestained,
Is that thou mayst the better understand　　　　[10]
How hardly Fortune hath for us ordained,
In whom her love and hate be whole contained,
For I am Richard, Prince Plantagenet,
The duke of York in royal race beget.

For Richard, earl of Cambridge, eldest son　　　　[15]
Of Edmund Langley, third son of King Edward,²⁴⁰
Engendered me of Anne, whose course did run
Of Mortimers to be the issue guard;
For when her brother Edmund died a ward,
She was sole heir by due descent of line,　　　　[20]
Whereby her rights and titles all were mine.²⁴¹

But mark me now, I pray thee Baldwin, mark,
And see how force oft overbeareth right.
Weigh how usurpers tyrannously wark

---

3. dust: remains.　**4. Of … trace:** of all those who follow her slippery track.　**11. hardly:** cruelly.　**18. issue guard:** keeper of the hereditary line.　**19. ward:** prisoner.

To keep by murder that they get by might.   [25]
And note what troublous dangers do alight
On such as seek to repossess their own,
And how through rigour right is overthrown.

The earl of Herford, Henry Bolingbroke,
Of whom Duke Mowbray told thee now of late,   [30]
When, void of cause, he had King Richard took,
He murdered him, usurpèd his estate
Without all right or title, saving hate
Of others' rule or love to rule alone;
These two excepted, title had he none.   [35]

The realm and crown was Edmund Mortimer's,
Whose father Roger was King Richard's heir,
Which causèd Henry and the Lancasters
To seek all shifts our households to appair,
For sure he was to sit beside the chair   [40]
Were we of power to claim our lawful right,
Wherefore to stroy us he did all he might.

His cursèd son ensued his cruel path
And kept my guiltless cousin straight in durance,
For whom my father hard entreated hath.   [45]
But, living hopeless of his life's assurance,
He thought it best by politic procurance
To prive the king and so restore his friend,
Which brought himself to an infamous end,²⁴²

For when King Henry of that name the Fift   [50]
Had tane my father in this conspiracy,
He, from Sir Edmund all the blame to shift,
Was fain to say the French king, his ally,
Had hired him this traitorous act to try,
For which condemnèd, shortly he was slain: [55]
In helping right this was my father's gain.²⁴³

---

25. **that**: that which.   29. **earl of Herford**: Henry Bolingbroke (d. 1413), first duke (not earl) of Hereford and, later, King Henry IV.   30. **Duke Mowbray**: Thomas Mowbray (d. 1399), first duke of Norfolk, speaker of Tragedy 4.   31. **King Richard**: King Richard II.   39. **appair**: damage, weaken.   40. **For … chair**: For he would certainly be removed from the throne.   44. **cousin**: near relative (i.e. Edmund, earl of March); **straight in durance**: closely held in prison.   48. **prive**: depose.   53. **fain to say**: willing to say (as the lesser of two evils).

Thus when the lin'age of the Mortimers
Were made away by this usurping line,
Some hanged, some slain, some pinèd prisoners,
Because the crown by right of law was mine, [60]
They gan as fast against me to repine,
In fear always lest I should stir them strife,
For guilty hearts have never quiet life.²⁴⁴

Yet at the last in Henry's days the Sixt,
I was restorèd to my father's lands, [65]
Made duke of York, wherethrough my mind I fixed
To get the crown and kingdom in my hands,²⁴⁵
For aid wherein I knit assurèd bands
With Neville's stock, whose daughter was my make,
Who for no woe would ever me forsake. [70]

Oh Lord, what hap had I through marrìage!
Four goodly boys in youth my wife she bore,
Right valiant men, and prudent for their age.
Such brethren she had and nephews still in store
As none had erst nor any shall have more. [75]
The earl of Salisbury and his son of Warwick
Were matchless men from Barbary to Berwick, ²⁴⁶

Through help of whom and Fortune's lovely look,
I undertook to claim my lawful right
And, to abash such as against me took, [80]
I raisèd power at all points prest to fight,
Of whom the chief that chiefly bare me spite
Was Somerset the duke, whom to annoy
I alway sought, through spite, spite to destroy.

And maugre him, so choice, lo, was my chance, [85]
Yea, though the queen that all ruled took his part,
I twice bare stroke in Normandy and France

---

69. Neville's stock: the family of Ralph Neville (d. 1425), first earl of Westmorland; **make**: mate. **71. hap**: good fortune. **72. four goodly boys**: see explanatory note 246. **77. Were … Berwick**: i.e. were men who had no match anywhere in the world. **81. prest**: ready, eager. **84. I … destroy**: I ever sought through hostile action to destroy the duke of Somerset's own spite towards me. **87. bare stroke**: held chief authority.

[87] *1563*: bare rule in

And last lieutenant in Ireland, where my heart
Found remedy for every kind of smart,
For through the love my doings there did breed, [90]
I had their help at all times in my need.[247]

This spiteful duke, his silly king and queen,
With armèd hosts I thrice met in the field:
The first unfought through treaty made between,
The second joined, wherein the king did yield, [95]
The duke was slain, the queen enforced to shield
Herself by flight. The third the queen did fight,
Where I was slain, being overmatched by might.[248]

Before this last were other battles three,
The first the earl of Salisbury led alone [100]
And fought on Blore Heath and got the victory.
In the next was I and my kinsfolk every chone,
But, seeing our soldiers stale unto our foen,
We warely brake our company on a night,
Dissolved our host and took ourselves to flight.[249] [105]

This boy and I in Ireland did us save;
Mine eldest son with Warwick and his father
To Calais got, whence by the rede I gave
They came again to London and did gather
Another host, whereof I spake not rather, [110]
And met our foes, slew many a lord and knight,
And took the king and drave the queen to flight.[250]

This done, came I to England all in haste
To make my claim unto the realm and crown,
And in the house while parliament did last [115]
I in the king's seat boldly sat me down
And claimèd it, whereat the lords did frown.
But what for that? I did so well proceed
That all at last confessed it mine indeed.

96. **the duke**: the duke of Somerset. 102. **every chone**: everyone. 103. **foen**: foes. 104. **warely**: prudent-ly. 106. **This boy**: Edmund (d. 1460), styled earl of Rutland. 110. **rather**: earlier.

[101] *1563*: got victory

But sith the king had reignèd now so long,   [120]
They would he should continue till he died,
And to the end that then none did me wrong
Protector and heir apparent they me cried.
But sith the queen and others this denied,
I sped me toward the north, where then she lay,   [125]
In mind by force to cause her to obey.²⁵¹

Whereof she warned prepared a mighty power
And, ere that mine were altogether ready,
Came bold to Bosworth and besieged my bower,²⁵²
Where, like a beast, I was so rash and heady   [130]
That out I would – there could be no remedy –
With scant five thousand soldiers to assail
Four times so many encamped to most avail,

And so was slain at first, and while my child
Scarce twelve year old sought secretly to part,   [135]
That cruel Clifford, lord, nay lorel wild,
While the infant wept and prayed him rue his smart,
Knowing what he was, with his dagger clave his heart.²⁵³
This done, he came to the camp where I lay dead,
Despoiled my corpse and cut away my head.   [140]

And when he had put a paper crown thereon,
As a gauring-stock he sent it to the queen,
And she for spite commanded it anon
To be had to York, where that it might be seen.
They placèd it where other traitors been.   [145]
This mischief Fortune did me after death,
Such was my life and such my loss of breath.²⁵⁴

Wherefore see Baldwin that thou set it forth
To the end the fraud of Fortune may be known,
That eke all princes well may weigh the worth   [150]
Of things for which the seeds of war be sown.

---

120. **sith**: since. 133. **most avail**: greatest advantage. 134. **at first**: immediately. 135. **part**: depart (the field of battle). 136. **lorel**: blackguard, scoundrel. 137. **infant**: child; **rue his smart**: pity his pain. 138. **Knowing … heart**: Knowing him to be who he was (i.e. the duke of York's son), he cleaved his heart with his dagger. 142. **gauring-stock**: gazing stock.

[129] *1563*: Came swift to Sandal and

No state so sure but soon is overthrown;
No worldly good can counterpoise the price
Of half the pains that may thereof arise.

Far better it were to lose a piece of right   [155]
Than limbs and life in sousing for the same;
It is not force of friendship nor of might
But God that causeth things to fro or frame.
Not wit but luck doth wield the winner's game.
Wherefore, if we our follies would refrain,   [160]
Time would redress all wrongs, we void of pain.

Wherefore warn princes not to wade in war
For any cause except the realm's defence;
Their troublous titles are unworthy far
The blood, the life, the spoil of innocence.   [165]
Of friends and foes behold my foul expense
And never the near; best therefore tarry time,
So right shall reign and quiet calm each crime.

153. **counterpoise**: balance out.   156. **sousing**: fighting, exchanging blows.   158. **fro**: go frowardly, be unsuccessful; **frame**: be successful.   161. **void of pain**: free from suffering, free from having to make an effort.   166. **expense**: loss.   168. **near**: nearer.

[Prose 14]

With this, Master Ferrers shook me by the sleeve, saying 'why, how now, man, do you forget yourself? Belike you mind our matters very much!' 'So I do indeed', quoth I, 'for I dream of them.' And when I had rehearsed my dream, we had long talk concerning the natures of dreams, which to stint
5   and to bring us to our matter again, thus said one of them, 'I am glad it was your chance to dream of Duke Richard, for it had been pity to have overpassed him.[255] And as concerning this Lord Clifford, which so cruelly killed his son, I purpose to give you notes, who, as he well deserved, came shortly after to a sudden death, and yet too good for so cruel a tyrant.[256]
10 Wherefore as you thought you saw and heard the headless duke speak through his neck, so suppose you see this Lord Clifford all armed save his head, with his breastplate all gore blood running from his throat, wherein an headless arrow sticketh, through which wound he sayeth thus:

4. **stint**: leave off.   12. **all … throat**: covered in blood that runs from his throat.

[4] *1563*: nature

How the Lord Clifford, for his Strange and Abominable Cruelty,
Came to as Strange and Sudden a Death

Open confession asketh open penance,
And wisdom would a man his shame to hide.
Yet, sith forgiveness cometh through repentance,
I think it best that men their crimes ascried,
For nought so secret but at length is spied,   [5]
For cover fire and it will never lin
Till it break forth: in like case shame and sin.

As for myself, my faults be out so plain
And publishèd so broad in every place,
That though I would I cannot hide a grain;   [10]
All care is bootless in a cureless case.
To learn by others' grief, some have the grace,
And, therefore, Baldwin, write my wretched fall,
The brief whereof I briefly utter shall.

I am the same that slew Duke Richard's child,   [15]
The lovely babe that beggèd life with tears,
Whereby my honour foully I defiled.
Poor silly lambs the lion never tears,
The feeble mouse may lie among the bears,
But wrath of man his rancour to requite   [20]
Forgets all reason, ruth, and virtue quite.[257]

I mean by rancour the parental wreak
Surnamed a virtue, as the vicious say,
But little know the wicked what they speak

---

3. sith: since. **4. ascried**: divulged. **6. lin**: desist. **10. a grain**: (even) the smallest bit. **14. brief**: report.
20. But ... requite: But a man's fit of rage to avenge that which has caused him rancour. **22. parental wreak**:
revenge taken on behalf of a parent.

In 'bold'ning us our en'mies' kin to slay.   [25]
To punish sin is good, it is no nay;
They wreak not sin but merit wreak for sin
That wreak the father's faults upon his kin.

Because my father Lord John Clifford died,
Slain at St Albans in his prince's aid,   [30]
Against the duke my heart for malice fried
So that I could from wreak no way be stayed,
But to avenge my father's death assayed
All means I might the duke of York to annoy
And all his kin and friends to kill and stroy.²⁵⁸   [35]

This made me with my bloody dagger wound
His guiltless son that never against me stirred,
His father's body lying dead on ground
To pierce with spear, eke with my cruel sword
To part his neck and with his head to bourd,   [40]
Invested with a paper royal crown,
From place to place to bear it up and down.²⁵⁹

But cruelty can never scape the scourge
Of shame, of horror, and of sudden death.
Repentance self, that other sins may purge,   [45]
Doth fly from this, so sore the soul it slayeth.
Despair dissolves the tyrant's bitter breath,
For sudden vengeance suddenly alights
On cruel heads, to quite their cruel spites.

This find I true, for as I lay in stale   [50]
To fight against Duke Richard's eldest son,
I was destroyed not far from Dintingdale,
For as I would my gorget have undone
To event the heat that had me nigh undone,
An headless arrow strake me through the throat,   [55]
Wherethrough my soul forsook his filthy coat.²⁶⁰

---

26. **it is no nay**: that is undeniable.   **27–8. They … kin**: Those who revenge the acts of a father on his kin deserve punishment themselves for such a sinful deed.   **40. bourd**: play.   **41. Invested**: Clothed in the insignia of a new office (used ironically).   **45. Revenge … purge**: Repentance itself, which can free one from other sins.   **47. dissolves**: removes from existence.   **49. quite**: repay.   **50. in stale**: in battle array.   **51. Duke Richard's eldest son**: King Edward IV.   **53. gorget**: neck-guard.   **54. event**: cool.

Was this a chance? No, sure, God's just award,
Wherein due justice plainly doth appear.
An headless arrow paid me my reward
For heading Richard lying on the bier. [60]
And as I would his child in nowise hear,
So sudden death bereft my tongue the power
To ask for pardon at my dying hour.

Wherefore, good Baldwin, warn the bloody sort
To leave their wrath, their rigour to refrain. [65]
Tell cruel judges horror is the port
To which they sail through shame and sudden pain.
Hell haleth tyrants down to death amain.
Was never yet nor shall be cruel deed
Left unrewarded with as cruel meed. [70]

---

57. **chance**: chance event.　68. **haleth**: drags; **amain**: quickly, with violence.

[Prose 15]

When this tragedy was ended, 'oh Lord', quoth another, 'how horrible a
thing is division in a realm! To how many mischiefs is it the mother, what
vice is not thereby kindled, what virtue left unquenched? For what was the
cause of the duke of York's death and of the cruelty of this Clifford, save
5　the variance between King Henry and the house of York, which at length,
besides millions of the commons, brought to destruction all the nobility?
For Edward, the duke's eldest son, immediately after his father was slain,
through help of the Nevilles, gave the king a battle whereat, besides this
Clifford and thirty-six thousand other soldiers, were slain their captains
10　the earls of Northumberland and Westmorland, with the Lords Dacres
and Welles; the winning of which field brought Edward to the crown, and
the loss drave King Henry and his wife into Scotland.[261] But as few reigns
begin without blood, so King Edward, to keep order, caused the earls of
Devonshire and Oxford, with divers other his enemies, to be attainted
15　and put to death. And, shortly after, he did execution upon the duke of
Somerset and the Lords Hungerford and Ros, whom he took prisoners at
Hexham field, for thither they came with King Henry out of Scotland,

---

8. **the Nevilles**: Edward Hall mentions several Nevilles fighting on the Yorkist side at the Battle of Towton (1461), chief among them Richard Neville (d. 1471), sixteenth earl of Warwick; and William Neville (d. 1463), sixth Baron Fauconberg.　14. **attainted**: convicted; often used specifically to mean condemned to death with corruption of blood and forfeit of all rights and possessions.

with an army of Scots, and fought a battle, which was lost and most part
of the army slain. And because these are all noble men, I will leave them
20   to Baldwin's discretion. But seeing the earl of Worcester was the chief instrument whom King Edward used as well in these men's matters as in like
bloody affairs, because he should not be forgotten, ye shall hear what I
have noted concerning his tragedy.[262]

[19] *1563*: of them slain

The Infamous End of Lord John Tiptoft, Earl of Worcester, for Cruelly Executing his Prince's Butcherly Commandments

The glorious man is not so loath to lurk
As the infamous glad to lie unknown,
Which maketh me, Baldwin, disallow thy work,
Where princes' faults so openly be blown.
I speak not this alonely for mine own,   [5]
Which were my prince's (if that they were any),
But for my peers, in number very many.

Or might report uprightly use her tongue,
It would less grieve us to augment thy matter,
But sure I am thou shalt be forced among   [10]
To 'frain the truth, the living for to flatter,
And otherwhiles in points unknown to smatter,
For time never was, nor ever I think shall be,
That truth unshent should speak in all things free.

This doth appear, I dare say, by my story,   [15]
Which divers writers diversely declare.
But story writers ought for neither glory,
Feare, nor favour, truth of things to spare.
But still it fares as alway it did fare:
Affection, fear, or doubts that daily brew   [20]
Do cause that stories never can be true.

---

3. **disallow**: discommend.   10. **among**: at this time.   11. **'frain**: refrain, hold back.   12. **otherwhiles**: sometimes; **smatter**: to speak ignorantly or superficially.   14. **unshent**: unspoiled.   18. **Feare**: Fear (disyllabic).

[Title] *1563*: Lord Tiptoft

Unfruitful Fabyan followèd the face
Of time and deeds but let the causes slip,
Which Hall hath added, but with double grace,
For fear, I think, lest trouble might him trip.   [25]
'For this or that', sayeth he, 'he felt the whip';
Thus story writers leave the causes out
Or so rehearse them as they were in doubt.[263]

But seeing causes are the chiefest things
That should be noted of the story writers   [30]
That men may learn what end all causes brings,
They be unworthy the name of chroniclers
That leave them clean out of their registers
Or doubtfully report them, for the fruit
Of reading stories standeth in the suit.   [35]

And therefore, Baldwin, either speak upright
Of our affairs or touch them not at all.
As for myself, I weigh all things so light
That nought I pass how men report my fall;
The truth whereof yet plainly show I shall,   [40]
That thou mayst write and other thereby read
What things I did, whereof they should take heed.

Thou hast heard of Tiptofts, earls of Worcester;
I am that John that lived in Edward's days
(The Fourth) and was his friend and counsellor   [45]
And butcher too, as common rumour says.
But people's voice is neither shame nor praise,
For whom they would alive devour today,
Tomorrow, dead, they will worship what they may.

But though the people's verdict go by chance,   [50]
Yet was there cause to call me as they did,

---

22. **face**: outer surface. 24. **grace**: favour; seemliness. 28. **as**: as if. 35. **in the suit**: in the sequence (of cause and effect). 49. **they … may**: they perhaps may worship (the person they had previously hated).

[44] *1563*: that Lord that
[51] *1563*: Yet had they cause

For I, enforced by mean of governance,
Did execute whatever my king did bid.
From blame herein myself I cannot rid,
But fie upon the wretched state that must   [55]
Defame itself to serve the prince's lust!

The chiefest crime wherewith men do me charge
Is death of the earl of Desmond's noble sons,
Of which the king's charge doth me clear discharge
By straight commandment and injunctions,   [60]
Th'effect whereof so rigorously runs
That either I must procure to see them dead
Or for contempt as a traitor lose my head.[264]

What would mine enemies do in such a case,
Obey the king or proper death procure?   [65]
They may well say their fancy for a face,
But life is sweet and love hard to recure.
They would have done as I did I am sure,
For seldom will a wealthy man at ease
For others' cause his prince in aught displease.   [70]

How much less I, which was lieutenant then
In the Irish isle, preferrèd by the king?
But who for love or dread of any man
Consents to accomplish any wicked thing,
Although chief fault thereof from other spring,   [75]
Shall not escape God's vengeance for his deed,
Who scuseth none that dare do ill for dread.

This in my king and me may well appear,
Which for our faults did not escape the scourge,
For when we thought our states most sure and clear,   [80]

---

52. **by mean of governance**: by the agency of (royal) authority.   65. **proper**: their own.   66. **They … face**: They may well utter their groundless assertions for appearance's sake.   67. **recure**: regain.   80. **clear**: free, without limitation.

[80] *1563*: our state most

The wind of Warwick blew up such a surge
As from the realm and crown the king did purge,
And me both from mine office, friends, and wife,
From good report, from honest death and life.

For th'earl of Warwick, through a cankered grudge [85]
Which to King Edward causeless he did bear,
Out of his realm by force did make him trudge
And set King Henry again upon his chair.²⁶⁵
And then all such as Edward's lovers were,
As traitors tane, were grievously oppressed, [90]
But chiefly I, because I loved him best.

And for my goods and livings were not small,
The gapers for them bare the world in hand
For ten years' space that I was cause of all
The executions done within the land. [95]
For this did such as did not understand
My en'mies' drift think all reports were true
And so to hate me worse than any Jew.²⁶⁶

For seldom shall a ruler lose his life
Before false rumours openly be spread, [100]
Whereby this proverb is as true as rife,
That rulers rumours hunt about ahead.
Frown Fortune once all good report is fled,
For present show doth make the many blind,
And such as see dare not disclose their mind. [105]

Through this was I King Edward's butcher named
And bare the shame of all his cruel deeds.
I clear me not; I worthily was blamed,
Though force was such I must obey him needs.
With highest rulers seldom well it speeds, [110]

---

93. **bare the world in hand**: led the world to believe. 102. **rulers rumours hunt about ahead**: An obscure phrase, perhaps meaning 'rumours hunt for rulers unrestrainedly'.

For they be ever nearest to the nip,
And fault who shall, for all feel they the whip.

For when I was by parliament attainted,
King Edward's evils all were counted mine.²⁶⁷
No truth availed, so lies were fast and painted,   [115]
Which made the people at my life repine,
Crying '*crucifige*, kill that butcher's line!'²⁶⁸
That when I should have gone to Blockam feast,
I could not pass, so sore they on me pressed.

And had not been the officers so strong,   [120]
I think they would have eaten me alive;
Howbeit, hardly halèd from the throng,
I was in the Fleet fast shrouded by the shrive.
Thus one day's life their malice did me give,
Which when they knew, for spite the next day after,   [125]
They kept them calm, so suffered I the slaughter.²⁶⁹

Now tell me Baldwin, what fault dost thou find
In me that justly should such death deserve?
None sure, except desire of honour blind
Which made me seek in offices to serve.   [130]
What mind so good that honours make not swerve?
So mayst thou see, it was only my state
That caused my death and brought me so in hate.

Warn therefore all men wisely to beware
What offices they enterprise to bear.   [135]
The highest alway most malignèd are
Of people's grudge and princes' hate in fear;
For princes' faults, his fautors all men tear.
Which to avoid, let none such office take,
Save he that can for right his prince forsake.   [140]

---

112. And … whip: No matter who is at fault, they receive the punishment. **115. fast**: firmly fixed in place. **118. Blockham feast**: the chopping block. **122. hardly haled**: dragged with difficulty. **123. fast shrouded by the shrive**: securely sheltered by the sheriff. **132. state**: office, high position. **135. enterprise**: take in hand. **138. faults**: defects, offences; **fautors**: adherents.

[Prose 16]

This earl's tragedy was not so soon finished but one of the company had provided for another of a notable person, Lord Tiptoft's chief enemy, concerning whom he said, 'Lord God, what trust is there in worldly chances? What stay in any prosperity? For see the earl of Warwick, which caused
5   the earl of Worcester to be apprehended, attainted, and put to death,²⁷⁰ triumphing with his old imprisoned and new unprisoned prince King Henry, was by and by after (and his brother with him) slain at Barnet Field by King Edward, whom he had beforetime damaged divers ways,²⁷¹ as first by his friends at Banbury Field, where, to revenge the death of his cousin
10   Harry Neville, Sir John Conyers and John Clapham his servants slew five thousand Welshmen and beheaded their captains the earl of Pembroke and Sir Richard Herbert his brother after they were yielded prisoners, of whom Sir Richard Herbert was the tallest gentleman both of his person and hands that ever I read or heard of.²⁷²
15   'At which time also Robin of Redesdale, a rebel of the earl of Warwick's raising, took the Earl Rivers, King Edward's wife's father, and his son John, at his manor of Grafton and carried them to Northampton and there, without cause or process, beheaded them. Which spites to requite, King Edward caused the Lord Stafford of Southwick, one of Warwick's chief
20   friends, to be taken at Brent March and headed at Bridgewater.²⁷³ This caused the earl shortly after to raise his power to encounter the king, which came against him with an army beside Warwick, at Woulney, where he won the field, took the king prisoner and kept him a while at Yorkshire in Middleham Castle, whence, as some say, he released him again, but other
25   think he corrupted his keepers and so escaped.²⁷⁴ Then through the lords the matter was taken up between them and they brought to talk together, but because they could not agree, the earl raised a new army, whereof he made captain the Lord Welles's son, which broil King Edward, minding to appease by policy, foully distained his honour, committing perjury, for he
30   sent for the Lord Welles and his brother Sir Thomas Dymoke under safe conduct, promising them upon his faith to keep them harmless, but, after, because the Lord Welles's son would not dissolve his army, beheaded them

---

9. **Banbury Field**: the Battle of Edgecote Moor (July 1469). **13–14. tallest ... hands**: the tallest and most doughty man. **26. they**: the earl of Warwick and Edward IV. **29. policy**: trickery.

[26] *1563*: earl araised [**araised**: raised]

both and went with his power down into Lincolnshire and there fought
with Sir Robert Welles and slew ten thousand of his soldiers (yet ran they
35 away so fast that the casting of their clothes for the more speed caused it to
be called Losecoat Field) and took Sir Robert and other and put them to
death in the same place.[275]

'This misfortune forced the earl of Warwick to sail into France, where
he was well entertained of the king awhile and, at last, with such poor help
40 as he procured there of Duke Rainer and other, he came into England
again and increased such a power in King Henry's name that, as the Lord
Tiptoft said in his tragedy, King Edward, unable to abide him, was fain to
fly over the Washes in Lincolnshire to get a ship to sail out of his kingdom
to his brother-in-law the Duke of Burgoyne – so was King Henry restored
45 again to the kingdom.[276]

'All these despites and troubles the earl wrought against King Edward,
but Henry was so infortunate that ere half a year was expired, King Edward
came back again and imprisoned him and gave the earl a field, wherein he
slew both him and his brother.[277] I have recounted thus much beforehand
50 for the better opening of the story, which, if it should have been spoken in his tragedy, would rather have made a volume than a pamphlet,
for I intend only to say in the tragedy what I have noted in the earl of
Warwick's person, wishing that these other noblemen, whom I have by the
way touched, should not be forgotten.

55 'And therefore imagine that you see this earl lying with his brother in
Paul's Church in his coat armour, with such a face and countenance as he
beareth in the portraiture over the door in Paul's at the going down to Jesus
Chapel fro the south end of the choir stairs, and saying as followeth':[278]

---

43. **the Washes**: the fordable part of the estuary between Lincolnshire and Norfolk.   48. **gave the earl a field**: met
the earl in battle.   56. **coat armour**: a vest displaying colours or insignia designed to identify the wearer while he
was in armour; **countenance**: facial expression.   57. **portraiture**: painting (not necessarily a portrait of a single
individual).

[Tragedy 16]

How Sir Richard Neville, Earl of Warwick, and his Brother John Lord Marquess Montagu through their too-much Boldness were Slain at Barnet Field

Among the heavy heap of happy knights
Whom Fortune stalled upon her stayless stage,
Oft hoist on high, oft pight in wretched plights,
Behold me, Baldwin, 'A *per se*' of my age:
Lord Richard Neville, earl by marrìage   [5]
Of Warwick duchy, of Sarum by descent,
Which erst my father through his marriage hent.[279]

Wouldst thou behold false Fortune in her kind,
Note well my life: so shalt thou see her naked,
Full fair before but too, too foul behind,   [10]
Most drowsy still when most she seems awaked.
My fame and shame her shift full oft hath shaked,
By interchange alow and up aloft,
The lizard like that changeth hue full oft.

For while the duke of York in life remained   [15]
Mine uncle dear, I was his happy hand;
In all attempts my purpose I attained,
Though king and queen and most lords of the land
With all their power did often me withstand,
For God gave fortune, and my good behaviour   [20]
Did from their prince steal me the people's favour.[280]

---

1. **happy knights**: knights subject to fortune.   2. **stalled**: placed; **stayless stage**: ever-moving place on Fortune's wheel.   3. **pight in**: pitched into.   4. **A *per se*** the person most excellent or pre-eminent.   6. **Sarum**: Salisbury.   7. **hent**: obtained.   8. **kind**: true nature.   14. **The lizard like**: Like the lizard (i.e. the chameleon).   16. **happy hand**: successful agent.   20. **gave fortune**: gave me good luck.

[7] *1563*: through this

So that through me in fields right manly fought
By force mine uncle took King Henry twice,
And for my cousin Edward so I wrought,
When both our sires were slain through rash advice, [25]
That he achieved his father's enterprise,
For into Scotland king and queen we chased,
By mean whereof the kingdom he embraced.²⁸¹

Which after he had enjoyed in quiet peace
(For shortly after was King Henry take [30]
And put in prison), his power to increase,
I went to France and matched him with a make,
The French king's daughter, whom he did forsake,
For while with pain I brought his suit to pass,
He to a widow rashly wedded was.²⁸² [35]

This made the French king shrewdly to suspect
That all my treaties had but ill pretence,
And when I saw my king so bent to lust
That with his faith he passed not to dispense
(Which is a prince's honour's chief defence), [40]
I could not rest till I had found a mean
To mend his miss or else to mar him clean.²⁸³

Wherefore I allied me with his brother George,
Incensing him his brother to malign
Through many a tale I did against him forge,²⁸⁴ [45]
So that, through power we did from Calais bring
And found at home, we frayèd so the king
That he to go to Frieslandward amain,
Whereby King Henry had the crown again.²⁸⁵

Then put we the earl of Worcèster to death, [50]
King Edward's friend, a man too foul defamed,²⁸⁶

---

22. **fields**: battles. 32. **make**: spouse. 42. **mend his miss**: correct his wrongdoing, end his sinfulness. 44. **malign**: regard with hatred. 48. **That … amain**: That he was forced to flee toward Friesland in great haste.

[36] *1563*: to mistrust

And in the while came Edward into breath,
For with the duke of Burgoyne so he framed
That, with the power that he to him had named,
Unlookèd for he came to England straight   [55]
And got to York and took the town by sleight.

And after through the sufferance of my brother,
Which like a beast occasion foully lost,
He came to London safe with many other
And took the town to good King Harry's cost,   [60]
Which was through him from post to pillar tossed,
Till the earl of Oxford, I, and other more
Assembled power, his freedom to restore.[287]

Whereof King Edward, warnèd, came with speed
And campèd with his host at Barnet Town,   [65]
Where we right fierce encountered him indeed
On Easter day right early, on the down.
There many a man was slain and stricken down
On either side, and neither part did gain,
Till I and my brother both at length were slain.   [70]

For we, to hearten our overmatchèd men,
Forsook our steeds and in the thickest throng
Ran pressing forth on foot and fought so then
That down we drave them, were they never so strong.
But, ere this luck had lasted very long,   [75]
With number and force we were so foully cloyed,
And rescue failed, that quite we were destroyed.[288]

Now tell me Baldwin, hast thou heard or read
Of any man that did as I have done?
That in his time so many armies led   [80]
And victory at every voyage won?

---

52. **came ... into breath**: regained his strength, abilities (lit. was no longer out of breath).   54. **named**: assigned.
67. **down**: open field.   76. **cloyed**: obstructed, impeded.   81. **voyage**: martial undertaking.

[60] *1563*: King Henry's cost   [65] *1563*: host in Barnet
[61] *1563*: Who was

Hast thou ever heard of subject under sun
That placed and based his sovèreigns so oft
By interchange, now low and then aloft?

Perchance thou think'st my doings were not such   [85]
As I and other do affirm they were,
And in thy mind I see thou musest much
What means I used that should me so prefer.
Wherein, because I will thou shalt not err,
The truth of all I will at large recite: [90]
The short is this, I was no hypocrite.[289]

I never did nor said save what I meant;
The commonweal was still my chiefest care.
To private gain or glory I was not bent.
I never passed upon delicious fare;   [95]
Of needful food my board was never bare.
No creditor did curse me day by day;
I usèd plainness: ever pitch and pay.

I heard old soldiers and poor workmen whine,
Because their duties were not duly paid.   [100]
Again, I saw how people did repine
At those through whom their payments were delayed.
And proof did oft assure (as scripture said)
That God doth wreak the wretched people's griefs:[290]
I saw the polls cut off fro polling thieves.   [105]

This made me alway justly for to deal,
Which, when the people plainly understood,
Because they saw me mind the commonweal,
They still endeavoured how to do me good,
Ready to spend their substance, life and blood   [110]
In any cause whereto I did them move,
For sure they were it was for their behove,

---

83. **based**: brought low.   89. **will**: desire.   95. **passed upon**: cared about.   96. **board**: table.   98. **ever pitch and pay**: [I] always paid immediately for any purchase.   100. **duties**: fees, charges.   103. **assure**: make certain.   104. **wreak**: avenge, requite.   105. **I … thieves**: I saw the hands cut off of robbing thieves.   112. **behove**: benefit.

And so it was. For when the realm decayed
By such as good King Henry sore abused,
To mend the state I gave his en'mies aid,[291]   [115]
But when King Edward sinful pranks still used
And would not mend, I likewise him refused
And holp up Henry, the better of the twain,
And in his quarrel (just, I think,) was slain.

And therefore, Baldwin, teach by proof of me   [120]
That such as covet people's love to get
Must see their works and words in all agree,
Live liberally and keep them out of debt,
On commonweal let all their care be set.
For upright dealing, debts paid, poor sustained   [125]
Is mean whereby all hearts are throughly gained.[292]

126. **throughly**: thoroughly.

[Prose 17]

As soon as the earl had ended his admonition, 'sure', quoth one, 'I think
the earl of Warwick, although he were a glorious man, hath said no more
of himself than what is true, for if he had not had notable good virtues
or virtuous qualities and used laudable means in his trade of life, the
5 people would never have loved him as they did. But God be with him
and send his soul rest, for sure his body never had any.[293] And although
he died, yet civil wars ceased not, for immediately after his death came
Queen Margaret with a power out of France, bringing with her her young
son Prince Edward, and, with such friends as she found here, gave King
10 Edward a battle at Tewkesbury, where both she and her son were tak-
en prisoners, with Edmund, duke of Somerset, her chief captain, whose
son Lord John and the earl of Devonshire were slain in the fight, and the
duke himself with divers other immediately beheaded, whose infortunes
are worthy to be remembered, chiefly Prince Edward's, whom the king,

2. **were**: may be; **glorious**: proud, boastful.

[1] *1563*: ended this

15 for speaking truth, cruelly struck with his gauntlet and his brothers tyrannously murdered.[294]

    'But, seeing the time so far spent, I will pass them over and, with them,
Fauconbridge that jolly rover, beheaded at Southampton, whose commotion made in Kent was cause of seely Henry's destruction.[295] And seeing
20 King Henry himself was cause of the destruction of many noble princes,
being of all other most unfortunate himself, I will declare what I have noted in his unlucky life, who, wounded in prison with a dagger, may lament
his wretchedness in manner following.'[296]

---

15. **gauntlet**: armoured glove; **brothers**: George (d. 1478), first duke of Clarence, and Richard (d. 1485), first duke of Gloucester. **18**. **jolly**: gallant; excessively self-confident; **rover**: pirate. **19**. **seely**: helpless; innocent; simple minded.

How King Henry the Sixth, a Virtuous Prince, was after Many Other Miseries Cruelly Murdered in the Tower of London

If ever woeful wight had cause to rue his state
Or by his rueful plight to move men moan his fate,
My piteous plaint may press my mishaps to rehearse,
Whereof the least most lightly heard, the hardest heart may pearce.

What heart so hard can hear of innocence oppressed   [5]
By fraud in worldly goods but melteth in the breast?
When guiltless men be spoiled, imprisoned for their own,
Who waileth not their wretched case to whom the cause is known?

The lion licketh the sores of seely wounded sheep;
The dead man's corpse may cause the crocodile to weep;[297]   [10]
The waves that waste the rocks refresh the rotten reeds:
Such ruth the wrack of innocence in cruel creature breeds.

What heart is then so hard but will for pity bleed
To hear so cruel luck so clear a life succeed,
To see a silly soul with woe and sorrow soused,   [15]
A king deprived, in prison pent, to death with daggers doused?

Would God the day of birth had brought me to my bier,
Then had I never felt the change of Fortune's cheer.
Would God the grave had gripped me in her greedy womb,
When crown in cradle made me king, with oil of holy thumb.   [20]

4. **pearce**: pierce. 6. **wordly goods**: personal possessions. 9. **seely**: weak, innocent. 14. **clear**: blameless; **succeed**: follow in the course of events. 16. **doused**: struck.

Would God the rueful tomb had been my royal throne,
So should no kingly charge have made me make my moan.
Oh that my soul had flown to heaven with the joy,
When one sort cried 'God save the king'; another, '*vive le roy*'![298]

So had I not been washed in waves of worldly woe, [25]
My mind, to quiet bent, had not been tossèd so,
My friends had been alive, my subjects unoppressed,
But death or cruel destiny denièd me this rest.

Alas, what should we count the cause of wretches' cares?
'The stars do stir them up', astronomy declares; [30]
'Or humours', saith the leech; the double true divines,
To the will of God or ill of man the doubtful cause assigns.

Such doltish heads as dream that all things drive by haps
Count lack of former care for cause of afterclaps,
Attributing to man a power fro God bereft, [35]
Abusing us and robbing him, through their most wicked theft.

But God doth guide the world and every hap by skill;
Our wit and willing power are peisèd by his will.
What wit most wisely wards and will most deadly irks,
Though all our power would press it down, doth dash our warest works. [40]

Then destiny, our sin, God's will, or else his wreak
Do work our wretched woes, for humours be too weak,
Except we take them so as they provoke to sin,
For through our lust by humours fed all vicious deeds begin.

So sin and they be one, both working like effect [45]
And cause the wrath of God to wreak the soul infect.

31. **leech**: physician; **double**: doubly.   33. **haps**: chance events.   34. **afterclaps**: undesirable results, consequences.   37. **hap**: occurrence; **skill**: a sense of what is right or proper.   38. **wit**: consciousness, intellect; **willing power**: will; **peised**: counterbalanced; weighed down.   39. **wards**: protects; **irks**: loathes.   40. **warest works**: most careful actions.   41. **wreak**: vengeance.   42–4. **for … begin**: for bodily humours are too weak [to bring about our tragic actions] unless we allow them to lead us to pursue our illicit appetites, the beginning of all sinful deeds.   46. **wreak**: punish; **infect**: tainted.

[27] *1563*: not oppressed   [31] *1563*: Our humours

Thus wrath and wreak divine, man's sins and humours ill,
Concur in one, though in a sort, each doth a course fulfil.

If likewise such as say the welkin fortune warks
Take fortune for our fate and stars thereof the marks,   [50]
Then destiny with fate and God's will all be one,
But if they mean it otherwise, scathe-causers skies be none.²⁹⁹

Thus of our heavy haps chief causes be but twain,
Whereon the rest depend and, underput, remain:
The chief, the will divine, called destiny and fate;   [55]
The other sin, through humours' holp, which God doth
    highly hate.

The first appointeth pain for good men's exercise;
The second doth deserve due punishment for vice;
This witnesseth the wrath and that the love of God;
The good for love, the bad for sin, God beateth with his rod.³⁰⁰   [60]

Although my sundry sins do place me with the worst,
My haps yet cause me hope to be among the first:
The eye that searcheth all and seèth every thought
Doth know how sore I hated sin and after virtue sought.

The solace of the soul my chiefest pleasure was;   [65]
Of worldly pomp, of fame, or game, I did not pass.
My kingdoms nor my crown I prizèd not a crumb:
In heaven were my riches heaped, to which I sought to come.³⁰¹

Yet were my sorrows such as never man had like,
So divers storms at once so often did me strike.   [70]
But why – God knows, not I, except it were for this:
To show by pattern of a prince how brittle honour is.

47–8. **Thus ... fulfil:** Thus divine wrath, divine vengeance, sins, and malign humours all come together in one person, though each in its own way has a determined course of action that it accomplishes. 49. **such ... warks:** those who say that the heavenly bodies bring about one's fortune on earth. 50. **marks:** signs, indications. 52. **scathe-causers:** causers of harm; **skies:** the stars and heavenly bodies. 54. **underput:** placed beneath. 57. **exercise:** training with the goal of spiritual improvement. 62. **haps:** things that befell me in life. 66. **game:** amusement, diversion.

[64] Is judge how

Our kingdoms are but cares, our state devoid of stay,
Our riches ready snares to hasten our decay,
Our pleasures privy pricks our vices to provoke, [75]
Our pomp a pump, our fame a flame, our power a smould'ring
    smoke.

I speak not but by proof, and that may many rue.
My life doth cry it out; my death doth try it true.
Whereof I will in brief rehearse my heavy hap,
That Baldwin in his woeful warp my wretchedness may wrap. [80]

In Windsor born I was and bare my father's name,
Who won by war all France, to his eternal fame,
And left to me the crown, to be received in peace,
Through marriage made with Charles his heir, upon his life's decease.

Which shortly did ensue, yet died my father first, [85]
And both their realms were mine, ere I a year were nursed. [302]
Which, as they fell too soon, so faded they as fast,
For Charles and Edward got them both, or forty years were past.[303]

This Charles was eldest son of Charles my father-in-law,
To whom as heir of France, the Frenchmen did them draw. [90]
But Edward was the heir of Richard, duke of York,
The heir of Roger Mortimer, slain by the kern of Cork.[304]

Before I came to age, Charles had recovered France
And killed my men of war, so lucky was his chance,
And through a mad contract I made with Rainer's daughter, [95]
I gave and lost all Normandy, the cause of many a slaughter:[305]

First of mine Uncle Humphrey, abhorring sore this act,
Because I thereby brake a better pre-contract,
Then of the flatt'ring duke that first the marriage made:
The just reward of such as dare their princes ill persuade.[306] [100]

---

76. **pump**: a sink of vice.   77. **proof**: experience.   80. **warp**: narrative work (lit. the threads that issue lengthwise from the loom).   83. **the crown**: the French crown.   84. **Charles his**: Charles's.   89. **father-in-law**: the poet's mistake for 'grandfather'.   92. **kern**: Irish foot soldiers.   99. **the flattering duke**: William de la Pole (d. 1450), first duke of Suffolk.

[79] *1563*: rehearse the heavy

And I, poor seely wretch, abode the brunt of all:
My marriage lust so sweet was mixed with bitter gall.
My wife was wise and good, had she been rightly sought,
But our unlawful getting it may make a good thing nought.

Wherefore warn men beware how they just promise break,   [105]
Lest proof of painful plagues do cause them wail the wreak.
Advise well ere they grant, but what they grant, perform,
For God will plague all doubleness, although we feel no worm.

I, falsely borne in hand, believèd I did well,
But all things be not true that learnèd men do tell.   [110]
My clergy said a prince was to no promise bound,
Whose words to be no gospel though, I, to my grief, have found.[307]

For after marriage joined Queen Margaret and me,
For one mishap afore, I daily met with three.
Of Normandy and France, Charles got away my crown;   [115]
The duke of York and other sought at home to put me down.

Bellona rang the bell at home and all abroad,
With whose mishaps amain fell Fortune did me load:
In France I lost my forts, at home the foughten field,
My kindred slain, my friends oppressed, myself enforced to yield.   [120]

Duke Richard took me twice and forced me to resign
My crown and titles, due unto my father's line,
And kept me as a ward, did all things as him list,
Till time my wife, through bloody sword, had tane me from his fist.[308]

But though she slew the duke, my sorrows did not slake,   [125]
But, like to hydra's head, still more and more awake,
For Edward, through the aid of Warwick and his brother,
From one field drave me to the Scots and took me in another.

---

101. abode: suffered.   102. marriage lust: pleasure in marriage.   104. But … nought: But the unlawful achieve-
ment of something can make it worthless.   106. wreak: punishment.   108. worm: mental pain.   109. borne
in hand: misled.   117. Bellona: the goddess of war.   118. amain: quickly.   119. foughten field: battlefield.
126. awake: come into being (it was said of the mythological Hydra that if one of its heads were cut off, two more
would grow in its place).   127. Warwick and his brother: Richard Neville (d. 1471), sixteenth earl of Warwick, and
John Neville (d. 1471), first Baron Montagu.

Then went my friends to wrack, for Edward ware the crown,
Fro which for nine-years' space his prison held me down. [130]
Yet thence through Warwick's work I was again released
And Edward driven fro the realm to seek his friends by east.[309]

But what prevaileth pain or providence of man
To help him to good hap, whom destiny doth ban?
Who moileth to remove the rock out of the mud [135]
Shall mire himself and hardly scape the swelling of the flood.

This all my friends have found, and I have felt it so,
Ordained to be the touch of wretchedness and woe,
For ere I had a year possessed my seat again,
I lost both it and liberty; my helpers all were slain. [140]

For Edward, first by stealth and sith by gathered strength,
Arrived and got to York and London at the length,
Took me and tied me up, yet Warwick was so stout,
He came with power to Barnet Field, in hope to help me out

And there alas was slain, with many a worthy knight: [145]
Oh Lord, that ever such luck should hap in helping right!
Last came my wife and son, that long lay in exile,
Defied the king and fought a field, I may bewail the while.

For there mine only son, not thirteen year of age,
Was tane and murdered straight by Edward in his rage, [150]
And shortly I myself, to stint all further strife,
Stabbed with his brother's bloody blade, in prison lost my life.[310]

Lo here the heavy haps which happened me by heap,
See here the pleasant fruits that many princes reap,
The painful plagues of those that break their lawful bands, [155]
Their meed which may and will not save their friends fro bloody hands.

God grant my woeful haps, too grievous to rehearse,
May teach all states to know how deeply dangers pierce,
How frail all honours are, how brittle worldly bliss,
That, warnèd through my fearful fate, they fear to do amiss. [160]

---

129. **wrack**: harm. 135. **moileth**: toils. 138. **touch**: touchstone, proof. 141. **sith**: subsequently. 155. **bands**: moral or spiritual bonds of union (as in 'marriage bands').

[Prose 18]

This tragedy ended, another said, 'either you or King Henry are a good philosopher, so narrowly to argue the causes of misfortunes! But there is nothing to experience which taught or might teach the king this lesson. But to proceed in our matter, I find mention here shortly after the death
5   of this king of a duke of Exeter found dead in the sea between Dover and Calais. But what he was or by what adventure he died, Master Fabyan hath not showed, and Master Hall hath overskipped him, so, that except we be friendlier unto him, he is like to be double drowned, both in the sea and in the gulf of forgetfulness.'[311]
10   About this matter was much talk, but because one took upon him to seek out that story, that charge was committed to him. And, to be occupied the meanwhile, I found the story of one drowned likewise and that so notably, though privily, that all the world knew of it; wherefore, I said, 'because night approacheth and that we will lose no time, ye shall hear what I
15   have noted concerning the duke of Clarence, King Edward's brother, who, all-to bewashed in wine, may bewail his infortune after this manner.'[312]

---

16. **all-to bewashed**: completely soaked.

How George Plantagenet, Third Son of the Duke of York, was by his Brother King Edward Wrongfully Imprisoned and by his Brother Richard Miserably Murdered

The fowl is foul, men say, that files the nest,
Which maketh me loath to speak now, might I choose,
But seeing time unburdened hath her breast,
And fame blown up the blast of all abuse,
My silence rather might my life accuse   [5]
Than shroud our shame, though fain I would it so,
For truth will out, though all the world say no.

And therefore, Baldwin, heartily I thee beseech
To pause awhile upon my heavy plaint,
And though uneath I utter speedy speech,   [10]
No fault of wit or folly maketh me faint;
No heady drinks have given my tongue attaint
Through quaffing craft, yet wine my wits confound:
Not which I drank of, but wherein I drowned.[313]

What prince I am, although I need not show,   [15]
Because my wine bewrays me by the smell,
For never was creature soused in Bacchus' dew
To death but I, through Fortune's rigour fell.
Yet, that thou mayst my story better tell,
I will declare as briefly as I may   [20]
My wealth, my woe, and causers of decay.

---

1. **files**: defiles. 4. **And ... abuse**: And since public report has trumpeted out all the insults laid against me. 10. **uneath**: with difficulty. 12. **given my tongue attaint**: overpowered my tongue. 17. **soused ... dew**: immersed in wine. 18. **rigour fell**: malign cruelty.

The famous house sournamed Plantagenet,
Whereat Dame Fortune frowardly did frown,
While Bolingbroke unjustly sought to set
His lord King Richard quite beside the crown,   [25]
Though many a day it wanted due renown,
God so preserved by providence and grace
That lawful heirs did never fail the race.[314]

For Lionel, King Edward's elder child,
Both uncle and heir to Richard issueless, [315]   [30]
Begot a daughter, Philip, whom unfiled
The earl of March espoused and God did bless
With fruit assigned the kingdom to possess:
I mean Sir Roger Mortimer, whose heir
The earl of Cambridge married – Anne the fair.[316]   [35]

This earl of Cambridge, Richard cleped by name,
Was son to Edmund Langley, duke of York,
Which Edmund was fifth brother to the same
Duke Lionel, that all this line doth cork,
Of which two houses joinèd in a fork,   [40]
My father Richard, prince Plantagenet,
True duke of York was lawful heir beget.

Who took to wife, as you shall understand,
A maiden of a noble house and old,
Ralph Neville's daughter, earl of Westmoreland,   [45]
Whose son Earl Richard was a baron bold
And had the right of Salisbury in hold,
Through marriage made with good Earl Thomas' heir,
Whose earnèd praises never shall appair.[317]

22. **sournamed**: surnamed, with likely pun on **sour**: extremely distasteful, unpleasant.   **29–30. For ... issue-less**: see explanatory note 315.   **31–5. Begot ... fair**: see explanatory note 316 (**unfiled**: undefiled).   **36. cleped**: called.   **37. Edmund Langley**: Edmund of Langley (d. 1402), first duke of York.   **39. Duke ... cork**: Duke Lionel, who upholds this whole line of succession (**cork**: a float used to help swimmers stay buoyant).   **49. appair**: decay.

[22] *1563*: surnamed   [43] *1563*: as ye shall
[29] *1563*: Edward's eldest child

The duke my father had by this his wife   [50]
Four sons, of whom the eldest Edward hight,
The second, John, who lost in youth his life
At Wakefield slain by Clifford, cruel knight.
I George am third, of Clarence duke by right;
The fourth, born to the mischief of us all,   [55]
Was duke of Gloucester, whom men Richard call.³¹⁸

Whenas our sire in suit of right was slain
(Whose life and death himself declarèd erst),
My brother Edward plied his cause amain
And got the crown, as Warwick hath rehearsed.   [60]
The pride whereof so deep his stomach pierced
That he forgot his friends, despised his kin,
Of oath and office passing not a pin.

Which made the earl of Warwick to malign
My brother's state and to attempt a way   [65]
To bring from prison Henry, seely king,
To help him to the kingdom if he may.
And, knowing me to be the chiefest stay
My brother had, he did me undermine
To cause me to his treasons to incline.   [70]

Whereto I was preparèd long before,
My brother had been to me so unkind,
For sure no canker fretteth flesh so sore
As unkind dealing doth a loving mind.
Love's strongest bands unkindness doth unbind;   [75]
It moveth love to malice, zeal to hate,
Chief friends to foes, and brethren to debate.³¹⁹

And though the earl of Warwick, subtle sire,
Perceived I bare a grudge against my brother,

57. **Whenas**: At the time at which.   58. **declared erst**: i.e. in Tragedy 13 (**erst**: earlier).   59. **plied**: applied himself to; **amain**: with full force, with all speed.   60. **as Warwick hath rehearsed**: as the ghost of Richard Neville (d. 1471), sixteenth earl of Warwick, has already related (in Tragedy 16).   63. **office**: duty; **not a pin**: not a bit.   66. **seely**: simple, helpless.   72. **unkind**: hurtful, unnatural (not befitting a kinsman).   73. **canker**: unhealing sore.   77. **debate**: strife.

Yet toward his feat to set me more on fire,   [80]
He kindled up one firebrand with another,
For, knowing fancy was the forcing rother
Which steereth youth to any kind of strife,
He offered me his daughter to my wife.

Wherethrough, and with his crafty filèd tongue,   [85]
He stale my heart that erst unsteady was,
For I was witless, wanton, fond, and young,
Whole bent to pleasure, brittle as the glass:
I cannot lie, *in vino veritas.*
I did esteem the beauty of my bride   [90]
Above myself and all the world beside.

These fond affections joint with lack of skill
(Which trap the heart and blind the eyes of youth
And prick the mind to practise any ill)
So tickled me that, void of kindly truth   [95]
(Which, where it wants, all wickedness ensueth),
I stinted not to persecute my brother
Till time he left his kingdom to another.³²⁰

Thus carnal love did quench the love of kind,
Till lust were lost through fancy fully fed,   [100]
But when at length I came unto my mind
I saw how lewdly lightness had me led
To seek with pain the peril of my head,
For had King Henry once been settled sure,
I was assured my days could not endure.   [105]

And therefore, though I bound myself by oath
To help King Henry all that ever I might,
Yet at the treaty of my brethren both

---

82. fancy: amorous desire; **forcing rother**: guiding rudder.   **85. filed**: smooth.   **86. erst**: already.   **89.** *in vino veritas*: in wine [there is] truth. A proverbial saying.   **92. skill**: reason, discernment.   **95. kindly truth**: loyalty to kin.   **97. I stinted not to persecute**: I did not leave off persecuting.   **99. kind**: kin.   **102. lewdly lightness**: wickedly wantonness, fickleness.   **108. treaty**: entreaty.

[96] *1563*: (Which, if it want, all wretchedness ensueth)

(Which reason granted to require but right),
I left his part, whereby he perished quite,
And reconciled me to my brethren twain,
And so came Edward to the crown again.³²¹ [110]

This made my father-in-law to fret and fume,
To stamp and stare and call me false forsworn
And, at the length, with all his power presume [115]
To help King Henry utterly forlorn.
Our friendly proffers still he took in scorn,
Refusèd peace and came to Barnet Field
And there was killed, because he would not yield.

His brother also there with him was slain, [120]
Whereby decayed the keys of chivalry,
For never lived the matches of them twain
In manhood, power, and martial policy,
In virtuous thews and friendly constancy
That, would to God, if it had been his will, [125]
They might have turned to us and livèd still.³²²

But what shall be, shall be; there is no choice:
Things needs must drive as destiny decreeth,
For which we ought in all our haps rejoice,
Because the eye eterne all thing forseeth [130]
Which to no ill at any time agreeth,
For ills too ill to us be good to it,
So far his skills exceed our reach of wit.

The wounded man which must abide the smart
Of stitching up or searing of his sore [135]
As thing too bad reproves the surgeon's art,
Which notwithstanding doth his health restore.
The child, likewise, to science plièd sore
Counts knowledge ill, his teacher to be wood,
Yet surgery and sciences be good. [140]

109. **Which ... right**: Which request reason acknowledged that for them to ask was only right.   121. **keys**: mainstays, key men of.   124. **thews**: practices.   129. **haps**: chances, occurrences.   132–3. **For ... wit**: For ills that seem too ill to us are good to God's eye, so far are his reasons for action beyond the reach of our comprehension.   138. **science**: knowledge acquired by study; **plied sore**: made to apply himself with great exertion.

But as the patient's grief and scholar's pain
Cause them deem bad such things as sure be best,
So want of wisdom causeth us to complain
Of every hap, whereby we seem oppressed.
The poor do pine for pelf, the rich for rest,   [145]
And whenas loss or sickness us assail,
We curse our fate, our fortune we bewail.

Yet for our good God worketh everything,
For through the death of those two noble peers
My brother lived and reigned a quiet king,   [150]
Who, had they lived perchance in course of years,
Would have delivered Henry from the breres
Or holp his son to enjoy the careful crown,
Whereby our line should have be quite put down.

'A careful crown' it may be justly named,   [155]
Not only for the cares thereto annexed
To see the subject well and duly framed
(With which good care few kings are greatly vexed),
But for the dread wherewith they are perplexed
Of losing lordship, liberty, or life,   [160]
Which woeful wracks in kingdoms happen rife.

The which to shun (while some too sore have sought),
They have not spared all persons to suspect
And to destroy such as they guilty thought,
Though no appearance provèd them infect.   [165]
Take me for one of this wrong-punished sect:
Imprisoned first, accusèd without cause,
And done to death, no process had by laws.

Wherein I note how vengeance doth aquite
Like ill for ill, how vices virtue quell: [170]

---

145. **pelf**: money.   152. **breres**: briers.   159. **But**: but also.   161. **wracks**: disasters.   162. **while ... sought**: although some have too vigorously sought to come to such disasters.   165. **infect**: tainted, corrupt.   169. **aquite**: repay.

[154] *1563*: have been quite

For as my marriage love did me excite
Against the king my brother to rebel,
So love to have his children prosper well
Provokèd him, against both law and right,
To murder me, his brother and his knight.   [175]

For by his queen two goodly sons he had
Born to be punished for their parents' sin,
Whose fortunes calkèd made their father sad,
Such woeful haps were found to be therein,
Which to avouch, writ in a rotten skin,   [180]
A prophecy was found, which said a 'G'
Of Edward's children should destruction be.[323]

Me to be G, because my name was George,
My brother thought and therefore did me hate,
But woe be to the wicked heads that forge   [185]
Such doubtful dreams to breed unkind debate,
For God, a glaive, a gibbet, grate, or gate,
A Grey, a Griffith, or a Gregory,
As well as George are written with a G.

Such doubtful riddles are no prophecies,   [190]
For prophecies, in writing though obscure,
Are plain in sense; the dark be very lies:
What God foreshoweth is evident and pure.
Truth is no herald nor no sophist sure.
She noteth not men's names, their shields, nor crests,   [195]
Though she compare them unto birds and beasts.

But whom she doth foreshow shall rule by force
She termeth a wolf, a dragon or a bear;
A wilful prince: a reinless ranging horse;
A bold: a lion; a coward much in fear: [200]

---

178. calked: reckoned astrologically. **180. avouch**: prove. **186. unkind**: unnatural. **187. glaive**: lance, spear. **194. herald**: a member of the Heralds' College, the official body tasked with deciding matters relating to armorial bearings; **sophist**: specious reasoner.

[176] *1563*: two prince-like sons   [197] *1563*: shall reign by
[178] *1563*: made the father

A hare or hart; a crafty: prickèd ear;
A lecherous: a bull, a goat, a foal;
An underminer: a moldwarp or a mole.

By knowen beasts thus truth doth plain declare
What men they be of whom she speaks before.   [205]
And whoso can men's properties compare
And mark what beast they do resemble more
Shall soon discern who is the grisly boar,[324]
For God by beasts expresseth men's conditions
And not their badges, heralds' superstitions.   [210]

And learnèd Merlin, whom God gave the sprite
To know and utter princes' acts to come
Like to the Jewish prophets, did recite
In shade of beasts their doings all and some,
Expressing plain by manners of the dumb   [215]
That kings and lords such properties should have
As had the beasts whose name he to them gave.[325]

Which while the foolish did not well consider,
And seeing princes gave, for difference
And knowledge of their issues mixed together,   [220]
All manner beasts for badges of pretence,
They took those badges to express the sense
Of Merlin's mind and those that gave the same
To be the princes noted by their name.

And hereof sprang the false-named prophecies   [225]
That go by letters, cyphers, arms, or signs,
Which all be foolish, false, and crafty lies
Devised by guess or guile's untrue divines:
For when they saw that many of many lines
Gave arms alike, they wist not which was he   [230]
Whom Merlin meant the noted beast to be.

---

201. **crafty**: a cunning, underhanded person.   204. **knowen**: familiar.   208. **grisly**: horrible, fearsome.   211. **sprite**: spirit, power.

[217] *1563*: As have the

For all the brood of Warwicks give the bear;
The Buckinghams do likewise give the swan.
But which bear-bearer should the lion tear,
They were as wise as Goose the ferryman.[326]   [235]
Yet in their skill they ceasèd not to scan
And, to be deemèd of the people wise,
Set forth their glosses upon prophecies.

And whom they doubted openly to name
They darkly termed or by some letter meant,   [240]
For so they mought, however the world did frame,
Preserve themselves from shame or being shent.
For howsoever contrary it went
They might expound their meaning otherwise,
As haps in things should newly still arise.   [245]

And thus there grew of a mistaken truth
An art so false as made the true suspect,
Whereof hath come much mischief, more the ruth,
That errors should our minds so much infect.
True prophecies have foully been reject;   [250]
The false, which breed both murder, war, and strife,
Believed to the loss of many a good man's life.[327]

And therefore, Baldwin, teach men to discern
Which prophecies be false and which be true,
And for a ground this lesson let them learn,   [255]
That all be false which are devisèd new.
The age of things is judgèd by the hue:
All riddles made by letters, names, or arms
Are young and false, far worse than witches' charms.

I know thou musest at this lore of mine,   [260]
How I, no student, should have learnèd it,
And dost impute it to the fume of wine

---

239. doubted: feared.   **241. mought**: might; **world did frame**: whatever might come to pass.   **242. shent**: disgraced.   **257. hue**: form.

[259] *1559*: for worse (corrected in *1563* to 'far worse')

That stirs the tongue and sharpeneth up the wit.
But hark! A friend did teach me every whit,
A man of mine in all good knowledge rife,   [265]
For which he, guiltless, lost his learnèd life.[328]

This man abode my servant many a day
And still in study set his whole delight,
Which taught me more than I could bear away
Of every art, and by his searching sight   [270]
Of things to come he could foreshow as right
As I rehearse the pageants that were past:
Such perfectness God gave him at the last.

He knew my brother Richard was the boar
Whose tusks should tear my brother's boys and me   [275]
And gave me warning thereof long before,
But wit nor warning can in no degree
Let things to hap which are ordained to be.
Witness the painted lioness, which slew
A prince imprisoned, lions to eschew.[329]   [280]

He told me too my yokefellow should die
(Wherein would God he had been no divine)
And, after her death, I should woo earnestly
A spouse, whereat my brother should repine
And find the means she should be none of mine,   [285]
For which such malice should among us rise
As, save my death, no treaty should decise.[330]

And, as he said, so all things came to pass,
For when King Henry and his son were slain
And every broil so throughly quenchèd was   [290]
That the king my brother quietly did reign,

---

267. **abode my servant**: remained in residence as my servant.   278. **Let things to hap**: Prevent things from happening.   281. **yokefellow**: wife.   282. **divine**: diviner.   287. **save**: save for; **decise**: settle, resolve.   289. **King Henry and his son**: Henry VI and his son Prince Edward (both d. 1471).   290. **throughly**: thoroughly.

[271] *1563*: he would for show   [285] *1563*: none mine
[281] *1563*: told me, eke, my

I, reconcilèd to his love again,
In prosperous health did lead a quiet life
For five years' space with honours laden rife.

And to augment the fullness of my bliss [295]
Two lovely children by my wife I had,
But froward hap, whose manner ever is
In chiefest joy to make the happy sad,
Bemixed my sweet with bitterness too bad,
For while I swam in joys on every side [300]
My loving wife, my chiefest jewel, died,

Whose lack, when sole I had bewailed a year,
The Duke of Burgoyne's wife, Dame Margaret
My loving sister, willing me to cheer,
To marry again did kindly me entreat [305]
And wished me matchèd with a maiden neat,
A step-daughter of hers, Duke Charles his heir,
A noble damsel, young, discreet, and fair,

To whose desire, because I did incline,
The king my brother, doubting my degree [310]
Through prophecies, against us did repine,
And at no hand would to our wills agree,
For which such rancour pierced both him and me
That face to face we fell to flat defiance,
But were appeased by friends of our alliance. [315]

Howbeit my marriage utterly was dashed,
Wherein, because my servant said his mind,
A mean was sought whereby he might be lashed
And, for they could no crime against him find,
They forged a fault, the people's eyes to blind [320]
And told he should by sorceries pretend
To bring the king unto a speedy end,

---

297. **froward hap**: perverse fortune. 303. **Duke of Burgoyne's**: Charles (d. 1477), duke of Burgundy's. 306. **neat**: comely. 308. **discreet**: tactful. 310–11. **The king ... repine**: My brother King Edward, led by prophecies to fear the status I would achieve (as the husband of the Duke of Burgundy's heir), complained about the marriage scheme. 317. **Wherein**: In respect of which. 321. **pretend**: intend, plan.

Of all which points he was as innocent
As is the babe that lacketh kindly breath,
And yet condemnèd by the king's assent   [325]
Most cruelly put to a shameful death.
This fired my heart as fouldre doth the heath,
So that I could not but exclaim and cry
Against so great and open an injury.

For this I was commanded to the Tower,   [330]
The king my brother was so cruel hearted,
And when my brother Richard saw the hour
Was come, for which his heart so sore had smarted,
He thought best take the time before it parted,
For he endeavoured to attain the crown,   [335]
From which my life must needs have held him down,³³¹

For though the king within a while had died
(As needs he must, he surfeited so oft),
I must have had his children in my guide,
So Richard should beside the crown have coft;   [340]
This made him ply the while the wax was soft
To find a mean to bring me to an end,
For realm-rape spareth neither kin nor friend.

And when he saw how reason can assuage
Through length of time my brother Edward's ire,   [345]
With forgèd tales he set him new in rage,
Till at the last they did my death conspire,
And though my truth sore troubled their desire,
For all the world did know mine innocence,
Yet they agreed to charge me with offence.   [350]

And covertly within the Tower they called
A quest to give such verdict as they should,
Who, what with fear and what with favour thralled,

---

324. **kindly breath**: natural breathing (as with a baby so newly born that it needs help to respire on its own).
327. **fouldre**: lightning.   337. **though**: if.   338. **surfeited**: excessively indulged in food and drink.   339–40. **I … coft**: I would have been obliged to have his children under my direction; otherwise, in that manner [i.e. control of the children] Richard should have acquired the crown.   343. **realm-rape**: seizure of a realm by force; plundering of the realm.   348. **truth**: loyalty; integrity.   352. **quest**: a body of men called to hold an inquest.

Durst nought pronounce but as my brethren would,
And, though my false accusers never could   [355]
Prove ought they said, I, guiltless, was condemned:
Such verdicts pass where justice is contemned.³³²

This feat achieved, yet could they not for shame
Cause me be killed by any common way,
But like a wolf the tyrant Richard came   [360]
(My brother, nay, my butcher I may say)
Unto the Tower, when all men were away
Save such as were provided for the feat,
Who in this wise did strangely me entreat.

His purpose was with a preparèd string   [365]
To strangle me, but I bestirred me so
That by no force they could me thereto bring,
Which causèd him that purpose to forgo;
Howbeit, they bound me whether I would or no
And in a butt of malmsey standing by   [370]
New christened me, because I should not cry.³³³

Thus drowned I was, yet for no due desert,
Except the zeal of justice be a crime,
False prophecies bewitched King Edward's heart,
My brother Richard to the crown would climb: [375]
Note these three causes in thy rueful rhyme
And boldly say they did procure my fall
And death, of deaths most strange and hard of all.

And warn all princes prophecies to eschew
That are too dark or doubtful to be known;   [380]
What God hath said, that cannot but ensue,
Though all the world would have it overthrown.
When men suppose by fetches of their own
To fly their fate, they further on the same
Like quenching blasts, which oft revive the flame. [385]

---

371. because: so that.   **383. fetches**: schemes, stratagems.

[380] *1563*: dark and doubtful

Will princes therefore not to think by murder
They may avoid what prophecies behight,
But by their means their mischiefs they may further
And cause God's vengeance heavier to alight.
Woe worth the wretch that strives with God's foresight!   [390]
They are not wise but wickedly do arr,
Which think ill deeds due destinies may bar.

For if we think that prophecies be true,
We must believe it cannot but betide
Which God in them foreshoweth shall ensue,   [395]
For his decrees unchangèd do abide,
Which, to be true, my brethren both have tried,
Whose wicked works warn princes to detest
That others' harms may keep them better blessed.

387. **behight**: promise, foretell.   391. **arr**: err.   392. **bar**: prevent.   394. **betide**: happen.

[Prose 19]
By that this tragedy was ended, night was so near come that we could
not conveniently tarry together any longer, and therefore said Master
Ferrers, 'it is best my masters to stay here, for we be come now to the end
of Edward the Fourth his reign, for the last whom we find unfortunate
5   therein was this duke of Clarence, in whose behalf I commend much that
which hath be noted. Let us therefore for this time leave with him and
this day seven nights hence, if your business will so suffer, let us all meet
here together again. And you shall see that in the mean season I will not
only devise upon this myself but cause divers other of my acquaintance
10   which can do very well to help us forward with the rest.' To this every man
gladly agreed; 'howbeit', quoth another, 'seeing we shall end at Edward the
Fourth's end, let himself make an end of our day's labour with the same
oration which Master Skelton made in his name, the tenor whereof, so far
as I remember, is this':

1. **By that**: By the time that.   6. **leave**: leave off.

[3] *1563*: be now come

[Tragedy 19]

How King Edward, through his Surfeiting and Untemperate Life, suddenly Died in the Mids of his Prosperity[334]

Miseremini mei, ye that be my friends,[335]
This world hath formed me down to fall.
How may I endure when that everything ends?
What creature is born to be eternal?
Now there is no more but pray for me all.   [5]
Thus say I, Edward, that late was your king,
And twenty-three years ruled this imperial,[336]
Some unto pleasure, and some to no liking;
Mercy I ask of my misdoing.
What availeth it, friends, to be my foe,   [10]
Sith I cannot resist nor amend your complaining,
Quia ecce nunc in pulvere dormio?[337]

I sleep now in mould, as it is natural,
As earth unto earth has his reverture.
What ordained God to be terrestrial   [15]
Without recourse to the earth by nature?
Who to live ever may himself assure?
What is it to trust on mutability,
Sith that in his world nothing may endure?
For now am I gone that was late in prosperity;   [20]
To presume thereupon is but a vanity
Not certain, but as a cherry-fair, full of woe.

1. *Miseremini mei*: Have pity on me. 7. **imperial**: imperial realm. 11. **Sith**: since. 12. *Quia ecce nunc in pulvere dormio*: For behold, now I sleep in the dust. 13. **mould**: dirt, earth. 14. **earth unto earth**: the material of the human body to the soil (see Genesis 3:19); **reverture**: return. 16. **recourse**: return. 22. **cherry-fair**: an often boisterous fair held in a cherry orchard; in late medieval literature 'a frequent symbol of the shortness of life and the fleeting nature of its pleasures' (*OED*, 'cherry-fair, *n.*').

[1] *1563*: *Siseremini mei* [an uncorrected error for '*Miseremini*']   [18] *1563*: trust to mutability?

Reigned not I of late in great prosperity?
Et ecce nunc in pulvere dormio.

Where was in my life such an one as I,   [25]
While Lady Fortune with me had continuance?
Granted not she me to have victory,
In England to reign and to contribute France?[338]
She took me by the hand and led me a dance,
And with her sugared lips on me she smiled,   [30]
But what for her dissembled countenance
I could not beware till I was beguiled.
Now from this world she hath me exiled,
When I was loathest hence for to go
And am in age as who sayeth but a child.[339]   [35]
Et ecce nunc in pulvere dormio.

I had enough; I held me not content,
Without remembrance that I should die,
And, moreover, to encroach ready was I bent;
I knew not how long I should it occupy.   [40]
I made the Tower strong, I wist not why;
I knew not to whom I purchased Tattersall.
I amended Dover on the mountain high
And London I provoked to fortify the wall.
I made Nottingham a place full royal,   [45]
Windsor, Eltham, and many other mo,
Yet at the last, I went from them all,
Et ecce nunc in pulvere dormio.[340]

Where is now my conquest and victory,
Where is my riches and royal array,   [50]
Where be my coursers and my horses high,
Where is my mirth, my solace, and play?

---

24. **Et ecce nunc in pulvere dormio**: And behold, now I sleep in the dust.   28. **contribute**: levy a tribute on.   39. **encroach**: take in an usurping manner the territory or possessions of others.   40. **occupy**: engage in.   41. **wist**: know.   42. **to**: for.

[31] *1563*: for dissembled   [52] *1563*: my solace, and my play?
[43] *1563*: I mended Dover

As vanity to nought all is withered away.
Oh Lady Bess, long for me may you call,
For I am departed until doomèsday,   [55]
But love you that Lord that is sovereign of all.
Where be my castles and buildings royal?
But Windsor alone, now have I no mo,
And of Eton the prayers perpetual,
Et ecce nunc in pulvere dormio.[341]   [60]

Why should a man be proud or presume high?
Saint Bernard thereof nobly doth treat,
Saying a man is but a sack of stercory
And shall return unto wormès' meat.[342]
Why, what became of Alexander the Great   [65]
Or else of strong Samson – who can tell?
Were not wormès ordained their flesh to freat?
And of Solomon, that was of wit the well?
Absalom proffered his hair for to sell,[343]
Yet, for all his beauty, wormès eat him also,   [70]
And I but late in honour did excel,
Et ecce nunc in pulvere dormio.

I have played my pageant; now am I past.
Ye wote well all, I was of no great eld.
This all thing concluded shall be at the last;   [75]
When death approacheth, then lost is the field.
Then, seeing this world me no longer upheld,
For nought would conserve me here in my place,
In manus tuas, Domine, my spirit up I yield,[344]
Humbly beseeching thee, oh God, of thy grace.   [80]
Oh you courteous commons, your hearts embrace
Benignly now to pray for me also,
For right well you know your king I was,
Et ecce nunc in pulvere dormio.

---

54. Lady Bess: Queen Elizabeth (d. 1492), Edward IV's wife. **63. stercory**: excrement. **64. wormes' meat**: food for worms. **67. freat**: gnaw, devour. **73. pageant**: part in life (lit. my dramatic performance). **74. wote**: know. **79. *In manus tuas, Domine***: Into your hands, Lord. **81. courteous commons**: politely respectful common people; **embrace**: undertake.

[77] *1563*: lenger [**lenger**: longer]
[78] *1563*: in any place

[80] *1559*: Humby [a misprint for 'Humbly' corrected in the 1563 edition]

[Prose 20]

When this was said, every man took his leave of other and departed, and I, the better to acquit my charge, recorded and noted all such matters as they had willed me.

FINIS.

[FINIS] *1563*: Thus endeth the first part.

ℭ The second Part of The Mirror for Magistrates
William Baldwin
to the Reader

The time being come when, according to our former appointment, we should meet together again to devise upon the tragical affairs of our English rulers, I, with such stories as I had procured and prepared, went to the place wherein we had debated the former part. There found I the
5 printer and all the rest of our friends and furtherers assembled and tarrying for us, save Master Ferrers, who shortly after, according to his promise, came thither.³⁴⁵

    When we had blamed him for his long tarrying, he satisfied us fully with this reasonable excuse: 'I have been letted', quoth he, 'divers ways,
10 but chiefly in tarrying for such tragedies as many of our friends, at mine instance, undertook to discourse, whereof I am sure you will be right glad, for mo wits are better than one, and diversity of device is alway most pleasant. And although I have presently brought but a few because no mo are ready, yet shall you be sure hereafter to have all the rest, which notable
15 men have undertaken, whereof some are half done, some more, some less, some scarce begun, which maketh me think that the diversity of brains in devising is like the sundriness of beasts in engendering, for some wits are ready and dispatch many matters speedily like the coney, which littereth every month; some other are slow like the elephant, scarce delivering any
20 matter in ten years. I dispraise neither of these births, for both be natural, but I commend most the mean, which is neither too slow nor too swift, for that is lion-like and therefore most noble. For the right poet doth neither through haste bring forth swift, feeble rabbits, neither doth he weary men in looking for his strong, jointless elephants, but in reasonable time
25 he bringeth forth a perfect and lively lion, not a bear-whelp that must be longer in licking than in breeding – and yet I know many that do highly like that lumpish delivery.³⁴⁶ But every man hath his gift, and the diversity of our minds maketh everything to be liked. And, therefore, while the elephants are in breeding (to whom I have therefore given the latter stories),

---

3. stories: historical narratives.   **9. letted**: hindered.   **11. instance**: entreaty.

30   I have brought you such as are already done, to be published in the mean
season, wherein there needeth no further labour but to place them in due
order.

   'Lo, you Baldwin, here is of mine own the duke of Somerset slain at St
Albans with other, which I promised, whom I wish you should place last.[347]
35   There is also Shore's wife, trimly handled by Master Churchyard, which
I pray you place where you think most convenient. Here are other also of
other men's, but they are rabbits: do with them as you think best. I would
tarry with a good will and help you in the order, save that my business is
great and weighty. But I know you can do it well enough and, therefore,
40   till we meet again, I will leave you.' Then delivered he the tragedies unto
me and departed.

   Divers of the rest, liking his device, used the like manner, for the printer
delivered unto me the 'Lord Hastings', penned by Master Dolman, and
'King Richard the Third' compiled by Francis Segars. Then said I, 'well,
45   my masters, sith you think it good to charge me with the order, I am contented therewith, for as you have done so have I likewise procured some of
my friends to aid us in our labour. For Master Sackville hath aptly ordered
the duke of Buckingham's oration, and Master Cavell the Blacksmith's,
50   and other.' 'I pray you', quoth one of the company, 'let us hear them.'
'Nay, soft', quoth I; 'we will take the chronicles and note their places and,
as they come, so will we orderly read them all.' To this they all agreed.

   Then one took the chronicle, whom therefore we made and call the
reader, and he began to read the story of Prince Edward called the fifth
55   king of that name and, when he came to the apprehending of the Lord
Rivers, 'stay there, I pray you', quoth I, 'for here is his complaint. For the
better understanding whereof, you must imagine that he was accompanied
with the Lord Richard Grey and with Haute and Clapham, whose infortunes he bewaileth after this manner':[348]

---

33. **duke of Somerset, slain at St. Albans**: (see Tragedy 26). **35. Shore's wife**: (see Tragedy 25); **trimly**: neatly,
effectively. **36. convenient**: suitable. **43. Master Dolman**: John Dolman. **44. Francis Segars**: Francis Seager.
45. sith: since. **47. Master Sackville**: Thomas Sackville. **49. the duke of Buckingham's oration**: see Tragedy
22b; **Master Cavell**: Humphrey Cavell; **the Blacksmith**: see Tragedy 27. **51. soft**: be silent. **53. the chronicle**:
Edward Hall's *Union of the Two Noble and Illustre Fameles of Lancastre & Yorke* (see Prose 24, n. 502).

[Tragedy 20]

How Sir Anthony Woodville, Lord Rivers and Scales, Governor of
Prince Edward, was with his Nephew Lord Richard Grey and other
Causeless Imprisoned and Cruelly Murdered

As silly suitors letted by delays
To show their prince the meaning of their mind,
That long have bought their brokers' yeas and nays
And, never the nigher, do daily wait to find
The prince's grace from weighty affairs untwined,   [5]
Which, time attained by attending all the year,
The wearied prince will then no suitors hear:

My case was such not many days ago.
For after bruit had blazèd all abroad
That Baldwin, through the aid of other mo,   [10]
Of fame or shame fallen princes would unload,
Out from our graves we got without abode
And pressèd forward with the rueful rout
That sought to have their doings bolted out.

But when I had long attended for my turn   [15]
To tell my tale as divers others did,
In hope I should no longer-while sojourn
But from my suits have speedily been rid,
When course and place both orderly had bid
Me show my mind and I prepared to say –   [20]
The hearers paused, arose, and went their way.349

These doubtful doings drave me to my dumps,
Uncertain what should move them so to do.
I fearèd lest affection's loathly lumps

3. **brokers'**: middlemen's, intermediaries'. **12. abode**: delay. **14. bolted out**: brought out (like an arrow from a bow); examined. **18. suits**: pending supplications. **19. course**: course of time. **22. drave me to my dumps**: led me to muse; made me melancholy. **24. affection's loathly lumps**: animosity's hateful excrescences.

Or inward grudge had driven them thereto,   [25]
Whose wicked stings all stories' truth undo,
Oft causing good to be reported ill
Or drowned in suds of Lethe's muddy swill.

For hitherto sly writers' wily wits,
Which have engrossèd princes' chief affairs   [30]
Have been, like horses, snaffled with the bits
Of fancy, fear, or doubt's full-deep despairs,
Whose reins enchainèd to the chiefest chairs
Have been so strained of those that bare the stroke
That truth was forced to chew or else to choke.   [35]

This causèd such as loathèd loud to lie
To pass with silence sundry princes' lives:
Less fault it is to leave than lead awry,
And better drowned than ever bound in gyves,
For fatal fraud this world so fondly drives   [40]
That whatsoever writers' brains may brew,
Be it never so false, at length is tane for true.

What harm may hap by help of lying pens,
How written lies may lewdly be maintained,
The loathly rites, the devilish idols' dens   [45]
With guiltless blood of virtuous men bestained
Is such a proof, as all good hearts have plained.
The tally grounds of stories throughly tries;
The death of martyrs vengeance on it cries.

Far better, therefore, not to write at all   [50]
Than stain the truth for any manner cause,

28. **suds**: muck; **Lethe's muddy swill**: the muddy, polluted water of the classical river of forgetfulness.   30. **engrossed**: written about.   31. **snaffled**: restrained.   32. **fancy**: imagination; arbitrary notions.   34. **bare the stroke**: bore rule.   36. **loud**: flagrantly.   38. **leave**: leave off.   39. **And ... gyves**: And it is better to be lost completely than to live ever in thrall to another's will.   43. **hap**: chance, come about.   48–9. **The ... cries**: The reckoning [of the harm caused by lying pens] thoroughly proves the bases of historical accounts; the death of martyrs cries vengeance on such harm.   51. **manner cause**: type of cause.

[39] *1563*: that ever [apparently an uncorrected printer's error]

'For this they mean to let my story fall',
Thought I, 'and ere my time their volume close'.
But after I knew it only was a pause
Made purposely, most for the readers' ease,   [55]
Assure thee, Baldwin, highly it did me please.³⁵⁰

For freshest wits I know will soon be weary
In reading long whatever book it be,
Except it be vain matter, strange or merry,
Well sauced with lies and glarèd all with glee.   [60]
With which because no grave truth may agree,
The closest style for stories is the meetest;
In rueful moans the shortest form is sweetest.

And sith the plaints already by thee penned
Are brief enough, the number also small,   [65]
The tediousness, I think, doth none offend,
Save such as have no lust to learn at all.
Regard none such, no matter what they brawl.
Warn thou the wary, lest they hap to stumble;
As for the careless, care not what they mumble.   [70]

My life is such as (if thou note it well)
May cause the witty-wealthy to beware.
For their sakes, therefore, plainly will I tell
How false and cumbrous worldly honours are,
How cankered foes bring careless folk to care,   [75]
How tyrants suffered and not quelled in time
Do cut their throats that suffer them to climb.

Neither will I hide the chiefest point of all,
Which wisest rulers least of all regard,
That was and will be cause of many a fall.   [80]
This cannot be too earnestly declared,
Because it is so seld and slackly heard:
The abuse and scorning of God's ordinances
Is chiefest cause of care and woeful chances.

---

60. **glared**: burnished; **glee**: jests, mockery. 62. **closest**: most succinct. 64. **sith**: since. 68. **brawl**: clamour. 69. **hap**: chance. 72. **witty-wealthy**: those well supplied with wisdom, good judgement. 74. **cumbrous**: trouble filled. 75. **cankered**: malignant.

God's holy orders highly are abused   [85]
When men do change their ends for strange respects;
They scornèd are when they be clean refused,
For that they cannot serve our fond affects.
The one our shame, the other our sin detects:
It is a shame for Christians to abuse them,   [90]
But deadly sin for scorners to refuse them.

I mean not this all only of degrees
Ordained by God for people's preservation,
But of his law, good orders, and decrees
Provided for his creatures' conservation.   [95]
And specially the state of procreation,
Wherein we here the number of them increase
Which shall in heaven enjoy eternal peace.

The only end why God ordainèd this
Was for the increasing of that blessèd number   [100]
For whom he hath prepared eternal bliss;
They that refuse it for the care or cumber,
Being apt thereto, are in a sinful slumber.
No fond respect, no vain-devisèd vows
Can quit or bar what God in charge allows.   [105]

'It is not good for man to live alone',
Said God, and therefore made he him a make.
'Sole life', said Christ, 'is granted few or none':[351]
All seed-shedders are bound like wives to take,
Yet not for lust, for lands or riches' sake   [110]
But to beget and foster so their fruit
That heaven and earth be storèd with the suit.[352]

But as this state is damnably refused
Of many apt and able thereunto,

---

86. **respects**: aims, concerns.   88. **For ... affects**: Because they cannot serve our foolish inclinations.   89. **The ... sin**: Our abuse of God's decrees divulges our shame; our scorn of them exposes our sin.   92. **all only**: solely; **degrees**: social ranks.   100. **blessèd number**: the elect predestined for salvation.   102. **They ... cumber**: Those who refuse to procreate because of its attendant burdens or trouble.   103. **apt thereto**: able to procreate.   105. **quit or bar**: abandon or obstruct; **in charge**: by command.   107. **make**: mate.   109. **seed-shedders**: sexually potent men; **like wives**: wives similar to them.   112. **stored with the suit**: furnished with the offspring.

So is it likewise wickedly abused   [115]
Of all that use it as they should not do.
Wherein are guilty all the greedy who
For gain, for friendship, lands, or honours wed,
And these pollute the undefiled bed.

And therefore God, through justice, cannot cease   [120]
To plague those faults with sundry sorts of whips,
As disagreement, health's or wealth's decrease,
Or loathing sore the never-likèd lips.
Disdain also with rigour sometime nips
Presuming mates unequally that match: [125]
Some bitter leaven sours the musty batch.³⁵³

We worldly folk account him very wise
That hath the wit most wealthily to wed.
By all means, therefore, always we devise
To see our issue rich in spousals sped.   [130]
We buy and sell rich orphans; babes scant bred
Must marry ere they know what marriage means;
Boys marry old trots; old fools wed young queans.³⁵⁴

We call this wedding, which in any wise
Can be no marriage, but pollution plain: [135]
A new-found trade of human merchandise,
The devil's net, a filthy, fleshly gain,
Of kind and nature an unnatural stain,
A foul abuse of God's most holy order,
And yet allowed almost in every border.   [140]

Would God I were the last that shall have cause
Against this creeping canker to complain,
That men would so regard their maker's laws
That all would leave the lewdness of their brain,
That holy orders holy might remain,   [145]

---

119. **And these**: And as a consequence these wicked people.   126. **Some … batch**: Some disagreeable leaven ferments the batch of new dough.   133. **old trots**: old, decrepit women; **young queans**: young women (with the disparaging sense of 'young hussies').   139. **God's most holy order**: that is, the order to Adam and Eve to populate the earth.   142. **canker**: cancer.

That our respects in wedding should not choke
The end and fruit of God's most holy yoke!

The sage King Solon, after that he saw
What mischiefs follow missought marriages,
To bar all baits establishèd this law: [150]
No friend nor father shall give heritages,
Coin, cattle, stuff, or other carriages
With any maid for dowry or wedding sale
By any mean, on pain of banning bale.³⁵⁵

Had this good law in England been in force,   [155]
My father had not so cruelly been slain,
My brother had not causeless lost his corpse,
Our marriage had not bred us such disdain,
Myself had lacked great part of grievous pain.
We wedded wives for dignity and lands   [160]
And left our lives in envy's bloody hands.

My father hight Sir Richard Woodville; he
Espoused the duchess of Bedford and by her
Had issue males my brother John and me,
Called Anthony. King Edward did prefer   [165]
Us far above the state wherein we were,
For he espoused our sister Elizabeth,
Whom Sir John Grey made widow by his death.³⁵⁶

How glad were we, think you, of this alliance,
So nearly coupled with so noble a king?   [170]
Who durst with any of us be at defiance,
Thus made of might the mightiest to wring?
But fie! What cares do highest honours bring,
What carelessness ourselves or friends to know,
What spite and envy both of high and low!   [175]

---

147. **yoke**: union.   150. **baits**: enticements.   152. **carriages**: pieces of moveable property.   154. **banning bale**: grievous interdiction.   165. **prefer**: promote.   172. **Thus ... wring?**: Thus made through might (of the king) able to harm even the mightiest?

Because the king had made our sister queen,
It was his honour to prefer her kin,
And, sith the readiest way, as wisest ween,
Was first by wedding wealthy heirs to win,
It pleased the prince by like mean to begin. [180]
To me he gave the rich Lord Scales his heir,
A virtuous maid, in mine eye very fair.[357]

He joinèd to my brother John the old
Duchess of Norfolk, notable of fame;
My nephew Thomas, who had in his hold [185]
The honour and rights of Marquess Dorset's name,
Espousèd Cicely, a right wealthy dame,
Lord Bonville's heir, by whom he was possessed
In all the rights wherethrough that house was blessed.[358]

The honours that my father attained were diverse: [190]
First chamberlain then constable he was.
I do omit the gainfulest, earl Rivers.[359]
Thus glistered we in glory clear as glass:
Such miracles can princes bring to pass
Among their lieges whom they mind to heave [195]
To honours false, who all their guests deceive.

Honours are like that cruel king of Thrace
With new-come guests that fed his hungry horses,
Or like the tyrant Busiris, whose grace
Offered his gods all strangers' strangled corpses.[360] [200]
To foreigners so hard false honour's force is
That all her boarders, strangers, either guests
She spoils to feed her gods and greedy beasts.

Her gods be those whom God by law or lot
Or kind by birth doth place in highest rooms. [205]
Her beasts be such as greedily have got
Office or charge to guide the seely grooms.

189. **rights**: titles, claims, privileges.   **196. who**: which.   **201. foreigners**: outsiders, those not native born to honour.   **202. either**: or.   **205. kind**: naturally.   **207. seely grooms**: innocent or naive stable hands.

These officers in law or charge are brooms
That sweep away the sweet from simple wretches
And spoil the enrichèd by their crafty fetches.   [210]

These pluck down those whom princes set aloft,
By wresting laws and false conspiracies;
Yea kings themselves by these are spoilèd oft.
When wilful princes carelessly despise
To hear the oppressèd people's heavy cries   [215]
Nor will correct their polling thieves, then God
Doth make those reeves the reckless princes' rod.

The second Richard is a proof of this,
Whom crafty lawyers by their laws deposed.[361]
Another pattern good King Henry is,   [220]
Whose right by them hath diversely been glosed:
Good while he grew, bad when he was unrosed.
And as they foaded these and divers other,
With like deceit they used the king my brother.

While he prevailed they said he owed the crown;   [225]
All laws and rights agreèd with the same.
But when by drifts he seemèd to be down,
All laws and right extremely did him blame:
Nought save usurping traitor was his name.
So constantly the judges construe laws,   [230]
That all agree still with the stronger cause.

These, as I said, and other like in charge
Are honour's horses, whom she feeds with guests;
For all whom princes frankly do enlarge
With dignities these bark at in their breasts.   [235]

---

210. **spoil the enrichèd**: rob the wealthy; **fetches**: tricks.   213. **spoiled**: despoiled.   217. **Doth ... rod**: [Then God] makes those plundering officers rods with which to punish irresponsible monarchs (**reeves**: crown officers, with an echo of 'reave', meaning 'to rob, plunder').   219. **lawyers**: men versed in the law (not solely attorneys and solicitors).   220. **King Henry**: Henry VI.   221. **glosed**: glossed (with a suggestion of 'glose', n., 'flattery, deceit'). 222. **unrosed**: Not in *OED*; the meaning perhaps is 'no longer in high esteem', derived from *OED* 'rose' *n.*, 5: 'a peerless or matchless person'. There may be an allusion as well to the English rose as a symbol of the monarchy (cf. Tragedy 9, line 49).   223. **foaded**: beguiled.   225. **owed**: owned.   231. **stronger**: mightier.   232. **in charge**: in office; in authority.   234. **frankly**: liberally.

Their spite, their might, their falsehood never rests
Till they devour them, sparing neither blood,
Ne limb, nor life, and all to get their good.

The earl of Warwick was a prancing courser;
That haughty heart of his could bear no mate. [240]
Our wealth through him waxed many a time the worser,
So canker'dly he had our kin in hate.
He troubled oft the king's unsteady state
And that because he would not be his ward
To wed and work, as he should list award. [245]

He spited us because we were preferred
By marrìage to dignities so great,
But craftily his malice he deferred
Till traitorously he found means to entreat
Our brother of Clarence to assist his feat. [250]
Whom, when he had by marriage to him bound,
Then wrought he straight our lin'age to confound.³⁶²

Through slanderous bruits he brewèd many a broil
Throughout the realm against the king my brother,
And raisèd traitorous rebels thirsting spoil [255]
To murder men, of whom among all other
One Robin of Redesdale many a soul did smother.
His rascal rabble, at my father wroth,
Took sire and son and quick beheaded both.³⁶³

This heinous act, although the king detested, [260]
Yet was he fain to pardon, for the rout
Of rebels all the realm so sore infested
That, every way assailed, he stood in doubt.
And though he were of courage high and stout,
Yet he assayed by fair means to assuage [265]
His enemies' ire, revealed by rebels' rage.

238. **good**: possessions, benefits.   240. **mate**: equal in status.   241. **wealth**: happiness, prosperity.   242. **canker'dly**: malignantly.   245. **To … award**: To wed and act in whatever manner Warwick should be pleased to determine.   250. **our brother Clarence**: George (d. 1478), first duke of Clarence, our relative (considered such because of the marriage of Clarence's brother Edward IV to Rivers's sister Elizabeth).   265. **fair**: gentle.   266. **revealed**: made manifest.

But Warwick was not pacifièd thus;
His constant rancour causeless was extreme.
No mean could serve the quarrel to discuss,
Till he had driven the king out of the realm.   [270]
Neither would he then be waked from his dream,
For when my brother was come and placed again,
He stinted not till he was stoutly slain.[364]

Then grew the king and realm to quiet rest,
Our stock and friends still flying higher an higher;   [275]
The queen with children fruitfully was blessed;
I governed them: it was the king's desire.
This set their uncles furiously on fire
That we, the queen's blood, were assigned to govern
The prince, not they, the king's own blood and brethren.[365]   [280]

This caused the duke of Clarence so to chafe
That with the king he brainless fell at bate.
The council, warily for to keep him safe
From raising tumults as he did of late
Imprisoned him, wherethrough his brother's hate   [285]
He was condemned and murdered in such sort,
As he himself hath truly made report.[366]

Was none abhorred these mischiefs more than I,
Yet could I not be therewith discontented,
Considering that his rancour touched me nigh,   [290]
Else would my conscience never have consented
To wish him harm, could he have been contented.
But fear of hurt, for safeguard of our state,
Doth cause more mischief than desert or hate.

Such is the state that many wish to bear   [295]
That either we must with others' blood be stained
Or lead our lives continually in fear.
You mounting minds behold here what is gained
By cumbrous honour painfully attained:

269. **discuss:** settle.   273. **stinted:** ceased.   275. **stock:** kindred; **an:** and.   282. **bate:** contention.

A damnèd soul for murd'ring them that hate you, [300]
Or doubtful life in danger lest they mate you.

The cause, I think, why some of high degree
Do deadly hate all seekers to ascend
Is this: the cloyne contented cannot be
With any state, till time he apprehend [305]
The highest top, for thereto climbers tend,
Which seldom is attained without the wrack
Of those between that stay and bear him back.

To save themselves, they therefore are compelled
To hate such climbers and with wit and power [310]
To compass means wherethrough they might be quelled
Ere they ascend, their honours to devour.
This caused the duke of Clarence frown and lour
At me and other whom the king promoted
To dignities, wherein he madly doted, [315]

For seeing we were his dear allìed friends,
Our furtherance should rather have made him glad
Than en'my-like to wish our woeful ends.
We were the nearest kinsfolk that he had:
We joyed with him; his sorrow made us sad. [320]
But he esteemed so much his painted sheath
That he disdained the love of all beneath.

But see how sharply God revengeth sin:
As he malignèd me and many other
His faithful friends and kindest of his kin, [325]
So Richard, duke of Gloucester, his natural brother,
Malignèd him and beastly did him smother.
A devilish deed, a most unkindly part,
Yet just revenge for his unnatural heart.

---

301. **mate**: defeat.   304. **cloyne**: cloyner, grasping, greedy person.   313. **lour**: scowl.   315. **wherein he madly doted**: in which behaviour Clarence acted madly and foolishly.   321. **painted sheath**: outward show, ostentatious presentation.   328. **unkindly**: morally unnatural, especially in treatment of kin.   329. **unnatural**: lacking normal human feelings, especially in regard to family members.

Although this brother-queller, tyrant fell,   [330]
Envied our state as much and more than he,
Yet did his cloaking flattery so excel
To all our friends-ward, chiefly unto me,
That he appeared our trusty stay to be,
For outwardly he wrought our state to further,   [335]
Where inwardly he minded not save murder.

Thus in appearance who but I was blessed?
The chiefest honours heapèd on my head.
Beloved of all, enjoying quiet rest,
The forward prince by me alone was led,   [340]
A noble imp to all good virtues bred.
The king my liege without my counsel known
Agreèd nought, though wisest were his own.367

But quiet bliss in no state lasteth long
Assailed still by mischief many ways,   [345]
Whose spoiling batt'ry, glowing hot and strong,
No flowing wealth, no force nor wisdom stays.
Her smokeless poulder beaten soldiers slays.
By open force foul mischief oft prevails;
By secret slight, she seld her purpose fails.   [350]

The king was bent too much to foolish pleasure;
In banqueting he had too great delight.
This made him grow in grossness out of measure,
Which as it kindleth carnal appetite
So quencheth it the liveliness of sprite,   [355]
Whereof ensue such sickness and diseases
As none can cure, save death that all displeases.368

Through this fault, furthered by his brother's fraud
(Now God forgive me if I judge amiss),
Or through that beast his ribald or his bawd   [360]
That larded still those sinful lusts of his,

---

330. brother-queller: brother-killer.   **333. To all our friends-ward**: toward all of our friends.   **340. forward**: precocious.   **343. Agreed nought**: assented to no course of action; **his own**: his own thoughts, counsel.   **346. spoiling batt'ry**: destructive bombardment.   **348. poulder**: explosive powder.   **360. ribald**: coarse companion; **bawd**: procurer.   **361. larded**: enriched.

He suddenly forsook all worldly bliss.
That loathèd leech, that never-welcome death,
Through spasmous humours stoppèd up his breath.[369]

That time lay I at Ludlow, Wales his border,   [365]
For with the prince the king had sent me thither,
To stay the robberies, spoil, and foul disorder
Of divers outlaws gathered there together,
Whose banding tended no man wist well whither.
When these by wisdom safely were suppressed,   [370]
Came woeful news, our sovereign was deceased.

The grief whereof, when reason had assuaged,
Because the prince remainèd in my guide,
For his defend great store of men I waged,
Doubting the storms which at such times betide.   [375]
But while I there thus warely did provide,
Commandment came to send them home again
And bring the king thence with his household train.

This charge sent from the council and the queen,
Though much against my mind I best obeyed.   [380]
The devil himself wrought all the drift I ween,
Because he would have innocents betrayed,
For ere the king were half his way conveyed,
A sort of traitors falsely him betrapped –
I caught afore and close in prison clapped.[370]   [385]

The duke of Gloucester, that incarnèd devil,
Confedered with the Duke of Buckingham,
With eke Lord Hastings, hasty both to evil,
To meet the king in mourning habit came
(A cruel wolf, though clothèd like a lamb)   [390]
And at Northampton, whereas then I bated,
They took their inn, as they on me had waited.

363. **leech**: physician.   365. **Wales his border**: on the Welsh border.   369. **Whose … whither**: The end to which their joining in league tended no man certainly knew.   376. **warely**: prudently.   384. **sort**: band.   391. **bated**: stopped.

The king that night at Stony Stratford lay,
A town too small to harbour all his train
(This was the cause why he was gone away,   [395]
While I with other did behind remain).
But will you see how falsely fiends can feign?
Not Sinon sly, whose fraud best fame rebukes,
Was half so subtle as these double dukes.³⁷¹

First to mine inn cometh in my brother false,   [400]
Embraceth me, 'Well met, good brother Scales!',
And weeps withal. The other me enhalse
With 'welcome cousin, now welcome out of Wales;
Oh happy day, for now all stormy gales
Of strife and rancour utterly are swaged,   [405]
And we your own to live or die unwaged'.

This proffered service, sauced with salutations
Immoderate, might cause me to suspect:
For commonly in all dissimulations
The excess of glavering doth the guile detect.   [410]
Reason refuseth falsehood too direct;
The will, therefore, for fear of being spied,
Exceedeth mean, because it wanteth guide.

This is the cause why such as feign to weep
Do howl outright, or, wailing, cry 'ah!',   [415]
Tearing themselves and straining sighs most deep;
Why such dissemblers as would seem to laugh
Breathe not 'tee hee!' but bray out 'hah hah hah!';
Why beggars, feigning bravery, are the proudest;
Why cowards bragging boldness wrangle loudest.   [420]

For commonly all that do counterfeit
In anything exceed the natural mean
And that for fear of failing in their feat,
But these conspirers couchèd all so clean

---

398. **best fame**: report of the best.   399. **double**: two; duplicitous.   400. **brother**: i.e. Gloucester.   402. **the other**: Buckingham; **enhalse**: clasps around the neck.   405. **swaged**: pacified.   410. **glavering**: flattery; **detect**: expose.   413. **mean**: moderation; **wanteth guide**: lacks guidance.   416. **Tearing themselves**: emitting piercing cries.   424. **couched**: expressed; **clean**: adroitly.

Through close demeanour that their wiles did wean   [425]
My heart from doubts, so many a false device
They forgèd fresh to hide their enterprise.

They supped with me, propounding friendly talk
Of our affairs, still giving me the praise,
And ever among the cups to me-ward walk.   [430]
'I drink to you, good coz', each traitor says;
Our banquet done, when they should go their ways,
They took their leave, oft wishing me good night
As heartily as any creature might.

A noble heart, they say, is lion-like: [435]
It cannot couch, dissemble, crouch nor feign.
How villainous were these and how unlike,
Of noble stock the most ignoble stain?
Their wolvish hearts, their traitorous foxly brain,
Either prove them base, of rascal race engendered,   [440]
Or from haut lin'age bastard-like degendered.

Such polling heads as praise for prudent policy
False practices I wish were packed on poles.
I mean the bastard law brood, which can mollify
All kind of causes in their crafty nolls.   [445]
These undermine all virtue: blind as moles,
They bolster wrong, they rack and strain the right
And praise for law both malice, fraud, and might.

These quench the worthy flames of noble kind,
Provoking best born to the basest vices;   [450]
Through crafts, they make the boldest courage blind,
Disliking highly valiant enterprises
And praising vilely villainous devices.
These make the boar a hog, the bull an ox,
The swan a goose, the lion a wolf or fox.[372]   [455]

---

425. **close demeanour**: hidden practice; **wean**: draw, detach.   428. **propounding**: proposing.   430. **to me-ward**: toward me.   431. **coz**: friend (lit. cousin).   436. **couch**: hide; **crouch**: cower.   440. **rascal**: low born.   441. **degendered**: degenerated.   443. **packed on poles**: placed closely together on poles, in the manner that heads of executed traitors were displayed as warnings to others.   444. **mollify**: represent in favourable terms.   445. **nolls**: heads.   448. **praise for**: proclaim as.   451. **crafts**: tricks.

The lawyer Catesby and his crafty feers,
A rout that never did good in any realm,
Are they that had transformed these noble peers:
They turned their blood to melancholic phlegm,
Their courage haut to cowardly extreme,   [460]
Their force and manhood into fraud and malice,
Their wit to wiles, stout Hector into Paris.

These glaverers gone, myself to rest I laid
And, doubting nothing, soundly fell asleep.
But suddenly my servants, sore afraid,   [465]
Awakèd me and, drawing sighs full deep,
'Alas', quoth one, 'my Lord, we are betrayed!'
'How so?' quoth I. 'The dukes are gone their ways;
They have barred the gates and borne away the keys.'

While he thus spake, there came into my mind   [470]
This fearful dream, whereout I wakèd was:
I saw a river stopped with storms of wind,
Wherethrough a swan, a bull, and boar did pass,
Franching the fish and fry with teeth of brass.
The river dried up, save a little stream,   [475]
Which at the last did water all the realm.373

My thought this stream did drown the cruel boar
In little space, it grew so deep and broad,
But he had killed the bull and swan before.
Besides all this, I saw an ugly toad   [480]
Crawl toward me, on which me thought I trode.
But what became of her or what of me,
My sudden waking would not let me see.374

These dreams considered with this sudden news,
So divers from their doings overnight,   [485]
Did cause me not a little for to muse.
I blessed me and rise in all the haste I might.

---

456. feers: men who take fees (lawyers).   459. phlegm: the bodily humour associated with apathy and indo-
lence.   463. glaverers: flatterers.   474. Franching: devouring.   477. My thought: me thought.   479. he: the
boar.

By this, Aurora spread abroad the light
Which fro the ends of Phoebus' beams she took,
Who then the Bull's chief gallery forsook.[375]   [490]

When I had opened the window to look out,
There might I see the streets each-where beset,
My inn on each side compassèd about
With armèd watchmen, all escapes to let,
Thus had these Neroes caught me in their net.   [495]
But to what end I could not throughly guess,
Such was my plainness, such their doubleness.

My conscience was so clear I could not doubt
Their deadly drift, which less apparent lay,
Because they caused their men return the route   [500]
That yode toward Stony Stratford, as they say,
Because the dukes will first be there today.
For this, thought I, they hinder me in jest,
For guiltless minds do eas'ly deem the best.[376]

By this the dukes were come into mine inn,   [505]
For they were lodgèd in another by.
I got me to them, thinking it a sin
Within my chamber cowardly to lie,
And merrily I asked my brother why
He used me so. He, stern in evil sadness,   [510]
Cried out 'I arrest thee, traitor, for thy badness!'

'How so?', quoth I. 'Whence riseth your suspicion?'
'Thou art a traitor', quoth he; 'I thee arrest.'
'Arrest?', quoth I, 'why, where is your commission?'
He drew his weapon, so did all the rest,   [515]
Crying 'yield thee, traitor!' I was sore distressed,
Made no resistance, but was sent to ward,
None save their servants assignèd to my guard.

---

490. **the Bull's chief gallery**: the zodiacal sign of Taurus. 492. **each-where beset**: everywhere occupied to prevent passing. 496. **throughly**: thoroughly. 497. **plainness**: honesty. 498. **doubt**: feel doubt about. 501. **yode**: went. 509. **brother**: i.e. Richard of Gloucester. 510. **sadness**: gravity. 517. **sent to ward**: put into custody, incarcerated.

This done, they sped them to the king in post
And, after their humble reverence to him done,   [520]
They traitorously began to rule the roast.
They picked a quarrel to my sister's son
Lord Richard Grey. The king would not be won
To agree to them, yet they, against all reason,
Arrested him (they said) for heinous treason.   [525]

Sir Thomas Vaughàn and Sir Richard Haute,
Two worthy knights, were likewise apprehended;[377]
These were all guilty in one kind of fault:
They would not like the practice then pretended.
And, seeing the king was herewith sore offended,   [530]
Back to Northampton they brought him again,
And thence dischargèd most part of his train.

There, lo, Duke Richard made himself protector
Of king and realm by open proclamation,
Though neither king nor queen were his elector.   [535]
Thus he presumed by lawless usurpation.
But will you see his deep dissimulation?
He sent me a dish of dainties from his board
That day and, with it, this false friendly word:

'Commend me to him; all things shall be well.   [540]
I am his friend; bid him be of good cheer.'
These news I prayed the messenger go tell
My nephew Richard, whom I loved full dear.
But what he meant by 'well', now shall you hear:
He thought it well to have us quickly murdered,   [545]
Which not long after thoroughly he furthered.[378]

For straight from thence we closely were conveyed,
From jail to jail northward we wist not whither,
Where after we had a while in sunder strayed,

519: **in post**: quickly.   **521. rule the roast**: take on chief authority.   **525. him**: Richard Grey.   **535. his elector**: the one who chose him.   **543. My nephew Richard**: Sir Richard Grey.

At last we met at Pomfret all together.   [550]
Sir Richard Ratcliffe had us welcome thither,
Who openly, all right and law contemned,
Beheaded us before we were condemned.[379]

My cousin Richard could not be content
To leave his life, because he wist not why   [555]
(Good, gentle man that never harm had meant!);
Therefore he askèd wherefore he should die.
The priest, his ghostly father, did reply
With weeping eyes, 'I know one woeful cause:
The realm hath neither righteous lords nor laws.'   [560]

Sir Thomas Vaughàn, chafing, crièd still
'This tryant Gloucester is the graceless "G"
That will his brother's children beastly kill!'
And lest the people through his talk might see
The mischiefs toward and thereto not agree,   [565]
Our tormentor, that false perjurèd knight,
Bade stop our mouths with words of high despite.[380]

Thus died we guiltless, process heard we none,
No cause alleged, no judge, nor yet accuser,
No quest empanelled passèd us upon.   [570]
That murderer Ratcliffe, law and right's refuser,
Did all to flatter Richard, his abuser,
Unhappy both that ever they were born
Through guiltless blood that have their souls forlorn.

In part I grant I well deservèd this,   [575]
Because I caused not speedy execution
Be done on Richard for that murder of his,
When first he wrought King Henry's close confusion,
Nor for his brother's hateful persecution.
These cruel murders painful death deserved,   [580]
Which had he suffered, many had been preserved.

Warn therefore all that charge or office bear
To see all murderers speed'ly executed

---

565. **mischiefs toward**: coming acts of wickedness.   570. **No … upon**: No empanelled jury passed judgement upon us.   572. **abuser**: misuser.   574. **forlorn**: brought to ruin.

And spare them not for favour or for fear.
By guiltless blood the earth remains polluted;   [585]
For lack of justice kingdoms are transmuted.
They that save murderers from deservèd pain
Shall through those murderers miserably be slain.[381]

[Prose 22]

When I had read this, they liked it very well. One wished that the combat
which he had with the Bastard of Burgoyne and the honour which he
won both with spear and axe should not be forgotten.[382] Another moved
a question about a great matter, and that is the variance of the chronicles
about the Lord Thomas Grey, Marquess Dorset, whom Fabyan everywhere
calleth the queen's brother. Sir Thomas More and Hall call him the queen's
son. Fabyan sayeth he was governor of the prince and had the conveyance
of him from Ludlow towards London. The other, whom we follow, say he
was then at London with the queen providing for the king's coronation
and took sanctuary with her as soon as he heard of the apprehending of his
uncle.[383] This disagreeing of writers is a great hindrance of the truth and no
small cumbrance to such as be diligent readers, besides the harm that may
happen in succession of heritages. It were therefore a worthy and a good
deed for the nobility to cause all the records to be sought and a true and
perfect chronicle thereout to be written, unto which we refer the deciding
of this and of all other like controversies, giving this to understand in the
meantime, that no man shall think his title either better or worse by anything that is written in any part of this treatise, for the only thing which
is purposed herein is by example of others' miseries to dissuade all men
from all sins and vices. If by the way we touch anything concerning titles,
we follow therein Hall's chronicle. And where we seem to swerve from
his reasons and causes of divers doings, there we gather upon conjecture
such things as seem most probable, or at the least most convenient for the
furtherance of our purpose.
    When the reader would have proceeded in the chronicle, which straight
entreateth of the villainous destruction of the Lord Hastings, I willed him
to surcease, because I had there his tragedy very learnedly penned. 'For the
better understanding whereof, you must imagine that you see him newly
crept out of his grave and speaking to me as followeth':

---

2. **Burgoyne**: Burgundy.   7. **the prince**: Edward (d. *c.* 1483), prince of Wales, the future Edward V.   9. **king's**: that
of Edward V.   13. **heritages**: inheritances.

How the Lord Hastings was Betrayed by Trusting too much to his Evil Counsellor Catesby and Villainously Murdered in the Tower of London by Richard, Duke of Gloucester

'Hastings I am, whose hastened death who knew
My life with praise, my death with plaint, pursue.
With others, fearing lest my headless name
Be wronged by partial bruit of flattering fame,
Cleaving my tomb the way my fame forewent   [5]
(Though bared of loans which body and Fortune lent
Erst my proud vaunt), present present to thee
My honour, fall, and forcèd destiny.

Ne fear to stain thy credit by my tale:
In Lethe's flood, long since, in Stygian vale   [10]
Self-love I drenched. What time hath fined for true
And ceaseth not, though stale, still to renew
Recount I will, whereof be this the proof:
That blaze I will my praise and my reproof.
We naked ghosts are but the very man,   [15]
Ne of ourselves more than we ought we scan.

But doubt distracteth me, if I should consent
To yield mine honoured name a martyred saint.
If martyrdom rest in the miser's life
Through torments wrongly reft by fatal knife,   [20]

1–2. whose … pursue: those who knew of my early death consider my life with praise and my demise with lamentation.   **4. partial bruit**: prejudicial report; **fame**: public talk.   **5. Cleaving … forewent**: Breaking out of my tomb in the manner my public reputation went out into the world before me.   **6. bared of loans**: stripped of things loaned.   **7. present present to thee**: in thy presence present to thee.   **9. Ne**: do not; **credit**: trust, willingness to believe.   **10. Lethe**: the classical river of forgetting; **Stygian vale**: the underworld.   **11. drenched**: drowned; **fined for true**: purified to leave only the truth.   **14. blaze**: divulge.   **15. very man**: the man in himself, in his essence.   **16. Ne … scan**: We do not judge ourselves more than we should.   **18. yield**: acknowledge.   **19. the miser's**: the miserable person's.   **20. reft**: taken from life.

How Fortune's nursling, I, and dearest babe
Ought thereto stoop none may me well persuade,
For how may miser-martyrdom betide
To whom in cradle Fortune was affied?

See how this grossest air infecteth me since: [25]
Forgot have I of loyalty to my prince
My happy meed is "martyr" to be named?
And what the heavens embrace, the world ay blamed,
For men's unjustice wreaked but God's just ire,
And, by wrong end, turned wreak to justice' hire.   [30]
Oh judgements just, by unjustice justice dealt!
Who doubteth of me may learn, the truth who felt.

So, therefore, as my fall may many stay,
As well the prince from violent headlong sway
Of noble peers from honour's throne to dust   [35]
As nobles less in tickle state to trust,
Shunning those sins that shake the golden leaves
Perforce from boughs, ere Nature bare the greaves,
So, what my life professed my death here teacheth
And, as with word, so with example preacheth.   [40]

The hilly heavens and valley earth below
Yet ring his fame, whose deeds so great did grow.
Edward the Fourth ye know unnamed I mean,
Whose noble nature so to me did lean
That I his staff was, I his only joy,   [45]
And even what Pandare was to him of Troy,
Which moved him first to create me chamberlain
To serve his sweets to my most sour pain.[384]

---

21. **How**: how it is that. 22. **stoop**: lower myself. 23. **miser-martyrdom**: the martyrdom of a miserable, wretched person; **betide**: happen. 24. **affied**: bound to, committed to. 25. **grossest**: densest, thickest; **infecteth me since**: corrupts me, leads me to wrongful beliefs since the time of my death. 26–7. **Forgot … name**: Have I forgotten that, because of my loyalty to my prince, my happy reward is to be named a martyr? (**happy**: fortunate; pleasant). 28. **ay**: ever. 29. **wreaked but**: only gave expression to. 30. **wreak**: punishment, harm; **to justice' hire**: to the service of justice. 31–2. **Oh … felt**: Oh how just are those unjust judgements by which justice is actually done! Anyone who doubts this may learn it from me, who felt the statement's truth. 34. **sway**: forcing down. 36. **tickle**: uncertain, changeable. 38. **Perforce**: forcibly; **bare the greaves**: make bare the branches (subjunctive mood).

[26] *1563*: foyaltye (an uncorrected misprint)

Wherein, too justly praised for secretness
(For now my guilt with shrieking I confess), [50]
To him too true, too untrue to the queen,
Such hate I won as lasted long between
Our families. Shore's wife was my nice cheat,
The holy whore, and eke the wily peat:
I fed his lust with lovely pieces, so [55]
That God's sharp wrath I purchased, my just woe.[385]

See here of nobles new the divers source:
Some virtue raiseth; some climb by sluttish sorts.
The first, though only of themselves begun,
Yet circlewise into themselves do run. [60]
Within their fame their force united so
Both endless is and stronger gainst their foe.
For when endeth it that never hath begun?
Or by what force may circled knot be undone?[386]

Th'òther, as by wicked means they grew [65]
And reigned by flattery or violence, so soon rue.
First tumbling step from honours old is vice,
Which, once descended, some linger, none arise
To former type but they catch virtue's spray,
Which mounteth them that climb by lawful way. [70]
Beware to rise by serving princely lust:
Surely to stand, one mean is rising just.[387]

Which learn by me, whom let it help to excuse
That, ruthful now, myself I do accuse
And that my prince I ever pleased with such [75]
As harmèd none and him contented much.
In vice some favour or less hate let win
That I ne wryed to worser end my sin

53. nice cheat: my wanton paramour (lit. piece of plunder). **54. peat**: young woman; sweetheart. **58. sluttish sorts**: immoral methods. **59–64. The … undone**: see explanatory note 386. **62. gainst**: against. **65–72. Th'other … just**: see explanatory note 387 ('Th'òther' in line 65, though spelled 'Thother' in the original, is evidently meant to be pronounced as three syllables). **69. spray**: slender branches. **70. mounteth**: raise in honour or rank; cause to ascend. **73–6. Which … much**: Learn this by me, and let it help to excuse me that I, ruthful now, accuse myself and also that I pleased my prince ever with such things [i.e. concubines] as harmed no one and contented him greatly. **78. wryed**: turned.

But used my favour to the safety of such
As fury of later war to live did grutch.[388]   [80]

For as on dirt, though dirty, shineth the sun,
So, even amidst my vice, my virtue shone.
Myself I spared with any his cheat to stain,
For love and reverence so I could refrain.
Gisippus' wife erst Titus would desire   [85]
With friendship's breach; I quenched that brutish fire.[389]
Manly it is to loathe the fawning lust,
Small vaunt to fly what of constraint thou must.

These therefore raised, if thou mine office scan,
Lo, none I hurt but furthered every man.   [90]
My chamber England was, my staff the law,
Whereby sauns rigour all I held in awe.[390]
So loving to all, so beloved of all
As what ensued upon my bloody fall,
(Though I ne felt, yet surely this I think)   [95]
Full many trickling tear their mouths did drink.

Disdain not, princes, easy access, meek cheer;
We know than angels statelier port ye bear
Of God himself, too massy a charge for sprites.[391]
But then, my lords, consider he delights   [100]
To vail his grace to us poor earthly wants,
To simplest shrubs and to the dunghill plants.
Express him then in might and mercy's mean,
So shall ye win, as now you wield, the realm.

But all too long, I fear, I do delay   [105]
The many means whereby I did bewray
My zealous will to earn my prince's grace,

---

80. **grutch**: begrudge.   83. **any his cheat**: any one of Edward IV's mistresses.   92. **sauns**: without; **held in awe**: inspired proper respect in.   93–6. **So ... drink**: Just as I was loving to all, so I was beloved by all, to the point that, at the time of my bloody death, many tasted their own tears (though I never experienced this posthumous reaction, I certainly believe it occurred).   97. **cheer**: countenance, disposition.   98–9. **We ... sprites**: We know that God himself has given you a bearing or rank more magnificent than that of the angels, too heavy a charge for spirits.   101. **vail**: lower; **wants**: moles.   103. **Express**: Be a likeness of; **mean**: instigation.   106. **bewray**: make manifest.

Lest thou differ to think me kind percase.
As nought may last, so Fortune's weathery cheer
With pouting looks gan lour on my sire [110]
And on her wheel advanced high in his room
The Warwick Earl, mace of Christendom.³⁹²

Besides the tempting prowess of the foe,
His traitor brother did my prince forgo.
The cause was liked; I was his linked ally. [115]
Yet, nor the cause nor brother's treachery,
Nor en'my's force, ne band of mingled blood
Made Hastings bear his prince other mind than good.
But tane and scaped from Warwick's gripping paws,
With me he fled through Fortune's froward'st flaws.³⁹³ [120]

To London come, at large we might have seemed,
Had we not then the realm a prison deemed.
Each bush a bar, each spray a banner splayed,
Each house a fort our passage to have stayed.
To Lynn we leap, where while we await the tide, [125]
My secret friends in secret I supplied
In mouth to maintain Henry Sixth their king,
By deed to devoir Edward to bring in.³⁹⁴

The restless tide to bare the empty bay
With waltering waves roams wambling forth. "Away!", [130]
The merry mariner hails. The bragging boy
To mast's high top up hies. In sign of joy
The wavering flag is vanced. The subtle seas
Their swelling cease; to calmest even peace
Sinketh down their pride. With drunkenness, gainst all care, [135]
The seamen armed await their noble fare.

On board we come. The massy anchors weighed,
One English ship, two hulks of Holland aid

---

108. **differ**: disagree; **percase**: perhaps. 109. **weathery**: changeable (like the weather). 113. **tempting**: afflicting. 115. **The cause was liked**: the people favoured Warwick's cause. 117. **ne band**: nor bond. 119. **tane**: taken by. 120. **froward'st flaws**: most contrary blasts of wind. 123. **splayed**: displayed. 126. **supplied**: begged. 127. **In mouth**: in their words. 128. **devoir**: endeavour. 130. **waltering**: rolling; **wambling**: unsteadily (with a sense of inducing nausea). 132. **hies**: climbs speedily. 133. **vanced**: upraised. 134. **to calmest even**: to their most calm, even state. 136. **fare**: passenger.

In such a pinch. So small, though, was the train,
Such his constraint, that now that one with pain   [140]
Command he might, who erst mought many mo
Than brought the ghastly Greeks to Tenedo.[395]
So nought is ours that we by hap may lose;
What nearest seems is farthest off in woes.

As banished wights, such joys we mought have made,   [145]
Eased of ay-threat'ning death that late we dread,
But once our country's sight (not care) exempt,
No harbour showing that mought our fear relent,
No covert cave, no shrub to shroud our lives,
No hollow wood, no flight that oft deprives   [150]
The mighty his prey, no sanctuary left
For exiled prince, that shrouds each slave from theft.

In prison pent, whose woody walls to pass
Of no less peril than the dying was,
With ocean moated, battered with the waves   [155]
As, chained at oars, the wretched galley slaves
At mercy sit of sea and en'mies' shot
And shun with death what they with flight may not;
But greenish waves and desert, louring skies,
All comfort else foreclosed our exiled eyes.   [160]

Lo, lo! From highest top the slavish boy,
Sent up with sight of land our hearts to joy,
Descries at hand whole fleet of Easterlings,
As then hot en'mies of the British kings.[396]
The mouse may sometime help the lion in need;   [165]
The beetle-bee once split the eagle's breed:[397]
Oh princes, seek no foes; in your distress
The earth, the seas conspire your heaviness.

---

140. **one:** i.e., the one English ship.   141. **erst mought many mo:** who earlier might command many more.   142. **Tenedo:** Tenedos.   143–4. **So … woes:** So nothing is truly ours that may be lost by chance; what we once thought closest to us is proved farthest away when we are in woe.   147. **exempt:** cut off from.   153–4. **whose … was:** i.e., to go beyond the wooden walls of the ship would bring about no less a danger than death.   159–60. **But … eyes:** Our exiled eyes excluded all comfort save greenish waves and empty louring skies. **desert:** desolate, lonely.   163. **Easterlings:** ships belonging to the members of the Hanseatic League.   166. **beetle-bee:** humming beetle.

Our foe descried, by flight we shun in hast
And lade with canvas now the bending mast.   [170]
The ship was racked to try her sailing then:
As squirrels climb the troops of trusty men;
The steersman seeks a readier course to run;
The soldier stirs; the gunner hies to gun;
The Flemings sweat; the English ship disdains   [175]
To wait behind to bear the Flemings' trains.³⁹⁸

Forth flyeth the bark, as from the violent gun
The pellet pierceth all stays and stops eftsoon,
And swift she swimmeth, as oft in sunny day
The dolphin fleets in seas in merry May.   [180]
As we for lives, so th'Easterlings for gain
Thwack on the sails and after make amain.
Though laden they were and of burden great,
A king to master yet, what swain nould sweat?

So mid the vale, the greyhound, seeing start   [185]
His fearful foe, pursueth before she flirteth
And, where she turneth, he turneth her there to bear:
The one prey pricketh, the other safety's fear.
So were we chased, so fled we afore our foes:
Bet flight than fight, in so uneven close.   [190]
I end. Some think, perhaps, "too long he stay'th
In peril present, showing his fixèd faith".

This ventured I, this dread I did sustain
To try my truth; my life I did disdain.
But, lo!, like trial against his civil foe: [195]
Faith's worst is trial, which is reserved to woe.
I pass our scape and sharp returning home,

---

169. hast: haste.   **172. As … men**: As squirrels climb so did the troops of trusty men.   **178. pellet**: bullet; **stays and stops**: all hindrances and impediments soon after (being fired).   **180. fleets**: swims.   **181. As … lives**: In the same manner as we did to save our lives.   **182. Thwack on**: set quickly in place; **after make amain**: make after us at full speed.   **184. nould**: would be unwilling to.   **186. foe**: i.e. a hare; **flirteth**: darts.   **188. The … fear**: The one is spurred in the chase by its desire for prey; fear of safety impels the other.   **190. Bet**: better; **close**: an encounter.   **193. dread**: proper awe or respect for a monarch.   **194. try my truth**: prove my loyalty.   **195. But … foe**: But see a similar trial of my loyalty against a foe from Edward's own country.   **196. Faith's … woe**: The most painful part of loyalty is the trying of it, a matter which is given over to woe.   **197. scape**: escape (from the pursuing ships).

Where we were welcomed by our wonted foen.
To battle main descends the empire's right;
At Barnet join the hosts in bloody fight.³⁹⁹   [200]

There joined three battles ranged in such array,
As mought for terror Alexander fray.
What should I stay to tell the long discourse?
Who won the palm? Who bare away the worse?
Sufficeth to say by my reservèd band   [205]
Our enemies fled; we had the upper hand.⁴⁰⁰
My iron army held her steady place
My prince to shield, his fearèd foe to chase.

The like success befell me in Tewkesbury field,
My furious force there forced perforce to yield   [210]
The traitor foe and render to my king
Her only son, lest he more bate might bring.⁴⁰¹
Thus hast thou a mirror of a subject's mind,
Such as perhaps is rare again to find:
The carving cuts that cleave the trusty steel   [215]
My faith and due allegiance could not feel.

But out alas! what praise may I recount
That is not spiced with spot that doth surmount
My greatest vaunt? For bloody war too feat
A tiger was I, all for peace unmeet.   [220]
A soldier's hands must oft be dyed with gore
Lest, stark with rest, they finewed wax and hoar.
Peace could I win by war, but peace not use;
Few days enjoy he, who warlike peace doth choose.

When Crofts, a knight, presented Henry's heir   [225]
To this our prince, in furious mood enquire
Of him he gan, what folly or frenzy vain
With armès forced him to invade his realm?

---

199. main: mighty; **descends**: comes down, falls. **201. battles**: battalions. **202. Alexander**: Alexander the Great. **210. perforce**: by force. **212. bate**: discord. **213. mirror**: model, exemplar. **219. too feat**: all too fitting. **222. Lest … hoar**: Lest, made stiff with rest, they become decrepit (**finewed**: vinnied, decrepit). **228. armès**: arms.

Whom answering that he claimed his father's right
With gauntlet smit, commanded from his sight, [230]
Clarence, Gloucester, Dorset, and I, Hastings, slew,
The guilt whereof we shortly all did rue.[402]

Clarence, as Cyrus, drowned in blood-like wine;
Dorset I furthered to his speedy pine.[403]
Of me, myself am speaking precedent, [235]
Nor easier fate the bristled boar is lent.
Our bloods have paid the vengeance of our guilt;
His fried bones shall broil for blood he hath spilt.
Oh wlatsome murder that attaineth our fame!
Oh horrible traitors wanting worthy name:[404] [240]

Who more mischievously of all states deserve
As better they who first did such preserve?
If those for gifts we reckon heavenly wights,
These may we well deem fiends and damnèd sprites
And (while on earth they walk) disguisèd devils, [245]
Sworn foes of virtue, factors for all evils,
Whose bloody hands torment their gorèd hearts.
Through bloodshed's horror, in soundest sleep he starts!

Oh happy world, were the lions men:
All lions should at least be sparèd then.[405] [250]
No surety now, no lasting league is blood.
A meacock is, who dreadeth to see bloodshed.
Stale is the pattern; the fact must needs be rife.
While two were armies two, the issues of first wife,
With armèd heart and hand th'one bloody brother [255]
With cruel chase pursueth and murd'reth th'other.

---

234. pine: torment; anguish.   235. Of ... precedent: I myself (in my ghostly state) am the speaking indication of the consequences of my guilty action (the killing of Prince Edward).   236. boar: Richard, duke of Gloucester (whose badge was the boar).   238. fried bones: cooked by frying (as the meat of a boar might be); tortured by fire (as Richard will be in hell).   239. wlatsome: loathsome (a Chaucerian archaism).   241–2. Who ... preserve: Who more appropriately deserves greater harm from members of all social classes than those who originally sought to preserve such people?   243. those: those who sought to protect the people.   246. factors: agents.   247. their: the referent is unclear: it is perhaps men and women of 'all states' (line 241) or 'those' who seek to aid such men and women (line 243); gored: pierced, stabbed.   248. he: he who sheds blood.   252. meacock: coward, weakling.   253. Stale: Old, worn out.   254. While ... wife: During the time that two armies were composed of two men only, the children of the world's first wife (i.e. Eve's sons Cain and Abel).

Which who defieth not? Yet who ceaseth to sue?
The bloody Cains their bloody sire renew.
The horror yet is like in common frays,
For in each murder, brother brother slays.   [260]
Traitors to nature, country, kin and kind,
Whom no band serveth in brothers' zeal to bind.
Oh simple age, when slander slaughter was!
The tongue's small evil how doth this mischief pass?

Hopest thou to cloak thy covert mischief wrought?   [265]
Thy conscience, caitiff, shall proclaim thy thought.
A vision, Chaucer showeth, disclosed thy crime;[406]
The fox descry the crows and chattering pyen.
And shall thy fellow felons not bewray
The guiltless death, whom guilty hands do slay?   [270]
Unpunished scaped for heinous crime some one,
But unavenged in mind or body none.

Vengeance on mind the fretting furies take;
The sinful corpse, like earthquake, agues shake.
Their frowning looks their frouncèd minds bewray;   [275]
In haste they run and mids their race they stay,
As gidded roe. Amidst their speech they whist;
At meat they muse. Nowhere they may persist
But some fear nettleth them. Ay hang they so:
So never wanteth the wicked murderer woe.   [280]

An infant rent with lion's ramping paws?
Why slander I lions? They fear the sacred laws
Of princes' blood. Ay me, more brute than beast
With princes' sides – Lycaon's pie – to feast?[407]
Oh tyrant tigers! Oh insatiable wolves!   [285]

---

257. **Which … sue?**: Who does not despise such a thing, yet who ceases to follow it?   261. **kind**: natural disposition; kindred.   262. **zeal**: ardent love.   263–4. **Oh … pass?**: Oh innocent age, when slander was the only slaughter! How far does the wicked act of murder surpass the tongue's minor transgression?   268. **The … pyen**: Crows and chattering magpies make known the presence of a fox (**pyen**: a pseudo-archaic plural for 'pies', magpies).   271. **some one**: a limited few.   273. **fretting**: gnawing, wasting.   274. **The … shake**: Agues shake the sinner's body like an earthquake.   275. **frounced**: hostile (lit. frowning).   277. **gidded roe**: deer made suddenly giddy; **whist**: fall silent.   278. **meat**: a meal.   279. **Ay … so**: They always remain in such an unsettled state.   281. **infant**: youth of noble birth; **ramping**: rampant, fiercely extended.   283. **more brute than beast**: you who are more brutish than a beast.   284. **sides**: both halves of a body prepared for eating (as in 'side of beef').

Oh English courtesy, monstrous maws and gulfs!
My death shall forthwith preach my earnèd meed,
If first to one like murder I proceed.

While Edward lived, dissembled discord lurked
In double hearts, yet so his reverence worked.   [290]
But when succeeding tender feeble age
Gave open gap to tyrants' rushing rage,
I holp the Boar and Buck to captivate
Lord Rivers, Grey, Sir Thomas Vaughan, and Haute.
If land would help the sea, well earned that ground   [295]
Itself to be with conquering waves surround.

Their speedy death by privy doom procured
At Pomfret; though my life short while endured,
Myself I slew, when them I damned to death.
At once my throat I rived and reft them breath,   [300]
For that self day, afore or near the hour
That withered Atropos nipped the springing flower
With violent hand of their forth-running life,
My head and body in Tower twinned like knife.⁴⁰⁸

By this my pattern all ye peers beware: [305]
Oft hangeth he himself, who others weeneth to snare.
Spare to be each other's butcher; fear the kite
Who soareth aloft, while frog and mouse do fight,
In civil combat grappling, void of fear
Of foreign foe at once all both to bear,⁴⁰⁹   [310]
Which plainer by my pitied plaint to see,
Awhile anew your list'ning lend to me.

Too true it is two sundry assemblies kept
At Crosby's Place and Baynard's Castle set.
The dukes at Crosby's, but at Baynard's we: [315]

---

286. gulfs: voracious appetites.   **288. like**: similar.   **290. yet**: at that time.   **293. Boar and Buck**: Richard, duke of Gloucester, and Henry Stafford (d. 1483), second duke of Buckingham.   **297. privy**: secret.   **300. At … breath**: At once I cut my own throat and took from them their breath.   **302. Atropos**: one of the classical fates; **springing**: growing.   **304. My … knife**: A similar knife severed my head from my body in the Tower of London.   **306. weeneth**: intends.   **310. all both to bear**: both to bear away.   **315. the dukes**: Gloucester and Buckingham.

The one to crown a king, the other to be.
Suspicious is secession of foul friends,
When either's drift to other's mischief tends.
I feared the end; my Catesby, being there,
Discharged all doubts. Him held I most entire,[410]   [320]

Whose great preferment by my means I thought
Some spur to pay the thankfulness he ought.
The trust he ought me made me trust him so
That privy he was both to my weal and woe.
My heart's one half, my chest of confidence,   [325]
My treasure's trust: my joy dwelt in his presence.
I loved him, Baldwin, as the apple of mine eye;
I loathed my life when Catesby would me die.[411]

Fly from thy channel, Thames, forsake thy streams!
Leave the adamant iron; Phoebus lay thy beams!   [330]
Cease heavenly spheres at last your weary wark;
Betray your charge, return to chaos dark.
At least some ruthless tiger hang her whelp,
My Catesby so with some excuse to help
And me to comfort that I alone ne seem   [335]
Of all Dame Nature's works left in extreme.[412]

A golden treasure is the trièd friend,
But who may gold from counterfeits defend?
Trust not too soon, ne all too light mistrust:
With th'one thyself, with th'other thy friend thou hurt'st.   [340]
Who twineth betwixt and steereth the golden mean
Nor rashly loveth nor mistrusteth in vain.[413]
For friendship poison, for safety mithridate,
It is thy friend to love as thou wouldst hate.

Of tickle credit ne had been the mischief,   [345]
What needed Virbius miracle-doubled life?[414]

---

323. **ought**: owed.   330. **adamant**: lodestone; **lay**: lay aside.   331. **wark**: work.   335. **ne**: do not.   336. **in extreme**: at the farthest point away from.   341–2. **Who … vain**: He who proceeds between the two extremes of trust and mistrust and who is guided by the golden mean neither too rashly loves nor vainly mistrusts.   343. **mithridate**: a panacea.   345. **Of … mischief**: Had it not been for the harm of facile trust.

Credulity surnamed first the Aegean seas;[415]
Mistrust doth treason in the trustiest raise.
Suspicious Romulus stained his walls first reared
With brother's blood, whom for light leap he feared.[416]   [350]
So not in brotherhood jealousy may be borne;
The jealous cuckold wears the infamous horn.

A beast may preach by trial, not foresight.
Could I have shunned this credit, ne'er had light
The dreaded death upon my guilty head.   [355]
But fools ay wont to learn by after-rede:
Had Catesby kept unstained the truth he plight,
Yet had ye enjoyed me, and I yet the light.
All Derby's doubts I clearèd with his name;
I knew no harm could hap us sauns his blame.[417]   [360]

But see the fruits of fickle light belief:
The ambitious dukes corrupt the traitor thief
To grope me if allured I would assent
To been a partner of their cursed intent.
Whereto, when neither force nor friendship vailed,   [365]
By tyrant force their purpose they assailed
And summoned shortly a council in the Tower
Of June the fifteenth, at appointed hour.[418]

Alas, are councils wryed to catch the good?
Is no place now exempt from shedding blood,   [370]
Sith councils that were careful to preserve
The guiltless good are means to make them starve?
What may not mischief of mad man abuse?
Religion's cloak someone to vice doth choose
And maketh God protector of his crime: [375]
Oh monstrous world, well ought we wish thy fine!

---

354. **light**: lighted.   356. **after-rede**: consideration, deliberation that only comes after an event.   357. **truth he plight**: loyalty he pledged.   358. **Yet ... light**: You would even now have been able to have the pleasure of having me present and I the enjoyment of the light (as someone who still lived).   360. **hap us**: happen to us.   361. **light**: unthinking.   363. **grope**: examine, sound out.   365. **vailed**: availed.   369. **wryed**: perverted.   371. **that were**: that once were.   373. **mad man**: madman; crazed humankind.   374. **to vice**: to cover vice.   376. **fine**: end.

The fatal skies roll on the blackest day,
When doubled bloodshed my blood must repay.
Others none forceth; to me Sir Thomas Howard
As spur is buckled to provoke me forward.[419]　　　　　　[380]
Derby, who feared the parted sittings yore,
Whether much more he knew by experience hoar
Or, unaffected, clearer truth could see,
At midnight dark this message sends to me:

"Hastings away! In sleep the gods foreshow　　　　　　[385]
By dreadful dream fell fates unto us two.
Me thought a boar with tusk so razed our throat
That both our shoulders of the blood did smoke.
Arise to horse, straight homeward let us hie,
And sith our foe we may not mate, oh fly!　　　　　　[390]
Of Chauntecleer you learn dreams' sooth to know;
Thence wisemen conster more than the cock doth crow".[420]

While thus he spake, I held within mine arm
Shore's wife, the tender piece, to keep me warm.
Fie on adultery, fie on lecherous lust!　　　　　　[395]
Mark in me, ye nobles all, God's judgements just:
A pander, murderer, and adulterer thus,
Only such death I die, as I ne blush.
Now, lest my dame mought fear appal my heart,
With eager mood up in my bed I start.　　　　　　[400]

"And is this thy lord", quoth I, "a sorcerer?
A wise man now become? A dream reader?
What though so Chauntecleer crowed? I reck it not.
On my part pleadeth as well Dame Pertelote;
Unjudged hang'th yet the case betwixt them tway,　　　　　　[405]
Ne was his dream cause of his hap, I say.[421]
Shall dreaming doubts from prince my service slack?
Nay, then mought Hastings life and living lack".

---

378. **doubled bloodshed my blood must repay**: my own death must pay for my two acts of bloodshed (i.e. Hastings's killing of Prince Edward and his hand in the condemnation of Rivers, Grey, Vaughn, and Haute). 383. **unaffected**: free from outside influence. 390. **mate**: defeat. 391. **sooth**: truth. 392. **conster**: construe. 397. **thus**: in this way. 398. **Only … blush**: An obscure line, perhaps suggesting 'It is this sort of death alone I die (one brought by God's judgement), I am not ashamed to admit'. 399. **Now … heart**: Now, lest my lady might fear my heart grow faint. 403. **I reck it not**: I don't concern myself for it. 405. **tway**: two. 406. **his hap**: what befell him.

He parteth; I sleep, my mind, surcharged with sin
As Phoebus' beams by misty clouds kept in,   [410]
Ne could misgive ne dream of my mishap;
As block I tumbled to mine enemies' trap.
Security causeless through my careless friend
Reft me foresight of my approaching end.
So Catesby clawed me, as when the cat doth play   [415]
Dallying with mouse, whom straight he minds to slay.

The morrow come, the latest light to me,
On palfrey mounted to the Tower I hie,
Accompanied with that Howard my mortal foe,
To slaughter led – thou, God, wouldst have it so.   [420]
Oh deep dissemblers, honouring with your cheer,
Whom in hid heart ye traitorously tear!
Never had realm so open signs of wrack
As I had showed me of my heavy hap.

The vision first of Stanley late descried,   [425]
Then mirth so extreme that near for joy I died – ⁴²²
Were it that swan-like I foresung my death
Or merry mind foresaw the loose of breath
That long it coveted from this earth's annoy!
But even as sicker as th'end of woe is joy,   [430]
And glorious light to obscure night doth tend,
So extreme mirth in extreme moan doth end,

For why extremes are haps racked out of course
By violent might far swingèd forth perforce,
Which as they are piercing'st while they violent'st move   [435]
(For near'st they cleave to cause that doth them shove),
So soonest fall from that their highest extreme
To th'other contrary that doth want of mean.

409–11. **my ... mishap**: my mind, overburdened by sin in the manner that the sun's beams are occluded by misty clouds, could neither have misgivings nor imagine in a dream my impending misfortune.   **412. block**: log, piece of wood; **tumbled**: fell helplessly.   **413. careless friend**: friend who did not care about me.   **421. cheer**: countenance.   **428. loose**: setting free from the body.   **430. sicker**: certain.   **433. For ... course**: Because extremes are occurrences pulled out of their normal course.   **434. swinged**: driven forcefully.   **435. piercing'st**: most intensely affecting.   **436. cleave**: adhere; **shove**: drive, propel.   **438. doth want of mean**: lacks any quality of moderation.

So laughed he erst, who laughèd out his breath;
So laughed I, when I laughed myself to death.   [440]

The pleasing'st means bode not the luckiest ends.
Not ay found treasure to like pleasure tends.
Mirth means not mirth all time; thrice happy hire
Of wit to shun the excess that all desire.
But this I pass; I hie to other like.   [445]
My palfrey in the plainest pavèd street
Thrice bowed his bones, thrice kneelèd on the floor,
Thrice shunned (as Balaam's ass) the dreaded Tower.[423]

What, should I think he had sense of after-haps,
As beasts foreshow the drought or rainy drops   [450]
As humours in them want or else abound
By influence from the heavens or change of ground?[424]
Or do we interpret by success each sign
And as we fancy of each hap divine,
And make that cause that kin is to th'effect,   [455]
Not having ought of consequence respect?

Bucephalus kneeling only to his lord
Showed only he was monarch of the world.[425]
Why may not then the steed foreshow by fall
What casual hap the sitter happen shall?   [460]
Darius' horse by braying brought a realm,[426]
And what letteth why he ne is, as the ass, God's mean
By speaking sign to show his hap to come
Who is deaf hearer of his speaking dumb?

---

439. **So ... breath**: So at first laughed the man who eventually laughed so much that he lost all his breath (thus exchanging his extreme mirth for extreme sorrow).   443. **all time**: at all times; for one's entire life; **hire**: service.   445. **hie**: move quickly.   449–52. **What ... ground?**: see explanatory note 424.   453–4. **Or ... divine?**: Or do we interpret each sign by what succeeded it and explain the nature of each occurrence by the power of our imagination?   455–6. **And ... respect**: And make that which is related to the effect its cause, without having any respect to the actual working of cause and effect.   460. **What ... shall?**: What unplanned-for occurrence shall befall the sitter?   462–4. **And ... dumb?**: And what prevents a horse from being God's medium (as is the ass) for showing in the form of an expressive sign what will happen to him who is deaf to the horse's silent speaking?

But forward yet: in Tower Street I stayed, [465]
Where (could I have seen), lo, Howard all bewrayed,
For as I commoned with a priest I met,
"Away my lord", quoth he; "your time ne is yet
To take a priest". Lo, Sinon might be seen
Had Troyans ears as they had hares' fool eyen.[427] [470]
But whom thou God allotted hast to die
Some grace it is to die with wimpled eye.

Ne was this all, for even at Tower wharf,
Near to those walls within whose sight I starfe,
Where erst in sorrow soused and deep distress [475]
I imparted all my pining pensiveness
With Hastings (so my pursuivant men call),
Even there the same to meet it did me fall,
Who gan to me most dolefully renew
The woeful conference had erst in that *lieu*. [480]

"Hastings", quoth I, "according now they fare
At Pomfret this day dying, who caused that care.
Myself have all the world now at my will,
With pleasures cloyed, engorgèd with the fill".
"God grant it so", quoth he. "Why doubtest thou though?", [485]
quoth I. And all in chafe to him gan show
In ample wise our drift with tedious tale
And entered so the Tower, to my bale.[428]

What should we think of signs? They are but haps.
How may they then be signs of afterclaps? [490]
Doth every chance foreshow or cause some other

469–70. **Lo ... eyen**: Lo, Sinon's trickery might have been perceived by the Trojans had they the ears of hares in the same way they had hares' foolish eyes (hares are famously short sighted but have excellent hearing).   471. **whom**: to whom.   472. **wimpled**: veiled.   474. **starfe**: died.   477. **pursuivant**: a junior heraldic officer attendant on a nobleman.   480. *lieu*: place (French).   481. **according**: fittingly.   486. **chafe**: vexation.   489. **haps**: chance occurrences.   490. **afterclaps**: ensuing events.

Or, ending at itself, extendeth no further?
As th'overflowing flood some mount doth choke,
But to his aid some other flood it yoke,
So, if with signs thy sins once join, beware,   [495]
Else whereto chances tend ne'er curious care.

Had not my sin deserved my death as wreak,
What might my mirth have hurt? Or horse's beck?
Or Howard's bitter scoff? Or Hastings' talk?
What mean then fool astrologers to calk   [500]
That twinkling stars fling down the fixèd fate
And all is guided by the starry state?
Pardie, a certain tax assigned they have
To shine and times divide, not fate to grave!

But grant they somewhat give: is at one instant   [505]
Of every babe the birth in heaven so scanned
That they that restless roll and never stay
Should in his life bear yet so violent sway
That not his actions only next his birth
But even last fine and death be swayed therewith?   [510]
How may one motion make so sundry effects,
Or one impression tend to such respects?

Some rule there is yet, else why were deferred
Till now these plagues, so long ere now deserved?
If for they are trifles they ne seem of care,   [515]
But toys with God the stateliest sceptres are.
Yet in them too plain doth appear foreset
The certain rule and fatal limits set.
Yet think we not this sure foresetting fate,
But God's fast providence for each princely state.   [520]

493–6. **As ... care**: Perhaps: Just as an overflowing river smothers a hillock yet aids, through its flooding, another river by joining with it, so if signs conjoin with your sins, beware; otherwise, never be curious about where chances might tend.   **498. beck**: mute signal.   **500. calk**: reckon astrologically.   **503. Pardie**: without a doubt; **tax**: task. **504. grave**: engrave, fix indelibly.   **505. But ... give**: But grant that the stars do play something of a role in human fate.   **507. they**: the heavenly bodies.   **509. next**: immediately succeeding.   **510. last fine**: extreme end of his life.   **515. for**: because.   **517. foreset**: determined beforehand.   **519. sure foresetting**: assured predetermination. **520. fast**: firmly fixed.

And hath he erst restrained his providence?
Or is he niggard of his free dispense?
Or is he uncertain, foreset drifts to drive,
That not Dame Chance but he all goods may give?
A heathen god they hold, who fortune keep [525]
To deal them haps, while God they ween asleep.
Mock gods they are, and many gods induce,
Who fortune feign to father their abuse.

How so be it, it mought have warnèd me,
But what I could not, that in me see ye: [530]
Who run in race the honour like to win,
Whose fairest form nought may deform but sin.
Alas, when most I did defy all dread,
By single hair death's sword hung over my head,
For hark the end and listen now my fall: [535]
This is the last and this is the fruit of all.

To council chamber come, awhile we stayed
For him, without whom nought was done or said.[429]
At last he came and courteously excused
For he so long our patience had abused [540]
And pleasantly began to paint his cheer,
And said, "My lord of Ely, would we had here
Some of the strawberries whereof you have store.
The last delighted me as nothing more".

"Would what so ye wish, I mought as well command, [545]
My lord", quoth he, "as those". And out of hand
His servant sendeth to Ely Place for them.
Out goeth from us the restless devil again,
Belike, I think, scarce yet persuaded full
To work the mischief that thus maddeth his skull. [550]
At last determined of his bloody thought
And force ordained to work the wile he sought,

---

525. **keep**: maintain. 527. **induce**: introduce, bring in. 531. **the honour like to win**: apparently about to win the glory. 542. **my lord of Ely**: John Morton (d. 1500), bishop of Ely. 545–6. **Would … those**: If only I could command to be done whatsoever you might wish, my lord, as well as I can command the supplying of those. 546. **out of hand**: immediately. 552. **force ordained**: i.e. armed men ordered.

Frowning he enters, with so changèd cheer
As for mild May had chopped foul Januere.
And louring on me with the goggle eye,   [555]
The whetted tusk, and furrowed forehead high,
His crooked shoulder bristle-like set up,
With frothy jaws, whose foam he chawed and supped,
With angry looks that flamèd as the fire,
Thus gan at last to grunt the grimmest sire.   [560]

"What earnèd they who me, the kingdom's stay,
Contrived have counsel traitorously to slay?"
Abashed all sat. I thought I mought be bold
For conscience' clearness and acquaintance old.
"Their hire is plain", quoth I; "be death the least   [565]
To whoso seeketh your grace so to molest".
Withouten stay: "the queen and the whore Shore's wife
By witchcraft", quoth he, "seek to waste my life.

"Lo here the withered and bewitchèd arm
That thus is spent by those two sorceress' charm".   [570]
And bared his arm and showed his swinish skin:
Such cloaks they use that seek to cloud their sin.
But out, alas, it serveth not for the rain;⁴³⁰
To all the house the colour was too plain.
Nature had given him many a maimèd mark   [575]
And it amongs, to note her monstrous wark.

My doubtful heart distracted this reply:
For th'one I cared not; th'other nipped so nigh
That whist I could not but forthwith brake forth.
"If so it be, of death they are doubtless worth".   [580]
"If traitor?" quoth he. "Playest thou with ifs and ands?
I'll on thy body avow it with these hands!"
And therewithal he mightily bounced the board.
In rushed his billmen; one himself bestirred

---

554. **chopped**: exchanged itself for.   555. **goggle**: protuberant.   558. **supped**: swallowed.   560. **sire**: lord; male parent of a quadruped (such as a boar).   561. **What earned they**: what sort of punishment do they deserve.   569. **Lo**:
see.   574. **colour**: pretext.   576. **And ... wark**: And it among, to denote her monstrous work.   577. **My ...
reply**: This reply drew my doubtful heart in two directions.   578. **th'one**: i.e. the queen.   582. **avow**: affirm.   583. **bounced the board**: thumped the table.

Laying at Lord Stanley, whose brain he had surely cleft [585]
Had not he down beneath the table crept.
But Ely, York, and I were taken straight:
Imprisoned they; I should no longer wait
But charged was to shrive me and shift with haste;
My lord must dine and now midday was past. [590]
The boar's first dish not the boar's head should be,
But Hastings' head the boarish beast would see.

Why stay I his dinner? Unto the chapel joineth
A greenish hill that body and soul oft twinneth.[431]
There on a block my head was stricken off: [595]
John Baptist's dish for Herod, bloody gnoff.
Thus lived I, Baldwin; thus died I; thus I fell.
This is the sum which all at large to tell
Would volumes fill, whence yet these lessons note,
Ye noble lords, to learn and ken by rote. [600]

By filthy rising fear your names to stain,
If not for virtue's love, for dread of pain.
Whom so the mind's unquiet state upheaves,
Be it for love or fear, when fancy reaves
Reason his right by mocking of the wit, [605]
If once the cause of this affection flit
Reason prevailing on the unbridled thought,
Down trotteth who by fancy clomb aloft.

So hath the riser foul no stay of fall,
No, not of those that raised him first of all. [610]
His surety stands in maintaining the cause
That heaved him first, which reft by reason's saws,
Not only fall'th he to his former state
But liveth forever in his prince's hate.
And mark my lords: God for adultery slay'th, [615]
Though ye it think too sweet a sin for death.

---

587. York: Thomas Rotherham (d. 1500), archbishop of York.   **589. shift**: arrange my matters.   **593. dinner**: midday meal.   **594. twinneth**: separates.   **596. gnoff**: churl, lout.   **598. all at large**: fully.   **600. ken**: learn, become familiar with.   **604. reaves**: removes.   **606–8. If ... aloft**: If once the cause of this feeling [i.e. the upheaval occasioned by an unquiet mind] removes reason from controlling the unbridled thought, down trots he who by imagination climbed aloft.   **609. So ... fall**: So has the foul riser nothing to prevent his fall.   **612. reft by reason's saws**: taken away by the dictates of reason.

Serve truly your prince and fear no rebel's might:
On princes' halves the mighty God doth fight.
Oh, much more than foreswear a foreign foe
Who seeketh your realm and country to undo!   [620]
Murder detest; have hands unstained with blood.
Ay with your succour do protect the good;
Chase treason where trust should be; wed to your friend
Your heart and power to your lives' last end.

"Fly tickle credence; shun alike distrust":   [625]
Too true it is, and credit it you must.
The jealous nature wanteth no stormy strife;
The simple soul ay leadeth a sour life.
Beware of flatterers, friends in outward show;
Best is of such to make thine open foe.   [630]
What all men seek, that all men seek to feign;
Some such to be, some such to seem, them pain.

Mark God's just judgements, punishing sin by sin
And slippery state wherein aloft we swim.
The proverb "all day up, if we ne fall"   [635]
Agreeth well to us high-heaved worldlings all.
From dunghill couch upstart in honour's weed
We shine, while Fortune false – whom none erst feed
To stand with stay and foreswear tickleness –
Souseth us in mire of dirty brittleness.   [640]

And learn ye princes by my wrongèd sprite
Not to misconster what is meant aright.
The wingèd words too oft prevent the wit,
When silence ceaseth afore the lips to sit.
Alas, what may the words yield worthy death?   [645]
The word's worst is, the speaker's stinking breath.
Words are but wind; why cost they then so much?
The guilty kick, when they too smartly touch.

---

618. On princes' halves: on the princes' side.   **623. Chase**: drive away.   **632. Some ... pain**: Some take pains to be such; some take pains to seem to be such.   **637. couch**: bed, lounge; **weed**: clothing.   **638–9. whom ... tickleness**: whom none before has bribed to stand without change and to foreswear inconstancy (**feed**: bribed; employed).   **642. misconster**: misconstrue.   **643. prevent**: act more quickly than.   **645. Alas ... death?**: Alas, what might words produce that is worthy of the penalty of death?   **648. they**: words; **touch**: reprove; 'hit' by some apt or smart saying.

Forth irreturnable flyeth the spoken word,
Be it in scoff, in earnest, or in bourd, [650]
Without return and unreceived it hangs
And at the taker's mercy or rigour stands.
Which, if he sourly wrest with wrathful cheer,
The shivering word turns to the speaker's fear.
If friendly courtesy do the word resolve, [655]
To the speaker's comfort sweetly it dissolveth.

Even as the vapour which the fire repels
Turns not to earth but in mid-air dwells,
Where, while it hangeth, if Boreas' frosty flaws
With rigour rattle it, not to rain it thaws [660]
But thunder, lightnings, rattling hail and snow
Sends down to earth, whence first it rose below,
But if fair Phoebus, with his countenance sweet,
Resolve it, down the dew or manna fleeteth

(The manna dew that in the eastern lands [665]
Excelleth the labour of the bees' small hands),
Else for her Memnon grey Aurora's tears
On the earth it stilleth, the partner of her fears,⁴³²
Or sendeth sweet showers to glad their mother earth,
Whence first they took their first inconstant birth, [670]
To so great griefs, ill-taken wind doth grow;
Of words well taken, such delights do flow.

This learnèd, thus be here at length an end;
What since ensued, to thee I will commend.
Now farewell, Baldwin, shield my torn name [675]
From scandalous tromp of blasting black defame.
But, ere I part, hereof thou record bear:
I claim no part of virtues reckoned here.
My vice myself but God my virtues take,
So hence depart I as I ent'red, naked.'⁴³³ [680]

---

650. **bourd**: jest. 655. **resolve**: explain, make clear. 656. **it dissolveth**: it (i.e. the speaker's fear) vanishes.
657. **vapour**: steam. 659. **Boreas' frosty flaws**: the north wind's frosty squalls. 663–8. **The … fears**: But if the
fair sun with its sweet face condenses it, the vapour trickles to earth as the manna dew (which in eastern lands exceeds the work of bees) or it distils on earth – as partner to Aurora's fears – Aurora's tears for her son, grey Memnon.
674. **commend**: entrust.

Thus ended Hastings, both his life and tale,
Containing all his bliss and world's bale.
Happy he lived, too happy but for sin;[434]
Happy he died, whom right his death did bring.
Thus ever happy, for there rests no mean   [685]
Twixt blissful life's and baleful death's extreme.
Yet fearèd not his foes to head his name
And by these sclaunders to procure his shame.

In rusty armour as in extreme shift,
They clad themselves to cloak their devilish drift   [690]
And forthwith for substantial citizens sent,
Declaring to them Hastings' forged intent
Was to have slain the duke and to have seized
The king's young person, slaying whom he had pleased,
But God of justice had withturned that fate,   [695]
Which, where it ought, light on his proper pate.[435]

Then fed they fame by proclamation spread
Nought to forget that mought defame him dead,
Which was so curious and so clerkly penned,
So long withal, that when some did attend   [700]
His death so young they saw that long afore
The shroud was shaped, then babe to die was bore.
So wonteth God to blind the worldly wise
That not to see that all the world espies.[436]

One hearing it cried out 'A goodly cast   [705]
And well contrived foul cast away for haste,'
Whereto another gan in scoff reply,
'First penned it was by inspiring prophecy.'
So can God reap up secret mischiefs wrought
To the confusion of the worker's thought.   [710]

---

683. **too**: exceedingly.   684. **whom right his death did bring**: to whom doing right (the defending of innocent women against Gloucester's false accusations) brought death.   687. **foes**: i.e. Gloucester and Buckingham; **head his name**: kill his reputation.   688. **sclaunders**: slanders.   699. **curious**: carefully.   700. **attend**: note.   701. **young**: recent.   702. **then**: at the time.   703. **wonteth**: is accustomed.   705. **cast**: device.   706. **foul cast away**: badly squandered.   709. **reap up**: rip up.

[686] *1563*: Twice (apparently an uncorrected misprint for 'Twixt', to which it was altered in the edition of 1574)

My lords, the tub that drowned the Clarence duke
Drowned not his death ne yet his death's rebuke.

Your politic secrets guard with trusty loyalty,
So shall they lurk in most assurèd secrety.
By Hastings' death and after-fame ye learn   [715]
The earth for murder crieth out vengeance stern.
Fly from his faults and spare his quitted fame;
The eager hounds forbear their slainè game.
'Dead, dead! Avaunt, curs, from the conquered chase!';
Ill mought he live who loveth the dead to race.   [720]

Thus lived this lord; thus died he; thus he slept,
Mids forward race when first to rest he stepped.
Envious Death, that bounceth as well with mace
At Caesar's courts, as at the poorest gates,
When nature seemed too slow, by art's slope mean   [725]
Conveyed him sooner to his life's extreme.
Happy, in preventing woes that after happed,
In slumber sweet his living lights he lapped.

Whose thus untimely death, if any grieve,
Know he, he lived to die and died to live.   [730]
Untimely never comes the life's last met:
In cradle death may rightly claim his debt.
Straight after birth due is the fatal bier;
By death's permission the agèd linger here.
Even in thy swath-bands out commission goeth,   [735]
To loose thy breath, that yet but youngly bloweth.

Happy, thrice happy, who so loseth his breath,
As life he gaineth by his living death
As Hastings here, whom time and truth agree
To engrave by fame in strong eternity.   [740]

---

717. **quitted fame**: exonerated reputation.   718. **slaine**: slain (disyllabic).   720. **race**: tear, lacerate.   722. **Mids forward race**: In the midst of rushing forward.   723. **bounceth**: knocks; **mace**: sceptre (showing death's ultimate power over all humans).   725. **slope**: sloped, slanting.   727. **preventing**: acting before.   728. **lights**: eyes; **lapped**: enfolded (with an echo of the phrase 'lap in lead': to entomb).   731. **met**: portion, measure.   735. **swath-bands**: swaddling clothes; **commission**: command, order.

Who spareth not spitting, if he spit but blood?
Yet this our lord spared not, for others' good,
With one sweet breath his present death to speak
Against the usurper boar, that hellish freak.

Worthy to live, who lived not for himself   [745]
But prized his fame more than this worldly pelf;
Whose name and line, if any yet preserve,
We wish they live like honour to deserve.[437]
Whether thou seek by martial prowess praise,
Or Pallas' policy high thy name to raise,   [750]
Or trusty service just death to attain,
Hastings forled: trace here his bloody train.

---

741. **Who … blood?**: Who does not refrain from spitting, if he spits only blood?   746. **pelf**: junk, trash.   752. **forled**: led before.

[Prose 23]

When I had read this, one said it was very dark and hard to be understood, except it were diligently and very leisurely considered. 'I like it the better', quoth another, 'for that shall cause it to be the oftener read and the better remembered. Considering also that it is written for the learned (for all such
5   magistrates are or should be), it cannot be too hard, so long as it is sound and learnedly written.'
        Then said the reader, 'the next here whom I find miserable are King Edward's two sons, cruelly murdered in the Tower of London; have you their tragedy?' 'No, surely', quoth I; 'the Lord Vaux undertook to pen it,
10 but what he hath done therein I am not certain, and therefore I let it pass till I know farther.[438] I have here "The Duke of Buckingham", King Richard's chief instrument, written by Master Thomas Sackville.' 'Read it we pray you', said they. 'With a good will', quoth I, 'but first you shall hear his preface or induction.' 'Hath he made a preface?' quoth one; 'what
15 meaneth he thereby, seeing none other hath used the like order?' 'I will tell you the cause thereof', quoth I, 'which is this: after that he understood that some of the council would not suffer the book to be printed in such order as we had agreed and determined, he purposed with himself to have gotten

---

8. two sons: King Edward V and Richard, first duke of York (both d. 1483?).

at my hands all the tragedies that were before the duke of Buckingham's,
20 which he would have preserved in one volume. And, from that time back-
ward even to the time of William the Conqueror, he determined to continue and perfect all the story himself, in such order as Lydgate, following
Bochas, had already used.[439] And, therefore, to make a meet induction into
the matter, he devised this poesy, which in my judgement is so well penned
25 that I would not have any verse thereof left out of our volume.

'Now that you know the cause and meaning of his doing, you shall also
hear what he hath done. His induction beginneth thus':

[Tragedy 22a]

The Induction

The wrathful winter, proaching on apace,
With blustering blasts had all ybared the treen,[440]
And old Saturnus with his frosty face
With chilling cold had pierced the tender green,[441]
The mantles rent, wherin enwrappèd been   [5]
The gladsome groves that now lay overthrown,
The tapets torn, and every bloom down blown.[442]

The soil that erst so seemly was to seen
Was all despoilèd of her beauty's hue,
And soot fresh flowers (wherewith the summer's queen   [10]
Had clad the earth) now Boreas' blasts down blew.
And small fowls flocking in their song did rue
The winter's wrath, wherewith each thing defaced
In woeful wise bewailed the summer past.

Hawthorne had lost his motley livery;   [15]
The naked twigs were shivering all for cold
And, dropping down the tears abundantly,
Each thing, me thought, with weeping eye me told
The cruel season, bidding me withhold
Myself within, for I was gotten out   [20]
Into the fields whereas I walked about.

1. **proaching on apace**: quickly approaching. 5. **mantles rent**: coverings (lit. cloaks) torn. 7. **tapets**: coverings (lit. ornamented tapestries). 10. **soot**: sweet.

[Title]: *1563 setting 2*: Master Sackville's Induction

[7]: *1563 setting 2*: every tree down blown

When, lo, the night with misty mantles spread
Gan dark the day and dim the azure skies,
And Venus in her message Hermes sped
To bloody Mars, to will him not to rise,   [25]
While she herself approached in speedy wise,
And Virgo, hiding her disdainful breast,
With Thetis now had laid her down to rest.[443]

Whiles Scorpio, dreading Sagittarius' dart,
Whose bow prest bent in sight the string had slipped,   [30]
Down slid into the ocean flood apart.
The bear that in the Irish seas had dipped
His grisly feet with speed from thence he whipped,
For Thetis, hasting from the virgin's bed,
Pursued the bear that ere she came was fled.[444]   [35]

And Phaeton now near-reaching to his race,
With glistering beams, gold-streaming where they bent,
Was prest to enter in his resting place;
Erythius that in the cart first went
Had even now attained his journey's stint   [40]
And fast declining hid away his head,
While Titan couched him in his purple bed.

And pale Cynthia, with her borrowed light
Beginning to supply her brother's place,
Was past the noonstead six degrees in sight   [45]
When sparkling stars amid the heavens' face
With twinkling light shone on the earth apace,
That while they brought about the nightès' chair
The dark had dimmed the day ere I was ware.

And sorrowing I to see the summer flowers,   [50]
The lively green, the lusty leas forlorn,
The sturdy trees so shattered with the showers,

---

23. Gan dark: began to darken.   **24. Hermes**: the planet Mercury.   **28. With Thetis**: In the ocean (**Thetis**: a sea nymph in Homer's *Iliad*).   **29–30. Whiles ... slipped**: While Scorpio, in fear of the arrow that had flown from the string of Sagittarius's ready-bent bow in sight.   **38. prest**: ready, eager.   **40. stint**: stopping point.   **48. nightès' chair**: night's chariot (here and elsewhere, 'nightes' is disyllabic).   **51. lusty leas**: pleasant meadows.

The fields so fade that flourished so beforne,
It taught me well all earthly things be born
To die the death, for nought long time may last: [55]
The summer's beauty yields to winter's blast.

Then looking upward to the heavens' leams,
With nightès' stars thick powdered everywhere,
Which erst so glistened with the golden streams
That cheerful Phoebus spread down from his sphere,   [60]
Beholding dark oppressing day so near,
The sudden sight reducèd to my mind
The sundry changes that in earth we find.

That musing on this worldly wealth in thought,
Which comes and goes more faster than we see   [65]
The flickering flame that with the fire is wrought,
My busy mind presented unto me
Such fall of peers as in this realm had be
That oft I wished some would their woes descrive
To warn the rest whom fortune left alive.   [70]

And straight forth stalking with redoubled pace,
For that I saw the night drew on so fast,
In black all clad there fell before my face
A piteous wight, whom woe had all forwaste.
Forth from her eyen the crystal tears outbrast,   [75]
And, sighing sore, her hands she wrung and fold,
Tare all her hair, that ruth was to behold.

Her body small forwithered and forspent,
As is the stalk that summer's drought oppressed,
Her welkèd face, with woeful tears besprent,   [80]
Her colour pale and, as it seemed her best,
In woe and plaint reposèd was her rest,
And, as the stone that drops of water wears,
So dented were her cheeks with fall of tears.

53. **fade**: withered.   57. **leams**: lights.   62. **reduced**: returned.   64. **That**: so that.   74. **forwaste**: enfeebled.
77. **Tare**: tore.   78. **forwithered**: withered; **forspent**: worn out.   80. **welked**: withered, dried up; **besprent**: sprin-
kled.   82. **reposed**: placed.

Her eyes swollen with flowing streams afloat, [85]
Wherewith her looks thrown up full piteously,
Her forceless hands together oft she smote,
With doleful shrieks that echoed in the sky,
Whose plaint such sighs did straight accompany
That in my doom was never man did see [90]
A wight but half so woebegone as she.

I stood aghast, beholding all her plight,
Tween dread and dolour so distrained in heart
That while my hairs upstarted with the sight
The tears outstreamed for sorrow of her smart. [95]
But when I saw no end that could apart
The deadly dool which she so sore did make,
With doleful voice then thus to her I spake.

'Unwrap thy woes whatever wight thou be
And stint betime to spill thyself with plaint. [100]
Tell what thou art and whence, for well I see
Thou canst not dure with sorrow thus attaint.'
And with that word of sorrow all forfaint
She lookèd up and, prostrate as she lay,
With piteous sound, lo, thus she gan to say: [105]

'Alas, I, wretch, whom thus thou seest distrained
With wasting woes that never shall aslake,
Sorrow I am, in endless torments pained
Among the Furies in the infernal lake,
Where Pluto god of hell so grisly black [110]
Doth hold his throne and Letheus' deadly taste
Doth reave remembrance of each thing forepast.445

Whence come I am, the dreary destiny
And luckless lot for to bemoan of those
Whom Fortune, in this maze of misery, [115]

---

90. **doom**: judgement. 93. **distrained**: distressed. 96. **apart**: set aside. 97. **dool**: mourning. 100. **And …
plaint**: And in good time leave off killing yourself with wailing. 102. **Thou … attaint**: You cannot last long
afflicted as you are by sorrow. 103. **forfaint**: very faint. 107. **aslake**: diminish. 112. **reave**: take away; **forepast**:
that has previously occurred.

Of wretched chance most woeful mirrors chose,
That when you seest how lightly they did lose
Their pomp, their power, and that they thought most sure,
Thou mayst soon deem no earthly joy may dure.'

Whose rueful voice no sooner had out-brayed   [120]
Those woeful words wherewith she sorrowed so
But out, alas, she shright and never stayed,
Fell down and all-to dashed herself for woe.
The cold pale dread my limbs gan overgo,
And I so sorrowed at her sorrows eft   [125]
That what with grief and fear my wits were reft.

I stretched myself, and straight my heart revives
That dread and dolour erst did so appale.
Like him that with the fervent fever strives
When sickness seeks his castle health to scale,   [130]
With gathered spirits so forced I fear to avale,
And, rearing her, with anguish all fordone,
My spirits returned and then I thus begun:

'Oh Sorrow, alas, sith Sorrow is thy name,
And that to thee this drear doth well pertain,   [135]
In vain it were to seek to cease the same,
But as a man himself with sorrow slain,
So I, alas, do comfort thee in pain
That here in sorrow art forsunk so deep
That at thy sight I can but sigh and weep.'   [140]

I had no sooner spoken of a sike
But that the storm so rumbled in her breast
As Aeolus could never roar the like,
And showers down rainèd from her eyen so fast
That all bedrent the place, till at the last   [145]
Well easèd they the dolour of her mind,
As rage of rain doth swage the stormy wind.

---

116. **most woeful mirrors chose**: chose to be the most woeful exemplars. **122. shright**: shrieked. **123. all-to dashed**: utterly beat. **125. eft**: once more. **128. appale**: make pale. **130. castle health**: castle of his health. **131. avale**: yield. **132. rearing her**: raising her up; **fordone**: exhausted. **139. forsunk**: submerged. **141. sike**: sigh (an archaism). **145. all bedrent**: completely drenched. **147. swage**: pacify.

Far-forth she pacèd in her fearful tale:
'Come, come', quoth she, 'and see what I shall show;
Come, hear the plaining and the bitter bale   [150]
Of worthy men by Fortune overthrow.
Come thou and see them rueing all in row.
They were but shades that erst in mind thou rolled.
Come, come with me; thine eyes shall them behold!'

What could these words but make me more aghast   [155]
To hear her tell whereon I mused whilere?
So was I mazed therewith, till at the last,
Musing upon her words and what they were,
All suddenly well lessened was my fear,
For to my mind returnèd how she telled   [160]
Both what she was and where her wone she held,

Whereby I knew that she a goddess was,
And therewithal resorted to my mind
My thought that late presented me the glass
Of brittle state, of cares that here we find,   [165]
Of thousand woes to silly men assigned,
And how she now bid me come and behold,
To see with eye that erst in thought I rolled.

Flat down I fell and with all reverence
Adorèd her, perceiving now that she,   [170]
A goddess sent by godly providence,
In earthly shape thus showed herself to me
To wail and rue this world's uncertainty,
And while I honoured thus her godhead's might,
With plaining voice these words to me she shright: [175]

'I shall thee guide first to the grisly lake
And thence unto the blissful place of rest,
Where thou shalt see and hear the plaint they make
That whilom here bare swinge among the best.

---

148. Far-forth: To a great distance.   **150. bale**: mental suffering.   **153. They ... rolled**: Those you earlier recorded in your mind were but unreal images (see lines 67–8).   **156. whilere**: a while ago.   **157. mazed**: bewildered.   **161. wone**: dwelling-place.   **164–5. glass of brittle state**: the true description of unreliable standing, condition.   **179. bare swinge**: bore rule.

This shalt thou see, but great is the unrest   [180]
That thou must bide before thou canst attain
Unto the dreadful place where these remain.'

And with these words as I upraisèd stood
And gan to follow her that straight forth paced,
Ere I was ware, into a desert wood   [185]
We now were come, where, hand in hand embraced,
She led the way and through the thick so traced
As but I had been guided by her might
It was no way for any mortal wight.

But lo, while thus amid the desert dark   [190]
We passèd on with steps and pace unmeet,
A rumbling roar confused with howl and bark
Of dogs shook all the ground under our feet
And stroke the din within our ears so deep
As half distraught unto the ground I fell,   [195]
Besought return and not to visit hell.

But she forthwith, uplifting me apace,
Removed my dread and with a steadfast mind
Bade me come on, for here was now the place,
The place where we our travail end should find,   [200]
Wherewith I arose and to the place assigned
Astoynde I stalk, when straight we approached near
The dreadful place that you will dread to hear.

An hideous hole all vast, withouten shape,
Of endless depth, o'erwhelmed with ragged stone,   [205]
With ugly mouth and grisly jaws doth gape
And to our sight confounds itself in one.
Here entered we and, yeding forth, anon
An horrible loathly lake we might discern,
As black as pitch, that clepèd is Averne.[446]   [210]

---

185. **ware**: aware. 187. **thick**: dense forest. 188. **but**: except that. 191. **unmeet**: unevenly matched. 202. **Astoynde**: astonied (dazed, bewildered). 207. **confounds itself in one**: makes its different elements difficult to distinguish from one another. 208. **yeding**: going (a pseudo-archaism).

A deadly gulf where nought but rubbish grows,
With foul black swelth in thickened lumps that lies,
Which up in the air such stinking vapours throws
That over there may fly no fowl but dies,
Choked with the pestilent savours that arise.   [215]
Hither we come, whence forth we still did pace,
In dreadful fear amid the dreadful place.

And first within the porch and jaws of hell
Sat deep Remorse of Conscience, all besprent
With tears, and to herself oft would she tell   [220]
Her wretchedness and, cursing, never stint
To sob and sigh but ever thus lament
With thoughtful care, as she that, all in vain,
Would wear and waste continually in pain.

Her eyes unsteadfast, rolling here and there,   [225]
Whirled on each place as place that vengeance brought,
So was her mind continually in fear
Tossed and tormented with the tedious thought
Of those detested crimes which she had wrought.
With dreadful cheer and looks thrown to the sky,   [230]
Wishing for death, and yet she could not die.

Next saw we Dread all trembling, how he shook
With foot uncertain proffered here and there,
Benumbed of speech, and with a ghastly look
Searched every place all pale and dead for fear.   [235]
His cap borne up with staring of his hair,
Stoynde and amazed at his own shade for dreed
And fearing greater dangers than was need.

And next within the entry of this lake
Sat fell Revenge gnashing her teeth for ire,   [240]
Devising means how she may vengeance take,
Never in rest till she have her desire,

---

211. **rubbish**: worthless matter.   212. **swelth**: foul water.   223. **as she that**: as she who.   224. **Would**: wished to.
228. **tedious**: wearying.   230. **dreadful cheer**: a visage expressing dread.   236. **staring**: the standing upright.
237. **Stoynde**: Stunned; **dreed**: dread.

But frets within so far-forth with the fire
Of wreaking flames that now determines she
To die by death, or venged by death to be.   [245]

When fell Revenge with bloody foul pretence
Had showed herself as next in order set,
With trembling limbs we softly parted thence,
Till in our eyes another sight we met:
When fro my heart a sigh forthwith I fet,   [250]
Rueing, alas, upon the woeful plight
Of Misery that next appeared in sight.

His face was lean and somedeal pined away,
And eke his hands consumèd to the bone,
But what his body was I cannot say,   [255]
For on his carcass raiment had he none,
Save clouts and patches piecèd one by one,
With staff in hand and scrip on shoulders cast,
His chief defence against the winter's blast.

His food for most was wild fruits of the tree,   [260]
Unless sometime some crumbs fell to his share,
Which in his wallet long, God wot, kept he,
As on the which full daint'ly would he fare.
His drink the running stream, his cup the bare
Of his palm closed, his bed the hard, cold ground: [265]
To this poor life was Misery ybound.

Whose wretched state when we had well beheld,
With tender ruth on him and on his fears,
In thoughtful cares forth then our pace we held
And, by and by, another shape appears   [270]
Of Greedy Care, still brushing up the breres,
His knuckles knobbed, his flesh deep dented in,
With tawèd hands and hard ytannèd skin.

---

243. **so far-forth**: to such a degree.   244. **wreaking**: revenging.   246. **pretence**: ostentatious display.   250. **fet**:
fetched.   257. **clouts**: bits of fabric.   258. **scrip**: beggar's bag.   262. **Which … he**: Which he kept for long periods
in his bag, God knows.   271. **breres**: briars.   273. **tawed**: beaten (as if to be made into leather).

The morrow grey no sooner hath begun
To spread his light even peeping in our eyes,   [275]
When he is up and to his work yrun,
But let the night's black misty mantles rise
And with foul dark never so much disguise
The fair bright day, yet ceaseth he no while
But hath his candles to prolong his toil.   [280]

By him lay Heavy Sleep, the cousin of Death,
Flat on the ground and still as any stone,
A very corpse save yielding forth a breath.
Small keep took he whom Fortune frownèd on
Or whom she lifted up into the throne   [285]
Of high renown; but as a living death
So, dead alive, of life he drew the breath.

The body's rest, the quiet of the heart,
The travail's ease, the still night's fere was he,
And of our life in earth the better part,   [290]
Reaver of sight, and yet in whom we see
Things oft that tide and oft that never be,
Without respect esteeming equally
King Croesus' pomp and Irus' poverty.447

And next in order sad Old Age we found,   [295]
His beard all hoar, his eyes hollow and blind,
With drooping cheer still poring on the ground
As on the place where nature him assigned
To rest, when that the sisters had untwined
His vital thread and ended with their knife   [300]
The fleeting course of fast-declining life.

There heard we him, with broken and hollow plaint,
Rue with himself his end approaching fast,
And all for nought his wretched mind torment
With sweet remembrance of his pleasures past   [305]
And fresh delights of lusty youth forwaste,

---

286. but: merely. **289. fere**: companion. **291. Reaver**: robber. **292. tide**: happen. **299. the sisters**: the Fates. **306. forwaste**: used up.

Recounting which, how would he sob and shriek
And to be young again of Jove beseek!

But and the cruel fates so fixèd be
That time forepassed cannot return again,   [310]
This one request of Jove yet prayèd he:
That in such withered plight and wretched pain
As eld (accompanied with his loathsome train)
Had brought on him, all were it woe and grief,
He might awhile yet linger forth his lief   [315]

And not so soon descend into the pit
Where death, when he the mortal corpse hath slain,
With reckless hand in grave doth cover it,
Thereafter never to enjoy again
The gladsome light but in the ground ylain   [320]
In depth of darkness waste and wear to nought,
As he had never into the world been brought.

But who had seen him sobbing, how he stood
Unto himself and how he would bemoan
His youth forepassed – as though it wrought him good   [325]
To talk of youth, all were his youth foregone –
He would have mused and marvelled much whereon
This wretched Age should life desire so fain
And knows full well life doth but length his pain.

Crookbacked he was, toothshaken, and blear-eyed,   [330]
Went on three feet and sometime crept on four,
With old lame bones that rattled by his side,
His scalp all pilled, and he with eld forlore.
His withered fist still knocking at death's door,
Fumbling and drivelling as he draws his breath: [335]
For brief, the shape and messenger of death.

308. **beseek**: beseech.   309. **and**: if.   310. **forepassed**: that has previously passed.   313. **eld**: old age.   314. **all were**: even though.   315. **lief**: life.   318. **reckless**: indifferent, uncaring.   322. **as**: as if.   328. **fain**: eagerly. 330. **toothshaken**: afflicted with loosened teeth.   331. **Went ... four**: He travelled with a cane and sometimes crawled on all fours.   333. **pilled**: bereft of hair;   **forlore**: brought to ruin.

And fast by him pale Malady was placed
Sore sick in bed, her colour all forgone,
Bereft of stomach, savour, and of taste,
Ne could she brook no meat but broths alone –   [340]
Her breath corrupt, her keepers every one
Abhorring her, her sickness past recure,
Detesting physic and all physic's cure.

But, oh, the doleful sight that then we see!
We turned our look and on the other side   [345]
A grisly shape of Famine mought we see,
With greedy looks and gaping mouth that cried
And roared for meat as she should there have died.
Her body thin and bare as any bone,
Whereto was left nought but the case alone,   [350]

And that, alas, was gnawn on everywhere,
All full of holes, that I ne mought refrain
From tears to see how she her arms could tear
And with her teeth gnash on the bones in vain
When, all for nought, she fain would so sustain   [355]
Her starven corpse, that rather seemed a shade
Then any substance of a creature made.

Great was her force whom stone wall could not stay,
Her tearing nails snatching at all she saw,
With gaping jaws that by no means ymay   [360]
Be satisfied from hunger of her maw
But eats herself as she that hath no law,
Gnawing, alas, her carcass all in vain,
Where you may count each sinew, bone, and vein.

On her while we thus firmly fixed our eyes   [365]
That bled for ruth of such a dreary sight,
Lo, suddenly she shright in so huge wise
As made hell gates to shiver with the might,
Wherewith a dart we saw how it did light

---

339. stomach: appetite; **savour:** relish (for something).   **348. meat:** food.   **350. case:** hide, skin.

Right on her breast, and therewithal pale Death   [370]
Enthrilling it to reave her of her breath.[448]

And by and by a dumb dead corpse we saw,
Heavy and cold, the shape of Death aright,
That daunts all earthly creatures to his law,
Against whose force in vain it is to fight.   [375]
Ne peers, ne princes, nor no mortal wight,
No towns, ne realms, cities, ne strongest tower,
But all perforce must yield unto his power.

His dart anon out of the corpse he took,
And in his hand, a dreadful sight to see,   [380]
With great triumph eftsoons the same he shook:
That most of all my fears affrayèd me.
His body dight with nought but bones pardie,
The naked shape of man there saw I plain,
All save the flesh, the sinew, and the vein.   [385]

Lastly stood War in glittering arms yclad,
With visage grim, stern looks, and blackly hued.
In his right hand a naked sword he had
That to the hilts was all with blood imbrued,
And in his left (that kings and kingdoms rued)   [390]
Famine and fire he held, and therewithal
He razèd towns and threw down towers and all.

Cities he sacked, and realms that whilom flowered
In honour, glory, and rule above the best
He overwhelmed and all their fame devoured,   [395]
Consumed, destroyed, wasted, and never ceased
Till he their wealth, their name, and all oppressed.
His face forhewed with wounds, and by his side
There hung his targe with gashes deep and wide,

In mids of which, depainted there we found   [400]
Deadly Debate all full of snaky hair

---

370. **therewithal**: with that. 371. **Enthrilling**: piercing; **reave**: rob. 374. **daunts**: subjects. 378. **perforce**: necessarily. 382. **affrayed**: terrified. 383. **His ... pardie**: His body arrayed with nothing but bones, by God. 398. **forhewed**: hewed. 399. **targe**: shield. 400. **depainted**: depicted. 401. **Deadly Debate**: Deadly Strife.

That with a bloody fillet was ybound,
Outbreathing nought but discord everywhere,
And round about were portrayed here and there
The hugy hosts, Darius and his power, [405]
His kings, princes, his peers, and all his flower,

Whom great Macedo vanquished there in sight
With deep slaughter, despoiling all his pride,
Pierced through his realms and daunted all his might.449
Duke Hannibal beheld I there beside, [410]
In Canna's field victor how he did ride,
And woeful Romans that in vain withstood
And Consul Paullus covered all in blood.450

Yet saw I more the fight at Trasimene
And Trebey field, and eke when Hannibal [415]
And worthy Scipio last in arms were seen
Before Carthago gate to try for all
The world's empire, to whom it should befall.451
There saw I Pompey and Caesar clad in arms,
Their hosts allied and all their civil harms, [420]

With conquerors' hands forbathed in their own blood,
And Caesar weeping over Pompey's head.452
Yet saw I Scilla and Marius where they stood,
Their great cruelty and the deep bloodshed
Of friends.453 Cyrus I saw and his host dead, [425]
And how the queen with great despite hath flung
His head in blood of them she overcome.454

Xerxes the Persian king yet saw I there
With his huge host that drank the rivers dry,
Dismounted hills, and made the vales uprear. [430]
His host and all yet saw I slain, pardie; 455
Thebès I saw all razed, how it did lie
In heaps of stones, and Tyrus put to spoil,
With walls and towers flat evened with the soil.456

---

402. **fillet**: head-band.   405. **hugy**: huge.   406. **flower**: choicest men.   410. **Duke**: General.   421. **forbathed**: fully bathed.

But Troy, alas (methought), above them all   [435]
It made mine eyes in very tears consume:
When I beheld the woeful weird befall
That by the wrathful will of gods was come,
And Jove's unmovèd sentence and foredoom
On Priam King and on his town so bent,   [440]
I could not lin but I must there lament,[457]

And that the more sith destiny was so stern
As force perforce there might no force avail
But she must fall, and by her fall we learn
That cities, towers, wealth, world, and all shall quail.   [445]
No manhood, might, nor nothing mought prevail:
All were there prest full many a prince and peer,
And many a knight that sold his death full dear.

Not worthy Hector, worthiest of them all,
Her hope, her joy: his force is now for nought.   [450]
Oh Troy, Troy, there is no boot but bale!
The hugy horse within thy walls is brought,
Thy turrets fall, thy knights that whilom fought
In arms amid the field are slain in bed,
Thy gods defiled, and all thy honour dead.   [455]

The flames upspring and cruelly they creep
From wall to roof, till all to cinders waste.
Some fire the houses where the wretches sleep;
Some rush in here, some run in there as fast:
In everywhere or sword or fire they taste.   [460]
The walls are torn, the towers whirled to the ground;
There is no mischief but may there be found.

Cassandra yet there saw I how they haled
From Pallas' house with sparkled tress undone,

---

437. weird: fate.   **439. unmoved**: fixed; **foredoom**: judgement establishing a later destiny.   **440. Priam King**: Priam, legendary king of Troy during the Trojan war.   **441. lin**: leave off.   **443. force perforce**: by force of circumstances.   **447. All ... peer**: Even though there had been many a prince and peer ready for action.   **449. Hector**: Troy's greatest defender in Homer's *The Iliad*.   **451. boot**: remedy.   **460. or sword or fire**: either sword or fire.   **463. Cassandra**: Trojan princess killed by the Greeks during the sack of Troy; **haled**: pulled.   **464. Pallas' house**: Minerva's temple; **sparkled**: dishevelled.

Her wrists fast bound and with Greeks' rout impaled, [465]
And Priam eke in vain how he did run
To arms, whom Pyrrhus with despite hath done
To cruel death and bathed him in the bain
Of his son's blood before the altar slain.⁴⁵⁸

But how can I descrive the doleful sight [470]
That in the shield so lifelike fair did shine?
Sith in this world I think was never wight
Could have set forth the half not half so fine.
I can no more but tell how there is seen
Fair Ilium fall in burning red gleeds down [475]
And from the soil great Troy, Neptunus' town.⁴⁵⁹

Herefrom, when scarce I could mine eyes withdraw
That filled with tears as doth the springing well,
We passèd on so far forth till we saw
Rude Acheron, a loathsome lake to tell, [480]
That boils and bubs up swelth as black as hell,
Where grisly Charon at their fixèd tide
Still ferries ghosts unto the farther side.

The agèd god no sooner Sorrow spied
But, hasting straight unto the bank apace, [485]
With hollow call unto the rout he cried
To swerve apart and give the goddess place.
Straight it was done, when to the shore we pace,
Where, hand in hand as we then linkèd fast,
Within the boat we are together placed, [490]

And forth we launch full fraughted to the brink,
When with the unwonted weight the rusty keel
Began to crack as if the same should sink.
We hoise up mast and sail, that in a while
We fet the shore, where scarcely we had while [495]
For to arrive but that we heard anon
A three-sound bark confounded all in one.

465. **impaled**: surrounded.   468. **bain**: bath water.   475. **gleeds**: embers.   476. **soil**: face of the earth.   481. **bubs up swelth**: brings bubbling up foul water.   482. **tide**: time.   491. **fraughted**: laden.   492. **unwonted**: unaccustomed; **rusty keel**: decrepit boat.   494. **hoise**: raise aloft.   495. **fet**: arrived at; **while**: time.

We had not long forth passed but that we saw
Black Cerberus the hideous hound of hell,
With bristles reared and with a three-mouthed jaw   [500]
Fordinning the air with his horrible yell
Out of the deep dark cave where he did dwell.
The goddess straight he knew and, by and by,
He peased and couched while that we passèd by.

Thence come we to the horror and the hell,   [505]
The large great kingdoms and the dreadful reign
Of Pluto in his throne where he did dwell,
The wide waste places and the hugy plain,
The wailings, shrikes, and sundry sorts of pain,
The sighs, the sobs, the deep and deadly groan,   [510]
Earth, air, and all resounding plaint and moan.

Here puled the babes, and here the maids unwed
With folded hands their sorry chance bewailed;
Here wept the guiltless slain and lovers dead
That slew themselves when nothing else availed.   [515]
A thousand sorts of sorrows here that wailed
With sighs and tears, sobs, shrikes, and all yfere
That (oh alas!) it was a hell to hear.

We stayed us straight and with a rueful fear
Beheld this heavy sight, while from mine eyes   [520]
The vapoured tears down stillèd here and there,
And Sorrow eke in far more woeful wise
Took on with plaint, upheaving to the skies
Her wretched hands, that with her cry the rout
Gan all in heaps to swarm us round about.   [525]

'Lo here', quoth Sorrow, 'princes of renown
That whilom sat on top of Fortune's wheel
Now laid full low, like wretches whirlèd down
Even with one frown that stayed but with a smile.

---

501. **Fordinning**: Filling with noise. 504. **peased and couched**: quieted and lay down. 509. **shrikes**: shrieks. 512. **puled**: whined, cried out plaintively. 513. **sorry chance**: misfortune. 517. **yfere**: together. 519. **We stayed us straight**: We stopped immediately. 521. **vapoured**: moist; **down stilled**: trickled down. 528–9. **Now ... smile**: Now fully laid low, brought down on Fortune's wheel like wretches by a single frown from Fortune, who had once kept them in place solely by her smiling upon them.

And now behold the thing that thou, erewhile,   [530]
Saw only in thought, and what thou now shalt hear,
Recompt the same to kaiser, king, and peer.'

Then first came Henry, duke of Buckingham,
His cloak of black all pilled and quite forworn,[460]
Wringing his hands and Fortune oft doth blame,   [535]
Which of a duke hath made him now her scorn.
With ghastly looks, as one in manner lorn,
Oft spread his arms, stretched hands he joins as fast,
With rueful cheer and vapoured eyes upcast.

His cloak he rent, his manly breast he beat,   [540]
His hair all torn about the place it lay,
My heart so molt to see his grief so great,
As feelingly me thought it dropped away.
His eyes they whirled about withouten stay,
With stormy sighs the place did so complain   [545]
As if his heart at each had burst in twain.

Thrice he began to tell his doleful tale,
And thrice the sighs did swallow up his voice,
At each of which he shrikèd so withal
As though the heavens rivèd with the noise,   [550]
Till at the last, recovering his voice,
Supping the tears that all his breast berained,
On cruel Fortune weeping thus he plained:

---

532. **Recompt**: recount; **kaiser**: emperor.   534. **pilled**: threadbare; **forworn**: worn out.   536. **of**: from.   537. **lorn**: lost, ruined.   542. **molt**: melted.   543. **feelingly**: with emotion.   545. **place did so complain**: did so fill with expressions of sorrow.   546. **each**: each sigh.   550. **rived**: split.

[Tragedy 22b]

The Complaint of Henry, Duke of Buckingham

'Who trusts too much in honour's highest throne
And warely watch not sly Dame Fortune's snare,
Or who in court will bear the sway alone
And wisely weigh not how to wield the care,
Behold he me and by my death beware,   [5]
Whom flattering Fortune falsely so beguiled
That, lo, she slew where erst full smooth she smiled.

And Sackville, sith in purpose now thou hast
The woeful fall of princes to descrive,
Whom Fortune both uplift and gain down cast,   [10]
To show thereby the unsurety in this life,
Mark well my fall, which I shall show belive,
And paint it forth that all estates may know:
Have they the warning and be mine the woe.

For noble blood made me both prince and peer,   [15]
Yea peerless too, had reason purchased place,
And God with gifts endowed me largely here,
But what avails his gifts where fails his grace?
My mother's sire, sprung of a kingly race,
And called was Edmund, duke of Somerset,   [20]
Bereft of life ere time by nature set.[461]

Whose faithful heart to Henry Sixth so wrought
That never he him in weal or woe forsook,
Till lastly he at Tewkesbury Field was caught

8. sith: since.   **10. gain**: back again.   **12. belive**: immediately.   **16. purchased place**: obtained its proper place.

Where with an axe his violent death he took.[462]   [25]
He never could King Edward's party brook,
Till by his death he vouched that quarrel good
In which his sire and grandsire spilt their blood.[463]

And such was erst my father's cruel chance,
Of Stafford earl by name that Humphrey hight,   [30]
Who, ever prest, did Henry's part advance
And never ceased till at St Albans' fight
He lost his life, as then did many a knight,
Where eke my grandsire duke of Buckingham
Was wounded sore and hardly scaped untane.[464]   [35]

But what may boot to stay the sisters three
When Atropos perforce will cut the thread?
The doleful day was come when you might see
Northampton field with armèd men o'erspread,
Where fate would algates have my grandsire dead.   [40]
So, rushing forth amidst the fiercest fight,
He lived and died there in his master's right.[465]

In place of whom, as it befell my lot,
Like on a stage so stepped I in straight way,
Enjoying there but woefully, God wot,   [45]
As he that had a slender part to play,
To teach thereby in earth no state may stay,
But as our parts abridge or length our age,
So pass we all while others fill the stage.

For of myself the dreary fate to plain,   [50]
I was sometime a prince withouten peer;
When Edward Fifth began his rueful reign,
Ay me!, then I began that hateful year
To compass that which I have bought so dear.
I bare the swinge, I and that wretched wight,   [55]
The duke of Gloucèster that Richard hight.

---

27. **vouched**: certified.   35. **untane**: untaken.   36. **But … three**: But what may avail to stop the three sisters (i.e. the Fates).   37. **Atropos**: one of the three mythological Fates; **perforce**: unavoidably.   40. **algates**: by all means.   51. **sometime**: once.

For when the Fates had reft that royal prince
Edward the Fourth, chief mirror of that name,
The duke and I fast joinèd ever since
In faithful love, our secret drifts to frame.   [60]
What he thought best to me so seemed the same,
Myself not bent so much for to aspire
As to fulfil that greedy duke's desire,

Whose restless mind, sore thirsting after rule,
When that he saw his nephews both to been   [65]
Through tender years as yet unfit to rule
And rather rulèd by their mother's kin,
There sought he first his mischief to begin,
To pluck from them their mother's friends assigned,
For well he wist they would withstand his mind.[466]   [70]

To follow which, he ran so headlong swift,
With eager thirst of his desired draught,
To seek their deaths that sought to dash his drift,
Of whom the chief the queen's allies he thought,
That bent thereto, with mounts of mischief fraught,   [75]
He knew their lives would be so sore his let,
That in their deaths his only help he set.

And I, most cursèd caitiff that I was,
Seeing the state unsteadfast how it stood,
His chief complice to bring the same to pass,   [80]
Unhappy wretch, consented to their blood.[467]
Ye kings and peers that swim in worldly good,
In seeking blood the end advert you plain
And see if blood ay ask not blood again.

Consider Cyrus in your cruel thought,   [85]
A makeless prince in riches and in might,
And weigh in mind the bloody deeds he wrought

---

57. **reft**: taken. 58. **chief mirror of that name**: paragon of all who bore the name Edward. 59. **fast**: firmly. 72. **draught**: scheme. 75. **with mounts of mischief fraught**: laden with heaps of wickedness. 76. **sore
his let**: so greatly his hindrance. 77. **That**: in consequence of which. 81. **Unhappy**: Unfortunate. 83. **the end
advert you plain**: take clear notice of the result. 84. **ay**: always. 86. **makeless**: matchless.

In shedding which he set his whole delight.
But see the guerdon lotted to this wight:
He whose huge power no man might overthrow   [90]
Tomyris Queen with great despite hath slowe.

His head dismembered from his mangled corpse
Herself she cast into a vessel fraught
With clottered blood of them that felt her force,
And with these words a just reward she taught: [95]
"Drink now thy fill of thy desired draught!"⁴⁶⁸
Lo, mark the fine that did this prince befall;
Mark not this one but mark the end of all.

Behold Cambyses and his fatal day,
Where murder's mischief mirror-like is left: [100]
While he his brother Mergus cast to slay,
A dreadful thing, his wits were him bereft.
A sword he caught, wherewith he piercèd eft
His body gored, which he of life benooms:
So just is God in all his dreadful dooms.⁴⁶⁹   [105]

Oh bloody Brutus, rightly didst thou rue,
And thou, Cassius, justly came thy fall,
That with the sword wherewith thou Caesar slew
Murd'rest thyself and reft thy life withal.⁴⁷⁰
A mirror let him be unto you all   [110]
That murderers be of murder to your meed,
For murder crieth out vengeance on your seed.

Lo Bessus, he that armed with murderer's knife
And trait'rous heart against his royal king,
With bloody hands bereft his master's life.   [115]
Advert the fine his foul offence did bring
And, loathing murder as most loathly thing,
Behold in him the just deservèd fall
That ever hath and shall betide them all!

---

91. **slowe**: slain. 94. **clottered**: clotted. 97. **fine**: end. 100. **mirror-like**: as an example. 101. **cast**: contrived. 103. **caught**: took hold of; **eft**: afterwards. 104. **gored**: stabbed; **benooms**: benims, deprives (an archaism). 113. **Lo**: behold. 116. **advert**: Take heed of.

What booted him his false, usurpèd reign, [120]
Whereto by murder he did so ascend?
When, like a wretch, led in an iron chain,
He was presented by his chiefest friend
Unto the foes of him whom he had slain,
That even they should venge so foul a guilt [125]
That rather sought to have his blood yspilt.⁴⁷¹

Take heed ye princes and ye prelates all
Of this outrage, which though it sleep awhile
And not disclosed, as it doth seld befall,
Yet God that suff'reth silence to beguile [130]
Such guilts, wherewith both earth and air ye file,
At last descries them to your foul deface:
You see the examples set before your face.

And deeply grave within your stony hearts
The dreary dool that mighty Macedo [135]
With tears unfolded, wrapped in deadly smarts,
When he the death of Clitus sorrowed so,
Whom erst he murdered with the deadly blow
Wrought in his rage upon his friend so dear,
For which, behold, lo!, how his pangs appear.⁴⁷² [140]

The lancèd spear he writhes out of the wound,
From which the purple blood spins on his face:
His heinous guilt when he returnèd found,
He throws himself upon the corpse, alas,
And in his arms how oft doth he embrace [145]
His murdered friend? And, kissing him in vain,
Forth flow the floods of salt repentant rain.

His friends, amazed at such a murder done,
In fearful flocks begin to shrink away
And he, thereat, with heaps of grief fordone, [150]

---

126. rather: earlier. **131. guilts:** offences; **file:** pollute. **132.descries:** reveals; **deface:** discredit. **135. dool:** grief; **Macedo:** 'The Macedonian', i.e. Alexander the Great (d. 323 BC). **136. unfolded:** displayed. **143. His ... found:** When he discovered his heinous crime after returning to his senses. **147. salt repentant rain:** salty tears of repentance. **150. fordone:** overcome.

Hateth himself, wishing his latter day.
Now he himself perceivèd in like stay,
As is the wild beast in the desert bred,
Both dreading others and himself adread.

He calls for death and, loathing longer life, [155]
Bent to his bane, refuseth kindly food
And, plunged in depth of death and dolour's strife,
Had quelled himself, had not his friends withstood.473
Lo he that thus had shed the guiltless blood,
Though he were king and kaiser over all, [160]
Yet chose he death to guerdon death withal.

This prince whose peer was never under sun,
Whose glistening fame the earth did overglide,
Which with his power well-nigh the world had won,
His bloody hands himself could not abide [165]
But fully bent with famine to have died:
The worthy prince deemèd in his regard
That death for death could be but just reward.

Yet we that were so drownèd in the depth
Of deep despair to drink the guiltless blood, [170]
Like to the wolf with greedy looks that leap'th
Into the snare to feed on deadly food,
So we delighted in the state we stood,
Blinded so far in all our blinded train
That blind we saw not our destruction plain. [175]

We sparèd none whose life could aught forlet
Our wicked purpose to his pass to come:
Four worthy knights we headed at Pomfret
Guiltless, God wot, withouten law or doom.
My heart even bleeds to tell you all and some, [180]
And how Lord Hastings, when he fearèd least,
Dispiteously was murdered and oppressed.474

---

151. **latter**: ultimate.   152. **stay**: state of arrested motion.   154. **dreading**: terrifying; **adread**: overcome with fear.   156. **kindly**: proper, natural.   158. **quelled**: killed.   160. **kaiser**: Caesar, emperor.   161. **guerdon**: repay.   174. **train**: trickery.   176. **aught forlet**: to any extent hinder.   177. **his pass to come**: to come to pass.   180. **all and some**: one and all.   182. **Dispiteously**: Without pity.

These rocks upraught that threatened most our wreck
We seemed to sail much surer in the stream.
And Fortune, faring as she were at beck,   [185]
Laid in our lap the rule of all the realm.
The nephews straight deposèd were by the eme,
And we advanced to that we bought full dear:
He crownèd king, and I his chiefest peer.[475]

Thus having won our long-desired prey,   [190]
To make him king that he might make me chief,
Downthrow we straight his seely nephews tway
From prince's pomp to woeful prisoner's life,
In hope that now stint was all further strife.
Sith he was king, and I chief stroke did bear,   [195]
Who joyed but we, yet who more cause to fear?

The guiltless blood which we unjustly shed,
The royal babes divested from their throne,
And we like traitors reigning in their stead,
These heavy burdens pressèd us upon,   [200]
Tormenting us so by ourselves alone,
Much like the felon that, pursued by night,
Starts at each bush as his foe were in sight.[476]

Now doubting state, now dreading loss of life,
In fear of wreck at every blast of wind,   [205]
Now start in dreams through dread of murd'rer's knife,
As though even then revengement were assigned.
With restless thought so is the guilty mind
Turmoiled and never feeleth ease or stay,
But lives in fear of that which follows ay.   [210]

Well gave that judge his doom upon the death
Of Titus Clelius that in bed was slain,
When every wight the cruel murder layeth

---

183. **upraught**: drawn up.   184. **sail**: navigate.   185. **And ... beck**: And Fortune, behaving as if she were at our command.   187. **eme**: uncle.   190. **prey**: plunder, booty.   192. **seely**: innocent, helpless; **tway**: two.   194. **stint**: ceased.   195. **stroke**: influence.   203. **as**: as if.   209. **stay**: self-control.

To his two sons that in his chamber lain.
The judge, that by the proof perceiveth plain   [215]
That they were found fast sleeping in their bed,
Hath deemed them guiltless of this blood yshed.

He thought it could not be, that they which brake
The laws of God and man in such outrage
Could so forthwith themselves to sleep betake;   [220]
He rather thought the horror and the rage
Of such an heinous guilt could never swage
Nor never suffer them to sleep or rest
Or dreadless breathe one breath out of their breast.⁴⁷⁷

So gnaws the grief of conscience evermore,   [225]
And in the heart it is so deep ygrave,
That they may neither sleep nor rest therefore,
Ne think one thought but on the dread they have.
Still to the death fortossèd with the wave
Of restless woe in terror and despair,   [230]
They lead a life continually in fear.

Like to the deer that stricken with the dart
Withdraws himself into some secret place
And, feeling green the wound about his heart,
Startles with pangs till he fall on the grass   [235]
And in great fear lies gasping there a space,
Forth braying sighs as though each pang had brought
The present death which he doth dread so oft,

So we, deep wounded with the bloody thought
And gnawing worm that grieved our conscience so,   [240]
Never took ease but as our heart forth brought
The strainèd sighs in witness of our woe:
Such restless cares our fault did well beknow,
Wherewith of our deservèd fall the fears
In every place rang death within our ears.   [245]

---

222. **swage**: abate.   229. **fortossed**: painfully tossed.   234. **green**: greenly, naively.   243. **Such … beknow**: Our restless cares well acknowledged our culpability.   244–5. **Wherewith … ears**: by reason of which, the fears we harboured of our deserved fall repeatedly proclaimed death to us everywhere we went.

And as ill grain is never well ykept,
So farèd it by us within a while.
That which so long with such unrest we reaped
In dread and danger by all wit and wile,
Lo, see the fine! When once it felt the wheel   [250]
Of slipper Fortune, stay it mought no stowne:
The wheel whirls up, but straight it whirleth down.

For having rule and riches in our hand
Who durst gainsay the thing that we averred?
Will was wisdom; our lust for law did stand,   [255]
In sort so strange that who was not afeared
When he the sound but of "King Richard" heard?
So hateful waxed the hearing of his name
That you may deem the residue by the same.

But what availed the terror and the fear,   [260]
Wherewith he kept his lieges under awe?
It rather won him hatred everywhere
And feignèd faces forced by fear of law,
That but while Fortune doth with favour blaw
Flatter through fear, for in their heart lurks ay   [265]
A secret hate that hopeth for a day.

Recordeth Dionysius the king
That with his rigour so his realm oppressed
As that he thought by cruel fear to bring
His subjects under as him likèd best.[478]   [270]
But lo the dread wherewith himself was stressed
And you shall see the fine of forcèd fear
Most mirror-like in this proud prince appear.

All were his head with crown of gold ysprad,
And in his hand the royal sceptre set,   [275]
And he with princely purple richly clad,

---

248. **That**: i.e., chief power in the realm.   251. **slipper**: wavering, deceitful; **stay it mought no stowne**: it could not remain in place even for a moment.   254. **Who ... averred?**: Who dared to contradict that which we asserted? 256. **sort so strange**: in a manner so extreme, abnormal.   259. **residue**: remainder.   264. **blaw**: blow.   266. **a day**: a time when it may exercise dominant power.   274. **ysprad**: covered.

Yet was his heart with wretched cares o'erfret
And inwardly with deadly fear beset
Of those whom he by rigour kept in awe
And sore oppressed with might of tyrant's law.　　　[280]

Against whose fear no heaps of gold and glee,
Ne strength of guard, nor all his hired power,
Ne proud high towers that pressèd to the sky
His cruel heart of safety could assure
But, dreading them whom he should deem most sure,　　　[285]
Himself his beard with burning brand would sear,
Of death deserved so vexèd him the fear.[479]

This might suffice to represent the fine
Of tyrants' force, their fears, and their unrest,
But hear this one, although my heart repine　　　[290]
To let the sound once sink within my breast,
Of fell Phereus, that above the rest
Such loathsome cruelty on his people wrought
As (oh, alas!) I tremble with the thought.

Some he encasèd in the coats of bears,　　　[295]
Among wild beasts devoured so to be,
And some for prey unto the hunters' spears
Like savage beasts withouten ruth to die.
Sometime to increase his horrible cruelty,
The quick with face to face ingravèd he,　　　[300]
Each other's death that each mought living see.[480]

Lo, what more cruel horror mought be found
To purchase fear, if fear could stay his reign?
It booted not; it rather strake the wound
Of fear in him to fear the like again,　　　[305]
And so he did full oft and not in vain,
As in his life his cares could witness well,
But most of all his wretched end doth tell.

---

277. o'erfret: worn down. 279. awe: fear. 281. glee: exalted state. 300. The ... he: He buried the living face to face. 301. mought: might. 303. stay: prop up. 305. again: in return.

His own dear wife, whom as his life he loved,
He durst not trust, nor proach unto her bed,   [310]
But, causing first his slave with naked sword
To go before, himself with trembling dread
Straight followeth fast and, whorling in his head
His rolling eyen, he searcheth here and there
The deep danger that he so sore did fear.[481]   [315]

For not in vain it ran still in his breast
Some wretched hap should hale him to his end,
And therefore alway by his pillow prest
Had he a sword, and with that sword he wend
In vain, God wot, all perils to defend,   [320]
For, lo, his wife, forirkèd of his reign,
Sleeping in bed this cruel wretch hath slain.[482]

What should I more now seek to say in this
Or one jot farther linger forth my tale
With cruel Nero or with Phalaris,   [325]
Caligula, Domitian, and all
The cruel rout, or of their wretched fall?[483]
I can no more but in my name advert
All earthly powers beware of tyrant's heart.

And as our state endurèd but a throw,   [330]
So best in us the stay of such a state
May best appear to hang on overthrow
And better teach tyrants' deservèd hate
Than any tyrant's death tofore or late.
So cruel seemed this Richard Third to me,   [335]
That, lo, myself now loathed his cruelty.

For when, alas, I saw the tyrant king
Content not only from his nephews twain
To rive world's bliss but also all world's being,
Sauns earthly guilt ycausing both be slain,   [340]

---

317. **hap**: unlucky event; **hale**: hasten. 319. **wend**: supposed. 321. **forirked of**: disgusted by. 328. **advert**: warn. 330. **a throw**: a brief while. 331. **stay**: support. 332. **hang on**: adhere closely to. 334. **tofore or late**: earlier or recently. 339. **rive**: tear.

My heart agrised that such a wretch should reign,
Whose bloody breast so savaged out of kind
That Phalaris had never so bloody a mind.[484]

Ne could I brook him once within my breast,
But with the thought my teeth would gnash withal,   [345]
For though I erst were his by sworn behest,
Yet when I saw mischief on mischief fall
So deep in blood to murder prince and all,
Ay then thought I, "alas and wellaway!",
And to myself thus mourning would I say: [350]

"If neither love, kindred, ne knot of blood,
His own allegiance to his prince of due,
Nor yet the state of trust wherein he stood,
The world's defame, nor nought could turn him true,
Those guiltless babes – could they not make him rue?   [355]
Nor could their youth nor innocence withal
Move him from reaving them their life and all?"

Alas, it could not move him any jot
Ne make him once to rue or wet his eye,
Stirred him no more than that that stirreth not,   [360]
But as the rock or stone that will not ply,
So was his heart made hard to cruelty
To murder them. Alas, I weep in thought,
To think on that which this fell wretch hath wrought!

That now when he had done the thing he sought   [365]
And, as he would, complished and compassed all
And saw and knew the treason he had wrought
To God and man to slay his prince and all,
Then seemed he first to doubt and dread us all

341. **agrised**: shuddered with horror.   342. **Whose ... kind**: Whose bloody breast was so unnaturally cruel.
344. **Ne ... breast**: Nor could I endure the idea of him even once in my private thoughts.   349. **Ay**: continually.   352. **of due**: as a matter of duty.   354. **true**: loyal.   357. **reaving**: robbing from.   360. **Stirred ... not**:
Moved him no more than it could an inanimate object.   361. **ply**: bend, yield.   366. **complished and compassed**:
accomplished and achieved.

And me in chief, whose death all means he might   [370]
He sought to work by malice and by might.[485]

Such heaps of harms upharboured in his breast,
With envious heart my honour to deface
(As knowing he that I, which wottèd best
His wretched drifts and all his cursèd case,   [375]
If ever sprang within me spark of grace
Must needs abhor him and his hateful race)
Now more and more can cast me out of grace,

Which sudden change, when I by secret chance
Had well perceived by proof of envious frown   [380]
And saw the lot that did me to advance
Him to a king that sought to cast me down,
Too late it was to linger any stowne,
Sith present choice lay cast before mine eye:
To work his death or I myself to die.   [385]

And as the knight in field among his foes
Beset with swords must slay or there be slain,
So I, alas, lapped in a thousand woes,
Beholding death on every side so plain,
I rather chose by some sly secret train   [390]
To work his death and I to live thereby
Than he to live and I of force to die.

Which heavy choice so hastened me to choose
That I in part aggrieved at his disdain,
In part to wreak the doleful death of those   [395]
Two tender babes, his silly nephews twain,
By him, alas, commanded to be slain,
With painted cheer humbly before his face
Straight took my leave and rode to Brecknock place.[486]

---

372. **upharboured**: stored.   374. **wotted**: knew.   375. **case**: condition.   378. **can**: did.   381–2. **And … down**: And saw the destiny that caused me to advance to the kingship him who sought to cast me down.   383. **stowne**: stound, moment.   384. **cast**: thrown; calculated.   392. **of force**: by necessity.   395. **wreak**: avenge.   398. **painted cheer**: feigned cheerfulness; false countenance.

And there, as close and covert as I might,   [400]
My purposed practice to his pass to bring,
In secret drifts I lingered day and night,
All how I might depose this cruel king.
That seemed to all so much desired a thing,
As thereto trusting I emprised the same,   [405]
But too much trusting brought me to my bane,

For while I now had Fortune at my beck,
Mistrusting I no earthly thing at all,
Unwares, alas, least looking for a check,
She mated me in turning of a ball;   [410]
When least I feared, then nearest was my fall,
And when whole hosts were prest to stroy my foen,
She changed her cheer and left me post alone.

I had upraised a mighty band of men
And marchèd forth in order of array,   [415]
Leading my power amid the forest Dean
Against that tyrant banner to display,
But, lo, my soldiers cowardly shrank away,
For such is Fortune, when she list to frown:
Who seems most sure, him soonest whirls she down.[487]   [420]

Oh let no prince put trust in commonty,
Nor hope in faith of giddy people's mind,
But let all noble men take heed by me
That by the proof too well the pain do find.
Lo, what is truth or trust, or what could bind   [425]
The vain people but they will swerve and sway
As chance brings change to drive and draw that way?

Rome, thou that once advancèd up so high
Thy stay, patron, and flower of excellence,
Hast now thrown him to depth of misery,   [430]

---

405. thereto trusting: i.e. trusting to the desire of all for Richard's deposition; **emprised**: undertook.   **407. beck**: absolute command.   **409. Unwares**: Unwary; **check**: evil turn (with a concomitant sense of 'check' in chess).   **410. mated**: defeated; checkmated; **turning of a ball**: in an instant.   **413. cheer**: disposition; **post alone**: entirely alone.   **421. commonty**: the common people.   **425. truth**: loyalty.   **429. stay**: prop.

Exilèd him that was thy whole defence,
Ne comptest it not an horrible offence
To riven him of honour and of fame
That won it thee when thou hadst lost the same.[488]

Behold Camillus, he that erst revived   [435]
The state of Rome that dying he did find,
Of his own state is now, alas, deprived,
Banished by them whom he did thus debt-bind,
That cruel folk, unthankful and unkind,
Declarèd well their false inconstancy   [440]
And Fortune eke her mutability.[489]

And thou, Scipio, a mirror mayst thou be
To all nobles, that they learn not too late
How they once trust the unstable commonty.
Thou that recured'st the torn, dismembered state,   [445]
Even when the conqueror was at the gate,
Art now exiled, as though thou not deserved
To rest in her, whom thou hadst so preserved.

Ingrateful Rome hast showed thy cruelty
On him by whom thou livest yet in fame,   [450]
But not thy deed nor his desert shall die,
But his own words shall witness ay the same,
For, lo, his grave doth thee most justly blame
And with disdain in marble says to thee,
"Unkind country, my bones shalt thou not see".[490]   [455]

What more unworthy than this his exile?
More just than this the woeful plaint he wrote.
Or who could show a plainer proof the while
Of most false faith than they that thus forgot
His great deserts that so deservèd not?   [460]
His cinders yet, lo, doth he them deny
That him denied amongst them for to die.[491]

---

432. **Ne comptest it not**: Nor regards it.   433. **riven**: have robbed.   438. **debt-bind**: bind by obligation (a nonce-word).   444. **How they once trust**: To what extent they at any time have confidence in.   445. **recured'st**: restored.   458. **the while**: in time.

Milciades, oh happy hadst thou be
And well rewarded of thy countrymen,
If in the field, when thou hadst forced to flee [465]
By thy prowess three hundred thousand men,
Content they had been to exile thee then
And not to cast thee in depth of prison so,
Laden with gyves to end thy life in woe.

Alas, how hard and steely hearts had they [470]
That, not contented there to have thee die
With fettered gyves in prison where thou lay,
Increased so far in hateful cruelty
That burial to thy corpse they eke deny,
Ne will they grant the same till thy son have [475]
Put on thy gyves to purchase thee a grave.⁴⁹²

Lo, Hannibal, as long as fixèd fate
And brittle Fortune had ordainèd so,
Whoever more advanced his country state
Than thou that lived'st for her and for no mo? [480]
But when the stormy waves began to grow,
Without respect of thy deserts erewhile,
Art by thy country thrown into exile.⁴⁹³

Unfriendly Fortune, shall I thee now blame,
Or shall I fault the fates that so ordain? [485]
Or art thou, Jove, the causer of the same,
Or cruelty herself doth she constrain?
Or on whom else, alas, shall I complain?
Oh trustless world, I can accusen none
But fickle faith of commonty alone. [490]

The polypus nor the chameleon strange
That turn themselves to every hue they see,
Are not so full of vain and fickle change
As is this false, unsteadfast commonty.

---

463. Milciades: Miltiades (d. 489 BC), Athenian military leader. **be**: been. **469. gyves**: shackles. **479. country state**: country's condition, standing. **482. erewhile**: some time ago. **491. polypus**: cuttlefish.

Lo, I, alas, with mine adversity   [495]
Have tried it true, for they are fled and gone,
And of an host there is not left me one.

That I, alas, in this calamity
Alone was left and to myself mought plain
This treason and this wretched cowardy,   [500]
And eke with tears beweepen and complain
My hateful hap, still looking to be slain,
Wand'ring in woe and to the gods on high
Cleping for vengeance of this treachery.

And as the turtle that hath lost her mate,   [505]
Whom gripping sorrow doth so sore attaint,
With doleful voice and sound which she doth make,
Mourning her loss, fills all the grove with plaint,
So I, alas, forsaken and forfaint,
With restless foot the wood roam up and down,   [510]
Which of my dole all shivering doth resowne.

And being thus alone and all forsake
Amid the thick, forwandered in despair
As one dismayed, ne wist what way to take
Until at last gan to my mind repair   [515]
A man of mine named Humphrey Bannister,
Wherewith me feeling much recomforted,
In hope of succour to his house I fled.[494]

Who being one whom erst I had upbrought
Even from his youth and loved and likèd best,   [520]
To gentry state advancing him from nought,
And had in secret trust above the rest,
Of special trust now being thus distressed,
Full secretly to him I me conveyed,
Not doubting there but I should find some aid.   [525]

---

502. **still looking:** always expecting. 504. **Cleping:** Calling. 505. **turtle:** turtle-dove. 506. **attaint:** affect. 509. **forfaint:** very weak. 510. **wood:** forest. 511. **dole:** grief; **resowne:** resound. 513. **thick:** densest part of the forest; **forwandered in despair:** wandering far and wide in my despairing state. 515. **repair:** return. 522. **had in secret trust:** held in trust of my most private affairs. 523. **Of ... distressed:** Now thus robbed of all in whom I might have close trust.

But out, alas, on cruel treachery!
When that this caitiff once an inkling heard
How that King Richard had proclaimed that he
Which me descried should have for his reward
A thousand pounds and farther be preferred,   [530]
His truth so turned to treason all distained
That faith quite fled, and I by trust was trained.

For by this wretch I being straight betrayed
To one John Mytton, sheriff of Shropshire then,
All suddenly was taken and conveyed   [535]
To Salisbury with rout of harnessed men,
Unto King Richard, there encampèd then,
Fast by the city with a mighty host,
Withouten doom where head and life I lost.'495

And with these words, as if the axe even there   [540]
Dismembered had his head and corpse apart,
Dead fell he down, and we in woeful fear
Stood mazèd when he would to life revert,
But deadly griefs still grew about his heart
That still he lay, sometime revived with pain,   [545]
And with a sigh becoming dead again.

Midnight was come, and every vital thing
With sweet, sound sleep their weary limbs did rest.
The beasts were still; the little birds that sing
Now sweetly slept besides their mothers' breast;   [550]
The old and all were shrouded in their nest.
The waters calm, the cruel seas did cease;
The woods, the fields, and all things held their peace.

The golden stars were whirled amid their race
And on the earth did laugh with twinkling light,   [555]
When each thing nestled in his resting place

---

529. Which me descried: Who treacherously revealed me. **530. preferred**: raised in rank or status. **531. distained**: sullied. **532. faith**: loyalty; **trained**: trapped. **534. John Mytton**: Hall's error for the historical Thomas Mytton. **536. harnessed**: armed, in armour. **542. we**: i.e. Sackville and his guide, Sorrow. **543. mazed**: confused; **to life revert**: regain consciousness.

Forgot day's pain with pleasure of the night.
The hare had not the greedy hounds in sight;
The fearful deer of death stood not in doubt;
The partridge dreamt not of the falcon's foot.   [560]

The ugly bear now minded not the stake
Nor how the cruel mastiffs do him tear;
The stag lay still, unrousèd from the brake;
The foamy boar feared not the hunter's spear.
All thing was still in desert, bush, and brear;   [565]
With quiet heart now from their travails rest,
Soundly they slept in midst of all their rest.

When Buckingham, amid his plaint oppressed
With surging sorrows and with pinching pains,
In sort thus sound, and with a sigh he ceased   [570]
To tellen forth the treachery and the trains
Of Bannister, which him so sore distrains,
That from a sigh he falls into a sound,
And from a swound lieth raging on the ground.

So twitching were the pangs that he assayed,   [575]
And he so sore with rueful rage distraught
To think upon the wretch that him betrayed,
Whom erst he made a gentleman of naught,
That more and more aggrievèd with this thought
He storms out sighs and, with redoubled sore,   [580]
Stroke with the Furies, rageth more and more.

Whoso hath seen the bull chasèd with darts
And with deep wounds forgalled and gorèd so,
Till he, oppressèd with the deadly smarts,

---

563. **brake**: thicket.   565. **desert**: wilderness; **brear**: briar.   570. **In sort**: In this company (of other resting creatures); **sound**: fell into a swoon.   572. **distrains**: distresses.   573. **sound**: swoon.   574. **from**: coming out of.   575. **assayed**: had experience of.   580. **sore**: suffering.   581. **Stroke with**: blasted by.   583. **forgalled**: thoroughly harassed by arrows.

[560] *1563*: drept (an uncorrected error for 'dreampt')

Fall in a rage and run upon his foe, [585]
Let him, I say, behold the raging woe
Of Buckingham, that in these grips of grief
Rageth gainst him that hath betrayed his life!

With blood-red eyen he stareth here and there,
Frothing at mouth, with face as pale as clout, [590]
When, lo, my limbs were trembling all for fear,
And I, amazed, stood still in dread and doubt,
While I mought see him throw his arms about
And gainst the ground himself plunge with such force
As if the life forthwith should leave the corpse. [595]

With smoke of sighs sometime I might behold
The place all dimmed, like to the morning mist,
And, straight again, the tears how they down rolled
Alongst his cheeks, as if the rivers hissed,
Whose flowing streams ne were no sooner whist [600]
But to the stars such dreadful shouts he sent
As if the throne of mighty Jove should rent.

And I the while with spirits well-nigh bereft
Beheld the plight and pangs that did him strain
And how the blood his deadly colour left [605]
And straight returned with flaming red again,
When, suddenly amid his raging pain,
He gave a sigh, and with that sigh he said
'Oh Bannister!', and straight again he stayed.

Dead lay his corpse, as dead as any stone, [610]
Till swelling sighs storming within his breast
Upraised his head, that downward fell anon
With looks upcast and sighs that never ceased.
Forth streamed the tears, records of his unrest,
When he with shrikes thus grovelling on the ground, [615]
Ybrayed these words with shrill and doleful sound:

590. **clout**: cloth.   592. **amazed**: terrified, lost in wonder.   596. **smoke**: vapour; **sometime**: at times.   600. **whist**: quieted.

'Heaven and earth and ye eternal lamps
That, in the heavens wrapped, will us to rest,
Thou, bright Phoebe, that clearest the nightès' damps,
Witness the plaints that, in these pangs oppressed,   [620]
I, woeful wretch, unlade out of my breast,
And let me yield my last words ere I part –
You, you, I call to record of my smart.

And thou, Allecto, feed me with thy food,
Let fall thy serpents from thy snaky hair,   [625]
For such relief well sits me in this mood
To feed my plaint with horror and with fear
While rage afresh thy venomed worm arear.
And thou, Sibylla, when thou seest me faint,
Address thyself the guide of my complaint.⁴⁹⁶   [630]

And thou, oh Jove, that with thy deep foredoom
Dost rule the earth and reign above the skies,
That wreckest wrongs and givest the dreadful doom
Against the wretch that doth thy throne despise,
Receive these words and wreak them in such wise   [635]
As heaven and earth may witness and behold
Thy heaps of wrath upon this wretch unfold.

Thou Bannister, gainst thee I clepe and call
Unto the gods that they just vengeance take
On thee, thy blood, thy stainèd stock and all.   [640]
Oh Jove, to thee above the rest I make
My humble plaint; guide me that what I speak
May be thy will upon this wretch to fall,
On thee Bannister, wretch of wretches all.

Oh would to God that cruel dismal day   [645]
That gave me light first to behold thy face
With foul eclipse had reft my sight away;
The unhappy hour, the time, and eke the place,

619. **Phoebe:** i.e. the moon; **nightes':** night's (disyllabic). 621. **unlade:** unload. 628. **worm:** serpent; **arear:** stirs up. 630. **Address thyself:** Devote yourself to being. 631. **foredoom:** judgement pronounced before an event; creation of destiny. 633. **wreckest:** avenges. 635. **wreak:** carry out (in the form of punishment). 638. **clepe:** appeal.

The sun and moon, the stars, and all that was
In their aspects helping in ought to thee, [497]   [650]
The earth, the air, and all accursèd be.

And thou, caitiff, that like a monster swerved
From kind and kindness, hast thy master lorn,
Whom neither truth nor trust wherein thou served,
Ne his deserts could move nor thy faith sworn.   [655]
How shall I curse but wish that thou unborn
Had been, or that the earth had rent in tway
And swallowed thee in cradle as thou lay?

To this did I even from thy tender youth
Witsafe to bring thee up? Did I herefore   [660]
Believe the oath of thy undoubted truth,
Advance thee up and trust thee evermore,
By trusting thee that I should die therefore?
Oh wretch and worse than wretch, what shall I say,
But clepe and curse gainst thee and thine for ay.   [665]

Hated be thou, disdained of every wight,
And pointed at wherever that thou go;
A traitorous wretch unworthy of the light
Be thou esteemed, and, to increase thy woe,
The sound be hateful of thy name also,   [670]
And in this sort with shame and sharp reproach,
Lead thou thy life till greater grief approach.

Dole and despair, let those be thy delight,
Wrappèd in woes that cannot be unfold
To wail the day and weep the weary night   [675]
With rainy eyen and sighs cannot be told,
And let no wight thy woe seek to withhold
But compt thee worthy, wretch, of sorrow's store
That, suff'ring much, oughtest still to suffer more.

---

650. **aspects**: relative positions at Bannister's nativity; **helping in ought**: favourable in anything.   653. **kind**: nature; **lorn**: doomed, abandoned.   660. **Witsafe**: vouchsafe, agree graciously.   665. **ay**: ever.   676. **told**: counted.   678. **compt**: count.

Deserve thou death, yea be thou deemed to die   [680]
A shameful death, to end thy shameful life:
A sight longed for, joyful to every eye,
When thou shalt be arraignèd as a thief,
Standing at bar and pleading for thy life,
With trembling tongue in dread and dolour's rage,   [685]
Lade with white locks and fourscore years of age.⁴⁹⁸

Yet shall not death deliver thee so soon
Out of thy woes, so happy shalt thou not be,
But to the eternal Jove this is my boon,
That thou may live thine eldest son to see   [690]
Reft of his wits and in a foul boar's sty
To end his days in rage and death distressed:
A worthy tomb where one of thine should rest.

And after this, yet pray I more, thou may
Thy second son see drownèd in a dike   [695]
And in such sort to close his latter day,
As heard or seen erst hath not been the like,
Ystrangled in a puddle not so deep
As half a foot, that such hard loss of life
So cruelly chanced may be thy greater grief.   [700]

And not yet shall thy hugy sorrows cease;
Jove shall not so withhold his wrath fro thee
But, that thy plagues may more and more increase,
Thou shalt still live that thou thyself mayst see
Thy dear daughter strocken with leprosy,   [705]
That she that erst was all thy whole delight
Thou now mayst loath to have her come in sight.

And after that, let shame and sorrow's grief
Feed forth thy years continually in woe,
That thou mayest live in death and die in life   [710]

---

686. Lade: Laden.   **695. dike:** ditch.   **698. Ystrangled:** Drowned.   **701. hugy:** great.   **705. strocken:** stricken.

And, in this sort forwailed and wearied so,
At length thy ghost to part thy body fro:
This pray I, Jove, and with this latter breath
Vengeance I ask upon my cruel death.'

This said, he flung his reckless arms abroad   [715]
And grovelling flat upon the ground he lay,
Which with his teeth he all-to gnashed and gnawed.
Deep groans he fet, as he that would away,
But, lo, in vain he did the death assay,
Although I think was never man that knew   [720]
Such deadly pains where death did not ensue.

So strove he thus a while as with the death,
Now pale as lead and cold as any stone,
Now still as calm, now storming forth a breath
Of smoky sighs, as breath and all were gone,   [725]
But everything hath end, so he anon
Came to himself, when, with a sigh outbrayed,
With woeful cheer these woeful words he said:

'Ah, where am I? What thing or whence is this?
Who reft my wits, or how do I thus lie?   [730]
My limbs do quake; my thought aghasted is.
Why sigh I so, or whereunto do I
Thus grovel on the ground?' And by and by
Upraised he stood, and with a sigh hath stayed,
When to himself returnèd, thus he said,   [735]

'Sufficeth now this plaint and this regret,
Whereof my heart his bottom hath unfraught,
And of my death let peers and princes weet
The world's untrust, that they thereby be taught.
And in her wealth, sith that such change is wrought,   [740]
Hope not too much, but in the mids of all
Think on my death and what may them befall.

---

711. **forwailed**: overwhelmed with wailing. 717. **all-to**: thoroughly. 718. **fet**: drew forth; **would away**: would die. 719. **assay**: endeavour after. 725. **as breath and all were gone**: as if breath and life were completely forced out. 737. **unfraughted**: unloaded. 738. **weet**: know. 739. **untrust**: untrustworthiness.

So long as Fortune would permit the same,
I lived in rule and riches with the best
And passed my time in honour and in fame   [745]
That of mishap no fear was in my breast,
But false Fortune, when I suspected least,
Did turn the wheel and with a doleful fall
Hath me bereft of honour, life, and all.

Lo, what avails in riches' floods that flows,   [750]
Though she so smiled as all the world were his?
Even kings and kaisers biden Fortune's throws,
And simple sort must bear it as it is.
Take heed by me that blithed in baleful bliss:
My rule, my riches, royal blood, and all,   [755]
When Fortune frowned the feller made my fall.

For hard mishaps that happens unto such
Whose wretched state erst never felt no change
Aggrieve them not in any part so much,
As their distress to whom it is so strange,   [760]
That all their lives ne passèd pleasure's range:
Their sudden woe that ay wield wealth at will
Algates their heart more piercingly must thrill.

For of my birth, my blood was of the best,
First born an earl, then duke by due descent: [765]
To swing the sway in court among the rest.
Dame Fortune me her rule most largely lent,
And kind with courage so my corpse had blent
That, lo, on whom but me did she most smile?
And whom but me, lo, did she most beguile?   [770]

Now hast thou heard the whole of my unhap,
My chance, my change, the cause of all my care:

---

750. **Lo … flows**: an obscure line. Perhaps, 'Lo, what avails him who flows in riches' floods'.   752. **biden**: endure, suffer; **throws**: turns (of her wheel).   754. **blithed**: made merry (an archaism).   756. **feller**: more terrible.   761. **ne passed pleasure's range**: never went beyond the boundaries of a pleasurable life.   763. **Algates**: Altogether; **thrill**: pierce.   767. **rule**: power.   768. **kind**: nature; **blent**: mixed.   771. **unhap**: misfortune.

[758] *1563*: fell (an uncorrected error for 'felt'

In wealth and woe how Fortune did me wrap
With world at will to win me to her snare.
Bid kings, bid kaisers, bid all states beware, [775]
And tell them this from me that tried it true:
Who reckless rules, right soon may hap to rue.'

777. **reckless**: heedlessly; **hap**: chance.

[775] *1563*: by all (an uncorrected error for 'bid')

[Prose 24]

'How like you this, my masters?' quoth I. 'Very well', said one. 'The tragedy excelleth, the invention also of the induction, and the descriptions are notable. But whereas he feigneth to talk with the princes in hell, that I'm sure will be misliked, because it is most certain that some of their souls
5 be in heaven. And, although he herein do follow allowed poets in their description of hell, yet it savoureth so much of purgatory, which the papists have digged thereout, that the ignorant may thereby be deceived.'[499] 'Not a whit, I warrant you', quoth I. 'For he meaneth not by his hell the place either of damned souls or of such as lie for their fees,[500] but rather the
10 grave, wherein the dead bodies of all sorts of people do rest till time of the resurrection, and in this sense is hell taken often in the scriptures and in the writings of learned Christians. And so, as he himself hath told me, he meaneth and so would have it taken.'[501] 'Tush', quoth another, 'what stand we here upon? It is a poesy and no divinity, and it is lawful for poets to
15 feign what they list, so it be appertinent to the matter. And, therefore, let it pass even in such sort as you have read it.'

'With a good will', quoth I. 'But whereas you say a poet may feign what he list, in deed my think it should be so and ought to be well taken of the hearers, but it hath not at all times been so allowed.' 'Ye say troth',
20 quoth the reader, 'for here followeth in the story that after the death of this duke, one called Collingbourne was cruelly put to death for making of a rhyme.'[502] 'I have his tragedy here', quoth I; 'for the better perceiving whereof, you must imagine that you see him a marvellous well-favoured man, holding in his hand his own heart, newly ripped out of his breast
25 and smoking forth the lively spirit and, with his other hand, beckoning to and fro, as it were to warn us to avoid, and with his faint tongue and voice saying as courageously as he may these words that follow':

18. **my think**: methinks. 23. **well-favoured**: handsome. 25. **smoking**: steaming. 27. **courageously**: bravely (but with a pun on the noun 'courage', meaning 'heart').

How Collingbourne was Cruelly Executed for Making a Foolish Rhyme

Beware, take heed, take heed, beware, beware,
You poets you that purpose to rehearse
By any art what tyrants' doings are!
Erinys' rage is grown so fell and fierce
That vicious acts may not be touched in verse.[503] [5]
The Muses' freedom, granted them of eld,
Is barred; sly reasons treasons high are held.

Be rough in rhyme and then they say you rail –
Though Juvenal so be, that makes no matter.[504]
With Jeremy you shall be had to jail [10]
Or forced with Martial Caesar's faults to flatter.[505]
Clerks must be taught to claw and not to clatter:
Free Helicon and frank Parnassus' hills
Are helly haunts and rank pernicious ills.[506]

Touch covertly in terms and then you taunt, [15]
Though praisèd poets alway did the like.
'Control us not, else traitor vile avaunt;
What pass we what the learnèd do mislike?
Our sins we see, wherein to swarm we seek;
We pass not what the people say or think. [20]
Their shittle hate maketh none but cowards shrink.

'We know', say they, 'the course of Fortune's wheel,
How constantly it whirleth still about,
Arrearing now, while elder headlong reel,

---

5. touched: reproved, censured. **7. reasons:** remarks. **12. Clerks:** Learned men; **claw:** flatter; **clatter:** chatter. **15. Touch covertly in terms:** Reprove allusively. **21. shittle:** inconstant, flighty. **24. Arrearing:** Drawing back; **elder:** older persons.

How all the riders alway hang in doubt. [25]
But what for that? We count him but a lout
That sticks to mount and, basely like a beast,
Lives temperately for fear of blockham feast.

Indeed, we would of all be deemèd gods,
Whatever we do, and, therefore, partly hate [30]
Rude preachers that dare threaten us plagues and rods
And blaze the blots whereby we stain our state,
But nought we pass what any such do prate:
Of course and office they must say their pleasure,
And we, of course, must hear and mend at leisure.[507] [35]

But when these pelting poets in their rhymes
Shall taunt and jest or paint our wicked works
And cause the people know and curse our crimes,
This ugly fault no tyrant lives but irks.
And therefore loathe we taunters worse than Turks: [40]
They mind thereby to make us know our miss
And so to amend, but they but dote in this.

We know our faults as well as any other,
We also doubt the dangers for them due,
Yet still we trust so right to guide the rother [45]
That scape we shall the surges that ensue.
We think we know mo shifts than other knew;
In vain, therefore, for us are counsels writ:
We know our faults and will not mend a whit.'

These are the affections of the wicked sort [50]
That press for honours, wealth, and pleasure vain.
Cease, therefore, Baldwin, cease thee I exhort,
Withdraw thy pen, for nothing shalt thou gain
Save hate, with loss of paper, ink, and pain.[508]
Few hate their sins; all hate to hear them touched, [55]
How covertly soever they be couched.

---

27. sticks: scruples.   **28. blockham feast**: execution.   **32. blaze**: make known.   **34. Of course**: As a matter of due order.   **35. of course**: as might be expected.   **36. pelting**: contemptible; passionate.   **42. dote**: act foolishly.   **44. doubt**: fear.   **45. rother**: rudder.

Thy intent I know is godly, plain, and good:
To warn the wise, to fray the fond fro ill.
But wicked worldlings are so witless wood
That to the worst they all things construe still.   [60]
With rigour oft they recompense good will;
They rack the words till time their sinews burst
In doubtful senses, straining still the worst.

A painful proof taught me the truth of this,
Through tyrant's rage and Fortune's cruel turn.   [65]
They murdered me for met'ring things amiss.
For wott'st thou what? I am that Collingbourne
Which rhymèd that which made full many mourn:
'The Cat, the Rat, and Lovell our Dog,
Do rule all England under a Hog.'⁵⁰⁹   [70]

Whereof the meaning was so plain and true
That every fool perceivèd it at first.
Most likèd it, for most that most things knew
In hugger-mugger muttered what they durst.
The king himself of most was held accursed,   [75]
Both for his own and for his faultors' faults,
Of whom were three, the naughtiest of all naughts.

The chief was Catesby, whom I called a cat,
A crafty lawyer catching all he could.
The second, Ratcliffe, whom I named a rat,   [80]
A cruel beast to gnaw on whom he should.
Lord Lovell barked and bit whom Richard would,
Whom therefore rightly I did term our dog,
Wherewith to rhyme I cleped the king a hog.⁵¹⁰

Till he usurped the crown, he gave the boar,   [85]
In which estate would God he had deceased!
Then had the realm not ruinèd so sore,

58. **the fond**: the foolish.   59. **worldlings**: people devoted to worldly pleasure.   62. **rack**: stretch (as on a rack); **time**: the time.   63. **straining still the worst**: ever construing the meaning of words to the worst.   66. **met'ring things amiss**: constructing a metrical poem in a faulty manner; putting into metre things that are amiss.   67. **wott'st**: wottest, know.   74. **hugger-mugger**: secrecy.   76. **faultors**: fautors, adherents.   77. **naughtiest of all naughts**: wickedest of all wicked people.   84. **cleped**: called.   85. **gave**: bore as his armorial device.   86. **estate**: rank (i.e. duke of Gloucester, in which rank he displayed the boar as his badge).

His nephew's reign should not so soon have ceased,
The noble blood had not been so decreased.
His Rat, his Cat, and Bloodhound had not noyed   [90]
So many thousands as they have destroyed.⁵¹¹

Their lawless dealings all men did lament,
And so did I, and therefore made the rhymes
To show my wit, how well I could invent,
To warn withal the careless of their crimes.   [95]
I thought the freedom of the ancient times
Stood still in force. *Ridentem dicere verum*
*Quis vetat?*⁵¹² None, save climbers still in *ferrum*.

Belike no tyrants were in Horace' days,
And therefore poets freely blamèd vice.   [100]
Witness their satire sharp and tragic plays,
With chiefest princes chiefly had in price.
They name no man; they mix their gall with spice.
No more do I: I name no man outright
But, riddle-wise, I mean them as I might.⁵¹³   [105]

When bruit had brought this to their guilty ears
Who rudely named were noted in the rhyme,
They all conspired like most greedy bears
To charge me with most heinous, trait'rous crime
And damnèd me the gallow-tree to climb   [110]
And, strangled first, in quarters to be cut,
Which should on high over London gates be put.

This wicked judgement vexèd me so sore
That I exclaimed against their tyranny.
Wherewith incensed, to make my pain the more,   [115]
They practisèd a shameful villainy:
They cut me down alive and cruelly
Ripped up my paunch and bulk to make me smart
And lingered long ere they took out my heart.

---

90. **noyed**: troubled.   **97–8.** *Ridentem ... vetat?*: Who prevents me from speaking truth with a laugh?   **98. None ... ferrum** [properly '*ferro*']: None excepting the ambitious, who are ever in iron shackles.   **102. price**: esteem.   **118. bulk**: torso.

Here tyrant Richard played the eager hog: [120]
His grashing tusks my tender gristles shore.
His bloodhound Lovell played the ravening dog:
His wolvish teeth my guiltless carcass tore.
His Rat and Cat did what they might and more:
Cat Catesby clawed my guts to make me smart;   [125]
The Rat Lord Ratcliffe gnawed me to the heart.

If Jews had killed the justest king alive,
If Turks had burned up churches, gods, and all,
What greater pain could cruel hearts contrive
Than that I suffered for this trespass small?   [130]
I am not prince nor peer, but yet my fall
Is worthy to be thought upon for this,
To see how cankered tyrants' malice is,

To teach also all subjects to take heed
They meddle not with magistrates' affairs   [135]
But pray to God to mend them if it need,
To warn also all poets that be strayers
To keep them close in compass of their chairs
And, when they touch things which they wish amended,
To sauce them so, that few need be offended,   [140]

And so to mix their sharp rebukes with mirth
That they may pierce, not causing any pain,
Save such as followeth every kindly birth,
Requited straight, with gladness of the gain.
A poet must be pleasant, not too plain,   [145]
No flatterer, no bolsterer of vice,
But sound and sweet, in all things ware and wise.

The Greeks do paint a poet's office whole
In Pegasus, their feignèd horse with wings,
Whom, shapèd so, Medusa's blood did foal,   [150]
Who with his feet strake out the Muses' springs

121. **His ... shore**: His gnashing tusks sheared my tender cartilage.   133. **cankered**: depraved.   136. **mend them if it need**: to correct them, if they need correcting.   138. **compass**: due limits; **chairs**: proper seats or situations of authority.   140. **To sauce them so**: To prepare them in such a way as to reduce their severity.   143. **kindly**: natural.   147. **ware**: prudent.   148. **office**: set of duties; official position with defined duties.

Fro flinty rocks to Helicon that clings
And then flew up unto the starry sky
And there abides among the heavens high.⁵¹⁴

For he that shall a perfect poet be   [155]
Must first be bred out of Medusa's blood.
He must be chaste and virtuous as was she,
Who, to her power, the Ocean god withstood.⁵¹⁵
To th'end also his doom be just and good,
He must, as she had, have one only eye,   [160]
Regard of truth, that nought may lead awry.⁵¹⁶

In courage eke he must be like a horse;
He may not fear to register the right.
And, that no power or fancy do him force,
No bit nor rein his tender jaws may twight.   [165]
He must be armed with strength of wit and sprite
To dash the rocks, dark causes and obscure,
Till he attain the springs of truth most pure.

His hooves must also pliant be and strong,
To rive the rocks of lust and errors blind   [170]
In brainless heads that alway wander wrong.
These he must bruise with reasons plain and kind,
Till springs of grace do gush out of the mind,
For till affections from the fond be driven,
In vain is truth told or good counsel given.   [175]

Like Pegasus, a poet must have wings
To fly to heaven, thereto to feed and rest.
He must have knowledge of eternal things;
Almighty Jove must harbour in his breast.
With worldly cares he may not be oppressed;   [180]
The wings of skill and hope must heave him higher
That all the joys which worldly wits desire.

He must be also nimble, free, and swift,
To travel far to view the trades of men –

---

158. to her power: to the best of her ability. **165. twight**: jerk, pull at. **170. rive**: split. **172. bruise**: crush. **182. That**: Than.

Great knowledge oft is gotten by the shift.   [185]
Things notable he must be quick to pen,
Reproving vices sharply now and then.
He must be swift when touchèd tyrants chafe,
To gallop thence to keep his carcass safe.

These properties, if I had well considered,   [190]
Especially that which I touchèd last,
With speedy flight my feet should have delivered
My feeble body from the stormy blast.
They should have caught me, ere I had be cast.
But, trusting vainly to the tyrant's grace,   [195]
I never shrunk nor changèd port or place.

I thought the poet's ancient liberties
Had been allowèd plea at any bar.
I had forgot how newfound tyrannies
With right and freedom were at open war,   [200]
That lust was law, that might did make and mar,
That with the lewd save this no order was,
Sic volo, sic iubeo, stet pro ratione voluntas.[517]

Where this is law, it booteth not to plead:
No privilege or liberties avail.   [205]
But with the learned whom law and wisdom lead,
Although through rashness poets hap to rail,
A plea of dotage may all quarrels quail.
Their liberties their writings to expound
Doth quit them clear from faults by Momus found.   [210]

This ancient freedom ought not be debarred
From any wight that speaketh ought or writeth.
The author's meaning should of right be heard;
He knoweth best to what end he inditeth.
Words sometime bear more than the heart behighteth.   [215]

---

185. **shift**: movement from one place to another.   194. **caught**: hastened; **had be cast**: had been condemned.   203. *Sic...voluntas*. Thus I will, thus I command: let will stand for a reason.   207. **hap**: chance.   208. **dotage**: foolishness.
209–10. **Their ... found**: Their liberty to interpret their own writings' meanings excuses them fully from any faults found in their work by Momus (**Momus**: an epithet for a carping critic, derived from the name of the Greek God of censure and ridicule).   214. **inditeth**: writes.   215. **behighteth**: lit. promises, but evidently used here as a synonym of 'highteth' in its meaning of 'intends'.

Admit, therefore, the author's exposition:
If plain, for truth; if forced, for his submission.

Of slanderers, just laws require no more
Save to amend that seemèd evil said,
Or to unsay the slanders said afore   [220]
And ask forgiveness for the hasty braid.
To heretics no greater pain is laid
Than to recant their errors or retract:
And worse than these can be no writer's act.[518]

'Yes', quoth the Cat, 'thy railing words be treason,   [225]
And treason is far worse than heresy.'
Then must it follow by this foolish reason
That kings be more than God in majesty,
And souls be less than bodies in degree,
For heretics both souls and God offend;   [230]
Traitors but seek to bring man's life to end.[519]

I speak this not to abase the heinous fault
Of trait'rous acts, abhorred of God and man,
But to make plain their judgement to be naught
That heresy for lesser sin do ban.   [235]
I curse them both as deep as any can
And alway did, yet, through my foolish rhyme,
They arraigned and stained me with that shameful crime.

I never meant the king or counsel harm,
Unless to wish them safety were offence.   [240]
Against their power I never lifted arm,
Neither pen nor tongue for any ill pretence.
The rhyme I made, though rude, was sound in sense,
For they therein whom I so fondly named
So rulèd all that they were foul defamed.   [245]

This was no treason but the very troth.
They rulèd all; none could deny the same.

---

216. exposition: interpretation.   **232. abase**: diminish.   **235. That ... ban**: Who curse heresy as a lesser sin (than treason).

What was the cause then why they were so wroth?
What, is it treason in a rhyming frame
To clip, to stretch, to add or change a name?   [250]
And this reserved, there is no rhyme or reason
That any craft can clout to seem a treason,

For where I meant the king by name of hog,
I only alluded to his badge, the boar;
To Lovell's name I added more 'our dog',   [255]
Because most dogs have born that name of yore.
These metaphors I use with other more,
As cat and rat, the half names of the rest
To hide the sense which they so wrongly wrest.

I pray you now, what treason find you here?   [260]
'Enough: you rubbed the guilty on the gall;
Both sense and names do note them very near.'
I grant that was the chief cause of my fall,
Yet can you find therein no treason at all.
There is no word against the prince or state   [265]
Nor harm to them whom all the realm did hate.

But sith the guilty always are suspicious
And dread the ruin that must sue by reason,
They cannot choose but count their counsel vicious
That note their faults and therefore call it treason: [270]
All grace and goodness with the lewd is geason.
This is the cause why they good things detest,
Whereas the good take ill things to the best.

And therefore, Baldwin, boldly to the good
Rebuke thou vice, so shalt thou purchase thanks.   [275]
As for the bad, thou shalt but move his mood,
Though pleasantly thou touch his sinful pranks.
Warn poets, therefore, not to pass the banks
Of Helicon but keep them in the streams;
So shall their freedom save them from extremes.   [280]

---

252. **clout**: join awkwardly together.   261. **gall**: sore point.   268. **sue**: follow.   271. **geason**: scarce.   277. **touch**: write about; censure; **pranks**: tricks.

[Prose 25]

'God's blessing on his heart that made this', said one, 'specially for reviving our ancient liberties, and I pray God it may take such place with the magistrates that they may ratify our old freedom.'

'Amen', quoth another, 'for that shall be a mean both to stay and uphold
5   themselves from falling, and also to preserve many kind, true, zealous, and well-meaning minds from slaughter and infamy. If King Richard and his counsellors had allowed or at the least but winked at some such wits, what great commodities might they have taken thereby? First, they should have known what the people misliked and grudged at (which no one of
10 their flatterers either would or durst have told them) and so mought have found mean, either by amendment, which is best, or by some other policy to have stayed the people's grudge, the forerunner commonly of rulers' destructions. *Vox populi, vox Dei*: in this case is not so famous a proverb as true.⁵²⁰ The experience of all times doth approve it. They should also have
15 been warned of their own sins, which call continually for God's vengeance, which never faileth to fall on their necks suddenly and horribly, unless it be stayed with hearty repentance. These weighty commodities mought they have taken by Collingbourne's vain rhyme. But, as all things work to the best in them that be good, so best things heap up mischief in the
20 wicked, and all to hasten their utter destruction, for after this poor wretch's lamentable persecution (the common reward of best endeavours) straight followed the eternal destruction both of this tyrant and of his tormenters, which I wish might be so set forth, that they might be a warning forever to all in authority to beware how they usurp or abuse their offices.'
25 'I have here', quoth I, 'King Richard's tragedy.' 'Read it we pray you', quoth they. 'With a good will', quoth I: 'for the better understanding whereof, imagine that you see him tormented with Dives⁵²¹ in the deep pit of hell and thence howling this that followeth':

---

4. **stay**: support.   7. **winked at**: pretended not to notice.   10. **mought**: might.   13. *vox populi, vox Dei*: the voice of the people is the voice of God (a familiar saying).

How Richard Plantagenet, Duke of Gloucester, Murdered his
Brother's Children, Usurping the Crown and, in the third Year of
his Reign, was Most Worthily Deprived of Life and Kingdom in
Bosworth Plain by Henry, Earl of Richmond, after called King
Henry the Seventh

What heart so hard but doth abhor to hear
The rueful reign of me, the third Richard?
King unkindly called, though I the crown did wear,
Who entered by rigour but right did not regard,
By tyranny proceeding in killing King Edward,   [5]
Fifth of that name, right heir unto the crown,
With Richard his brother, princes of renown.

Of trust they were committed unto my governance,
But trust turned to treason, too truly it was tried,
Both against nature, duty, and allegiance,   [10]
For through my procurement most shamefully they died.⁵²²
Desire for a kingdom forgeteth all kindred,
As after by discourse it shall be showèd here,
How cruelly these innocents in prison murdered were.

The Lords and Commons all with one assent   [15]
Protector made me both of land and king,⁵²³
But I therewith, alas, was not content,
For, minding mischief, I meant another thing,
Which to confusion in short time did me bring.
For I, desirous to rule and reign alone,   [20]
Sought crown and kingdom, yet title had I none.

To all peers and princes a precedent I may be,
The like to beware how they do enterprise,
And learn their wretched falls by my fact to foresee,

3. **unkindly**: unnaturally. **18. minding mischief**: turning my mind to evil-doing; **meant**: intended. **19. confusion**: ruin.

Which rueful stand, bewailing my chance before their eyes,   [25]
As one clean bereft of all felicities,
For right through might I cruelly defaced,
But might helped right and me again displaced.

Alas, that ever prince should thus his honour stain
With blood of innocents, most shameful to be told,   [30]
For these two noble imps I caused to be slain,
Of years not full ripe as yet to rule and reign,
For which I was abhorred both of young and old.
But as the deed was odious in the sight of God and man,
So shame and destruction in the end I wan.   [35]

Both God, nature, duty, allegiance all forgot:
This vile and heinous act unnaturally I conspired,
Which horrible deed done, alas, alas, God wot,
Such terrors me tormented and my spirits fired,
As unto such a murder and shameful deed required.   [40]
Such broil daily felt I breeding in my breast,
Whereby more and more increased my unrest.⁵²⁴

My brother's children were right heirs unto the crown,
Whom nature rather bound to defend than destroy,
But I, not regarding their right nor my renown,   [45]
My whole care and study to this end did employ,
The crown to obtain and them both to put down,
Wherein I God offended, provoking just his ire
For this my attempt and most wicked desire.

To cruel cursèd Cain compare my careful case,   [50]
Which did unjustly slay his brother just Abel.
And did I not in rage make run that rueful race
My brother duke of Clarence, whose death I shame to tell,
For that so strange it was, as it was horrible?
For sure he drenchèd was and yet no water near,   [55]
Which strange is to be told to all that shall it hear.⁵²⁵

---

40. **required**: were fittingly called forth.   48. **just his ire**: his just wrath.

The butt he was not whereat I did shoot,
But yet he stood between the mark and me,
For had he lived, for me it was no boot
To tempt the thing that by no means could be,   [60]
For I third was then of my brethren three,
But yet I thought the elder being gone,
Then needs must I bear the stroke alone.[526]

Desire to rule made me, alas, to rue;
My fatal fall, I could not it foresee.   [65]
Puffed up in pride so haughty then I grew
That none my peer I thought now could be,
Disdaining such as were of high degree.
Thus daily rising and pulling other down,
At last I shot how to win the crown.[527]   [70]

And daily devising which was the best way
And mean how I might my nephews both devour,
I secretly then sent without further delay
To Brackenbury, then lieutenant of the Tower,
Requesting him by letters to help unto his power   [75]
For to accomplish this, my desire and will,
And that he would secretly my brother's children kill.[528]

He answered plainly with a flat nay,
Saying that to die he would not do that deed,
But finding then a proffer ready for my prey,   [80]
'Well worth a friend', quoth I, 'yet in time of need.'
James Tyrell hight his name, whom with all speed
I sent again to Brackenbury, as you heard before,
Commanding him to deliver the keys of every door.[529]

The keys he rendered but partaker would not be   [85]
Of that flagitious fact. 'Oh happy man!', I say,
And as you heard before, he rather chose to die

---

59. boot: good. **60. tempt:** attempt. **63. the stroke:** rule. **70. shot:** suddenly thought. **80. proffer:** means (not listed as a definition in the *OED*, but cf. Seager's inspiration for this line, Tragedy 10, line 22). **81. yet:** now. **86. flagitious fact:** heinous, wicked action; **happy:** fortunate.

Than on those silly lambs his violent hands to lay.
His conscience him pricked, his prince to betray:
Oh constant mind, that wouldst not condescend, [90]
Thee may I praise and myself discommend!

What though he refused, yet be sure you may,
That other were as ready to take in hand the thing,
Which watched and waited as duly for their prey
As ever did the cat for the mouse-taking, [95]
And how they might their purpose best to pass bring,
Where Tyrell he thought good to have no bloodshed,
Becast them to kill by smothering in their bed.[530]

The wolves at hand were ready to devour
The silly lambs in bed, whereas they lay, [100]
Abiding death and looking for the hour,
For well they wist they could not scape away.
Ah, woe is me that did them thus betray
In assigning this vile deed to be done
By Miles Forrest and wicked John Dighton, [105]

Who privily into their chamber stale
In secret-wise somewhat before midnight
And gan the bed together tug and hale,
Bewrapping them, alas, in rueful plight,
Keeping them down by force, by power and might, [110]
With haling, tugging, turmoiling, torn and tossed
Till they of force were forcèd yield the ghost.

Which when I heard, my heart I felt was eased
Of grudge, of grief, and inward deadly pain.
But with this deed the nobles were displeased [115]
And said, 'Oh God, shall such a tyrant reign
That hath so cruelly his brother's children slain?'
Which bruit, once blown in the people's ears,
Their dolour was such that they brast out in tears.[531]

---

89. His ... betray: The thought of betraying his prince (i.e. Edward V) caused Brackenbury's conscience to trouble him. **90. constant**: steadfast. **94. Which**: Who. **108. And ... hale**: And together began to tug and pull on the bed. **119. brast**: burst.

But what thing may suffice unto the bloody man?   [120]
The more he bathes in blood, the bloodier he is alway.
By proof I do this speak, which best declare it can,
Which only was the cause of this prince's decay:
The wolf was never greedier than I was of my prey,
But who so useth murder, full well affirm I dare,   [125]
With murder shall be quit, ere he thereof be ware.

And mark the sequel of this begun mischief,
Which shortly after was cause of my decay,
For high and low conceivèd such a grief
And hate against me, which sought day by day   [130]
All ways and means that possible they may
On me to be revengèd for this sin,
For cruel murdering unnaturally my kin.⁵³²

Not only kin but king the truth to say,
Whom unkindly of kingdom I bereft,   [135]
His life also from him I raught away
With his brother's, which to my charge were left.
Of ambition, behold the work and weft,
Provoking me to do this heinous treason
And murder them against all right and reason.   [140]

After whose death thus wrought by violence,
The lords, not liking this unnatural deed,
Began on me to have great diffidence,
Such brinning hate gan in their hearts to breed,
Which made me in doubt and sore my danger dread,   [145]
Which doubt and dread proved not in vain
By that ensued, alas, unto my pain.

For I supposing all things were as I wished
When I had brought these silly babes to bane,
But yet in that my purpose far I missed,   [150]

---

123. **Which ... decay**: Who alone was the cause of Edward V's downfall.   126. **With ... ware**: He will be requited
with murder himself, before he is aware of it.   136. **raught**: took.   138. **work and weft**: the woven product and the
pattern of its weaving.   143. **diffidence**: doubt, misgiving.   144. **brinning**: burning.   145. **sore**: pain.

For as the moon doth change after the wane,
So changed the hearts of such as I had tane
To be most true, to troubles did me turn,
Such rage and rancour in boiling breasts do burn.

And suddenly a bruit abroad was blown   [155]
That Buckingham, the duke both stern and stout,
In field was ready with divers to me known
To give me battle if I durst come out,
Which daunted me and put me in great doubt,
For that I had no army then prepared,   [160]
But after that, I little for it cared.

But yet remembering that oft a little spark
Suffered doth grow unto a great flame,
I thought it wisdom wisely for to wark,
Mustered then men in every place I came,   [165]
And marching forward daily with the same
Directly towards the town of Salisbury,
Where I gat knowledge of the duke's army.

And as I passed over Salisbury down,
The rumour ran the duke was fled and gone,   [170]
His host dispersed besides Shrewsbury town
And he dismayed was left there post alone,
Bewailing his chance and making great moan,
Towards whom I hasted with all expedition,
Making due search and diligent inquisition.533   [175]

But at the first I could not of him hear,
For he was scaped by secret byways
Unto the house of Humphrey Bannister,
Whom he had much preferred in his days
And was good lord to him in all assays,   [180]
Which he full evil requited in the end,
When he was driven to seek a trusty friend,

---

168. gat: got.   **169. down**: plain.   **172. post alone**: completely alone.   **173. chance**: bad luck, misfortune.   **180. all assays**: everything he endeavoured to do.

For it so happened to his mishap, alas,
When I no knowledge of the duke could hear,
A proclamation by my commandment was   [185]
Published and cried through every shire
That whoso could tell where the duke were
A thousand mark should have for his pain:
What thing so hard but money can obtain?

But were it for money, meed or dread,   [190]
That Bannister thus betrayed his guest.
Divers have diversely divined of this deed,
Some deem the worst and some judge the best,
The doubt not dissolved nor plainly expressed,
But of the duke's death he doubtless was the cause,   [195]
Which died without judgment or order of laws.

Lo, this noble duke I brought thus unto the bane,
Whose doings I doubted and had in great dread;
At Bannister's house I made him to be tane
And without judgement be shortened by the head,   [200]
By the shrive of Shropshire to Salisbury led,
In the marketplace upon the scaffold new,
Where all the beholders did much his death rue.[534]

And after this done, I broke up my host,
Greatly applauded with this happy hap,   [205]
And forthwith I sent to every sea coast
To foresee all mischiefs and stop every gap
Before they should chance and light in my lap,
Giving them in charge to have good regard
The sea coast to keep with good watch and ward,   [210]

Directing my letters unto every shrive,
With straight commandment under our name
To suffer no man in their parts to arrive
Nor to pass forth of the same,

---

187. were: might be (subjunctive mood).   **188. mark**: marks (a monetary unit worth two-thirds of a pound sterling).   **201. shrive**: sheriff.   **205. Greatly ... hap**: Receiving great approval with this fortunate event.

As they tendered our favour and void would our blame,   [215]
Doing therein their pain and industry
With diligent care and vigilant eye.[535]

And thus setting things in order as you hear
To prevent mischiefs that might then betide,
I thought myself sure and out of all fear   [220]
And for other things began to provide.
To Nottingham castle straight did I ride,
Where I was not very long space,
Strange tidings came, which did me sore amaze.

Reported it was, and that for certainty,   [225]
Th'earl of Richmond landed was in Wales,
At Milford Haven, with an huge army,
Dismissing his navy, which were many sails,
Which at the first I thought fleeing tales,
But in the end did otherwise prove,   [230]
Which not a little did me vex and move.[536]

Thus fawning Fortune began on me to frown
And cast on me her scornful louring look.
Then gan I fear the fall of my renown;
My heart it fainted, my sinews sore they shook,   [235]
This heavy hap a scourge for sin I took,
Yet did I not then utterly despair,
Hoping storms passed, the weather should be fair.

And then, with all speed possible I might,
I caused them muster throughout every shire,   [240]
Determining with the earl speedily to fight
Before that his power much increasèd were
By such as to him great favour did bear
(Which were no small number, by true report made,
Daily repairing him for to aid),   [245]

215. **void**: avoid.   229. **fleeing tales**: rumours.

Directing my letters to divers noble men,
With earnest request their power to prepare
To Nottingham castle whereas I lay then,
To aid and assist me in this weighty affair.
Where straight to my presence did then repair   [250]
John, duke of Norfolk, his eldest son also,
With th'earl of Northumberland and many other mo.[537]

And thus being furnished with men and munition,
Forward we marched in order of battle-ray,
Making by scouts every way inquisition   [255]
In what place the earl with his camp lay,
Towards whom directly we took then our way,
Evermore minding to seek our most avail,
In place convenient to give to him battayle.

So long we laboured, at last our armies met   [260]
On Bosworth plain besides Leicester town,
Where sure I thought the garland for to get
And purchase peace or else to lose my crown,
But fickle Fortune, alas, on me did frown,
For when I was encampèd in the field   [265]
Where most I trusted I soonest was beguiled.[538]

The brand of malice, thus kindling in my breast
Of deadly hate which I to him did bear,
Pricked me forward and bade me not desist
But boldly fight and take at all no fear   [270]
To win the field and the earl to conquer.
Thus hoping glory great to gain and get,
My army then in order did I set.

Betide me life or death, I desperately ran
And joined me in battle with this earl so stout,   [275]
But Fortune so him favoured that he the battle wan;

247. **prepare**: make ready to go. 248. **whereas**: where. 254. **battle-ray**: arrangement for battle. 268. **him**:
Henry, earl of Richmond. 274. **Betide**: Befall.

With force and great power I was beset about,
Which when I did behold in mids of the whole rout,
With dent of sword I cast me on him to be revengèd,
Where in the midst of them my wretched life I ended.⁵³⁹ [280]

My body it was hurried and tugged like a dog
On horseback, all naked and bare as I was born.
My head, hands, and feet down hanging like a hog,
With dirt and blood besprent, my corpse all-to torn,
Cursing the day that ever I was born, [285]
With grievous wounds bemangled most horrible to see,
So sore they did abhor this, my vile cruelty.⁵⁴⁰

Lo, here you may behold the due and just reward
Of tyranny and treason, which God doth most detest,
For if unto my duty I had taken regard, [290]
I might have lived still in honour with the best,
And had I not attempt the thing that I ought lest.
But desire to rule, alas, did me so blind,
Which caused me to do against nature and kind.

Ah cursed caitiff! Why did I climb so high, [295]
Which was the cause of this my baleful thrall?
For still I thirsted for the regal dignity,
But hasty rising threateneth sudden fall.
Content yourselves with your estates all
And seek not right by wrong to suppress, [300]
For God hath promised each wrong to redress.

See here the fine and fatal fall of me
And guerdon due for this my wretched deed,
Which to all princes a mirror now may be
That shall this tragical story after read, [305]
Wishing them all by me to take heed
And suffer right to rule as it is reason,
For time trieth out both truth and also treason.

---

278. rout: crowd. **279. dent**: blow, strike. **284. besprent**: besprinkled; **all-to**: completely. **292. And ... lest**: And I would not have attempted that which I least should have done. **296. baleful thrall**: hateful distress. **302. fine**: end. **303. guerdon**: recompense.

[Prose 26]

When I had read this, we had much talk about it, for it was thought not vehement enough for so violent a man as King Richard had been. The matter was well-enough liked of some, but the metre was misliked almost of all. And when divers therefore would not allow it, 'what', quoth one,
5   'you know not whereupon you stick, else you would not so much mislike this because of the uncertain metre. The comeliness called by the rhetoricians decorum is specially to be observed in all things. Seeing, then, that King Richard never kept measure in any of his doings, seeing also that he speaketh in hell, whereas is no order, it were against the decorum of his
10 personage to use either good metre or order. And, therefore, if his oration were far worse, in my opinion it were more fit for him. Mars and the muses did never agree; neither is it to be suffered that their mild, sacred art should seem to proceed from so cruel and profane a mouth as his, seeing they themselves do utterly abhor it, and although we read of Nero that
15 he was excellent both in music and in versifying, yet do not I remember that I ever saw any song or verse of his making – Minerva justly providing that no monument should remain of any such unjust usurpation.[541] And, therefore, let this pass even as it is, which the writer I know both could and would amend in many places, save for keeping the decorum, which he
20 purposely hath observed therein.'

    'Indeed', quoth I, 'as you say, it is not meet that so disorderly and unnatural a man as King Richard was should observe any metrical order in his talk, which, notwithstanding, in many places of his oration is very well kept. It shall thus pass therefore even as it is, though too good for so ill
25 a person. And to supply that which is lacking in him, here I have Shore's wife, an eloquent wench, which shall furnish out both in metre and matter that which could not comelily be said in his person. Mark, I pray you, what she sayeth and tell me how you like it.'

---

9. whereas: where there.   **27. comelily**: in a comely, attractive manner.

How Shore's Wife, Edward the Fourth's Concubine, was by King Richard Despoiled of all her Goods and Forced to Do Open Penance

Among the rest by Fortune overthrown,
I am not least that most may wail her fate.
My fame and bruit abroad the world is blown;
Who can forget a thing thus done so late?
My great mischance, my fall and heavy state,   [5]
Is such a mark whereat each tongue doth shoot
That my good name is plucked up by the root.

This wand'ring world bewitchèd me with wiles
And won my wits with wanton sugared joys.
In Fortune's freaks, who trusts her when she smiles   [10]
Shall find her false and full of fickle toys.
Her triumphs all but fill our ears with noise;
Her flattering gifts are pleasures mixed with pain;
Yea, all her words are thunders threat'ning rain.

The fond desire that we in glory set   [15]
Doth thirl our hearts to hope in slipper hap.
A blast of pomp is all the fruit we get
And, under that, lies hid a sudden clap.
In seeking rest, unwares we fall in trap;
In groping flowers, with nettles stung we are;   [20]
In labouring long, we reap the crop of care.

Oh dark deceit, with painted face for show!
Oh poisoned bait that makes us eager still!
Oh feignèd friend deceiving people so!

---

10. freaks: sudden changes of mind. **11. toys**: acts of toying (with someone); tricks. **16. thirl**: subject, bind; **slipper hap**: unstable chance. **18. clap**: stroke of misfortune (lit. a stroke of lightning).

Oh world, of thee we cannot speak too ill,   [25]
Yet fools we are that bend so to thy skill.
The plague and scourge that thousands daily feel
Should warn the wise to shun thy whirling wheel.

But who can stop the stream that runs full swift
Or quench the fire that crept is in the straw?   [30]
The thirsty drinks: there is no other shift.
Perforce is such that need obeys no law.
Thus bound we are in worldly yokes to draw
And cannot stay nor turn again in time,
Nor learn of those that sought too high to climb.   [35]

Myself for proof, lo, here I now appear,
In woman's weed with weeping, watered eyes,
That bought her youth and her delights full dear,
Whose loud reproach doth sound unto the skies
And bids my corpse out of the grave to rise,   [40]
As one that may no longer hide her face
But needs must come and show her piteous case.

The sheet of shame wherein I shrouded was
Did move me oft to plain before this day,
And in mine ears did ring the trump of brass,   [45]
Which is defame that doth each vice bewray.
Yea, though full dead and low in earth I lay,
I heard the voice of me what people said,
But then to speak, alas, I was afraid.

And now a time for me I see prepared;   [50]
I hear the lives and falls of many wights.
My tale, therefore, the better may be heard,
For at the torch the little candle lights.
Where pageants be, small things fill out the sights.
Wherefore give ear, good Baldwin, do thy best   [55]
My tragedy to place among the rest.

---

26. **skill**: art, practice. 32. **Perforce is such**: It is inevitable. 45. **trump**: trumpet. 46. **bewray**: expose. 48. **voice of**: words about.

Because that truth shall witness well with thee,
I will rehearse in order as it fell
My life, my death, my doleful destiny,
My wealth, my woe, my doing everydeal,   [60]
My bitter bliss, wherein I long did dwell.
A whole discourse of me, Shore's wife by name,
Now shalt thou hear as thou hadst seen the same.[542]

Of noble blood I cannot boast my birth,
For I was made out of the meanest mould.   [65]
Mine heritage but seven foot of earth;
Fortune ne gave to me the gifts of gold,
But I could brag of nature if I would,
Who filled my face with favour fresh and fair,
Whose beauty shone like Phoebus in the air.   [70]

My shape, some said, was seemly to each sight,
My countenance did show a sober grace,
Mine eyes in looks were never provèd light,
My tongue in words were chaste in every case.
Mine ears were deaf and would no lovers place,   [75]
Save that (alas!) a prince did blot my brow:
Lo, there the strong did make the weak to bow.

The majesty that kings to people bear,
The stately port, the awful cheer they show,
Doth make the mean to shrink and couch for fear,   [80]
Like as the hound that doth his master know.
What then? Since I was made unto the bow,
There is no cloak can serve to hide my fault,
For I agreed the fort he should assault.

The eagle's force subdues each bird that flies;   [85]
What metal may resist the flaming fire?
Doth not the sun dazzle the clearest eyes
And melt the ice and make the frost retire?

---

60. **everydeal**: in every respect.   65. **made out of the meanest mould**: came from the lowest of origins.   73. **proved light**: judged to be wanton.   75. **place**: put in place; assign a place to.   76. **blot**: sully.   79. **awful cheer**: awe-inspiring countenance.   80. **couch**: crouch.   82. **made unto the bow**: led into the yoke.

Who can withstand a puissant king's desire?
The stiffest stones are piercèd through with tools; [90]
The wisest are with princes made but fools.

If kind had wrought my form in common frames
And set me forth in colours black and brown,
Or beauty had been parched in Phoebus' flames,
Or shamefast ways had plucked my feathers down, [95]
Then had I kept my name and good renown,
For nature's gifts was cause of all my grief;
A pleasant prey enticeth many a thief.

Thus, woe to thee that wrought my peacock's pride
By clothing me with nature's tapestry! [100]
Woe worth the hue wherein my face was dyed,
Which made me think I pleasèd every eye.
Like as the stars make men behold the sky,
So beauty's show doth make the wise full fond
And brings free hearts full oft to endless bond. [105]

But clear from blame my friends cannot be found;
Before my time, my youth they did abuse:
In marrìage a prentice was I bound,
When that mere love I knew not how to use.543
But wellaway, that cannot me excuse: [110]
The harm is mine, though they devised my care,
And I must smart and sit in sland'rous snare.

Yet give me leave to plead my case at large.
If that the horse do run beyond his race,
Or anything that keepers have in charge [115]
Do break their course, where rulers may take place,
Or meat be set before the hungry's face,
Who is in fault – the offender, yea or no,
Or they that are the cause of all this woe?

92. **kind**: nature. **116. Do ... place**: an uncertain line, meaning perhaps 'cross the path of rulers presumptuously during a hunt' or 'proceed to tear apart their prey (rather than simply bring it to bay), wherever rulers have precedence in killing a hunted beast'.

Note well what strife this forcèd marriage makes,   [120]
What loathèd lives do come where love doth lack,
What scratting briers do grow upon such brakes,
What commonweals by it are brought to wrack.
What heavy load is put on patience's back,
What strange delights this branch of vice doth breed,   [125]
And mark what grain springs out of such a seed.

Compel the hawk to sit that is unmanned,
Or make the hound untaught to draw the deer,
Or bring the free against his will in band,
Or move the sad a pleasant tale to hear: [130]
Your time is lost, and you are never the near.
So love ne learns of force the knot to knit;
She serves but those that feel sweet fancy's fit.

The less defame redounds to my dispraise:
I was enticed by trains and trapped by trust.   [135]
Though in my power remainèd yeas and nays,
Unto my friends yet needs consent I must
In everything, yea, lawful or unjust.
They brake the boughs and shaked the tree by sleight
And bent the wand that might have grown full straight.   [140]

What help in this? The pale thus broken down,
The deer must needs in danger run astray.
At me, therefore, why should the world so frown?
My weakness made my youth a prince's prey.
Though wisdom should the course of nature stay,   [145]
Yet, try my case who list, and they shall prove,
The ripest wits are soonest thralls to love.

What need I more to clear myself too much?
A king me won and had me at his call.
His royal state, his princely grace was such,   [150]
The hope of will (that women seek for all),

---

122. **scratting**: scratching; **brakes**: bushes.   127. **unmanned**: untamed.   128. **draw**: search out.   134. **The ... dispraise**: The lesser disgrace contributes to my disparagement.   135. **trains**: tricks, stratagems.   140. **wand**: branch.   141. **pale**: fence.   145. **stay**: restrain.   147. **ripest**: must mature in judgement.   151. **will**: undue assertion of one's own will.

The ease and wealth, the gifts which were not small
Besiegèd me so strongly round about,
My power was weak; I could not hold him out.

Duke Hannibal in all his conquest great,   [155]
Or Caesar yet, whose triumphs did exceed,
Of all their spoils which made them toil and sweat
Were not so glad to have so rich a meed
As was this prince, when I to him agreed
And yielded me a prisoner willingly,   [160]
As one that knew no way away to flee.

The nightingale, for all his merry voice,
Nor yet the lark that still delights to sing,
Did never make the hearers so rejoice
As I with words have made this worthy king.   [165]
I never jarred; in tune was every string:
I tempered so my tongue to please his ear
That what I said was current everywhere.⁵⁴⁴

I joined my talk, my gestures, and my grace
In witty frames that long might last and stand,   [170]
So that I brought the king in such a case
That to his death I was his chiefest hand.
I governed him that rulèd all the land.
I bare the sword, though he did wear the crown;
I strake the stroke that threw the mighty down.   [175]

If justice said that judgement was but death,
With my sweet words I could the king persuade
And make him pause and take therein a breath,
Till I with suit the faulter's peace had made;
I knew what way to use him in his trade.   [180]
I had the art to make the lion meek;
There was no point wherein I was to seek.⁵⁴⁵

---

155. **Duke**: General; **Hannibal**: Hannibal Barca (d. *c.* 182 BC), Carthaginian conqueror of much of Italy in the Second Punic War. 156. **Caesar**: Julius Caesar. 170. **frames**: forms. 172. **to**: up to the time of; **hand**: agent. 179. **suit**: supplication; **the faulter's**: the offender's. 182. **was to seek**: at a loss.

If I did frown, who then did look awry?
If I did smile, who would not laugh outright?
If I but spake, who durst my words deny?   [185]
If I pursued, who would forsake the flight?
I mean my power was known to every wight.
On such a height good hap had built my bower,
As though my sweet should never have turned to sour.

My husband then, as one that knew his good,   [190]
Refused to keep a prince's concubine,
Foreseeing the end and mischief as it stood,
Against the king did never much repine.
He saw the grape whereof he drank the wine,
Though inward thought his heart did still torment,   [195]
Yet outwardly he seemed he was content.

To purchase praise and win the people's zeal,
Yea, rather bent of kind to do some good,
I ever did uphold the commonweal;
I had delight to save the guiltless blood.   [200]
Each suitor's cause, when that I understood,
I did prefer as it had been mine own
And helped them up that might have been o'erthrown.

My power was prest to right the poor man's wrong;
My hands were free to give where need required.   [205]
To watch for grace I never thought it long;
To do men good I need not be desired,
Nor yet with gifts my heart was never hired.
But when the ball was at my foot to guide,
I played to those that Fortune did abide.   [210]

My want was wealth, my woe was ease at will,
My robes were rich and braver than the sun,
My fortune then was far above my skill,
My state was great, my glass did ever run,

---

198. bent of kind: naturally disposed. **204. prest:** ready. **206. watch for grace:** to wait for the king to offer favour, benevolence. **207. desired:** asked. **210. fortune did abide:** did await (the judgement or decree of) fortune. **212. braver:** more splendid.

My fatal thread so happily was spun   [215]
That then I sat in earthly pleasures clad,
And for the time a goddess' place I had.

But I had not so soon this life possessed
But my good hap began to slip aside,
And fortune then did me so sore molest   [220]
That unto plaints was turnèd all my pride.
It booted not to row against the tide:
Mine oars were weak, my heart and strength did fail,
The wind was rough; I durst not bear a sail.

What steps of strife belong to high estate?   [225]
The climbing up is doubtful to endure,
The seat itself doth purchase privy hate,
And honour's fame is fickle and unsure.
And all she brings is flow'rs that be unpure,
Which fall as fast as they do sprout and spring,   [230]
And cannot last, they are so vain a thing.

We count no care to catch that we do wish,
But what we win is long to us unknown.
Till present pain be servèd in our dish,
We scarce perceive whereon our grief hath grown.   [235]
What grain proves well that is so rashly sown?
If that a mean did measure all our deeds,
Instead of corn we should not gather weeds.

The settled mind is free from Fortune's power;
They need not fear who look not up aloft,   [240]
But they that climb are careful every hour,
For when they fall they light not very soft.
Examples hath the wisest warnèd oft
That where the trees the smallest branches bear,
The storms do blow and have most rigour there.   [245]

---

215. **happily**: fortunately. 219. **hap**: fortune, lot in life. 232. **We ... wish**: We think on no trouble to attain that which we wish. 237–8. **If ... weeds**: If a happy medium regulated all our deeds, we would not reap weeds instead of wheat.

Where is it strong but near the ground and root?
Where is it weak but on the highest sprays?
Where may a man so surely set his foot
But on those boughs that groweth low always?
The little twigs are but unsteadfast stays: [250]
If they break not, they bend with every blast.
Who trusts to them shall never stand full fast.

The wind is great upon the highest hills;
The quiet life is in the dale below.
Who treads on ice shall slide against their wills;   [255]
They want no care that curious arts would know.
Who lives at ease and can content him so
Is perfect wise and sets us all to school.
Who hates this lore may well be called a fool.

What greater grief may come to any life   [260]
Than after sweet to taste the bitter sour?
Or after peace to fall at war and strife,
Or after mirth to have a cause to lour?
Under such props false Fortune builds her bower;
On sudden change her flitting frames be set,   [265]
Where is no way for to escape her net.

The hasty smart that Fortune sends in spite
Is hard to brook where gladness we embrace.
She threatens not but suddenly doth smite.
Where joy is most, there doth she sorrow place.   [270]
But sure, I think, this is too strange a case
For us to feel such grief amid our game
And know not why until we taste the same.

As erst I said, my bliss was turned to bale;
I had good cause to weep and wring my hands   [275]
And show sad cheer with countenance full pale,
For I was brought in sorrow's woeful bands.

---

247. **sprays**: twigs.   256. **want no care**: lack no mental suffering; **curious arts**: matters that one does not have a right to know.

A pirrie came and set my ship on sands.
What should I hide or colour care and noye?
King Edward died, in whom was all my joy.   [280]

And when the earth receivèd had his corpse,
And that in tomb this worthy prince was laid,
The world on me began to show his force:
Of troubles then my part I long assayed,
For they, of whom I never was afraid,   [285]
Undid me most and wrought me such despite
That they bereft from me my pleasure quite.

As long as life remained in Edward's breast,
Who was but I? Who had such friends at call?
His body was no sooner put in chest   [290]
But well was him that could procure my fall.
His brother was mine enemy most of all,
Protector then, whose vice did still abound
From ill to worse till death did him confound.[546]

He falsely feigned that I of counsel was   [295]
To poison him, which thing I never meant,[547]
But he could set thereon a face of brass,
To bring to pass his lewd and false intent.
To such mischief this tyrant's heart was bent.
To God ne man he never stood in awe,   [300]
For in his wrath he made his will a law.

Lord Hastings' blood for vengeance on him cries
And many mo that were too long to name,
But most of all, and in most woeful wise,
I had good cause this wretched man to blame.   [305]
Before the world I suffered open shame:
Where people were as thick as is the sand,
I penance took with taper in my hand.[548]

---

278. pirrie: squall, storm.   **279. noye**: distress.   **284. assayed**: had proof of.   **289. Who was but I?**: Who else was there but I?   **290. chest**: coffin.   **297. But ... brass**: He could be insensible to shame.   **300. To ... awe**: He never stood in awe of either God or man.

Each eye did stare and look me in the face;
As I passed by, the rumours on me ran. [310]
But patience then had lent me such a grace,
My quiet looks were praised of every man.
The shamefast blood brought me such colour then
That thousands said, which saw my sober cheer,
'It is great ruth to see this woman here.' [315]

But what prevailed the people's pity there?
This raging wolf would spare no guiltless blood.
Oh wicked womb that such ill fruit did bear!
Oh cursèd earth that yieldeth forth such mud!
The hell consume all things that did thee good; [320]
The heavens shut their gates against thy sprite;
The world tread down thy glory under feet!

I ask of God a vengeance on thy bones;
Thy stinking corpse corrupts the air, I know.
Thy shameful death no earthly wight bemoans, [325]
For in thy life thy works were hated so
That every man did wish thy overthrow.
Wherefore I may, though partial now I am,
Curse every cause whereof thy body came.

Woe worth the man that fathered such a child; [330]
Woe worth the hour wherein thou were begat;
Woe worth the breasts that have the world beguiled
To nourish thee that all the world did hate!
Woe worth the gods that gave thee such a fate
To live so long, that death deserved so oft; [335]
Woe worth the chance that set thee up aloft!

Ye princes all and rulers everychone,
In punishment beware of hatred's ire.
Before you scourge, take heed, look well thereon:
In wrath's ill will, if malice kindle fire, [340]

---

314. **sober cheer**: solemn expression. 317. **this raging wolf**: i.e. Richard of Gloucester. 332. **beguiled**: cheated. 337. **everychone**: everyone.

Your hearts will burn in such a hot desire
That in those flames the smoke shall dim your sight;
Ye shall forget to join your justice right.

You should not judge till things be well discerned;
Your charge is still to maintain upright laws.   [345]
In conscience' rules ye should be throughly learned,
Where clemency bids wrath and rashness pause
And further sayeth 'strike not without a cause'.
And when ye smite, do it for justice' sake,
Then in good part each man your scourge will take.   [350]

If that such zeal had moved this tyrant's mind
To make my plague a warning for the rest,
I had small cause such fault in him to find:
Such punishment is usèd for the best.
But by ill will and power I was oppressed;   [355]
He spoiled my goods and left me bare and poor,
And causèd me to beg from door to door.[549]

What fall was this: to come from prince's fare
To watch for crumbs among the blind and lame?
When alms was dealt, I had a hungry share,   [360]
Because I knew not how to ask for shame,
Till force and need had brought me in such frame
That starve I must or learn to beg an alms
With book in hand and say St. David's psalms.[550]

Where I was wont the golden chains to wear,   [365]
A pair of beads about my neck was wound,
A linen cloth was lapped around my hair,
A ragged gown that trailed on the ground.
A dish that clapped and gave a heavy sound,
A staying staff and wallet therewithal   [370]
I bear about as witness of my fall.

---

346. throughly: thoroughly.   **366. beads**: prayer beads.   **369. A dish that clapped**: A clap-dish, i.e. a wooden dish with a lid that beggars would clatter to gain the attention of potential alms-givers.   **370. staying staff and wallet**: a staff to keep her up and a beggar's bag.

I had no house wherein to hide my head;
The open street my lodging was perforce.
Full oft I went all hungry to my bed:
My flesh consumed, I lookèd like a corpse,   [375]
Yet in that plight who had on me remorse?⁵⁵¹
Oh God, thou knowest my friends forsook me then;
Not one holp me, that succoured many a man.

They frowned on me that fawned on me before,
And fled from me that followed me full fast.   [380]
They hated me, by whom I set much store;
They knew full well my fortune did not last.
In every place I was condemned and cast:
To plead my cause at bar it was no boot,
For every man did tread me under foot.   [385]

Thus long I lived, all weary of my life,
Till death approached and rid me of that woe.
Example take by me both maid and wife,
Beware, take heed, fall not to folly so!
A mirror make of my great overthrow.   [390]
Defy this world and all his wanton ways;
Beware by me that spent so ill her days.

---

380. **full fast**: very closely.   383. **cast**: rejected.   384. **To … boot**: It availed me nothing to plead openly my case.

[Prose 27]

This was so well liked that all together exhorted me instantly to procure Master Churchyard to undertake and to pen as many mo of the remainder as might by any means be attainted at his hands.⁵⁵²

And when I had promised I would do my diligence therein, they asked me if I had any mo tragedies yet unread, for the evening was now at hand and there were enough already read to make a handsome volume.⁵⁵³ 'Indeed', quoth I, 'I purpose here to end the second part of this volume, for here endeth the cruel reign of King Richard the Third, and, in another volume hereafter, to discourse the residue from the beginning of King

---

3. **attainted at**: attained from.

10   Henry the Seventh to the end of this king and queen's reign (if God so long
      will grant us life). And I beseech you all that you will diligently perform
      such stories as you have undertaken and procure your friends such as be
      learned to help us with the rest, for there is in this part matter enough to
      set all the poets in England in work, and I would wish that every fine, apt
15   wit would at the least undertake one, for so would it be a notable volume.
      For my part, I intend to be so impudent and importunate a suitor to so
      many as I knew or may hereafter be acquainted with, that no excuse shall
      serve to shake me off, and I desire you all to be as earnest.
          'And to occupy the time while we now be together, I will read unto you
20   "Edmund the Duke of Somerset", which must be placed in the first part,
      and then "The Blacksmith", which must serve for the third volume, to the
      end I may know your judgement therein.' 'Do so, we pray you', quoth
      they.

          [21] *1563*: for third volume

The Tragedy of Edmund, Duke of Somerset, Slain at the First Battle at Saint Albans, in the Time of Henry VI

Some, I suppose, are born unfortunate,
Else good endeavours could not ill succeed.
What shall I call it, ill fortune or fate,
That some men's attempts have never good speed,
Their travail thankless, all bootless their heed, [5]
Where other unlike in working or skill
Outwrestle the world and wield it at will?

Of the first number I count myself one,
To all mishap, I ween, predestinate.
Believe me, Baldwin, there be few or none [10]
To whom Fortune was ever more ingrate.
Make thou, therefore, my life a caveat,
That whoso with force will work against kind
Saileth, as who sayeth, against the stream and wind.

For I of Somerset, which Duke Edmund hight, [15]
Extract by descent from Lancaster line,
Were it by folly or Fortune's fell despite
Or by ill aspect of some crooked sign,
Of my works never could see a good fine.
Whatso I began did seldom well end. [20]
God from such fortune all good men defend!

Where I sought to save most part did I spill,
For good hap with me was alway at war.

---

6. **working or skill**: actions or ability.   13. **whoso**: whoever; **against kind**: contrary to one's nature or natural quality derived from birth; against one's kinsmen.   14. **as who sayeth**: as they say.   18. **ill aspect of some crooked sign**: the unfavourable placement in the heavens of a perverse astrological sign (at the time of my birth).   20. **whatso**: whatever.   23. **hap**: luck.

The lin'age of York, whom I bare so ill,
By my spite became bright as the morning star.   [25]
Thus somewhiles men make when fain they would mar.
The more ye lop trees, the greater they grow;
The more ye stop streams, the higher they flow.

By malice of me, his glory grew the more,
And mine, as the moon in the wane, waxed less.   [30]
For having the place which he had before,
Governor of France, needs I must confess,
That lost was Normandy without redress.
Yet wrought I all ways that wit might contrive,
But what doth it boot with the stream to strive?⁵⁵⁴   [35]

Born was I neither to war nor to peace,
For Mars was malign to all my whole trade.
My birth, I believe, was in Jove's decrease,
When Cancer in his course being retrograde⁵⁵⁵
Declined from Sol to Saturnus' shade.   [40]
Where aspects were good, opposites did mar,
So grew mine unhap both in peace and war.⁵⁵⁶

A strange nativity in calculation,
As all my life's course did after declare,
Whereof, in a brief to make relation   [45]
That other by me may learn to beware,
Overlight credence was cause of my care,
And want of foresight in giving assent
To condemn Humphrey, the duke innocent.⁵⁵⁷

Humphrey I mean that was the protector,   [50]
Duke of Gloucester of the royal blood.
So long as he was England's director,
King Henry's title to the crown was good.

---

24. lin'age of York: descendants of Richard (d. 1460), third duke of York. 26. Thus ... mar: Thus sometimes men help that which they desired to harm. 29. his: the duke of York's. 38. Jove's decrease: the period when the planet Jupiter is moving south from its northernmost latitude in the heavens (measured with reference to the supposed orbit of the sun). 41. Where ... mar: Wherever the relative positions of heavenly bodies were favourable at my birth, the planets in opposition to them countered their effect. 42. unhap: misfortune. 43. A ... calculation: A strange, exceptional birth, when judged according to astrology.

This prince as a pillar most steadfastly stood,
Or like to a prop set under a vine,   [55]
In state to uphold all Lancaster's line.⁵⁵⁸

Oh heedless trust, unware of harm to come!
Oh malice, headlong swift to serve fond will!
Did ever madness man so much benumb
Of prudent forecast, reason, wit, and skill,   [60]
As me, blind Bayard, consenting to spill
The blood of my cousin, my refuge and stay,
To my destruction making open way?⁵⁵⁹

So long as the duke bore the stroke and sway,
So long no rebels' quarrels durst begin.   [65]
But when that the post was once pulled away
Which stood to uphold the king and his kin,
York and his banders proudly pressèd in
To challenge the crown and title of right,
Beginning with law and ending with might.⁵⁶⁰   [70]

Abroad went bruits in country and in town
That York of England was the heir true,
And how Henry usurpèd had the crown
Against all right, which all the realm may rue.
The people then, embracing titles new,   [75]
Irksome of present and longing for a change,
Assented soon, because they love to range.⁵⁶¹

True is the text which we in scripture read,
Ve terrae illi cuius rex est puer,
'Woe to the land whereof a child is head!'⁵⁶²   [80]
Whether child or childish, the case is one sure.
Where kings be young we daily see in ure
The people, aweless, wanting one to dread,
Lead their lives lawless by weakness of the head.

---

60. **skill**: the power of discrimination.   61. **blind Bayard**: a byword in early modern England for someone who does not assess the probable consequences before acting.   64. **bore the stroke and sway**: held chief authority.   79. *Ve ... puer*: translated in the next line.

And no less true is this text again,   [85]
Beata terra cuius rex est nobilis.
Blessed is the land where a stout king doth reign,
Where in good peace each man possesseth his,
Where ill men fear to fault or do amiss,
Where the prince prest hath always sword in hand,   [90]
At home and abroad his enemies to withstand.⁵⁶³

In case King Henry had been such a one,
Hardy and stout as his fathers afore,
Long mought he have sat in the royal throne,
Without any fear of common uproar.   [95]
But daily his weakness showed more and more,
And that gave boldness to the adverse band
To spoil him at last both of life and land.⁵⁶⁴

His humble heart was nothing unknown
To the gallants of York and their retinue;   [100]
A ground lying low is soon overflown,
And shored houses cannot long continue.
Joints cannot knit whereas is no sinew,
And so a prince, not dread as well as loved,
Is from his place by practice soon removed.   [105]

Well mought I see, had I not wanted brain,
The work begun to undermine the state,
When the chief link was loosed fro the chain,
And that men durst upon blood royal grate,
How tickle a hold had I of mine estate?   [110]
When the head post lay flat upon the floor,
Mought not I think my staff next the door?

So mought also Dame Margaret the queen,
By mean of whom this mischief first began.

---

86. Beata ... nobilis: Blessed is the land in which the king is of noble birth.   **90. prest:** prepared, ready for action.   **94. mought:** might.   **102. shored:** propped up.   **103. whereas:** where there.   **104. dread:** feared; held in awe.   **105. practice:** scheming; conspiracy.   **109. grate:** strike against.   **110. tickle:** insecure.   **111. head post:** most important support (i.e. Duke Humphrey).   **112. my staff next the door:** I would be the next to succumb (a reference to the proverbial saying 'when thy neighbour's house is afire, thy staff standeth next the door').

Did she, trow ye, herself not overween, [115]
Death to procure to such a noble man,
Which she and hers afterward did ban,
On whom did hang, as I before have said,
Her husband's life, his honour and his aid?[565]

For whilst he lived which was our stable stay, [120]
York and his imps were kept as under yoke.
But when our post removèd was away,
Then burst out flame that late before was smoke.
The traitor covert then cast off his cloak,
And he that lay hid came forth in open light, [125]
With titles blind which he set forth for right.[566]

Which thing to compass, him first behooved
The king and his kin asunder to set,
Who being per force or practice removed,
Then had they avoided the principal let [130]
Which kept the sought prey so long from the net.
The next point after was themselves to place
In highest authority about his grace.

Therefore, he wrought straight me to displace,
No cause pretending but the commonweal. [135]
The crown of England was the very case
Why to the commons they burnèd so in zeal.
My faults were cloaks their practice to conceal.
In counsel hearing, consider the intent,
For by pretence of truth treason oft is meant.[567] [140]

So their pretence was only to remove
Counsel corrupt from place about the king.
But, oh ye princes, you it doth behoove
This case to construe as no feignèd thing,
That never traitor did subdue his king [145]

---

115. **Did … overween**: Did she not, do you believe, think too highly of herself. 117. **Which … ban**: Which action she and those allied with her later cursed. 121. **imps**: malicious allies. 126. **titles blind**: false claims of entitlement (to the crown). 128. **his kin**: i.e. Somerset, the king's first cousin once removed. 130. **avoided**: cleared away. 134. **straight**: immediately. 145–7. **That … made**: No traitor ever sought to overthrow his king without commencing his plot with an attack on the king's allies.

But for his plat, ere he would further wade,
Against his friends the quarrel first he made.

And if by hap he could so bring about
Them to subdue at his own wish and will,
Then would he wax so arrogant and stout,   [150]
That no reason his outrage might fulfil
But to proceed upon his purpose still,
Till king and counsel brought were in one case:
Lo to a rebel what it is to give place!

So for the fish casting forth his net,   [155]
The next point was in driving out his plat:
Common dolts to cause furiously to fret
And to rebel, I cannot tell for what,
Requiring redress of this and of that,
Who, if they speed, he, standing at receipt,   [160]
Grasp would the prey that long he did await.[568]

Then by surmise of something pretended
Such to displace as they may well suspect
Like to withstand their practices intended
And in their rooms their banders to elect,   [165]
The adverse party proudly to reject,
And then with reports the simple to abuse,
And when these helps fail, open force to use.

So this duke's trains were covert and not seen,
Which nought less meant than he most pretended,   [170]
Like to a serpent covert under green,
To the weal public he seemed wholly bended.
Zealous he was and would have all thing mended,
But by that mendment nothing else he meant
But to be king: to that mark was his bent.   [175]

---

148. hap: chance.   154. Lo: see.   156. driving out his plat: forwarding his plot.   165. rooms: offices, places at court.   168. when: if.   170. Which ... pretended: Which were nonetheless what he meant rather than that which he offered as a pretext.

For had he been plain, as he meant indeed,
Henry to depose from the royal place,
His haste had been waste and much worse his speed,
The king then standing in his people's grace.
This duke, therefore, set forth a goodly face, [180]
As one that meant no quarrel for the crown;
Such as bear rule he only would put down.

But all for nought, so long as I bear stroke,
Servèd these drifts and provèd all vain.
Then did he attempt the people to provoke [185]
To make commotion and uproars amain,
Which to appease, the king himself was fain
From Blackheath in Kent to send me to the Tower,
Such was the force of rebels that hour.[569]

The tempest yet therewith was not ceased, [190]
For York was bent his purpose to pursue,
Who seeing how soon I was released
And ill success of sufferance to ensue,
Then, like a Judas unto his lord untrue,
Esteeming time lost longer to defer, [195]
By Warwick's aid proclaimèd open war.[570]

At St Albans town both our hosts did meet,
Which to try a field was no equal place:
Forced we were to fight in every lane and street;
No fear of foes could make me shun the place. [200]
There I and Warwick fronted face to face
At an inn door – The Castle was the sign –
Where with a sword was cut my fatal line.

Oft was I warned to come in castle none
But thought no whit of any common sign. [205]
I did imagine a castle built with stone,
For of no inn I could the same divine.

193. **sufferance**: forbearance.   200. **try a field**: attempt a battle.   205. **no whit**: not at all.

In prophet's skill my wit was never fine:
A fool is he that such vain dreams doth dread
And more fool of both that will by them be led.⁵⁷¹   [210]

My life I lost in that unlucky place,
With many lords that leanèd to my part.
The Earl Percy had there no better grace;
Clifford, for all his courage, could not shun the dart.
Stafford, although stout, free went not from this mart;   [215]
Babthorpe the attorney for all his skill in law,
In this point of pleading was found very raw.⁵⁷²

So thus this poor king, disarmed of his bands,
His friendès slain, wanting all assistance,
Was made a prey unto his enemies' hands,   [220]
Prived of power and princely reverence,
And as a pupil void of all experience,
Innocent plain, and simply witted,
Was as a lamb to the wolf committed.⁵⁷³

A parliament then was called with speed.   [225]
A parliament? Nay, a plain conspiracy.
When all in post it was by act decreed
That after the death of the sixth Henry
York should succeed unto the regaly
And, in his life, the charge and protection   [230]
Of king and realm at the duke's discretion.⁵⁷⁴

And thus was York declarèd protector.
Protector, said I? Nay, proditor plain,
A rank rebel the prince's director,
A liege to lead his lord and sovereign.   [235]
What honest heart would not conceive disdain
To see the foot appear above the head?
A monster is in spite of nature bred.

---

213. **Earl Percy**: Henry Percy, second earl of Northumberland.   214. **Clifford**: Thomas, eighth Baron Clifford; **the dart**: death's dart (proverbial).   219. **friendès**: friends.   223. **plain**: entirely.   227. **in post**: in haste.   230. **his**: Henry VI's.   233. **proditor**: traitor.

Some haply here will move a farther doubt
And for York's part allege an elder right.   [240]
Oh brainless heads, that so run in and out!
When length of time a state hath firmly pight,
And good accord hath put all strife to flight,
Were it not better such titles should sleep
Than all a realm for their trial to weep?   [245]

From the heir female came York and his lede,
And we of Lancaster from the heir male.
Of whom three kings in order did succeed
By just descent: this is no feignèd tale.
Who would have thought that any storm or gale   [250]
Our ship could shake, having such anchor hold?
None, I think sure, unless God so would.[575]

After this hurl, the king was fain to flee
Northward in post for succour and relief.
Oh blessèd God, how strange it was to see   [255]
A rightful prince pursuèd as a thief![576]
To thee, oh England, what can be more reprief
Than to pursue thy prince with armèd hand?
What greater shame may be to any land?

Traitors did triumph; true men lay in the dust;   [260]
Reaving and robbing roisted everywhere.
Will stood for skill, and law obeyèd lust;
Might trod down right: of king there was no fear.
All thing was tried only by shield and spear.
All which unhaps, that they were not foreseen,   [265]
I was in fault, or some about the queen.

Thou lookest, Baldwin, I should myself accuse
Of some subtle drift or other like thing,

---

239. **haply**: perhaps.   242. **state**: particular state of affairs; claim to right of possession; **pight**: fixed.   245. **trial**: testing, determination.   246. **lede**: people, race.   253. **hurl**: tumult; **fain**: glad under the circumstances.   257. **more reprief**: a greater cause for censure.   261. **Reaving … everywhere**: Unrestrained pillaging and robbing occurred everywhere.   262. **Will … lust**: Wilfulness took the place of reason; law obeyed illicit desire.   265. **All … foreseen**: For all these mishaps, because they were not foreseen.

Wherein I should my prince's ears abuse,
To the duke's foes overmuch adhering.   [270]
Though some men's practice did me thereto bring,
My fault only consisted in consent:
Forgive it me, for sore I did repent.

If I, at first, when brands began to smoke,
The sparks to quench by any way had sought,   [275]
England had never felt this mortal stroke,
Which now, too late lamenting, helpeth nought.
Two points of wit too dearly have I bought:
The first, that better is timely to foresee
Than after over-late a counsellor to be.   [280]

The second point, not easily to assent
To advice given against thy faithful friend,
But of the speaker ponder the intent,
The meaning full, the point, and final end.
A saint in show in proof is found a fiend;   [285]
The subtle man, the simple to abuse,
Much pleasant speech and eloquence doth use.

And so was I abused, and other mo,
By Suffolk's slights, who sought to please the queen,
Forecasting not the misery and woe   [290]
Which thereof came and soon was after seen.
With glozing tongue he made us fools to ween
That Humphrey did to England's crown aspire,
Which, to prevent, his death they did conspire.[577]

What should I more of mine unhaps declare,   [295]
Whereof my death at last hath made an end?
Not I alone was cause of all this care;
Some besides me there were that did offend.
None I accuse, nor yet myself defend:
Faults I know I had, as none lives without;   [300]
My chief fault was folly, I put thee out of doubt.

---

270. **the duke's foes**: Duke Humphrey's foes.   292. **glozing**: lying but persuasive.

Folly was the chief; the naughty time was next,
Which made my fortune subject to the chief.
If England then with strife had not been vexed,
Glory might have grown whereas ensuèd grief.   [305]
Yet one thing to me is comfort and relief,
Constant I was in my prince's quarrel
To die or live and spared for no peril.

What though Fortune envious was my foe?
A noble heart ought not the sooner yield   [310]
Nor shrink aback for any weal or woe,
But for his prince lie bleeding in the field.
If privy spite at any time me held,
The price is paid, and grievous is my guerdon.
As for the rest, God, I trust, will pardon.   [315]

---

303. **the chief**: i.e. my own folly.   307–8. **Constant ... peril**: I remained constant in my decision to live or die in my prince's cause, and no peril ever led me to abandon that constancy.   314. **guerdon**: recompense.

[Prose 28]

When they had said their minds herein, allowing it very well, they willed me also to read 'The Blacksmith'. 'With a good will', quoth I, 'but first you must imagine that you see him standing on a ladder, overshrined with the Tyburn, a meet throne for all such rebels and traitors, and there cour-
5   ageously saying as follows':

---

3. **overshrined with**: covered over by.   4. **the Tyburn**: the gallows at Tyburn, London.   4–5. **courageously**: boldly.

The Wilful Fall of Blacksmith, and the Foolish
End of the Lord Audley

Who is more bold than is the blind Bayard?
Where is more craft than in the clouted shoen?
Who catch more harm than such as nothing feared?
Where is more guile than where mistrust is none?
No plasters help before the grief be known: [5]
So seems by me, who could no wisdom lere,
Until such time I bought my wit too dear.

Who, being boisterous stout and brainless bold,
Puffed up with pride, with fire and furies fret,
Incensed with tales so rude and plainly told,   [10]
Wherein deceit with double knot was knit,
I trappèd was as seely fish in net,
Who, swift in swimming, not doubtful of deceit,
Is caught in gin wherein is laid no bait.

Such force and virtue hath this doleful plaint,   [15]
Set forth with sighs and tears of crocodile.[578]
Who seems in sight as simple as a saint
Hath laid a bait the wareless to beguile
And, as they weep, they work deceit the while,
Whose rueful cheer the rulers so relent   [20]
To work in haste that they at last repent.

---

1. blind Bayard: the proverbial impetuous bay horse whose name was used as a byword for someone who acts without considering the consequences. **2. craft**: guile; **clouted shoen**: shoes soled with an iron plate or studded with iron nails (worn by rural commoners). **3. catch**: could receive. **5. plasters**: medicines. **6. lere**: learn. **12. seely**: naive, thoughtless. **14. gin**: trap. **17. Who**: he who. **18. wareless**: unwary. **20-1. Whose ... repent**: Whose rueful demeanour so softens rulers that they act without deliberation, which they end up regretting.

Take heed, therefore, ye rulers of the land,
Be blind in sight and stop your other ear,
In sentence slow till skill the truth hath scanned,
In all your dooms both love and hate forbear, [25]
So shall your judgement just and right appear:
It was a soothfast sentence long ago
That hasty men shall never lack much woe.

Is it not truth? Baldwin, what sayest thou?
Say on thy mind, I pray thee, muse no more. [30]
Me think thou starest and lookest I wote not how,
As though thou never sawest a man before.
Belike thou musest why I teach this lore
Else what I am that here so boldly dare
Among the press of princes to compare. [35]

Though I be bold, I pray thee blame not me,
Like as men sow, such corn needs they must reap,
And nature hath so planted in each degree
That crabs like crabs will kindly crawl and creep,
The subtle fox unlike the silly sheep. [40]
It is according to mine education
Forward to press in rout and congregation.

Behold my coat burnt with the sparks of fire,
My leather apron filled with horseshoe nails,
Behold my hammer and my pincers here, [45]
Behold my looks, a mark that seldom fails:
My cheeks declare I was not fed with quails.
My face, my clothes, my tools with all my fashion,
Declare full well a prince of rude creation.

A prince, I said; a prince, I say again, [50]
Though not by birth, by crafty usurpation.

---

24. **sentence**: official judgement; **skill**: reason.   35. **princes**: governors, men of high standing (the Blacksmith employs the rhetoric of the title under which Baldwin's collection was originally conceived, *A Memorial of Such Princes*).   39. **kindly**: according to their kind, nature.   41. **according**: in accordance with; **education**: upbringing.   42. **rout**: mob; **congregation**: assemblage.   47. **quails**: game birds usually consumed only by the upper classes.

Who doubts but some men princehood do obtain
By open force and wrongful domination,
Yet while they rule are had in reputation.
Even so by me, the while I wrought my feat,   [55]
I was a prince – at least in my conceit.

I dare the bolder take on me the name,
Because of him whom here I lead in hand,
Tuchet, Lord Audley, a lord of birth and fame,
Which with his strength and power served in my band.[579]   [60]
I was a prince while that I was so manned:
His butterfly still underneath my shield
Displayèd was from Wells to Blackheath field.

But now behold, he doth bewail the same,
Thus after-wits their rashness do deprave.   [65]
Behold, dismayed, he dare not speak for shame;
He looks like one that late came from the grave,
Or one that came forth of Trophonius' cave,[580]
For that in wit he had so little pith,
As he, a lord, to serve a traitor smith.   [70]

Such is the courage of the noble heart,
Which doth despise the vile and baser sort:
He may not touch that savours of the cart.
Him listeth not with each Jack lout to sport;
He lets him pass for pairing of his port.   [75]
The jolly eagles catch not little fleas;
The courtly silks match seld with homely frieze.

But surely Baldwin, if I were allowed
To say the truth, I could somewhat declare,
But clerks will say, 'this smith doth wax too proud,   [80]
Thus in precepts of wisdom to compare.'

---

62. **butterfly**: the badge of the Lords Audley. 65. **after-wits**: those who gain wisdom only after an event has occurred, when it is too late to benefit from it; **deprave**: decry. 69. **pith**: substance. 74. **Jack lout**: common lout. 75. **pairing of his port**: diminishing his dignity. 76. **jolly**: high-hearted; large. 77. **homely frieze**: humble coarse-spun wool cloth. 80. **clerks**: learned men.

But smiths must speak that clerks for fear ne dare.
It is a thing that all men may lament,
When clerks keep close the truth lest they be shent.

The hostler, barber, miller and the smith [85]
Hear of the saws of such as wisdom ken
And learn some wit, although they want the pith
That clerks pretend, and, yet, both now and then,
The greatest clerks prove not the wisest men.
It is not right that men forbid should be [90]
To speak the truth, all were he bond or free.

And for because I have used to fret and foam,
Not passing greatly whom I should displease,
I dare be bold a while to play the mome,
Out of my sack some others' faults to lease [95]
And let my own behind my back to pease,
For he that hath his own before his eye
Shall not so quick another's fault espy.

I say, was never no such woeful case
As is when honour doth itself abuse. [100]
The noble man that virtue doth embrace
Represseth pride and humbleness doth use,
By wisdom works and rashness doth refuse.
His wanton will and lust that bridle can
Indeed is gentle both to God and man. [105]

But where the nobles want both wit and grace,
Regard no rede, care not but for their lust,
Oppress the poor, set will in reason's place,
And in their words and dooms be found unjust,
Wealth goeth to wrack till all lie in the dust. [110]
There Fortune frowns and spite beginn'th to grow,
Till high and low and all be overthrow.

---

82. **that**: that which. 84. **shent**: reproached, harmed. 88. **pretend**: profess to have. 92. **foam**: vent vehement rage. 94. **mome**: carping critic. 95. **lease**: gather. 96. **to pease**: to become silent. 104. **that**: who. 105. **gentle**: noble in spirit; of high social rank. 107. **rede**: counsel, advice.

Then, sith that virtue hath so good reward
And after vice so duly waiteth shame,
How happ'th that princes have no more regard [115]
Their tender youth with virtue to inflame?
For lack whereof their wit and will is lame,
Infect with folly, prone to lust and pride,
Not knowing how themselves or theirs to guide.

Whereby it happen'th to the wanton wight [120]
As to a ship upon the stormy seas,
Which lacking stern to guide itself aright
From shore to shore the wind and tide do tease,
Finding no place to rest or take his ease,
Till at the last it sink upon the sand: [125]
So fare they all that have not virtue canned.

The ploughman first his land doth dress and turn
And makes it apt or ere the seed be sow,
Whereby he is full like to reap good corn,
Where otherwise no seed but weed would grow. [130]
By which example men may easily know,
When youth have wealth before they can well use it,
It is no wonder though they do abuse it.

How can he rule well in a commonwealth
Which knoweth not himself in rule to frame? [135]
How should he rule himself in ghostly health,
Which never learned one lesson for the same?
If such catch harm, their parents are to blame,
For needs must they be blind and blindly led
Where no good lesson can be taught or read. [140]

Some think their youth discreet and wisely taught
That brag and boast and wear their feather brave,
Can roist and rout, both lour and look aloft,
Can swear and stare and call their fellows knave,

---

115. **happ'th**: does it happen. 122. **stern**: rudder and helm. 123. **tease**: pull. 126. **canned**: come to know. 127. **dress**: prepare. 136. **ghostly**: spiritual. 141. **discreet**: marked by sound judgement. 143. **roist**: behave uproariously; **rout**: roar.

Can pill and poll and catch before they crave,   [145]
Can card and dice, both cog and foist at fare,
Play on unthrifty, till their purse be bare.

Some teach their youth to pipe, to sing and dance,
To hawk, to hunt, to choose and kill their game,
To wind their horn and with their horse to prance,   [150]
To play at tennis, set the lute in frame,
Run at the ring and use other such game,
Which feats, although they be not all unfit,
Yet cannot they the mark of virtue hit.

For noble youth, there is nothing so meet   [155]
As learning is, to know the good from ill,
To know the tongues and perfectly indite,
And of the laws to have a perfect skill,
Things to reform as right and justice will,
For honour is ordainèd for no cause   [160]
But to see right maintainèd by the laws.⁵⁸¹

It spites my heart to hear when noblemen
Cannot disclose their secrets to their friend
In safeguard sure with paper, ink, and pen,
But first they must a secretary find,   [165]
To whom they show the bottom of their mind,
And be he false or true, a blab or close,
To him they must their counsel needs disclose.

And where they rule that have of law no skill,
There is no boot; they needs must seek for aid.   [170]
Then ruled are they and rule as others will,
As he that on a stage his part hath played,
But he was taught nought hath he done or said.
Such youth, therefore, seek science of the sage,
As think to rule when that ye come to age.   [175]

---

145. pill and poll: rob and plunder; **catch before they crave**: take before they ask.   **146. cog**: attempt to throw dice unfairly so that certain numbers come up; **foist**: replace a true die with a hidden false one immediately before making one's throw; **fare**: a dice game.   **151. set in frame**: put in proper order.   **152. Run at the ring**: a game in which horsemen attempt to carry off a small hanging ring by taking it with a lance.   **157. indite**: write.   **160. honour**: office; exalted status.   **167. close**: a keeper of secrets.   **173. hath he**: (that) he has.   **174. science**: knowledge.

Where youth is brought up in fear and obedience,
Kept from ill company, bridled of their lust,
Do serve God duly and know their allegiance,
Learn godly wisdom, which time nor age can rust,
There prince, people, and peers needs prosper must,   [180]
For happy are the people and blessèd is that land
Where truth and virtue have got the overhand.

I speak this Baldwin of this rueful lord,
Whom I perforce do here present to thee.
He faints so sore he may not speak a word;   [185]
I plead his cause without reward or fee
And am enforced to speak for him and me.
If in his youth he had been wisely taught,
He should not now his wit so dear have bought.

For what is he that hath but half a wit   [190]
But may well know that rebels cannot speed?
Mark well my tale and take good heed to it;
Recount it well and take it for good rede.
If it prove untrue, I will not trust my creed.
Was never rebel before the world nor since   [195]
That could or shall prevail against his prince.

For ere the subject beginneth to rebel,[582]
Within himself let him consider well,
Foresee the danger and beat well in his brain
How hard it is his purpose to obtain,   [200]
For if he once be entered to the briers
He hath a raging wolf fast by the ears.

And when he is once entered to rule the beastly rout,
Although he would, he can no way get out;
He may be sure none will to him resort   [205]
But such as are the vile and rascal sort.
All honest men, as well the most as lest,
To taste of treason will utterly detest.

---

182. **overhand**: mastery.   193. **rede**: counsel.   201. **entered to the briers**: entered into trouble.   207. **lest**: least.

Then let him weigh how long he can be sure,
Where faith nor friendship may no while endure.　　　[210]
He whom he trusteth most, to gain a groat,
Will fall him from and assay to cut his throat.
Among the knaves and slaves where vice is rooted,
There is no other friendship to be lookèd.

With slashers, slaves, and snuffers, so falsehood is in price　[215]
That simple faith is deadly sin and virtue counted vice.
And where the quarrel is so vile and bad,
What hope of aid then is there to be had?
Thinks he that men will run at this or that,
To do a thing they know not how or what　　　[220]

Nor yet what danger may thereof betide,
Where wisdom would they should at home abide
Rather than seek and know not what to find?
Wise men will first debate this in their mind:
Full sure they are if that they go to wreck,　　　[225]
Without all grace they lose both head and neck,

They lose their lands and goods, their child and wife[583]
With sorrow and shame shall lead a woeful life.
If he be slain in field, he dieth accursed,
Which of all wrecks we should accompt the worst,　　　[230]
And he that dieth defending his liege lord
Is blessed and blessed again by God's own word.[584]

And where the soldiers' wages is unpaid,
There is the captain slenderly obeyed,
And where the soldier is out of fear and dread,　　　[235]
He will be lack when that there is most need,
And privately he seeks his ease and leisure,
And will be ruled but at his will and pleasure.

---

215. snuffers: those who scorn others; **in price**: held in esteem.　**230. wrecks**: disasters.　**235. out of fear and dread**: without proper fear and respect of authority.　**236. lack**: wanting.

And where some draw forth, and other do draw back,
There in the end must needs be woe and wrack: [240]
To hope for aids of lords, it is but vain,
Whose foretaught wit of treason knoweth the pain.
They know what power a prince hath in his land
And what it is with rebels for to stand.[585]

They know by treason honour is defaced,   [245]
Their offspring and their progeny disgraced,
They know to honour is not so worthy a thing
As to be true and faithful to their king.
Above cognizance or arms or pedigree afar,
An unspotted coat is like a blazing star.[586]   [250]

Therefore the rebel is accursed and mad
That hopeth for that which rebel never had,
Who trusting still to tales doth hang in hope,
Till at the last he hang fast by the rope,
For though that tales be told that hope might feed,   [255]
Such foolish hope hath still unhappy speed.

It is a custom that never will be broken:
In broils the bag of lies is ever open.
Such lying news men daily will invent
As can the hearers' fancy best content,   [260]
And as the news do run and never cease,
So more and more they daily do increase.

And as they increase, they multiply as fast,
That ten is ten hundred, ten thousand at the last.
And though the rebel had once got the field,   [265]
Thinks he thereby to make his prince to yield?
A prince's power within his own region
Is not so soon brought unto confusion,

---

242. **pain**: painful consequences.   247. **is not**: nothing is.   249. **cognizance**: heraldic crest or badge; **arms**: heraldic insignia.   250. **coat**: coat of arms.   258. **broils**: tumults.

For kings by God are strong and stoutly hearted,
That they of subjects will not be subverted; [270]
If kings would yield, yet God would them restrain,
Of whom the prince hath grace and power to reign,[587]
Who straightly chargeth us above all thing
That no man should resist against his king.

Who that resisteth his dread sovereign lord [275]
Doth damn his soul by God's own very word.
A Christian subject should with honour due
Obey his sovereign though he were a Jew.
Whereby assured when subjects do rebel,
God's wrath is kindled and threateneth fire and hell. [280]

It is soon known when God's wrath is kindled,
How they shall speed with whom he is offended.
If God give victory to whom he liketh best,
Why look they for it whom God doth most detest?
For treason is hateful and abhorred in God's sight, [285]
(Example of Judas, that most wicked wight),

Which is the chief cause no treason prevails,
For ill must he speed whom God's wrath assails.
Let traitors and rebels look to speed then,
When God's mighty power is subject to men. [290]
Much might be said that goeth more near the pith,
But this suffiseth for a rural smith.

Baldwin, when thou hearest my reason in this case,
Belike thou thinkest I was not very wise
And that I was accursed or else lacked grace, [295]
Which, knowing the end of my fond enterprise
Would thus presume against my prince to rise.
But as there is a cause that moveth every woe,
Somewhat there was whereof this sore did grow.

And to be plain and simple in this case, [300]
The cause why I such matter took in hand

286. **Example of**: Exemplified by.

Was nothing else but pride and lack of grace,
Vain hope of help and tales both false and fond,
By mean whereof my prince I did withstand,
Denied the tax assessed by convocation   [305]
To maintain war against the Scottish nation,[588]

Whereat the Cornishmen did much repine
For they of gold and silver were full bare
And livèd hardly digging in the mine.
They said they had no money for to spare,   [310]
Began first to grudge and then to swear and stare,
Forgot their due obeisance and rashly fell to raving
And said they would not bear such polling and such shaving.[589]

They first accused the king as author of their grief
And then the Bishop Morton and Sir Reynold Bray,   [315]
For they then were about the king most chief.
Because they thought the whole fault in them lay,
They did protest to rid them out of the way.
Such thank have they that rule about a prince:
They bear the blame of others men's offence.[590]   [320]

When I perceived the commons in a roar,
Then I and Flamoke consulted both together,
To whom the people resorted more and more,
Lamenting and crying 'help us now or never!
Break this yoke of bondage; then are we free forever!'   [325]
Whereat we, enflamed in hope to have us a fame,
To be their captains took on us the name.[591]

Then might you hear the people make a shout
And cry 'God save the captains and send us all good speed!',
Then he that fainted was counted but a lout,   [330]
The ruffians ran abroad to sow seditious seed,
To call for company then there was no need,
For every man laboured another to entice
To be partaker of his wicked vice.

---

305. **convocation**: parliament.   309. **hardly**: with hardship.   313. **shaving**: complete stripping of funds.

Then all such news as made for our avail   [335]
Was brought to me, but such as sounded ill
Was none so bold to speak or yet bewail.
Everich was so wedded unto his will
That 'forth!' they cried with bowès, sword and bill.
And what the ruffler spake, the lout took for a verdit,   [340]
For there the best was worst, the worst was best regarded,

For when men go a-madding, there still the viler part
Conspire together and will have all the sway,
And be it well or ill they must have all the port
As they will do; the rest must needs obey.   [345]
They prattle and prate as doth the popinjay;
They cry and command the rest to keep th'array,
Whiles they may range and rob for spoil and prey.

And when we had preparèd everything,
We went to Taunton with all our provision,   [350]
And there we slew the provost of Penryn,
For that on the subsidy he sat in commission.⁵⁹²
He was not wise nor yet of great discretion
That durst approach his enemies in their rage,
When wit nor reason could their ire assuage.   [355]

From thence we went to Wells, where we were received
Of this Lord Audley as of our chief captain –
And so had the name, but yet he was deceived,
For I indeed did rule the clubbish train.
My cartly knights true honour did disdain,   [360]
For like doth love his like, it will be none other,
A churl will love a churl before he will his brother.

Then from Wells to Winchester and so to Blackheath field,
And there we encamped, looking for more aid,
But when none came, we thought ourselves beguiled.   [365]

---

338. **Everich**: everybody.   339. **bowes**: bows.   340. **ruffler**: swaggering braggart; **verdit**: authoritative pronouncement.   344. **port**: high rank.   346. **popinjay**: parrot.   347. **th'array**: the proper arrangement in military forma-
tion.   348. **prey**: plunder.   352. **subsidy**: i.e., the tax granted by parliament.   357. **as of**: as if by.   359. **clubbish**:
boorish, rough.   360. **cartly knights**: knights more fit for the cart than for battle (a play, perhaps, on 'carpet
knights').

Such Cornishmen as knew they were betrayed
From their fellows by night away they strayed;
There might we learn how vain it is to trust
Our feignèd friends in quarrels so unjust.

But we the sturdy captains that thought our power was strong   [370]
Were bent to try our fortune, whatever should betide;
We were the bolder, for that the king so long
Deferrèd battle, which so increased our pride
That sure we thought the king himself did hide
Within the city; therefore, with courage hault,   [375]
We did determine the city to assault.

But he, working contrary to our expectation,
Was fully minded to let us run our race,
Till we were from our domestical habitation
Where that of aid or succour was no place,   [380]
And then to be plagued as it should please his grace.
But all doubtful points, however they did sound,
To our best vail we alway did expound.

When that the king saw time, with courage bold
He sent a power to circumvent us all,   [385]
Where we, enclosed as simple sheep in fold,
Were slain and murdered as beasts in butcher's stall.
The king himself, whatever chance might fall,
Was strongly encamped within Saint George's Field,
And there abode till that he heard us yield.[593]   [390]

Then down we kneeled and cried to save our life;
It was too late our folly to bewail:
There we were spoiled of armour, coat, and knife,
And we, which thought with pride the city to assail,
Were led in prisoners, naked as my nail.   [395]
But of us two thousand they had slain before,
And we of them three hundred and no more.

---

371. **betide**: happen.   375. **hault**: high, haughty.   380. **Where … place**: To a location at which there was no opportunity to receive aid or succour from our homeland.   383. **vail**: profit.   389. **Saint George's Field**: St George's Fields, near London in Southwark.

This my lord and we, the captains of the west,
Took our inn at Newgate, fast in fetters tied,
Where after trial we had but little rest: [400]
My lord through London was drawn on a slide
To Tower Hill, where with axe he died,
Clad in his coat armour painted all in paper,
All torn and reversed in spite of his behaviour.[594]

And I, with Thomas Flamoke and other of our bent, [405]
As traitors at Tyburn our judgement did obey;
The people looked I should my fault lament,
To whom I boldly spake that for my fond assay
I was sure of fame that never should decay,
Whereby ye may perceive vainglory doth inflame [410]
As well the meaner sort as men of greater name.

But as the sickly patient, sometime hath desire
To taste the things that physic hath denied,
And hath both pain and sorrow for his hire,
The same to me right well might be applied, [415]
Which, while I wrought for fame, on shame did slide
And, seeking fame, brought forth my bitter bane,
As he that fired the temple of Diane.[595]

I tell thee, Baldwin, I muse right oft to see
How every man for wealth and honour gapeth, [420]
How every man would climb above the sky,
How every man th'assurèd mean so hateth,
How froward Fortune oft their purpose mateth,
And, if they hap their purpose to attain,
Their wealth is woe, their honour care and pain. [425]

We see the servant more happy than his lord,
We see him live, when that his lord is dead,
He sleepeth sound, is merry at his board,
No sorrow in his heart doth vex his head;

---

401. **slide**: sled, a conveyance traditionally used to drag prisoners to execution. 404. **in spite of**: to spite. 406. **Tyburn**: the site of execution for common criminals in London. 414. **hire**: recompense. 416. **wrought**: worked. 422. **mean**: middle way. 424. **hap**: chance.

Happy then is he that poverty can wed.   [430]
What gain the mighty conquerors, when they be dead,
By all the spoil and blood that they have shed?

The terrible tower, where honour hath his seat
Is high on rocks more slipper than the ice,
Where still the whirling wind doth roar and beat,   [435]
Where sudden qualms and pirries still arise,
And is beset with many sundry vice
So strange to men when first they come thereat,
They be amazed and do they wot not what.

He that prevails and to the tower can climb   [440]
With trouble and care must needs abridge his days,
And he that slides may curse the hour and time
He did attempt to give so fond assays,
And all his life to sorrow and shame obeys.
Thus slide he down or to the top ascend,   [445]
Assure himself repentance is the end.

Wherefore, good Baldwin, do thou record my name
To be ensample to such as credit lies,
Or thirst to suck the sugared cup of fame,
Or do attempt against their prince to rise   [450]
And charge them all to keep within their size.
Who doth assay to wrest beyond his strength,
Let him be sure he shall repent at length.

And at my request admonish thou all men
To spend well the talent which God to them hath lent,   [455]
And he that hath but one, let him not toil for ten,
For one is too much, unless it be well spent.[596]
I have had the proof; therefore I now repent.
And happy are those men, and blessed and blissed is he,
As can be well content to serve in his degree.   [460]

---

432. **spoil**: plunder.   433. **terrible**: awe-inspiring.   436. **qualms**: disasters; **pirries**: blasts of wind.   444. **obeys**: subjects himself.   448. **credit**: believe.   451. **size**: proper limits.   455. **talent**: biblical coin.

[Prose 29]

'It is pity', quoth one, 'that the metre is no better, seeing the matter is so good; you may do very well to help it, and a little filing would make it formal.' 'The author himself', quoth I, 'could have done that, but he would not and hath desired me that it may pass in such rude sort as you have heard it, for he observeth therein a double decorum, both of the Smith and of himself, for he thinketh it not meet for the Smith to speak nor for himself to write in any exact kind of metre.'

    'Well', said another, 'the matter is notable to teach all people, as well officers as subjects, to consider their estates and to live in love and obedience to the highest powers, whatsoever they be, whom God, either by birth, law, succession, or universal election, doth or shall authorize in his own room to execute his laws and justice among any people or nation, for by all these means God placeth his deputies.⁵⁹⁷ And in my judgement, there is no mean so good either for the common quiet of the people or for God's free choice as the natural order of inheritance by lineal descent, for so it is left in God's hands to create in the womb what prince he thinketh meetest for his purposes. The people also know their princes, and therefore the more gladly and willingly receive and obey them. And although some realms more careful than wise have entailed their crown to the heir male, thinking it not meet for the feminine sex to bear the royal office, yet, if they consider all circumstances and the chiefest uses of a prince in a realm, they shall see how they are deceived, for princes are God's lieutenants or deputies to see God's laws executed among their subjects, not to rule according to their own lusts or desires but by the prescript of God's laws.⁵⁹⁸ So that the chiefest point of a prince's office consisteth in obedience to God and to his ordinances, and what should let but that a woman may be as obedient unto God as a man?

    'The second point of a prince's office is to provide for the impotent, needy, and helpless, as widows, orphans, lame and decrepit persons, and seeing women are by nature tender hearted, mild, and pitiful, who may better than they discharge the duty? Yea, but a woman lacketh courage, boldness, and stomach to withstand the adversary, and so are her subjects an open spoil to their enemies – Deborah, Jael, Judith, Tomyris, and other

---

11. **universal election**: general agreement to elect by those eligible to vote; **room**: office. 19. **entailed their crown**: established that the office of monarch may be passed on only to a specific class or set of persons. 26. **let but**: prevent it.

[17–18] *1563*: theefore (an uncorrected error); obey thr (an uncorrected error for 'the[m]')

do prove the contrary.[599] But grant it were so: what harm were that, seeing victory consisteth not in wit or force but in God's good pleasure? I am sure
35   that whatsoever prince doth his duty in obeying God and causing justice to be ministered according to God's laws shall not only lack war (be he man, woman or child) but also be a terror to other princes. And if God suffer any at any time to be assailed, it is for the destruction of the assailer, whether he be rebel or foreign foe, and to the honour and profit of the virtuous prince,
40   in whose behalf, rather than he shall miscarry, God himself will fight with infections and earthquakes from the land and waters, and with storms and lightnings from the air and skies. Mo wars have been sought through the wilful and haughty courages of kings and greater destructions happened to realms thereby, than by any other means. And as for wisdom and policy,
45   seeing it consisteth in following the counsel of many godly, learned and long-experienced heads, it were better to have a woman who, considering her own weakness and inability, should be ruled thereby, than a man which, presuming upon his own fond brain, will hear no advice save his own.

     'You muse, peradventure, wherefore I say this. The frantic heads which dis-
50   able our queen because she is a woman and our king because he is a stranger to be our princes and chief governors hath caused me to say thus much. For whatsoever man, woman, or child is by the consent of the whole realm estab- lished in the royal seat, so it have not been injuriously procured by rigour of sword and open force but quietly by title, either of inheritance, succession,
55   lawful bequest, common consent, or election, is undoubtedly chosen by God to be his deputy. And whosoever resisteth any such, resisteth against God himself and is a rank traitor and rebel, and shall be sure to prosper as well as this blacksmith and other such have done. All resist that wilfully break any law, not being against God's law, made by common consent for the wealth
60   of the realm and commanded to be kept by the authority of the prince, or that deny to pay such duties as by consent of the high court of parliament are appointed to the prince for the defence and preservation of the realm.'

     'You have said very truly herein', quoth I, 'and I trust this terrible example of the Blacksmith will put all men in mind of their duties and teach them
65   to be obedient to all good laws and lawful contributions. The scriptures do forbid us to rebel or forcibly to withstand princes, though they command unjust things. Yet, in any case, we may not do them but receive quietly at the

---

49–50. **disable**: disparage; **our queen**: Mary I; **our king**: Philip of Spain.   61. **duties**: taxes, charges on transactions owed to the crown.   65. **contributions**: taxes or other government-imposed levies.

prince's hand whatsoever punishment God shall suffer to be laid upon us for our refusal. God will suffer none of his to be tempted above their strength.[600]

70   'But, because the night is come, I will trouble you no longer. I have certain rabbits here, but they are not worth the reading. I will cause these which you have allowed to be printed as soon as I may conveniently.'[601]

This said, we take leave each of other and so departed.

---

71. rabbits: Baldwin's term for the hastily and poorly composed tragedies he received from some would-be contributors (see Prose 21).

A Mirror for Magistrates: 1578 Additions

[Prose 30, First Version]⁶⁰²

When this was said, 'let King Jamie go', said Master Ferrers, 'and return we to our own story and see what broils were among the nobility in the king's minority: how the Cardinal Beaufort maligneth the state of Duke Humphrey, the king's uncle and protector of the realm, and by what drifts
5 he first banisheth his wife from him, and, lastly, how the said duke is murderously made away through conspiracy of Queen Margaret and other – both whose tragedies I have here joined together, for they be notable.' 'That will do very well', said another, 'but take heed ye stay not too long upon them.' 'I warrant you', quoth I,⁶⁰³ 'and, therefore, I would that first
10 of all ye give ear what the duke himself doth say, as followeth':⁶⁰⁴

1. **King Jamie**: James I (d. 1437), king of Scots, the speaker of the previous tragedy in the 1578 *Mirror* (Tragedy 10).
1–2. **our own story**: i.e. English history.

[Prose 30, Second Version]⁶⁰⁵

When this was said, quod one of the company, 'let pass those Scottish matters and return we to our English stories, which minister matter enough of tragedy without seeking or travelling to foreign countries. Therefore, return we to the rest of the tragical troubles and broils which happened in
5 this realm during the minority of King Henry VI, and the sundry falls and overthrows of great princes and other noble persons happening thereby.'

'Well said', quoth Master Ferrers, 'and, as it happeneth, I have here ready penned two notable tragedies, the one of Humphrey, duke of Gloucester, the other of the Duchess Eleanor his wife, which as, me seemeth, be two of
10 the most memorable matters fortuning in that time. But whether of them is first to be placed in the order of our book, I somewhat stand in doubt, for, albeit the said duke's death happened before the decease of the duchess, yet was her fall first, which finally was cause of overthrow to both.'

'Why should you doubt then?', quod the rest of the company. 'For see-
15 ing the cause doth always go before the effect and sequel of anything, it is good reason you should begin with the first. And, therefore, we pray you let us hear first what she hath to say, for all this while we have not heard the complaint of any lady or other woman.'

1–2. **quod**: quoth; **Scottish matters**: i.e. the life and death of James I (d. 1437), king of Scots, the speaker of the previous poem in the 1578 *Mirror* (Tragedy 10).   10. **whether**: which.

How Dame Eleanor Cobham, Duchess of Gloucester, for Practising Witchcraft and Sorcery Suffered Open Penance and After was Banished the Realm into the Isle of Man

If a poor lady, damnèd in exile,
Amongst princes may be allowèd place,
Then, gentle Baldwin, stay thy pen awhile
And of pure pity ponder well my case:
How I, a duchess, destitute of grace,   [5]
Have found by proof, as many have and shall,
The proverb true, that pride will have a fall.⁶⁰⁶

A noble prince, extract of royal blood,
Humphrey sometime Protector of this land,
Of Gloucester duke, for virtue called 'the good'⁶⁰⁷ –   [10]
When I but base beneath his state did stand,
Vouchsafed with me to join in wedlock's band,
Having in court no name of high degree
But Eleanor Cobham as parents left to me.

And though by birth of noble race I was,   [15]
Of barons' blood, yet was I thought unfit
So high to match, yet so it came to pass,
Whether by grace, good fortune, or by wit,
Dame Venus' lures so in mine eyes did sit,
As this great prince, without respect of state,   [20]
Did worthy me to be his wedded mate.⁶⁰⁸

His wife I was and he my true husband,
Though for a while he had the company
Of Lady Jaquet, the duchess of Holland,
Being an heir of ample patrimony,   [25]

---

5. **grace**: favour.   11. **state**: estate, rank.

But that fell out to be no matrimony,
For after war, long suit in law, and strife,
She provèd was the duke of Brabant's wife.⁶⁰⁹

Thus of a damsel a duchess I became,
My state and place advancèd next the queen,   [30]
Whereby me thought I felt no ground but swam,
For in the court mine equal was not seen,
And so possessed with pleasure of the spleen
The sparks of pride so kindled in my breast,
As I in court would shine above the rest.⁶¹⁰   [35]

Such gifts of nature God in me hath graft,
Of shape and stature, with other graces mo,
That by the shot of Cupid's fiery shaft,
Which to the heart of this great prince did go,
This mighty duke with love was linkèd so   [40]
As he, abasing the height of his degree,
Set his whole heart to love and honour me.

Grudge who so would, to him I was most dear
Above all ladies advanced in degree;
The queen except, no princess was my peer   [45]
But gave me place, and lords with cap and knee
Did all honour and reverence unto me.
Thus hoisted high upon the rolling wheel,
I sat so sure me thought I could not reel,

And weening least that fortune hath a turn,   [50]
I looked aloft and would not look a-low,
The brands of pride so in my breast did burn
As the hot sparks burst forth in open show,
And more and more the fire began to glow
Without quenching and daily did increase,   [55]
Till Fortune's blasts with shame did make it cease,

For, as 'tis said, pride passeth on afore
And shame follows for just reward and meed.

---

33. **pleasure of the spleen**: amusement, delight (the spleen was understood to be the producer of laughter and mirth).   48. **wheel**: the wheel of Fortune.   56. **blasts**: blasts of wind; pernicious actions.

Would God ladies, both now and evermore,
Of my hard hap which shall the story read   [60]
Would bear in mind and trust it as their creed,
That pride of heart is a most hateful vice
And lowliness a pearl of passing price,[611]

Namely in queens and ladies of estate,
Within whose minds all meekness should abound,   [65]
Since high disdain doth always purchase hate,
Being a vice that most part doth redound
To their reproach in whom the same is found,
And seldom gets good favour or good fame
But is, at last, knit up with worldly shame.   [70]

The proof whereof I found most true indeed,
That pride afore hath shame to wait behind.
Let no man doubt, in whom this vice doth breed
But shame for pride by justice is assigned,
Which well I found, for truly, in my mind,   [75]
Was never none whom pride did more inflame,
Nor never none receivèd greater shame,

For not content to be a duchess great,
I longèd sore to bear the name of queen,
Aspiring still unto a higher seat   [80]
And with that hope myself did overween,
Since there was none which that time was between
Henry the king and my good duke his eme,
Heir to the crown and kingdom of this realm.[612]

So near to be was cause of my vain hope   [85]
And long await when this fair hap would fall.
My studies all were tending to that scope;
Alas the while!, to counsel I did call
Such as would seem by skill conjectural
Of art magic and wicked sorcery   [90]
To deem and divine the prince's destiny,[613]

---

60. **hap**: lot, fortune. 63. **lowliness**: humility; **passing**: surpassing. 67. **redound**: contribute greatly. 72. **wait**: attend. 74. **But**: nought but. 81. **did overween**: think too highly. 83. **eme**: uncle. 89. **skill conjectural**: skill in interpreting signs and making prognostications.

Among which sort of those that bare most fame,
There was a beldame called the witch of Eye,
Old Mother Madge her neighbours did her name,
Which wrought wonders in countries. By hearsay, [95]
Both fiends and fairies her charming would obey,
And dead corpses from grave she could uprear;
Such an enchantress as that time had no peer.⁶¹⁴

Two priests also, the one hight Bolingbroke,
The other Southwell, great clerks in conjuration: [100]
These two chaplains were they that undertook
To cast and calk the king's constellation
And then to judge by deep divination
Of things to come and who should next succeed
To England's crown, all this was true indeed.⁶¹⁵ [105]

And further sure they never did proceed,
Though I confess that this attempt was ill.
But for my part, for anything indeed
Wrought or else thought by any kind of skill,
God is my judge I never had the will [110]
By any enchantment, sorcery or charm
Or otherwise to work my prince's harm.⁶¹⁶

Yet, nonetheless, when this case came to light,
By secret spies to Caiphas our cardinal,
Who long in heart had borne a privy spite [115]
To my good duke, his nephew natural,
Glad of the chance so fitly forth to fall
His long-hid hate with justice to colour,
Usèd this case with most extreme rigour,⁶¹⁷

And causèd me with my complices all [120]
To be cited by process peremptory,
Before judges, in place judicial,

---

93. **Eye**: Ebury, a village near Westminster.   95. **countries**: rural areas.   100. **clerks**: scholars.   101. **chaplains**: chapel priests, often used specifically for those who minister privately to high-ranking persons.   102. **calk the king's constellation**: reckon astrologically the position of the heavenly bodies at Henry VI's birth (the 'stars' which were believed to influence the course of his life).   114. **Caiphas**: Caiaphas, the high priest who antagonized Christ and urged that he be turned over to the Roman authorities for execution; **our cardinal**: Cardinal Henry Beaufort (d. 1447). 116. **natural**: by nature (but not by law, since Beaufort was born a bastard).   121. **cited**: ordered to appear; **process peremptory**: summons that allows no resistance or delay.

Whereas Caiphas, sitting in his glory,
Would not allow my answer dilatory,
Ne doctor or proctor to allege the laws   [125]
But forcèd me to plead in mine own cause.[618]

The king's counsel were callèd to the case,
My husband then shut out for the season,
In whose absence I found but little grace,
For lawyers turned our offence to treason.   [130]
And so with rigour, without ruth or reason,
Sentence was given that I for the same
Should do penance and suffer open shame.[619]

Nay, the like shame had never wight I ween –
Duchess, lady, ne damsel of degree –   [135]
As I that was a princess next the queen,
Wife to a prince, and none so great as he,
A king's uncle, Protector of his country,
With taper burning, shrouded in a sheet,
Three days a row to pass in open street   [140]

Bare legg'd and bare foot, to all the world's wonder,[620]
Yea, and as though such shame did not suffice,
With more despite then to part asunder
Me and my duke, which traitors did devise
By statute law in most unlawful wise,   [145]
First sending me with shame into exile,
Then murd'ring him by treachery and guile.[621]

Yea, and besides this cruel banishment –
Far from all friends to comfort me in care –
And husband's death, there was by parliament   [150]
Ordained for me a mess of coarser fare.
For they to bring me to beggar's state most bare,
By the same act from me did then withdraw
Such right of dower as widows have by law.[622]

---

124. answer dilatory: plea to delay legal proceedings. **125. Ne doctor or proctor**: Neither a doctor of laws nor a canon-law attorney; **allege the laws**: cite the law as an authority (on Eleanor's behalf). **128. for the season**: for this occasion. **136. princess**: wife of a prince (Duke Humphrey was the son of a king, Henry IV). **145. devise**: separate; order. **151. mess**: meal. **154. dower**: the portion of a husband's estate that the law allows to be enjoyed by his widow during her lifetime.

Death, as 'tis said, doth set all things at rest, [155]
Which fell not so in mine unhappy case,
For since my death, mine en'mies made a jest
In minstrels' rhyme, mine honour to deface,
And then to bring my name in more disgrace,
A song was made in manner of a lay [160]
Which old wives sing of me unto this day.⁶²³

Yet with these spites their malice did not end,
For shortly after, my sorrows to renew,
My loyal lord, which never did offend,
Was called in haste, the cause he little knew, [165]
To a parliament, without summons due,
Whereas his death was cruelly contrived,
And I, his wife, of earthly joys deprived.⁶²⁴

For all the while my duke had life and breath,
So long I stood in hope of my restore, [170]
But when I heard of his most causeless death,
Then the best salve for my recureless sore
Was to despair of cure for evermore
And, as I could, my careful heart to cure
With patìence most painful to endure. [175]

Oh traitors fell, which in your hearts could find
Like fiends of hell the guiltless to betray!
But ye chiefly his kinsmen most unkind,
Which gave consent to make him so away
That unto God with all my heart I pray [180]
Vengeance may light on him that causèd all:
Beaufort, I mean, that cursèd cardinal,⁶²⁵

Which bastard priest of the house of Lancaster,
Son to Duke John, surnamèd John of Gaunt,
Was first create bishop of Winchester, [185]
For no learning whereof he might well vaunt
Ne for virtue, which he did never haunt,

---

158. minstrels' rhyme: likely tail rhyme, a stanza form frequently employed by medieval minstrels for narrative verse.   **172. recureless**: incurable.   **184. Duke John**: John of Gaunt (d. 1399), first duke of Lancaster; **surnamed**: also called.

But for his gold and sums that were not small
Paid to the pope, was made a cardinal.[626]

Proud Lucifer, which from the heavens on high   [190]
Down to the pit of hell below was cast,
And, being once an angel bright in sky,
For his high pride in hell is chainèd fast
In deep darkness that evermore shall last,
More haut of heart was not before his fall   [195]
Than was this proud and pompous cardinal,

Whose life, good Baldwin, paint out in his pickle,
And blaze this Baal and belly-god most blind
An hypocrite, all faithless and fickle,
A wicked wretch, a kinsmen most unkind,   [200]
A devil incarnate, all devilishly inclined,
And, to discharge my conscience all at once,
The devil him gnaw both body, blood, and bones![627]

The spiteful priest would needs make me a witch,
As would to God I had been for his sake!   [205]
I would have clawed him where he did not itch;
I would have played the Lady of the Lake
And, as Merlin was, closed him in a brake,
Yea, a meridian to lull him by daylight
And a nightmare to ride on him by night.[628]   [210]

The fiery fiends with fevers hot and frenzy,
The airy hags with stench and carrion savours,
The watery ghosts with gouts and with dropsy,
The earthly goblins with aches at all hours,
Furies and fairies with all infernal powers   [215]
I would have stirred from the dark dungeon
Of hell centre, as deep as Demogorgon.

---

197. pickle: condition, situation. **198. blaze:** describe; **belly-god:** glutton. **200. unkind:** unnatural; cruel.
207. Lady of the Lake: Nyneve (or Nymue), the chief Lady of the Lake in Sir Thomas Malory's *Le Morte d'Arthur*.
208. brake: cage; trap. **209. meridian:** midday nap. **210. nightmare:** female spirit said to alight on sleepers
and to cause feelings of suffocation and distress. **211. frenzy:** crazy. **212. hags:** evil spirits in female form.
217. Demogorgon: a mythological god or demon of the underworld.

Or had I now the skill of Dame Erichto,
Whose dreadful charms, as Lucan doth express,
All fiends did fear, so far forth as Prince Pluto   [220]
Was at her call for dread of more distress,[629]
Then would I send of hellhounds more and less
A legion at least at him to cry and yell,
And with that chirm harry him down to hell,

Which neèd not, for sure I think that he   [225]
Who here in earth leads Epicurus' life
As far from God as possible may be,
With whom all sin and vices are most rife,
Using at will both widow, maid, and wife,
But that some devil his body doth possess: [230]
His life is such, as men can judge no less.

And God forgive my wrath and wreakful mind,
Such is my hate to that most wicked wretch;
Die when he shall, in heart I could well find
Out of the grave his corpse again to fetch   [235]
And rack his limbs as long as they would stretch,
And take delight to listen every day,
How he could sing a mass of 'wellaway'!

The Isle of Man was the appointed place
To penance me forever in exile.   [240]
Thither in haste they posted me apace
And, doubting scape, they pinned me in a pile
Close by myself in care, alas the while!
There felt I first poor prisoner's hungry fare:
Much want, things scant, and stone walls hard and bare.[630]   [245]

The change was strange, from silk and cloth of gold
To rugged frieze my carcass for to clothe,
From princes' fare and dainties hot and cold

---

223. **A legion**: A multitude. **224. chirm**: noise, din. **226. Epicurus' life**: a life devoted to personal indulgence. **232. wreakful**: vengeful. **240. to penance**: to punish; to impose a penance on. **241. they posted me apace**: they swiftly dispatched me. **242. doubting scape**: fearing I might escape; **pinned me in a pile**: imprisoned me in a stronghold.

To rotten fish and meats that one would loathe.
The diet and dressing were much alike both,   [250]
Bedding and lodging were all alike fine:
Such down it was, as servèd well for swine.

Neither do I mine own case thus complain,
Which I confess came partly by desert.
The only cause which doubleth all my pain,   [255]
And that which most near goeth now unto my heart,
Is that my fault did finally revert
To him that was least guilty of the same,
Whose death it was, though I abode the shame.⁶³¹

Whose fatal fall when I do call to mind,   [260]
And how by me his mischief first began,
So oft I cry on fortune most unkind,
And my mishap most bitterly do ban
That ever I to such a noble man,
Who from my crime was innocent and clear,   [265]
Should be a cause to buy his love so dear.

Oh, to my heart how grievous is the wound,
Calling to mind this dismal, deadly case!
I would I had been dolven underground,
When he first saw or lookèd on my face,   [270]
Or took delight in any kind of grace
Seeming in me that did him stir or move
To fancy me or set his heart to love.

Farewell Greenwich, my palace of delight,
Where I was wont to see the crystal streams   [275]
Of royal Thames, most pleasant to my sight!
And farewell Kent, right famous in all realms,
A thousand times I mind you in my dreams
And, when I wake, most grief it is to me
That never more again I shall see you.⁶³²   [280]

---

250. **dressing**: clothing; items of culinary seasoning, such as a sauce.   257. **revert**: return.   263. **ban**: curse.
266. **so dear**: at such a high cost.   269. **dolven**: buried.   274. **Greenwich**: Humphrey and Eleanor's palace
Plesaunce in Greenwich, Kent (now London).

In the night time when I should take my rest,
I weep, I wail, I wet my bed with tears
And, when dead sleep my spirits hath oppressed,
Troubled with dreams I fantasy vain fears.
Mine husband's voice then ringeth at mine ears   [285]
Crying for help, 'Oh, save me from the death!
These villains here do seek to stop my breath!'

Yea, and sometimes methinks his dreary ghost
Appears in sight and shows me in what wise
Those fell tyrants with torments had embossed   [290]
His wind and breath to abuse people's eyes,
So as no doubt or question should arise
Among rude folk which little understand
But that his death came only by God's hand.

I plain in vain, where ears be none to hear   [295]
But roaring seas and blust'ring of the wind,
And of redress am ne'er a whit the near
But with waste words to feed my mournful mind,
Wishing full oft, the Parcas had untwined
My vital strings, or Atropos with knife   [300]
Had cut the line of my most wretched life.[633]

Oh that Neptune and Aeolus also,
Th'one god of seas, the other of weather,
Ere mine arrival into that isle of woe
Had sunk the ship wherein I sailed thither   [305]
(The shipmen saved), so as I together
With my good duke mought have been dead afore
Fortune had wroken her wrath on us so sore,

Or else that God, when my first passage was
Into exile along Saint Albans town,   [310]
Had never let me further for to pass
But in the street with death had struck me down.

289. **wise**: manner.   290. **embossed**: made short (apparently an unusual use of **emboss**: to run a hunted animal until it is desperately short of breath or foaming from the mouth from exhaustion).   299. **Parcas**: Parcae, the three Fates of Roman mythology.   300. **vital strings**: the natural cords (ligaments, nerves) that compose a human body; **Atropos**: one of the three Fates who in mythology draw out (and eventually cut off) the thread that determines an individual's lifespan.   307. **mought**: might.   308. **wroken**: wreaked.   310. **along**: by way of.

Then had I sped of my desired boon,
That my poor corpse mought there have lyen with his
Both in one grave, and so have gone to bliss.[634]   [315]

But I – alas, the greater is my grief! –
Am passed that hope to have my sepulchre
Near unto him, which was to me most lief,
But in an isle and country most obscure
To pine in pain, whilst my poor life will dure,   [320]
And, being dead, all honourless to lie
In simple grave, as other poor that die.[635]

My tale is told and time it is to cease
Of troubles past, all which have had their end.
My grave, I trust, shall purchase me good peace   [325]
In such a world where no wight doth contend
For highest place, whereto all flesh shall wend.
And so I end, using one word for all,
As I begin, that pride will have a fall.[636]

FINIS, quod G. F.

---

313. **sped of**: achieved.   318. **lief**: beloved.   328. **word**: statement.

[Prose 31, 1578 Cancel Edition]

'Surely', said one of the company, 'this lady hath done much to move
the hearers to pity her and hath very well knit up the end of her tragedy
according to the beginning, but I marvel much where she learned all this
poetry touched in her tale, for in her days learning was not common but a
rare thing, namely in women.' 'Yes', quod Master Ferrers, 'that might she
very well learn of the duke her husband, who was a prince so excellently
learned as the like of his degree was nowhere to be found, and not only so,
but was also a patron to poets and orators much like as Maecenas was in the
time of Augustus Caesar. This duke was founder of the divinity school in
Oxford, whereas he caused Aristotle's works to be translated out of Greek
into Latin and caused many other things to be done for advancement of

---

8. **Maecenas**: Gaius Maecenas (d. 8 BC), patron of Virgil and other Roman poets.

learning, having always learned men near about him.[637] No marvel, therefore, though the duchess brought some piece away.'

15   'Methinks', quod another, 'she passeth bounds of a lady's modesty to in-
veigh so cruelly against the Cardinal Beaufort.' 'Not a whit', quod another,
'having such cause as she had, and somewhat ye must bear with wom-
en's passions. Therefore, leave we her to eternal rest, and let us hear what
Master Ferrers will say for the duke her husband, whose case was the more
lamentable, in that he suffered without cause. And, surely, though the
20   Cardinal against nature was the duke's mortal foe,[638] yet the chief causers of
his confusion was the queen and William de la Pole, earl of Suffolk and afterwards duke, whose counsel was chiefly followed in the contriving of this
noble man's destruction: she through ambition to have sovereignty and
rule, and he through flattery to purchase honour and promotion, which
25   as he in short time obtained, so in as short time he lost again and his life
withal by the just judgement of God, receiving such measure as he before
mete to this good prince. This drift of his turned to the utter overthrow of
the king himself, the queen his wife, and Edward their son, a most goodly
prince, and to the subversion of the whole house of Lancaster, as you may
30   see at large in the chronicles.[639] But now, let us hear what the duke will say.'

---

13. **though**: if. **15**. **Cardinal Beaufort**: Henry Beaufort (d. 1447), cardinal and bishop of Winchester.
28. **Edward**: Edward (d. 1471), Lancastrian Prince of Wales.

How Humphrey Plantagenet, Duke of Gloucester, Protector of
England During the Minority of his Nephew King Henry the
Sixth, Commonly Called the good Duke, by the Practice of his
Enemies was Brought to Confusion[640]

As highest hills with tempests been most touched,
And tops of trees most subject unto wind,
And as great towers with stone strongly couched
Have heavy falls when they be undermined,
Even so, by proof, in worldly things we find   [5]
That such as climb the top of high degree
From peril of falling never can be free.

To prove this true, good Baldwin, hearken hither,
See and behold me, unhappy Humphrey,
England's Protector and duke of Gloucester,   [10]
Who, in the time of the sixth King Henry,
Rulèd this realm yearès mo than twenty.[641]
Note well the cause of my decay and fall
And make a mirror for magistrates all

In their most weal to beware of unhap   [15]
And not to sleep in slumb'ring sickerness,
Whilst Fortune false doth lull them in her lap,
Drownèd in dreams of brittle blessedness,
But then to fear her freaks and fickleness,
Accompting still the higher they ascend   [20]
More nigh to be to danger in the end,

And that vain trust in blood or royal race
Abuse them not with careless assurance
To trust Fortune but, weighing well my case,

---

1. **been**: are. 3. **couched**: laid in place. 9. **unhappy**: unfortunate. 15. **most weal**: greatest happiness; **unhap**: misfortune. 16. **sickerness**: sense of security. 19. **freaks**: sudden changes of mind. 20. **Accompting still**: Ever considering.

When she most smileth, to have in remembrance [25]
My sudden fall, who, in all appearance
Having most stays which man in state maintain,
Have found the same untrusty and most vain.

Better than I none may the same affirm,
Who, trusting all in height of high estate, [30]
Led by the ears with false flattery's chirm,
Which never prince could banish from his gate,
Did little think on such a sudden mate,
Not heeding, less dreading, all unaware,
By foes least feared was trapped into a snare. [35]

If noble birth or high authority,
Number of friends, kindred or alliance,
If wisdom, learning or worldly policy
Mought have been stayers to Fortune's variance,
None stood more strong in worldly countenance, [40]
For all these helps had I to avail me
And yet, in fine, all the same did fail me.

Of King Henry the Fourth, fourth son I was,
Brother to King Henry the fifth of that name,
And uncle to Henry the Sixth but, alas, [45]
What cause had I to presume on the same
Or, for vainglory advancing my fame,
Myself to call in records and writings
The son, brother and uncle unto kings?

This was my boast, which lastly was my bane, [50]
Yet not this boast was it that brought me down.
The very cause which made my weal to wane,
So near of kin that I was to the crown:
That was the rock that made my ship to drown.
A rule there is not failing but most sure: [55]
Kingdom no kin doth know ne can endure.

---

27. **stays**: supports. 31. **chirm**: chatter. 33. **mate**: checkmate, defeat. 38. **policy**: shrewdness; political prudence. 39. **Mought**: Might. 40. **countenance**: estimation, credit. 42. **in fine**: in the end.

For after my brother the fifth Henry
Won by conquest the royal realm of France
And of two kingdoms made one monarchy,
Before his death, for better obeisance   [60]
To his young son, not ripe to governance,
Protector of England I was by testament
And John my brother in France made regent,⁶⁴²

To whom if God had lent a longer life
Our house to have kept from storms of inward strife,   [65]
Or it had been the Lord Almighty's will,
Plantagenet's name in state had standen still,
But deadly discord, which kingdoms great doth spill,
Bred by desire of high domination,
Brought our whole house to plain desolation.   [70]

It is for truth in an history found
That Henry Plantagenet, first of our name,⁶⁴³
Who callèd was King Henry the Second,
Son of Dame Maud, the empress of high fame,
Would oft report that his ancient grandam,   [75]
Through seeming in shape a woman natural
Was a fiend of the kind that *succubae* some call.⁶⁴⁴

Which old fable, so long time told before,
When the king's sons against him did rebel,⁶⁴⁵
He called to mind and, being grievèd sore,   [80]
'Lo!, now', quoth he, 'I see and prove full well
The story true, which folk of old did tell,
That from the devil descended all our race,
And now my children do verify the case.'⁶⁴⁶

Whereof to leave a long memorial   [85]
In mind of man evermore to rest,
A picture he made and hung it in his hall
Of a pelican sitting on his nest

---

62. testament: formal declaration (not necessarily in writing) of a dying person's wishes for his or her property; a will.   **63. John my brother**: John (d. 1435), first duke of Bedford.   **67. Plantagenet's ... still**: The Plantagenet name would have remained in high place.   **74. Maud**: Maud (or Matilda) of England (d. 1167), wife first of Emperor Heinrich V and then of Count Geoffrey of Anjou.   **75. ancient grandam**: female ancestor from long past.   **77. succubae**: Latin plural of *succuba*; demons in female form that were said to have sexual intercourse with sleeping men.

With four young birds, three pecking at his breast
With bloody beaks and, further, did devise [90]
The youngest bird to peck the father's eyes.[647]

Meaning hereby his rebel children three,
Henry and Richard, who beat him on the breast
(Geoffrey only from that offence was free).[648]
Henry died of England's crown possessed; [95]
Richard lived his father to molest;
John the youngest pecked still his father's eye,
Whose deeds unkind the sooner made him die.[649]

This king, some write, in his sickness last
Said, as it were by way of prophecy, [100]
How that the devil a darnel grain had cast
Among his kin to increase enmity,
Which should remain in their posterity
Till mischief and murder had spent them all,
Not leaving one to piss against the wall.[650] [105]

And yet from him in order did succeed
In England here of crownèd kings fourteen
Of that surname and of that line and seed,
With dukes and earls and many a noble queen,
The number such as all the world would ween [110]
So many imps could never so be spent
But some heir male should be of that descent.

Which to be true, if any stand in doubt,
Because I mean not further to digress,
Let him peruse the stories throughout [115]
Of English kings whom practice did oppress,
And he shall find the cause of their distress
From first to last unkindly to begin
Always by those that next were of the kin.

Was not Richard, of whom I spake before, [120]
A rebel plain until his father died,

---

113. Which: evidently a reference to the prophecy of lines 101–5.   **118. unkindly**: unnaturally, cruelly.

And John likewise an en'my evermore
To Richard again and for a rebel tried?[651]
After whose death, it cannot be denied,
Against all right this John most cruelly   [125]
His brother's children causèd for to die,

Arthur and Isabel, I mean, that were
Geoffrey's children, then duke of Britaine,
Henry's third son, by one degree more near
Than was this John, as stories show most plain,   [130]
Which two children were famished or else slain
By John their eme, called *Sans-terre* by name,
Of whose foul act all countries speak great shame.[652]

Edward and Richard, second both by name,
Kings of this land, fell down by fatal fate.   [135]
What was the cause that princes of such fame
Did leese at last their honour, life, and state?
Nothing at all but discord and debate,
Which when it haps in kindred or in blood,
Erynis' rage was never half so wood.[653]   [140]

Be sure, therefore, ye kings and princes all,
That concord in kingdoms is chief assurance
And that your families do never fall,
But where discord doth lead the doubtful dance
With busy brawls and turns of variance,   [145]
Where malice is minstrel, the pipe ill report,
The masque mischief, and so ends the sport.

But now to come to my purpose again,
Whilst I my charge applied in England,
My brother in France long time did remain.   [150]
Cardinal Beaufort took proudly in hand
In causes public against me to stand,
Who of great malice so much as he might
Sought in all things to do me despite.[654]

123. **for a rebel tried**: submitted to judgement on a charge of rebellion.   128. **Britaine**: Brittany.   132. **eme**: uncle; *Sans-terre*: the French version of Prince John's familiar cognomen 'Lackland'.   137. **leese**: lose.   139. **haps**: chances. 140. **Erynis' rage**: A fury's rage; the rage of Erynis, a vengeful goddess in some Roman writings.   146. **the pipe ill report**: the (metaphoric) musical instrument is slander, ill repute.   147. **The masque mischief**: The entertainment is evil-doing, injury; **sport**: entertainment.

Which proud prelate to me was bastard eme, [155]
Son to Duke John of Gaunt, as they did feign,[655]
Who, being made high chancellor of the realm,
Not like a priest but like a prince did reign,
Nothing wanting which might his pride maintain.
Bishop besides of Winchester he was, [160]
And cardinal of Rome, which angels brought to pass.

Not God's angels but angels of old gold
Lift him aloft, in whom no cause there was
By just desert so high to be extolled
(Riches except), whereby this golden ass [165]
At home and abroad all matters brought to pass,
Namely at Rome, having no mean but that
To purchase there his crimson cardinal hat.

Which thing the king my father him forbad,
Plainly saying that he could not abide [170]
Within his realm a subject to be had
His prince's peer, yet such was this man's pride
That he forthwith, after my father died,
The king then young, obtainèd of the pope
That honour high, which erst he could not hope.[656] [175]

Whose proud attempts, because that I withstood,
My bounden duty the better to acquite,
This holy father waxèd well near wood,
Of mere malice devising day and night
To work to me dishonour and despite, [180]
Whereby there fell between us such a jar,
As in this land was like a civil war.

My brother John, which lay this while in France,
Heard of this hurl and passed the seas in haste,
By whose travail this troublesome distance [185]
Ceased for a while, but netheless in waste,
For rooted hate will hardly be displaced

---

156. feign: make out, fable. **161. angels**: English coins worth about 10 shillings each in the mid-Tudor period. **165. golden ass**: wealthy fool, with a reference to the ancient Roman author Apuleius's famous prose narrative *The Golden Ass*. **171. to be had**: to be brought into the state of. **177. acquite**: fulfil. **184. hurl**: strife. **185. distance**: dissension. **186. netheless**: nevertheless. **187. hardly**: not easily.

Out of high hearts and namely where debate
Happeneth amongst great persons of estate.[657]

For like as a match doth lie and smoulder   [190]
Long time before it commeth to the train,
But yet when fire hath caught in the poulder,
No art is able the flames to restrain,
Even so the sparks of envy and disdain
Out of the smoke burst forth in such a flame   [195]
That France and England yet may rue the same.

So when of two realms the regiment royal
Between brothers was parted equally,
One placed in France for affairs martial
And I at home for civil policy,   [200]
To serve the state we both did so apply
As honour and fame to both did increase:
To him for the war, to me for the peace.

Whence envy sprang and specially because
This proud prelate could not abide a peer   [205]
Within the land to rule the state by laws,
Wherefore, sifting my life and acts most near,
He never ceased until, as you shall hear,
By practice foul of him and his allies
My death was wrought in most unworthy wise.[658]   [210]

And first he sought my doings to defame
By rumours false, which he and his did sow:
Letters and bills to my reproach and shame
He did devise and all about bestow,
Whereby my troth in doubt should daily grow,   [215]
In England first and afterward in France,
Moving all means to bring me to mischance.[659]

One quarrel was that where by common law
Murder and theft been punished all alike,

---

190. **match**: fuse.   191. **train**: line of gunpowder.   192. **poulder**: gunpowder.

So as manslears, which bloody blades do draw, [220]
Suffer no more than he that doth but pick.
Me thought the same no order politic
In setting pains to make no difference
Between the lesser and greater offence.

I, being seen somewhat in civil law, [225]
The rules thereof reputed much better,
Wherefore to keep offenders more in awe
Like as the fault was smaller or greater,
So set I pains more easier or bitter,
Weighing the quality of every offence [230]
And so according prounounced sentence.⁶⁶⁰

Amongst my other *delicta juventutis,*
Whilst rage of youth my reason did subdue,
I must confess as the very truth is,
Driven by desire fond fancies to ensue, [235]
A thing I did whereof great trouble grew,
Abusing one to my no small rebuke,
Which wife was then to John of Brabant, duke.

Callèd she was Lady Jaquet the Fair,
Delightful in love like Helen of Troy, [240]
To the duke of Bavier sole daughter and heir.
Her did I marry to my great annoy,
Yet, for a time, this dame I did enjoy
With her whole lands, withholding them by force,
Till Martin the pope between us made divorce.⁶⁶¹ [245]

Yet all these blasts not able were to move
The anchor strong, whereby my ship did stay;
Some other shift to seek him did behove,
Whereto ere long ill fortune made the way,
Which finally was cause of my decay [250]
And cruel death, contrivèd by my foes,
Which fell out thus, as now I shall disclose.

---

220. **manslears**: man-slayers, murderers.   221. **pick**: steal.   222. **politic**: judicious, sensible.   225. **seen**: versed.
232. ***delicta juventutis***: youthful offences.   235. **ensue**: follow.   241. **Bavier**: Bavaria.

Eleanor my wife, my duchess only dear,
I know not how, but as the nature is
Of women all, ay curious to enquire   [255]
Of things to come (though I confess in this
Her fault not small and that she did amiss),
By witches' skill, which sorcery some call,
Would know of things which after should befall.⁶⁶²

And for that cause made herself acquainted   [260]
With Mother Madge, called the witch of Eye,
And with a clerk that after was attainted
(Bolingbroke he hight) that learnèd was that way,
With other mo, which famous were that day,
As well in science, called mathematical,   [265]
As also in magic and skill supernatural.

These cunning folks she set on work to know
The time how long the king should live and reign,
Some by the stars and some by devils below,
Some by witchcraft sought knowledge to attain   [270]
With like fancies, frivolous, fond, and vain,
Whereof, though I knew least of any man,
Yet by that mean my mischief first began.⁶⁶³

Yet besides this there was a greater thing,
How she in wax by counsel of the witch   [275]
An image made, crownèd like a king,
With sword in hand, in shape and likeness such
As was the king, which daily they did pitch
Against a fire, that as the wax did melt
So should his life consume away unfelt.⁶⁶⁴   [280]

My duchess thus accusèd of this crime
As she that should such practice first begin,
My part was then to yield unto the time,
Giving her leave to deal alone therein.
And since the cause concernèd deadly sin   [285]

255. ay: ever.   261. Mother: used here as a term of address for an elderly woman; Madge: the reputed witch Margery Jourdemayne (d. 1441).   262. attainted: condemned.   265. mathematical: astrological.

Which to the clergy only doth pertain,
To deal therein I plainly did refrain[665]

And suffered them her person to accite
Into their courts to answer and appear,
Which to my heart was sure the greatest spite   [290]
That could be wrought and touchèd me most near,
To see my wife, my lady lief and dear,
To my reproach and plain before my face
Entreated so, as one of sort most base.

The clergy, then examining her cause,   [295]
Convincèd her as guilty in the same
And sentence gave according to their laws
That she and they whom I before did name
Should suffer death or else some open shame,
Of which penance my wife by sentence had   [300]
To suffer shame – of both the two more bad.

And first she must by days together three
Through London streets pass all along in sight
Barelegg'd and barefoot that all the world might see,
Bearing in hand a burning taper bright   [305]
And, not content with this extreme despite,
To work me woe, in all they may or can,
Exiled she was into the Isle of Man.[666]

This heinous crime and open worldly shame,
With such rigour showed unto my wife,   [310]
Was a fine fetch further things to frame
And nothing else but a preparative
First from office and finally from life
Me to deprive and, so passing further
What law could not, to execute by murder,   [315]

Which by sly drifts and windlasses aloof
They brought about, persuading first the queen

288. **accite**: summon.   **292. lief**: beloved.   **296. Convinced**: Convicted.   **301. of both the two more bad**: the worst of the two.   **311. fetch**: contrivance, trick.   **316. windlasses aloof**: round-about actions performed at a distance or apart (from their victim Humphrey).

That in effect it was the king's reproof
And hers also to be exempted clean
From princely rule, or that it should be seen   [320]
A king of years still governèd to be
Like a pupil that nothing could foresee.[667]

The danger more, considering the king
Was without child, I being his next heir
To rule the realm as prince in everything   [325]
Without restraint and all the sway to bear
With people's love, whereby it was to fear
That my haut heart, unbridled in desire,
Time would prevent and to the crown aspire.[668]

These with such like were put into her head,   [330]
Who, of herself, was thereto soon inclined.
Other there were that this ill humour fed,
To neither part which had good will or mind:
The duke of York, our cousin most unkind,
Who, keeping close a title to the crown,   [335]
Lancaster's house did labour to pull down.[669]

The stay whereof he took to stand in me,
Seeing the king of courage nothing stout,
Neither of wit great peril to foresee.
So, for purpose, if he could bring about   [340]
Me to displace, then did he little doubt
To gain the goal for which he drove the ball:
The crown I mean, to catch ere it should fall.

This hope made him against me to conspire
With those which foes were to each other late.   [345]
The queen did ween to win her whole desire,
Which was to rule the king and all the state
If I were rid, whom therefore she did hate,
Forecasting not, when that was brought to pass,
How weak of friends the king her husband was.   [350]

328–9: That … aspire: My haughty heart, unchecked in its desire, would lead me to act as if the time of King Henry's death had already come and spur me to seek the crown. **334. unkind:** wicked, unnatural. **340. for purpose:** for his ultimate intention. **342. for which he drove the ball:** for which he aimed (a turn of phrase derived from the medieval game of football).

The dukès two, of Exeter and Buckingham,
With the Marquis Dorset therein did agree,
But namely the marquis of Suffolk, William,
Contriver chief of this conspiracy,
With other mo that sat still and did see [355]
Their mortal foes on me to whet their knives,
Which turned at last to loss of all their lives.[670]

But vain desire of sovereignty and rule,
Which otherwise ambition hath to name,
So stirred the queen that, wilful as a mule, [360]
Headlong she runs from smoke into the flame,
Driving a drift, which after did so frame
As she, the king, with all their line and race,
Deprivèd were of honour, life and place.[671]

So for purpose she thought it very good [365]
With former foes in friendship to confeder;
The duke of York and other of his blood
With Nevilles all knit were then together,
And de la Pole, friend afore to neither.
The cardinal also came within this list, [370]
As Herod and Pilate to judge Jesu Christ.[672]

This cursèd league too late discovered was
By Bayards blind, that, linkèd in the line,
The queen and cardinal brought it so to pass,
With Marquis Suffolk, master of this mine, [375]
Whose ill advice was counted very fine,
With other mo which finely could disguise
With false visors my mischief to devise.

Concluding thus, they point without delay
Parliament to hold in some unhaunted place [380]
Far from London, out of the common way,
Where few or none should understand the case
But whom the queen and cardinal did embrace,

---

352. Marquis: Marquess.   **366. confeder**: ally.   **373. Bayards blind**: 'blind as Bayard' was a proverbial expression that could denote someone ignorant of the true circumstances surrounding him or her.   **375. mine**: act designed to undermine.   **378. visors**: masks; outward appearances.   **379. point**: appoint, fix.

And so for place they chose St. Edmundsbury,
Since when, some say, England was never merry.[673]   [385]

Summons was sent this company to call,
Which made me muse that in so great a case
I should no whit of counsel be at all,
Who yet had rule and next the king in place;
Me thought nothing my state could more disgrace   [390]
Than to bear name and in effect to be
A cipher in algrim, as all men mought see.

And though just cause I had for to suspect
The time and place appointed by my foes,
And that my friends most plainly did detect   [395]
The subtle train and practice of all those
Which against me great treasons did suppose,
Yet trust of truth, with a conscìence clear,
Gave me good heart, in that place to appear.[674]

Upon which trust, with more haste than good speed,   [400]
Forward I went to that unlucky place,
Duty to show and no whit was in dread
Of any train but bold to show my face
As a true man, yet so fell out the case
That after travail, seeking for repose,   [405]
An armèd band my lodging did enclose.

The Viscount Beaumont, who for the time supplied
The office of high constable of the land,
Was with the queen and cardinal allied,
By whose support he stoutly took in hand   [410]
My lodging to enter with an armèd band
And for high treason my person did arrest
And laid me that night where him seemèd best.[675]

Then shaking and quaking for dread of a dream,
Half waked, all naked in bed as I lay,   [415]

---

392. cipher in algrim: a zero in algorism (the decimal system of numbering); the phrase was a byword for a person of no consequence.   **396. train:** trickery.   **397. suppose:** allege.   **403. train:** treachery.

What time strake the chime of mine hour extreme.
Oppressed was my rest with mortal affray;
My foes did unclose, I know not which way,
My chamber doors and boldly they in brake
And had me fast before I could awake.   [420]

Thou lookest now that of my secret murder
I should at large the manner how declare.
I pray thee, Baldwin, ask of me no further,
For speaking plain, it came so at unware
As I myself, which caught was in the snare,   [425]
Scarcely am able the circumstance to show,
Which was kept close and known but unto few.

But be thou sure by violence it was
And no whit bred by sickness or disease
That felt it well before my life did pass,   [430]
For when these wolves my body once did seize,
Usèd I was but smally to mine ease,
With torments strong, which went so near the quick
As made me die before that I was sick.

A palsy, they said, my vital sprites oppressed,   [435]
Bred by excess of melancholy black.
This for excuse to lay them seemèd best,
Lest my true friends the cause might further rack
And so perhaps discover the whole pack
Of the conspirers, whom they might well suspect   [440]
For causes great, which after took effect.

Dead was I found by such as best did know
The manner how the same was brought to pass,
And then my corpse was set out for a show
By view whereof nothing perceivèd was,   [445]
Whereby the world may see as in a glass
The unsure state of them that stand most high,
Which then dread least when danger is most nigh.[676]

---

416. **What ... extreme**: When the chime marking my last hour struck.   417. **affray**: terror.   433. **the quick**: the central part of someone's being.   436. **melancholy black**: deep sadness; the humour black bile, believed to cause melancholy.

And also see what danger they live in
Which next their king are to succeed in place,　　　　　[450]
Since kings, most part, be jealous of their kin,
Whom I advise, forewarnèd by my case,
To bear low sail and not too much embrace
The people's love, for as Senec saith truly,
O quam funestus est favor populi![677]　　　　　　　　[455]

FINIS, G. F.

---

455. *O quam funestus est favor populi!*: Oh how fatal is the favour of the people!

[Prose 32]

The good duke having ended his woeful tragedy, after much talk had concerning dissension among those that be magistrates, 'Good Lord', quoth one, 'what mischief and destruction doth privy grudge and malice raise among all sorts of people, both high and low, but especially among magis-
5　trates, being the head and guide of the commonwealth? For what mischief did the dissension between these two persons, being both of high estate, bring afterward to both the realms, yea, and the utter ruin of most part of them that were the chief workers of this duke's death!'

'You say troth', quoth I,[678] 'and now for that, if I may crave your patience
10　awhile, you shall hear what I have noted in the duke of Suffolk's doings, one of the chief procurers of Duke Humphrey's destruction, who by the providence of God came shortly after in such hatred of the people that the king himself could not save him from a strange and notable death.[679] For being banished the realm for the term of five years to appease the con-
15　tinual rumours and inward grudges that not only the commons but most part of the nobility of England bare towards him for the death of the said duke,[680] he, sailing toward France, was met with a ship of Devonshire and beheaded forthwith the first day of May, Anno 1450, and the dead corpse thrown up at Dover upon the sands, which may lament his death after this
20　manner':[681]

---

3. **privy**: personal; secret.　6. **these two persons**: Duke Humphrey of Gloucester and Cardinal Henry Beaufort (see Tragedy 29).　10. **duke of Suffolk's doings**: the actions of William de la Pole (d. 1450), first duke of Suffolk (whose tragedy follows Prose 32 in the 1578 edition).

APPENDICES

APPENDIX I

Printer's Note to A Memorial of Such Princes *(1554)*

The Printer to the Reader

While I attended the queen's highness's pleasure in setting forth an uniform primer to be used of her subjects, for the printing whereof it pleased her highness (which I beseech God long to preserve) to give me a privilege under her letters patent, I thought it good to employ and occupy my print
5 and servants for that purpose provided about some necessary and profitable work. And because that sundry gentlemen very well learned commended much the works of Lydgate, chiefly *The Fall of Princes*, which he drew out of Bochas, whereof none were to be got, after that I knew the council's pleasure and advice therein, I determined to print it and, for that purpose,
10 caused the copy to be read over and amended in divers places where it was before, either through the writer's or printer's fault, corrupted, for very few names were true besides much matter displaced, as to the conferrers may appear. Yet is it not so thoroughly well corrected as I would have wished it, by means of lack of certain copies and authors which I could not get by
15 any mean, and yet I doubt not, gentle reader, but thou shalt find it as clear as any other heretofore set forth. To which I have added a continuation of that argument concerning the chief princes of this island, penned by the best clerks in such kind of matters that be this day living, not unworthy to be matched with Master Lydgate, whose doings do praise themselves, as to
20 the indifferent reader shall appear.

Title: **Printer**: John Wayland. **1. attended**: waited on; **queen's highness's**: Queen Mary I's. **2. primer**: private devotional manual for the use of lay people. **3. privilege**: right exclusively to print. **7. Lydgate**: John Lydgate (d. *c.* 1450). **8. Bochas**: Giovanni Boccaccio (d. 1375), author of the source text for Lydgate's *Fall of Princes*.

Wherefore, I beseech thee, good reader, to take in worth these my endeavours and to judge and report of them as they do deserve. And, as I shall be encouraged herein, so will I proceed to cause other notable works to be penned and translated, which I trust shall be to the weal of the whole country and to the singular profit of every subject, and so imprint the queen's highness's primer, when I shall get the copy, as shall content her and all the realm.

APPENDIX 2

Table of Contents, A Mirror for Magistrates (1559)

❦ King Henry the Sixth murdered
❦ George, duke of Clarence, drowned.
❦ King Edward the Fourth surfeited.

Finis .

Additional Table of Contents, A Mirror for Magistrates (1563)

A Mirror

¶ The contents of the second part

FINIS

[15] FINIS does not appear in all copies of the 1563 *Mirror*

APPENDIX 4

Principal Battles of the Wars of the Roses

Date	Battle	Victory
1455 (22 May)	First Battle of St Albans	Yorkist
1459 (23 September)	Blore Heath	Yorkist
1460 (10 July)	Northampton	Yorkist
1460 (30 December)	Wakefield	Lancastrian
1461 (2 February)	Mortimer's Cross	Yorkist
1461 (17 February)	Second Battle of St Albans	Lancastrian
1461 (28–30 March)	Towton and related skirmishes, including the Battle of Ferrybridge	Yorkist
1464 (25 April)	Hedgeley Moor	Yorkist
1464 (15 May)	Hexham	Yorkist
1469 (26 July)	Edgecote Moor (Banbury)	Lancastrian
1470 (12 March)	Losecote Field (Empingham)	Yorkist
1471 (14 April)	Barnet	Yorkist
1471 (4 May)	Tewkesbury	Yorkist
1485 (22 August)	Bosworth	Lancastrian

GLOSSARY

'False Friends' and Archaic Past-tense Verb Forms

Gathered below are many of the most common 'false friends' (words with meanings distinctly different in the early modern period from their most familiar modern connotations) and archaic past-tense verb forms in *A Mirror for Magistrates*. Not all such words are listed here. Some terms have remained in the glosses, either because they may easily be misinterpreted (e.g. 'treaty' is glossed in the text when it means 'entreaty' rather than 'formal pact') or because the term is used in a wide and often changing variety of ways in the text (e.g. 'kind', 'skill', and 'happy').

'False Friends'

affection	powerful or controlling emotion; feeling; partiality
brother	brother-in-law
careful	full of care; woeful
careless	unwary; negligent; unconcerned; unheeding
chance	luck, lot, fortune, situation
clean	completely
courage	the heart as the seat of feeling and thought; spirit; liveliness; boldness
cousin	any familial relation beyond one's immediate family, whether by blood or by marriage
debate	strife, contention
doom	judgement
dread	awe, reverence, proper respect for a monarch, reverential fear
drift	scheme, stratagem, plot, plotting; aim, intention
estate	social rank, place in society; dignity
fond	foolish; overly credulous; unreasoning
fray	frighten
let (v.)	hinder, check, prevent
let (n.)	hindrance, obstacle
lewd	wicked
lust	desire, pleasure

329

meet	fitting
mischief	wickedness; harm, calamity
naught	nothing; naughty, wicked
nought	nothing; wicked; worthless
or	before
ought	anything
pass	care; concern myself
plain	lament; complain; wail
plaint	complaint; wailing
poll	rob, plunder; cheat
process	legal trial
race (n.)	course, path
rigour	harmful action; harshness; cruelty
shift (n.)	trick, stratagem
silly	innocent, simple; weak, harmless; thoughtless
speed (v.)	prosper; succeed; fare
speed (n.)	success, fortune
spill	destroy
sprite	spirit, ghost; soul
stay (v.)	stop
still	ever; constantly
story	non-fictional historical account
strange	unfamiliar, foreign, outlandish; surprising
stranger	foreigner
stream	current; river
suffer	allow, permit
try	prove; judge
vicious	wicked, vice-ridden
want	lack
whereas	where
wherefore	for this reason; for which; why
wood	insane; frenzied, violently angry

Archaic Past-tense Verb Forms

bare	bore
be	been
brake	broke
drave	drove
durst	dared

gan	began
holp	helped
stale	stole
strake	struck
tane	taken
trode	trod
wan	won
ware	wore

EXPLANATORY NOTES

[Baldwin's Dedication]

42 Baldwin paraphrases a dictum included in his own collection of classical maxims *A Treatise of Moral Philosophy*, which ascribes to Plato the sentence 'The city is wel ordered, where ambicious men desire to have no offices' (Baldwin, *A Treatise of Morall Phylosophie* (London, 1547 [i.e. 1548]; *STC* 1253), sig. N3v).

43 For the biblical exhortation to pray for one's governors, see 1 Timothy 2:1–2.

44 For God as the ordainer of offices, see Romans 13:1–2; for hypocrites who will not dispense justice, see Matthew 23:23.

45 Baldwin echoes Psalm 82:6–7, which warns wicked officers 'ye are Goddes, and ye all are chyldren of the moost hyest. But ye shall dye lyke men, and fall lyke one of the princes' (Great Bible).

46 For the origin of *A Mirror for Magistrates* as a supplement to Giovanni Boccaccio's ('Bochas's') fourteenth-century text *De Casibus Virorum Illustrium*, as translated and adapted by John Lydgate (*The Fall of Princes*), see the introduction to this edition.

47 The contents of the 1559 *Mirror* were originally composed, compiled, and printed in 1554 as a supplement to the printer John Wayland's new edition of Lydgate's *Fall of Princes*. Titled *A Memorial of Such Princes*, this early version of *A Mirror for Magistrates* was prohibited before publication by Mary I's lord chancellor, Stephen Gardiner (d. 1555). Baldwin's use of 'four year ago' to mean 1554 suggests that he is writing between 1 January and 25 March 1559, a period still considered under the widely used legal calendar to be part of the year 1558.

48 Despite his words in this passage, there is no evidence that Baldwin commissioned any poems in 1554 handling figures who met their tragic ends after the death of King Edward IV (April 1483), the last ghostly speaker in the 1559 *Mirror*. Later in Mary's reign, Baldwin began a new attempt to expand the work chronologically, adding poems presenting figures who endured their downfalls in the 1480s and 1490s. Despite his stated desire to extend the scope of the work to Queen Mary I's reign, he apparently received no poems on figures from the sixteenth century he deemed worthy of publication. See Prose sections 21, 27, and 29.

49 In 1560 Baldwin left the print trade to become a minister in the Elizabethan church and, by at least 1561, chaplain to Henry, Lord Stafford. For the printing

of these unpublished Marian tragedies in the 1563 *Mirror*, as well as for Baldwin's commissioning of new, Elizabethan poems to supplement them, see the Introduction.

[Prose 1]

50 King Edward III's reign ended in 1377; following his source, Boccaccio's *De Casibus Virorum Illustrium*, Lydgate concludes his *Fall of Princes* with the tragedy of King John II of France, who died Edward III's captive in 1364. The chronicle works 'there present' at the authors' first meeting were apparently those that served as the bases for the great majority of the *Memorial of Such Princes* poems, namely Robert Fabyan's *Fabyan's Chronicle* (printed 1516, 1533, and 1542) and Edward Hall's *Union of the Two Noble and Illustre Families of Lancaster and York* (published in 1548 and 1550).

51 Fabyan records that England's King Richard I (d. 1199) met his end by a poisoned arrow (Fabyan, 309). Later, he offers two accounts of the death of King John (d. 1216). In the first, John dies of dysentery; in the second, he dies from poison administered by a vindictive monk (ibid., 322).

52 In his zeal to recount the falls of Sir Robert Tresilian (d. 1388) and other judges of Richard II's reign (1377–99), Ferrers ignores the company's decision to begin at about the time of Boccaccio's last narrative, the 1360s.

53 Ferrers's words here initiate the conceit, continued throughout all the prose sections of the 1559 *Mirror*, that the poets extemporaneously compose their poems while reading through the chronicles at their meeting. Nevertheless, his remark that he relies on his own 'memory and judgement' for Tragedy 1, 'Robert Tresilian', and not on any history work present at the gathering undercuts this fiction, calling attention as it does to Ferrers's reliance on a single non-chronicle source for this poem, the rolls of the 1388 parliament.

54 Fabyan portrays the pseudonymous Jack Straw as the principal leader of the widespread Peasants' Revolt of 1381 (Fabyan, 530–1). As with his defence of Sir Robert Tresilian's non-princely status below, Ferrers's words reflect that this prose passage was originally designed to introduce not a work titled *A Mirror for Magistrates* but *A Memorial of Such Princes*.

[Tragedy 1] 'Robert Tresilian'

Author: George Ferrers. **Historical subjects:** Sir Robert Tresilian (d. 1388), chief justice of the king's bench and royal counsellor, and other judges of King Richard II's reign. **Principal source:** The parliament rolls of the February 1388 parliament. (NA C 65/46–8). **Contemporary literary treatments:** Sir Robert Tresilian appears as one of the chief villains in the anonymous drama *Thomas of Woodstock* (c. 1592 or later). Samuel Daniel touches on the Lords Appellant's rising and the condemnation of Richard II's chief judges in his narrative poem *Civil Wars* (first published in 1595 (*STC* 6244); later released in a revised and expanded version in 1609 (*STC* 6245)).

55 Early Roman consuls had the first written laws of the Roman republic (the famous Twelve Tables of Law) engraved in brass or bronze and displayed so that they might remain before the eyes of the people for perpetuity (Livy, *History of Rome*, 2:195).

56 Sir Robert Tresilian was made chief justice of the king's bench in 1381; soon after, he became one of Richard II's closest advisors, taking his place among a group of royal favourites widely hated in the realm. In the parliament of February 1388 (called the Merciless Parliament), Tresilian and several other prominent legal men were charged with falsely advising the king in August 1387 that two actions of the previous parliament – the impeachment of royal favourite Michael de la Pole (d. 1389), first earl of Suffolk, and the granting of control of Richard's government to a council of state – were illegal and, furthermore, that those nobles who created the new state council could be dealt with as if they were traitors. The charges brought against the judges in the Merciless Parliament claimed the jurists' August 1387 opinions were the true acts of treason, since they aided Richard's corrupt counsellors in traitorously turning the king against his own subjects (see *PROME*, 7:91–5). The practice that Ferrers claims led to Tresilian and his fellows' condemnation, namely maliciously wresting the clear sense of the law when making judicial rulings, was never one historically lodged against Richard II's jurists. It was, however, precisely the accusation made against the legal men of Queen Mary I's reign who notoriously offered unprecedented interpretations of current treason law in a bid to help the crown bring the evangelical courtier (and Ferrers's acquaintance) Sir Nicholas Throckmorton to execution (April 1554). For a reading of 'Tresilian' as a topically allusive work designed to move readers to condemn the actions of Throckmorton's judges, see Lucas, 'A Mirror for Magistrates', 176–89.

57 Tresilian had gone into hiding before the Merciless Parliament convened on 3 February 1388. He was thus found guilty of treason (13 February) *in absentia*. Six days later Tresilian was apprehended and presented to parliament. When asked if he had anything to offer that could convince parliamentarians not to proceed with his execution, Tresilian 'had nothing to say or claim for himself' (*PROME*, 7:103).

58 With Tresilian, the judges John Lockton (fl. 1388), Sir John Holt (d. 1418/19), and Sir Robert Bealknap (d. 1401) were those whom Richard II summoned in 1387 for their opinions concerning the legality of the 1386 parliament's restraint of Richard's powers. It was not for corruption but for their determination that Richard's royal prerogative superseded parliamentary decrees, as well as their decision that the nobles in parliament who tried to restrain Richard's prerogative should be treated as traitors, that Lockton, Holt, and Bealknap were condemned by the Merciless Parliament on 6 March 1388. Tresilian was not condemned with his fellow judges for his participation in their counsel since he had already been hanged for other crimes (*PROME*, 7:103–11).

59 Until the nineteenth century, common-law judges were selected only from those barristers who had achieved the elevated rank of serjeant at law. At the time of their appointment, new serjeants swore an oath to serve 'well and truly' both the monarch and the people; the mandate to interpret laws correctly that Ferrers's Tresilian claims to exist is in fact only implied in the oath. See Sir William Dugdale, *Origines Juridiciales*, 3rd edn (London, 1680), 138.

60 A proverbial expression.

61 Until Mary I's reign, judges of the king's bench, the highest secular law court, rode on mules to the court sessions at Westminster (Dugdale, *Origines Juridiciales*, 38).

62 Historically, the rising against King Richard's counsellors was the work not of the entire 'barony' and the commons but of five powerful nobles known as the Lords Appellant, so called because their stated goal was to appeal (to accuse and seek to prove before the king) King Richard's favourites of treason. These lords' victory at Radcot Bridge in Oxfordshire (20 December 1387) over royal forces led by Richard's chief ally Robert de Vere (d. 1392), first duke of Ireland, gave them the power to compel the king to call parliament. Despite Ferrers's words in this and the next stanza, the Appellant Lords did not themselves convoke the February 1388 parliament, and its members did not debate changes to the rights of the ruler or the state of the commonweal. Instead, this session focused itself primarily on the punishment of Richard's hated chief counsellors (*PROME*, 7:55–120). For an interpretation of this passage, see Lucas, "'Let none such office take'", 104.

63 On 13 February 1388 parliament condemned as traitors Richard's close counsellors Robert de Vere, duke of Ireland; Michael de la Pole, earl of Suffolk; and Alexander Neville (d. 1392), archbishop of York. While they were stripped of their secular offices and titles, none was executed, since each had fled before parliament was convened. Nicholas Brembre (d. 1388), royal advisor and former mayor of London, did not escape; instead, he was tried for treason and executed on 20 February (*PROME*, 7:101–4).

64 The Appellant Lords appealed Tresilian in the upper house of parliament as one of the court favourites whom they accused of treasonously accroaching (taking illegally for themselves) royal power and alienating King Richard from his own subjects. Parliament thus tried and condemned Tresilian with the other royal counsellors and not, as Ferrers implies here, with the justices who gave allegedly false judicial opinions to their monarch. Because of the difference in the charges against them, Tresilian's fellow judges were not indicted by means of appeal, as the favourites were, but impeached by members of the lower house. Tried separately from Tresilian and his fellow counsellors, the judges ultimately suffered only exile for offering their supposedly treasonous legal advice, while Tresilian was hanged for a variety of high crimes (*PROME*, 7:83–111, 117–18). As Ferrers suggests in the following stanza, Tresilian was indeed accused of malfeasance and bribe-taking; the charges, however, make it clear that he committed these crimes in his role as a corrupt royal counsellor and not in that of a justice of the king's bench (ibid., 7:87).

[Prose 2]

65 Baldwin's reference to those 'touched' (a term meaning 'written of' but also 'reproved') in Ferrers's tragedy may be to the historical Tresilian and his fellows or to those 'some in latter days' (Tragedy 1, line 141) who continue to practise the corrupt actions Ferrers ascribes to Richard II's judges. See Tragedy 1, n. 56.

66 The speaker, Lord Henry Stafford, follows Fabyan in incorrectly placing the death of Roger Mortimer, fourth earl of March, in the London mayoral year of October 1385–October 1386 rather than in the calendar year 1398 (Fabyan, 533). Since Fabyan places Tresilian's death in the mayoral year 1387/8, Stafford could well conclude that Mortimer and Tresilian died about one year apart (ibid., 534).

[Tragedy 2] 'The Two Rogers'

Author: Henry, tenth Baron Stafford. **Historical subjects:** (1) Sir Roger Mortimer (1287–1330), first earl of March; (2) Sir Roger Mortimer (1328–1360), second earl of March; (3) Sir Roger Mortimer (1374–1398), fourth earl of March and sixth earl of Ulster (Stafford inadvertently combines the latter two Roger Mortimers into a single figure in the poem). **Principal sources:** *Fabyan's Chronicle*; the parliament roll of the April 1354 parliament (NA C 65/18); Jean Froissart, *Chronicles*. **Contemporary literary treatments:** Early modern literary works that handle the first earl of March's final years of life under Edward III include Michael Drayton's *Mortimeriados* (1596), its revision, *The Barons' Wars* (1603), and Ben Jonson's drama *Mortimer his Fall* (printed 1641).

67 In January 1327, the powerful soldier and political magnate Sir Roger Mortimer (d. 1330) and his lover Queen Isabella arranged the deposition of Isabella's husband, King Edward II, in favour of Edward and Isabella's son, Edward III. The new king was a minor, and between 1327 and 1330 Mortimer and Isabella held all real power in the realm.

68 Edward III created Roger Mortimer the first earl of March in 1328. According to the chronicler Fabyan, it was after his elevation to this new rank that Mortimer took for himself and Isabella all authority in the realm, thereby excluding the group of powerful nobles who had previously counselled the king (Fabyan, 440).

69 March was arrested on charges of treason in October 1330. In the next month, parliament condemned and attainted him by a process known as conviction by notoriety, which allowed judgement without trial based on the assumption that the accused's crimes were so well known that no further proving of them was needed. He was soon after drawn and hanged (Fabyan, 441; *PROME*, 5:95–7).

70 The accusation that Mortimer caused Edward III to yield English-held towns to the Scots is apparently Stafford's invention. The 'charter called Ragman' was the document by which Scottish nobles in 1291 acknowledged the king of England's lordship over them. In 1328, in order to conclude a peace, Edward III surrendered this charter to the Scots. According to Fabyan, the outraged

people of England blamed Mortimer and Isabella for this 'unprofetable and dishonorable peace', and parliament later formally charged Mortimer with being in the pay of the Scots (Fabyan, 439, 441).

71 'Sir Edward of Carnarvan' was the title given to the former King Edward II after his deposition. In September 1327, Edward II's keepers announced that the former ruler had died at Berkeley Castle of natural causes. Despite the official pronouncement, Edward II was widely believed to have been murdered at the behest of Roger Mortimer. For the charge of 'polling' the king and commons, Stafford expands on Fabyan's claim that Mortimer wrongly acquired and misspent royal funds (Fabyan, 438, 441).

72 Stafford's speaker is chiefly modelled on Roger Mortimer (d. 1398), fourth earl of March, who was actually the great-great-grandson of the executed first earl. Stafford, however, confuses this Roger Mortimer with the first earl's grandson, also named Roger Mortimer (d. 1360), second earl of March. It was the second earl whom parliament restored in blood, not (as the poem suggests) the fourth earl (*PROME*, 5:89, 94–8).

73 The fourth earl of March was the son of Edmund Mortimer (d. 1381), third earl of March, and Philippa (or 'Phylyp', as Fabyan calls her) of Clarence (d. 1378), daughter of Edward III's second surviving son Lionel (see Fabyan, 533). Roger's claim in the poem that his father was the 'true' earl of March is occasioned by Stafford's confusion of the fourth earl (d. 1398) with his grandfather, the second earl (d. 1360). In his supplication to parliament to annul the first earl's treason conviction, the second earl referred to his father, Edmund Mortimer (d. 1331), as 'late earl of March', despite the fact that Edmund had never held that title (*PROME*, 5:95). The second earl's warrant in so calling his father was his belief that the judgement against the first earl was never valid and that thus the Mortimer family had never lost the earldom.

74 A ferle (ferule) was the rod or cane schoolmasters used to discipline students. Stafford's speaker may mean that Edmund Mortimer was such a paragon of knighthood that he stood superior to other knights in the same way a teacher does to young students.

75 As a consequence of his condemnation for treason, the first earl of March was attainted, which entailed the forfeiture of all his titles, honours, offices, and wholly owned possessions. His heirs, furthermore, were forbidden from inheriting any Mortimer family titles and properties that would normally have descended to them. In 1354 the first earl's grandson Roger Mortimer (d. 1360) petitioned parliament to invalidate his grandfather's 1330 conviction without trial, successfully arguing that condemning a free Englishman to death without arraignment or the opportunity to answer the charges against him violated the legally recognized liberties of English subjects. With the annulment of the first earl's conviction, the elder Roger Mortimer's attainder was also annulled and his heirs were thus restored to the Mortimer family inheritance, including to the right to bear the title earl of March (*PROME*, 5:98).

76 It was less Mortimer's titles than his mother Philippa's royal blood that led observers to consider the fourth earl of March to be heir presumptive to the

childless King Richard (Fabyan and other chroniclers' claim that Richard
declared Mortimer his heir apparent in the parliament of October 1385 is
without historical foundation).

77 Stafford draws on Fabyan for Mortimer's reason for journeying to Ireland
(Fabyan, 533). Historically, Earl Roger became lord lieutenant of Ireland in
1395 and spent most of the rest of his life there. March died in July 1398,
fighting the native Irish in County Carlow, far to the south of Ulster.

78 Stafford takes his description of the 'wild' Irish and their vicious battlefield
practices from Jean Froissart's *Chronicles* (*c.* 1404). See Froissart, vol. 2, fos.
256r–58r.

79 'Bodoh' is apparently Stafford's anglicized rendering of the Gaelic *bodach*
(genitive and nominative plural both *bodaigh*), meaning 'churl', 'peasant'.
According to Richard Stanyhurst, the Irish commonly used the term *bobdeagh*
(*bodaigh*) as a term of contempt for those of English stock, a practice which may
have led Stafford to believe the word meant 'enemy' rather than 'low born'. See
Richard Stanyhurst, 'A Treatise Containing a Plain and Perfect Description of
Ireland', in Raphael Holinshed, *The First Volume of the Chronicles of England,
Scotland, and Ireland* (London, 1577; *STC* 13568), fos. 27v–28r.

80 Fabyan asserts that the wild Irish came upon Mortimer and his men 'in
noumbre' (Fabyan, 533).

81 The fourth earl of March was married to Eleanor Holland (d. 1405), daughter
of the earl of Kent. As Fabyan notes, their eldest son Edmund (d. 1425) became
the fifth earl, while their eldest daughter Anne (d. 1411) became wife of Richard
(d. 1415), first earl of Cambridge, and, thereafter, mother to Richard (d. 1460),
third duke of York, founder of the Yorkist faction in the Wars of the Roses and
father of King Edward IV and King Richard III (Fabyan, 533).

[Prose 3]

82 Robert Fabyan writes that in November 1393 several Scottish nobles and
knights challenged their English counterparts to a tourney in London. One of
the Scots, 'Lord Morif' (John Dunbar, first earl of Moray), died of a wound
received from Thomas Mowbray (d. 1399), first earl of Nottingham (Fabyan,
538). Historically, Moray died in 1391 or 1392, of uncertain causes.

83 Fabyan notes that several people, including the prior of the friary at Tiptree,
Essex, were crushed to death by crowds attending Queen Isabella's January 1395
(historically 1397) coronation entrance into London (Fabyan, 541). Ferrers's
description of the prior as fat is his own anti-clerical addition.

[Tragedy 3] 'Thomas of Woodstock'

Author: George Ferrers. **Historical subject:** Sir Thomas of Woodstock
(1355–1397), first duke of Gloucester, prince, constable of England, and uncle
to King Richard II. **Principal sources:** *Fabyan's Chronicle*; Jean Froissart,
Chronicles; *Hardyng's Chronicle*; *Hall's Chronicle*; the parliament rolls of the 1388
parliament (NA C 65/46–8). **Possible further source:** The parliament rolls of

the September 1397 'Revenge' parliament (NA C 65/57–61). **Contemporary literary treatments:** Woodstock is the titular subject of the anonymous drama *Thomas of Woodstock* (*c.* 1592 or after), and Samuel Daniel recounts Duke Thomas's part in the Lords Appellant's rising and the circumstances leading to his death in the first book of his *Civil Wars* (first printed 1595; revised and expanded 1609). Although Woodstock is not a character in Shakespeare's *Richard II* (*c.* 1595), his death is spoken of in the drama several times as one of King Richard's most heinous crimes.

84 Edward III's son Thomas was called Thomas of Woodstock after the place of his birth, Woodstock, in Oxfordshire. Woodstock's 10-year-old nephew Richard II made Thomas earl of Buckingham in 1377.

85 Ferrers follows the incorrect genealogy given by Edward Hall at the opening of his chronicle (Hall, 2). Woodstock was in fact the last-born of King Edward's eight sons (only seven of whom survived infancy). The eldest was the famous military leader Edward (d. 1376), called the Black Prince, father of Richard II.

86 Ferrers magnifies Robert Fabyan's and Jean Froissart's accounts of Woodstock's exploits during his 1380 expedition into France (see Fabyan, 530; Froissart, vol. 1, fos. 236v–441). As Froissart records, Woodstock's martial exploits were not notably successful, and none of Ferrers's sources claims that Gloucester received his dukedom (granted historically in 1385) as a reward for his French campaign (see Hardyng, 341; Fabyan, 533; Froissart, vol. 2, fo. 80v). For an argument that this and other unhistorical interpolations into the poem are designed to evoke for mid-Tudor readers not primarily the career of the fourteenth-century Thomas of Woodstock but that of the recently deceased military hero and political leader Edward Seymour (d. 1552), first duke of Somerset, see Lucas, '*A Mirror for Magistrates*', 106–28.

87 Woodstock received the constable's office, one of the great offices of state, in 1376, by means of his marriage to Eleanor (d. 1399), daughter and co-heir of Humphrey de Bohun (d. 1373), seventh earl of Hereford, whose family possessed hereditary claim to the constableship. Woodstock only became duke of Gloucester later, in 1385. Ferrers may have been misled in his chronology by ambiguous wording in John Hardyng's chronicle; see Hardyng, 341.

88 As constable, Woodstock was not chief officer of the realm in the period leading up to the Lords Appellant's rising (for which, see note 92); Richard II's chancellor and royal favourite Michael de la Pole (d. 1389), first earl of Suffolk, was superior to Woodstock both in the hierarchy of the great offices of state and in the amount of power he wielded. Ferrers's presentation of Woodstock and his actions against his royal nephew's counsellors recalls the plans of Ferrers's former patron Edward Seymour, duke of Somerset, who in 1551 considered himself to be England's chief officer (he did not deem his deposition from the office of protector of the realm in 1549 to be legal) and sought means – whether through parliament, an armed rising, or both – to reassert his authority and to purge his nephew Edward VI's closest counsellors. See Lucas, '*A Mirror for Magistrates*', 106–9, 119.

89 By 1386, the powerful nobles Gloucester, Richard Fitzalan (d. 1397), fourth earl of Arundel, and Thomas Beauchamp (d. 1401), twelfth earl of Warwick, had come to despise Richard II's chief counsellors Suffolk and Robert de Vere (d. 1392), first duke of Ireland. In the parliament of 1386, Gloucester and Arundel in particular helped to further the commons members' successful attempt to remove Chancellor de la Pole from office and to establish a council of state to oversee the royal government (see Nigel Saul, *Richard II* (New Haven, Conn.: Yale University Press, 1997), 157–64). Despite Ferrers's words, Gloucester never had an overarching plan to replace Richard's hand-picked counsellors, since neither he nor any of the other lords had the authority to do so.

90 In this stanza and the next, Ferrers imperfectly remembers the episode of the 'Rat of Renown' in William Langland's *Piers Plowman* (*c.* 1370–90), a work which had only recently made its first appearance in print. In Langland's poem, mice and rats at court gather to discuss what could be done about a cat that constantly catches and toys with them. A wise 'rotton [rat] of renowne' suggests belling the cat, so they could know whenever he was near. The rats obtain a bell, but no rat is brave enough to put it around the cat's neck. A mouse then speaks up, arguing that it is better to suffer a cat that merely torments them than to risk having it replaced with one that will actually eat them (William Langland, *The Vision of Pierce Plowman* (London, 1550; *STC* 19906), sigs. A3r–4r).

91 While the term 'liege' suggests a vassal bound to offer feudal service and allegiance to a lord himself, it is noteworthy that Ferrers modifies this sense by having Woodstock state that a subject's proper obedience is to the 'prince's laws'. Cf. William Baldwin's similar qualification at the end of Prose 29.

92 In August 1387, Richard II received advice from a panel of judges that the council put in place by the 1386 parliament to oversee his government was illegal and that those who conceived of it could be punished in the manner of traitors (see Tragedy 1). Fearing for their lives, Gloucester, Arundel, and Warwick took up arms in November 1387 and appealed (accused of treason) Richard II's closest adherents, including de la Pole and de Vere. In response, de Vere gathered an army, an action that led Henry Bolingbroke (d. 1413), third earl of Derby, and Thomas Mowbray (d. 1399), first earl of Nottingham, to join the other lords in their armed appeal. These five men, known as the Lords Appellant, met de Vere's soldiers on 20 December 1387 at Radcot Bridge, Oxfordshire, where they routed the royal army and forced de Vere to flee the realm (Hardyng, 341; Fabyan, 534; Froissart, vol. 2, fos. 111v–131r; Saul, *Richard II*, 176–88).

93 None of Ferrers's sources states that anyone but Richard II called this parliament. In asserting that Woodstock had the power to summon parliament by means of his office of constable of England, Ferrers may draw on the claims of Thomas Starkey's manuscript work 'A Dialogue Between Pole and Lupset' (*c.* 1532). In this text, the humanist Starkey portrays his friend Reginald Pole as proposing a number of innovations to the sixteenth-century English constitution. One of them is the revival of what Starkey's Pole characterizes

as the ancient authority of England's constable to counter the actions of a tyrannous king. According to the Pole of the 'Dialogue', the office of constable was established by England's 'old aunceturys … to conturpayse [counterpoise] the authoryte of the prynce and tempur the same, gyvyng hym authoryte to cal a parlyament in such case as the prynce wold run in to any tyranny' (Thomas Starkey, *A Dialogue between Pole and Lupset*, ed. T. F. Mayer, Camden Society 4th series, 37 (London: Royal Historical Society, 1989), 121). Ferrers could have encountered Starkey and his political thought when both men were servants of Thomas Cromwell in the 1530s.

94 Hardyng notes that the Lords Appellant came armed to parliament in order to compel the punishment of Richard's hated counsellors (Hardyng, 342). Neither he nor any other source suggests, however, that the Lords Appellant remained armed in parliament or used physical threats rather than parliamentary procedure to condemn the royal favourites.

95 On 3 February 1388 the Lords Appellant formally appealed five of King Richard's favourites in the high court of parliament. All were found guilty and condemned either to death or exile. Parliament soon after impeached and executed or exiled several other of King Richard's adherents. See *PROME*, 7:83–118; Saul, *Richard II*, 191–4; Tragedy 1, nn. 63 and 64. Woodstock's ghost refers readers to the last of the three parliament rolls of the February 1388 parliament, in which the judgements against the convicted men were recorded (*PROME*, 7:99–118).

96 Ferrers apparently offers his own version of a historically unsubstantiated episode included by Froissart in his *Chronicles*. According to Froissart, at some time before the Lords Appellant's rising, a group of Londoners came to Gloucester to urge him to take control of crown finances, since the people had no knowledge of how funds raised by heavy taxes and levies laid upon them were being spent. Gloucester urged the Londoners to join with citizens of other English towns and to come before King Richard to request an immediate reckoning of royal income and expenditures. As the townsmen met with the king at Windsor, Gloucester spoke in support of their plea, and Richard in response established a commission to inquire into his own financial affairs (Froissart, vol. 2, fos. 105v–7r). Froissart, however, does not suggest that Gloucester led this delegation of townsmen, that the mayor of London was present, or that King Richard was displeased by their request.

97 In 1342, Edward III established an English garrison in the city of Brest, in Brittany, which until 1397 maintained almost constant control over the town (Michael Jones, *Ducal Brittany, 1364–1399* (Oxford University Press, 1970), 143). In his chronicle, Fabyan writes that King Richard returned Brest to John IV (d. 1399), duke of Brittany, in 1396 (historically June 1397), in exchange for payments owed to the English crown. Gloucester learned of the return of Brest only in February 1397, Fabyan asserts, when he saw homeless soldiers of the Brest garrison taking residence in a room at Westminster Hall. Furious, Gloucester confronted Richard, denouncing the fact that the Brest

soldiers were now unemployed and poverty-stricken. Although the king promised to see the soldiers properly recompensed, Gloucester continued with his denunciation, accusing Richard of basely selling Brest. As a result of Gloucester's intemperate words, 'such rancoure and malyce kyndelyd atwene the kynge and [Gloucester], that it ceasyd not tyll the sayd duke was put to deth by murdre unlefullye [unlawfully]' (Fabyan, 541). For Ferrers's reshaping of his sources in this stanza, see Lucas, '*A Mirror for Magistrates*', 124.

98 None of Ferrers's chronicle sources claims that King Richard harboured continual hate for his uncle Gloucester in the wake of the 1387–8 Lords Appellant's rising. Fabyan dates Richard's resentment of Gloucester only to 1397, and Froissart, for his part, claims that it was Gloucester who hated Richard and not (at least until matters reached a crisis) the other way around. Both Fabyan and Froissart claim the king had Gloucester arrested in 1397 (as the poem narrates below) only to prevent Duke Thomas from striking against Richard first, either through a new conspiracy to control the government (Fabyan) or a bid to kill his royal nephew (Froissart). See Fabyan, 541–2; Froissart, vol. 2, fos. 284r, 287v; see also Hardyng, who offers no reason at all for Richard's move against Gloucester (344–5). Notably, Ferrers telescopes the events of Richard's reign to suggest that Gloucester's arrest came relatively soon after the Lords Appellant's rising. To do so, he omits from his work both King Richard's resumption of rule over the realm in 1388 and Fabyan's charge of a second attempt by Gloucester (in 1397) to remove Richard's counsellors.

99 Although they differ on the specifics, all of Ferrers's chronicle sources record the story that King Richard came in person to Woodstock's principal residence of Pleshey Castle, Essex, to arrest his uncle. Ferrers draws on Hardyng's chronicle for the claims that Woodstock lodged at Pleshey rather than at court at this time because of illness and that Richard brought a cohort of servants to the castle to seize Duke Thomas (Hardyng, 345). For his assertion that Richard came to visit Woodstock under 'colour of kindness', Ferrers apparently expands on Froissart's assertion that Richard suddenly appeared at Pleshey one afternoon, feigning that he had been hunting nearby and desired food and drink. After dining at Pleshey, the king, Froissart writes, lured Woodstock into accompanying him to a village near the Thames, where a 'bande' of men led by Lord Marshal Thomas Mowbray, earl of Nottingham, arrested Gloucester, took him to a ship, and transported him immediately to Calais. Woodstock died while in captivity in Calais, the victim of what Ferrers's chronicle sources uniformly assert was a murder (Froissart, vol. 2, fos. 287v–8r, 293v–4r; Fabyan, 542; Hardyng, 345).

100 It is Hardyng who records that, after Woodstock's death, Richard II circulated a document purporting to be Gloucester's confession to '.ix. poyntes fayned' of treason (Hardyng, 345). Although not mentioned in chronicle sources, Woodstock did indeed receive 'doom after death' (posthumous conviction for treason) in the high court of parliament. Ferrers could have gained this

information from the September 1397 parliament rolls; since nothing else in 'Woodstock' suggests that Ferrers ever consulted this parliament's records, however, his source remains uncertain (see *PROME*, 7:411–12).

101 For two different interpretations of the concluding stanzas of this poem, see Henry A. Kelly, *Divine Providence in the England of Shakespeare's Histories* (Cambridge, Mass.: Harvard University Press, 1970), 168–9; and Lucas '*A Mirror for Magistrates*', 117–28.

[Prose 4]

102 Thomas Mowbray (d. 1399), first earl of Nottingham, was captain of Calais in 1397, and it was under his supervision that Richard II's uncle Thomas of Woodstock (d. 1397), first duke of Gloucester, died in captivity. This connection to Woodstock's death, however, is not mentioned in *A Mirror for Magistrates* or in Baldwin's two known historical sources for Tragedy 4, 'Lord Mowbray'. It thus appears that by characterizing Mowbray as 'the chief worker of the duke's destruction', Baldwin refers not to Nottingham's presence in Calais at the time of Woodstock's death but to Fabyan's claim that in 1397 Mowbray informed Richard II of a plot by Gloucester and others to strip him of his favourite counsellors, a revelation that led directly to Richard's decision to strike against his uncle (Fabyan, 541–2).

[Tragedy 4] 'Lord Mowbray'

Author: William Baldwin. **Historical subject:** Sir Thomas Mowbray (1366–1399), first earl of Nottingham, first duke of Norfolk, and earl marshal of England. **Principal sources:** *Fabyan's Chronicle*; *Hall's Chronicle*. **Contemporary literary treatments**: The dispute between Mowbray and Henry Bolingbroke and its aftermath are portrayed in Thomas Deloney's 'A Song of the Banishment of the Two Dukes, Hereford and Norfolk' (*c.* 1593), Shakespeare's *Richard II* (*c.* 1595), and book 1 of Samuel Daniel's *Civil Wars* (first printed 1595; revised and expanded 1609).

103 Historically, Richard II created Thomas Mowbray earl of Nottingham in 1383 and made him marshal – one of the great officers of state – two years later, though Fabyan records Richard bestowing both titles simultaneously on Mowbray in 1385 (Fabyan, 533).

104 Baldwin's account of the Lords Appellant's rising of 1387 bears little resemblance to that of his source, Robert Fabyan (for the historical Lords Appellant's revolt, see Saul, *Richard II*, 176–88; see also the explanatory notes to Tragedy 1, 'Robert Tresilian', and Tragedy 3, 'Thomas of Woodstock', above). Fabyan names the Appellant Lords themselves as the originators of their armed challenge to King Richard's chief counsellors and makes no mention of discontent among the people. Furthermore, he correctly implies that Mowbray was the least of the five lords who appealed (accused of treason) Richard II's court favourites, placing Mowbray's name last among the men who took arms and stating only that Nottingham worked 'with' the three

leaders of the rising (Fabyan, 534). While Baldwin's presentation of the Lords Appellant's revolt does not match that of his historical source, it does serve to exemplify John Calvin's claim that duly appointed magistrates charged with protecting the people are permitted and even duty-bound to resist tyranny in the realm. See Calvin, *Institutes*, 2:1493–4, 1518–19. For Baldwin's Calvinist political thought, see Andrew Hadfield, *Literature, Politics and National Identity* (Cambridge University Press, 1994), 98–9; and, for its application to 'Mowbray', Scott Lucas, '"Let none such office take"', 98–102.

105 As Fabyan has it, the Appellant Lords in 1387 gathered an army and marched it to London, where they compelled Richard II to call a parliament and to permit the arrest of his hated royal favourites (Fabyan, 534). Among those the parliament of 1388 found guilty of treason were Sir Robert Tresilian (d. 1388), royal counsellor and chief justice of the king's bench; Sir John Beauchamp of Holt (d. 1388), steward of Richard's household; and Michael de la Pole (d. 1389), first earl of Suffolk and lord chancellor of England. The first two were executed; the last fled the realm before parliament gathered and died in exile.

106 Baldwin's account of Mowbray's career as Richard's chief counsellor is completely his own invention, created to add exemplary force to his poem's later admonition to officers against strict obedience to princes (see Lucas, '*A Mirror for Magistrates*', 189–95). The chronicler Edward Hall's description of Mowbray as a 'depe dissimuler and a pleasaunte flaterer' gave Baldwin warrant for his otherwise unprecedented portrait of England's earl marshal in the wake of the Lords Appellant's rising (Hall, 3).

107 According to Fabyan, in February 1397 King Richard's powerful uncle Thomas (d. 1397), first duke of Gloucester, denounced his royal nephew for 'selling' to the duke of Brittany the English-held fortified city of Brest and for throwing its garrison's long-underpaid soldiers into poverty. Soon after this confrontation, Gloucester concluded that Richard was being misled by his chief counsellors and began a plot to drive Richard's advisors from his side. Among the conspirators, according to Fabyan, were four of the five former Appellant Lords: Gloucester; Richard Fitzalan (d. 1397), fourth earl of Arundel; Thomas Beauchamp (d. 1401), twelfth earl of Warwick; and Mowbray (Fabyan, 541–2). Historically, there is no evidence for this alleged plot of 1397.

108 According to Fabyan, Mowbray revealed Gloucester's plot to the king; the claims, however, that Mowbray did so in order to win royal favour and that he became duke of Norfolk in reward for his perfidy are Baldwin's creations. The leaders of Gloucester's plot, as Fabyan tells it, were indeed 'shent': Gloucester was murdered in captivity, while the others were either executed or exiled (Fabyan, 542–3).

109 Baldwin now abandons his first source Fabyan, who repeats the story that it was Henry Bolingbroke (d. 1413), first duke of Hereford, who reported to King Richard words spoken against the monarch by the recently created duke of Norfolk, Mowbray, in late 1397 (Fabyan, 544). For the remainder of the poem, Baldwin instead takes up Edward Hall's unhistorical version of the exchange

and its aftermath, which makes Bolingbroke the man who voiced concern about Richard's rule and Mowbray the one who reported Bolingbroke's words (and others Bolingbroke did not say) to the king (Hall, 3).

110 Ancient writers claimed that the palm tree was not only unharmed by heavy weights attached to it but even thrived under such impediments (see, among others, Aulus Gellius, *Attic Nights*, 3 vols., trans. John Rolfe (London: Heinemann, 1927), 255).

111 Baldwin incorrectly refers to the future Henry IV as earl of Hereford ('Harforde') rather than duke of Hereford, even though both Hall and Fabyan identify him correctly as duke of Hereford at the time of his fateful conversation with Mowbray. The mistake appears three times more in the *Mirror* (see Tragedies 5, 9 and 13), and its repetition in the collection perhaps led Shakespeare to make the same error in 2 *Henry IV* (4.1).

112 As Hall tells it, after he learned that Norfolk had falsely imputed to him treasonous words, Bolingbroke called Duke Thomas a seditious liar and offered to prove his own innocence through trial by combat. Mowbray accepted Bolingbroke's challenge, and the two men met to do battle in August (historically September) 1398 (Hall, 3–5).

113 Just before Bolingbroke and Mowbray sought to commence their battle, King Richard halted the trial and instead ended their dispute by sentencing both men to banishment, Hereford to ten-years' exile and Norfolk to banishment for life. The king also took for his own the annual income of Mowbray's lands up to the amount Richard claimed Duke Thomas had improperly diverted from funds meant for soldiers in Calais (Hall, 5).

114 Baldwin incorrectly assumes that Mowbray was attainted by King Richard at the time he was sent into exile, an action that would have entailed the loss for Mowbray and his family of all possessions, offices, titles, and legal rights, including the right of inheritance. While the Mowbrays indeed lost much of their land and wealth as a result of Norfolk's condemnation, Mowbray's teenaged son Thomas (d. 1405) remained his father's legal heir and was thus able to inherit the title earl of Nottingham (but not that of duke of Norfolk) in the wake of the elder Mowbray's September 1399 death.

115 In this and the following stanzas, Baldwin expands upon Hall's brief statement that Mowbray 'was sore repentant of his enterprise, and departed sorowfully out of the realme into Almaine, and at the laste came to Venice where he for thought and Melancolye desceassed' (Hall, 5).

116 Bolingbroke returned from exile in July 1399; he seized Richard II in August and soon after imprisoned him in the Tower of London. By the end of September, Richard was said to have resigned the crown to Bolingbroke, and the new ruler Henry IV was crowned in October. Historically, Mowbray died in Venice on 22 September 1399, though this date is unmentioned in Baldwin's sources.

[Prose 5]

117 Compare Hall, 3, and Fabyan, 544. Fabyan's claim that Henry Bolingbroke (d. 1413), first duke of Hereford, 'appealed' (accused of treason) Thomas Mowbray (d. 1399), first duke of Norfolk, is the historically correct one.

118 As those charged with settling issues of noble precedence, the heralds could be expected to have great familiarity with historical records involving England's peers.

119 The speaker – whom the sole surviving leaf of text from the suppressed 1554 *Memorial* shows to be Sir Thomas Chaloner – follows here Fabyan's account of the Epiphany Rising of January 1400, through which Richard II's half-brother John Holland (d. 1400), first earl of Huntingdon (formerly duke of Exeter), and other nobles planned to assassinate Henry IV during a masque (a disguised entertainment), so that Richard could be restored to the throne (Fabyan, 567–8; see also Hall, 16).

120 Chaloner's striking setting for his ghostly speaker's address is suggested to him by Fabyan, who writes that King Richard met his death from several men armed with axes (cf. Hall's account, which asserts that Richard either died of starvation or was killed with a single blow from a pole axe (Hall, 20)). Fabyan then notes that Richard's corpse was soon after brought to St Paul's cathedral, 'open visaged', so all could see he was dead (Fabyan, 568). Chaloner's claim that the deposed monarch's corpse was dumped on the floor and displayed naked is the poet's own invention.

[Tragedy 5] 'King Richard II'

> **Author:** Sir Thomas Chaloner. **Historical subject:** King Richard II of England (1367–1400; reigned 1377–99). **Principal sources:** *Fabyan's Chronicle*, *Hall's Chronicle*. **Contemporary literary treatments:** Richard II's career forms the basis of the anonymous play *Thomas of Woodstock* (*c.* 1592) and of Shakespeare's *Richard II* (*c.* 1595). King Richard's last years are also handled in the first three books of Samuel Daniel's *Civil Wars* (1595–1609).

121 For King Richard's self-indulgent behaviour, Chaloner draws on material added to the 1542 edition of *Fabyan's Chronicle* (Fabyan, 544).

122 The articles of deposition against King Richard, as recorded by Hall, accused him of imposing numerous unjust levies on his subjects as well as demanding loans that he never intended to repay. Hall and Fabyan both note as well the unprecedented and illegal oaths Richard compelled many of those under him to swear. If he judged that an oath-taker had not upheld his pledge, King Richard would, Hall writes, quickly seize the monetary bond the oath-taker had been compelled to offer as surety, to 'the great undoyng of many honest men'. Finally, Fabyan refers to Richard's hated 'blank charters' (*cartes blanches*), which were documents that gave the king full power over the lives and possessions of certain subjects (Hall, 9–11; Fabyan, 543–5). For these and similar oppressive actions by King Richard during his last years in power,

see Caroline Barron, 'The Tyranny of Richard II', *Bulletin of the Institute of Historical Research* 41 (1968): 1–18.

123 For Richard II's 1397 'selling' of the English-held city of Brest to the duke of Brittany and the angry words this act elicited from his uncle Thomas of Woodstock (d. 1397), first duke of Gloucester, see Tragedy 3, n. 97. Fabyan claims that Duke Thomas's chastisement of his nephew sparked Richard's undying anger. After learning soon after that Gloucester was plotting to purge his chosen counsellors, Richard struck against his uncle and his co-conspirators, placing Gloucester in the captivity in which he was subsequently murdered and executing or exiling his allies (Fabyan, 541–3; see also Hall, 9).

124 In September 1398, Richard II exiled Henry Bolingbroke (d. 1413), first duke of Hereford, initially for a space of ten years (see Tragedy 4). In May 1399, King Richard led a military expedition into Ireland. According to the chronicler Hall, it was at this point that unnamed political and religious leaders sent a letter into France urging Bolingbroke to return to England to put an end to Richard's tyrannous rule. When Hereford landed on English soil in late June or early July 1399, a number of powerful men, including Henry Percy (d. 1408), first earl of Northumberland, and his son Sir Henry (called Hotspur) Percy (d. 1403) came immediately to his side (Hall, 6–8). No medieval or early modern source, however, claims that either Richard II's uncle Edmund of Langley (d. 1402), first duke of York, or the Percies ever plotted secretly to contact Bolingbroke to have him return to challenge Richard.

125 As lord steward, Thomas Percy (d. 1403), first earl of Worcester, was King Richard's chief household officer. By publicly shattering the staff that was the symbol of his office, Worcester openly communicated his withdrawal of obedience from his sovereign (see Fabyan, 546; Hall, 9).

126 Hall writes that 'diverse lordes whiche wer kyng Richardes frendes, outwardly dissimuled that whiche thei inwardly conspired and determined, to confounde this kyng Henry ... and set up their old lorde and frend kyng Richard the second' (Hall, 15). Among these were the men who became the leaders of the Epiphany Rising of January 1400, a conspiracy whose goals were the assassination of Henry IV and the reinstatement of Richard II (see Prose 5). Chaloner's explanation of the Epiphany plotters' primary impetus for rebellion – that Henry IV would not accept their control of him – does not comport with the chief motive for the historical Epiphany revolt (whose fomenters had never sought to work with King Henry); it matches more closely the catalyst (as Edward Hall describes it) for the Percy family's 1403 rising against Henry IV. See Hall, 16, 27.

127 According to Fabyan, the attempt on Henry's life by the Epiphany conspirators was planned to take place during a 'mumming' or masked entertainment; Chaloner evidently understood this to mean that the assassins too would be masked. The Epiphany plot, Fabyan continues, was exposed to Henry before it could take place and its ringleaders were soon after executed. To ensure

that there would be no future conspiracies on Richard's behalf, Henry IV decided that England's former monarch would have to die (Fabyan, 567–8).

128   Both Fabyan and Hall mention the claim that a knight named Sir Piers of Exton brought about Richard's murder at Pomfret (Pontefract) Castle, Yorkshire. There is no evidence that such a man existed. As Hall notes, other early writers claimed that Richard met his death through starvation. See Fabyan, 568; Hall, 20, 30.

[Prose 6]

129   Baldwin refers in this passage to the conspirators behind the Epiphany Rising of January 1400. See Prose 5, n. 119.

130   'Martin Hundred' is perhaps a colloquial name for Castlemartin Hundred, a jurisdictional unit of Pembrokeshire located in the Anglophone area of Wales known as Little England beyond Wales. In a section of this passage included in the 1554 edition, Baldwin notes that he has been led to understand that his ancestors are Welsh in origin (see textual notes). 'Martin Hundred' may thus refer to the area of Wales from which he believes they originated.

[Tragedy 6] 'Owen Glendour'

Author: William Baldwin (no evidence supports the unique ascription of this tragedy to the poet Thomas Phaer (d. 1560) in the 1578 edition of the *Mirror*). **Historical subject:** Owain Glyn Dŵr [or Glyndŵr] (*c.* 1359– *c.* 1416), magnate and leader of the Welsh revolt against King Henry IV. **Principal source:** *Hall's Chronicle.* **Contemporary literary treatments**: As Owen Glendower, Glyn Dŵr appears prominently in Shakespeare's *1 Henry IV* (*c.* 1597). Samuel Daniel briefly relates Owain Glyn Dŵr's revolt in book IV of his poem *Civil Wars* (first published 1595; revised and expanded 1609).

131   Baldwin's claim that Glendour was poorly bred is his own creation, one that allows him to promote the humanist credos that 'good bringing up' makes the person and that true nobility is found only in character and not in blood.

132   According to the Welsh author Geoffrey of Monmouth's fanciful but influential twelfth-century history of early Britain, *Historia Regum Britanniae*, the Welsh are the progeny of the original Britons, whose line commenced with Trojans brought to Britain by their leader Brute. One of the early Britons was the wizard Merlin, who was fathered by an incubus (Geoffrey of Monmouth, *History of the Kings of Britain*, trans. Lewis Thorpe (Harmondsworth: Penguin, 1966), 65–74, 167–8, 284).

133   In 1399, Henry Bolingbroke (d. 1413), first duke of Hereford, deposed King Richard II to become King Henry IV. As a result, the heir presumptive to the throne (the heir apparent, according to Edward Hall (Hall, 27)) was no longer Edmund Mortimer (d. 1425), fifth earl of March, but the new king's eldest son Prince Henry (d. 1422). Glendour's claim that Henry IV's subjects attempted to 'put him down' is apparently a reference to the Epiphany Rising of January 1400 (see Prose 5, n. 119).

134   In 1402, Owain Glyn Dŵr captured Lord Reynold Grey (d. 1440) of
      Ruthin (or Rithin), Wales. Following Hall, Baldwin mistakenly claims that
      Glyn Dŵr kept Grey in long captivity and forced him to marry one of his
      daughters. Hall is also the source for Baldwin's conflation of the wealthy
      landowner Sir Edmund Mortimer (d. 1409), whom Glyn Dŵr captured in
      the same year as Lord Grey, with Sir Edmund's nephew Edmund Mortimer,
      fifth earl of March, the young nobleman who held the strongest rival claim
      to Henry IV's throne (Hall, 23). In later years, Holinshed's *Chronicles* and
      Shakespeare's history plays would similarly follow Hall's erroneous claim that
      the earl of March was the man captured by Glyn Dŵr.

135   In this and the following five stanzas, Baldwin describes events of 1404–5
      (as related by Hall, who places them in the year 1402), including the French
      king Charles VI's desire to aid the Welsh against Henry IV; the unsuccessful
      attempt by Jacques (called James by Hall) de Bourbon (d. 1438), count of la
      Marche, to reach Glyn Dŵr with aid; the landing of 12,000 French troops at
      Milford Haven, Wales; Glyn Dŵr's and the king's abortive confrontation at
      Woodbury Hill, Worcestershire; the demoralizing loss of English provisions
      during the pursuit of Glyn Dŵr; and King Henry's decision to end his Welsh
      campaign before winter approached (see Hall, 25–6).

136   In 1402, Sir Henry Percy (d. 1403), called 'Hotspur', won a great victory
      over invading Scottish forces, taking as his prisoners a number of Scottish
      earls. Expecting to ransom these nobles back to the Scots, Hotspur and his
      powerful father Henry Percy (d. 1408), first earl of Northumberland, were
      outraged when King Henry claimed their prisoners as his own. As Hall tells
      it, Northumberland and Hotspur ignored their monarch's demand for the
      prisoners and instead dispatched Northumberland's brother Thomas Percy
      (d. 1403), first earl of Worcester, to the king to insist that he raise forces to
      rescue their kinsman the earl of March, whom Glyn Dŵr held prisoner. King
      Henry had no interest in freeing Richard II's heir apparent (and thus his
      chief rival for the throne), and he therefore refused (Hall, 24–5, 27–8).

137   Furious (Hall writes) at King Henry's refusal to aid the earl of March, the
      Percies went directly to Owain Glyn Dŵr, who freed Mortimer and plotted
      with his new-found allies to depose Henry IV. In this and the following
      stanzas, Baldwin follows Hall for the tripartite indenture Hall describes,
      uniquely among early commentators, as being made before rather than after
      the Battle of Shrewsbury (21 July 1403) and between Glyn Dŵr, Sir Henry
      'Hotspur' Percy, and the earl of March, rather than between Glyn Dŵr,
      Northumberland, and Sir Edmund Mortimer (Hall, 28). Hall's idiosyncratic
      account of the tripartite pact would influence not only the poems of the 1559
      Mirror but also Holinshed's *Chronicles* and Shakespeare's *1 Henry IV*.

138   The prophet's characterization of Henry IV as Gogmagog is Baldwin's
      invention. According to Geoffrey of Monmouth, Gogmagog was the only
      one of the original Albion race of giants not slain by Brute and his men in
      their conquest of Britain (*History of the Kings of Britain*, 72–3). In August
      1554, just at the time Baldwin and his fellow authors were composing their

poems, London officials placed a statue of Gogmagog at the entrance to London Bridge as part of the pageantry welcoming Queen Mary I and her new husband Philip of Spain on their first joint royal entry into the city. Baldwin bases his characterization of Gogmagog as 'accursed of God' not on Geoffrey's narrative but on the words of Revelation 20:8, which identify Gog and Magog as agents of Satan.

139   King Henry's forces defeated those of Hotspur and Worcester at the Battle of Shrewsbury. Hotspur died in combat and Worcester was captured. After his victory, King Henry had Worcester executed and his head sent to London for public display (see Hall, 31).

140   Baldwin follows Hall in suggesting that Glyn Dŵr died of starvation after the Battle of Shrewsbury; the horrific details of Glyn Dŵr's end, however, are Baldwin's own creation (Hall, 31).

[Prose 7]

141   The unnamed speaker is correct in his supposition that all three titles derived from words meaning borderland. Edward III had the earldom of March specifically created for Sir Roger Mortimer (d. 1330), whose base of power was in Wales and its bordering English counties (the Marches). In Scotland, the title 'earl of March' arose as an alternate name for the title held by the earls of Dunbar, whose locus of power was the marches (frontier) of Scotland. Baldwin's 'Lord James of Bourbon' was the historical Jacques de Bourbon (d. 1438), count of la Marche, whose title derived from the French county of La Marche, situated on Aquitaine's eastern frontier (Georges Thomas, 'Les Comtes de la Marche de la Maison de Charroux (Xe siècle–1177)', *Mémoires de la Société des Sciences Naturelles et Archéologiques de la Creuse* 23 (1925–7): 562–6).

142   George Ferrers here attempts to reconcile the differing accounts offered by Robert Fabyan and Edward Hall of the northern revolt of 1405. According to Fabyan, this rising in Yorkshire was the sole work of Richard Scrope (d. 1405), archbishop of York, and Thomas Mowbray (d. 1405), second earl of Nottingham (Fabyan, 572). Hall, by contrast, casts Henry Percy (d. 1408), first earl of Northumberland, as the mastermind behind a larger rising of which York and Nottingham's planned action was but a part (Hall, 34–5). Ferrers takes the names 'Baynton and Blinkinsops' from Hall's account of the aftermath of Northumberland's revolt (ibid., 35). Sir Henry Boynton and Alexander Blenkinsop were both executed in 1405 for assisting Northumberland in his abortive rising. For Boynton, see M. H. Keen, 'Treason Trials under the Law of Arms', *Transactions of the Royal Historical Society* 12 (1962): 85–7; for Blenkinsop, see Andy King, '"They have the Hertes of the People by North": Northumberland, the Percies and Henry IV, 1399–1408', *Henry IV: The Establishment of the Regime, 1399–1406*, ed. Gwilym Dodd and Douglas Biggs (Woodbridge: York Medieval Press and Boydell Press, 2003), 151. As Ferrers suggests, Northumberland himself fled into Scotland after the failure of his revolt (Hall, 35).

[Tragedy 7] 'Henry Percy, Earl of Northumberland'

Author(s): Unknown (Sir Thomas Chaloner and William Baldwin?).
Historical subject: Sir Henry Percy (1341–1408), first earl of Northumberland,
magnate and rebel to King Henry IV. **Principal source:** *Hall's Chronicle*.
Contemporary literary treatments: Northumberland plays prominent
roles in Shakespeare's plays *Richard II* (c. 1595), *1 Henry IV*, and *2 Henry
IV* (both *c.* 1597), as well as in Samuel Daniel's narrative poem *Civil Wars*
(1595–1609).

143 'Moral Senec' is John Lydgate's preferred epithet in *The Fall of Princes* for
the Roman dramatist and philosopher Lucius Annaeus Seneca (d. AD 65).
See Lydgate, *Tragedies*, sigs. C2v, L5v. The poet offers in this stanza a general
expression of Seneca's stoic sentiments.

144 Under Richard II, Northumberland's younger brother Thomas Percy (d.
1403), first earl of Worcester, rose to become lord steward, the chief officer of
the royal household (Hall, 9; see also Tragedy 5, 'King Richard II').

145 The poet mistakenly construes Hall's statement that 'Lord Henry Percy' wed
Eleanor Mortimer to mean that it was the earl of Northumberland rather
than Northumberland's son Sir Henry Percy (d. 1403) who married a member
of the Mortimer family (Hall, 27). The younger Percy, called Hotspur by his
Scottish opponents for his 'haut and valiant corage' (ibid., 24), wed Elizabeth
(not, as Hall has it, Eleanor) Mortimer, sister of Sir Edmund Mortimer
(d. 1408/9), the English magnate captured by Welsh rebel leader Owain
Glyn Dŵr (d. *c.* 1416). Later in this poem, the author will follow Hall in
erroneously conflating Sir Edmund Mortimer with Sir Edmund's nephew
Edmund Mortimer (d. 1425), fifth earl of March (ibid., 27).

146 For these matters, the poet draws on Hall's brief, apparently unhistorical
statement that Thomas Percy bore malice toward Richard II, because Richard
had proclaimed Percy's brother Northumberland to be a traitor (Hall, 9; cf.
Hall's source, Froissart, vol. 2, fos. 306v–7r, where Richard's accusation is
dated May 1399).

147 That the Percies plotted with Edmund of Langley (d. 1402), first duke of
York, to give power to Henry Bolingbroke (d. 1413), first duke of Hereford
(the future King Henry IV), is the same unusual and entirely unprecedented
claim made by Sir Thomas Chaloner in Tragedy 5, 'King Richard II' (see
Tragedy 5, n. 124). Its presence here may point to Chaloner as the author of
this anonymous tragedy or possibly as the person who gathered historical
matter for it, so that Baldwin would 'know what to say' in the poem when
he put its contents into verse (see Prose 7).

148 Hall records that Northumberland and the other northern lords who came
to Bolingbroke's side in 1399 made Bolingbroke swear an oath not to do
bodily harm to King Richard. That Henry IV broke that oath was one of
the charges the Percies lodged against the king before the July 1403 Battle of
Shrewsbury (Hall, 8, 30).

149 For the Percies' capture of Scottish prisoners in 1402, King Henry IV's demand that they turn those prisoners over to him, and the Percies' angry defiance of that command, see Tragedy 6, n. 136.

150 Historically, it was Hotspur and not Northumberland who was the uncle of Edmund Mortimer (d. 1425), fifth earl of March. According to Edward Hall, in the first year of Henry IV's reign Owen Glendour (the Welsh rebel leader Owain Glyn Dŵr) seized and held captive the earl of March (Hall's mistake for the man whom Glyn Dŵr actually captured, March's uncle Sir Edmund Mortimer (d. 1408/9)). The Percies, feigning deep concern for their kinsman, demanded that King Henry effect Mortimer's release. The motivation behind their demand, however, was not strong devotion to March but a desire to 'prove and tempt' a monarch whose authority the Percies had come to envy. The king, Hall continues, had no interest in freeing Mortimer, since March had been Richard II's heir apparent and thus stood as Henry's greatest rival for the throne. Henry therefore refused to act on behalf of Hotspur's nephew and instead falsely declared March to be a traitor, a turncoat who allowed himself to be taken so he could join Glendour's rebellion. The king's answer drove the Percies into such a fury that they began to plot the monarch's overthrow (Hall, 23, 27–8).

151 Hall writes that it was Owen Glendour, 'Lord Henry Percy' (by whom he means Sir Henry Percy), and the earl of March who made the famous tripartite agreement to divide the rule of England and Wales amongst themselves. As he did in construing Northumberland to be the earl of March's uncle, the poet erroneously construes Hall's use of the courtesy title 'the Lord Percy' here to indicate Northumberland rather than Hotspur (Hall, 28). On Hall's idiosyncratic but influential presentation of this 'tripartite indenture', see Tragedy 6, n. 137.

152 King Henry, Hall records, quickly learned of the machinations of Owen, Hotspur, and March, and he thus led forces toward Wales to engage Glendour's rebels. In response, Northumberland and Hotspur marshalled forces in the north and made a pact with their Scottish prisoners to gain their support. Before the combined English and Scottish forces could move south, however, Northumberland fell ill and Hotspur was forced to go on without him. Combining his forces with those of his uncle the earl of Worcester, Hotspur continued to Shrewsbury, where he and Worcester engaged the royal army on 21 July 1403 (1402 according to Hall). The Percies were defeated: Hotspur was killed in battle and Worcester was captured and executed. In the wake of his victory, Henry IV sent a large army into Wales to suppress Glendour's rising and to re-establish English rule. He also received the earl of Northumberland, who professed to have had no knowledge of his son and brother's rising. Although suspicious, Henry accepted Northumberland's excuse and allowed him to remain free (Hall, 28–32).

153 In Hall's telling, Northumberland in 1405 began to commune with several northern leaders about resistance to Henry IV, including the titular Earl Marshal Thomas Mowbray (d. 1405), second earl of Nottingham (son of

the exiled speaker of *Mirror* Tragedy 4); Thomas (d. 1408), fifth Baron Bardolf; the knights (not lords) Sir Ralph Hastings and Sir John Fauconberg (both d. 1405); and Archbishop Richard Scrope of York (d. 1405), a man Hall claims was spurred in his hostility towards the king by Henry's 1399 beheading of Scrope's brother (historically his cousin) William Scrope, first earl of Wiltshire (for these men, see Hall, 34–5; see also Simon Walker, 'The Yorkshire Risings of 1405: Texts and Contexts', *Henry IV: The Establishment of the Regime, 1399–1406*, 161–84).

154 Henry IV, Hall relates, learned of the planned Yorkshire rising as it was still developing; he thus speedily took an army north, where he captured and executed all of the chief rebel leaders save Northumberland and Bardolf, who fled into Scotland. Thereafter, Earl Henry and Lord Bardolf travelled to the Continent in a bid to gain support from foreign monarchs. Rebuffed, they returned to Scotland (Hall, 35). In 1408, Northumberland finally decided to invade England, allied only with Bardolf and his old friend George Dunbar (d. between 1416 and 1423), the Scottish earl of March. Crossing the border, Northumberland's forces soon attracted numerous common supporters to their side and captured many of the former Percy possessions that King Henry had earlier seized (ibid., 39).

155 Since the ancient period, storks had been understood to be particularly kind and loyal birds (see, for instance, St Ambrose, *Hexameron, Paradise, and Cain and Abel*, trans. John Savage, *The Fathers of the Church: A New Translation* (Washington, DC: Catholic University of America Press, 1961), 42:204–5).

156 As Hall narrates it, Northumberland's invading forces engaged those of Rafe Rekesby (the historical Sir Thomas Rokeby) at Bramham Moor, Yorkshire. Rekesby and his men won the battle and executed Northumberland and Bardolf, sending their heads to the king at London (Hall, 39). Historically, both Northumberland and Bardolf died of wounds received on the battlefield; they were only posthumously beheaded.

157 The Percy motto was *Esperance*, French for 'hope'.

[Prose 8]

158 Baldwin offers a more charitable understanding of the three leading members of the Percy family – Henry (d. 1408), first earl of Northumberland, his son Henry 'Hotspur' Percy (d. 1403), and Northumberland's brother Thomas (d. 1403), earl of Worcester – and their defiance of King Henry IV than does his chief source, Hall's chronicle. In Hall's telling, the Percies' stated desire to have King Henry rescue their kinsman Edmund Mortimer (d. 1425), fifth earl of March, from captivity by the Welsh rebel leader Owen Glendour (Owain Glyn Dŵr (d. *c.* 1416)) was in fact just a pretext with which to 'set al thynges in broile and uncerteintie' between themselves and their prince (Hall, 27; cf. the presentation of the Percies in Tragedies 6 and 7).

159 In 1407, Henry IV made Edmund Holland, seventh earl of Kent (d. 1408), admiral of the west and north, and he dispatched him in the next year to rid the English Channel of pirates. Kent pursued the Breton raiders to Île

de Bréhat ('Briake'), an island off the coast of Brittany. While assaulting its town, he was felled by an arrow (see Fabyan, 573; also Hall, 39–40). For Richard (d. 1415), first earl of Cambridge, and Henry (d. 1415), third Baron Scrope of Masham, see Tragedy 8.

[Tragedy 8] 'Richard, Earl of Cambridge'

Author: William Baldwin. **Historical subject:** Richard (1385–1415), first earl of Cambridge, magnate and conspirator against King Henry V. **Principal source:** *Hall's Chronicle.* **Contemporary literary treatments:** Cambridge's plotting is dramatized in the multi-author play *Sir John Oldcastle* (1599), while Shakespeare portrays the conspiracy's exposure and aftermath in *Henry V* (c. 1599). Samuel Daniel also narrates Cambridge's plot in his poem *Civil Wars* (1595–1609).

160 Richard, second son of Edward (d. 1402), first duke of York, and thus grandson of King Edward III, married in 1408 Anne Mortimer (d. 1411), eldest sister of Edmund Mortimer (d. 1425), fifth earl of March, heir presumptive to Richard II at the time of Richard's deposition. Many who opposed the rule of Henry IV and his son Henry V looked to March as England's rightful king. According to Hall, several sources affirm that Cambridge secretly supported Mortimer's claim to the throne in the hope that he or his children might one day inherit it from the impotent, childless March (Hall, 61). As he did in Tragedy 6 above, Baldwin follows Hall in conflating the fifth earl of March with his uncle, Sir Edmund Mortimer (d. 1408/9), the man actually captured in 1402 by the Welsh rebel leader 'Owen Glendour' (Owain Glyn Dŵr (d. c. 1416)).

161 Although Baldwin suggests plots against both Henry IV and Henry V, Hall correctly portrays Cambridge conspiring only against Henry V in 1415 (Hall, 60).

162 Cambridge's partners in his plot were the earl of March, Sir Thomas Grey of Heaton (d. 1415), and Henry (d. 1415), third Baron Scrope of Masham. Hall does not say who revealed Cambridge's plot; historically, it was exposed to Henry by the very man in whose name it was fomented, March.

163 Drawing on Polydore Vergil's *Anglica Historia* (Basel, 1534), Hall states that, upon exposure, the conspirators quickly admitted that the French King Charles VI had paid them to kidnap or kill King Henry. Hall then notes, however, that other writers (e.g. Hardyng, 374) assert that Cambridge actually undertook his plot on behalf of the earl of March. As does Hall, Baldwin combines both accounts, portraying the claim to serve Charles VI as a falsehood told by Cambridge to protect his brother-in-law Edmund Mortimer (Hall, 61).

[Prose 9]

164 Despite the July 1415 plot against the king undertaken by his younger brother Richard (d. 1415), earl of Cambridge, Edward, second duke of York, retained

Henry V's trust and travelled in August with the royal expedition to France. According to Edward Hall, it was at the Battle of Agincourt (25 October 1415) that York and Michael de la Pole, second earl of Suffolk, were killed on the battlefield (Hall, 72). Historically, only York lost his life in the conflict; Suffolk had succumbed to illness in the month previous.

165   Robert Fabyan claims that 'dyvers wryters' call Thomas Montagu (or Montacute) (d. 1428), fourth earl of Salisbury, 'the good earl', an epithet Fabyan himself adopts (Fabyan, 598). Neither he nor any other of the *Mirror* authors' sources, however, mentions any domestic action by which Salisbury might have earned such an appellation.

[Tragedy 9] 'Thomas Montague, Earl of Salisbury'

Author: Unknown. **Historical subject:** Thomas Montagu (or Montacute) (1388–1428), fourth earl of Salisbury, magnate and military leader. **Principal sources:** *Fabyan's Chronicle; Hall's Chronicle.* **Contemporary literary treatments:** Shakespeare dramatizes the earl of Salisbury's death in *1 Henry VI* (c. 1591–2), and he portrays Salisbury's father and the unravelling of the Epiphany Rising plot in *Richard II* (c. 1595).

166   Salisbury's father John Montagu (or Montacute) (d. 1400), third earl of Salisbury, was a participant in the Epiphany Rising of January 1400, in which several partisans of the deposed Richard II plotted to assassinate the new king Henry IV (see Prose 5). When the conspiracy was exposed, John Montagu escaped but was quickly taken and beheaded (Fabyan, 567–8). For an argument that this poet shapes Salisbury's presentation of his father's unjust posthumous reputation to evoke memories of that of a more recent fallen and discredited political leader, Edward Seymour (d. 1552), first duke of Somerset, see Lucas 'A Mirror for Magistrates', 67–9.

167   For the arrest and 'murder' of Thomas of Woodstock (d. 1397), first duke of Gloucester, and for his posthumous condemnation for treason, see Tragedy 3, nn. 99 and 100. Although many at the time believed Gloucester's death to have been an act of murder, no one could openly condemn the action until two years later, when Richard II lost his crown to Henry Bolingbroke (d. 1413), first duke of Hereford. The new king Henry IV's first parliament (October 1399) charged King Richard with arranging Gloucester's murder and made this accusation part of its justification for deposing him (Hall, 9).

168   Edward Hall records that the 'common fame' at the time of Richard II's demise was that his jailers had starved him to death (Hall, 20). As do the authors of Tragedies 4 and 5, the poet mistakenly refers to Henry Bolingbroke, who was duke of Hereford at the time of his challenge to Richard II, as 'Earl Henry'.

169   The 'Salisbury' author rewrites the accounts of the Epiphany Rising offered in his two sources, Fabyan's and Hall's chronicles. Most notably, the poet excludes Hall's claim that the abbot of Westminster rather than Richard II's half-brother John Holland (d. 1400), first earl of Huntingdon (and, until

he lost the title in November 1399, first duke of Exeter), was the originator of the plot, and he makes the starving of King Richard a catalyst for the Epiphany Rising, whereas Hall makes it clear that Richard's starvation was a consequence of that failed revolt. See Hall, 15–20; Fabyan, 567–8.

170 The poet follows Fabyan in making the conspirators plan their assassination attempt to take place during a disguised entertainment and in having Edward (d. 1415), first earl of Rutland – whom Fabyan names by his former title duke of Aumale – expose it to Henry IV (Fabyan, 567–8).

171 Upon learning that their plans had been revealed, the Epiphany plotters scattered and fled. John Montagu was soon after captured and executed by the townspeople of Cirencester, Gloucestershire (Fabyan, 568).

172 Although his father was posthumously attainted by the parliament of 1401, Thomas Montagu was permitted to assume the title earl of Salisbury when he came of age in 1409. Both Fabyan and Hall record that Salisbury took part in several military actions under Henry V; the poet's description of him personally leading assaults and winning 'holds' at this time, however, is his own invention. Similarly, the author builds on relatively slender evidence in his chronicle sources to claim that Salisbury took part in crafting 'all treaties' under Henry V (see Fabyan, 583; Hall, 95). For a topical approach to the often unhistorical presentation of Salisbury in this tragedy, see Lucas, *'A Mirror for Magistrates'*, 142–8.

173 By the treaty of Troyes (May 1420), England's Henry V became heir to the throne of France. Unfortunately, King Henry died on 31 August 1422, leaving his 9-month-old son Henry VI to succeed him as English monarch and heir to the French throne. Since Henry VI was a minor, his two paternal uncles assumed chief authority in his name. Humphrey (d. 1447), first duke of Gloucester, became protector of the realm in England and John (d. 1435), first duke of Bedford, took the office of regent of France. When the French king Charles VI died in October 1422, the infant Henry became (at least in English eyes) ruler of both England and France.

174 Here and later, in his presentation of Salisbury's alleged mildness in martial assaults, the poet imaginatively expands on Fabyan's bare comment that 'dyvers wryters' termed Salisbury 'the good erle' (Fabyan, 598). Neither Hall nor Fabyan makes any mention of Salisbury bearing rule in England or of holding the philosophy of governance ascribed to him in the poem. See Lucas, *'A Mirror for Magistrates'*, 142–5.

175 Hall notes that in 1428 two towns surrendered their keys to Salisbury on hearing that he offered citizens of a nearby city the opportunity to keep their property if they swore loyalty to Henry VI (see note 187 below). Otherwise, he presents Salisbury's career as one of nearly unceasing assaults and hostile sieges (Hall, 144). For enemy forces fleeing at the sound of his name, see lines 218–24 below.

176 In July 1423, Louis (d. 1446), count of Vendôme ('Vantadore'), and John Stewart (d. 1424), the Scottish earl of Buchan, laid siege to Cravant on the river Yonne in the Auxerrois district of Burgundy. Sent by Regent Bedford to

relieve the town, Salisbury and his Burgundian allies won a decisive victory on 31 July over the French and Scottish besiegers. The claim that Salisbury killed all who did not flee is the poet's invention. See Hall, 117–18; and 'Cravant, Battle of (1423)', in John A. Wagner, *Encyclopedia of the Hundred Years War* (Westport, Conn.: Greenwood Press, 2006), 104–5.

177　As a reward for the victory at Cravant, John of Bedford made Salisbury his vicegerent and lieutenant for Brie and Champagne. Salisbury then travelled to Brie to attack the Château Montaiguillon, a fortress that withstood his siege for five months before surrendering completely (Hall, 119).

178　Hall describes Arthur (d. 1458), younger brother to John (d. 1442), duke of Brittany, as 'commonly called the earle of Richemond, havyng neither profite of the name nor of the countrey'. This Arthur, Hall continues, turned against his former English allies, 'notwithstandyng that king Henry the .v. had created him earle of Yvry in Normandy and gave him not onely a great pencion but the same toune of Yvry' (Hall, 121). Arthur of Brittany was indeed 'earl of Yvry' (count of Ivry) and lord of the Norman town and castle of the same name. He also laid claim to the title earl of Richmond, a Yorkshire earldom that had often been held by Bretons following the Norman conquest. Henry V, however, had bestowed that title and its privileges in 1414 on his own brother John of Bedford.

179　Hall relates that Duke John of Brittany, fearing that the English planned to put his dukedom under their control, switched his allegiance in 1424 from Henry VI to Dauphin Charles. His brother Arthur then stole away from Brittany to join the Dauphin, which emboldened the Bretons who commanded Arthur's castle and town of Ivry (Ivry-la-Battaille), Normandy, to defy the English and to harm the surrounding English-held lands. In August, Regent Bedford, with Salisbury and other English military leaders, assembled an army and laid siege to Ivry. The commanders of the castle negotiated terms with the English, in which they agreed to surrender the castle and town if the Dauphin did not dispatch an army to rescue them by an appointed day. On hearing of the plight of the men of Ivry, Dauphin Charles sent a force of 20,000 French, Breton, and Scottish fighters ('two thousand score' is a mistake by the poet) under the command of his young lieutenant-general, John (d. 1476), second duke of Alençon (Hall, 121–2).

180　Coming, Hall writes, within two miles of Ivry, Alençon suddenly ordered his troops to proceed to the English-held town of Verneuil (Verneuil-sur-Avre, Normandy). There, he told its garrison that his forces had destroyed the English army at Ivry and, by that falsehood, convinced the Verneuil soldiers to yield to him. When Alençon's forces did not appear at Ivry by the appointed day, the defenders of the town surrendered to Bedford, who then set off in pursuit of the dauphinist army. Alençon took his troops and met Bedford's men in the field before Verneuil on 17 August 1424 (27 August 1425, according to Hall), where the English forces delivered to the Dauphin's army a crushing defeat. Hall states that 1,800 English 'men of armes' and 8,000 other fighters slaughtered nearly 10,000 French and Scottish combatants on that day (Hall, 121–5).

181 After the victory at Verneuil, Bedford sent an army under Salisbury's command into Maine and Anjou. In August 1425, Salisbury's forces laid siege to Le Mans ('Mawns'), the strongly fortified capital of Maine. Hall names as the first of the city's three captains 'Baldwin of Champaigne lord of Toisse', the historical Baudouin of Champagne (d. b. 1466), seigneur de Tucé. Salisbury's artillery destroyed the walls and towers of the town, which thereafter surrendered (Hall, 126).

182 Hall notes that 'Baldwin' of Champagne and his fellow captains chose to defend Le Mans against Salisbury's army, because they had no inkling of the power of Salisbury's heavy guns. It was the townspeople and not Baldwin and the other captains, Hall records, who finally offered to surrender their city (Hall, 126).

183 The poet follows Hall for the Maine forts and towns captured by Salisbury in the wake of the 10 August 1425 surrender of Le Mans (see Hall, 126–7). Hall's own source for this sometimes garbled list of conquests is the detailed memoir of English actions in France preserved in College of Arms MS M.9.

184 Hall recounts how Arthur of Brittany, newly appointed constable of France, assembled an army of 40,000 and laid siege to the English garrison of fewer than 600 men at Saint-James de Beuvron, on the Breton–Norman border. One evening, the overmatched soldiers of Saint-James quietly issued forth and divided their attack, sending part of their force to the rear of Arthur's troops to surprise them with war cries of 'St George!' and 'Salisbury!' Thinking that the earl of Salisbury had arrived with an army of relief, Arthur's men panicked and were routed by their English opponents. By this means, the siege was broken, over 4,000 Breton, French, and Scottish troops were killed, and the soldiers of Saint-James seized much in the way of provisions left behind by the constable's fleeing forces (Hall, 129).

185 The public quarrel between Protector Gloucester and Henry Beaufort (d. 1447), bishop (later cardinal) of Winchester, which Hall places immediately after the March 1426 victory at Saint-James de Beuvron, occurred from about October 1425 to March 1426 (Hall, 130–8; Fabyan, 595–7). Despite the poet's claim, Salisbury was not among the lords who pledged to end Gloucester's and Beaufort's dispute (see Hall, 135).

186 Thomas Beaufort, first duke of Exeter, governor of the king's person, died on 31 December 1426. To replace him, Henry VI's minority council appointed John of Bedford's lieutenant in France, Richard Beauchamp (d. 1439), thirteenth earl of Warwick. Warwick took up his new position in June 1428; Salisbury – who had come to England at a date unmentioned by Hall – departed soon after for France with a new expeditionary force. On his return to the Continent, Salisbury 'began mervailously to phantesie' the capture of Orléans, a well-defended city on the Loire river. Knowing it to be a long and risky undertaking, he debated the idea at length with Bedford and his counsellors. Though the others found Salisbury's plan 'harde and straunge',

such was his influence at this time that they ultimately agreed to support it. With a force of 10,000 men, Salisbury departed Paris for Orléans in August 1428 (Hall, 138–9, 143–4).

187 To prepare for their siege of Orléans, Salisbury and his forces took the dauphinist towns of Janville ('Yainvile' in Hall), where some of the defenders were put to death 'for certain causes', and Beaugency. In the case of the latter town, Salisbury allowed every citizen who swore fealty to Henry VI to keep his goods and rights of inheritance. Hearing of Salisbury's generous offer, the leaders of the nearby towns of Meung-sur-Loire ('Mewne') and Jargeau ('Jargeman') offered to surrender their towns to him if he would offer them similar conditions (Hall, 144).

188 Hall relates how John (d. 1468), called the Bastard of Orléans, was born to a beautiful woman who was both the wife of the 'lord of Cauny' (Aubert le Flamenc, seigneur de Cany) and the mistress of Louis, duke of Orléans. When Cany's wife gave birth to John, it was not known if the child was Cany's or Orléans's. Pressed at eight years old to declare himself Cany's child and thereby to claim an inheritance worth 4,000 crowns a year, John stoutly declared that he would be 'more glad' to be known as the duke of Orléans's bastard 'with a meane livyng, then the lawfull sonne of that coward cuckolde Cauny, with his foure thousande crounes' (Hall, 144–5).

189 After enduring three weeks of siege, the Bastard of Orléans led a sortie out of the fortified bridgehead that guarded the Loire-side entrance to Orléans. His men were beaten back, and in the process the English took the bridgehead and its towers (which Hall speaks of as a single tower). While the newly won possession brought Orléans into the range of Salisbury's heavy guns, it also left the English who occupied it exposed to French artillery. See Hall, 145.

190 On the fifty-ninth day of the siege (historically 27 October 1428), Salisbury and several of his captains went to the highest chamber in one of the captured bridge towers to view the condition of Orléans. A French gunner caught sight of the men and fired his cannon, shattering an iron grate that tore away one of Salisbury's eyes and cheeks. Salisbury succumbed to his injuries eight days later (Hall, 145).

[Prose 10]

191 On 7 May 1429, French forces from Orléans successfully assaulted the English-held bridgehead in which Thomas Montagu (d. 1428), fourth earl of Salisbury, had earlier received his mortal wound (see Tragedy 9). Among those who died in the battle, Hall writes, were 'Lorde Morlyns, and the lorde Pownynges' (Hall, 148). The men to whom Hall refers are Sir William Molyens and Sir Richard Poynings (Paul Charpentier and Charles Cuissard, eds., *Journal du Siège D'Orléans* (Orléans, 1896), 3, 87).

192 The English military leader John Fitzalan, seventh earl of Arundel, died from a gunshot wound received during a June 1435 attempt to take Gerberoy castle, located in the Beauvaisis (now Oise), France (Hall, 173).

[Tragedy 10] 'King James I'

Author: Unknown. **Historical subject:** James I (1394–1437), King of Scots. **Principal source:** *Hall's Chronicle.* **Contemporary literary parallels**: Sir David Lyndsay employs key events from King James I's life as a warning to his own monarch, James V, in his poem *Testament and Complaint of our Sovereign Lord's Papingo* (1530). George Pettie includes lines 111–12 of 'James I' in the dedicatory epistle to his *A Petite Palace of Pettie his Pleasure* (1576).

193 James's father King Robert III (d. 1406), son of Robert II, the founder of the Stewart royal line, came to power in 1390; physical disabilities, however, left him unable to overmaster the most powerful nobles of his realm. Edward Hall describes Robert as 'sicke and unapt to rule' and notes that by 1400 real power in the realm was wielded not by the king but by a governor, whom Hall initially (and correctly) identifies as Robert Stewart (d. 1420), first duke of Albany (Hall, 24).

194 The poet combines two historical figures in his character of Walter, governor of the realm during the time of Robert III. The poet's source, Hall's chronicle, first identifies King Robert's governor of Scotland as Robert, duke of Albany, but it then later incorrectly terms him Walter, duke of Albany (Hall, 24, 37). Like Robert III, Robert of Albany was the son of King Robert II and his first wife, Elizabeth (Robert III's baptismal name was John). Under Robert II, Robert Stewart became a powerful figure in Scottish politics as guardian of Robert II's kingdom. At the accession of his brother Robert III (1390), Stewart remained guardian of the realm until 1393. Thereafter, he became duke of Albany in 1398 and lieutenant of the realm in 1402 (not governor in 1400, as Hall has it). Walter Stewart (d. 1437), created first earl of Atholl in 1404, was the son of Robert II by his second wife, Euphemia. While politically influential, Walter was never lieutenant or governor. Although Hall later clearly distinguishes Albany and Atholl from one another in his account of James I's career (see ibid., 187), the poet continues throughout the entirety of his tragedy to conflate King James's two royal uncles under the single name Walter.

195 Robert III, Hall states, became convinced that his son and heir Davy (1378–1402), first duke of Rothesay, spent his days in lust and adultery. Robert therefore sent Davy to his brother the duke of Albany (identified as Walter in this part of Hall's chronicle) for counsel and correction. Albany, however, harboured ambitions for the crown; he therefore seized Davy and, after moving him repeatedly between various strongholds, starved him to death in Falkland castle, where he also executed a woman who had tried to feed the emaciated prince through a reed with milk pumped from her breasts (Hall, 37).

196 In Hall's telling, after Rothesay's death was revealed, Albany attempted to shift blame by accusing other men of the crime. King Robert, however, still suspected his brother, and he thus decided to send his 9-year-old son James to safety in France. Unfortunately, James's ship was blown off course to England. Since England and Scotland were at war, the king's council decided

to treat Prince James as a prisoner. He would remain in English keeping (albeit with many liberties) for the next eighteen years; his father, however, lasted only a few months before dying of grief over his son's capture (Hall, 37–9). Historically, James was 12 years old at the time he departed for France in March 1406, four years after Rothesay's death. King Robert died within days of learning of his son's capture (Stephen Boardman, *The Early Stewart Kings: Robert II and Robert III, 1371–1406* (East Linton: Tuckwell Press, 1996), 291–7).

197 James I became king of the Scots on 4 April 1406. While the English, Hall writes, would have ransomed their captive for a relatively small amount of money, 'the Scottes were neither able [to pay] nor offered no summe convenient'. James thus remained in England for the next eighteen years, first as a prisoner under Henry IV and then as a member of Henry V's and Henry VI's court. During his youth, James was taught to excel 'in all poynctes of Marciall feates, Musicall instrumentes, Poeticall artes and liberal sciences. In so muche that at his returne from captivitee, he furnished his realme bothe with good learnyng and civill policie, whiche before was barbarous, savage, rude and without all good nurtur' (Hall, 119, 39).

198 As Hall records it, James I was wed in 1424 to Jane (historically Joan) (d. 1445), daughter of John Beaufort (d. 1410), first earl of Somerset. Jane was 'cosyn germayne' to the 2-year-old Henry VI, and the match was made by Protector of the Realm Humphrey (d. 1447), first duke of Gloucester, in order to forge a tie between Scotland and England that James would be loath to break. King Henry's minority council also greatly reduced James's ransom, which permitted James to return to Scotland after swearing (so the chauvinistic Hall claims, following the propaganda of his own king, Henry VIII) an oath of fealty recognizing Henry VI as Scotland's true overlord (Hall, 119, 186). James entered Scotland and assumed power in April 1424.

199 The poet continues his conflation of two of James I's uncles, Robert, first duke of Albany, and Walter, first earl of Atholl. Albany, governor of the realm during most of James's captivity and the man widely accused of murdering David, duke of Rothesay, died in 1420, four years before James returned to Scotland. The claims that 'Walter' of Albany was the governor who turned over Scotland to James I (it was in fact Robert of Albany's eldest son Murdoch (or Murdo) Stewart (d. 1425), second duke of Albany) and that this Walter accused Duke Murdo of killing Davy of Rothesay are the poet's inventions. Historically, it was James I himself and not Walter of Atholl who determined in 1425 that Duke Murdoch should be arrested and tried for treason (see Michael Brown, *James I* (Edinburgh: Cannongate, 1994), 40–67; cf. Hall, 187).

200 According to Hall, James created an alliance with the French solely out of his naturally perverse Scottish nature, which led him to reject all proper feelings of gratitude for the kindness England had shown him (Hall, 119–20). Walter of Albany's role in James's repudiation of the English, as well as the poem's claim that James invaded England, are entirely the poet's own creations. For a reading of the 'James I' poet's narrative choices in the context of the

long-running contention between the Scots and the English in the 1540s (known as the 'Rough Wooing'), see Lucas, *A Mirror for Magistrates*, 148–57.

201 Medieval and early modern physicians believed that the physical substance *spiritus* (breath or air, but also spirit, soul) mixed with blood in the heart to produce and distribute the vital heat that creatures needed to stay alive. The 'vital spirits' were also key to perceiving sensations. Some understood insensibility to pain resulting from illness to be the effect of the vital spirits rushing from the diseased parts of the body to the heart in order to defend it from the attacking malady. See, for instance, William Drummond, 'A Cypresse Grove', in *Flowres of Sion* (Edinburgh, 1623; *STC* 7247), 57–8.

202 Hall relates how Walter of Atholl, eager for the crown, suborned his nephew Robert Stewart (or Stuart) and his kinsman Robert Graham, as well as 'diverse other' to assassinate King James. In February 1437, the assassins came to Perth ('Pertho'), where the king was lodged, and burst suddenly into his privy chamber, killing King James and several of his servants and wounding Queen Jane, who herself killed one of her assailants (Hall, 187).

[Prose 11]

203 The 1559 edition's table of contents (apparently based on that of the suppressed 1554 edition) shows that George Ferrers's tragedy 'Humphrey, Duke of Gloucester, and Elianor Cobham his Wife' was once intended to follow this prose link. It did not appear, however, in the 1559 *Mirror*, nor did it appear in its original form in any subsequent edition. On the absence of Ferrers's poem from the 1559 *Mirror* and its reworking for the edition of 1578, see Introduction, p. xxi; Prose 30, First Version; and Lucas, *A Mirror for Magistrates*, 21–2, 240–1.

[Tragedy 11] 'William de la Pole, Earl of Suffolk'

Author: Unknown. **Historical subject:** William de la Pole (1396–1450), military and political leader. **Principal source:** *Hall's Chronicle*. **Contemporary literary treatments:** Shakespeare dramatizes Suffolk's military career in *1 Henry VI* and his political actions and downfall in *2 Henry VI* (both plays *c.* 1591–2). In *England's Heroical Epistles* (1597), Michael Drayton creates for Suffolk and Queen Margaret verse letters supposedly exchanged at the time of Suffolk's banishment; later, Drayton would rehearse Suffolk's career from the time of Margaret of Anjou's marriage contract to Suffolk's murder in his poem *The Miseries of Queen Margarite* (1627). Finally, in *Civil Wars* (1595–1609), Samuel Daniel narrates Suffolk's last years, including his downfall and death.

204 'Poole' was a familiar alternate spelling and pronunciation of the family name 'Pole'.

205 At age 19, William de la Pole took part in Henry V's 1415 expedition into France. He became fourth earl of Suffolk in that year, after the death of his elder brother, and was made knight of the Garter in 1421.

206 Hall records that Joan of Arc ('Pucelle Joan') was captured in May 1430 by English and Burgundian forces under the commands of the duke of Burgundy ('Burgoyne'), Burgundy's lieutenant John of Luxembourg, and the earls of Arundel and Suffolk. Hall does not in fact credit Suffolk with her capture; instead, he correctly identifies John of Luxembourg as the leader of the force that took Joan, and prints a letter issued in Henry VI's name praising Burgundy for taking her (Hall, 156–9). Historically, Burgundian forces alone captured Joan.

207 Following an error introduced into printed versions of Enguerrand de Monstrelet's chronicle, Hall incorrectly ascribes to Suffolk rather than to Humphrey (d. 1460), sixth earl of Stafford, the July 1430 capture of Aumale ('Aumerle'), Normandy, a town whose fortified castle had withstood twenty-four 'great assau[l]tes' before its captain André, seigneur de Rambures, capitulated (Hall, 156).

208 Hall describes the spring 1444 diplomatic meeting at Tours as arranged not by the pope but by 'all the princes of Christendom'. There, he writes, Suffolk, 'Robert lorde Roos' (Sir Robert Roos (d. 1448)), and 'diverse other' met with Duke Charles (d. 1465) of Orléans and his fellow French representatives. Acting as mediators were ambassadors representing Spain, Denmark, Hungary, and the Holy Roman Emperor (Hall, 203).

209 Although their bid for a lasting settlement failed, the English and French representatives did agree, Hall writes, to conclude an eighteen-month truce. While negotiating this truce, the earl of Suffolk, 'extendyng his commission to the uttermost', secretly decided to pursue a 'perfite peace' by means of a French marriage for his monarch (ibid.).

210 Margaret of Anjou (1430–1482) was the daughter of René (or Rainièr), duke of Anjou, titular king of Jerusalem, Naples, and Sicily. According to Hall, Suffolk, either corrupted by bribes or simply blinded by his zeal for a French marriage, consented at Tours to turn over to René the hard-won English possessions of Maine and Anjou; he also agreed to forgo a dowry for Henry VI's intended bride. While Hall describes the future Queen Margaret as beautiful and excellent in 'wit and pollicie', the 'Suffolk' poet's praise for her disposition and learning is his own additon. Of Margaret's personality, Hall offers only the single comment that she was in 'stomack and corage [spirit and vigour], more like to a man, then a woman' (Hall, 204–5).

211 As Hall tells it, in 1442 or 1443 Henry VI made by proxy a marriage contract with the daughter (but not heir) of John, fourth count of Armagnac. Unfortunately, John and his daughters were soon after taken prisoner by Charles VII's son Louis, so the marriage was never formally concluded. Upon learning of Suffolk's 1444 Anjou marriage proposal, Henry VI's uncle Humphrey (d. 1447), first duke of Gloucester, vigorously opposed the plan, holding that the earlier pre-contract between King Henry and the daughter of the recently freed count of Armagnac was a true marriage in the eyes of God and, thus, to repudiate it would be an act of sin (Hall, 202–4). Despite the claims of Hall and other early chroniclers, the 1442–3 Armagnac marriage

plan never proceeded beyond initial negotiations. See Bertram Wolffe, *Henry VI* (New Haven, Conn.: Yale University Press, 2001), 159–61.

212 Hall records Suffolk's September 1444 elevation to the rank of marquess, though he does not describe it as a reward for making the Anjou marriage pact. After Suffolk's elevation, Hall continues, Suffolk travelled to France and stood proxy for his king in a wedding ceremony with Margaret of Anjou; he returned to England with Henry's bride in April 1445 (Hall, 204–5).

213 Hall identifies Queen Margaret as the originator of the 1446–7 actions that led to Duke Humphrey's death. Margaret was jealous of Gloucester's power over her husband; she thus permitted Gloucester's enemies to foment a conspiracy against him. A group of Humphrey's opponents, led by the marquess of Suffolk, falsely accused Gloucester of multiple crimes. In February 1447 the conspirators arrested Humphrey and imprisoned him. He was found dead on the next morning, murdered, Hall claims, by his foes (Hall, 208–9). In asserting that the conspirators moved against Gloucester to end his complaints about the adulterous nature of the Anjou marriage, the poet builds upon Hall's comment that Humphrey's early opposition to the marriage initiated a chain of events that led ultimately to his death (ibid., 204).

214 In 1445 (according to Hall, 1446), Suffolk appeared before both houses of parliament to extol his creation of a truce and a marriage for his king. At Suffolk's urging, a delegation from the House of Commons, joined by members of the upper house kneeling in supplication, successfully petitioned Henry VI to allow Suffolk's recent deeds to be recorded in the parliament rolls for posterity. It was in this way, Hall continues, that Suffolk mounted up to 'fortunes t[h]rone', becoming first the dominant figure in the English government and then, in 1448, a duke (Hall, 206–7, 210).

215 The English surrendered the county of Maine and its fortified capital Le Mans ('Mauntes') in March 1448, though Hall suggests that the surrender came shortly after Suffolk's commendation in parliament (Hall, 207). The 'Suffolk' poet has Charles VII render the ceded territories to Anjou to reconcile the initial claim in Hall's chronicle that the lands were given to Anjou with the text's subsequent statement that they were turned over to King Charles. Historically, Charles served as Anjou's agent in the conveyance (ibid., 205, 207; Wolffe, *Henry VI*, 172). Hall identifies both the loss of Anjou and Maine ('the very stayes, and backstandes to the Duchy of Normandy') and the bellicose Duke Humphrey's death as key factors in Charles VII's decisions in August 1449 to break Suffolk's truce and to attack Normandy (Hall, 205, 212).

216 Hall writes that by late 1449 the French had won numerous victories in Normandy and that the people of England began openly to execrate Suffolk for misruling the realm and causing English losses in France. That the populace cursed specifically Henry VI's marriage to Queen Margaret and that parliament was called to quiet the resultant unrest are the poet's own additions to his source. In early 1450, Commons members impeached Suffolk

of treason and other offences; in response, the queen, fearful of an uprising if she did not seem to act against her accused favourite, ordered Suffolk committed to the Tower of London. After keeping the duke imprisoned for a month, Queen Margaret allowed his release. Her action caused a great uproar among the people, who began to form themselves into companies under a rebel leader called Bluebeard. Only the prompt capture of the leaders of the revolt prevented an armed uprising (Hall, 216–19). Historically Bluebeard's disturbance in Canterbury in January 1450 had nothing to do with de la Pole's release from the Tower, which occurred only in March.

217 In Hall's telling, the queen, fearing Suffolk's destruction, moved parliament in late 1449 from London to Leicester, where the populace might better be controlled. When few of the nobility would come to that session, she transferred it to Westminster, where the Commons presented its formal articles of impeachment. After Suffolk was released from prison and Bluebeard's rising was quieted, the queen moved parliament farther from London, returning it to Leicester. When King Henry and Margaret arrived at Leicester with the newly restored Suffolk, the House of Commons reacted with such fury that Henry VI was forced to banish his wife's favourite for a period of five years (Hall, 217–19). For the complex set of parliamentary events that led to the historical duke of Suffolk's impeachment and banishment from the realm, see *PROME*, 12:71–7.

218 While sailing towards France, Suffolk's ship met the armed vessel *Nicholas of the Tower*, whose captain (commander of the ship's soldiers) took Suffolk from his boat and beheaded him near Dover (Hall, 219). The captain's rehearsing of Suffolk's 'faults' of murdering Duke Humphrey and contracting an unlawful marriage is the poet's invention. Whether intentionally or unintentionally, the poet changes Hall's claim that the *Nicholas of the Tower* was a ship belonging to Henry Holland (d. 1475), second duke of Exeter, into an assertion that it was controlled by Thomas Courtenay (d. 1458), thirteenth earl of Devon. Neither statement is correct: on the *Nicholas of the Tower* and Suffolk's demise, see Roger Virgoe, 'The Death of William de la Pole, Duke of Suffolk', *Bulletin of the John Rylands Library* 47.2 (1965): 495–6.

219 For a reading of this poem in the context of mid-Tudor politics, see Lucas, *'A Mirror for Magistrates'*, 157–71.

[Tragedy 12] 'Jack Cade'

Author: Unknown. **Historical subject:** Jack Cade (d. 1450), rebel leader. **Principal sources:** *Hall's Chronicle*; *Fabyan's Chronicle*. **Contemporary literary treatments:** Shakespeare famously portrays Cade and his rebellion in *2 Henry VI* (c. 1591–2). In narrative verse, Samuel Daniel makes Cade's rising a chief subject of the fifth book of his *Civil Wars*, which in 1599 was added to the original four books of the collection published in 1595 (this is book VI in the revised and expanded version of 1609). It is also recounted in Michael Drayton's *Miseries of Queen Margarite* (1627).

220 This stanza may be paraphrased, 'Though appetite be strong and the will inclined to wickedness (the one being forced upon us by the mixture of our bodily humours and the other by the movement of the heavens), yet through the power of moral discernment that God has incorporated into the faculty of reason and given to humankind, there is no impetus of appetite or desire that cannot be suppressed or abated in such a way that renders it unable to make us work our own harm or to depart from proper human behaviour.'

221 Edward Hall writes that in 1450 a 'certayn yongman of a goodely stature, and pregnaunt wit, was entised to take upon him the name of Jhon Mortymer, all though his name were Jhon Cade'. Cade adopted the name Mortymer, so that adherents of the once powerful Mortimer family would believe him to be of that stock (Hall, 220). As Hall relates it, Richard II had designated Edmund Mortimer (d. 1425), fifth earl of March, his heir apparent (ibid., 27). After deposing Richard, Henry IV laboured to keep his potential rival March in 'thrall', first by refusing to seek his release when he was captured by the Welsh rebel leader Owen Glendour (Owain Glyn Dŵr (d. *c.* 1416)) and thereafter by restricting him to court and placing him under the watchful eye of a keeper (ibid., 23, 27–8; see also Tragedies 6 and 7). March's heir was his nephew Richard (d. 1460), third duke of York, and Hall claims that Cade's rising was secretly the work of York's allies, who sought to help Duke Richard exercise the Mortimer claim to the English crown (ibid., 219–20). Notably, the 'Cade' poet suppresses all sense of a Yorkist hand in Cade's revolt, casting Cade's decision to rise as solely his own.

222 Rousing the people of Kent by denouncing recent taxes and levies, Cade marched his followers to Blackheath, near London (June 1450). The leaders of the rising then sent a bill to Henry VI accusing his high officers of corruption and oppression. The king and his allies refused to countenance Cade's bill and instead sent an army to Blackheath. In response, Cade retreated to Sevenoaks ('Senock'), Kent, and laid a trap for the royal forces (Hall, 220).

223 On learning of Cade's retreat from Blackheath, Henry VI's wife Queen Margaret ordered an armed party led by Sir Humphrey Stafford and his kinsman William Stafford to engage the Cade rebels at Sevenoaks, in Kent; in the ensuing skirmish, Cade's forces were victorious and the two Staffords were slain. Hearing of the shocking defeat of the Staffords' party, members of the royal army began openly to 'grudge and murmure' against Henry, Margaret, and their counsellors, some even affirming the justice of Cade's protests (Hall, 220).

224 In response to the growing fury in his own ranks, Henry VI felt compelled to send the hated lord treasurer James Fiennes (d. 1450), first Baron Saye and Sele, to the Tower. Cade and his followers soon returned to Blackheath, where their numbers were swelled by new adherents. Henry VI then sent a delegation to entreat with Cade. Whereas the poet suggests that the delegation offered Cade and his men concessions ('grants'), Hall records that Cade refused to speak with anyone but King Henry himself. In response to the failure of negotiations, Henry VI fled north, leaving the veteran fighter

Thomas (d. 1460), seventh Baron Scales, to defend the Tower of London (Hall, 220–1).

225 Hearing that King Henry had fled, Cade brought his men to London and took Lord Saye from prison. At a hastily convened hearing at Guildhall on 3 July, Lord Saye demanded his right to trial by his peers. Cade responded by ordering Saye beheaded at Cheapside. He then had Saye's son-in-law James (historically William) Cromer, sheriff of Kent, executed in similar fashion and mocked the two men's heads in the manner the poet describes (Hall, 221).

226 Cade, Hall continues, established his centre of operations in Southwark, sending men each day into London. When the rebels begin to rob London citizens, the city's fathers went to Lord Scales and requested assistance. A joint party of city and royal fighters prohibited Cade's followers from crossing London Bridge, sparking a lengthy battle during which numerous bridge residences were burned. Eventually, the two sides called a truce and Cade's men returned to Southwark. It was then that Cade sought to augment his forces by opening Southwark (but not London) jails (Hall, 221–2).

227 Lord Chancellor John Cardinal Kemp (d. 1454), who had remained in the Tower of London during the assault on the city, offered a pardon to any of Cade's men who would leave the rebel camp and return to their homes. The rebels, demoralized after failing to take London Bridge, gladly accepted the pardon and abandoned Cade, who soon after fled into Sussex (Hall, 222). That Cade's men were 'half gone' even before the issuance of the pardon is the poet's invention.

228 The poet embellishes Hall's simple statement that Iden 'manfully' slew Cade after discovering him (Hall, 222).

229 The poet draws on Fabyan's chronicle for his account of the disposition of Cade's corpse (Fabyan, 625). The bodies of medieval and early modern rebel leaders were often parboiled, quartered, and set up at various parts of London as warnings to others.

[Prose 13]

230 Although the term 'gentleman' primarily denoted someone of gentle birth and/or of landed wealth, some learned men were also afforded this title (see Sir Thomas Smith, *De Republica Anglorum* (London, 1583; *STC* 22857), 27).

231 Through his comparison of the 'Cade' poet to a divine, the speaker calls attention to the close relation between the closing stanzas of the previous tragedy, 'Jack Cade', and the sentiments of the familiar 1547 sermon 'Exhortation, Concerning Good Order and Obedience', one of the twelve homilies of the English church that, under Edward VI, non-preaching ministers were required to offer to parishioners each Sunday. Although it directed men not to obey any ungodly command issued by an officer, the 'Exhortation' strictly forbade violent resistance to governors, no matter how wicked their crimes might be. See *Certain Sermons, or Homilies* (London, 1547; *STC* 13638.5), sigs. N1r–P2r.

232 While the homily on obedience does not suggest that God installs evil rulers to punish evil people, a number of Edwardian churchmen asserted that view. See, for instance, John Veron, 'Prologue', in Heinrich Bullinger, *A most necessary and frutefull dialogue*, trans. John Veron (Worcester, 1551; STC 4068), sigs. A3r–4v; and Thomas Lever, *A fruitfull sermon made in Poules churche* (London, 1550; STC 15543), sigs. C2v–3r. Given his further comments, however, the speaker is likely drawing primarily on John Calvin's words about obedience to unjust rulers in his *Institutes of the Christian Religion* (Calvin, *Institutes*, 2:1512–13).

233 The speaker echoes John Calvin, who asserts that God sometimes stirs up popular risings in order to punish wicked rulers. Participants in such rebellions are vehicles of God's justice, even though the rioters themselves 'planned in their minds to do nothing but an evil act' (Calvin, *Institutes*, 2:1517).

234 Neither Hall nor Fabyan makes any mention of corruption on the part of Lord Treasurer James Fiennes (d. 1450), first Baron Saye and Sele, though both chroniclers note that Henry VI's own forces wanted Saye imprisoned and, later, Cade had Saye arraigned on unstated charges and executed (see Hall, 220–1; Fabyan, 622–4). Similarly, both Hall and Fabyan record the death of William Aiscough (d. 1450), bishop of Salisbury, killed at the time of Cade's rising; neither chronicler, however, claims that Aiscough was proud and covetous, nor does either one make any connection between Aiscough's death in Wiltshire and Cade's rebellion in Kent (see Fabyan, 625–6; Hall, 222–3).

235 The speaker is George Ferrers, author of the tragedy 'Somerset', which was completed too late to be included in the 1554 *Memorial*. Ferrers here follows Edward Hall's assertion, omitted by the 'Cade' poet, that a cabal of 'frendes, kinsmen and alyes [allies]' of Richard (d. 1460), third duke of York, secretly suborned Cade to start his rising in Kent (Hall, 219–20).

236 Ferrers looks forward to events of 1455, when, in the words of Robert Fabyan, York, 'beynge in the marchys of Walys … gathered a stronge hoost of people, and than in the moneth of Apryll toke his journey towarde London'. In response, Henry VI marshalled his own adherents and, on 23 May 1455, met York's party at St Albans, Hertfordshire. While the king's representatives approached Duke Richard to negotiate a peace treaty, York's confederate Richard Neville (d. 1471), sixteenth earl of Warwick, suddenly attacked from the rear, routing the royal forces. Among those of the king's party killed were Edmund Beaufort, first duke of Somerset; Henry Percy, second earl of Northumberland; and Thomas, eighth Baron Clifford (Fabyan, 629; see also Hall, 232–3). In the wake of this battle, York was named protector of England (November 1455); nevertheless, through the urging of Queen Margaret, a council soon stripped him of the title (February 1456). Several years of further strife between the king's men and York's partisans resulted, until Duke Richard assembled yet another army in Wales to challenge Henry VI's rule (October 1459). When key supporters abandoned him near

Ludlow in the face of advancing royal troops, York decided to flee to Ireland, while his eldest son Edward (d. 1483) and his allies the earl of Warwick and Warwick's father, Richard Neville (d. 1460), fifth earl of Salisbury, went to Calais (Fabyan, 629–35; Hall, 233–42).

237   In June 1460, Duke Richard's son Edward and the Yorkist earls of Salisbury and Warwick invaded England. They quickly took London from Lancastrian forces and then met the king and his army at the Battle of Northampton (10 July 1460). There, according to Fabyan's account, the earl of Salisbury (Warwick, in Hall's telling) led the victory over the royal army, capturing in the process King Henry and slaying numerous Lancastrian leaders. Among those dead were Humphrey Stafford, first duke of Buckingham; John Talbot, second earl of Shrewsbury; John, first Viscount Beaumont; and Thomas Percy, first Baron Egremont (Fabyan, 636; see also Hall, 243–4).

238   Ferrers completed his 'Somerset' poem too late for inclusion in the 1554 *Memorial*, and the copy of it Baldwin received *c.* 1556 was evidently unavailable to him when the 1559 *Mirror* went to press. The tragedy would not appear until the edition of 1563. See Prose 21 and Tragedy 26, as well as Lucas, '*A Mirror for Magistrates*', 241–4, 246.

239   The manicule that begins this paragraph, unique in *A Mirror for Magistrates*, calls attention to another unique feature of this part of the 1559 *Mirror*, Baldwin's presentation of his poem 'Richard Duke of York' as a dream vision rather than as an extemporaneously created, intentional work of art. The manicule has been often noted by *Mirror* scholars; it may, however, have been printed accidentally. As mentioned above, George Ferrers had not completed 'Edmund Duke of Somerset' by the time the *Memorial of Such Princes* went to press. Ferrers clearly intended to include 'Somerset' in the 1554 *Memorial*, and his lengthy recital of English history in this prose passage calls attention to the odd absence of any tragedy covering the fall of even one notable figure between Cade's death in July 1450 and York's in December 1460. Even if Baldwin held out hope of obtaining Ferrers's poem in time for inclusion in the 1554 *Memorial*, he could not have written a prose passage to follow it based on his fellow authors' discussion of the work, because 'Somerset' had never been presented to them. His dream-vision gambit for introducing 'York' provided him with means both of transitioning from 'Somerset' to 'York', if he received Ferrers's poem before the *Memorial* went to the press, and of transitioning from Prose 13 directly to 'York' if he did not receive the work. If Ferrers had given him the poem for the 1554 *Memorial*, Baldwin could have explained the authors' lack of recorded discussion of it with the claim that he had fallen asleep. Similarly, if he had been unable to obtain 'Somerset' (as was the case), he could abruptly move readers to 'York' by claiming the 'York' poem suddenly came to him as a dream. It is possible that this unique manicule may have begun its life as an aid to memory drawn by Baldwin on the printed copy of the 1554 *Memorial* he had marked up for the printers of the 1559 *Mirror*. The manicule reminded him, if he were able to obtain the 'Somerset' poem, to end Prose 13 at the point Ferrers says 'I

mind to say somewhat of this duke of Somerset' and to place the 'Somerset' tragedy there. The printer Marshe's compositor may have mistakenly taken the manicule to be part of Baldwin's revision of the 1554 text and included it for that reason in the *Mirror* itself.

[Tragedy 13] 'Richard Plantagenet, Duke of York'

Author: William Baldwin. **Historical subject:** Richard (1411–1460), third duke of York, magnate, military leader, and claimant of the English crown. **Principal sources:** *Hall's Chronicle*, *Fabyan's Chronicle*. **Contemporary literary treatments:** Duke Richard appears in all three of Shakespeare's *Henry VI* plays (*c.* 1591–2). Additionally, Samuel Daniel narrates York's career in his poem *Civil Wars* (1595–1609), and Michael Drayton makes York's quest for the crown central to his verse narrative *The Miseries of Queen Margarite* (1627).

240 Edmund of Langley (d. 1402), first duke of York and father of Richard (d. 1415), first earl of Cambridge, was King Edward III's fifth son. Baldwin confuses him with Lionel (d. 1368), first duke of Clarence, who was Edward III's third son and the grandfather of Anne Mortimer, Cambridge's wife and the mother of Richard of York (see Hall, 2). Baldwin also errs in making Richard, earl of Cambridge, Edmund of Langley's eldest son; Cambridge's brother Edward (d. 1415), second duke of York, held that distinction. Since Edward of York died after Cambridge and without children, his title duke of York passed directly to Cambridge's son Richard (ibid., 60–1, 138).

241 According to Hall, the last Mortimer earl of March, Edmund (d. 1425), was held long in captivity and died in the third year of Henry VI's reign, leaving no children. His claim to the throne (see note 242) passed to Richard of York, by means of Duke Richard's late mother Anne Mortimer, March's eldest sister (Hall, 27–8, 128).

242 Robert Fabyan claims that parliament in 1385 formally recognized Roger Mortimer (d. 1398), fourth earl of March, as Richard II's heir apparent (Fabyan, 533). At this earl's death, the Mortimer claim to the throne devolved to his son, Edmund (d. 1425), the fifth earl of March. Baldwin then turns to Edward Hall to assert that Henry IV ever kept March 'restrained from his liberty', a practice Hall implies continued under Henry V (Hall, 128). That Richard of York's father Cambridge pleaded for March's release is Baldwin's own addition.

243 For Richard of Cambridge's unsuccessful plot against Henry V, see Tragedy 8 and Hall, 60–1.

244 York's claims in this poem of the execution of Mortimer family members, of his own persecution for his Mortimer blood, and of the Lancastrian kings' feelings of guilt for their deposition of Richard II are unprecedented in Baldwin's sources.

245 Baldwin follows Hall's mistaken statement that Richard became third duke of York in 1426, under Henry VI, rather than in 1415 under Henry V (Hall, 138). According to Hall, furthermore, it was only in the twenty-sixth year of

Henry VI's reign (1447–8) that Richard of York began plotting for the crown, a date long after that which York's ghost asserts in the poem (see Hall, 210).

246 York's marriage to Cecily Neville (d. 1495) was made for him while he was a minor; his close alliance with her family would later prove key in his bid to take chief power in England. York's sons by Cecily were Edward (d. 1483), fourth duke of York (the future Edward IV); Edmund (d. 1460), styled earl of Rutland; George (d. 1478), first duke of Clarence; and Richard (d. 1485), first duke of Gloucester (the future Richard III). York's powerful supporters Richard Neville (d. 1460), fifth earl of Salisbury, and Salisbury's son Richard Neville (d. 1471), sixteenth earl of Warwick, were Cecily's brother and nephew respectively (see Hall, 231).

247 York, Hall writes, first served as regent of France in 1436–7; he was opposed in this office by Edmund Beaufort (d. 1455), first duke of Somerset, who envied York's advancement. Somerset's resentment was the initial cause of the two men's long-running enmity. York was again named regent of France in 1441, and he held the position until 1445, when he was replaced, to his displeasure, by Somerset. Duke Richard then took up residency in Ireland in 1449 as its lieutenant, where he won the deep love of the Irish people (Hall, 179, 191, 206, 213). Historically, York was never regent: his offices on the Continent were lieutenant-general and governor of France and Normandy. It was in these posts that Somerset replaced him in 1447 (not 1445). Furthermore, despite Baldwin's words, Margaret of Anjou could not have opposed York's appointments in France, since she was not even in England before April 1445.

248 York refers to his armed confrontation of King Henry in Kent (February–March 1452), the First Battle of St Albans (May 1455) and the Battle of Wakefield (December 1460). Margaret was not in fact at the First Battle of St Albans, nor did she flee from Duke Richard in its aftermath. See Hall, 225–6, 232–3, 250–1.

249 After Queen Margaret demanded the imprisonment of one of the earl of Warwick's servants (an act seen by the Nevilles as a preliminary strike against them), Warwick's father Salisbury gathered an army and won a victory over royal forces at Blore Heath, Shropshire (September 1459). In the next month, York himself, aided by his eldest sons and the Nevilles, sought to engage a Lancastrian army near Ludlow, Shropshire. The defection of key supporters as the king's forces approached, however, forced the Yorkists to break up their camp. Duke Richard and his second son Edmund, styled earl of Rutland, fled into Ireland, while York's eldest son Edward, called earl of March, and the Nevilles sought refuge in Calais (Hall, 239–42).

250 In June 1460 the Nevilles and March left Calais for London, where they assembled a force to confront the king and queen, who had gone to Coventry. On 10 July, March and Warwick defeated Henry and Margaret's army at the town of Northampton, where they seized the king and forced Margaret and her allies to flee to the north (Hall, 243–5).

251 After his supporters' victory at Northampton, York left Ireland, Hall writes, to attend parliament. There, York shocked the upper house by seating

himself on the throne to deliver a speech advancing his claim to sovereignty
(Hall, 245). While its members would not support his bid to supplant King
Henry, parliament did on 31 October 1460 name York protector of England
and heir apparent. Knowing that Margaret would reject parliament's actions
and would continue to support the claim of her and Henry's young son to
be his father's successor, York travelled north in December 1460 with his son
Rutland and his brother-in-law Salisbury to confront Margaret's forces in
Yorkshire (Hall, 249–50).

252 'Bosworth' in Leicestershire is where York's son Richard III lost his life in
1485. Its mention here is Baldwin's slip of the pen for Wakefield, Yorkshire,
near to which York installed himself in his stronghold of Sandal Castle ('my
bower') in December 1460. In the 1563 *Mirror*, Baldwin corrected this line.

253 On 30 December, York and his allies rashly issued forth from Sandal to
engage the much larger Lancastrian army. York was slain within half an hour
of commencing battle. According to Hall (who is the only known source for
the story), a priest attempted to help York's 12-year-old son Edmund, called
earl of Rutland, to escape, but the two were stopped and Rutland was cruelly
slain by John (d. 1461), ninth Baron Clifford (Hall, 250–1). Rutland was in
fact 17 years old in 1460 and likely died fighting against Clifford during the
rout of York's forces (see Tragedy 14).

254 See Hall, 251.

[Prose 14]

255 The unnamed speaker's expression of relief that the story of Richard (d.
1460), third duke of York, was not left out of the collection may suggest
either that 'York' was not one of the tragedies originally chosen for inclusion
in *A Memorial of Such Princes* (and that Baldwin added it later to be sure
that it was not 'overpassed') or that another poet had promised the work but
never delivered it, leaving Baldwin hastily to compose something of his own
to make up for the other author's negligence.

256 The speaker's unusual statement that he will supply Baldwin not with a poem
but with 'notes' may suggest that he brought to Baldwin only information
about Lord Clifford, leaving Baldwin himself to compose Tragedy 14 based
on that material.

[Tragedy 14] 'Lord Clifford'

Author(s): Unknown (and William Baldwin?). **Historical subject:** John
(1435–1461), ninth Baron Clifford, Lancastrian magnate and soldier.
Principal source: *Hall's Chronicle.* **Contemporary literary treatments:**
Shakespeare makes Baron Clifford one of the most prominent characters in
3 Henry VI (c. 1591–2), dramatizing both his killing of Rutland and Clifford's
own demise. In narrative verse, Samuel Daniel and Michael Drayton each
record Clifford's participation in the Battle of Wakefield and his slaying of
Rutland, Daniel in the 1609 edition of *Civil Wars* and Drayton in his *Miseries*

of Queen Margarite (1627). Drayton bases his poem's account of Clifford's mutilation of York's body specifically on this tragedy.

257 After his supporters defeated Henry VI's forces and captured the king at the Battle of Northampton (10 July 1460), Richard (d. 1460), third duke of York, had parliament name him lord protector and heir apparent. He was still opposed by King Henry's wife Margaret of Anjou, however, who assembled a large army in the north. Taking his second son Edmund, styled earl of Rutland, with him, York travelled to Yorkshire in December 1460, where his overmatched forces were routed by those of Margaret in the Battle of Wakefield (30 December 1460). According to Hall, York's son Rutland was at the time a boy 'sca[r]ce of the age of 12 yeres, a faire gentleman and a maydenlike person'. While he was being led from the fighting by a kindly priest, Rutland was overtaken by Clifford, who, Hall writes, cruelly put the boy to death while Rutland silently pleaded for mercy, fear having robbed him of his ability to speak (Hall, 251). Historically, Rutland was not 12 but 17 years old in 1460, and almost certainly participated in the battle.

258 At the First Battle of St Albans (1455), Yorkists killed Thomas (not John), eighth Baron Clifford, father of this tragedy's speaker. According to Hall, the younger Clifford exclaimed to Rutland just before killing him, 'by Gods blode, thy father slew myne, and so wil I do the[e] and all thy kin' (Hall, 251).

259 Hall relates that Clifford ordered York's head to be stricken from his corpse. He then put a paper crown on it, fixed it on a pole, and presented it to Queen Margaret (Hall, 251). Further details in this stanza are the poet's embellishments.

260 Clifford died on 28 March 1461, the day before the Battle of Towton, Yorkshire. Resting, Hall writes, at a place called Dintingdale after an earlier skirmish with forces loyal to the newly installed King Edward IV, Clifford removed his gorget and was soon after killed by an arrow shot into his neck. 'Some say', Hall continues, that the arrow was headless (Hall, 255).

[Prose 15]

261 The speaker of this passage follows Edward Hall's account of the losses experienced during three days of fighting between Lancastrian and Yorkist forces near Towton, Yorkshire, on 28–30 March 1461. The speaker departs from Hall, however, in suggesting that Edward IV became king after the Yorkist victory at the Battle of Towton instead of immediately before it (see Hall, 254–6). The Lancastrian leaders slain in the combat in and around Towton were Henry Percy, third earl of Northumberland; John, ninth Baron Clifford; Randolph, first Baron Dacre (or Dacres); and Leo, sixth Baron Welles. Ralph Neville (d. 1484), second earl of Westmorland, was not present at the battle; it was his brother John, first Baron Neville, who died there.

262 Thomas Courtenay, fourteenth earl of Devon, was captured at the Battle of Towton and beheaded shortly thereafter. John de Vere, twelfth earl of

Oxford, was convicted of high treason in the constable's court and executed in February 1462, though Hall mistakenly claims that Oxford was condemned by means of parliamentary attainder. Later, after the victory of the Yorkist leader John Neville (d. 1471), first Baron Montagu, at the Battle of Hexham (15 May 1464), the Lancastrians Henry Beaufort, second duke of Somerset; Robert, third Baron Hungerford; and Thomas, ninth Baron Ros, were all put to death (Hall, 256, 258, 260). Neither Hall nor Fabyan depicts John Tiptoft (d. 1470), first earl of Worcester and constable of England, as taking part in any of these condemnations. Historically, however, it was indeed Worcester who as constable passed sentence on Oxford in the court over which he presided (which handled crimes alleged to have occurred during times of martial conflict), and it is likely that he condemned those captured at Hexham as well. It is unknown, however, if the 'Worcester' poet was aware that Tiptoft had served as Edward IV's constable, since that fact is not mentioned either by Fabyan or Hall.

[Tragedy 15] 'John Tiptoft, Earl of Worcester'

Author: Unknown. **Historical subject:** John Tiptoft (1427–1440), first earl of Worcester, magnate, lord high constable of England, and successively deputy lieutenant and lieutenant in Ireland. **Principal sources:** *Fabyan's Chronicle*; *Hall's Chronicle*. **Contemporary literary treatments:** While the historical John Tiptoft was a humanist, translator, and the patron of several fifteenth-century writers, he himself is apparently not the subject of any extant work of Tudor or early Stuart fiction other than his poem in *A Mirror for Magistrates*.

263   Worcester may be specifically complaining here of his own treatment by the chroniclers Fabyan and Hall. Fabyan records that the people of England called Worcester the 'bochier [butcher] of Englande', but he never mentions the precise misdeeds that earned Worcester this title (Fabyan, 659). For his part, Hall notes that the 'fame went' that Worcester cruelly killed the sons of Thomas Fitzgerald (d. 1468), seventh earl of Desmond (the crime to which his ghost confesses below), but Hall indicates that he is unsure if it had been for actual 'treason to him layed or [for] malice against him conceyved' by his Lancastrian enemies that Worcester was executed (Hall, 286).

264   Following the account he found in the manuscript history 'The Great Chronicle of London', Hall relates that Worcester, while serving as Edward IV's lieutenant in Ireland, was rumoured to have exercised 'extreme crueltie' while in office, 'in especial on two enfantes, being sonnes to the erle of Desmond' (ibid.). Worcester's claim in the poem that he executed Desmond's children on Edward IV's orders may arise from the characterization in Hall's chronicle of Worcester as 'Jhon Typtoft, erle of Worcester lieuetenant, for king Edward in Ireland exercising there more extreme crueltie (as the fame went) then princely pity' (ibid.). The comma after 'lieuetenant' could make the phrase suggest not 'lieutenant on King Edward's behalf in Ireland, who exercised there extreme cruelty', but instead 'lieutenant, who exercised in

Ireland extreme cruelty on behalf of King Edward'. Historically, John Tiptoft came to Ireland in September 1467 as lord deputy, not lieutenant. Within months of his arrival, the Irish parliament attainted Desmond, Worcester's predecessor in his office, on a charge of aiding Irish opponents to English rule (February 1468). Desmond was quickly beheaded. Thereafter, rumour spread that Worcester had ordered the beheading of two of Desmond's younger sons, children 'soo tendyr of age' that one of them was unable to understand what was happening to him (*The Great Chronicle of London*, ed. A. H. Thomas and I. D. Thornley (London: George W. Jones, 1938), 213). There is, however, no extant evidence that Edward IV ever ordered Desmond's condemnation and execution, let alone the destruction of two of Desmond's children. See Art Cosgrove, 'The Execution of the Earl of Desmond, 1468', *Journal of the Kerry Archaeological and Historical Society* 8 (1975): 11–27; and John Ashdown-Hill and Annette Carson, 'The Execution of the Earl of Desmond', *The Ricardian* 14 (2005): 1–15.

265 After helping King Edward IV to the throne in 1461, the powerful Yorkist Richard Neville (d. 1471), sixteenth earl of Warwick, undertook negotiations to marry his sovereign to the French monarch's sister-in-law. King Edward, however, decided instead to wed Elizabeth Grey (May 1464), an act he kept secret from Warwick for many months. Furious at what he saw as Edward's betrayal of him, Warwick turned against his former ally, aligning himself with the Lancastrian leader Margaret of Anjou and, in October 1470, driving King Edward out of the realm. In the wake of his victory, Warwick freed the captive Henry VI and placed him once more on the throne. See Hall, 263–6, 269–86; see also Tragedy 16. The poet has Worcester speak here in character: Hall, in fact, offers numerous reasons why Warwick decided to rise against Edward IV.

266 Here and in the following stanzas, the poet evidently expands on Fabyan's laconic comment that the people hated Worcester as a 'butcher' (Fabyan, 659). It is possible, however, that the poet was aware that Worcester was constable of England under Edward IV, in which role, as head of the constable's court, he indeed put into effect King Edward's summary capital judgements against many of his enemies. On Worcester's juridical actions as England's constable, see Prose 15, n. 262, and J. G. Bellamy, 'Justice Under the Yorkist Kings', *American Journal of Legal History* 9.2 (1965): 139–40.

267 The poet follows Hall's unhistorical claim that Worcester was condemned by a parliamentary bill of attainder (Hall, 286).

268 In the Vulgate Bible, the Jews cry out 'crucifige eum' ('crucify him!') after Pilate proposes that Jesus be released (Mark 15:13–14; John 19:15).

269 On 17 October 1470, so many people pressed into the streets of London to see the hated Worcester executed that the sheriff was unable to bring his prisoner to the block. Tiptoft was lodged in Fleet prison overnight and beheaded the next day (Fabyan, 659).

[Prose 16]

270 The speaker evidently draws for this claim on the recently recited Tragedy 15, which suggests that it was 'the wind of Warwick' – i.e. the actions of Richard Neville (d. 1471), sixteenth earl of Warwick – that brought Worcester to his death. Edward Hall, by contrast, claims a parliamentary act demanding 'extreme punishment' for all of Edward IV's partisans was the occasion of Worcester's arrest and execution (Hall, 286).

271 As Hall tells it, in 1463 (historically 1465) Henry VI, who had escaped to Scotland after his defeat at the Battle of Towton (March 1461), inexplicably returned to England in disguise. He was quickly recognized, captured, and brought to Edward IV, who placed him in perpetual imprisonment. In September 1470, King Edward's former-ally-turned-opponent the earl of Warwick managed to drive Edward from the realm. Warwick triumphantly entered London in October, freeing Henry VI and restoring him to the kingship (Hall, 261, 285). In March 1471, Edward IV returned to England from the Low Countries; Warwick and his brother John Neville, first Marquess Montagu, soon after engaged Edward's forces in the Battle of Barnet (April 1471), where the two Nevilles lost their lives (ibid., 290, 296).

272 In July 1469, William Herbert, first earl of Pembroke, and his brother Sir Richard Herbert marshalled troops to support King Edward against rebel forces allied with the earl of Warwick. The two sides met on 26 July at Edgecote Moor, near Banbury, Oxfordshire, and during the fighting the Herberts' Welsh soldiers captured and put to death Warwick's cousin Sir Henry Neville. When Warwick's allies broke the Welsh line, their men, furious at Sir Henry's execution, proceeded to slaughter more than 5,000 Welshmen as they fled the field. The Neville retainers Sir John Conyers and John Clapham soon after oversaw the execution of Pembroke and his brother (Hall, 273–4). While Hall praises the executed Sir Richard Herbert of Coldbrook's prodigious fighting ability, neither he nor any of the other known source employed by the *Memorial-Mirror* authors makes any mention of Herbert's physical stature. Sir Richard's Welsh contemporaries, however, knew him as 'Risiart Herbert *hir*', or Richard Herbert the Tall (George Sandford, 'The Herberts During the Wars of the Roses', *Collections Historical and Archaeological Relating to Montgomeryshire and its Borders* 22 (1888): 226).

273 The rebel leader Robin of Redesdale (fl. 1469), whose men defeated the Herberts at Edgecote Moor, followed his victory over King Edward's allies by putting to death Queen Elizabeth's father Richard Woodville, first Earl Rivers, and his second son Sir John. Outrage over the defeat at Edgecote Moor and his father-in-law's death then led Edward IV to order the execution of Humphrey Stafford, first Baron Stafford of Southwick and first earl of Devon, who had refused to support the Herberts at Edgecote after quarrelling with them (Hall, 274–5).

274 The victors at Edgecote Moor travelled to Warwickshire, Hall writes, where they joined with the forces of the earl of Warwick and George (d. 1478), first duke of Clarence, who had allied himself with Warwick in rebellion against

his brother Edward IV. King Edward brought a large army against them, but before battle could be joined, Warwick and a small band of his men sneaked into Edward's camp at Woulney, Warwickshire, killed the watchmen, and captured the king. Warwick placed King Edward under guard at Middleham Castle, Yorkshire, but Edward somehow soon regained his freedom, either, Hall states, by permission of Warwick himself (an idea Hall later in his chronicle rejects) or by the corruption or laxity of the Middleham captors (Hall, 275–6). Hall's account of Edward's capture is unhistorical; it was not in fact Earl Richard but his brother George (d. 1476), archbishop of York, who seized Edward IV as the king travelled south near Olney, Buckinghamshire (Ross, *Edward IV*, 132).

275 After his escape from Middleham to London, the king began a round of negotiations with Warwick and Clarence. When their talks collapsed, Warwick travelled to Lincolnshire, where he made the soldier Sir Robert Welles commander of a new fighting force. In response to this move, King Edward called to him Sir Robert's father Richard, seventh Baron Welles, who came with his brother-in-law Sir Thomas Dymoke under a promise of protection. King Edward commanded Lord Welles to write to his son to dissolve his army; when the younger Welles did not comply, the king, in a fit of anger, had Baron Welles and Sir Thomas executed. Soon after, Edward's forces met Sir Robert's on the battlefield near Empingham, Rutland (12 March 1470). After a lengthy fight, royal forces captured Sir Robert; on hearing of the loss of their captain, Welles's men panicked and ran, shedding their coats as they fled in order to run more quickly. For this reason, Hall declares, the clash near Empingham has been ever known as the Battle of Losecote Field (Hall, 277).

276 After the defeat of their supporters at Losecote Field, Warwick and Clarence fled the realm. Turned away at Calais, the two men sailed to France, where they were welcomed by King Louis XI (April–May 1470). While in France, Warwick and Clarence made a pact with Henry VI's wife Margaret of Anjou to restore King Henry to the throne. With material support from King Louis and Margaret's father Rene (or Rainièr), duke of Anjou, Warwick and Clarence returned to England in September 1470. Declaring their intention to restore King Henry, they drew to their side numerous supporters, gathering such a large force that King Edward chose to escape to Holland, which was ruled by his brother-in-law Duke Charles of Burgundy ('Burgoyne'), rather than risk a battle. Thereafter, Warwick entered London in triumph, freeing Henry VI from imprisonment and restoring him to the throne (October 1470). For these events, see Hall, 277–85; Ross, *Edward IV*, 145–55.

277 Edward IV returned to England in March 1471. He quickly reconciled with Clarence and together the brothers entered London in April and incarcerated King Henry. On 14 April, Edward's troops met those of Warwick and Montagu at Barnet Field, Hertfordshire (now London), where both the Neville brothers were slain in battle (Hall, 290–7).

278 The speaker asks the company to picture Warwick and Montagu as he imagines they looked at the time their bodies were displayed 'open visaged' in St Paul's cathedral to prove that they were dead (Hall, 297; cf. Fabyan, 661). Jesus Chapel was in the eastern portion of the crypt directly underneath the choir of St Paul's. The 'portraiture' of Warwick was likely devotional in theme and apparently removed during the Reformation: in his *Survey of London* (1598), John Stow makes no mention of it, and it does not appear in Wenceslaus Hollar's seventeenth-century engraving of the old cathedral's choir steps (see William Dugdale, *History of St. Pauls Cathedral* (London: T. Warren, 1658), 168).

[Tragedy 16] 'Richard Neville, Earl of Warwick'

Author: Unknown. **Historical subject:** Richard Neville (1428–1471), sixteenth earl of Warwick and sixth earl of Salisbury, magnate and military leader, called 'The Kingmaker'. **Principal source:** *Hall's Chronicle.* **Contemporary literary treatments:** Warwick plays important roles in Shakespeare's *2* and *3 Henry VI* (*c.* 1591–2). He also features prominently in the last book of Samuel Daniel's *Civil Wars* (added to the original poem in 1609), in Thomas Sampson's *Mirror*-style verse tragedy *Fortune's Fashion* (1613), and in Michael Drayton's *Miseries of Queen Margarite* (1627). William Herbert (or Harbert) invents a speech supposedly delivered by Warwick at Banbury Field (i.e. the Battle of Edgecote Moor) in *The Prophecy of Cadwallader* (1604), while George Daniel has Warwick's ghost rehearse, in the manner of the *Mirror*, Earl Richard's entire career during the Wars of the Roses in the manuscript poem 'Vervicensis' (1639).

279 The poet follows Hall for the genealogy and titles of Warwick and his father, Richard Neville the elder, fifth earl of Salisbury (Hall, 231). The younger Richard Neville became earl of Warwick through his wife's right in 1449 and sixth earl of Salisbury in the wake of his father's 1460 death.

280 Richard (d. 1460), third duke of York, was the husband of Warwick's aunt Cecily Neville. Hall identifies Warwick's participation in the First Battle of St Albans (22 May 1455) as his initial service to York. It was Warwick's personal charisma, as well as his 'abundant liberalitie, and plentifull house kepynge', Hall writes, that inspired the common people's fierce devotion to him (Hall, 231–2).

281 With Warwick's aid, Richard of York took control of Henry VI after the First Battle of St Albans (22 May 1455) and again following the Battle of Northampton (10 July 1460). On 30 December 1460, York lost his life at the Battle of Wakefield; his ally Salisbury was captured in the same conflict and soon put to death. Warwick, who had not been at Wakefield, turned his support to York's son Edward, who claimed the crown as Edward IV on 4 March 1461. The new king and Warwick thereafter defeated the Lancastrian army at the Battle of Towton, Yorkshire (29 March 1461). As a result of their loss, Henry

VI and his wife Margaret of Anjou fled into Scotland. See Hall, 232–3, 244–5, 250–6.

282 According to Hall, in 1463 Henry VI foolishly decided to return to England in disguise. He was quickly captured and imprisoned in the Tower of London. In early 1464, Warwick began negotiations to wed King Edward to Lady Bona of Savoy, sister-in-law (not daughter) to the French King Louis XI. While Warwick was pursuing this marriage treaty, however, Edward IV secretly married the widow Elizabeth Grey, née Woodville (d. 1492), rendering Warwick's work meaningless (Hall, 261, 263–4).

283 Upon learning that all his efforts in creating a French marriage for Edward IV had been done in vain, an angry Warwick concluded that Edward was an 'inconstant prince, not worthy of such a kyngly office' and decided to depose him (Hall, 265). While the poet makes Warwick's moral outrage at Edward IV's behaviour the sole catalyst for Earl Richard's departure from his monarch, Hall lists numerous other practical and personal reasons for Warwick's break (ibid., 265, 269–70).

284 Bringing first his powerful brothers John (d. 1471), first earl of Northumberland, and George (d. 1468), archbishop of York, into his conspiracy, Warwick next went to Edward IV's disaffected sibling George (d. 1478), first duke of Clarence, who was already enraged at his elder brother for a host of perceived injuries (Hall, 271). Clarence needed no coaxing, Hall relates; the poet's claim here that Warwick fabricated tales to win over Clarence is his own addition.

285 In 1469 the discontented Warwick and Clarence travelled to Calais, where they began preparations for an invasion of England. The poet now conflates Warwick and Clarence's return to England from Calais in July 1469 with the two men's second invasion of England from France in September 1470. In so doing, he omits the various changes in fortune between King Edward and his two noble enemies in 1469 and early 1470, including Warwick and Clarence's alliance with the exiled Lancastrian leader Queen Margaret of Anjou (for these events, see Prose 16). So many people rallied to Warwick and Clarence during their September invasion that King Edward found himself forced to flee to the Low Countries on 2 October, landing in Alkmaar, West Friesland. Warwick triumphantly entered London four days later and restored Henry VI to power. See Hall, 272–86; Ross, *Edward IV*, 126–55.

286 None of the *Mirror* poets' known sources mentions any particular friendship between John Tiptoft (d. 1470), first earl of Worcester, and King Edward IV, nor do any of the sources suggest that Worcester – popularly known as the Butcher of England for his cruelty – was 'defamed' to an excessive degree. Both claims, however, are made by Tiptoft himself in *Mirror* Tragedy 15.

287 In early 1471, Duke Charles of Burgundy ('Burgoyne') assigned to Edward IV ships for an invasion of England. Edward landed in Yorkshire in March, and he soon gained control of the city of York through false promises. King Edward and a small band then began to march south, passing by the forces of Warwick's brother John, now first Marquess Montagu, who made no

effort stop the returned king, much to Warwick's anger. Attracting his now reconciled brother Clarence and many others to his side, Edward arrived in London on 11 April 1471, where he seized and imprisoned Henry VI. Hearing that Warwick, Montagu, and John de Vere (d. 1513), thirteenth earl of Oxford, had assembled men and were camped in the village of Barnet, north of London, Edward IV gathered forces of his own and took them north, along with the captive King Henry, to encounter the threatening army (Hall, 290–5).

288 Warwick's and King Edward's forces clashed at Barnet on Easter Sunday, 14 April 1471. As Hall tells it, late in the battle Warwick sought to inspire his weary troops by leading them on foot against the enemy. He was quickly slain by Edward's soldiers. Seeking to aid his brother, Montagu followed Warwick into the melee and was cut down as well. The Nevilles' forces soon abandoned the fight, leaving the victory to King Edward (Hall, 296).

289 Warwick's description here and in the following three stanzas of the secrets of his success are entirely the poet's invention.

290 See, for instance, Psalm 140:12: 'Sure I am, that the Lorde wyll avenge the poore, and mainteyne the cause of the helplesse' (Great Bible).

291 According to Hall, the duke of York initially won supporters in his opposition to Henry VI by complaining that the king allowed royal favourite Edmund Beaufort (d. 1455), first duke of Somerset, to rule the realm and lead it into ruin (Hall, 231).

292 For an argument concerning the political thought that shapes this poem, see Lucas, '"Let none such office take"', 104–6.

[Prose 17]

293 Edward Hall notes Warwick's demise by observing that death brought him the things he had never experienced in life, namely 'rest, peace, quietnes, tranquillitie, whiche his life ever abhorred, and could not suffre nor abide' (Hall, 296).

294 The exiled Edward IV returned to England in March 1471 and began to gather men to challenge Henry VI's rule. On hearing of Edward's return, Henry VI's wife, Queen Margaret, assembled forces in France in order to oppose him. Storms, however, delayed her journey to England, so that by the time she and her soldiers arrived, Edward IV had already defeated Warwick's army at Barnet (14 April 1471) and made himself king once more (see Tragedy 16). With some reluctance, Margaret, Hall writes, decided to engage King Edward in battle. Under the joint direction of Edmund Beaufort, called by the Lancastrians third duke of Somerset; John Beaufort, Somerset's brother (not, as the speaker of this passage has it, son); and John Courtenay, fifteenth earl of Devon, the Lancastrians engaged King Edward's soldiers on 4 May 1471 near Tewkesbury, Gloucestershire, where they were defeated and their army's leaders killed or taken prisoner. On being presented to Edward IV, Queen Margaret's captured son Edward, the Lancastrian Prince of Wales, defiantly asserted his family's right to the throne. Some say, writes Hall, that

King Edward slapped the Lancastrian prince in response; all agree, however, that the king's brothers and two other men fell on Henry VI's outspoken heir and stabbed him to death (Hall, 297–301; see also Tragedy 21).

295 Thomas Neville (d. 1471), called the Bastard of Fauconbridge (or Fauconberg), was the illegitimate son of William Neville, Lord Fauconberg, uncle to the sixteenth earl of Warwick. After restoring Henry VI, Warwick made Thomas Neville vice-admiral. On learning of Warwick's death at Barnet, Fauconbridge took to piracy. With captured ships, he landed at Kent, raised the commons, and marched on London with the stated intention of freeing Henry VI. The Londoners, however, repulsed Fauconbridge and his men. After eluding the authorities for a time, Fauconbridge was eventually captured near Southampton and executed (Hall, 301–2; see also Fabyan, 662–3).

296 Henry VI was stabbed to death with a dagger in the Tower of London shortly after the Battle of Tewkesbury. The 'constant fame ranne', Hall writes, that his murderer was Edward IV's brother Richard (d. 1485), first duke of Gloucester – the future Richard III (Hall, 303; see also Fabyan, 662).

[Tragedy 17] 'King Henry VI'

Author: Unknown. **Historical subject:** Henry VI (1421–1471), king of England (reigned 1422–61; 1470–1). **Principal source:** *Hall's Chronicle.* **Contemporary literary treatments:** King Henry appears in Shakespeare's three *Henry VI* plays (*c.* 1591–2). The unfortunate monarch's story is also told by Samuel Daniel in *Civil Wars* (1595–1609) and forms the background for Michael Drayton's *Miseries of Queen Margarite* (1627). In a letter of 1609, Sir John Harington sent Henry, prince of Wales, metrically altered versions of this tragedy's lines 73–6 and 135–6, claiming that they were composed by Henry VI himself (see Thomas Park, ed., *Nugae Antiquae*, 2 vols. (London, 1792), 2:145).

297 Some ancient and medieval authors asserted that crocodiles wept while eating the bodies of humans they had killed.

298 Henry VI was 9 months old when he became king of England (31 August 1422). In 1429, King Henry underwent the English coronation ritual, during which he was anointed with holy oil ('oil of holy thumb'). Two years later, he was taken to Paris to be crowned king of France (16 December 1431). See Hall, 153, 160–1.

299 The poet denies that the heavenly bodies themselves guide worldly events, since fate and fortune are but expressions of divine will. If the stars seem to predict fate, they act only as signs of God's intentions. Compare the similar sentiments expressed in Tragedy 12, 'Jack Cade', lines 8–14.

300 The author expresses the Christian belief that God often afflicts the good for their own improvement.

301 See Matthew 6:19–20.

302 In 1420, King Charles VI of France disinherited his son Charles and declared England's Henry V his successor to the French crown. The two monarchs

sealed their pact with Henry's marriage to Charles VI's daughter (but not heir) Catherine of Valois (d. 1437). In December 1421, Catherine gave birth to the future Henry VI. Prince Henry became king of England on his father's death in August 1422 and, two months later, king of France.

303   Despite being formally disinherited, the Dauphin Charles declared himself king of France on the death of his father (October 1422). After decades of warfare, Charles VII and his supporters in 1453 finally drove the English from the last (other than Calais) of their French possessions and ended any real claim Henry VI had to sovereignty over France. Later, a council assembled by Edward (d. 1483), fourth duke of York, declared Henry VI to be deposed and York to be the realm's true monarch (3 March 1461). Soon after, the newly created Edward IV's forces defeated those of Henry VI at the Battle of Towton (29 March). Henry was forced to flee the realm. See Hall, 116, 230–1, 253–6.

304   The author mentions Cork apparently for the sake of rhyme. Fabyan suggests that Roger Mortimer (d. 1398), fourth earl of March and Richard II's heir apparent (historically heir presumptive), died in defence of his lordship of Ulster in the Irish north (Fabyan, 533; see also Tragedy 2). The Mortimer claim to the throne eventually passed in 1425 to Richard (d. 1460), third duke of York, and, after his demise, to York's son Edward.

305   King Henry came of age in December 1442. By that time, Charles VII had retaken many of the French possessions once held by England. In the year 1448 (according to Hall, 1446), Henry VI surrendered control of the county of Maine to Charles VII's ally René (or Rainièr) (d. 1480), duke of Anjou. The ceding of Maine (and of English claims to the duchy of Anjou) was popularly believed to have been made as part of Henry's marriage pact with Anjou's daughter Margaret (d. 1482); it was soon after blamed for setting in motion England's subsequent loss of Normandy. See Hall, 204, 207, 217–18; Tragedy 11.

306   Hall writes that Henry VI's uncle Humphrey (d. 1447), first duke of Gloucester, opposed the king's Anjou marriage, because Henry had already made a formal pre-contract, binding according to God's law, to wed the Count of Armagnac's daughter. Hall suggests that Humphrey's opposition to Henry and Margaret's marriage led directly to Gloucester's death three years later (Hall, 204; see also Tragedies 11 and 29). In 1450, William de la Pole (d. 1450), first duke of Suffolk, was banished in the face of intense popular anger at the Anjou marriage he arranged and the subsequent English losses in France for which his marriage treaty was blamed. He was killed while sailing to France. See Hall, 203–5, 219; Tragedy 11.

307   That ecclesiastics told Henry VI he was not bound by his promises and was thus free to break the Armagnac marriage contract is the poet's own addition. For a similar charge, see William Tyndale, *The Practyse of Prelates* (London, 1548; *STC* 24466), sig. G7r–v.

308   Richard of York offered his first armed defiance of Henry VI in early 1452. Later, he captured the king in the wake of the Yorkist victory over royal forces

at the First Battle of St Albans (May 1455). The poet is mistaken in claiming that York forced Henry to resign his 'crown and titles'. Twice York took authority from King Henry; he did so, however, not by seizing the crown but by having himself named lord protector (in July 1455 and October 1460). In assuming the protectorship for a second time, York also had himself declared Henry's heir apparent. Soon after, Queen Margaret's victory over York at the Battle of Wakefield (December 1460), where Duke Richard met his end, and her defeat of York's allies at the Second Battle of St Albans (February 1461), allowed her once more to take control of her husband (Hall, 225–6, 233, 249, 252).

309 The newly crowned Edward IV and his ally Richard Neville (d. 1471), sixteenth earl of Warwick, defeated Henry VI and his supporters at the Battle of Towton (29 March 1461), forcing the Lancastrian monarch to flee to Scotland. Two years later Edward's allies captured Henry after he attempted to sneak back into England. Henry VI was kept in the Tower of London from the third year of Edward IV's rule until the ninth year (and not for nine years, as the poet has it) and was released in October 1470, after the earl of Warwick turned against his former ally and forced King Edward to flee to Holland (Hall, 254–6, 261, 283–4).

310 For Edward IV's return to England in 1471 and the historical events described in this and the previous stanza, see Tragedy 16, nn. 287, 288; Prose 17, nn. 294, 295; and Hall, 290–301. Hall correctly notes that Prince Edward was born in October 1453 and died in May 1471, making him age 17, not 12, at the time of his death (ibid., 230, 301).

[Prose 18]

311 See Fabyan, 663. Henry Holland (d. 1475), second duke of Exeter, fought on the Lancastrian side at Barnet (14 April 1471). He was imprisoned after the battle, but was released four years later so that he might accompany Edward IV on his expedition into France. He drowned on the voyage back to England, perhaps the victim of Yorkist foul play.

312 For the drowning of George (d. 1478), first duke of Clarence, in a butt of wine, see Hall, 326; Fabyan, 666; and Tragedy 18.

[Tragedy 18] 'George Plantagenet, Duke of Clarence'

Author: William Baldwin. **Historical subject:** George (1449–1478), first duke of Clarence, prince. **Principal sources:** *Hall's Chronicle*; Sir Thomas More, 'The History of King Richard III', in the version incorporated into Hall's chronicle. **Contemporary literary treatments:** In drama, Clarence appears in Shakespeare's *3 Henry VI* (*c.* 1591–2) and *Richard III* (*c.* 1592–3), as well as in Thomas Heywood's *2 Edward IV* (1599). Clarence's ghost, furthermore, opens the anonymous play *The True Tragedy of Richard III* (*c.* 1586). In poetry, Michael Drayton briefly tells of Clarence's break with Edward IV and his return to his brother's side in his poem *The Miseries of*

Queen Margarite (1627); the circumstances of Clarence's last division with Edward IV and his untimely death are rehearsed by the anonymous verse narrative *The First Book of the Preservation of King Henry the VII* (1599; *STC* 13076) and, more briefly, by Christopher Brooke's *Ghost of Richard the Third* (1614; *STC* 3830–3830.3).

313   Clarence was widely understood to have met his end by drowning in a butt of malmsey wine. See lines 369–72 below.

314   In 1399, Henry Bolingbroke (d. 1413), first duke of Hereford, brought down King Richard II from power and had himself installed as the new King Henry IV. Baldwin apparently has his Clarence reserve the use of the Plantagenet name solely for his own Yorkist branch of the English royal family. Edward Hall, by contrast, employs 'Plantagenet' as the common surname of all those legitimately born of royal blood – Lancastrian and Yorkist alike – who descended from King Henry II (d. 1189), founder of what came to be known as the Plantagenet dynasty in England (see Hall, 4, 13, 327). Historically, 'Plantagenet' was an epithet for Henry II's father, Geoffrey, count of Anjou. It was Clarence's father Richard (d. 1460), third duke of York, who revived and popularized the term as the surname of the English royal family. See 'Plantagenet, House of (1154–1485)', in Wagner, *Encyclopedia of the Wars of the Roses*, 206–7.

315   Lionel of Antwerp (1338–1368), first duke of Clarence, was the third of King Edward III's eight sons. Despite the claim of this stanza, Duke Lionel was never his childless ('issueless') nephew King Richard II's heir. Baldwin's use of the term 'elder' for Lionel of Clarence is likely intended to emphasize the fact that the Yorkist claim to the throne came through a son of Edward III older than the progenitor of the Lancastrian branch of the royal family, John (1340–1399), first duke of Lancaster (cf. Hall, 246).

316   Duke Lionel's heir was his daughter Philippa, who married Edmund Mortimer (d. 1381), third earl of March. Their eldest son was Roger (d. 1398), fourth earl of March. According to Robert Fabyan, Richard II named this Roger Mortimer his heir apparent in 1385 (Fabyan, 533). Anne Mortimer (d. *c.* 1411), wife of Richard (d. 1415), first earl of Cambridge, was never the heir of her father Roger, the fourth earl of March. Her brother Edmund, fifth earl of March, was his father's heir. When the fifth earl died without issue in 1425, the Mortimer titles and patrimony passed to Anne's son, Richard, third duke of York. By the 1450s, York understood his Mortimer inheritance to confer upon him the status of true heir to the English throne. See Hall, 246; cf. Baldwin's other accounts of York's ancestry and the descent of the Mortimer claim to the throne in Tragedies 8 and 13.

317   Clarence's father Richard became third duke of York at 4 years of age (October 1415). In 1424, Richard was married to Cecily Neville, daughter of Ralph (d. 1425), first earl of Westmorland. Through this union, York gained as a brother-in-law Richard Neville (d. 1460), fifth earl of Salisbury, a powerful magnate who became one of his most valuable supporters. Richard Neville

acquired his title earl of Salisbury by right of his wife, who was the heir of Thomas Montagu (d. 1428), fourth earl of Salisbury (the speaker of Tragedy 9).

318 York's four sons were Edward (d. 1483), the future King Edward IV; Edmund (not John) (d. 1460), styled earl of Rutland; George, the speaker of this tragedy; and Richard (d. 1485), the future Richard III. Rutland died at the Battle of Wakefield, supposedly at the hands of John (d. 1461), ninth Baron Clifford (see Hall, 251; and Tragedies 13 and 14). The 11-year-old George became duke of Clarence shortly after his brother Edward's accession to the throne in 1461; the 9-year-old Richard became first duke of Gloucester later in the same year.

319 As Hall tells it, after helping Edward IV to the throne, Warwick later broke with his former ally, complaining of just the sort of slights and misdeeds Clarence describes (see Hall, 269–71). In his anger over Edward IV's perceived transgressions, Warwick began to plot to depose Edward and to return Henry VI to the throne. To further his scheme, he approached Clarence, who bitterly complained to him that King Edward had been 'unkynd, and unnatural to me beynge his awne brother', particularly by granting favours to his wife Queen Elizabeth's Woodville relatives that Clarence insisted should have gone to Edward's own flesh and blood (ibid., 271).

320 After agreeing to ally against King Edward, Warwick and Clarence sealed their partnership with the July 1469 marriage of Clarence to Warwick's daughter Isabel. (Baldwin's suggestion that Clarence doted immoderately on his wife is his own addition.) For Warwick's and Clarence's campaign against Edward IV in 1469–70, including their driving him out of the realm and their restoration of Henry VI (October 1470), see Prose 16.

321 As Hall tells it, shortly after Warwick and Clarence made a pact with Queen Margaret to restore her husband Henry VI to the throne (July 1470), King Edward sent a 'damosell' to Clarence, who privately admonished him that it was both unnatural and personally perilous for a son of York to ally with his family's enemies (Hall, 281). From that point on, Clarence began to harbour doubts about his opposition to his brother. Clarence eventually switched sides, persuaded to do so by Richard of Gloucester in the wake of Edward IV's March 1471 return from exile to challenge the restored King Henry (ibid., 293).

322 Furious at Clarence's perfidy, Warwick ignored overtures from Edward and his brothers and vowed to continue his fight against them, even after the Yorkists had occupied London and deposed King Henry. Warwick met Edward, Clarence, and Gloucester at the Battle of Barnet (14 April 1471), where both he and his brother John, first Marquess Montagu, died in combat (Hall, 293–7).

323 In 1477 anger flared once again between King Edward and his brother Clarence. While, Hall declares, none has been able to identify with certainty the origin of their unexpected hostility, one contemporary rumour charged that the king, the queen, or both came to believe a prophecy that, in the

wake of Edward IV's death, 'after king Edward should reigne, one whose first letter of hys name shoulde be a G' (Hall, 326). The implication was, of course, that the king's two young sons Edward (b. 1470), prince of Wales, and Richard (b. 1473), first duke of York, would be harmed so that someone whose name started with 'G' (such as George, duke of Clarence) could take the throne.

324 The boar was the insignia of Clarence's brother Richard of Gloucester.

325 Since his first appearance in twelfth-century author Geoffrey of Monmouth's writings, Merlin had been associated with prophecies involving metaphorical beasts.

326 'Goose' was a byword for a foolish, simple-minded person.

327 Tudor governments dreaded just the sort of consequences of popularly disseminated prophecies that Clarence describes. In the 1540s alone, parliament passed two laws prohibiting the application of prophecies to specific high-born men and women based on their armorial insignias. See *Statutes of the Realm*, 11 vols., ed. Alexander Luders et al. (London, 1810–28), 3:850, 4:114–15.

328 Baldwin bases 'this learned man of mine' on Hall's report that, whether justly or unjustly, one of Clarence's servants was executed on a charge of 'poysonyng, sorcery, or inchauntment' (Hall, 326). All other details concerning this unnamed servant (historically Thomas Burdett (d. 1477), one of Clarence's gentleman retainers), including the reason for his death (see lines 321–2), are Baldwin's own creations.

329 One of Aesop's fables tells of a young man who was locked away to avoid death by a lion. He met his end by a nail protruding from a painted image of that beast (Aesop, 127–8).

330 Clarence's wife Isabel died in December 1476. When Duke Charles of Burgundy died in the succeeding month, his widow Margaret of York proposed her brother Clarence as a suitable husband for Charles's heir, Margaret's step-daughter Mary. Edward IV would not allow Clarence to make such an important union. Some say, Hall writes, that Edward's refusal made the earlier enmity between the two brothers flare once again, an enmity that ultimately led to Clarence's death (Hall, 326).

331 Hall relates that Clarence 'dayly did oppugne [attack with words]' the execution of his servant, to the point that an angry Edward IV had Clarence arrested and committed to the Tower (Hall, 326). In charging Richard of Gloucester with Clarence's death, Baldwin expands on material in Thomas More's 'History of King Richard III', in the version incorporated into Hall's chronicle. More notes that some believe Richard of Gloucester's 'drifte [plot] lacked not in helpynge furth his owne brother of Clarence to his death, which thyng in all apparaunce he resisted, although he inwardly mynded it'. Gloucester sought his elder brother's death, these men believe, so that he – expecting that Edward IV's poor diet would bring him to an early end – could be that much nearer to the succession to the throne (ibid., 343).

Although More makes it clear that the idea that Richard played a role in Clarence's death is only a conjecture, Baldwin treats it here as a certainty.

332 In this and the following stanzas, Baldwin elaborates on Hall's laconic comment that Clarence was 'cast into the Towre, where he beyng taken and adjudged for a Traytor, was prively drouned in a But of Malvesey [Malmsey]' (Hall, 326). Historically, Clarence was condemned by a parliamentary bill of attainder and executed, apparently by drowning in a butt of wine, on 18 February 1478.

333 Richard of Gloucester's presence in the Tower and his hand in Clarence's death are entirely Baldwin's invention. In *Richard III*, Shakespeare draws on this section of 'Clarence' in having Gloucester confess he fed false tales about Clarence to Edward IV. The anonymous author of the drama *The True Tragedy of Richard III* similarly follows this poem for his idea that Gloucester took a direct hand in murdering his brother.

[Tragedy 19] 'King Edward IV'

Author: John Skelton (with revisions made by either the unnamed *Mirror* contributor who in Prose 19 is credited with reciting Skelton's poem or by William Baldwin). **Historical subject:** Edward IV (1442–1483), king of England. **Principal source:** Skelton apparently relies on his own knowledge for the factual material in his poem. **Contemporary literary treatments:** Unsurprisingly, Edward IV appears in numerous works of early modern historical literature. Those dramatic works that treat his last years of life (*c*. 1473–83) include the anonymous *True Tragedy of Richard III* (*c*. 1586), Shakespeare's *Richard III* (*c*. 1592–3), and Thomas Heywood's *1 and 2 Edward IV* (1599). King Edward's attempts to capture his Lancastrian rival Henry (d. 1509), second earl of Richmond, and Edward's death are portrayed in the anonymous verse narrative *The First Book of the Preservation of King Henry the VII* (1599). Edward is also a key figure in Thomas Sampson's poem *Fortune's Fashion* (1613) and in George Daniel's 'Vervicensis' (1639). Michael Drayton composes a love letter from King Edward to his mistress Elizabeth Shore in *England's Heroical Epistles* (1597), and the king figures in a number of other poems relating to Shore (for these, see the headnote to Tragedy 25, 'Shore's Wife').

334 As with the names of the other tragedies in the collection, the lengthy title of 'Edward IV' is Baldwin's and not Skelton's. It draws on claims by Sir Thomas More and Edward Hall in Hall's chronicle that Edward IV indulged in an 'over liberall and wanton diet' and that the king's 'superfluous surfet (to the whiche he was muche geven)' may have led to the conditions that brought about his death (Hall, 345, 339). Baldwin's reference to Edward's 'untemperate' behaviour may refer as well to both Hall's and More's assertions that Edward had been given to lechery as a younger man, though More makes it clear that the king had abandoned such activities in his older age (ibid., 265, 345–6).

335 King Edward's first line is a variation of Job's cry in the Vulgate Bible (Job 19:21): 'Miseremini mei miseremini saltim vos amici mei quia manus Domini

tetigit me' ('Have mercie upon me, have mercie upon me, at the least you my frendes, because the hand of our Lord hath touched me' (Douay-Rheims Bible)).

336   Edward IV died on 9 April 1483, in the second month of his twenty-third regnal year.

337   King Edward's Latin words are a version of Job 7:21 (Vulgate Bible): 'ecce nunc in pulvere dormiam' ('behold, now I shal sleepe in the dust' (Douay-Rheims Bible)). The verse was familiar in the medieval period as part of the Catholic Church's ritual prayer the Office of the Dead.

338   Edward IV invaded France in July 1475. In the next month, France's Louis XI agreed to the treaty of Picquigny, which ended hostilities in exchange for annual payments to King Edward that the English characterized as tribute money (Ross, *Edward IV*, 233–5; Hall, 320).

339   Edward IV was 40 years old when he died.

340   During his reign, Edward IV refortified the Tower of London; John Stow, however, credits London's mayor rather than the king himself for the 1477 strengthening of the city wall (John Stow, *A Survey of London*, ed. C. S. Kingsford, 2 vols. (Oxford: Clarendon Press, 1908), 1:48, 10). In 1476 crown officials purchased on Edward IV's behalf the beautiful brick castle of Tattersall (or Tattershall) in Lincolnshire; five years later the king repaired Dover Castle at enormous expense. Also costly were his extensive improvements to the royal castles at Nottingham, Windsor, and Eltham. It is likely that Edward IV spent more on his residences than any king since Edward III.

341   Edward's ghost can claim to 'have' Windsor castle, in the sense that his body was interred there. Daily prayers for King Edward were held at Eton College in the years before his death, and Skelton evidently believes that the college's priests would feel obligated to offer perpetual prayers for his soul (Lionel Cust, *A History of Eton College* (New York, 1899), 19–22).

342   See *Meditationes Piissimae*, a work once ascribed to St Bernard of Clairvaux (d. 1153), in which the author claims that a human is little more than 'saccus stercorum, cibus vermium' ('a sack of excrement, food for worms'). See St Bernard, *Sancti Bernardi … Opera Omnia*, 4 vols., ed. Jean Mabillon (Paris, 1839), vol. 2, part 1, col. 668.

343   According to 2 Samuel 14:26, King David's son Absalom once cut his hair and found that it weighed 200 shekels. Since the term 'shekel' denoted a form of currency as well as a unit of weight, some medieval interpreters understood the passage to mean that Absalom had sold his hair for that amount.

344   Edward IV's macaronic cry echoes the words of Jesus on the cross in Luke 23:46.

[Prose 21]

345   This prose passage combines the words of an original introduction written *c.* 1556, when Baldwin attempted to produce a new version of *A Memorial of*

such Princes, with several Elizabethan additions and revisions. The printer to whom Baldwin refers here is the Elizabethan producer of his works, Thomas Marshe.

346 The claims that elephants had no leg joints and that bear cubs were born as lumps that were licked into shape by their mothers were common in medieval bestiaries.

347 Ferrers's words date from Mary's reign, *c.* 1556, when Baldwin was compiling the manuscript he would later partially revise as 'The Second Part of *A Mirror for Magistrates*'. Ferrers likely asked for 'Somerset' to be placed last in Baldwin's manuscript, so that it might be taken out and placed in the first part of the collection (where it belonged chronologically) without disrupting any of the prose links created for the second part of the *Memorial*. Ultimately, Baldwin placed 'Somerset' at the end of the poems he gathered for the 'second volume' of *Memorial* tragedies (covering Edward V's and Richard III's reigns). He then ended his *c.* 1556 manuscript with Tragedy 27, 'The Blacksmith', which he intended for a separate third volume of poems that would cover the Tudor period. For Baldwin's *c.* 1556 Marian manuscript, see Prose 27 and Introduction, p. xviii.

348 Sir Richard Grey, Queen Elizabeth Woodville's son by her first marriage, and Sir Richard Haute, Prince Edward of Wales's comptroller of the household, were put to death with Anthony Woodville, second Earl Rivers, in 1483 (see Tragedy 20). The fourth man executed with them was Sir Thomas Vaughn; 'Clapham' is evidently a slip of the pen.

[Tragedy 20] 'Anthony Woodville, Lord Rivers and Scales'

Author: William Baldwin. **Historical subject:** Anthony Woodville (*c.* 1440–1483), second Earl Rivers and, by right of his wife, Baron Scales, magnate. **Principal sources:** *Hall's Chronicle*; *Fabyan's Chronicle*; Sir Thomas More, 'History of King Richard III' (in the version incorporated into Hall's chronicle). **Contemporary literary treatments:** Rivers appears as a character in Thomas Legge's Latin drama *Richardus Tertius* (1579/80); the anonymous *True Tragedy of Richard III* (*c.* 1586); Shakespeare's *3 Henry VI* (*c.* 1591–2) and *Richard III* (*c.* 1592–3); and Thomas Heywood's *2 Edward IV* (1599).

349 In 'Rivers', Baldwin abandons the conceit of the 1559 *Mirror* that he and his fellow authors extemporaneously create their poetic tragedies after reading about their subjects in the chronicles. Instead, he presents Rivers as an actual ghost, following Thomas Sackville's treatment of the ghostly characters in his own 'Induction' and 'Henry, Duke of Buckingham' (see Tragedy 22).

350 Baldwin shapes Rivers's words to evoke thoughts of Queen Mary I's reign (1553–8), when Catholicism was restored and nearly 300 Protestants were executed for their faith. His final comments remind readers of the conclusion of the 1559 *Mirror*, in which the gathered authors promised to return in a week's time to continue their sharing of historical verse tragedies (see Prose 19). In fact, four years had passed before Baldwin returned to his *Mirror*

project to create a second part. For a reading of Rivers's comments here in the context of the Marian government's prohibition of Baldwin's two attempts to publish early versions of *A Mirror for Magistrates*, see Lucas 'A Mirror for Magistrates', 203–7.

351   For God's words in line 106, see Genesis 2:18. Baldwin's reference to Christ's utterance in this stanza is less certain, though his use of the term 'seed-shedder' points to Christ's enigmatic declarations in Matthew 19:11–12, which the editors of the Geneva Bible understood to assert that perpetual celibacy was possible for men only by means of physical incapability or by a direct gift from God. 'This gift is not commune for all men', a side note warns, 'but is verie rare, and given to fewe: therefore men may not rashly absteine from mariage' (Geneva Bible, sig. 2C3r).

352   See Genesis 1:28.

353   Baldwin echoes the Great Bible version of 1 Corinthians 5:6–7, in which St Paul rebukes a community that has tolerated an incestuous affair: 'Youre rejoysynge is not good: knowe ye not, that a lytle leven sowreth [leavens] the whole lompe of dowe? Pourge therfore the old leven that ye maye be new dowe, as ye are swete breed [unleavened bread]'.

354   The power of fathers over the marriage choices of their children in the early modern period was extensive, and parents often contracted unions based solely on what financial and/or social gains a marriage could bring to their families. Furthermore, a person of means could purchase from the crown the wardship of a wealthy young orphan and arrange for him or her to be wed to the guardian's own child. While 'babes scant bred' could not legally marry, informal contracts were often made for very young children, determining with whom the child would join as soon as he or she reached the age of consent (14 for boys and 12 for girls). See Joel Hurstfield, *The Queen's Wards: Wardship and Marriage under Elizabeth I* (London: Frank Cass, 1973), 18, 130–56.

355   According to Plutarch, the Athenian lawmaker Solon (d. *c.* 560 BC) allowed newly-wed brides to bring to their husbands only three changes of clothing and some household furniture (Plutarch, 'Life of Solon', *Plutarch's Lives*, 1:459). Baldwin himself included this example of Solon's wisdom in his *Treatise of Moral Philosophy* (*STC* 1253), sig. C6r.

356   Anthony Woodville was the son of Sir Richard Woodville (d. 1469), first Earl Rivers, and his wife Jacquetta (d. 1472), widow of John, first duke of Bedford. In addition to Anthony, Hall names two other of Sir Richard's fourteen children in his chronicle: Elizabeth (d. 1492), who after the death of her first husband Sir John Grey (d. 1461) married King Edward IV; and Sir John Woodville, whose fate Rivers describes below. See Hall, 264, 274.

357   Baldwin follows Hall in claiming that Anthony Woodville wed Elizabeth, heir of Thomas (d. 1460), seventh Baron Scales, only after his sister's 1464 union with King Edward. In fact, Woodville married his wife, a widow and not a maid, in 1460, gaining through her the right to her father's title (Hall, 264).

358 Fabyan records that Sir John Woodville 'hadde maried the olde duchesse of Norffolke', Katherine Neville, who was at least forty-five years older than Sir John at the time Queen Elizabeth arranged their 1465 union (Fabyan, 657). Baldwin follows Hall's error in claiming that, shortly after his mother's marriage to the king, Elizabeth's son Sir Thomas Grey (d. 1501) became marquess of Dorset and wed Cicely, heir to the estate of her powerful grandfather William, first Baron Bonville (Hall, 264). It was in fact Edward IV's niece Anne Holland whom Sir Thomas wed in 1466. Only after his first wife's death in the early 1470s did Grey marry Cicely Bonville, and it was only in the wake of this marriage that he was created first marquess of Dorset (1475).

359 Edward IV created Sir Richard Woodville first Earl Rivers and constable of England; as Fabyan notes, however, Woodville served in the royal household not as chamberlain but as treasurer (Hall, 264; Fabyan, 656).

360 One of Hercules' twelve labours was to steal the man-eating horses of the Thracian tyrant Diomedes. Later, Hercules killed the Egyptian Busiris, who sacrificed any stranger who entered his land (Diodorus Siculus, *Diodorus of Sicily*, 10 vols., trans. C. H. Oldfather (Cambridge, Mass.: Harvard University Press, 1935), 4:393, 401, 429). The claim that Busiris strangled his victims is Baldwin's addition.

361 For Richard II's fall from power, see Tragedy 5. By 'lawyers', Baldwin apparently means lawmakers, since it was parliamentarians and not attorneys who judged Richard worthy of deposition (see Hall, 9–11). See, however, Rivers's attack on attorneys beginning at line 444.

362 By impulsively marrying Rivers's sister Elizabeth in 1464 (Hall writes), Edward IV roused the fury of his powerful supporter Richard Neville (d. 1471), sixteenth earl of Warwick, whose painstaking plans to create a French marriage for his prince were ruined. As the years progressed, Warwick's anger was compounded by his belief that King Edward had given himself to ignoring his old friends and to 'preferryng to high estate, men discended of lowe bloud, and basse degree', an apparent reference to the Woodvilles and their rapid advancement in rank and power (Hall, 270). For Warwick's plotting with George (1478), first duke of Clarence, to depose Edward IV and for the two men's actions against their former royal ally, see Tragedies 16 and 18.

363 In 1469 the rebel Robin of Redesdale, who was aligned with Warwick, seized and beheaded both Anthony Woodville's father Richard, first Earl Rivers, and Anthony's brother Sir John (Hall, 274; see also Prose 16).

364 Fabyan records that Edward IV pardoned Robin of Redesdale and his rebels, even for the deaths of Earl Rivers and Sir John Woodville (Fabyan, 657). Tensions ran high between Warwick, Clarence, and Edward until October 1470, when the two nobles were successful in driving the king from England. Edward IV returned to the realm five months later, however, and, after winning Clarence to his side, he defeated Warwick and his brother John Neville, Marquess Montagu, at the Battle of Barnet in April 1471. See Hall, 275–97; Tragedy 16.

365 Queen Elizabeth bore ten children between 1466 and 1480, including, in 1470, Edward, prince of Wales. In 1473, Sir Anthony (who had become Earl Rivers in the wake of his father's death) was made governor of the young prince.

366 As a possible reason for the 'privy malice' that grew in 1477 between King Edward and his brother Clarence, both Hall and Sir Thomas More mention the Woodville family members' rancour against those of the king's blood; they do not, however, mention any opposition by Clarence towards Rivers's governance of Prince Edward (Hall, 326, 342). More also dates complaints about Rivers's control of young Edward made by Clarence's younger brother Richard (d. 1485), first duke of Gloucester, only to the 1480s (ibid., 347). For Baldwin's unprecedented claim that Gloucester arranged Clarence's death in the Tower of London, see Tragedy 18.

367 More depicts the duplicitous Gloucester as 'outwardely familier where he inwardely hated, not lettynge [refraining] to kisse whom he thought to kill'. Elsewhere, he praises Rivers as 'a wise, hardy and honourable personage, as valiaunte of handes [stalwart; brave in battle] as pollitique of counsaill' (Hall, 343, 347).

368 Both Hall and More comment on Edward IV's gluttony and how it endangered his health in his last years (Hall, 339, 343). For Edward IV's corpulence ('grossness'), see Hall, 345.

369 Baldwin's reference to Edward IV's 'ribald or his bawd' is apparently to two other texts' characterizations of the royal chamberlain William (d. 1483), first Baron Hastings. In his 'History of King Richard III', More claims that Queen Elizabeth detested Hastings because 'she thoughte hym familier with the kynge in wanton compaignie'. More also records Richard of Gloucester's charge that it was Hastings who enticed King Edward into licentious (ribald) behaviour (Hall, 344, 362). Accusations that Hastings (or anyone else in particular) had served as Edward IV's procurer are not found in Baldwin's chronicle sources; in Tragedy 21, however, John Dolman has Lord Hastings confess that he had performed just that service (see lines 43–56).

370 More relates that, soon after Edward IV's death, the conniving Richard of Gloucester convinced Queen Elizabeth that the new king Edward V should come to London from Wales accompanied only by a small company of 'frendes'. As Rivers relates in the following stanzas, Gloucester and his ally Henry Stafford (d. 1483), second duke of Buckingham, then rode to Northampton with an armed band to intercept the royal party. After imprisoning Earl Rivers and others of King Edward's household, the dukes then took control of the 12-year-old monarch, who had been lodged separately in Stony Stratford, Buckinghamshire (Hall, 348–9).

371 For the lying Greek Sinon, see Virgil, *Aeneid*, book 2. Baldwin's account of Rivers's interactions with Gloucester and Buckingham in the following stanzas are his own embellishments to More's brief statement that the two dukes offered Rivers 'frendly chere' before leaving him for the evening (Hall, 349).

372 Rivers alludes to the heraldic badges of Richard, duke of Gloucester (the boar); William, Baron Hastings (the bull); Henry, duke of Buckingham (the swan); and John (d. 1485), first Baron Howard (the lion, though historically the Howard family would not bear this badge until after Rivers's death). These were the chief men who removed Rivers's nephew Edward V from power. Rivers's attack in the next stanza on lawyers in general and on Gloucester's counsellor William Catesby in particular as those who turned the noblemen named above to vice is unprecedented in Baldwin's sources.

373 Woodville's ghost adds to his play on the badges of his enemies an allusion to his own title, Earl Rivers. The stream is Henry Tudor (d. 1509), second earl of Richmond and the future King Henry VII, who would defeat Richard III at Bosworth in 1485, two years after the deaths of Rivers, Buckingham, and Hastings. Baldwin's inspiration for Rivers's dream is likely Lord Thomas Stanley's nightmare of the bloody boar in More's 'History of King Richard III' (see Hall, 360–1).

374 The toad is perhaps a reference to the Lancastrian leader Queen Margaret of Anjou (d. 1482). Her end was unknown to Rivers, since she had left England once and for all after her forces' May 1471 defeat at the Battle of Tewkesbury (Hall, 301).

375 By having the sun rise in the zodiacal sign of Taurus ('the Bull'), Baldwin correctly indicates that Rivers's arrest occurred between 11 April and 12 May, the dates early astronomers understood the sun to occupy that sign (Rivers was historically arrested on 30 April 1483).

376 Compare More, who states that Rivers 'marveilously myslyked' the new state of affairs he discovered upon awakening (Hall, 349).

377 All the men arrested were members of the prince of Wales's household; Sir (not Lord) Richard Grey was as well the new king's half-brother.

378 For lines 519–46, Baldwin follows closely More's account, save that More has Duke Richard make himself de facto governor of Edward V after Rivers's arrest and not protector of the realm (see Hall, 349–50).

379 More writes that Gloucester arranged it so that Rivers, Grey, Vaughan, and Haute would be executed at Pomfret (Pontefract) Castle, Yorkshire, on the very day Gloucester brought his former ally Lord Hastings to his death (13 June 1483). Sir Richard Ratcliffe, a man 'as farre from pytie as from all feare of God', oversaw the public execution (which historically took place on 25 June), allowing the condemned men neither a trial nor a chance to speak before their beheading (Hall, 359, 364).

380 Although Vaughan's words are based on More's narrative, Grey's interaction with the priest is Baldwin's invention (Hall, 364).

381 The historical Earl Rivers had no constitutional authority to execute justice on Edward IV's brother, even if he wanted to, for his murders of Henry VI and (so Baldwin claims here and in Tragedy 18) George, duke of Clarence. It is possible that Baldwin meant his words in these final two stanzas to be applied to events of the mid-Tudor period.

[Prose 22]

382 Both Fabyan and Hall record the celebrated 1467 tournament in which Sir Anthony Woodville dominated Antoine, count of La Roche, the famous warrior known as the Bastard of Burgundy (Fabyan, 655–6; Hall, 268).

383 Fabyan mistakenly identifies Sir Thomas Grey (d. 1501), first marquess of Dorset, as the man charged with the governance of Edward, prince of Wales (Fabyan, 668, 670). As a result, he calls Dorset Queen Elizabeth's brother rather than her eldest son (he was the product of her first marriage to Sir John Grey). The governor of the future Edward V was Elizabeth's brother Anthony Woodville, second Earl Rivers, as Hall (in the material he incorporated into his chronicle from Sir Thomas More) correctly notes (Hall, 347).

[Tragedy 21] 'Lord Hastings'

Author: John Dolman. **Historical subject:** William, first Baron Hastings (*c.* 1430–1483), Yorkist ally and lord chamberlain of Edward IV's royal household (1461–83). **Principal sources:** *Hall's Chronicle*; Sir Thomas More, 'History of King Richard III' (in the version incorporated into Hall). **Probable additional source**: *Fabyan's Chronicle*. **Contemporary literary treatments**: William Hastings appears in Thomas Legge's neo-Latin drama *Richardus Tertius* (1579/80), the anonymous play *The True Tragedy of Richard III* (*c.* 1586), and Shakespeare's *3 Henry VI* (*c.* 1591–2) and *Richard III* (*c.* 1592–3).

384 In his 'History of King Richard III', Sir Thomas More observes that Edward IV's Queen Elizabeth disliked Hastings in part because 'she thoughte hym familier with the kynge in wanton compaignie'. More also records that the dubious proclamation justifying Hastings's execution in 1483 charged him with enticing the king into vicious living and abuse of his body (Hall, 344, 362). Nevertheless, Dolman's claims that Hastings certainly served as Edward IV's pander and that it was for that reason that the king made him lord chamberlain are not found in his sources. By 'Pandare', Dolman refers to the character Pandarus in Chaucer's *Troilus and Criseyde*, the licentious go-between who helps Criseyde and Troilus ('him of Troy') begin their love affair.

385 According to More, Edward IV often said that he had three concubines, 'one, the meriest, the other the wyliest, the thirde the holyest harlot in the realme' (Hall, 363). Elizabeth Shore (d. *c.* 1526/7), wife of a London citizen named Shore, was termed the 'merriest' of Edward IV's mistresses (see Tragedy 25). After Edward IV's death, she became Hastings's lover (ibid., 360).

386 Hastings's point seems to be that those who are raised to the nobility through their own merits depend only on themselves to gain and maintain their status and not on others. It is their 'force' and good report ('fame') combined that ensure they remain in rank and impervious to the attacks of those unfavourable to them.

387 This stanza may perhaps be paraphrased as 'The others, since they came to high rank by wicked means and exercised authority through flattery and

with violence, soon come to rue their actions. Indulgence in vice is the first step down and away from old honours; once it is undertaken, some linger in their reduced state, and none will rise except by grabbing hold of virtue's slender branches, which will serve to raise those who by proper means seek to ascend. Beware of gaining power through serving a prince's illicit desires; the one mean for staying sure in high estate is to come to one's position justly.'

388 The claim that Hastings used his favour with King Edward to protect others whom later wars put into danger of losing their lives is apparently Dolman's invention.

389 One of the tales in Boccaccio's *Decameron* is that of Titus and Gisippus, two boon companions whose friendship is put to the test when Titus falls madly in love with Gisippus' intended bride. More relates that Hastings had 'somwhat doted' on Elizabeth Shore during Edward IV's lifetime, but he reportedly refrained from pursuing her out of 'reverence towarde his kyng, or els of a certayne kynde of fidelitie towarde his frend' (Hall, 360).

390 Hastings plays on his office of royal chamberlain, the symbol of which was a white staff.

391 Dolman alludes to Psalm 82:6, in which the psalmist warns those in authority 'ye are gods' and are thus required to rule justly (Geneva Bible).

392 In July 1469, Richard Neville (d. 1471), sixteenth earl of Warwick, and Edward IV's brother George (d. 1478), first duke of Clarence, broke openly with the king. After several skirmishes, Warwick and Clarence drove King Edward into exile in October 1470 and restored Henry VI to the throne (see Prose 16). Hastings apparently employs metonymy in this line to praise Warwick's prowess as a fighter ('mace of Christendom').

393 Warwick and his partisans captured King Edward in July 1469 and held him prisoner. Edward managed to escape two months later and to reassert his authority, but the next year he and Hastings found themselves forced to flee England (Hall, 275, 283). Despite being Warwick's brother-in-law, Hastings remained loyal to King Edward even during the worst of his travails. The reference to Warwick's paws alludes to the Warwick badge of a bear with a ragged staff.

394 Dolman compresses the time between Edward IV's September 1469 escape from captivity and return with Hastings to London and his October 1470 flight from Lincolnshire to King's Lynn, Norfolk, the site from which he and Hastings embarked for exile in the Burgundian Low Countries (Hall, 276, 283).

395 According to myth, the Achaean fleet of 1,000 ships that left Greece to attack Troy stopped first at the island of Tenedos (Apollodorus, *Gods and Heroes of the Greeks: The Library of Apollodorus*, trans. Michael Simpson (Amherst: University of Massachusetts Press, 1976), 242).

396 Hostility between England and the towns of the Hanseatic League arose in the fifteenth century as a result of commercial disputes and English piracy. In 1468 the arrest of all Hansard merchants in England led to a complete

breakdown of relations and a state of war at sea between the two former trading partners (Ross, *Edward IV*, 361–2, 365–6).

397 Hastings refers to two of Aesop's fables, the first in which a mouse aids a lion by chewing through the net in which it is caught and the second in which a beetle takes revenge on an eagle by rolling the eagle's eggs out of the nest (Aesop, 7–8 and 130–1).

398 According to Hall, Edward IV set out on the sea with one English ship and two 'hulks of Holland'. The English ship was the fastest of the group, and it thus was able to outrace both its Hanseatic pursuers and the other ships of the convoy (Hall, 283–4).

399 Hastings now elides from his narrative his and his king's subsequent escape from the Easterlings, their safe landing in Holland, and their period of exile at the court of the duke of Burgundy (October 1470–March 1471). He also omits their return to England, King Edward's gathering of an army, Edward's reconciliation with Clarence, and the Yorkist prince's triumphant entrance into London (March–April 1471). Instead, he proceeds directly to the 'trial' he mentions in line 195, the Battle of Barnet Field, at which he aided King Edward in the defeat of his 'civil foe' the earl of Warwick (14 April).

400 At the Battle of Barnet, both Warwick and Edward divided their forces into three battalions. Hall states that Hastings had charge of the rearward division of the royal army; Dolman takes this to mean that Hastings commanded the company of fresh reserves that joined the battle late in the fighting and helped to turn the course of the conflict to Edward's side (Hall, 295–6).

401 After her ally Warwick's defeat at Barnet, Queen Margaret of Anjou and other Lancastrians met Edward IV's forces at Tewkesbury, Gloucestershire (4 May 1471). The Yorkists won a sweeping victory, capturing in the process not only Queen Margaret but also her son Edward, the Lancastrian prince of Wales (Hall, 300–1).

402 After his victory at the Battle of Tewkesbury, King Edward issued a proclamation promising to spare the life of Henry VI's son Prince Edward, if he were brought to him. Trusting the king's words, Sir Richard Croft (called 'Croftes' by Hall) presented the captive prince to King Edward, who demanded of him why he returned to England under arms. When the Lancastrian Edward boldly declared that he did so to fight for his family's right to the crown, an angry King Edward either pushed the prince away or struck him with his gauntlet. Immediately thereafter, Gloucester, Clarence, Thomas Grey (d. 1501), first marquess of Dorset, and Hastings all fell on the young man and murdered him (Hall, 301).

403 It is said, writes Herodotus, that Cyrus the Great (d. *c.* 529 BC) of Persia lost his life in battle with the Massagetai people of central Asia. After his death, the Massagetai queen Tomyris mocked him by dunking his severed head in a wineskin filled with blood (Herodotus, 1:261–9). For Clarence's death by drowning in a butt of malmsey wine, see Tragedy 18. Neither More nor Hall makes any mention of Hastings causing direct harm to Queen Elizabeth's

son Dorset, whom Hall notes had sought the protection of sanctuary at 'the begynnynge of Richardes daies' (Hall, 393). Dolman perhaps extrapolates on Fabyan's claim that during Edward V's brief reign Dorset 'escaypd many wonderfull daungers' (Fabyan, 670).

404 Hastings likely calls himself and his fellow murderers of Prince Edward traitors, both because as humans they betrayed one of their own kind (see line 261) and also because they slew a man their king had pledged he would preserve (Hall, 301).

405 An obscure couplet. The idea is perhaps that lions, no matter how vicious they may be, do not kill their own kind, unlike members of the sinful human race.

406 In Chaucer's *Nun's Priest's Tale*, the rooster Chauntecleer relates how a pilgrim learned through a dream of the secret murder of his friend (Geoffrey Chaucer, *The Nun's Priest's Tale*, *The Riverside Chaucer*, 3rd edn, ed. Larry D. Benson (Boston, Mass.: Houghton Mifflin, 1987), 255–6).

407 In Ovid's *Metamorphoses*, Jupiter decides to destroy the human race after a man named Lycaon, doubting Jupiter's divinity, attempts to serve him cooked human flesh. Versions of the story based on the influential medieval poem *Ovide Moralisé* claimed that Lycaon baked part of the meat into a pie.

408 In April 1483, Richard of Gloucester and Henry Stafford (d. 1483), second duke of Buckingham, arrested Queen Elizabeth's brother Anthony, second Earl Rivers, her son Sir Richard Grey, and the courtiers Sir Thomas Vaughan and Sir Richard Haute (all d. 1483), as they brought the young King Edward V from Wales to London after his father's death. Hastings, Sir Thomas More states, consented to the arrest of these innocent men. Two months later, Gloucester so arranged it that Hastings himself would be executed in London at nearly the same time that Rivers, Grey, Vaughan, and Haute were put to death in Pomfret (Pontefract) Castle, Yorkshire (Hall, 364; see also Tragedy 20).

409 In one version of Aesop's fable 'Of the Mouse and the Frog', a frog and a mouse engage in fierce battle with one another. In the midst of their fight, a kite swoops down and takes them both (Aesop, 1–2).

410 Once he had his 12-year-old nephew Edward V in his possession, Gloucester – now lord protector – made an appearance of arranging for the boy's coronation. While he directed most of the lords to assemble at Baynard's Castle, London, he and his adherents met at Gloucester's own London residence, Crosby Place. Many worried, More records, about the implications of the separate gathering of the ambitious Gloucester and his close allies; Hastings, however, declared to Thomas (d. 1504), second Baron Stanley, that he was unconcerned about Gloucester's meeting, since his supposedly trustworthy servant William Catesby was there and would warn him if anything were said against him (Hall, 358–9).

411 Although Hastings had raised him to positions of status and power, William Catesby in June 1483 turned against his benefactor, convincing Gloucester, who had held Hastings to be an ally, that Hastings would stand against

Richard's bid for the crown and thus needed to be destroyed (Hall, 359). Soon after, Catesby became Gloucester's own creature.

412 The implication of lines 333–6 is perhaps that if a mother tiger would do something so seemingly unnatural as hang its own cub, then Catesby would have an excuse for his own seemingly unnatural act of turning against his patron Hastings. In turn, Hastings himself could take comfort that, if such actions as he has described earlier in the stanza are natural, then his suffering by means of Catesby's betrayal of him does not in fact place him, as it might seem, far from the experiences of all other of nature's works.

413 Dolman's metaphor of steering a vessel along the golden mean is inspired by Horace, *Odes*, 2:10.

414 Ovid relates how Theseus credulously believed his second wife Phaedra, when she falsely accused his son Hippolytus of attempting to sleep with her. Travelling into exile on his father's orders, Hippolytus was killed by a fall from his chariot. He was given new life, however, as the minor Roman forest god Virbius (Ovid, *Metamorphoses*, 2:400–3).

415 Aegeus, king of Athens, asked his son Theseus to signal that he had survived his attack on the minotaur of Crete by raising a white sail as he came into port. Theseus, however, forgot to display the sail, and his father, falsely believing his son to be dead, committed suicide. In his widely disseminated commentary on *The Aeneid*, Maurus Servius Honoratus claimed Aegeus died by throwing himself into the body of water that thereafter became known as the Aegean sea (Servius Honoratus, *Servii Grammatici ... in Vergilii Carmina Commentarii*, 3 vols., ed. Georgius Thilo and Hermanus Hagen (Leipzig, 1881–7), 1:352–3).

416 One explanation for Remus' death offered by the historian Livy is that Romulus slew his brother when Remus mocked his new Roman wall by leaping over it (Livy, *History of Rome*, 1:24–5). The claim that Romulus was both suspicious and jealous of Remus is likely to be influenced by a passage from Lucan's *Pharsalia* that Dolman evokes in this stanza. Early in his poem, Lucan asserts that the attempt by Julius Caesar, Pompey, and Crassus to rule together as the first triumvirate was bound to end in failure, since there may ever be only resentment and distrust between those who share rule. Romans need not look to foreign examples for proof of this fact, Lucan observes, since Rome's first walls were wetted with a brother's blood ('fraterno primi maduerunt sanguine muri'). See *Lucan, With an English Translation*, trans. J. D. Duff (Cambridge, Mass.: Harvard University Press, 1943), 9.

417 Dolman follows Fabyan's practice of referring to Thomas, second Baron Stanley, by the title earl of Derby, an honour Stanley would gain only in Henry VII's reign (cf. Fabyan, 668–9).

418 Gloucester and Buckingham asked Catesby to approach Hastings to see if he would join them in their plotting. It is unknown, More writes, if Catesby ever broached the subject to Hastings; all that is certain is that Catesby convinced Gloucester that Hastings was set against any of Gloucester's plans. Catesby then urged Duke Richard to bring Hastings to a quick death, an

action Richard determined to undertake at an upcoming council meeting called for Friday, 13 June ('June the fifteenth' is a slip of Dolman's pen) (Hall, 359).

419 On the morning of the 13th, Gloucester sent Sir Thomas Howard (d. 1524), eldest son of Gloucester's ally John (d. 1485), first Baron Howard, to ensure that Hastings came to the fatal council meeting (Hall, 361).

420 Thomas More notes that Stanley had sent to Hastings a messenger at midnight before the council meeting, warning him to flee. Stanley's proof of Hastings's danger was a dream he had had that a boar had 'rased them bothe by the heades' with its tusks. Stanley's reference to Chauntecleer in Chaucer's *Nun's Priest's Tale* is Dolman's addition (Hall, 360–1).

421 In *The Nun's Priest's Tale*, Chauntecleer grows fearful after dreaming of a fox in the hen yard. The hen Pertelote ridicules him for assuming that dreams may be prophetic. He, in turn, defends at length his belief in the truth of dreams. Neither side convinces the other, and Chauntecleer eventually abandons the argument and goes out into the yard, where a fox does indeed lie in wait for him (Chaucer, *Nun's Priest's Tale*, 255–61).

422 The oblivious Hastings 'was never merier', according to More, than when he rode to the fateful meeting at the Tower of London (Hall, 361).

423 More notes Hastings's unsteady horse and remarks that a horse's stumbling has long been understood to indicate 'a goyng toward mischiefe' (Hall, 361). For Balaam's ass, see Numbers 22:21–34.

424 Hastings wonders if the stumbling of his horse indicated that the beast knew the tragic events that would ensue at the Tower, in the way that other animals are able to foretell drought or rain by the unbalance of their bodily humours brought on by changes in the atmosphere or soil.

425 In his *History of Alexander the Great*, the Roman historian Quintus Curtius writes that the horse Bucephalus would kneel before its master Alexander the Great whenever he wished to mount it (Curtius, *History of Alexander*, 2:45).

426 Herodotus relates how Darius (d. 486 BC) and five other men, after putting down the king of Persia, entered into a pact whereby the next king would be the one among them whose horse neighed first at the next dawn. Darius' groom Oebares used a stratagem to ensure that Darius' horse was the first to call out (Herodotus, 2:113–15; see also Lydgate, *Tragedies*, sig. N5r).

427 On seeing Hastings pause on the way to the Tower meeting to chat with a priest, Sir Thomas Howard ironically asked him 'wherfore talke you so long with that priest[?] [Y]ou have no nede of a priest yet'. Hastings laughed with Howard at this seeming jest, unaware that he would be making his last confession to a priest later that day (Hall, 361). Hastings's reference to Sinon is to the duplicitous Greek in Virgil's *Aeneid*, book 2, who convinces the Trojans to accept the Trojan horse.

428 At Tower Wharf, Hastings met one of his pursuivants, John Walsh, popularly known as 'Hastings' from his title Hastings Pursuivant (Philip Schwyzer, *Shakespeare and the Remains of Richard III* (Oxford University Press, 2013), 136). The two recalled the last time they had met at Tower Wharf, when a

fearful Lord Hastings had been called before King Edward IV to answer accusations lodged against him by his foe Anthony, Earl Rivers. Knowing that Rivers and his allies were to be executed at Pomfret Castle that very day, Lord Hastings declared himself to his pursuivant to be 'never in my lyfe merrier nor never in so great surety'. The wary pursuivant Hastings replied with a fearful 'I praye God it prove so', dampening Lord Hastings' ebullient mood as he entered the Tower (Hall, 361–2).

429   For the events at the council meeting, Dolman follows closely Sir Thomas More (Hall, 359–60).

430   'A cloak for the rain': a proverbial expression meaning in this case a false excuse.

431   More notes that Hastings was taken to the green space near the chapel of St Peter ad Vincula at the Tower of London, where a nearby log was made to serve as an impromptu chopping block (Hall, 360). In having Hastings refer to a hill near the chapel, Dolman evidently conflates the familiar public location for executions, Tower Hill, with the flat, private space where Hastings was killed.

432   Ovid relates that Memnon, son of the goddess of the dawn Aurora, died at Achilles' hands during the Trojan War. His mother was so disconsolate that she has continued ever since to bathe the earth with her tears, which humans see as dew (*Metamorphoses*, 2:268–73). The punctuation in the original indicates that the adjective 'grey' modifies Memnon; it likely refers to the reduction of Memnon's body to ashes on his funeral pyre.

433   Unusually for the *Mirror*, Dolman now continues his speaker's complaint in his own voice.

434   Dolman echoes the earl of Surrey's estimation of Sir Thomas Wyatt as 'Happy, alas, too happy, but for foes' in the poem 'Wyatt Resteth Here'.

435   Within hours after executing Hastings, Gloucester and Buckingham called leading London citizens to the Tower, where they greeted them in old rusty armour. The two told the citizens that because they learned only at the council meeting that Hastings had plotted their murder, they were constrained to don whatever protection was at hand. The death planned for Gloucester and Buckingham instead lighted on him who had contrived it, the two dukes averred (Hall, 362).

436   Within two hours of Hastings's death, Gloucester released a proclamation declaring eloquently and at great length the alleged crimes for which he had been executed. More observes that this document was 'so curiously endyted [carefully composed] and so fayre writen ... that every chyld might perceyve that it was prepared and studyed before'. In the following stanza, Dolman paraphrases two responses More records to the protector's obviously precomposed proclamation (Hall, 362).

437   Dolman is evidently uncertain if the man holding the title of Baron Hastings in 1563, Henry Hastings (d. 1595), third earl of Huntingdon, be William Hastings's direct descendent.

[Prose 23]

438 Although the holder of the title Lord Vaux in 1563 was William Vaux (d. 1595), third Baron Vaux of Harrowden, he is not known to have ever written verse. The reference appears instead to be to Thomas (d. 1556), second Baron Vaux of Harrowden, one of the most celebrated poets of the mid-Tudor period. He died in September or October 1556; Baldwin's words about him appear to be left over from the manuscript of Marian post-suppression *Memorial* poems that Baldwin later partially revised for the 1563 *Mirror* (see Introduction, p. xviii and Prose 27).

439 Baldwin suggests that Sackville, after learning that the Marian privy council had prohibited Baldwin from printing his manuscript 'Second Part of *A Memorial of Such Princes*', undertook to compose his own version of the *Memorial*, in style closer to that of Lydgate's single-author *Fall of Princes* than that of Baldwin's multi-author collection. For Sackville's unfinished *de casibus* tragedy project, see Introduction, pp. xxviii–xxix.

[Tragedy 22a] The Induction

Author: Thomas Sackville. **Principal sources:** Virgil, *Aeneid*; Lydgate, *Tragedies*. **Contemporary literary parallels:** Sackville's 'Induction' became the inspiration for several later *Mirror* editors, who crafted their own Sackville-like openings for their additions to the *Mirror*. See John Higgins's 'The Author's Induction' in *The First Part of the Mirror for Magistrates* (1574); Thomas Blenerhasset's prose 'The Induction' in *The Second Part of the Mirror for Magistrates* (1578); and Richard Niccols's two separate 'Inductions' to his 'Winter's Night Vision' and 'England's Eliza' sections of the 1610 *Mirror for Magistrates*.

440 In emulation of Chaucer and other medieval poets, Sackville often adds the archaic prefix 'y-' to verbs and participles. Many of Sackville's terms preceded by the 'y-' prefix (which denoted accomplishment of an action) are of his own invention and were never used in middle English. Sackville's use of irregular plurals such as 'treen' for 'trees' are often similarly archaizing gestures.

441 That in astrological theory the planet Saturn was supposed to cause a coldness in disposition in those born under its influence may have led medieval and early modern poets to ascribe to it a part in creating cold weather.

442 Sackville's 'Induction' exists in two settings in the 1563 *Mirror*. The poem was originally printed with 'blome [bloom] downe blowen' in line 7 and 'fowles' misspelled as 'sowles' in line 13. In a stop-press correction, the press's corrector changed 'sowles' to the correct 'fowles', and he replaced 'blome' with 'tree'. It is likely the change from 'blome' to 'tree' was made because Sackville mentions the flowers being blown down in lines 10–11. The correction, however, was evidently made in error, for Sackville's partially autograph manuscript copy of the 'Induction' has 'blome' (see Thomas Sackville, *The Complaint of Henry Duke of Buckingham*, ed. Marguerite Hearsey (New Haven, Conn.: Yale University Press, 1936), 41). By employing a copy of the 'corrected' printing

of the 1563 edition as his copy-text, the editor of the 1571 *Mirror* helped to ensure that his and all future *Mirror* editions would have 'tree' rather than 'blome' as their reading.

443 In this lengthy description of the evening sky, Sackville appears to describe the planet Mercury as placed between Venus and Mars, with Mars not visible above the eastern horizon. The constellation Virgo has gone below the western horizon, followed soon after by Scorpio and Sagittarius. The 'feet' of the constellation Ursa Major ('the Bear') had dipped below the horizon but soon reascended. The sun (described as being driven across the skies by Phaeton, Apollo's son) was descending; part of it (Erythius, or more properly Erythraeus, the first horse in the mythological team that drives Phaeton's 'cart', i.e. the sun) had disappeared from view, and the sun-god Titan was already taking his rest in the purple of dusk. Meanwhile, the moon ('Cynthia') was replacing the sun; it had passed the meridian (the 'noonstead') by six degrees. This elucidation follows that of Walter Skeat in *Specimens of English Literature ... A.D. 1394–A.D. 1579* (Oxford, 1887), 463, with corrections by Jacobus Swart (*Thomas Sackville: A Study in Sixteenth-Century Poetry* (Groningen: Wolters, 1949), 33–7) and emendations of my own.

444 Paul Bacquet argues that Sackville, through his presentation of the heavenly bodies and their movements in this passage, indicates a specific date for his poem's events: 23 November 1560 (Bacquet, *Un Contemporain d'Elisabeth I: Thomas Sackville, l'homme et l'œuvre* (Geneva: Droz, 1966), 151–7).

445 In his short tract 'On Funerals', Lucian (d. after AD 180) describes Pluto's underworld kingdom as surrounded by water, including a lake formed by the wide, slow-moving river Acheron (Greek for 'river of woe'). On the inner bank of Lake Acheron, Pluto has his throne and the Furies do his bidding. Present there as well is the spring of Lethe ('Oblivion'), whose waters bring forgetfulness to whoever drinks them (*Lucian, with an English Translation*, 8 vols., trans. A. M. Harmon et al. (London: Heinemann, 1925), 4:115–17).

446 Ancient Romans understood Lake Avernus in southern Italy to be the entrance to the underworld (e.g. Virgil, *Aeneid*, 1:523). For this and many other details of his character's journey to the underworld, which Sackville calls 'hell', the poet draws on or finds inspiration from Virgil, *Aeneid*, book 6.

447 King Croesus of ancient Lydia was renowned for his wealth; Irus was an Ithacan beggar in Homer's *Odyssey*. In ancient literature, the two men's names were bywords for wealth and poverty.

448 Death's dart (a small spear) was a familiar part of allegorical images of death in the early modern period.

449 Darius III (d. 330 BC), the last Achaemenid king of Persia, was decisively defeated in 331 BC by Alexander the Great (Sackville's 'Macedo' (lit. The Macedonian)); Alexander then overran Darius' realm. Sackville's source for this and several other of his historical examples is Wayland's edition of Lydgate's *Fall of Princes* (see Sackville, *Complaint*, ed. Hearsey, 8–9, 91, 102; Sackville's note 'Bochas fo. lxiiii' in his manuscript is a specific reference to

Lydgate, *Tragedies*, sig. M1r). For Darius' defeat and Alexander's invasion of Persia, see Lydgate, *Tragedies*, sigs. S2v–4v. Sackville finds inspiration for Death's impossibly detailed shield in that of Aeneas described in *Aeneid*, book 8.

450 During the Second Punic War, the Carthaginian military leader Hannibal (d. 182 BC) won a crushing victory at Cannae ('Canna') in south-eastern Italy over a larger Roman army led by Lucius Aemilius Paullus and Gaius Terentius Varro (216 BC). The Roman historian Livy tells of how a stone flung in battle severely injured Paullus and covered him in blood; he died at the end of the conflict. On the morning after his victory, Hannibal and his officers rode among the tens of thousands of slaughtered Roman soldiers still strewn on the battlefield, a spectacle that even the exultant Carthaginians found horrific (Livy, *History of Rome*, 5:359–61, 369–71).

451 In 218 BC Hannibal surprised the Roman forces by crossing the Alps and invading Italy from the north. In December he met a large Roman army near the Trebia river ('Trebey') and defeated it. In the following year he won another great victory over the Roman forces at Lake Trasimene. After Hannibal's further decisive victory at Cannae (216 BC), the city of Rome itself was in danger of conquest. Hannibal, however, did not attack the city, and the Romans eventually compelled him in 203 BC to return to Carthage ('Carthago') to defend it against an invasion by the Roman general Publius Cornelius Scipio (d. 183 BC). Scipio defeated Hannibal's forces near Carthage at the Battle of Zama (202 BC), thus ending the Second Punic War and earning him the honorific epithet 'Scipio Africanus'. Sackville's most likely source for all these battles is Livy: see Livy, *History of Rome*, 5:159–69, 213–23, 8:489–99.

452 In 49–48 BC the generals Pompey (d. 48 BC) and Julius Caesar (d. 44 BC) fought a civil war for control of Rome. After a loss to Caesar at the Battle of Pharsalus (48 BC), Pompey fled to Egypt, where he was treacherously killed by the Egyptian king. Lydgate notes that Caesar burst into tears when he was handed the severed head of his old enemy (Lydgate, *Tragedies*, sig. *2r–v).

453 In *The Fall of Princes*, Lydgate recounts at length the cruelty of two Roman military and political leaders, Lucius Cornelius Sulla (d. 79 BC), whom Lydgate calls Scilla, and 'Gaius Marius', Lydgate's conflation of a father and son of the same name (d. 86 and 82 BC respectively). Sulla and Marius the elder fought a civil war for mastery of Rome in 88–87 BC. See Lydgate, *Tragedies*, sigs. &5v–W2r.

454 After defeating the powerful Persian king Cyrus II (d. 530 BC), Queen Tomyris of the Massagetai mocked Cyrus' head by dunking it in a wineskin (a small tun, according to Lydgate) filled with blood (Lydgate, *Tragedies*, sigs. L1v–2v; cf. Herodotus, 1:269).

455 According to Lydgate, the Persian king Xerxes the Great (d. 465 BC) gathered an army of 300,000 men, whose members 'Dried ryvers that they dyd attayne, / Karfe downe hylles, and made valeys playne'. Nevertheless, the

Persian king's forces were overcome in 480 BC by a small band of Greeks at the Battle of Thermopylae (Lydgate, *Tragedies*, sigs. O1r–2r).

456 In 335 BC, Alexander the Great destroyed 'Thebes the mighty towne' (Lydgate, *Tragedies*, sig. S3r). For the destruction of 'Tyrus' (the Phoenician city of Tyre), Sackville draws on Ezekiel 26:4, in which God warns that armies 'shal destroie the walles of Tyrus and breake downe her towers: I wil also scrape her dust from her, and make her like the toppe of a rocke' (Geneva Bible).

457 For the fall of Troy, Sackville follows book 2 of Virgil's *Aeneid*. For his borrowings from the Virgil translations of Gavin Douglas and Henry Howard, earl of Surrey, see Sackville, *Complaint*, ed. Hearsey, 104–5.

458 In the *Aeneid*, the ruthless Greek warrior Pyrrhus kills Priam's son Polites before his father's eyes; he then drags Priam through Polites' blood to a nearby altar, where he stabs the aged king to death (1:328–31).

459 Virgil calls Troy 'Neptune's city', since the ocean god had helped to build its walls (*Aeneid*, 1:337; see also Ovid, *Metamorphoses*, 2:135).

460 Sackville has Henry Stafford (d. 1483), second duke of Buckingham, wear the same 'pilled blacke cloke' in which he was placed by his captors after his aborted rebellion (Hall, 395).

[Tragedy 22b] 'Henry, Duke of Buckingham'

Author: Thomas Sackville. **Historical subject:** Henry Stafford (1455–1483), second duke of Buckingham, magnate and rebel. **Principal sources:** *Hall's Chronicle*; Sir Thomas More, 'History of King Richard III' (in the version incorporated into Hall's *Union*); Valerius Maximus, *Memorable Doings and Sayings* (for the poem's classical examples). **Contemporary literary treatments**: In drama, Buckingham appears in Thomas Legge's *Richardus Tertius* (1579/80), the anonymous play *The True Tragedy of Richard III* (c. 1586), Shakespeare's *Richard III* (c. 1592–3), and Thomas Heywood's *2 Edward IV* (1599). In verse, his story is told in Richard Johnson's 'The Life and Death of the Great Duke of Buckingham', printed in the first edition of his *Crown Garland of Golden Roses* (1612); Johnson later relates Buckingham's part in the seizing of Edward V and the destruction of Earl Rivers in 'An Excellent Song Made of the Successors of King Henry [i.e. Edward] the Fourth', in the second edition of the *Crown Garland* (1631). Richard Niccols has Richard III's ghost describe Buckingham's failed rebellion in 'The Tragical Life and Death of Richard III', a poem added to the 1610 edition of *A Mirror for Magistrates*. Similarly, in *The Ghost of Richard III* (1614), Christopher Brooke has Richard's spirit recall Buckingham's early service to him, the duke's rebellion, and his untimely death. Duke Henry's betrayal by Banister and its aftermath are the chief subjects of two anonymous poems, 'A Song of the Duke of Buckingham' (c. early 1600s; preserved in British Library Additional MS 15225), and the broadside ballad *A Most Sorrowful Song, Setting forth the Miserable End of Banister, Who Betrayed the Duke of Buckingham* (composed c. 1600; earliest surviving printed edition c. 1630; STC 1361.5).

461 Henry Stafford, second duke of Buckingham, was a 'prince' (a member of the royal family) in part by virtue of his mother Margaret (d. 1474), daughter of Edmund Beaufort (d. 1455), first duke of Somerset, who was a direct descendent of King Edward III.

462 Sackville confuses Buckingham's grandfather Edmund Beaufort, first duke of Somerset, with Buckingham's uncle, also named Edmund Beaufort (d. 1471), who was called by Lancastrians third duke of Somerset. It was the younger Edmund Beaufort who was captured and beheaded in the wake of the Battle of Tewkesbury (May 1471).

463 Edmund Beaufort, first duke of Somerset and the father ('sire') of the Lancastrian third duke, did indeed die of wounds received in Henry VI's cause at the First Battle of St Albans (May 1455); the third duke's 'grandsire', John Beaufort (d. 1410), first earl of Somerset, died, however, long before the Wars of the Roses.

464 Edward Hall writes that Humphrey (d. 1460), first duke of Buckingham, was wounded at the First Battle of St Albans (1455), while his son Humphrey the younger (d. 1458), called earl of Stafford, lost his life there (both Staffords in fact survived the conflict). See Hall, 233.

465 Duke Henry's grandfather Humphrey died fighting against Yorkist forces at the Battle of Northampton in July 1460 (Hall, 244). Since his father Humphrey Stafford the younger had already passed away, Henry Stafford became second duke of Buckingham on his grandfather's death.

466 At the time of Edward IV's demise (9 April 1483), the royal heir Edward, prince of Wales, was 12 years old, and his brother Richard, first duke of York, was aged 9 years. During his lifetime, Edward IV entrusted the care of his eldest son to his wife's brother Anthony Woodville (d. 1483), second Earl Rivers, and to others of the Woodville affinity. Queen Elizabeth herself retained control of her younger son Richard. Sir Thomas More asserts that, on Edward IV's death, Richard (d. 1485), first duke of Gloucester, initiated a bid to usurp the throne by plotting against those members of the Woodville family who surrounded the late king's children. The duke of Buckingham was the first to join the future Richard III in his scheming, motivated in part by his own deep hatred of the Woodvilles (Hall, 346–8).

467 In April 1483, Gloucester and Buckingham intercepted Earl Rivers and his party as they brought Edward V to London from Ludlow. The dukes' men arrested Rivers, Queen Elizabeth's son Sir Richard Grey, and two others of the Woodville affinity, thus separating the queen's adherents from the new king. The arrested men were executed two months later (Hall, 349–50, 364; see also Tragedy 20).

468 For this anecdote, see Tragedy 22a, n. 454.

469 Cambyses II (d. 522 BC) became king of Persia on the death of his father, Cyrus II. As Sackville's source Lydgate tells it, Cambyses dreamed that his brother Mergus would take the throne after him. Jealous of his brother, Cambyses began plotting Mergus' death. God, outraged, cast Cambyses

into madness; the deranged king died soon after when he accidently stabbed himself (Lydgate, *Tragedies*, sig. N4r).

470 Marcus Junius Brutus and Gaius Cassius Longinus (both d. 42 BC) were the chief conspirators in the assassination of Julius Caesar (d. 44 BC). After defeat in battle, both committed suicide, Cassius employing against himself the very weapon he used on Caesar (*Plutarch's Lives*, 7:605–9).

471 After his defeat in battle by Alexander the Great, the Persian king Darius III (d. 330 BC) fled from Alexander's forces. During the flight, the Bactrian satrap (provincial governor) Bessus turned on his monarch, mortally wounded him, and declared himself king in Darius' stead. Within a year, Bessus himself was betrayed by his closest companion, Spitamenes, who seized the self-proclaimed sovereign and brought him, led by an iron chain, before Alexander. The Macedonian leader immediately ordered Bessus crucified (Curtius, *History of Alexander*, 1:397–423, 2:169–77).

472 Alexander the Great's early biographer Quintus Curtius Rufus relates how in 328 BC Alexander gave the command of Sogdiana (historically, Bactria) to the veteran soldier Clitus (or Cleitus), a trusted companion who had once saved his life. That very evening, Alexander invited Clitus to a banquet, at which both men became drunk. After hearing Alexander disparage the accomplishments of his own father, Philip of Macedon, under whom Clitus had served, Clitus spoke intemperately to his friend and sovereign. In a fit of drunken anger, Alexander stabbed Clitus with a spear. Upon seeing what he had done, Alexander was overcome with horror and remorse; he even tried to stab himself with the very spear with which he had killed Clitus (Curtius, *History of Alexander*, 2:237–49). Sackville artfully expands here on Curtius' brief account of Alexander's immediate reaction to his crime.

473 For three days after Clitus' death, Alexander remained in seclusion, refusing food and contemplating suicide. It would be another week thereafter before he could overcome his shame and return to command (Curtius, *History of Alexander*, 2:251).

474 On 13 June 1483, Gloucester had executed at Pomfret (Pontefract) Castle, Yorkshire, the four men he and Buckingham had earlier arrested as they brought Edward V to London. At nearly the same time, he ordered beheaded the chamberlain of the royal household, Lord William Hastings. See Hall, 364; see also Tragedies 20 and 21.

475 By June 1483, Gloucester had become lord protector and had taken control of King Edward V and his brother Richard, whom he placed in the Tower of London. Soon after, Gloucester had the two boys declared bastards and assumed the crown for himself as Richard III. More paints Buckingham as Gloucester's closest ally, and he displays at length what he claims to be the artful rhetoric Buckingham employed in deluding English subjects into transferring their loyalty from Edward V to the scheming Richard (Hall, 358, 368–74).

476 Edward V was 12 years of age and his brother 9 when they were sent to the Tower. The fear and guilty conscience Sackville ascribes to Richard and

Buckingham in the wake of their seizing power are Sackville's own creations, though they resemble the mental suffering Richard allegedly later underwent after the murder of his nephews (Hall, 379).

477 In his manuscript of 'Buckingham', Sackville cites Valerius Maximus' *Memorable Doings and Sayings* (*Factorum ac Dictorum Memorabilium*) as his source for this anecdote of Titus Cloelius (fl. early first century BC) and his sons (Sackville, 'Complaint', 68; Valerius, 2:199–201). Sackville offers, however, Cicero's rather than Valerius' spelling of Cloelius' family name.

478 In his 'Life of Dion', Plutarch describes Dionysius I of Syracuse (d. 367 BC) as an oppressive tyrant, one who based his rule on 'fear and force and a multitude of ships and numberless barbarian body-guards' (*Plutarch's Lives*, 6:21–3). Sackville's grouping of the tyrants Dionysius I, Alexander of Pherae, and Phalaris in this and the following eight stanzas is likely inspired by Cicero's similar linking of the three men in his treatise *De Officiis*. Cicero marshalled them as proof of the assertion that 'those who wish to be feared cannot but themselves be afraid of the very men that fear them'. See Cicero, *On Duties*, ed. M. T. Griffin and E. M. Atkins (Cambridge University Press, 1991), 71–2.

479 In *Tusculan Disputations*, Cicero evokes the memory of Dionysius I as an example of how cruelty creates grief and paranoia in a leader. Despite being the ruler of a wealthy and beautiful city, Dionysius' brutal behaviour made him lead a wretched life, since he came to suspect all those around him. So fearful was he of attack that he surrounded himself with bodyguards and would only speak to his subjects from the safety of a high tower (Cicero, *Tusculan Disputations*, trans. J. E. King (Cambridge, Mass.: Harvard University Press, 1945), 483–91; for the anecdote of Dionysius' searing of his own hair, see Cicero, *On Duties*, 71). Sackville would also have known the similar accounts of Dionysius' paranoia in *Plutarch's Lives*, 6:19–21; and Valerius, 2:385.

480 In his 'Life of Pelopides', Plutarch describes the outrages of Alexander (d. *c.* 358 BC), tyrant of Pherae, Greece, including his practice of dressing men as animals to be torn apart or hunted down. While he notes Alexander's cruel punishment of live burial, Plutarch does not claim that Alexander forced his victims to watch each other die (*Plutarch's Lives*, 5:411–15).

481 Both Cicero and Valerius Maximus record this expression of Alexander's paranoia (*On Duties*, 71–2; Valerius, 2:383–5).

482 Sick of her husband's cruelty, Alexander's wife Thebe conspired with her three brothers to kill the tyrant in his sleep. She allowed them to attack Alexander in safety by taking away the sword he always kept hanging above his pillow (*Plutarch's Lives*, 5:431–3).

483 The ancient historians Tacitus and Suetonius in particular paint the Roman emperors Caligula (d. AD 41), Nero (d. AD 68), and Domitian (d. AD 96) as cruel despots. Each met a violent end: Caligula and Domitian were assassinated, while Nero committed suicide after the people of Rome turned against him. Phalaris (d. *c.* 554 BC), tyrant of Acragas in Sicily, was notorious

for his sadistic treatment of his own subjects, including roasting them alive in a hollow brazen bull. According to Cicero, at his overthrow the entire population of his long-afflicted city took a hand in putting him to death (*On Duties*, 72).

484   In the wake of his coronation on 6 July 1483, King Richard spread the word that Edward V and his brother Richard had died of natural causes in the Tower of London. More, however, expresses no doubt that Richard had the two princes murdered (Hall, 377–9). Neither of Sackville's two chief sources makes revulsion at the murder of Edward IV's children a primary emphasis for Buckingham's break with Richard. It is not mentioned at all in More's narrative and only briefly – in a self-serving oration by Buckingham himself – in Edward Hall's continuation of More's account. Instead, both authors credit above all Buckingham's ambition for advancement and his jealousy of Richard's supremacy as the spurs for Duke Henry's break with his former ally (Hall, 382–3, 386–7). Sackville may follow the chronicler Fabyan here, who makes the princes' murder a principal cause of Buckingham's rebellion (Fabyan, 670), or he may simply create such an impetus himself, choosing to treat Buckingham from this point on as a sympathetic figure for artistic purposes and/or out of respect for Buckingham's grandson, *Mirror* author Henry, tenth Baron Stafford, who remained close to the *Memorial–Mirror* project between 1554 and 1563. For Baron Stafford, see Introduction, pp. xxvi–xxvii.

485   Richard III's suspicion of Buckingham in the wake of the murder of the princes is Sackville's invention. Cf. Hall, 382.

486   More notes that while some claimed Buckingham was openly furious at the newly crowned Richard's refusal to grant him new lands, others saw no trouble between the duke and the king when Buckingham left Richard to travel to his residence in Brecknock, Wales (Hall, 382). In the following stanzas, Sackville completely passes over More's and Hall's lengthy descriptions of how John Morton (d. 1500), bishop of Ely, persuaded Buckingham to turn against King Richard (Hall, 382–90).

487   Buckingham, writes Hall, marshalled a rebel army of 'wilde Weleshmen', who were compelled by feudal obligation rather than by reward or personal desire to join his side. Duke Henry led the force out of Wales through the Forest of Dean in west Gloucestershire, but flooding prevented him from crossing the Severn river to join with other parties gathered to attack the king. After a long period of inaction in miserable weather, Buckingham's Welsh fighters returned to Wales. Buckingham was left 'almost post alone' and forced to flee for his life (Hall, 394).

488   For the following examples, Sackville draws on the section titled 'Of Ingrates' in Valerius Maximus' *Memorable Doings and Sayings* (1:475–93).

489   Marcus Furius Camillus (d. 365 BC) saved early Rome from defeat by conquering the Etruscans of Veii. Despite this and other victories, a political dispute later led Camillus' Roman enemies to charge him with appropriating for personal use goods taken from Veii. Rather than pay a humiliating fine,

Camillus chose exile. See Valerius, 1:477; and Plutarch, 'Life of Camillus', *Plutarch's Lives*, 2:95–125.

490 Valerius writes that after the Carthaginian general Hannibal's string of stunning early victories in Italy during the Second Punic War (216 BC), Rome 'was not only bruised and broken … but already almost bloodless and dying'. Although the courageous Roman general Publius Cornelius Scipio (d. 183 BC) saved his city and defeated the Carthaginians (202 BC), his domestic rivals later charged him and his family members with several crimes; as a result, Scipio left Rome for self-exile. Forced to live in 'an ignoble hamlet and a deserted swamp', the embittered saviour of his city had himself buried outside of Rome and had engraved on his tomb 'Ungrateful country, you do not even have my bones' (1:477).

491 Scipio 'denied his ashes to her [i.e. Rome] whom he had not let collapse into ash' (Valerius, 1:479).

492 In 490 BC the Athenian general Miltiades (d. 489 BC) led a small army of soldiers to victory at Marathon over the invading force – said by Valerius to number 300,000 men – of the Persian king Darius I (Valerius, 1:489). The Roman biographer Cornelius Nepos (d. *c.* 24 BC) relates that Miltiades shortly after embarked on an unsuccessful attack on the island of Paros (489 BC). On his return to Athens, Miltiades' political enemies charged him with treason, levied on him an enormous financial penalty, and put him in chains in prison, where he died. Sackville's chief source, Valerius Maximus, follows Nepos in observing that so ungracious were Miltiades' enemies that after his death they forced his son Cimon into prison until such time as he could pay his father's fine, but he adds to Nepos' account the claims that Cimon was compelled to wear the very same fetters in which his father had once been shackled and that Miltiades would not be given burial until Cimon took his place in prison. (Cornelius Nepos, *Cornelius Nepos, with an English Translation*, trans. John Rolfe (Cambridge, Mass.: Harvard University Press, 1984), 18–21, 56–7; Valerius, 1:489).

493 Sackville draws on Valerius' brief comment that the people of Carthage exiled Hannibal, despite all his service to his country (Valerius, 1:485).

494 Hall records that Buckingham, without provisions or allies, fled to the Shropshire home of his servant Humphrey (historically Richard) Bannister, 'whome he had tenderly broughte up, and whome he above all men loved, favoured and trusted'. Buckingham planned to hide at Bannister's residence until he could either form a new army or flee to Brittany to join King Richard's chief Lancastrian opponent, Henry (d. 1509), second earl of Richmond – the future Henry VII (Hall, 394).

495 Sackville follows Hall, 394–5; he does not include, however, Hall's opinion that Buckingham's death was a fitting 'reward' for his earlier assistance to King Richard in his crimes.

496 In book 7 of Virgil's *Aeneid*, the Fury Allecto takes one of the many venomous snakes that grow like hair from her head and uses it to drive Amata, queen of

the Latins, into a maddened frenzy. In book 6, the mysterious oracle known as the Sibyl of Cumae serves as Aeneas' guide through the underworld.

497 Drawing on the language of astrological determinism, Buckingham curses any of the heavenly bodies whose positions at Bannister's birth brought good fortune to him.

498 With some alterations, Sackville crafts Buckingham's curses out of the miseries that, according to Hall, did in fact befall Bannister in the wake of his betrayal of his former master. In his 'extreme age', Hall writes, Bannister was arraigned on a charge of murder, for which he escaped execution only by pleading benefit of clergy. His eldest son, furthermore, went insane and died in a boar's sty, his younger son drowned in a small puddle, and his daughter, once a beauty, became horribly disfigured by leprosy (Hall, 395).

[Prose 24]

499 In the medieval and early modern periods, authors used the term 'hell' to indicate both the classical underworld and the Christian place of punishment for sinners. The Elizabethan auditor speaking here incorrectly assumes that Sackville meant his depiction of the mythological underworld to be a description of the biblical place of the damned. Moreover, since Buckingham clearly represents himself as repentant for his crimes, the speaker fears that others will mistake Sackville's 'hell' for purgatory, the existence of which had been denied in the parliament of 1559 along with the authority of the Catholic church in England. On the inclusion of this speaker's concerns in this prose section, see Lucas, 'A Mirror for Magistrates', 206–9.

500 In the manner of many sixteenth-century evangelical Protestants, Baldwin suggests that the existence of purgatory is a lie maintained by Catholic priests in order to wring money ('fees') from those who believe paying for prayers for the dead can aid the souls of their loved ones in purgatory.

501 Whether dead souls went immediately to heaven or to hell or whether they remained in the grave or in some intermediary place until Judgement Day was a matter of enduring controversy among early Protestants. In the 1559 edition of his influential *Institutes of the Christian Religion*, John Calvin warned evangelical Christians against enquiring too much into the matter, since scripture did not answer the question with precision (Calvin, *Institutes*, 2:997). It appears evident that Sackville's answer here is one formulated not chiefly as a point of theology but as a means to deflect the accusations of suspicious readers. For the most part, the 1563 *Mirror* contributors show themselves to be unconcernedly imprecise about where their fictional ghosts reside, just as they are imprecise about the ontological status of those ghosts. For instance, Baldwin in Tragedy 20, Dolman in Tragedy 21, and Churchyard in Tragedy 25 all claim that their ghosts rise from the grave to tell their tales. In Prose 25, however, the auditors accept without demurral Francis Seager's conceit that Richard III's spirit narrates his tale from Christian hell (see Prose 25).

502   It is the chronicler Edward Hall who claims that William Collingbourne was executed solely for making a satirical rhyme against the king and his henchmen, a fact which indicates that 'the reader' mentioned here and in Prose 21 employs Hall's chronicle (and not Fabyan's, the source for Baldwin's version of Collingbourne's rhyme) as the historical text by whose chronology Baldwin orders his reading of the newly added *Mirror* poems (see Hall, 398; cf. Fabyan, 672).

[Tragedy 23] 'Collingbourne'

Author: William Baldwin. **Historical subject:** William Collingbourne (d. 1484), gentleman opponent of King Richard III. **Principal sources:** *Fabyan's Chronicle*; *Hall's Chronicle*; Sir Thomas More, 'History of King Richard III' (in the version incorporated into Hall's *Chronicle*). **Contemporary literary treatments**: None known.

503   While 'Erinys' is the Greek term for any one of the three mythological Furies, some Roman authors understood 'Erinys' to be the proper name of a goddess devoted to conflict and vengeance.

504   The Roman poet Juvenal (fl. *c.* AD 100) composed poems satirizing contemporary Roman society in an indignant, aggressive, and hyperbolic manner.

505   While Jerusalem was under siege by Babylonian forces, the prophet Jeremiah was sent to prison on a false charge of trying to slip away from the city to join its enemies (see Jeremiah 37). The Roman poet Martial (d. *c.* AD 103) wrote numerous poems flattering the Emperor Domitian ('Caesar'), a man widely held to have been a tyrant. Baldwin suggests that Martial did so out of fear rather than out of true admiration for Domitian or base desire for advancement.

506   In Greek mythology, Helicon and Parnassus are mountains sacred to the nine Muses. The phrase 'frank and free' here echoes the speaker of the House of Commons's familiar request to the monarch at the opening of parliament that Commons members 'might franckely and freely saye their minds in disputing of such matters as may come into question, and that without offence of his Majestie' (Sir Thomas Smith, *De Republica Anglorum* (Cambridge University Press, 1982), 80–1). For a similar use, see Tragedy 1, line 104.

507   Baldwin has his wicked rulers' imagined words in part echo those of the 'Argument' to the book of Exodus in the Geneva Bible, which relates how God visited the ungrateful Israelites he had freed from Egypt with 'sharpe roddes and plagues that by his corrections they might … repent them for their rebellions and wickednes' (sig. f4r). Collingbourne's words echo as well the complaints of a number of Edwardian clerics, who execrated those in power for listening to their admonitions but refusing to act on them. See Lucas, '*A Mirror for Magistrates*', 212–13.

508 Baldwin, of course, suffered all these consequences in 1554 when his topically allusive, politically interventionary *Memorial of such Princes* was suppressed and ordered destroyed before publication.

509 Baldwin's source for Collingbourne's couplet is Fabyan's chronicle, which renders the verse as 'The catte, the ratte, and Lovell our dogge, / Ruleth all Englande under a hogge' (Fabyan, 672). While he follows Fabyan's version of the poem, Baldwin suppresses Fabyan's claim that Collingbourne was condemned for 'sondry treasons' and, along with them, for his offensive rhyme (Fabyan, 672; cf. Hall, 398).

510 In his 'History of King Richard III' (in the version incorporated by Hall into his chronicle), Sir Thomas More describes Richard III's unscrupulous advisor William Catesby (d. 1485) as 'wel learned in the lawes of this lande', and he portrays Sir Richard Ratcliffe (d. 1485) as a man entirely without pity (Hall, 359–60, 364). It was Ratcliffe who on Richard's orders oversaw the June 1483 execution of two of King Edward V's innocent relatives (see Tragedy 20, n. 379). Francis (d. 1488 or after), first Viscount Lovell, was Richard III's chamberlain of the household and loyal servant (Hall, 375). Finally, as Collingbourne notes below, Richard of Gloucester's personal emblem was the white boar.

511 Baldwin's three sources (More, Hall, and Fabyan) brand Richard III a tyrant chiefly for his vicious treatment of his political rivals and not for his bringing any widespread harm to the English people (see Hall, 380–1). Baldwin has Collingbourne claim that Richard and his henchmen destroyed thousands of men during their time in power in order to darken the king's reputation, just as he had earlier unhistorically impugned Richard by having George (d. 1478), first duke of Clarence, claim that Richard not only orchestrated Clarence's death but also attempted to murder him with his own hands (see Tragedy 18).

512 With a change of pronoun from *quid* ('what') to *quis* ('who'), Collingbourne quotes Horace, *Satires*, 1.1.24–5.

513 Horace famously composed his satirical verse in a reserved and civil style, avoiding other Roman satirists' strategy of savage rhetoric and direct attacks on recognizable contemporary leaders.

514 Ovid, among others, tells of how Pegasus sprung fully formed out of the blood that gushed from Medusa's neck, after the Greek hero Perseus decapitated her. In his *Poetica Astronomica*, the mythographer Hyginus (fl. first century AD) relates that Pegasus created the Hippocrene fountain, the spring sacred to the Muses, by striking a rock with his hoof, and that immediately after doing so he flew to the heavens, where Jupiter made him a constellation (Ovid, *Metamorphoses*, 1:233 (see also 1:257); Hyginus, *The Myths of Hyginus*, trans. and ed. Mary Grant (Lawrence: University of Kansas Press, 1960), 206).

515 Baldwin builds on Ovid's story of Neptune's rape of Medusa (see Ovid, *Metamorphoses*, 1:235).

516 Baldwin mistakenly conflates Medusa's condition with that of the daughters of Phorcys, the twin sisters who possessed only one eye between them. Perseus encounters the daughters of Phorcys shortly before killing Medusa (Ovid, *Metamorphoses*, 1:233).

517 Baldwin's Latin quote is a slightly altered version of line 223 of Juvenal, *Satire 6*, in which a wife in a fit of anger demands that her husband crucify a slave without a hearing.

518 For much of the sixteenth century, the typical English form of redress for matters of slander involved compelling the slanderer publicly to repent his or her defamatory words and to apologize to the victim (M. Lindsay Kaplan, *The Culture of Slander in Early Modern England* (Cambridge University Press, 1997), 15). In both the pre- and post-Reformation English churches, heretics were generally allowed to continue on in the church if they would abandon their heretical opinions. Only those who refused to recant were persecuted further.

519 Whether words against the monarch unaccompanied by overt actions should fall under the definition of high treason was a matter of great controversy in the mid-Tudor period. Although Queen Mary's first parliament had repealed earlier statutes treating acts of speaking or writing as treasonous, her second parliament re-established as treason the denying in writing of the monarch's right to rule (1 & 2 Ph. & Mary c. 10). It was essentially this statute, altered in 1559 to speak of Elizabeth rather than of Philip and Mary, that remained in force in Elizabeth's early reign (1 Eliz. c. 5). On the mid-Tudor treason statutes and their varying treatments of verbal and written offences, see John Bellamy, *The Tudor Law of Treason: An Introduction* (London: Routledge & Kegan Paul, 1979), 9–62.

[Prose 25]

520 While this Latin saying was a common one, it is possible that the speaker has specifically in mind a manuscript poem titled '*Vox Populi, Vox Dei*', which sought to display to King Edward VI precisely the sort of social and economic ills that his subjects 'misliked and grudged at'. See F. J. Furnivall, ed., *Ballads from Manuscripts*, 2 vols. (London, 1868–73), 1:124–46.

521 Dives (Latin for 'wealthy man') was the popular name for the rich man sent to hell in Christ's parable of the rich man and Lazarus (Luke 16:19–31).

[Tragedy 24] 'Richard Plantagenet, Duke of Gloucester'

Author: Francis Seager. **Historical subject:** Richard Plantagenet (1452–1485), first duke of Gloucester and, between 1483 and 1485, King Richard III of England. **Principal sources:** *Hall's Chronicle*; Sir Thomas More, 'History of King Richard III' (in the version incorporated into *Hall's Chronicle*). **Contemporary literary treatments:** In drama, Richard III appears in Thomas Legge's *Richardus Tertius* (1579/80), the anonymous *True Tragedy of*

Richard III (c. 1586), Shakespeare's *2* and *3 Henry VI* (c. 1591–2) and *Richard III* (c. 1592–3), and Thomas Heywood's *2 Edward IV* (1599). In verse, he is the subject of three later *de casibus* poems: Giles Fletcher's 'The Rising to the Crown of Richard III' (1593); Christopher Brooke's *Ghost of Richard III* (1614); and Richard Niccols's 'The Tragical Life and Death of Richard III', which Niccols added to his 1610 edition of *A Mirror for Magistrates* in place of Seager's poem. Richard plays major roles in Thomas Sampson's *Fortune's Fashion* (1613) and in Richard Johnson's 'An Excellent Song made on the Successors of King Henry [i.e. Edward] the Fourth', included in the 1631 edition of Johnson's *Crown Garland of Golden Roses*. Richard's alleged arrangement of his brother Clarence's death is handled in the anonymous *First Book of the Preservation of King Henry the VII* (1599), while Sir John Beaumont narrates Richard's own demise in the poem *Bosworth Field* (1629).

522 King Edward IV died on 9 April 1483, leaving the crown to his 12-year-old son Edward V. By May, Edward V's ambitious uncle Richard, duke of Gloucester, had taken control of the young monarch and had himself declared protector of the realm. In June, Gloucester gained possession of Edward V's younger brother, Richard, first duke of York, as well. Thereafter, the protector had his supporters claim that the king and his brother were in fact bastards and thus ineligible for the throne. With this excuse, Gloucester, as Richard III, took the crown for himself, installed his royal nephews in the Tower of London, and, according to Sir Thomas More, arranged for their covert murder (see Hall, 342–79).

523 As More notes, it was in fact Edward V's council and not parliament that named Gloucester protector (Hall, 351).

524 Close observers of King Richard in the wake of his nephews' murder, More writes, claimed that the boys' deaths brought Richard no joy; instead, he was ever after fretful and plagued by insomnia and nightmares (Hall, 379).

525 Seager evidently follows William Baldwin's Tragedy 18, 'George Plantagenet, Duke of Clarence', for his unhistorical claim that Richard III had a direct hand in bringing his brother George (d. 1478), first duke of Clarence, to his death by drowning in a butt of malmsey wine (see Tragedy 18, lines 358–71).

526 During Edward IV's reign, Richard of Gloucester had two elder living brothers, the king and George, duke of Clarence. Seager likely draws on Baldwin's Tragedy 18 in claiming that Richard had begun aiming for the crown during Clarence's lifetime and sought Duke George's murder as part of his plot (see Tragedy 18; see also, however, Hall, 343, where More raises this possibility as a conjecture).

527 In the following stanzas, Seager alters the chronology found in his chief historical source, More's 'History of King Richard III'. Whereas More claims that Richard had his royal nephews declared bastards and immediately took the crown for himself, only later ordering their murder, Seager instead has Richard, while still duke of Gloucester, plot to kill Edward V and his brother as a means to seize the throne (cf. Hall, 367–79).

528 According to More, King Richard feared that his subjects would doubt the legitimacy of his rule so long as his nephews lived. He thus sent a servant to Sir Robert Brackenbury, constable of the Tower of London, to urge Brackenbury to kill Edward IV's sons, who were lodged there. Brackenbury, however, refused to commit such a deed (Hall, 377).

529 After Brackenbury refused Richard's request, one of the royal pages proposed that the ambitious courtier Sir James Tyrell act as Richard's agent. Richard sent the unscrupulous Tyrell to Brackenbury with a letter commanding Brackenbury to turn over to Tyrell all the keys of the Tower (Hall, 377–8).

530 In this and the following two stanzas, Seager follows closely More's account of the princes' murder in Hall, 378.

531 In a passage added to More's narrative, the chronicler Edward Hall writes that the rumour of the two princes' death spread quickly among the people of England, who bewailed the loss of the two boys and cursed Richard for his unnatural slaughter of innocent children (Hall, 379).

532 Seager ignores Hall's assertion that the common people, while still lamenting the deaths of the princes in the Tower, nevertheless soon came to reverence King Richard, since he played the role of a just ruler and was liberal with his bounty (Hall, 380–1). Hall, furthermore, names no nobleman who turned against Richard specifically because of his nephews' murder; Fabyan, for his part, identifies only Edward Stafford (d. 1483), second duke of Buckingham, as so motivated, though he also mentions that several unnamed gentlemen joined Buckingham in his break with Richard (Fabyan, 670).

533 For the October 1483 rebellion of Richard III's former ally Buckingham, the collapse of his rising, and King Richard's subsequent search for the fugitive duke, see Tragedy 22b, n. 487.

534 Abandoned by his forces, Buckingham fled to Shrewsbury to the house of his gentleman servant Humphrey (historically Ralph) Bannister, whom Hall states Buckingham had 'tendrely broughte up, and whome he above all men loved, favored and trusted'. After King Richard offered a thousand pounds (not marks) to anyone who would deliver to him Buckingham, Bannister betrayed his master, either for fear of punishment or for desire for riches. Arrested by the sheriff of Shrewsbury and denied a trial or formal sentence of death, Buckingham was publicly beheaded in Salisbury (where Richard had taken residence) shortly thereafter (Hall, 394–5).

535 Seager's Richard III now jumps ahead to 1485, when he ordered all nobles who resided near the sea to keep a strong watch on the coast, in order to prevent any landing by his exiled Lancastrian rival Henry Tudor (d. 1509), second earl of Richmond (Hall, 408–9). Richard's claim that he sent letters to England's sheriffs is the poet's own addition.

536 In August 1485 the earl of Richmond sailed with about 2,000 supporters from France to Milford Haven, in Wales. Learning of the landing while residing at Nottingham Castle, Richard, Hall writes, was initially unconcerned, but subsequent reports of Richmond's entry into England ultimately spurred the king to assemble troops (Hall, 412).

537 In response to the news of Richmond's landing, King Richard at first commanded three of his most trusted high-ranking supporters, John Howard (d. 1485), first duke of Norfolk; Norfolk's son Thomas Howard (d. 1524), styled earl of Surrey; and Henry Percy (d. 1489), fourth earl of Northumberland, to raise forces to meet Earl Henry. Growing more and more anxious, however, Richard ultimately decided to lead an army himself, joining his men to those of the Howards and Percy and marching to Bosworth Field, near Leicester (Hall, 412–14).

538 Richard III's and Henry of Richmond's forces engaged in battle at Bosworth Field (22 August 1485), during which time Thomas (d. 1504), second Baron Stanley, and his brother Sir William suddenly abandoned the king's side to fight on behalf of Richmond. Lord Stanley's troops joined with those of John de Vere (d. 1513), the Lancastrian thirteenth earl of Oxford, in breaking the royal army and forcing its soldiers to flee (Hall, 418–19).

539 After cutting his way to a face-to-face encounter with the earl of Richmond, King Richard was overwhelmed by Sir William Stanley's men and died 'manfully fyghtynge in the mydell of his enemies' (Hall, 419).

540 Richard's filthy and nearly naked corpse was trussed 'lyke a hogge or calfe', thrown over the back of a horse, and then left lying as a spectacle at the Grey Friars' church in Leicester (Hall, 421).

[Prose 26]

541 The Roman historian Suetonius records that the murderous Emperor Nero (d. AD 68) was proficient at both music and poetry. Only a few fragments of Nero's verse, however, survived the classical period.

[Tragedy 25] 'Shore's Wife'

Author: Thomas Churchyard. **Historical subject:** Elizabeth Shore (d. 1526/7), royal mistress. **Principal source:** Sir Thomas More, 'History of King Richard III' (in the version printed in *Hall's Chronicle*). **Contemporary literary treatments:** Churchyard's 'Shore's Wife' was an immediate sensation and remained its author's most beloved poem over the course of Churchyard's long life. As a result, its protagonist appeared in numerous later works of the early modern period. On the stage, Mistress Shore took her place in Thomas Legge's *Richardus Tertius* (1579/80), the anonymous *True Tragedy of Richard III* (c. 1586), and, with the unhistorical first name 'Jane', in Thomas Heywood's *1 and 2 Edward IV* (1599). She is frequently mentioned in Shakespeare's *Richard III* (c. 1592–3). In 1593, Churchyard himself offered an expanded version of his original poem in *Churchyard's Challenge*. In the same year Anthony Chute released *Beauty Dishonoured, Written under the Title of Shore's Wife* and Thomas Deloney composed 'A New Sonnet, Containing the Lamentation of Shore's Wife'. For *England's Heroical Epistles* (1597), Michael Drayton created an exchange of verse epistles between Shore and her lover Edward IV; later, an anonymous author drew on both Heywood's and Drayton's works for his ballad 'The Woeful Lamentation of Mistress Jane Shore' (*c.* 1600).

542 Churchyard, like Dolman in Tragedy 21, is unaware of Elizabeth Shore's first name, since it is not mentioned anywhere in Hall's chronicle. In later years Shore would become known as 'Jane', the name bestowed on her in Thomas Heywood's *1 and 2 Edward IV* (1599).

543 In his 'History of King Richard III', More writes that Elizabeth Shore was 'borne in London, well frended, honestly brought up, and very well maryed, savyng somewhat to[o] so[o]ne, her husbande an honest and a yong citizen, godly and of good substaunce, but forasmuche as they were coupled [before] she were well rype, she not very fervently loved for whom she never longed, which was the thyng (by chaunce) that the more easely made her to encline to the kynges appetite, when he required her' (Hall, 363).

544 Sir Thomas More describes Mistress Shore as a woman of 'proper wytte … mery in compaigny, redy and quicke of answere', one whose pleasant behaviour pleased men even more than did her beauty (Hall, 363).

545 According to More, 'where the king toke displeasure, [Shore's wife] would mitigate and apeace his mynde, where men were out of favour, she would bring them into his grace, for many that had highly offended, she obteyned pardon' (Hall, 363).

546 Edward IV died in April, 1483, leaving his 12-year-old son Edward V to rule. The new king's ruthless uncle Richard (d. 1485), first duke of Gloucester, soon after became protector of England. More does not characterize Gloucester as Shore's enemy; instead, he asserts, Duke Richard falsely claimed Shore was part of a June 1483 conspiracy against him chiefly in order to advance the destruction of Shore's lover William (d. 1483), first Baron Hastings (see Tragedy 21). Nevertheless, Gloucester continued to persecute her even after Hastings's death, stripping from her all of her substantial wealth 'as it were for anger and not for coveteous [covetousness]' (Hall, 363).

547 More claims that Duke Richard falsely charged Shore with using witchcraft against him and of being of 'secrete counsaill' in Hastings's alleged plot to kill him. The plan to use poison is Churchyard's addition (Hall, 360, 362).

548 Rather than have her tried for treason, Gloucester turned Shore over to the church to punish her for her adultery. The bishop of London forced Shore to perform a humiliating public penance that entailed walking before a cross through London in a loose gown, while carrying a candle (Hall, 363). The *Great Chronicle of London* observes that this sort of public shaming was one usually imposed on a 'comon harlott' (233).

549 More notes that Shore fell into poverty after her humiliation and was reduced to begging. Much of Churchyard's moving description of her later years is his own creation (Hall, 364).

550 More particularly notes that Elizabeth Shore was literate (Hall, 363). The book she carries is evidently a psalter.

551 The version of More's narrative in Hall's chronicle records that by the time she died in the eighteenth year of Henry VIII's reign, Shore looked solely like 'reveled [reviled] skynne and bone' (Hall, 363).

[Prose 27]

552 Baldwin's reference to 'this king and queen's reign' below shows that this prose link was not written or revised during Queen Elizabeth's rule (as all the links before it were) but dates from the time of Philip and Mary. Prose 27 and the poems and prose links that follow it in the 1563 *Mirror* were apparently taken verbatim from Baldwin's attempt *c.* 1556 to create a 'second part' and 'third volume' of *de casibus* tragedies in the manner of his original, suppressed *Memorial of Such Princes*. Baldwin's death in September 1563 probably prevented him from revising these unpublished Marian pieces to conform with the new Elizabethan offerings added to the second *Mirror* edition.

553 Other than Sackville's 'Buckingham', the tragedies that preceded 'Shore's Wife' in the Marian 'second part' and 'third volume' manuscript are not certainly known, since they were either revised or replaced in Elizabeth's reign.

[Tragedy 26] 'Edmund, Duke of Somerset'

Author: George Ferrers. **Historical subject:** Edmund Beaufort (*c.* 1406–1455), first duke of Somerset, magnate, and military leader. **Principal source:** *Hall's Chronicle.* **Contemporary literary treatments:** Shakespeare conflates Duke Edmund with his brother John (d. 1444) in the character of Somerset in *1 Henry VI*. The duke of Somerset in *2 Henry VI* is entirely based on Edmund Beaufort, and it is his head that is presented to Richard, third duke of York, at the opening of *3 Henry VI* (all three plays *c.* 1591–2). Samuel Daniel portrays Somerset's confrontations with York in the 1609 edition of *Civil Wars*, as does Michael Drayton in his verse narrative *The Miseries of Queen Margarite* (1627).

554 In late 1447, Edmund Beaufort, then marquess of Dorset, was made governor of France and Normandy, replacing as England's chief officer overseas Richard (d. 1460), third duke of York (Hall, 206). Beaufort held this post throughout the year 1449, during which time almost all of Normandy was overrun by the troops of Charles VII.

555 Somerset's statement that Cancer was in retrograde (moving opposite to its normal orbit) at the time of his birth reveals Ferrers's lack of expertise in astrological knowledge; it is the 'planets' (in astrology, a term comprising the sun, the moon, and the five planets visible to the naked eye) that become retrograde in their courses and not the fixed constellations identified as zodiacal signs.

556 Somerset asserts that heavenly bodies were in positions unfavourable to him at the time of his birth. Astrologers understood the planet Jupiter to

be a beneficial influence in one's life and Mars and Saturn to be malign influences. Somerset assumes that Jupiter was not ascendant (that is, above the eastern horizon) at his birth; had it been, it would have provided him with good fortune. Worse, it seems, the constellation Cancer had declined from being aligned with the neutral sun and instead stood aligned with the malignant Saturn. In addition, early modern astrologers held that not only the planets in ascendance in one's zodiac sign at the time of one's birth influenced a person's future but also planets in various specific longitudinal relations ('aspects') with those ascendant bodies. Heavenly bodies that stood at a 180-degree angle from the planets in ascendance were said to be in the aspect of 'opposition'. In the penultimate line of this stanza, Somerset claims that the effect of any favourable planetary aspects at his birth was undercut by the influence of malign aspects of opposition. For a concise explanation of these concepts, see J. D. North, *Chaucer's Universe* (Oxford: Clarendon Press, 1988), 209. As mentioned in the previous note, Ferrers's grasp of astrological thought is not precise.

557 Somerset's claim that he gave only 'assent' to others to strike against Henry VI's uncle Humphrey (d. 1447), first duke of Gloucester, is Ferrers's invention. Historically, Edmund Beaufort was an ally of his uncle Cardinal Henry Beaufort (d. 1447), Gloucester's fiercest opponent. Indeed, in Tragedy 29, Ferrers himself identifies Edmund Beaufort (at that time marquess of Dorset) as one of the conspirators who actively plotted against Duke Humphrey (line 352). For an argument that Ferrers shapes his unhistorical description of Somerset's interactions with his kinsman Gloucester here to evoke thoughts of those between the executed royal uncles Edward Seymour (d. 1552), first duke of Somerset, and Thomas (d. 1549), first Baron Seymour of Sudeley, see Lucas, *'A Mirror for Magistrates'*, 70–90.

558 In the wake of his brother Henry V's death in 1422, Duke Humphrey was made protector of England on behalf of his infant nephew, the new king Henry VI. As protector, he was the dominant figure in English politics, and he retained great influence in the realm even after leaving that office. Although historically Gloucester surrendered his protectorship at Henry VI's coronation in November 1429, Ferrers evidently follows Hall's understanding that Gloucester remained lord protector even as late as the year 1446 (Hall, 208).

559 Edmund Beaufort was Humphrey of Gloucester's half-cousin. Both men were grandsons of King Edward III's son John (d. 1399), first duke of Lancaster, though Somerset's father John (d. 1410), first marquess of Dorset, and Dorset's brother Henry (later Cardinal) Beaufort were born out of wedlock and were only later legitimated under the newly created Beaufort name.

560 Gloucester died in February 1447; York made his first open challenge for the crown through claims of 'title and right' only in the parliament of October 1460, though Hall suggests that machinations by York's supporters to assert

Duke Richard's right to the throne started as early as 1450 (Hall, 219). For the basis of York's claim to sovereignty, see Tragedy 13, nn. 240 and 241.

561 Hall insists that Jack Cade's 1450 rising in Kent was the secret work either of 'the duke of Yorke or his frendes', though he names economic redress and the purging of hated counsellors around Henry VI (and not the advance of York's title to the crown) as its participants' principal aims (Hall, 219–20).

562 Somerset's tag is a version of the Vulgate Bible's 'Vae tibi terra cuius rex est puer', 'woe to you, land, where a child is king' (Ecclesiastes 10:16).

563 A version of the Vulgate's 'Beata terra cuius rex nobilis est' (Ecclesiastes 10:17), which Ferrers turns to mean a strong and powerful king rather than one who 'is come of nobles' (Great Bible).

564 Hall describes the adult Henry VI as 'a man of a meke spirite, and of a simple witte, preferryng peace before warre [and] reste before businesse ... yet he was governed of them whom he should have ruled, and brideled of suche, whom he sharpely should have spurred' (Hall, 208).

565 It was Queen Margaret, Hall writes, who made the first move against Duke Humphrey, by purging him from her husband's government. Soon after, others created the conspiracy that brought Humphrey to his death, albeit with the queen's permission (Hall, 208–9).

566 Despite Somerset's words, Hall gives no indication that either York or his supporters ever plotted to overthrow King Henry during Humphrey's lifetime.

567 Hall writes that York began his open campaign for the crown in September 1450 by claiming that he sought to defend the commonwealth against the misrule of Henry VI's closest counsellors, most notably Somerset (Hall, 225).

568 Ferrers now unhistorically characterizes Jack Cade's rebellion of May–July 1450 as part of York's September–November 1450 campaign against the duke of Somerset. While Hall suggests Yorkists were behind Cade's rising, he makes it clear that the revolt was not against Somerset himself, since Duke Edmund was in France, not England, during this entire time (see Hall, 219–20; Tragedy 12). For a reading of Ferrers's unhistorical conflation of these events in the context of mid-Tudor politics, see Lucas 'A Mirror for Magistrates', 80–4.

569 In this and subsequent stanzas, Ferrers conflates various events of the period 1450 through 1455. As Hall tells it, York and his partisans began their campaign for supremacy in late 1450, gathering adherents by privately denouncing King Henry's chief counsellor Somerset, who they claimed had dangerously 'ruled the kynge [and] ordred the realme' ever since he returned from France in August 1450. Knowing that the people already hated Beaufort for his role in the loss of English-held Normandy, York and his allies in February 1452 formed an army in the marches of Wales and encamped at Brentheath (Dartford), Kent, claiming to seek on behalf of the people redress for Somerset's misrule of the realm (Hall, 225). In this stanza, Ferrers reshapes Hall's narrative. Drawing on matter from Hall's earlier account

of Cade's rebellion (ibid., 219–20), Ferrers invents the claim that it was a popular uprising spurred by Yorkist propaganda that caused Henry VI to send Somerset to the Tower from Blackheath, Kent, where the king and his forces had assembled to confront York's army. Historically, it was the threat of York's organized Brentheath forces that caused Henry VI to put Somerset under arrest at Blackheath. Somerset was not in fact sent from Blackheath to the Tower; instead, this happened to James Fiennes (d. 1450), first Baron Saye and Seale, during Cade's rising nearly two years earlier (see ibid., 226, 220).

570 York dissolved his army on 1 March 1452, only to discover that Henry VI had not only released Somerset from his brief captivity but returned him to his side (Hall, 226). Ferrers then proceeds to combine this event with occurrences of the years 1453–5, in which York, taking advantage of King Henry's onset of mental illness, arranged for Somerset to be imprisoned in the Tower of London on a charge of treason (November 1453). After Somerset languished for some time in captivity (historically until about January 1455), the newly recovered king ordered Somerset released. In response, an outraged York began to gather forces to wage open war against the crown (see ibid., 232).

571 York's forces met King Henry and his supporters at St Albans on 22 May 1455. As Hall records it, Somerset lost his life in battle at 'the sign of the Castle', that is, before the Castle Inn of St Albans. Somerset's place of death was notable, Hall writes, because he 'long before was warned to eschew all Castles' (Hall, 233). That Warwick personally slew Somerset is Ferrers's invention (see Lucas, *A Mirror for Magistrates*, 87–90).

572 Although Hall records that Humphrey Stafford (d. 1458), eldest son of the earl of Buckingham, died at St Albans, he in fact was only wounded there (Hall, 233). Hall does not mention Ralph Babthorpe among the battle's casualties; the St Albans native Ferrers would have been aware of Babthorpe's death from the memorial commemorating it in the Ferrers family's parish church of St Peter (John Weever, *Antient Funeral Monuments of Great Britain* (London, 1767), 342; for the Ferrers family's membership in St Peter parish, see Hertfordshire Archives and Local Studies AR228). It was not, however, Ralph but his uncle William Babthorpe who had served Henry V and VI as king's attorney (Cecil Foljambe, Baron Hawkesbury, 'Some East Riding Families', *Transactions of the East Riding Antiquarian Society* 7 (1899): 4).

573 Hall, in fact, declares that York treated King Henry 'with great honor and due reverance' after taking him at St Albans (Hall, 233).

574 Ferrers conflates here the actions of two different parliaments. After the First Battle of St Albans, a parliament summoned within days of York's victory made Duke Richard protector of England, a post he occupied for only three months. In 1460, following the defeat of Queen Margaret's forces at the Battle of Northampton, parliament once more named York protector and, with it, heir to the English throne (25 October 1460). See Hall, 233, 249.

575 Richard of York based his claim to the crown in part on his descent from Edward III's third son, Lionel (1338–1368), first duke of Clarence. Henry VI, by contrast, was a descendent only of Edward III's fourth son, John of Gaunt

(1340–1399), first duke of Lancaster. York's hereditary claim to the throne, however, came to him through two female ancestors, Lionel's daughter Philippa and Philippa's granddaughter Anne Mortimer (d. 1411), who was York's mother. Lancastrian supporters argued that Henry VI's claim to the crown was strongest, since his right came to him through a wholly male line of succession (see Hall, 2).

576 Ferrers now skips from events of 1460 to those of 1461. Richard of York died at the Battle of Wakefield (30 December 1460), leaving his title and claim to the crown to his son Edward (d. 1483), the new fourth duke of York. Duke Edward had himself declared King Edward IV on 4 March 1461; he soon after marched north to challenge Henry VI, Queen Margaret, and their Lancastrian allies. Edward won a decisive victory at the Battle of Towton (29 March 1461). In the wake of their defeat, Henry and Margaret fled north into Scotland.

577 While Somerset's words bear little resemblance to the historical Edmund Beaufort's feelings towards Humphrey of Gloucester, they could evoke for mid-Tudor readers thoughts of a later duke of Somerset, Edward Seymour, and what his supporters believed to be his sorrow over the loss of his executed brother Thomas. Similarly, the claim that Somerset was led to believe that Gloucester sought the crown is not in Ferrers's known historical sources (cf. Hall, 209; Fabyan, 619; Hardyng, 400); it evokes, rather, the treason charges against Thomas Seymour in the 1549 parliamentary attainder that led to his death. See Lucas, *'A Mirror for Magistrates'*, 73–80.

[Tragedy 27] 'The Blacksmith'

Authors: Humphrey Cavell (d. 1558), probable author of lines 197–292, and William Baldwin, probable author of the rest of the poem (see note 582). **Historical subject:** Michael Joseph (d. 1497), called 'An Gof' ('The Blacksmith' in Cornish), rebel leader. **Principal source:** *Hall's Chronicle*. **Possible additional source**: *Fabyan's Chronicle*. **Contemporary literary treatments**: None known. Michael Joseph's 1497 rising does, however, form the backdrop for Thomas Deloney's short prose piece 'A Speech Between Ladies, being Shepherds on Salisbury Plain', which concludes his posthumous poetry collection *Strange Histories* (1602).

578 Crocodiles were widely believed to cry and moan as if in sorrow to lure unsuspecting humans close enough to seize them.

579 Edward Hall records that two Cornishmen, Thomas Flamock (or Flamank), a member of the gentry, and Michael Joseph, a blacksmith, began the May–June 1497 rising against Henry VII's tax policies. After marching from Cornwall to Wells, Somerset, the protestors were joined by James Tuchet, seventh Baron Audley (d. 1497), who accompanied the rebels in their subsequent journey toward Blackheath, near London (Hall, 477–8). Although both Hall and Robert Fabyan indicate that Audley became the rebels' 'chiefe capiteyne' after joining the uprising, Baldwin diminishes

Audley's authority in the revolt relative to that of Michael Joseph (Hall, 478; Fabyan, 686).

580 In classical mythology, Trophonius was an oracle who lived in a terrifying cavern. Those who visited the cave were said never to smile again.

581 Baldwin addresses nobles' need for legal knowledge in filling the judicial offices incumbent upon their rank, such as presiders in manor courts, members of juridical commissions, justices of the peace, and the like.

582 Mike Pincombe persuasively argues that this and the following fifteen stanzas of rhymed couplets is the only section of 'The Blacksmith' actually written by the man named as the tragedy's author, 'Master Cavell'. William Baldwin is responsible for the rest (see Mike Pincombe, 'William Baldwin, Humphrey Cavell, and the Authorship of The Tragedy of the Blacksmith in the 1563 *Mirror for Magistrates*', *Notes & Queries* 56.4 (2009): 515–21).

583 Cavell's warning that rebels will lose their lands if they fail suggests that he does not have peasant rebels in mind but land-owning men of the gentlemen or at least yeoman class who, like Thomas Flamank during the Cornish rebellion, might use their superior rank to organize angry commoners. As Pincombe notes, Cavell may be thinking of the ferocious 1549 risings, popular revolts led in many places by gentlemen ('William Baldwin, Humphrey Cavell', 517). Cavell's native Cornwall was an epicentre of the 1549 risings.

584 Cavell echoes the familiar mid-Tudor rhetoric that resistance to one's ruler is resistance to God, while service to the monarch is service to God, whose lieutenant on earth he or she is. It found expression in Edward VI's reign in such works as the official homily 'An Exhortation, Concerning Good Order and Obedience' (*Certain Sermons, or Homilies*, STC 13638.5, sigs. N1r–P2r), and in Mary I's in texts such as John Christopherson's *An Exhortation to All Men to Take Heed and Beware of Rebellion* (London, 1554; *STC* 5207).

585 Cavell here does not betray any awareness of the actual circumstances of Michael Joseph's rebellion, a rising whose ranks, according to Hall, were quickly swelled by high-born men such as Lord Audely and 'diverse other of the nobilitee' (Hall, 478).

586 The implication is that that a noble's avoidance of the 'spot' of disloyalty to his monarch is worth much more than any other measure of the quality of his family and rank.

587 Given that the poems of *A Memorial of Such Princes* record several overthrows of reigning monarchs and at least one popular revolt (Jack Cade's rebellion) that won concessions from the prince, it appears unlikely that Cavell had read any of the other *Memorial* tragedies before composing these lines.

588 In 1496, James IV of Scotland led a brief invasion of England in support of Perkin Warbeck (d. 1499), who challenged Henry VII's right to the throne by claiming to be Edward IV's long-lost son Richard, first duke of York (see Tragedy 24, n. 522). In the wake of James's failed incursion, Henry VII asked parliament for funds with which to attack the Scots, and it was the onerous tax granted by parliament for this purpose that led to the Cornishmen's rebellion (Hall, 475–6; Fabyan, 685–6).

589 According to Hall, Michael Joseph and Thomas Flamock stirred their fellow Cornishmen against Henry VII's tax by reminding them that they were 'but poore men, and being in a sterile and unfruitefull countrey gate [got] their lyvyng hardly [with difficulty] by mining and digging tynne and metall oute of the grounde bothe day and night labouryng and turmoylyng'. Death would be better, they continued, than paying the grievous tax that would plunge them all into 'calamitee and wretchednes' (Hall, 477).

590 Baldwin adheres closely to Hall in this stanza (Hall, 477). Chancellor John Cardinal Morton (d. 1500), Archbishop of Canterbury, and Sir Reginald (or Reynold) Bray (d. 1503) were two of King Henry VII's closest advisors at the time of the rising.

591 While he presents the Cornishmen's legitimate complaints of oppressive taxation, Baldwin suggests that the Blacksmith's chief purpose for his rising was the boast he made shortly before his execution, namely that his audacious rising would grant him 'a name perpetual and a fame permanent and immortal' (Hall, 479).

592 John Oby (d. 1497), provost of Glassney collegiate church in Penryn, Cornwall, lost his life at Taunton, Somerset, because of his role as a commissioner assigned to collect the new tax (Hall, 477–8).

593 Baldwin closely follows Hall for his accounts of Michael Joseph's journey towards London, his encampment at Blackheath, Kent, and the rebels' ultimate defeat at nearby Deptford Bridge (17 June). He alters only Hall's claim that the Blacksmith's Cornishmen began deserting their leaders before reaching Blackheath and not after (cf. Hall, 478–80).

594 Hall notes that Audley was taken from Newgate prison to Tower Hill for his execution (Hall, 480); Baldwin assumes from this that the other two rebel leaders were also imprisoned in Newgate. All three rebel leaders were in fact kept in the Tower of London until their trial and convictions. Thereafter, Henry VII had Audley moved to Newgate, so that he might be drawn through the city to the derision of the crowds before his execution at Tower Hill (see the contemporary account in Charles Kingsford, ed., *Chronicles of London* (Oxford University Press, 1905), 215–16).

595 In a bid for fame, a Greek named Herostratus burned the temple of Artemis (or Diana) in Ephesus, one of the seven wonders of the world. He was tortured and executed for his crime. See Valerius Maximus, *Memorable Doings and Sayings*, 2:277–9. Herostratus' name became a byword for someone who does wrong in search of notoriety.

596 The Blacksmith refers to Christ's parable of the talents (Matthew 25:14–30). The implication here is that one should increase one's wealth and station only within the scope of one's rank and not seek to exceed it, for it is hard enough even for one with but little to use one's God-given worldly prosperity correctly.

[Prose 29]

597 'Universal election' was the process by which the body of German electors selected the King of the Romans, the only person eligible to become Holy Roman Emperor. It was by this means that King Philip's father Emperor Charles V had ascended to his imperial title.

598 France famously followed the long-standing Salic law of succession, which excluded women (and any male whose royal blood descended to him solely from a woman) from inheriting the crown.

599 Deborah, the only female judge in the Hebrew Bible, commanded her general Barak to free Israel from the oppression of the Canaanites and accompanied him on his expedition against the Canaanite commander Sisera's forces. After his defeat by the Hebrew army, Sisera took refuge in the tent of the Israelite woman Jael. Pretending to agree to hide him, Jael took a tent nail and drove it into Sisera's skull (Judges 4–5). The biblical book of Judith describes how King Nebuchadnezzar of Assyria (historically Babylon) sent his general Holofernes to persecute the people of Palestine, after they refused to fight against his enemies. Holofernes besieged Judea and cut off its water supply. In response, the brave and beautiful Israelite Judith came to Holofernes on a pretext of seeking to aid him. When he became drunk one night, Judith slew him, an act that broke the Assyrian siege. Tomyris (fl. 530 BC) was queen of the Massegetai people of central Asia. According to Herodotus, she and her forces triumphed over the powerful Persian army and killed its celebrated leader King Cyrus the Great (Herodotus, 1:261–9).

600 While he endorses the speaker's claim that subjects should never forcibly resist the prince, Baldwin nevertheless emphasizes in his own statement not a subject's duty to a ruler but instead to 'all good laws and lawful contributions'. He also qualifies the previous speaker's sweeping declaration by adding that one should never fulfil an unjust order. In so doing, Baldwin expands to considerations of secular justice John Calvin's admonition that no Christian may ever obey an ungodly command (Calvin, *Institutes*, 2:1520). Baldwin's final comment paraphrases 1 Corinthians 10:13.

601 The uncertainty Baldwin expresses here about when this new gathering of poems will be printed suggests that, unlike previously in 1554 and later in 1563, he does not yet have a printer ready to produce his text. In any event, as Baldwin himself notes, Mary's privy council forbade publication of this second attempt at a *de casibus* tragedy collection before its production could even begin (see Prose 23).

[Prose 30, First Version]

602 This prose link appears in the uncancelled version of the 1578 *Mirror*, replacing what was Prose 11 in the 1559 and 1563 editions of the text. It introduces 'Humphrey Duke of Gloucester', which follows it in this version of the 1578 *Mirror*. This prose was removed and replaced, however, in some 1578 copies by a cancel (new leaves of text inserted into an already completed

work) comprising Prose 30, Second Version, Tragedy 28, and Prose 31. For the historical events and figures mentioned in Prose 30, First Version, see Prose 11.

603 This slip of the pen shows that Ferrers is the author of this prose link. In all other prose sections, William Baldwin is understood to be the person speaking in the first person.

604 Ferrers's words here seem to confirm the implication of the 1559 edition's table of contents that Ferrers had originally told the tragedies of both Duke Humphrey and his wife Eleanor in a single poem. See Introduction, p. xx and Prose 11.

[Prose 30, Second Version]

605 This prose link appears in the second release of the 1578 *Mirror*, in which Prose 30, First Version, had been removed from the original printed volume and replaced with new leaves comprising Prose 30, Second Version; Tragedy 28; and Prose 31. As with the first version of Prose 30, the text of this prose link replaced what was Prose 11 in the 1559 and 1563 *Mirror* editions. Whereas George Ferrers was apparently the author of Prose 30, First Version, the composer of this section was the anonymous editor of the 1578 *Mirror*, probably John Higgins (see Introduction, p. xxi).

[Tragedy 28] 'Eleanor Cobham, Duchess of Gloucester'

Author: George Ferrers. **Historical subject:** Eleanor, née Cobham (*c.* 1400–1452), duchess of Gloucester, accused accessory to sorcery and witchcraft. **Principal sources:** *Hall's Chronicle*; the roll of the February 1447 parliament (NA C 65/98), apparently imperfectly remembered (see notes 621 and 622); the fifteenth-century poem 'The Lamentation of the Duchess of Gloucester', in a version similar to the one preserved in Oxford University, Balliol College MS 354, 360–2 (printed as 'The Lament of the Duchess of Gloucester' in Thomas Wright, ed., *Political Poems and Songs Relating to English History*, 2 vols. (London, 1861), 2:205–8; all further references to 'The Lamentation' will be to Wright's edition and under his title for the work). **Possible further sources**: the unknown fifteenth-century poem satirizing Cobham mentioned in lines 157–8. **Contemporary literary treatments:** Shakespeare portrays Duchess Eleanor's downfall in *2 Henry VI* (*c.* 1591–2), while Michael Drayton offers fictional verse epistles exchanged between Eleanor and her husband in the second edition of *England's Heroical Epistles* (1600). Eleanor's story is told as well in Richard Johnson's 'Lamentable Fall of the Great Duchess of Gloucester', which first appeared in the 1631 edition of his *Crown Garland of Golden Roses*.

606 In his moralizing of Cobham's fall, Ferrers follows the medieval complaint poem 'The Lament of the Duchess of Gloucester', which identifies pride as the ultimate cause of Eleanor's travails (Wright, ed., *Political Poems*, 2:206–8). Cf. Fabyan and Hall, who both suggest that Cobham's travails were chiefly

the result of plots against her husband Humphrey (d. 1447), first duke of Gloucester (Fabyan, 614; Hall, 202).

607 Duke Humphrey was the youngest son of King Henry IV. In the wake of the death of Henry V in 1422, he was made protector of England during the infancy of his nephew Henry VI, who was less than a year old when he came to the throne. Gloucester's admirers often called him 'the good duke' (Hall, 209).

608 Eleanor Cobham was the daughter of Sir Reginald Cobham (d. 1445), *de jure* third Baron Cobham of Sterborough, though the author of the 'Lament of the Duchess of Gloucester' has Eleanor claim that she 'was browght up of nowght [from poverty and/or low social status]' (Wright, ed., *Political Poems*, 2:205). Eleanor first came to Duke Humphrey's attention through her service as an attendant on Gloucester's first wife, Jacqueline (or Jaquet, as Edward Hall calls her) of Hainault (d. 1436). By the mid 1420s Cobham had become Gloucester's mistress. In January 1428, after Gloucester's marriage to Jacqueline was declared invalid, she became his wife (see Hall's account, 128–9).

609 In 1418, Jacqueline (Jaquet) of Hainault, daughter and heir to William, count of Holland (called duke by Hall (116)), married John, duke of Brabant, her first cousin. By 1421, Jacqueline had repudiated her marriage to John and had travelled to England, where she wed Duke Humphrey. In 1424, Humphrey took up arms to pursue his wife's claim to the rule of Hainault. John of Brabant, however, was supported by the powerful Duke Philip of Burgundy, and in the face of their combined threat Humphrey left Jacqueline in Hainault with a small body of armed men and returned to England to gather more troops. Jacqueline was taken by Burgundian forces; thereafter, Pope Martin V declared her earlier marriage to Brabant valid and her subsequent one to Humphrey illegitimate (January 1428). Hall suggests that Gloucester's keen disappointment in his first marriage helped spur him to seek quickly a new match, this time with his mistress Eleanor Cobham (Hall, 128–9).

610 If by 'the queen' he means Henry VI's queen, Margaret of Anjou (d. 1482), Ferrers shows himself confused about his dates, since Margaret did not arrive in England until almost four years after Eleanor's downfall. It is possible his reference is to the queen dowager, Catherine of Valois (d. 1437), Henry V's widow and mother of Henry VI.

611 Ferrers's language evokes Christ's parable of the pearl of great price, for which a merchant gladly gave all he had (Matthew 13:45–6).

612 By the late 1430s Duke Humphrey had become heir presumptive to his childless nephew Henry VI.

613 According to their 1441 indictment in the court of the king's bench, Duchess Eleanor had in the previous year encouraged three men of her affinity – Roger Bolingbroke, a learned cleric; Thomas Southwell, a canon of St Stephen's chapel in Westminster Palace; and John Home, her chaplain – to determine through necromancy when Henry VI would die. After employing magical items and summoning spirits and devils to prognosticate the king's

future, Bolingbroke and Southwell spread a prophecy claiming that the king would either lose his life or face some terrible bodily threat within the next two years (R. A. Griffiths, 'The Trial of Eleanor Cobham: An Episode in the Fall of Duke Humphrey of Gloucester', *Bulletin of the John Rylands Library* 51.2 (1968–9): 390–1; Jessica Freeman, 'Sorcery at Court and Manor: Margery Jourdemayne, the Witch of Eye Next Westminster', *Journal of Medieval History* 30.4 (2004): 348).

614   Ferrers's source for his description of Margery Jourdemayne (d. 1441), called 'the witch of Eye', as an elderly necromancer nicknamed 'Mother Madge' is unknown; his assertions about her may be his own inventions. Historically, it was Eleanor's male associates and not Jourdemayne who were formally charged with conjuring demons and evil spirits (Griffiths, 'Trial', 390; for the historical Margery Jourdemayne, see Freeman, 'Sorcery at Court and Manor', 343–57).

615   No extant fifteenth- or sixteenth-century chronicle states that Cobham's associates calculated the king's nativity, though the indictment and a surviving counter-horoscope show that they indeed did so. The two men's formal indictment also asserted that Cobham wished to learn from them when she might be queen of England (Griffiths, 'Trial', 390–1; Robert Ralley, 'Stars, Demons and the Body in Fifteenth-Century England', *Studies in History and Philosophy of Biological and Biomedical Sciences* 41.2 (2010): 114). Ferrers's specific source for this information is not known.

616   Ferrers has Cobham deny the assertion recorded by nearly every fifteenth- and sixteenth-century chronicler – and by Ferrers himself in Tragedy 29 – that Dame Eleanor and her associates sought to bring about the king's death by magic. Given that so many contemporaries note the charge, it likely was an early accusation against her. If so, the claim evidently could not be legally sustained, since the formal treason indictment against Cobham's servants ultimately accused them only of using necromancy to calculate the king's nativity and not of employing sorcery directly to harm the king. Bolingbroke and Southwell's precise treasonous act, according to the indictment, was communicating to the people their finding that Henry would sicken and likely die by 1442. The two men sought through their prophecy's publication, the indictment claimed, to alienate Henry VI from the love of his subjects and thus to lead the monarch into a fit of melancholy that would end in death (J. G. Bellamy, *The Law of Treason in England in the Later Middle Ages* (Cambridge University Press, 1970), 126–7, 236–7).

617   It is unknown who first brought news of Bolingbroke's and Southwell's activities to the authorities. Ferrers follows Hall in tying the accusations against Eleanor and her servants to the machinations of Duke Humphrey's enemies. Hall does not identify Gloucester's long-time rival for power Cardinal Henry Beaufort (d. 1447) as Eleanor's chief persecutor, but he does suggest that Humphrey's opponents were emboldened to seek means to harm 'the good duke' after Gloucester's failed attempt in 1440 to have

Cardinal Beaufort and his ally Cardinal John Kemp (d. 1454) punished for alleged corrupt practices (Hall, 197–202).

618 Ferrers could have learned of Cardinal Beaufort's presence on the first of the ecclesiastical commissions that interrogated Cobham from the 'Lament of the Duchess of Gloucester', in which Eleanor declares that she was tried before 'two cardynals, and byshoppis fyve'. Similarly, it may have been Eleanor's statement in the 'Lament' that she spoke directly to the commissioners that led Ferrers to assume she was refused legal counsel (Wright, ed., *Political Poems*, 2:207). The claim that Cobham sought to delay the ecclesiastical proceedings against her is apparently Ferrers's invention.

619 No source mentions the appearance of the king's body of legal advisors at Cobham's ecclesiastical hearings. Ferrers may have added them to make sense of ambiguous wording in Hall's chronicle, which seems to suggest that Cobham was tried by an ecclesiastical body on an accusation of treason – a secular charge that the church had no proper authority to adjudicate – and sentenced to a religious punishment, penance, for this civil crime (see Hall, 202). Historically, the ecclesiastical tribunal that ordered Cobham to perform public penance in November 1441 condemned her not for treason but for indulgence in sorcery and witchcraft (Hall, 202; Griffiths, 'Trial', 394; Freeman, 'Sorcery', 351).

620 Duchess Eleanor was ordered to make public penance in London on three consecutive market days (Griffiths, 'Trial', 394). While no known chronicler mentions that she was forced to do her penance bare-legged or in a sheet, such was a common state of presentation for public penitents in late medieval England. See Dave Postles, 'Penance and the Market Place: A Reformation Dialogue with the Medieval Church (*c.* 1250–*c.* 1600)', *Journal of Ecclesiastical History* 54.3 (2003): 445. Shakespeare likely drew on Ferrers's description for his own portrait of Eleanor performing penance clad in a sheet and barefoot in *2 Henry VI*.

621 Historically, two months after an ecclesiastical commission sentenced Cobham to her public penance, Henry VI ordered her perpetual imprisonment and, in July 1446, her placement on the Isle of Man (Griffiths, 'Trial', 395–7). Hall, by contrast, suggests it was not the king but a juridical body who condemned Eleanor to exile on the Isle of Man immediately after what he (incorrectly) claims was her conviction for treason (Hall, 202). Ferrers, for his part, seems to offer a third, unprecedented version of how the duchess got to the island, suggesting she was relegated there by an act of parliament, the same act that stripped her of her dower (see line 153 and note 622). For Duke Humphrey's death, see note 624.

622 While no parliamentary act condemned Eleanor to exile, a statute passed on 3 March 1447, eight days after Humphrey of Gloucester's death, did forbid her from 'having or claiming any dower of the endowment' of her late husband. Parliament directed that Cobham was to be treated in matters pertaining to the duke's possessions as if she were already dead (*PROME*, 12:23).

623 The former poem is unknown; the latter is likely the 'Lament of the Duchess of Gloucester'. Given that the words 'these spites' in line 162 refer to Cobham's exile and loss of dower mentioned in the stanza before this one, and given that this stanza's lines have Eleanor speak of occurrences after her death, despite the fact that all other lines in the poem suggest that she is still alive when making her complaint, it seems that Ferrers (or the editor of the 1578 *Mirror*) inserted lines 155–61 into 'Eleanor Cobham' after the surrounding matter of this tragedy had been composed.

624 Shortly after arriving at Bury St Edmunds, Suffolk, to attend the February 1447 parliament, Duke Humphrey was arrested by a group of powerful nobles. According to Edward Hall, on the next night (historically 23 February 1447, five days after his arrest), he was found dead in the room in which he was held. Although Humphrey's captors claimed that he died of an illness, Hall, like a number of other chroniclers, treats Gloucester's death as a clear case of murder (Hall, 209; see also Ferrers's Tragedies 26 and 29). Ferrers himself is evidently the creator of the claims that Humphrey was hastily and improperly called to parliament, that Gloucester's 1447 death occurred 'shortly after' Cobham's exile (at least as the condemnation to exile is presented by Hall and other chroniclers), and that Humphrey met his death after and not before the bill had passed stripping Eleanor of any right to her dower or his possessions.

625 According to Hall, it was the duke's high-ranking enemies William de la Pole (d. 1450), first marquess of Suffolk, and Humphrey Stafford (d. 1460), first duke of Buckingham, who led the plot against Duke Humphrey, though in doing so they were 'not unprocured by the Cardinall [Henry Beaufort] of Winchester', who was Humphrey's uncle (Hall, 209). In his mention of 'consent', Ferrers may refer to his earlier *Mirror* poem 'Somerset', in which Edmund Beaufort (d. 1455), first duke of Somerset, insists that he did not actively plot to bring about his kinsman Humphrey's death but only consented to it (see Tragedy 26).

626 Eleanor's words echo Hall's own assessments of Beaufort's character, though Hall does not specifically claim that Beaufort bribed his way to the office of cardinal (Hall, 210–11).

627 Eleanor's execration of Beaufort is likely inspired by Elizabeth Shore's cursing of the vindictive Richard (d. 1485), first duke of Gloucester, in Thomas Churchyard's 'Shore's Wife' (Tragedy 25).

628 In Sir Thomas Malory's *Morte d'Arthur* (1469/70), Merlin becomes infatuated by the chief Lady of the Lake, Nyneve (or Nymue), who learns his magic and imprisons him in what would be his living tomb (Malory, [*Le Morte d'Arthur*] (London, 1485; *STC* 801), sigs. f2v, f6r.

629 In Lucan's ancient Roman epic *Pharsalia*, Sextus Pompeius, son of the Roman general Pompey, consults the powerful witch Erictho, who revives a corpse so that it might prophesy the future for Pompey and his family (*Lucan, with an English Translation*, 340–65).

630 Ferrers follows Hall in characterizing the Isle of Man as Cobham's sole place of incarceration. Historically, she was kept under guard on the mainland for several years before finally being settled on the Isle of Man (Griffiths, 'Trial', 395–7). No extant chronicle describes the conditions of Cobham's residence there. Ferrers likely expands in these lines on the pained farewells the fallen Eleanor offers to all happiness, wealth, 'and the world so wide' in 'The Lament of the Duchess of Gloucester' (Wright, ed., *Political Poems*, 2:208).

631 Ferrers follows Hall, who suggests that Eleanor's persecution was an early instance of Gloucester's enemies' attacks on him, 'whiche in conclusion came so nere, that they bereft hym both of lyfe and lande' (Hall, 202).

632 Ferrers echoes Eleanor's similar farewells in 'The Lament of the Duchess of Gloucester' (Wright, ed., *Political Poems*, 2:207–8). The palace called *Plesaunce* in Greenwich, Kent (now London), was Humphrey and Eleanor's principal residence. Ferrers may also have known that Kent was Eleanor's place of birth and the traditional seat of the Cobhams. The lack of rhyme and the upset of the rhythm in the last two lines of this stanza are probably the result of a compositor accidently reversing the order of the words 'you' and 'see' in line 280 when setting the type.

633 Unusually for the *Mirror*, Ferrers wishes readers to imagine Eleanor as still living and imprisoned on the desolate Isle of Man as she speaks.

634 Ferrers could well imagine that Cobham journeyed through St Albans while travelling north into captivity, since the long-established primary road north-west from London passed through the town (Roy Porter, *London: A Social History* (Cambridge, Mass.: Harvard University Press, 1994), 15). After his death, Humphrey of Gloucester was buried in St Albans monastery, where he and Eleanor had been members of the abbey's confraternity.

635 While almost all early chroniclers suggest that Duchess Eleanor spent all her time in captivity on the Isle of Man, Cobham was in fact kept prisoner there only from 1446 to 1449. Thereafter, she was moved to Beaumaris Castle in Wales, where she died and was presumably interred in 1452.

636 Cf. 'The Lament of the Duchess of Gloucester': 'The syne of pryde wille have a falle; / Alle women may be ware by me' (Wright, ed., *Political Poems*, 2:207).

[Prose 31]

637 Duke Humphrey (d. 1447) of Gloucester patronized numerous erudite authors and was himself a student of classical and humanist learning. An important benefactor of Oxford University, Humphrey did not actually found its divinity school, but he promised great support for its creation. While there is no evidence that Gloucester had Aristotle's works translated from Greek into Latin at Oxford, he apparently did donate his manuscript of Leonardo Bruni's translation of Aristotle's *Ethics* to the university (for Humphrey's learning and acts of patronage, see Susanne Saygin, *Humphrey,*

Duke of Gloucester (1390–1447) and the Italian Humanists (Leiden: Brill, 2002)).

638 The speaker characterizes Cardinal Henry Beaufort (d. 1447) as Humphrey of Gloucester's enemy 'against nature', because Beaufort was Gloucester's blood relation.

639 Edward Hall writes that Henry VI's new queen, Margaret of Anjou (d. 1482), was jealous of Duke Humphrey's authority in the mid 1440s and sought any means to undermine it. She was encouraged in this action by the duke's noble enemies, and it was 'by her permission, and favor', that these nobles created a conspiracy against Humphrey's life, a plot headed chiefly by William de la Pole (d. 1450), first marquess of Suffolk, and Humphrey Stafford (d. 1460), first duke of Buckingham. The speaker further follows Hall in suggesting that the loss of Duke Humphrey was a root cause of the downfall and suffering of King Henry and his Lancastrian supporters in later years (Hall, 208–10).

[Tragedy 29] 'Humphrey Plantagenet, Duke of Gloucester'

Author: George Ferrers. **Historical subject:** Humphrey Plantagenet (1390–1447), first duke of Gloucester, prince, uncle to King Henry VI, and protector of England. **Principal known sources:** *Hall's Chronicle*; *Fabyan's Chronicle*; *Hardyng's Chronicle*; Giraldus Cambrensis (Gerald of Wales), *De Principis Instructione*. **Possible further source:** Giraldus Cambrensis (Gerald of Wales), *De Vita Galfridi Archiepiscopi Eboracensis*. **Contemporary literary treatments:** Gloucester appears as a character in Shakespeare's *Henry V* (*c.* 1599), and he plays central roles in *1* and *2 Henry VI* (*c.* 1591–2). Samuel Daniel includes Duke Humphrey in his *Civil Wars* (1595–1609), and Christopher Middleton portrays Gloucester's travails under Henry VI in his tragic poem *The Legend of Humphrey Duke of Gloucester* (1600). Later, Michael Drayton crafts verse epistles between Gloucester and his wife Eleanor Cobham for the second edition of *England's Heroical Epistles* (1598), and he recounts Humphrey's death in the poem *The Miseries of Queen Margarite* (1627).

640 Both Fabyan and Hall note that Humphrey of Gloucester's admirers termed him 'the good duke' (Fabyan, 619; Hall, 209).

641 Humphrey, youngest son of King Henry IV, became duke of Gloucester in 1414 and was made protector of England shortly after his infant nephew Henry VI succeeded to the throne in August 1422 (Hall, 115). While historically Duke Humphrey held the office of protector only until Henry VI's coronation in 1429, Ferrers follows Hall and Fabyan, who continue to characterize Gloucester as protector – and thus as England's chief domestic officer – until nearly the time of his death in 1447.

642 By the Treaty of Troyes (1420), Henry V and France's Charles VI established that their two kingdoms would, in the wake of Charles's death, be ruled by a single (English) monarch. Humphrey's elder brother John (d. 1435), first duke of Bedford, became regent of France on Henry VI's behalf at about the same time Gloucester became protector of England.

643　The 'history' to which Gloucester refers is *De Principis Instructione,* a thirteenth-century century work by Gerald of Wales (traditionally known as Giraldus Cambrensis) containing numerous anecdotes about England's Henry II (d. 1189) and his family. See *Giraldi Cambrensis Opera,* vol. 8, *De Principis Instructione Liber,* ed. J. S. Brewer, James Dimock, and George Warner (London, 1891); see also this work's sometimes unreliable translation, 'Concerning the Instruction of Princes', *The Church Historians of England,* vol. 5, part 1, ed. and trans. Joseph Stevenson (London, 1858), 133–241. The future King Henry II was born the son of Count Geoffrey of Anjou, who was called Geoffrey Plantagenet perhaps from the sprig of *Planta genista* (broom) he often wore in his helmet. When Geoffrey's son Henry claimed the English crown in 1154, he based his assertion of right on his descent from his mother, who was the daughter of England's Henry I. Despite sixteenth-century chroniclers' use of the Plantagenet name to identify Henry II and his descendants, the sobriquet was not in fact employed by members of the English royal family until Richard (d. 1460), third duke of York, began to style himself Richard Plantagenet in an attempt to bolster his claim to the English crown. See 'Plantagenet, House of (1154–1485)', in Wagner, *Encyclopedia of the Wars of the Roses,* 206–7.

644　Gerald of Wales relates that a count of Anjou, one of Henry II's ancestors, married a beautiful woman who would never hear Mass in church. When her husband one day forced her to remain for the ceremony, she revealed herself to be a demon and flew out one of the church's windows. According to Gerald, it was Henry II's son Richard the Lionheart and not King Henry himself who would often mention this tale (Giraldus, *De Principis,* 301–2; 'Concerning the Instruction of Princes', 224).

645　Henry II's four rebellious sons were Henry (d. 1183), called the Young King; Richard (d. 1199), nicknamed the Lionheart (the future Richard I); Geoffrey (d. 1186), duke of Brittany; and John (d. 1216), later king of England.

646　Here too Ferrers ascribes to Henry II sentiments Gerald credits to Richard the Lionheart (Giraldus, *De Principis,* 301–2; 'Concerning the Instruction of Princes', 224).

647　Gerald describes a painting Henry II commissioned of an eagle with three eaglets, two on his wings and another at his breast, digging their claws and beaks into their parent, while a fourth waited for its chance to peck out its father's eyes (Giraldus, *De Principis,* 295–6; for an accurate translation of this passage, see George Henderson, 'Giraldus Cambrensis: A Note on his Account of a Painting in the King's Chamber at Winchester', *Archaeological Journal* 118.1 (1961): 175). Ferrers replaces Gerald's eagle with a pelican, a bird said in medieval bestiaries to be plagued by its young pecking at its breast. Eventually, the pelican kills its ungrateful children but in a burst of pity sheds its own blood to bring them back to life. On the pelican legend in relation to the eagle painting described by Giraldus, see Henderson, 'Giraldus Cambrensis', 178–9.

648 While the context of the preceding matter would lead readers to expect here a reference to Henry II's often fiercely antagonistic son Geoffrey, duke of Brittany, Ferrers's words in this line seem to point instead to King Henry's illegitimate child Geoffrey Fitzroy (d. 1212), who became bishop elect of Lincoln and chancellor of the realm during Henry II's lifetime. Gerald of Wales attests to the deep love and support the future Archbishop of York Geoffrey bestowed on his father in his biographical account '*De Vita Galfridi Archiepiscopi Eboracensis*' (see *Giraldi Cambrensis Opera*, vol. 4, ed. J. S. Brewer (London, 1873), 370–1). The fact that Ferrers speaks of four birds attacking their father (line 89) but then of only three rebellious sons (line 92) may indicate error in the text.

649 In 1170, Henry II had his eldest surviving son, the 15-year-old Henry, crowned as his co-ruler. The often rebellious Young King died, however, in 1183, six years before his father. Later, King Henry's second son Richard broke with his father in 1188 and paid homage to King Philip of France. Philip agreed to help Richard seize territories from King Henry, 'from whence there arose an inexorable discord, and such an implacable dissension was excited as never ceased to fill his father with confusion to the last day of his life' (Giraldus, *De Principis*, 254; quotation from 'Concerning the Instruction', 197–8). Henry II's youngest son, John, betrayed his father only at the end of the king's life, transferring in 1189 his support from his parent to his defiant brother Richard. Gerald claims that Henry's anguish over John's betrayal hastened him to his death (*De Principis*, 295; 'Concerning the Instruction', 221).

650 This anecdote does not appear in the surviving manuscript of *De Principis Instructione*; it may be Ferrers's invention. The prophecy draws upon Matthew 13:24–30 and 36–43, in which Jesus tells of a farmer who sowed wheat in his field, only to have his enemy come at night and mix tares (seeds of the weed darnel) in among the wheat seed, forcing the farmer's servants, after the grain was grown, to separate the useless darnel from the good wheat. Christ explained that the 'the good sede, they are the children of the kingdome, and the tares are the children of the wicked, and the enemie that soweth them, is the devil' (Matthew 13:38–9, Geneva Bible). Ferrers's phrase 'not leaving one to piss against the wall' echoes 1 Kings 16:11, in which King Zimri of Israel slays the men of the former King Baasha's affinity, 'not leaving thereof one to pisse against a wall, ne[i]ther of his kinsfolkes nor of his friends' (Geneva Bible).

651 Richard was still allied with the French king against his father when Henry II died on 6 July 1189. In the next year, the new monarch Richard I left for the crusades; while returning to England in late 1192, he was captured by Duke Leopold of Austria and held prisoner. As the chronicler Fabyan tells it, on learning of Richard's captivity, France's King Philip encouraged Richard's brother John to take arms and claim the English throne for himself; John's rising, however, gained him only limited success. On his return to England in January 1194, Richard quickly re-established his authority and called a council of nobles, which condemned John. The brothers reconciled,

however, just a few months later, and John remained loyal to Richard for the rest of the reign (Fabyan, 304–6). Historically, Richard's council did not in fact try John for his rebellion but penalized him for failing to appear before it to answer charges.

652 Arthur (d. 1203), duke of Brittany, son of John's deceased elder brother Geoffrey of Brittany, was Henry II's sole legitimate grandson. As such, many understood him rather than John to be the proper heir to the English crown. When John took the throne in 1199, Arthur and his supporters began a military campaign in John's French territories to prosecute Arthur's right. In 1202, John's forces captured Arthur and his sister Eleanor at Mirebeau, France. Eleanor was sent to England, where she was kept in ward until her death in 1241. Arthur was held in Normandy and died the year after his capture. The exact cause of Arthur's death is unknown, but most early sources agree that John was responsible for his demise. Ferrers bases his specific treatment of the two imprisoned siblings on John Hardyng's account, which claims that John arranged miserable, early deaths for both Arthur and 'Isabell' (Hardyng's mistake for Eleanor) so that he might 'joy the crowne' without fear of rivals (Hardyng, 270). Hardyng only states that the siblings died in 'payne'; the manners of their deaths postulated by Gloucester are Ferrers's own additions.

653 In 1326, King Edward II's wife Isabella helped to depose her husband in favour of her son Edward III, after years of conflict between the elder Edward and his most powerful nobles. Soon after, Isabella's lover Roger, first earl of March, was said to have arranged the former monarch's death (see Tragedy 2). In 1399, Henry Bolingbroke, first duke of Hereford, overthrew his cousin King Richard II, and many believed that the newly crowned Bolingbroke then brought Richard to his death the following year (see Tragedy 5).

654 Gloucester and his powerful uncle Bishop (later Cardinal) Henry Beaufort of Winchester (d. 1447) began openly to feud in 1425, in a conflict, Hall writes, born either from Beaufort's envy of Humphrey's power or Gloucester's disdain for his wealthy, pompous uncle (Hall, 130).

655 Humphrey's father Henry IV was the son of the Lancastrian patriarch John of Gaunt, first duke of Lancaster, and his first wife Blanche. Henry Beaufort was also Gaunt's son, but he was born out of wedlock to Lancaster's mistress Katherine Swynford. Gaunt later married Swynford and legitimated their four children under the family name Beaufort. The Beauforts thereafter wielded great power in Lancastrian England, though they were barred from any place in the royal succession.

656 Bishop Beaufort served intermittently as chancellor under Henry IV, Henry V, and, from 1424–6, Henry VI. According to Hall, the ambitious Beaufort had long sought appointment as cardinal; Henry V, however, barred him from such a rank, since he feared that the proud Beaufort would use that office 'to presume to be egall [equal] with Princes'. Beaufort gained his cardinal's hat in 1427; while Hall does not suggest that Beaufort obtained the cardinal's office through bribery, he does suggest that the new cardinal

subsequently 'purchased' (a word that could mean either 'obtained' or 'bought') his legatine power (Hall, 139).

657 In October 1425 hostility between Gloucester and Beaufort had reached such a point that a group of Beaufort's armed adherents battled Londoners in a bid to enter the city to attack Gloucester's servants. Summoned by a letter from Beaufort, Bedford came to England in January 1426 to preside over parliament's attempt to reconcile the two feuding magnates (Fabyan, 595–6; Hall, 130–8). After the members of the upper house made peace between Gloucester and Beaufort, Hall writes, 'the greate fire of this discencion, betwene these twoo noble personages, was thus ... utterly quenched out', at least, Hall adds, according to the 'knowledge and judgement' of the parliamentarians (Hall, 138).

658 In 1440 public enmity between Gloucester and Beaufort flared again, after Gloucester made a formal complaint to Henry VI concerning alleged acts of misconduct by Beaufort. As Hall tells it, when King Henry and his council made no effort to investigate Gloucester's charges, Duke Humphrey's enemies felt emboldened to begin a covert campaign against Gloucester (Hall, 197–202).

659 None of Ferrers's known sources suggests that Beaufort or anyone else spread letters and bills against Gloucester. For an argument that Ferrers intends this and other unhistorical details in his poem to put readers in mind of the downfall of another, later lord protector of England, Ferrers's former patron Edward Seymour (d. 1552), first duke of Somerset, see Lucas, 'A Mirror for Magistrates', 94–105.

660 According to Hall, in the year 1446 Gloucester's opponents accused him of assigning to condemned men modes of execution more severe than English law prescribed. Hall states these acts of severity were born from Gloucester's detestation of crime and his knowledge of civil law procedure (Hall, 209). Ferrers's unhistorical claims of Gloucester's leniency towards certain malefactors and his suggestion that Gloucester was attacked for his alleged legal innovations earlier than 1446 are entirely his own inventions.

661 In 1422 or 1423, Humphrey married Jacqueline (or Jaquet, as Hall calls her) of Hainault (d. 1436), the daughter and heir to William (d. 1417), duke of Bavaria-Straubing and count of Hainault and Holland. Humphrey sought her hand after Jacqueline disavowed her earlier marriage to John (d. 1427), duke of Brabant (Hall, 116). For Humphrey's seizure of and unsuccessful attempt to hold Hainault in Jacqueline's name, and for Pope Martin V's subsequent invalidation of Gloucester's marriage, see Tragedy 28, n. 609. Despite Gloucester's claim in the poem that all this was an offence of his madcap youth, Gloucester was in fact in his early thirties and already protector of England when he wed Jacqueline.

662 After his previous union had been invalidated, in 1428 Duke Humphrey married his mistress Eleanor Cobham (d. 1452). In June 1441 accusations were brought against Duchess Eleanor that she encouraged persons associated with her to calculate the king's nativity (to reckon the position of the heavenly

bodies at the time of King Henry's birth and those bodies' influence on his future life). It was understood that Eleanor had the horoscope cast so she could see when her husband, the heir presumptive to the childless Henry VI, might become king. See Tragedy 28, nn. 613–15.

663 According to formal charges brought against them in the court of the king's bench, Cobham's associate Roger Bolingbroke (d. 1441), a learned cleric, summoned demons and used magical figures to help him calculate when Henry VI might die, while another priest, Thomas Southwell (d. 1441), chanted oaths from a book of necromancy. Margery Jourdemayne, known as 'the Witch of Eye', was not part of the king's bench indictment, though an ecclesiastical commission charged her with practising witchcraft and sorcery on Eleanor's behalf, with the intention of harming the king (Freeman, 'Sorcery', 350–1).

664 While Fabyan and Hall report that Cobham and her confederates made a wax image of Henry VI (Fabyan's chronicle is the earliest extant source for this story), neither describes the figure with the details Ferrers supplies; both claim Bolingbroke, Southwell, and Eleanor's chaplain John Home joined Jourdemayne in creating the wax figure; and both assert that Cobham's associates used sorcery and not fire slowly to destroy the image. See Fabyan, 614; Hall, 202; cf. Griffiths, 'Trial', 390.

665 Historically, Eleanor was examined both by secular and ecclesiastical commissions, though Hall, whom Ferrers follows here, mentions only her appearance before the church authorities and implies that it was ecclesiastical commissioners who sentenced her both to public penance in London and to exile in the Isle of Man (Hall, 202; cf. Fabyan, 614, and Ferrers's different account of Eleanor's actions, prosecution, and punishment in Tragedy 28, lines 85–154). Hall further states that in response to his wife and her adherents' troubles, the humiliated Gloucester 'toke all these thynges paciently, and saied litle' (Hall, 202).

666 Ferrers describes a mode of penance often imposed in the late medieval period (see Postles, 'Penance', 445). Historically, an ecclesiastical tribunal found Duchess Eleanor guilty of witchcraft and sorcery and sentenced her to walk barefoot through London on three separate market days, holding a candle; it was, however, the king himself who ordered first her perpetual imprisonment and, in 1446, her exile to the Isle of Man (Freeman, 'Sorcery', 351; Griffiths, 'Trial', 394–7).

667 In 1444, King Henry VI wed by proxy Margaret (d. 1482), daughter of René, duke of Anjou; his new bride arrived in England the following year. By 1446, Hall writes, Margaret had grown deeply to resent Duke Humphrey's power over her meek, simple husband. Describing her as 'a woman of greate witte, and yet of no greater witte, then of haute stomacke, desirous of glory, and covetous of honor', Hall states that Margaret yearned for chief power over King Henry and his government; she thus sought means to deprive Humphrey of all his authority. Ferrers alters his chronicle source, making Gloucester's enemies the ones who convince Margaret to join in their

attempts against Duke Humphrey; Hall, by contrast, makes it clear that the idea to ruin the former protector 'came first of her [i.e. Margaret's] awne high mind' and was subsequently taken up by others (Hall, 208). Historically, Gloucester had already lost much of his influence over the king to the royal favourite William de la Pole (d. 1450), first marquess of Suffolk, and his allies by the time Queen Margaret arrived in England.

668   Margaret's reasons here to act against Duke Humphrey are Ferrers's invention.

669   No chronicler suggests that the Richard (d. 1460), third duke of York, had any part in the actions against Gloucester or that he actively sought the crown at this early date.

670   Of these men, Hall names only Suffolk and Henry Stafford (d. 1460), first duke of Buckingham, as part of the alleged conspiracy against Humphrey (Hall, 209). Edmund Beafuort (d. 1455), first marquess of Dorset, was Cardinal Beaufort's nephew, so Ferrers may have assumed that he was one of Gloucester's enemies, as historically he was, even though Ferrers explicitly has Dorset (the future Edmund, first duke of Somerset) claim he was not part of the conspiracy in Tragedy 26, lines 267–73. Finally, no chronicler mentions John Holland (d. 1447), first duke of Exeter, as an opponent of Humphrey. It is possible that Ferrers attempted to evoke in readers' minds contemporary sixteenth-century figures through the inclusion of these and other unhistorical members in the conspiracy. See Lucas, 'A Mirror for Magistrates', 100–2.

671   Cf. Hall's similar comments (Hall, 210).

672   As with Richard of York, neither the two Nevilles most prominent in politics in Henry VI's reign – Richard Neville (d. 1460), fifth earl of Salisbury, and his son Richard Neville (d. 1471), sixteenth earl of Warwick – nor any of York's near kinsmen took part in opposition to Gloucester. Hall assigns leadership of the conspiracy against Duke Humphrey to Suffolk and Buckingham, but he also notes that the two men were 'not unprocured by the Cardinall of Winchester [i.e. Henry Beaufort] and the Archebishop of Yorke' (Hall, 209).

673   Humphrey's enemies arranged it, Hall writes, so that parliament was called for February 1447 in Bury St Edmunds, Suffolk, a town far from London, the city in which Humphrey's support was strongest (Hall, 209).

674   Contrary to Ferrers's claim, Hall makes it clear that Margaret had completely excluded Gloucester from the rule of the realm by the time this parliament was called. Similarly, Hall names no 'great treasons' of which Duke Humphrey was accused (Hall, 209). For mid-Tudor readers, Ferrers's stanzas could evoke thoughts not chiefly of the historical Humphrey of Gloucester but of Ferrers's former patron Edward Seymour, duke of Somerset, at the time of his 1549 fall from power. See Lucas, 'A Mirror for Magistrates', 28–30.

675   On 18 February 1447, Duke Humphrey was arrested, Hall writes, by the Lord Constable John (d. 1460), first Viscount Beaumont, accompanied by a group of Gloucester's enemies. The claims that Gloucester was taken at his lodgings and on a charge of high treason are Ferrers's addition to Hall's narrative,

though they correspond to several fifteenth-century accounts of Gloucester's arrest.

676 Hall writes that Gloucester was found dead in his bedchamber on the night after his arrest. His corpse, which bore no marks of violence, was 'shewed to the lordes and commons, as though he had died of a palsey or empostome [impostume, an abscess]: but all indifferent persons well knewe, that he died of no natural death but of some violent force', either strangulation, suffocation, or impalement through the rectum (Hall, 209). Ferrers has his Gloucester specifically refute the claim of the chronicler John Hardyng that Humphrey died naturally of a palsy brought on by melancholy (Hardyng, 400).

677 Gloucester's Latin quote is a paraphrase of lines from the anonymous Roman tragedy *Octavia*, ascribed in the Renaissance to the playwright Seneca (d. AD 65): 'O funestus multis populi / dirusque favor!', 'Oh, dire and deadly to many has the people's favour proved!' (Seneca, *Seneca's Tragedies with an English Translation*, 2 vols., trans. Frank Miller (London: Heinemann, 1929), 2:482–3). As with other matter in this poem, Ferrers's Latin tag bears little relation to the rise and fall of the historical Humphrey, duke of Gloucester; it is, by contrast, entirely appropriate to the career of the recently fallen Tudor nobleman Edward Seymour, duke of Somerset. See Lucas, '*A Mirror for Magistrates*', 23–30.

[Prose 32]

678 The editor of the 1578 edition, likely John Higgins, makes William Baldwin appear to be the speaker of the following passage and thus, by implication, the author of the succeeding Tragedy 11. By contrast, all previous editions ascribe the poem to an unnamed 'another' of the company (see Prose 11, which this prose replaces in the 1578 and 1587 *Mirror* editions).

679 The 1578 editor takes the remainder of this prose link almost verbatim from the version of Prose 11 offered in the 1571 *Mirror for Magistrates*.

680 Men and women of all classes grew to despise Henry VI's close counsellor William de la Pole (d. 1450), first duke of Suffolk, whom they accused of murdering Duke Humphrey of Gloucester (see Tragedies 11 and 29). So intense was the popular fury that in 1450 Henry VI reluctantly banished Suffolk for five years (Hall, 217–19).

681 According to Hall, the craft transporting Suffolk into exile was met by a warship belonging to Henry Holland (d. 1475), second duke of Exeter. Exeter's men boarded Suffolk's ship, beheaded the duke, and left his body on the sands of Dover (Hall, 219). The editor of the 1571 edition of *A Mirror for Magistrates* makes the vessel that intercepted Suffolk not one in service to a nobleman but an undistinguished ship from Devonshire, and it is that account that the 1578 editor reproduces here. The date of 1 May is supplied by Fabyan, who claims it was on that day that Suffolk's corpse was discovered (Fabyan, 622).

Appendix 2

682 The tragedies of Gloucester and his wife, listed as a single work here, did not appear in either the 1559 or 1563 editions. Omitted from the list of poems in the 1563 *Mirror*, their names reentered the table of contents of the 1571 *Mirror*, this time as two separate tragedies. Those works were not printed until the edition of 1578 (see Introduction, p. xxi and Tragedies 28 and 29). That the printer hoped to include the joint Gloucester–Cobham tragedy but did not know how long that poem might be could explain why his employees were not able to assign definite folio numbers to the two poems that were intended to follow it.